NOTE CONCERNING THE FLYLEAVES: The "time line" on the flyleaves sets forth in chronological order the most important figures, events, and movements of the Judaeo-Christian tradition. For reasons of space, some periods are extended and others shortened on the line, such as 1500-1600 A.D. and 1700-1300 B.C. In some cases it has seemed advisable to give the dates of a particular figure; in others, the date of a significant book. For details, consult the introductions to the main periods of the Judaeo-Christian tradition and the works cited in the bibliographies.

Pope Gregory I (the Great), 590-604

600

Mohammed and the rise of Islam

700

800 Coronation of Charlemagne, 800

900

Cluniac reform of monasticism, 927

1000 Final break between Roman Catholic and Greek Orthodox churches, 1054

Pope Gregory VII (Hildebrand), 1073-1085

Beginning of Crusades, 1096

Anselm of Canterbury, 1033-1109

1100 Moses Maimonides, 1135-1204

Pope Innocent III, 1198-1216

1200 Papal approval of the Dominicans, 1216

Papal approval of the Franciscans, 1223

Thomas Aquinas, 1225-1274

Roger Bacon, 1214-1292

1300 Papacy in Avignon, 1305-1417

Dante, 1265-1321

Spread of Renaissance

1400 John Hus executed, 1415

Fall of Constantinople to Turks, 1453

Columbus' discovery of America, 1492

1500 Luther's 95 theses, 1517

Diet of Worms, 1521

Rise of Anabaptists, ca. 1525

Papal authority abolished in England, 1534

First edition of Calvin's *Institutes,* 1536

Council of Trent ("Counter-Reformation"), 1545-1563

Elizabethan Settlement, 1559-1563

Presbyterianism established in Scotland, 1560

1600 King James (Authorized) Version of the Bible, 1611

Establishment of Plymouth colony by Pilgrims, 1620

Roger Williams' *Bloody Tenet,* 1644

Westminster Confession, 1646

George Fox, 1624-1691

1700 John Wesley and the Methodists at Oxford, 1726-1730

Jonathan Edwards, 1703-1758

David Hume's *Dialogues Concerning Natural Religion,* 1751

French Revolution and Emancipation of the Jews, 1789

1800 Unitarian Society formed in United States, 1820

Darwin's *Origin of Species,* 1859

Dogma of Papal Infallibility defined, 1870

Pittsburgh Platform of Reform Judaism, 1885

Sigmund Freud's *Studies on Hysteria,* 1895

Pope Leo XIII's encyclical *Rerum Novarum*

Theodor Herzl's *The Jewish State,* 1896

1900 Condemnation of "modernism" by Pope Piux X

Walter Rauschenbusch's *Theology for the Social Gospel,* 1917

First General Assembly of the World Council of Churches, 1948

Establishment of the State of Israel, 1948

Dogma of the Bodily Assumption of the Virgin defined, 1950

BASIC SOURCES OF THE JUDAEO-CHRISTIAN TRADITION

EDITORS

FRED BERTHOLD, JR.

Dean of the William Jewett Tucker Foundation and Professor of Religion, Dartmouth College

ALAN W. CARLSTEN

Chaplain and Associate Professor of Religion Florida Presbyterian College

KLAUS PENZEL

Instructor in the Department of Religion, Dartmouth College, 1956-1959

JAMES F. ROSS

Assistant Professor of Old Testament The Theological School Drew University

PRENTICE-HALL, INC. *Englewood Cliffs, N. J.* *1962*

BASIC SOURCES OF THE JUDAEO-CHRISTIAN TRADITION

Credits: Page 6, top, photo by Paul Lippman; bottom, Israel Office of Information. Page 7, photo published by permission of the Matson Photo Service, Los Angeles, California. Page 116, from *Cathédrales et Trésors Gothiques de France,* by Marcel Aubert, Arthaud Editeur, Paris, 1958; photo A. Trincano, exclusivité Arthaud. Page 117, top, photo Jean Roubier; bottom, copyright Soprintendenza ai Monumenti e Gallerie di Trieste. Pages 236 and 237, top, woodcut by Lucas Cranach, "Das Abendmahl der Evangelischen und der Hoellensturz der Papisten," reproduced in Max Geisberg, *Das deutsche Einblatt–Holzschnitt in der ersten Haelfte des 16. Jahrhunderts,* IX (Die Reformation), No. 29, Muenchen: Hugo Schmidt Verlag, 1929; John Calvin, from E. Doumergue, *Iconographie Calvinienne,* Lausanne: George Bridel, 1909 (Plate V); John Wesley, after a painting by N. Hone engraved by John Greenwood, courtesy of the New York Public Library, Prints Division. Page 303, courtesy of the New York Public Library, Rare Books Division. Page 324, top, courtesy Anshen & Allen, architects, and *Architectural Record,* Julius Shulman, photographer; bottom, Cornell Capa–Magnum, courtesy *Life* magazine. Page 325, top, George Miles Ryan Studios, Eero Saarinen and Associates, and Frederick A. Praeger, Inc.; bottom, The Bettmann Archive.

Library of Congress Catalog Card No.: 62-9946

Printed in the United States of America 06928-C

PREFACE

The selection of basic sources found in this book took place in connection with the teaching of an "introductory" course in Religion at Dartmouth College. Before their paths diverged, the four co-editors worked in this course with a great many undergraduates. One debt of gratitude which certainly must be acknowledged is to those students who so patiently read from mimeographed pages—as the manuscript was tried out and changed many times.

The editors were cautioned by many colleagues about the dangers of directing undergraduates to primary sources. There are, of course, difficulties—the most serious of which arises from the fact that many undergraduates lack any systematic historical knowledge. We can hardly pretend that the brief introductions provided for each selection overcome this deficiency, although we hope they may stimulate more serious students to search in the right direction.

In spite of this danger, however, the editors have been convinced by their own experience that the advantages of acquainting undergraduates with the sources far outweigh the disadvantages. The sources, we believe, are livelier than most secondary analyses. The analyst often feels compelled to use generalizations which may obscure the variety within the tradition; or his desire to be fair may result in constant qualification of statements to such an extent that novel or bold formulations are weakened. Confronted with novelty and variety, the student may experience a greater stimulus to his own thinking. It has been our experience, too, that the sources provide the student with material for dialogue with his instructor. However impartial he may seek to be, every instructor has a certain point of view. A significant number of the sources will challenge it. This seems to encourage many students to formulate their own critical questions.

A book of source readings obviously calls for supplementation. We have found it possible to provide for this largely through historical and systematic lectures. At Dartmouth almost all of the materials included in this volume have been read in a one-term course, meeting four days a week. We feel that this plan can be successfully modified in several ways: by using the book of readings over a longer period (two terms or a year) in connection with other books, or by assigning fewer selections in a one-term course while relying more heavily on lectures or on a supplementary textbook.

One valuable aid is a weekly "precept" or discussion group small enough to permit each student to raise questions for clarification or to request additional background information.

Students will find it helpful to consult some of the suggested readings cited at the end of each section. The extent to which this will be found necessary will vary in terms of the amount of historical and theological background they bring to the course.

Even in a relatively large book such as this, it has been necessary to be extremely selective. No thoughtful student will imagine that he has mastered the tradition when he finishes. It is our hope, however, that by reading sizable portions of a few of the most influential and representative authors he will be more conversant with the richness of our western religious history, and more eager to pursue certain aspects in greater depth.

The entire volume has received the attention of all four editors. Yet each editor has assumed primary responsibility for editing one section: James F. Ross, the Biblical Period; Alan W. Carlsten, the Early and Medieval Periods; Klaus Penzel, the Reformation Period; and Fred Berthold, Jr., the Modern Period.

CONTENTS

PART THREE THE REFORMATION

PART FOUR THE MODERN PERIOD

Introduction
The Judaeo-Christian Tradition

Today in the United States we find a bewildering variety of religious denominations among those calling themselves Christians and several distinguishable movements among the Jews. In view of this situation, can we rightly say that there is "a Judaeo-Christian tradition"? Are not the differences between many of these groups so decisive that it is more accurate to speak of a number of historically related, and perhaps overlapping, traditions?

This is in part a problem of definition, and it is characteristic of such a problem that equally well-informed persons may decide to use their terminology differently. Our purpose in this book is not to settle such questions for the reader but to set forth, within the inevitable limitations of space, some of the most important source materials relevant to an understanding of the religious heritage of the West. In spite of the diversity of religious groups among Christians and Jews, there are certain fundamental reasons for bringing together in one book of readings all of the movements represented in the following pages. There is the fact that all of these groups have, according to their own interpretations, a common origin: the covenant between God (Yahweh) and His people, a record of which is to be found in the Hebrew Bible (or Old Testament). In addition, there is the fact that each of these groups, in greater or lesser measure, has vitally affected the ideas and institutions of Western civilization. Whether their similarities or their differences be emphasized, all of these groups offer for our consideration an understanding of life's meaning and purpose rooted in religious faith, and for all of them it is a faith in the God of Abraham, Isaac and Jacob. In this respect they all stand in sharp contrast to the secular ideologies of modern times.

The Problem of Historical Context

The development of religious institutions and ideas takes place within, and reflects, the history of culture generally. Thus, in an introductory study of religion, as is perhaps the case with all introductory courses, we are faced with a pedagogical dilemma. In order to understand fully our religious heritage, it is necessary to have a grasp of Western cultural history. Yet "Western cultural history" is merely an abstraction standing for specific developments in religion, government, science, art, philosophy, and the like. The student must begin somewhere. He needs both specific information and a general interpretive framework. To some extent he must shuttle back and forth between the two demands.

The literature whose major types and periods we seek to illustrate is so vast that we feel constrained to give the bulk of our space to the primary texts themselves. We cannot provide here the broad historical framework which we acknowledge to be essential to the *full* and proper understanding of the texts. Our brief introductions, and our suggested supplementary readings, are primarily guides to further study, though we hope that they will also give a modicum of historical orientation to the student whose background is seriously deficient in this area. A simple *time line* is also given (see front and back endpapers) as a convenient reminder of the major strands which have contributed to our tradition.

Basis for Selection

Our attempt has been to bring together in a single volume selections representing the major periods *of,* the most important contributors *to,* and the most influential movements *within* the Judaeo-Christian tradition. The need for such a volume rests upon the growth of courses which seek to "introduce" the college student to the subject matter of religion by means of a study of the living religions of the West. For some years now students in one institution have read in a semester substantially all that is included in this book. The course of readings has been accompanied by a much fuller treatment, in lectures, of the historical and systematic contexts which shed light upon the texts. It has seemed to us that this volume might also be useful in a full year course, if supplemented by other readily available texts and even more extensive lectures.

The literature of this tradition, at a conservative estimate, spans almost 3,000 years. It is obvious, therefore, that we have had to be highly selective. No doubt it will seem to many that we have given too much space to this or that writer and not enough to some other; or that we have not chosen the most important representative of some particular movement. Wherever possible we have tried to select authors who are of first rank importance in their own right. Occasionally, however, it has seemed to us that an author of lesser reputation has stated a certain position with a brevity and clarity not found among its more famous exponents.

Considerations of space have forced us to concentrate, on the whole, upon the "classic" expressions of Judaism, Roman Catholicism, and Protestantism —rather than upon some of the interesting recent developments or, for example, upon peculiarly American phenomena. In our judgment, it is hardly possible to evaluate more recent trends without a foundation of understanding in the historically decisive events and documents—the Bible, the Talmud, St. Augustine, St. Thomas Aquinas, the continental Reformation, and the like. In the United States of America, to be sure, one finds a variety of vigorous movements today whose special "source" documents we have omitted. The student will find guidance in understanding these movements and in locating their source documents in any good history of American religion—for example, in Olmstead's *The History of Religion in America.*

Eastern Orthodoxy

The authors have especially regretted the necessity of omitting any special readings on Eastern Orthodoxy—or the so-called "Orthodox Churches." These Churches are very much alive today, not only in Greece, Russia and other nations of the Near East, but in the United States. Theologically, they are close to the Roman Catholic Church and to Anglicanism, though with unique emphases. The liturgical traditions of Orthodoxy are especially rich, as may be seen, for example, in the beautiful liturgies of St. John Chrysostom (died in 407). Indeed, it is the very richness of the Orthodox tradition which made it impossible even to make a beginning of representing it in these already overcrowded pages.

The Orthodox Churches share with the rest of Christendom the history of the early Church, and of the great ecumenical councils which, in the first centuries, hammered out the creeds which most Christians still regard as binding. In 1054 A.D. a decisive split occurred between Rome and the East, a split not yet healed, though as recently as 1959 Pope John XXIII announced that an ecumenical council would be held "in the near future" to see if the differences might be reconciled.

PART ONE

THE BIBLICAL PERIOD

Torah Scroll. PAUL LIPPMAN, PHOTOGRAPHER.

Nazareth.

Mt. Sinai.

An Introduction to the Study of the Bible

In some sense all three of the major branches of the Judaeo-Christian tradition regard the Bible as authoritative for faith and action. The Bible is not only a "source" of the tradition; it is also a "source of sources" for the thought of the church fathers, the medieval rabbis, and the Protestant reformers; modern theology also finds its origin in the biblical record of God's relationship with man and man's response to God.

Yet alongside this apparent unanimity as to the importance of the Bible there is considerable disagreement between the great religions and within each of them as to the precise significance of "Holy Writ." In the first place, there is no general agreement on the extent of the Bible. Judaism, of course, accepts only the thirty-nine books which Christians call the "Old Testament." Not only the Christian New Testament but also numerous writings from the last two centuries B. C. and the first two centuries A. D. were excluded from the "canon," or list of authoritative books, drawn up by the Palestinian Jews toward the end of the first century A. D. Christianity, while accepting the twenty-seven books of the New Testament, is divided on the question of whether or not to accept certain other Jewish works from the above-mentioned "intertestamental period." Roman Catholicism, following the practice of Alexandrine (Egyptian) Judaism, regards as "deutero-canonical" (authoritative in the second degree) some fourteen books which are called the "Apocrypha" by Protestants; the most important of these are I Maccabees, Tobit, Ecclesiasticus (Sirach), and the Wisdom of Solomon. The Protestant churches in turn regard the Apocrypha (literally, "hidden books") as "useful and good to read" (Martin Luther in his German translation of the Bible, 1534) or "[to be] read for example of life, and instruction of manners" (the Sixth Article of the Church of England) but of no authority in the establishment of doctrine.

Second, there is considerable disagreement on the nature of the authority to be vested in the documents regarded as canonical. The official position of the Roman Catholic church, as well as that of Orthodox Judaism, is that the biblical books are infallibly inspired by

God and therefore without error. This is a position shared by those Protestant groups which are commonly called fundamentalist. Seen in this light the Bible is, of course, absolutely authoritative, since it is the pronouncement of God himself. Nevertheless, Roman Catholicism allows for various "senses" of scripture; a given passage may be literally true, an allegory of a higher truth, or (in the case of many Old Testament stories) a foreshadowing or "type" of the history of Christ and the church. Indeed, a particular story or poem may be taken in more than one "sense"; the final decision must be left up to the Church as the only authoritative interpreter of scripture. In their turn, Orthodox Jews interpret the Hebrew scriptures in the light of the Talmud, which is itself a commentary on the Bible.

Many modern Protestants, however, do not start from the above assumption that the Bible is by its nature infallible in all its parts. They point out inner inconsistencies within the biblical record as well as statements attributed to God or leading figures in the Bible which are not in accord with our modern understanding of the nature of true religion. Furthermore, it is claimed that in the Bible there is an obvious development in the idea of God as well as in the view of man and his responsibility. It is to be concluded that there is a considerable human element in the divine word. The Bible is, to be sure, ultimately inspired by God, but this inspiration is not to be conceived after the pattern of an executive dictating a letter to a secretary. Rather, we are to assume that the lives of the Biblical authors were inspired; what they actually wrote is subject to much of the confusion and error of any human effort. Those who hold these views would say that the Bible is authoritative as the classic expression of "man's search for God"; it is not to be taken as a textbook of religious knowledge, nor as a scientific treatise, nor as a history of ancient times. Starting from these assumptions, "liberal" Protestants have engaged in the type of study known as "higher criticism," which raises questions concerning the date, authorship, unity, purpose, and historical background of the Biblical books or parts thereof.

Still other Protestants, whom we may call "neo-orthodox," share many of the assumptions of the "liberals" but feel that they have gone too far. They feel that judging the Bible in accord with our standards of religious truth actually deprives the Bible of any real authority. The Bible must be independent of any human norms or standards; it must stand as the "Word of God" over against the "word of man." The Bible challenges and inspires us; we do not presume to ask questions of it. The neo-orthodox do not, however, return to the position that the Bible is absolutely infallible and therefore beyond criticism. In many details it is still a human book, and questions of "higher criticism" must still be asked. But after the critics have had their say, the Bible still remains the only authoritative source of faith.

Questions such as these have divided the Judaeo-Christian tradition in the centuries past, and they are no less vigorously discussed at the present time. Yet the very fact that theological wars have been fought along these lines, and that new groups have been formed as a result, indicates that these issues are of central importance. To the question, "How can I know God and His will?" the answer has always been, "Read the Bible." In this the Judaeo-Christian tradition finds its unity.

Introduction to the Old Testament

The Old Testament, or the Hebrew Scriptures, consists of thirty-nine books; in the Jewish tradition, however, the twelve "minor" prophets are counted as one book. The following divisions are customary: (1) *the Pentateuch* ("five scrolls"—the first five books), (2) *the Prophets,* (a) former (Joshua through II Kings) and (b) latter (Isaiah through Malachi; in Christian Bibles Daniel is considered to be one of the prophetic books, while in Jewish Bibles it is in the next division), and (3) *the Writings* (the remaining books). It has already been noted that Roman Catholicism includes the Apocrypha as "deuterocanonical." The order of books is different in Jewish and Christian Bibles, the most notable difference being that the latter prophets come at the end in the Christian version.

Those who accept to one degree or another the assumptions and results of "higher criticism" (see above), hold that the books of the Old Testament were written over a period of almost a thousand years; the earliest portions (such as the "Song of Deborah," in Judges 5) come from the middle of the twelfth century B. C., and the latest book (Daniel) from the second quarter of the second century B. C. Furthermore, it is held that very few of the books are by one author only, although some have come down to us with only minor additions. On the other hand many modern biblical scholars claim that we must assume the existence of several "schools" or groups of writers who were responsible for both the writing and editing of a series of books. For example, it is said that the "Deuteronomists" not only produced the book of Deuteronomy, but also edited the early histories from Joshua through II Kings as well as some of the prophetic books. Similarly, the "Priestly school" provided the framework for and edited the first four books of the Old Testament, just as the "Chronicler(s)" produced I and II Chronicles, Ezra, and Nehemiah. In particular, the following results of higher criticism, although not universally agreed upon by all scholars, may be singled out for special attention.

The Pentateuch

As early as the seventeenth century, biblical scholars began to notice that the Pentateuch is not consistent in its use of terms for the Deity. Long sections use "Yahweh" (in the King James and Revised Standard versions, "the Lord"; in the Revised Version, "Jehovah"); other sections use simply "Elohim" (in all versions, "God"). It was thus suspected that those parts using "Yahweh" are from one author or school, and those using "Elohim" from another. Furthermore, scholars noticed that many stories are told twice or even three times, particularly in Genesis. Abraham expels Hagar twice; Jacob is given the name "Israel" twice; God reveals his name "Yahweh" to Moses twice; on three separate occasions a patriarch attempts to pass off his wife as his sister. In addition there are many apparent errors in chronology; according to a strict reading of the text Isaac was on his deathbed for eighty years! Finally, the style of various sections is radically different; there are lengthy genealogies and lists of cultic laws side by side with fresh, fast-moving narratives.

On the basis of this evidence the so-called Documentary Hypothesis was worked out in the nineteenth century, and is still accepted by most critics today, although with some reservations. Those portions using the term "Yahweh" are called the "Yahwist Epic"; those using "Elohim" are called the "Elohist Epic"; those using "Elohim" but showing a marked interest in the cult, chronologies, and genealogies are called the "Priestly Source"; and finally, the Book of Deuteronomy is simply called the "Deuteronomic

Source." The Yahwist Epic (with a conventional symbol, J) is the earliest—perhaps as early as 950 B.C. This was followed by its (northern) parallel, the Elohist (E) in approximately 750 B.C. The two were joined together and later added to the Book of Deuteronomy (D—621–550 B.C.). The whole (J + E + D) was finally edited and expanded by the priests in about 400 B.C. By far the largest portion of the strictly legal material in the Pentateuch comes from this Priestly Source (P). Of course, those who accept this analysis deny that Moses was the author of the Pentateuch; it is not "Mosaic," but "*a* mosaic." An extensive portion of the Yahwist Epic is included in this book (see below, p. (13ff.) as well as a narrative in which three of the major sources are to be found (see below, p. (21ff.).

The Latter Prophets

Most scholars claim that the books of the so-called "writing prophets" are largely the result of editorial work done by disciples of the prophets, in which the oracles of the master were written down and combined with biographical and autobiographical material. Furthermore it is said that most of the books contain major or minor additions from later writers. For example, the Book of Isaiah is usually attributed to at least three major authors. "First Isaiah" is to be found in chapters 1 to 39, although even here long sections (such as 24–27 and 36–39) come from a later period; the prophet himself was active in the last half of the eighth century B. C. "Second (or "Deutero-") Isaiah" consists of chapters 40 to 55. Whereas Isaiah spoke of judgment at the hands of the Assyrians, Second Isaiah promises comfort and redemption and speaks of the Persians. "Third (or "Trito-") Isaiah" (chapters 56 to 66) is commonly regarded as the work of Second Isaiah's disciples; whereas their master prophesied in the Babylonian Exile, their writings reflect the conditions in Palestine after the return.

The Writings

The results of critical work on these books may appear to be largely negative. For example, it is usually held that few, if any, of the Psalms were written by David; the very title usually translated "A Psalm of David" really means "A Psalm written in the manner or spirit of David." Actually, the Psalms are largely the cultic poetry of Israel prior to the Exile. Similarly, the Proverbs were not actually written by Solomon (it may be noted that there are other titles in the book, such as "The Words of Lemuel" and "Proverbs Collected by the Men of Hezekiah"); nevertheless, Solomon is the traditional source of "proverbial" wisdom (I Kings 4:29–34). Furthermore, a distinction is usually made between the prose prologue and epilogue to the Book of Job and the poetic dialogue between Job and his friends along with the reply from the Lord; there is little agreement, however, as to whether the prose precedes the poetry or vice versa.

In recent years another approach to the literature of the Old Testament has been developed which may be regarded as a valuable supplement to the views outlined in the preceding paragraphs. This is usually called "form criticism," because it concentrates on an analysis of the types and categories of literature to be found in the Old Testament rather than the more limited problems of date, authorship, unity, and the like. Scholars who use this approach search for the "situation in life" or religious and social context of particular passages; they investigate the ways in which a given author or school uses traditional forms and the points at which these are modified and changed. The detailed results of this approach cannot be given here, but it may be noted that at least four "forms" or "types" have been discovered in the Book of Psalms, and they are discussed in the prefaces to the following selections (pp. 46 to 50).

A. Narrative and History

1. *The Yahwist Epic*

The Yahwist, the name used for the author(s) of the Yahwist Epic, was probably a Judaean (that is, from southern Israel) living in the time of Solomon. This was an age of enlightenment; the conquest of the land was finished and Israel enjoyed a brief period of political and religious independence. The author proceeded to collect poems, stories, traditions, and laws from the patriarchal age and to combine these with the traditional account of the Exodus and the Conquest. To all of this he prefaced ancient traditions concerning the Creation and the beginnings of civilization (Genesis 2–11, in the main). Much of his material was relatively ancient; the Song of the Ark (Num. 10:35–36) is probably to be dated in the thirteenth century B. C. The religious significance of the Yahwist's work is that he provided the nucleus of a national religious epic; the Israelites were not to be regarded as late-comers on the scene of history, but were connected with ancient times; furthermore their God, Yahweh, created the heavens and the earth. The Yahwist is quite nationalistic; Yahweh's promise is that Israel shall inherit the whole of Palestine. Nevertheless, in Abraham "shall all the families of the earth be blessed."

The following selections, the story of creation and the history of Abraham, are typical of the Yahwist's style and thought. Other material from the epic will be found alongside E and P in Exodus 1–24. (See p. 21).

[GENESIS 2:4b–4:26 AND 12:1–25:12, FOLLOWING THE ANALYSIS OF S. R. DRIVER, *The Book of Genesis* (WESTMINSTER COMMENTARIES), 15TH EDITION, METHUEN AND CO., LTD., 1948.]

* (Ch. 2) In the day that the LORD God made the earth and the heavens, when no plant of the field was yet in the earth and no herb of the field had yet sprung up—for the LORD God had not caused it to rain upon the earth, and there was no man to till the ground; but a mist went up from the earth and watered the whole face of the ground—then the LORD God formed man of dust from the ground, and breathed into his nostrils the breath of life; and man became a living being. And the LORD God planted a garden in Eden, in the east; and there he put the man whom he had formed. And out of the ground the LORD God made to grow every tree that is pleasant to the sight and good for food, the tree of life also in the midst of the garden, and the tree of the knowledge of good and evil.

A river flowed out of Eden to water the garden, and there it divided and became four rivers. The name of the first is Pishon; it is the one which flows around the whole land of Havilah, where there is gold; and the gold of that land is good; bdellium and onyx stone are there. The name of the second river is Gihon; it is the one which flows around the whole land of Cush. And the name of the third river is Hiddekel, which flows east of Assyria. And the fourth river is the Euphrates.

The LORD God took the man and put him in the garden of Eden to till it and keep it. And the LORD God commanded the man, saying, "You may freely eat of every tree of the garden; but of the tree of the knowledge of good and evil you shall not eat, for in the day that you eat of it you shall die."

Then the LORD God said, "It is not good that the man should be alone; I will make him a helper fit for him." So out of the ground the LORD God formed every beast of the field and every bird of the air, and brought them to the man to see what he would call them; and whatever the man called every living creature, that was its name. The man gave names to all cattle, and to the birds of the air, and to every beast of the field; but for the man there was not found a helper fit for him. So the LORD God caused a deep sleep to fall upon the man, and while he slept took one of his ribs and closed up its place with flesh; and the rib which the LORD God had taken from the man he made into a woman and brought her to the man. Then the man said,

"This at last is bone of my bones
  and flesh of my flesh;
she shall be called Woman,
  because she was taken out of Man."

Therefore a man leaves his father and his mother and cleaves to his wife, and they become one flesh. And the man and his wife were both naked, and were not ashamed.

(Ch. 3) Now the serpent was more subtle than any other wild creature that the LORD God had made. He said to the woman, "Did God say, 'You shall not eat of any tree of the garden'?" And the woman said to the serpent, "We may eat of the fruit of the trees of the garden; but God said, 'You shall not eat of the fruit of the tree which is in the midst of the garden, neither shall you touch it, lest you die.' " But the serpent said to the woman, "You will not die. For God knows that when you eat of it your eyes will be opened, and you will be like God, knowing good and evil." So when the woman saw that the tree was good for food, and that it was a delight to the eyes, and that the tree was to be desired to make one wise, she took of its fruit and ate; and she also gave some to her husband, and he ate. Then the eyes of both were opened, and they knew that they were naked; and they sewed fig leaves together and made themselves aprons.

And they heard the sound of the LORD God walking in the garden in the cool of the day, and the man and his wife hid themselves from the presence of the LORD God among the trees of the garden. But the LORD God called to the man, and said to him, "Where are you?" And he said, "I heard the sound of thee in the garden, and I was afraid, because I was naked; and I hid myself." He said, "Who told you that you were naked? Have you eaten of the tree of which I commanded you not to eat?" The man said, "The woman whom thou gavest to be with me, she gave me fruit of the tree, and I ate." Then the LORD God said to the woman, "What is this that you have done?" The woman said, "The serpent beguiled me, and I ate." The LORD God said to the serpent,

"Because you have done this,
  cursed are you above all cattle,
  and above all wild animals;
upon your belly you shall go,
  and dust you shall eat
  all the days of your life.
I will put enmity between you and the woman,
  and between your seed and her seed;
he shall bruise your head,
  and you shall bruise his heel."

To the woman he said,

"I will greatly multiply your pain in childbearing;
  in pain you shall bring forth children,
yet your desire shall be for your husband,
  and he shall rule over you."

And to Adam he said,

"Because you have listened to the voice of your wife,
  and have eaten of the tree
of which I commanded you,
  'You shall not eat of it,'
cursed is the ground because of you;
  in toil you shall eat of it all the days of your life;
thorns and thistles it shall bring forth to you;
  and you shall eat the plants of the field.
In the sweat of your face
  you shall eat bread
till you return to the ground,
  for out of it you were taken;
you are dust,
  and to dust you shall return."

The man called his wife's name Eve, because she was the mother of all living. And the LORD God made for Adam and for his wife garments of skins, and clothed them.

Then the LORD God said, "Behold, the man has become like one of us, knowing good and evil; and now, lest he put forth his hand and take also of the tree of life, and eat, and live for ever"—therefore the LORD God sent him forth from the garden of Eden, to till the ground from which he was taken. He drove out the man; and at the east of the garden of

Eden he placed the cherubim, and a flaming sword which turned every way, to guard the way to the tree of life.

(Ch. 4) Now Adam knew Eve his wife, and she conceived and bore Cain, saying, "I have gotten a man with the help of the LORD." And again, she bore his brother Abel. Now Abel was a keeper of sheep, and Cain a tiller of the ground. In the course of time Cain brought to the Lord an offering of the fruit of the ground, and Abel brought of the firstlings of his flock and of their fat portions. And the LORD had regard for Abel and his offering, but for Cain and his offering he had no regard. So Cain was very angry, and his countenance fell. The LORD said to Cain, "Why are you angry, and why has your countenance fallen? If you do well, will you not be accepted? And if you do not do well, sin is couching at the door; its desire is for you, but you must master it."

Cain said to Abel his brother, "Let us go out to the field." And when they were in the field, Cain rose up against his brother Abel, and killed him. Then the LORD said to Cain, "Where is Abel your brother?" He said, "I do not know; am I my brother's keeper?" And the LORD said, "What have you done? The voice of your brother's blood is crying to me from the ground. And now you are cursed from the ground, which has opened its mouth to receive your brother's blood from your hand. When you till the ground, it shall no longer yield to you its strength; you shall be a fugitive and a wanderer on the earth." Cain said to the LORD, "My punishment is greater than I can bear. Behold, thou hast driven me this day away from the ground; and from thy face I shall be hidden; and I shall be a fugitive and a wanderer on the earth, and whoever finds me will slay me." Then the LORD said to him, "Not so! If any one slays Cain, vengeance shall be taken on him sevenfold." And the LORD put a mark on Cain, lest any who came upon him should kill him. Then Cain went away from the presence of the LORD, and dwelt in the land of Nod, east of Eden.

Cain knew his wife and she conceived and bore Enoch; and he built a city, and called the name of the city after the name of his son, Enoch. To Enoch was born Irad; and Irad was the father of Mehujael, and Mehujael the father of Methushael, and Methushael the father of Lamech. And Lamech took two wives; the name of the one was Adah, and the name of the other Zillah. Adah bore Jabal; he was the father of those who dwell in tents and have cattle.

His brother's name was Jubal; he was the father of all those who play the lyre and pipe. Zillah bore Tubal-cain; he was the forger of all instruments of bronze and iron. The sister of Tubal-cain was Naamah.

Lamech said to his wives:

"Adah and Zillah, hear my voice;
  you wives of Lambech, hearken to what I say:
I have slain a man for wounding me,
  a young man for striking me.
If Cain is avenged sevenfold,
  truly Lamech seventy-sevenfold."

And Adam knew his wife again, and she bore a son and called his name Seth, for she said, "God has appointed for me another child instead of Abel, for Cain slew him." To Seth also a son was born, and he called his name Enosh. At that time men began to call upon the name of the LORD.

(Ch. 12) Now the LORD said to Abram, "Go from your country and your kindred and your father's house to the land that I will show you. And I will make of you a great nation, and I will bless you, and make your name great, so that you will be a blessing. I will bless those who bless you, and him who curses you I will curse; and by you all the families of the earth will bless themselves." So Abram went, as the LORD had told him; and Lot went with him.

Abram passed through the land to the place at Shechem, to the oak of Moreh. At that time the Canaanites were in the land. Then the LORD appeared to Abram, and said, "To your descendants I will give this land." So he built there an altar to the LORD, who had appeared to him. Thence he removed to the mountain on the east of Bethel, and pitched his tent, with Bethel on the west and Ai on the east; and there he built an altar to the LORD and called on the name of the LORD. And Abram journeyed on, still going toward the Negeb.

Now there was a famine in the land. So Abram went down to Egypt to sojourn there, for the famine was severe in the land. When he was about to enter Egypt, he said to Sarai his wife, "I know that you are a woman beautiful to behold; and when the Egyptians see you, they will say, 'This is his wife'; then they will kill me, but they will let you live. Say you are my sister, that it may go well with me because of you, and that my life may be spared on your account." When Abram entered Egypt the Egyptians saw that the woman was very beautiful. And when the princes of Pharaoh saw her, they praised her to Pharaoh. And the woman was taken into Pharaoh's house. And for her sake he dealt well with Abram; and he had sheep, oxen, he-asses, menservants, maid servants, she-asses, and camels.

But the LORD afflicted Pharaoh and his house with great plagues because of Sarai, Abram's wife. So Pharaoh called Abram, and said, "What is this you have done to me? Why did you not tell me that she was your wife? Why did you say, 'She is my sister,' so that I took her for my wife? Now then, here is your wife, take her, and be gone." And Pharaoh gave men orders concerning him; and they set him on the way, with his wife and all that he had.

(Ch. 13) So Abram went up from Egypt, he and his wife, and all that he had, and Lot with him, into the Negeb.

Now Abram was very rich in cattle, in silver, and in gold. And he journeyed on from the Negeb as far as Bethel, to the place where his tent had been at the beginning, between Bethel and Ai, to the place where he had made an altar; and there Abram called on the name of the LORD. And Lot, who went with Abram, also had flocks and herds and tents.

There was strife between the herdsmen of Abram's cattle and the herdsmen of Lot's cattle. At that time the Canaanites and the Perizzites dwelt in the land.

Then Abram said to Lot, "Let there be no strife between you and me, and between your herdsmen and my herdsmen; for we are kinsmen. Is not the whole land before you? Separate yourself from me. If you take the left hand, then I will go to the right; or if you take the right hand, then I will go to the left." And Lot lifted up his eyes, and saw that the Jordan valley was well watered everywhere like the garden of the LORD, like the land of Egypt in the direction of Zoar; this was before the LORD destroyed Sodom and Gomorrah. So Lot chose for himself all the Jordan valley, and Lot journeyed east. Lot dwelt among the cities of the valley and moved his tent as far as Sodom. Now the men of Sodom were wicked, great sinners against the LORD.

The LORD said to Abram, after Lot had separated from him, "Lift up your eyes, and look from the place where you are, northward and southward and eastward and westward; for all the land which you see I will give to you and to your descendants for ever. I will make your descendants as the dust of the earth; so that if one can count the dust of the earth, your descendants also can be counted. Arise, walk through the length and the breadth of the land, for I will give it to you." So Abram moved his tent, and came and dwelt by the oaks of Mamre, which are at Hebron; and there he built an altar to the LORD.

(Ch. 15) And Abram said to the LORD, "Behold, thou hast given me no offspring; and a slave born in my house will be my heir. And behold, the word of the LORD came to him, "This man shall not be your heir; your own son shall be your heir." And he believed the LORD; and he reckoned it to him as righteousness.

And he said to him, "I am the LORD who brought you from Ur of the Chaldeans, to give you this land to possess." But he said, "O Lord GOD, how am I to know that I shall possess it?" He said to him, "Bring me a heifer three years old, a she-goat three years old, a ram three years old, a turtledove, and a young pigeon." And he brought him all these, cut them in two, and laid each half over against the other; but he did not cut the birds in two. And when birds of prey came down upon the carcasses, Abram drove them away.

As the sun was going down, a deep sleep fell on Abram; and lo, a dread and great darkness fell upon him. Then the LORD said to Abram, "Know of a surety that your descendants will be sojourners in a land that is not theirs, and will be slaves there, and they will be oppressed for four hundred years; but I will bring judgment on the nation which they serve, and afterward they shall come out with great possessions. As for yourself, you shall go to your fathers in peace; you shall be buried in a good old age. And they shall come back here in the fourth generation; for the iniquity of the Amorites is not yet complete."

When the sun had gone down and it was dark, behold, a smoking fire pot and a flaming torch passed between these pieces. On that day the LORD made a covenant with Abram, saying, "To your descendants I give this land, from the river of Egypt to the great river, the river Euphrates, the land of the Kenites, the Kenizzites, the Kadmonites, the Hittites, the Perizzites, the Rephaim, the Amorites, the Canaanites, the Girgashites and the Jebusites."

(Ch. 16) [Sarai] had an Egyptian maid whose name was Hagar; and Sarai said to Abram, "Behold now, the LORD has prevented me from bearing children; go in to my maid; it may be that I shall obtain children by her." And Abram hearkened to the voice of Sarai.

And he went in to Hagar, and she conceived; and when she saw that she had conceived, she looked with contempt on her mistress. And Sarai said to Abram, "May the wrong done to me be on you! I gave my maid to your embrace, and when she saw that she had conceived, she looked on me with contempt. May the LORD judge between you and me!" But Abram said to Sarai, "Behold, your maid is in your power; do to her as you please." Then Sarai dealt harshly with her, and she fled from her.

The angel of the LORD found her by a spring of water in the wilderness, the spring on the way to Shur. And he said, "Hagar, maid of Sarai, where have you come from and where are you going?" She said, "I am fleeing from my mistress Sarai." The angel of the LORD said to her, "Return to your mistress, and submit to her." The angel of the LORD also said to her, "I will so greatly multiply your descendants that they cannot be numbered for multitude." And the angel of the LORD said to her, "Behold, you are with child, and shall bear a son; you shall call his name Ishmael; because the LORD has given heed to your affliction. He shall be a wild ass of a man, his hand against every man and every man's hand against him; and he shall dwell over against all his kinsmen." So she called the name of the LORD who spoke to her, "Thou art a God of seeing"; for she said, "Have I really seen God and remained alive after seeing him?" Therefore the well was called Beer-lahai-roi; it lies between Kadesh and Bered.

(Ch. 18) And the LORD appeared to him by the oaks of Mamre, as he sat at the door of his tent in the heat of the day. He lifted up his eyes and looked, and behold, three men stood in front of him. When he saw them, he ran from the tent door to meet them, and bowed himself to the earth, and said, "My lord, if I have found favor in your sight, do not pass by your servant. Let a little water be brought, and wash your feet, and rest yourselves under the tree, while I fetch a morsel of bread, that you may refresh yourselves, and after that you may pass on—since you have come to your servant." So they said, "Do as you have said." And Abraham hastened into the tent to Sarai, and said, "Make ready quickly three measures of fine meal, knead it, and make cakes." And Abraham ran to the herd, and took a calf, tender and good, and gave it to the servant, who hastened to prepare it. Then he took curds, and milk, and the calf which he had prepared, and set it before them; and he stood by them under the tree while they ate.

They said to him, "Where is Sarai your wife?" And he said, "She is in the tent." He said, "I will surely return to you in the spring, and Sarai your wife shall have a son." And Sarai was listening at the tent door behind him. Now Abraham and Sarai were old, advanced in age; it had ceased to be with Sarai after the manner of women. So Sarai laughed to herself, saying, "After I have grown old, and my husband is old, shall I have pleasure?" The LORD said to Abraham, "Why did Sarai laugh, and say, 'Shall I indeed bear a child now that I am old?' Is anything too hard for the LORD? At the appointed time I will return to you, in the spring, and Sarai shall have a son." But Sarai denied, saying, "I did not laugh"; for she was afraid. He said, "No, but you did laugh."

Then the men set out from there, and they looked toward Sodom; and Abraham went with them to set them on their way. The LORD said, "Shall I hide from Abraham what I am about to do, seeing that Abraham shall become a great and mighty nation, and all the nations of the earth shall bless themselves by him? No, for I have chosen him, that he may charge his children and his household after him to keep the way of the LORD by doing righteousness and justice; so that the LORD may bring to Abraham what he has promised him." Then the LORD said, "Because the outcry against Sodom and Gomorrah is great and their sin is very grave, I will go down to see whether they have done altogether according to the outcry which has come to me; and if not, I will know."

So the men turned from there, and went toward Sodom; but Abraham still stood before the LORD. Then Abraham drew near, and said, "Wilt thou indeed destroy the righteous with the wicked? Suppose there are fifty righteous within the city; wilt thou then destroy the place and not spare it for the fifty righteous who are in it? Far be it from thee to do such a thing, to slay the righteous with the wicked so that the righteous fare as the wicked! Far be that from thee! Shall not the Judge of all the earth do right?" And the LORD said, "If I find at Sodom fifty righteous in the city, I will spare the whole place for their sake." Abraham answered, "Behold, I have taken upon myself to speak to the Lord, I who am but dust and ashes. Suppose five of the fifty righteous are lacking? Wilt thou destroy the whole city for lack of five?" And he said, "I will not destroy it if I find forty-five there." Again he spoke to him, and said, "Suppose forty are found there." He answered, "For the sake of forty I will not do it." Then he said, "Oh let not the Lord be angry, and I will speak. Suppose thirty are found there." He answered, "I will not do it, if I find thirty there." He said, "Behold, I have taken upon myself to speak to the Lord. Suppose twenty are found there." He answered, "For the sake of twenty I will not destroy it." Then he said, "Oh let not the Lord be angry, and I will speak again but this once. Suppose ten are found there." He answered, "For the sake of ten I will not destroy it." And the LORD went his way, when he finished speaking to Abraham; and Abraham returned to his place.

(Ch. 19) The two angels came to Sodom in the evening; and Lot was sitting in the gate of Sodom. When Lot saw them, he rose to meet them, and bowed himself with his face to the earth, and said, "My lords, turn aside, I pray you, to your servant's house and spend the night, and wash your feet; then you may rise up early and go on your way." They said, "No; we will spend the night in the street." But he urged them strongly; so they turned aside to him and entered his house; and he made them a feast, and baked unleavened bread, and they ate. But before they lay down, the men of the city, the men of Sodom, both young and old, all the people to the last man, surrounded the house; and they called to Lot, "Where are the men who came to you tonight? Bring them out to us, that we may know them." Lot went out of the door to the men, shut the door after him, and said, "I beg you, my brothers, do not act so wickedly. Behold, I have two daughters who have not known man; let me bring them out to you, and do to them as you please; only do nothing to these men, for they have come under the shelter of my roof." But they said, "Stand back!" And they said, "This fellow came to sojourn, and he would play the judge! Now we will deal worse with you than with them." Then they pressed hard against the man Lot, and drew near to break the door. But the men put forth their hands and brought Lot into the house to them, and shut the door. And they struck with blindness the men who were at the door of the house, both small and great, so that they wearied themselves groping for the door.

Then the men said to Lot, "Have you any one else here? Sons-in-law, sons, daughters, or any one you have in the city, bring them out of the place; for we are about to destroy this place, because the outcry against its people has become great before the LORD, and the LORD has sent us to destroy it." So Lot went out and said to his sons-in-law, who were to marry his daughters, "Up, get out of this place; for the LORD is about to destroy the city." But he seemed to his sons-in-law to be jesting.

When morning dawned, the angels urged Lot, saying, "Arise, take your wife and your two daughters who are here, lest you be consumed in the punishment of the city." But he lingered; so the men seized him and his wife and his two daughters by the hand, the LORD being merciful to him, and they brought him forth and set him outside the city. And when they had brought them forth, they said, "Flee for your life; do not look back or stop anywhere in the valley; flee to the hills, lest you be consumed." And Lot said to them, "Oh, no, my lords; behold, your servant has found favor in your sight, and you have shown me great kindness in saving my life; but I cannot flee to the hills, lest the disaster overtake me, and I die. Behold, yonder city is near enough to flee to, and it is a little one. Let me escape there—is it not a little one?—and my life will be saved!" He said to him, "Behold, I grant you this favor also, that I will not overthrow the city of which you have spoken. Make haste, escape there; for I can do nothing till you arrive there." Therefore the name of the city was called Zoar. The sun had risen on the earth when Lot came to Zoar.

Then the LORD rained on Sodom and Gomorrah brimstone and fire from the LORD out of heaven; and he overthrew those cities, and all the valley, and all the inhabitants of the cities, and what grew on the ground. But Lot's wife behind him looked back, and she became a pillar of salt. And Abraham went early in the morning to the place where he had stood before the LORD; and he looked down toward Sodom and Gomorrah and toward all the land of the valley, and beheld, and lo, the smoke of the land went up like the smoke of a furnace.

Now Lot went up out of Zoar, and dwelt in the hills with his two daughters, for he was afraid to dwell in Zoar; so he dwelt in a cave with his two daughters. And the firstborn said to the younger, "Our father is old, and there is not a man on earth to come in to us after the manner of all the earth. Come, let us make our father drink wine, and we will lie with him, that we may preserve offspring through our father." So they made their father drink wine that night; and the first-born went in, and lay with her father; he did not know when she lay down or when she arose. And on the next day, the first-born said to the younger, "Behold, I lay last night with my father; let us make him drink wine tonight also; then you go in and lie with him, that we may preserve offspring through our father." So they made their father drink wine that night also; and the younger arose, and lay with him; and he did not know when she lay down or when she arose. Thus both the daughters of Lot were with child by their father. The first-born bore a son, and called his name Moab; he is the father of the Moabites to this day. The younger also bore a son, and called his name Ben-ammi; he is the father of the Ammonites to this day.

(Ch. 21) The LORD visited Sarai as he had said. And Sarai conceived, and bore Abraham a son in his old age. . . . Abraham planted a tamarisk tree in Beer-sheba, and called there on the name of the LORD, the Everlasting God. . . .

(Ch. 22) Now after these things it was told Abraham, "Behold, Milcah also has borne children to your brother Nahor: Uz the first-born, Buz his brother, Kemuel the father of Aram, Chesed, Hazo, Pildash, Jidlaph, and Bethuel. Bethuel became the father of Rebekah. These eight Milcah bore to Nahor, Abraham's brother. Moreover, his concubine, whose name was Reumah, bore Tebah, Gaham, Tahash, and Maacah.

(Ch. 24) Now Abraham was old, well advanced in years; and the LORD had blessed Abraham in all things. And Abraham said to his servant, the oldest of his house, who had charge of all that he had, "Put your hand under my thigh, and I will make you swear by the LORD, the God of heaven and of the earth, that you will not take a wife for my son from the daughters of the Canaanites, among whom I dwell, but will go to my country and to my kindred, and take a wife for my son Isaac." The servant said to him, "Perhaps the woman may not be willing to follow me to this land; must I then take your son back to the land from which you came?" Abraham said to him, "See to it that you do not take my son back there. The LORD, the God of heaven, who took me from my father's house and from the land of my birth, and who spoke to me and swore to me, 'To your descendants I will give this land,' he will send his angel before you, and you shall take a wife for my son from there. But if the woman is not willing to follow you, then you will be free from this oath of mine; only you must not take my son back there." So the servant put his hand under the thigh of Abraham his master, and swore to him concerning this matter.

Then the servant took ten of his master's camels and departed, taking all sorts of choice gifts from his master; and he arose, and went to Mesopotamia, to the city of Nahor. And he made the camels kneel down outside the city by the well of water at the time of evening, the time when women go out to draw water. And he said, "O LORD, God of my master Abraham, grant me success today, I pray thee, and show steadfast love to my master Abraham. Behold, I am standing by the spring of water, and the daughters of the men of the city are coming out to draw water. Let the maiden to whom I shall say, 'Pray let down your jar that I may drink,' and who shall say, 'Drink, and I will water your camels'—let her be the one whom thou hast appointed for thy servant Isaac. By this I shall know that thou hast shown steadfast love to my master."

Before he had done speaking, behold, Rebekah, who was born to Bethuel the son of Milcah, the wife of Nahor, Abraham's brother, came out with her water jar upon her shoulder. The maiden was very fair to look upon, a virgin, whom no man had known. She went down to the spring, and filled her jar, and came up. Then the servant ran to meet her, and said, "Pray give me a little water to drink from your jar." She said, "Drink, my lord"; and she quickly let down her jar upon her hand, and gave him a drink. When she had finished giving him a drink, she said, "I will draw for your camels also, until they have done drinking." So she quickly emptied her jar into the trough and ran again to the well to draw, and she drew for all his camels. The man gazed at her in silence to learn whether the LORD had prospered his journey or not.

When the camels had done drinking, the man took a gold ring weighing a half shekel, and two bracelets for her arms weighing ten gold shekels, and said, "Tell me whose daughter you are. Is there room in your father's house for us to lodge in?" She said to him, "I am the daughter of Bethuel the son of Milcah, whom she bore to Nahor." She added, "We have both straw and provender enough, and room to lodge in." The man bowed his head and worshiped the LORD, and said, "Blessed be the LORD, the God of my master Abraham, who has not forsaken his steadfast love and his faithfulness toward my master. As for me, the LORD has led me in the way to the house of my master's kinsmen."

Then the maiden ran and told her mother's household about these things. Rebekah had a brother whose name was Laban; and Laban ran out to the man, to the spring. When he saw the ring, and the bracelets on his sister's arms, and when he heard the words of Rebekah his sister, "Thus the man spoke to me," he went to the man; and behold, he was standing by the camels at the spring. He said, "Come in, O blessed of the LORD; why do you stand outside? For I have prepared the house and a place for the camels." So the man came into the house; and Laban ungirded the camels, and gave him straw and provender for the camels, and water to wash his feet and the feet of the men who were with him. Then food was set before him to eat; but he said, "I will not eat until I have told my errand." He said, "Speak on."

So he said, "I am Abraham's servant. The LORD has greatly blessed my master, and he has become great; he has given him flocks and herds, silver and gold, menservants and maidservants, camels and asses. And Sarai my master's wife bore a son to my master when she was old; and to him he has given all that he has. My master made me swear, saying, 'You shall not take a wife for my son from the daughters of the Canaanites, in whose land I dwell; but you shall go to my father's house and to my kindred and take a wife for my son.' I said to my master, 'Perhaps the woman will not follow me.' But he said to me, 'The LORD, before whom I walk, will send his angel with you and prosper your way; and you shall take a wife for my son from my kindred and from my father's house; then you will be free from my oath, when you come to my kindred; and if they will not give her to you, you will be free from my oath.'

"I came today to the spring, and said, 'O LORD, the God of my master Abraham, if now thou wilt prosper the way which I go, behold, I am standing by the spring of water; let the young woman who comes out to draw, to whom I shall say, "Pray give me a little water from your jar to drink," and who will say to me, "Drink, and I will draw for your camels also," let her be the woman whom the LORD has appointed for my master's son.'

"Before I had done speaking in my heart,

behold, Rebekah came out with her water jar on her shoulder; and she went down to the spring, and drew. I said to her, 'Pray let me drink.' She quickly let down her jar from her shoulder, and said, 'Drink, and I will give your camels drink also.' So I drank, and she gave the camels drink also. Then I asked her, 'Whose daughter are you?' She said, 'The daughter of Bethuel, Nahor's son, whom Milcah bore to him.' So I put the ring on her nose, and the bracelets on her arms. Then I bowed my head and worshiped the LORD, and blessed the LORD, the God of my master Abraham, who had led me by the right way to take the daughter of my master's kinsman for his son. Now then, if you will deal loyally and truly with my master, tell me; and if not, tell me; that I may turn to the right hand or to the left."

Then Laban and Bethuel answered, "The thing comes from the LORD; we cannot speak to you bad or good. Behold, Rebekah is before you, take her and go, and let her be the wife of your master's son, as the LORD has spoken."

When Abraham's servant heard their words, he bowed himself to the earth before the LORD. And the servant brought forth jewelry of silver and of gold, and raiment, and gave them to Rebekah; he also gave to her brother and to her mother costly ornaments. And he and the men who were with him ate and drank, and they spent the night there. When they arose in the morning, he said, "Send me back to my master." Her brother and her mother said, "Let the maiden remain with us a while, at least ten days; after that she may go." But he said to them, "Do not delay me, since the LORD has prospered my way; let me go that I may go to my master." They said, "We will call the maiden, and ask her." And they called Rebekah, and said to her, "Will you go with this man?" She said, "I will go." So they sent away Rebekah their sister and her nurse, and Abraham's servant and his men. And they blessed Rebekah, and said to her, "Our sister, be the mother of thousands of ten thousands; and may your descendants possess the gate of those who hate them!" Then Rebekah and her maids arose, and rode upon the camels and followed the man; thus the servant took Rebekah, and went his way.

Now Isaac had come from Beer-lahai-roi, and was dwelling in the Negeb. And Isaac went out to meditate in the field in the evening; and he lifted up his eyes and looked, and behold, there were camels coming. And Rebekah lifted up her eyes, and when she saw Isaac, she alighted from the camel, and said to the servant, "Who is the man yonder, walking in the field to meet us?" The servant said, "It is my master." So she took her veil and covered herself. And the servant told Isaac all the things that he had done. Then Isaac brought her into the tent, and took Rebekah, and she became his wife; and he loved her. So Isaac was comforted after his mother's death.

(Ch. 25) Abraham took another wife, whose name was Keturah. She bore him Zimran, Jokshan, Medan, Midian, Ishbak, and Shuah. Joshan was the father of Sheba and Dedan. The sons of Dedan were Asshurim, Letushim, and Leummim. The sons of Midian were Ephah, Epher, Hanoch, Abida, and Eldaah. All these were the children of Keturah. Abraham gave all he had to Isaac. But to the sons of his concubines Abraham gave gifts, and while he was still living he sent them away from his son Isaac, eastward to the east country. And Isaac dwelt at Beer-lahai-roi.

[The Yahwist Epic continues with the stories of Isaac, Jacob, and Joseph; then follows the account of Moses and the Exodus (see below). Parts of Numbers and Judges (Chapter 1) are also from the Epic.]

2. *Moses and the Exodus*

The following account of the birth and call of Moses and the exodus of the Israelites from Egypt is a mixture of three of the Pentateuchal sources, J, E, and P. They are identified in square brackets; it will be noted that occasionally the sources cannot be distinguished from each other, and two or more symbols are used. The letter "R" stands for one of the editors who brought the sources together in their present form.

[Ex. 1:1–7:13; 11:10–19:26; 24, FOLLOWING THE ANALYSIS OF A. H. MCNEILE, *The Book of Exodus* (WESTMINSTER COMMENTARIES). LONDON: METHUEN & CO., LTD., 1908.]

(Ch. 1) [P] These are the names of the sons of Israel who came to Egypt with Jacob, each with his household: Reuben, Simeon, Levi, and Judah, Issachar, Zebulun, and Benjamin, Dan and Naphtali, Gad and Asher. All the offspring of Jacob were seventy persons; Joseph was already in Egypt. [J] Then Joseph died, and all his brothers, and all that generation. [P] But the descendants of Israel were fruitful and increased greatly; they multiplied and grew exceedingly strong; so that the land was filled with them.

[J] Now there arose a new king over Egypt, who did not know Joseph. And he said to his people, "Behold, the people of Israel are too many and too mighty for us. Come, let us deal shrewdly with them, lest they multiply, and, if war befall us, they join our enemies and fight against us and escape from the land." Therefore they set taskmasters over them to afflict them with heavy burdens; and they built for Pharaoh store-cities, Pithom and Raamses. But the more they were oppressed, the more they multiplied and the more they spread abroad. And the Egyptians were in dread of the people of Israel. [P] So they made the people of Israel serve with rigor, [J] and made their lives bitter with hard service, in mortar and brick, and in all kinds of work in the field; [R^P] in all their work they made them serve with rigor.

[E] Then the king of Egypt said to the Hebrew midwives, one of whom was named Shiphrah and the other Puah, "When you serve as midwife to the Hebrew women, and see them upon the birthstool, if it is a son, you shall kill him; but if it is a daughter, she shall live." But the midwives feared God, and did not do as the king of Egypt commanded them, but let the male children live. So the king of Egypt called the midwives, and said to them, "Why have you done this, and let the male children live?" The midwives said to Pharaoh, "Because the Hebrew women are not like the Egyptian women; for they are vigorous and are delivered before the midwife comes to them." So God dealt well with the midwives; [J] and the people multiplied and grew very strong. [E] And because the midwives feared God he gave them families. [J] Then Pharaoh commanded all his people, "Every son that is born to the Hebrews you shall cast into the Nile, but you shall let every daughter live."

(Ch. 2) [E] Now a man from the house of Levi went and took to wife a daughter of Levi. The woman conceived and bore a son; and when she saw that he was a goodly child, she hid him three months. And when she could hide him no longer she took for him a basket made of bulrushes, and daubed it with bitumen and pitch; and she put the child in it and placed it among the reeds at the river's brink. And his sister stood at a distance, to know what would be done to him. Now the daughter of Pharaoh came down to bathe at the river, and her maidens walked beside the river; she saw the basket among the reeds and sent her maid to fetch it. When she opened it she saw the child; and lo, the babe was crying. She took pity on him and said, "This is one of the Hebrews' children." Then his sister said to Pharaoh's daughter, "Shall I go and call you a nurse from the Hebrew women to nurse the child for you?" And Pharaoh's daughter said to her, "Go." So the girl went and called the child's mother. And Pharaoh's daughter said to her, "Take this child away, and nurse him for me, and I will give you your wages." So the woman took the child and nursed him. And the child grew, and she brought him to Pharaoh's daughter, and he became her son; and she named him Moses, for she said, "Because I drew him out of the water."

[J] One day, when Moses had grown up, he went out to his people and looked on their burdens; and he saw an Egyptian beating a Hebrew, one of his people. He looked this way and that, and seeing no one he killed the Egyptian and hid him in the sand. When he went out the next day, behold, two Hebrews were struggling together; and he said to the man that did the wrong, "Why do you strike your fellow?" He answered, "Who made you a prince and a judge over us? Do you mean to kill me as you killed the Egyptian?" Then Moses was afraid, and thought, "Surely the thing is known." When Pharaoh heard of it, he sought to kill Moses.

But Moses fled from Pharaoh, and stayed in the land of Midian; and he sat down by a well. Now the priest of Midian had seven daughters; and they came and drew water, and filled the troughs to water their father's flock. The shepherds came and drove them away; but Moses stood up and helped them, and watered their flock. When they came to their father Reuel, he said, "How is it that you have come so soon today?" They said, "An Egyptian delivered us out of the hand of the shepherds, and even drew water for us and watered the flock." He said to his daughters, "And where is he? Why have you left the man? Call him, that he may eat bread." And Moses was content to dwell with the man, and he gave Moses his daughter Zipporah. She bore a son and he called his name Gershom; for he said, "I have been a sojourner in a foreign land."

In the course of those many days the king of Egypt died. [P] And the people of Israel groaned under their bondage, and cried out for help, and their cry under bondage came up to God. And God heard their groaning, and God remembered his covenant with Abraham, with Isaac, and with Jacob. And God saw the people of Israel, and God knew their condition.

(Ch. 3) [E] Now Moses was keeping the flock of his father-in-law, Jethro, the priest of Midian; and he led his flock to the west side of the wilderness, and came to Horeb, the mountain of God. [J] And the angel of the LORD appeared to him in a flame of fire out of the midst of a bush; and he looked, and lo, the bush was burning, yet it was not consumed. And Moses said, "I will turn aside and see this great sight, why the bush is not burnt." When the LORD saw that he turned aside to see, [E] God called to him out of the bush, "Moses, Moses!" And he said, "Here am I." [J] Then he said, "Do not come near; put off your shoes from your feet, for the place on which you are standing is holy ground." [E] And he said, "I am the God of your father, the God of Abraham, the God of Isaac, and the God of Jacob." And Moses hid his face, for he was afraid to look at God.

[J] Then the LORD said, "I have seen the affliction of my people who are in Egypt, and have heard their cry because of their taskmasters; I know their sufferings, and I have come down to deliver them out of the hand of the Egyptians, and to bring them up out of that land to a good and broad land, a land flowing with milk and honey, to the place of the Canaanites, [R^{D}] the Hittites, the Amorites, the Perizzites, the Hivites, and Jebusites. [E] And now, behold, the cry of the people of Israel has come to me, and I have seen the oppression with which the Egyptians oppress them. Come, I will send you to Pharaoh that you may bring forth my people, the sons of Israel, out of Egypt." But Moses said to God, "Who am I that I should go to Pharaoh, and bring the sons of Israel out of Egypt?" He said, "But I will be with you; and this shall be the sign for you, that I have sent you: when you have brought forth the people out of Egypt, you shall serve God upon this mountain."

Then Moses said to God, "If I come to the people of Israel and say to them, 'The God of your fathers has sent me to you,' and they ask me, 'What is his name?' what shall I say to them?" God said to Moses, "I AM WHO I AM." And he said "Say this to the people of Israel, 'I AM has sent me to you.' " [R^{JE}] God also said to Moses, "Say this to the people of Israel, 'The LORD, the God of your fathers, the God of Abraham, the God of Isaac, and the God of Jacob, has sent me to you': this is my name for ever, and thus I am to be remembered throughout all generations. [J] Go and gather the elders of Israel together, and say to them, 'The LORD, the God of your fathers, the God of Abraham, of Isaac, and of Jacob, has appeared to me, saying, "I have observed you and what has been done to you in Egypt; and I promise that I will bring you up out of the affliction of Egypt, to the land of the Canaanites, the Hittites, the Amorites, the Perizzites, the Hivites, and the Jebusites, a land flowing with milk and honey." ' And they will hearken to your voice; and you and the elders of Israel shall go to the king of Egypt and say to him 'The LORD, the God of the Hebrews, has met with us; and now, we pray you, let us go a three days' journey into the wilderness, that we may sacrifice to the LORD our God.' [R^{JE}] I know that the king of Egypt will not let you go unless compelled by a mighty hand. So I will stretch out my hand and smite Egypt with all the wonders which I will do in it; after that he will let you go. [E] And I will give this people favor in the sight of the Egyptians; and when you go, you shall not go empty, but each woman shall ask of her neighbor, and of her who sojourns in her house, jewelry of silver and of gold, and clothing, and you shall put them on your sons and on your daughters; thus you shall despoil the Egyptians."

(Ch. 4) [J] Then Moses answered, "But behold, they will not believe me or listen to my voice, for they will say, 'The LORD did not appear to you.'" The LORD said to him, "What is that in your hand?" He said, "A rod." And he said, "Cast it on the ground." So he cast it on the ground, and it became a serpent; and Moses fled from it. But the LORD said to Moses, "Put out your hand, and take it by the tail"—so he put out his hand and caught it, and it became a rod in his hand—"that they may believe that the LORD, the God of their fathers, the God of Abraham, the God of Isaac, and the God of Jacob, has appeared to you." Again, the LORD said to him, "Put your hand into your bosom." And he put his hand into his bosom; and when he took it out, behold, his hand was leprous, as white as snow. Then God said, "Put your hand back into your bosom." So he put his hand back into his bosom; and when he took it out, behold, it was restored like the rest of his flesh. "If they will not believe you," God said, "or heed the first sign, they may believe the latter sign. If they will not believe even these two signs or heed your voice, you shall take some water from the Nile and pour it upon the dry ground; and the water which you shall take from the Nile will become blood upon the dry ground."

But Moses said to the LORD, "Oh, my Lord, I am not eloquent, either heretofore or since thou hast spoken to thy servant; but I am slow of speech and of tongue." Then the LORD said to him, "Who has made man's mouth? Who makes him dumb, or deaf, or seeing, or blind? Is it not I, the LORD? Now therefore go, and I will be with your mouth and teach you what you shall speak." [R^{JE}] But he said, "Oh, my Lord, send, I pray, some other person." Then the anger of the LORD was kindled against Moses and he said, "Is there not Aaron, your brother, the Levite? I know that he can speak well; and behold, he is coming out to meet you, and when he sees you he will be glad in his heart. And you shall speak to him and put the words in his mouth; and I will be with your mouth and with his mouth, and will teach you what you shall do. He shall speak for you to the people; and he shall be a mouth for you, and you shall be to him as God. [E] And you shall take in your hand this rod, with which you shall do the signs."

Moses went back to Jethro his father-in-law and said to him, "Let me go back, I pray, to my kinsmen in Egypt and see whether they are still alive." And Jethro said to Moses, "Go in peace." [J] And the LORD said to Moses in Midian, "Go back to Egypt; for all the men who were seeking your life are dead." So Moses took his wife and his sons and set them on an ass, and went back to the land of Egypt; [E] and in his hand Moses took the rod of God.

[R^{JE}] And the LORD said to Moses, "When you go back to Egypt, see that you do before Pharaoh all the miracles which I have put in your power; but I will harden his heart, so that he will not let the people go. And you shall say to Pharaoh, 'Thus says the LORD, Israel is my first-born son, and I say to you, "Let my son go that he may serve me"; if you refuse to let him go, behold, I will slay your first-born son.'"

[J] At a lodging place on the way the LORD met him and sought to kill him. Then Zipporah took a flint and cut off her son's foreskin, and touched Moses' feet with it, and said, "Surely you are a bridegroom of blood to me!" So he let him alone. Then it was that she said, "You are a bridegroom of blood," because of the circumcision.

[E] The LORD said to Aaron, "Go into the wilderness to meet Moses." So he went, and met him at the mountain of God and kissed him. And Moses told Aaron all the words of the LORD with which he had sent him, and all the signs which he had charged him to do. [J] Then Moses and Aaron went and gathered together all the elders of the people of Israel. And Aaron spoke all the words which the LORD had spoken to Moses, and did the signs in the sight of the people. And the people believed;

and when they heard that the LORD had visited the people of Israel and that he had seen their affliction, they bowed their heads and worshiped.

(Ch. 5) [E] Afterward Moses and Aaron went to Pharaoh and said, "Thus says the LORD, the God of Israel, 'Let my people go, that they may hold a feast to me in the wilderness.'" But Pharaoh said, "Who is the LORD, that I should heed his voice and let Israel go? I do not know the LORD, and moreover I will not let Israel go." [J] Then they said, "The God of the Hebrews has met with us; let us go, we pray, a three days' journey into the wilderness, and sacrifice to the LORD our God, lest he fall upon us with pestilence or with the sword." [E] But the king of Egypt said to them, "Moses and Aaron, why do you take the people away from their work? Get to your burdens." [J] And Pharaoh said, "Behold, the people of the land are now many and you make them rest from their burdens!" The same day Pharaoh commanded the taskmasters of the people and their foremen, "You shall no longer give the people straw to make bricks, as heretofore; let them go and gather straw for themselves. But the number of bricks which they made heretofore you shall lay upon them, you shall by no means lessen it; for they are idle; therefore they cry, 'Let us go and offer sacrifice to our God.' Let heavier work be laid upon the men that they may labor at it and pay no regard to lying words."

So the taskmasters and the foremen of the people went out and said to the people, "Thus says Pharaoh, 'I will not give you straw. Go yourselves, get your straw wherever you can find it; but your work will not be lessened in the least.'" So the people were scattered abroad throughout all the land of Egypt, to gather stubble for straw. The taskmasters were urgent, saying, "Complete your work, your daily task, as when there was straw." And the foremen of the people of Israel, whom Pharaoh's taskmasters had set over them, were beaten, and were asked, "Why have you not done all your task of making bricks today, as hitherto?"

Then the foremen of the people of Israel came and cried to Pharaoh, "Why do you deal thus with your servants? No straw is given to your servants, yet they say to us, 'Make bricks!' And behold, your servants are beaten; but the fault is in your own people." But he said, "You are idle, you are idle; therefore you say, 'Let us go and sacrifice to the LORD.' Go now, and work; for no straw shall be given you, yet you shall deliver the same number of bricks." The foremen of the people of Israel saw that they were in evil plight, when they said, "You shall by no means lessen your daily number of bricks." They met Moses and Aaron, who were waiting for them, as they came forth from Pharaoh; and they said to them, "The LORD look upon you and judge, because you have made us offensive in the sight of Pharaoh and his servants, and have put a sword in their hand to kill us."

Then Moses turned again to the LORD and said, "O LORD, why hast thou done evil to this people? Why didst thou ever send me? For since I came to Pharaoh to speak in thy name, he has done evil to this people, and thou hast not delivered thy people at all."

(Ch. 6) But the LORD said to Moses, "Now you shall see what I will do to Pharaoh; for with a strong hand he will send them out, yea, with a strong hand he will drive them out of his land."

[P] And God said to Moses, "I am the LORD. I appeared to Abraham, to Isaac, and to Jacob, as God Almighty, but by my name the LORD I did not make myself known to them. I also established my covenant with them, to give them the land of Canaan, the land in which they dwelt as sojourners. Moreover I have heard the groaning of the people of Israel whom the Egyptians hold in bondage and I have remembered my covenant. Say therefore to the people of Israel, 'I am the LORD, and I will bring you out from under the burdens of the Egyptians, and I will deliver you from their bondage, and I will redeem you with an outstretched arm and with great acts of judgment, and I will take you for my people, and I will be your God; and you shall know that I am the LORD your God, who has brought you out from under the burdens of the Egyptians. And I will bring you into the land which I swore to give to Abraham, to Isaac, and to Jacob; I will give it to you for a possession. I am the LORD.'" Moses spoke thus to the people of Israel; but they did not listen to Moses, because of the broken spirit and their cruel bondage.

And the LORD said to Moses, "Go in, tell Pharaoh king of Egypt to let the people of Israel go out of his land." But Moses said to the LORD, "Behold, the people of Israel have not listened to me; how then shall Pharaoh listen to me, who am a man of uncircumcised lips?" [R^P] But the LORD spoke to Moses and Aaron, and gave them a charge to the people of Israel and to Pharaoh king of Egypt to bring the people of Israel out of the land of Egypt.

These are the heads of their fathers' houses: the sons of Reuben, the first-born of Israel: Hanoch, Pallu, Hezron, and Carmi; these are the families of Reuben. The sons of Simeon: Jemuel, Jamin, Ohad, Jachin, Zohar, and Shaul, the son of a Canaanite woman; these are the families of Simeon. These are the names of the sons of Levi according to their generations: Gershon, Kohath, and Merari, the years of the life of Levi being a hundred and thirty-seven years. The sons of Gershon: Libni and Shimei, by their families. The sons of Kohath: Amram, Izhar, Hebron, and Uzziel, the years of the life of Kohath being a hundred and thirty-three years. The sons of Merari: Mahli and Mushi. These are the families of the Levites according to their generations. Amram took to wife Jochebed his father's sister and she bore him Aaron and Moses, the years of the life of Amram being one hundred and thirty-seven years. The sons of Izhar: Korah, Nepheg, and Zichri. And the sons of Uzziel: Mishael, Elzaphan, and Sithri. Aaron took to wife Elisheba, the daughter of Amminadab and the sister of Nahshon; and she bore him Nadab, Abihu, Eleazar, and Ithamar. The sons of Korah: Assir, Elkanah, and Abiasaph; these are the families of the Korahites. Eleazar, Aaron's son, took to wife one of the daughters of Putiel; and she bore him Phinehas. These are the heads of the fathers' houses of the Levites by their families.

These are the Aaron and Moses to whom the LORD said: "Bring out the people of Israel from the land of Egypt by their hosts." It was they who spoke to Pharaoh king of Egypt about bringing out the people of Israel from Egypt, this Moses and this Aaron.

On the day when the LORD spoke to Moses in the land of Egypt, the LORD said to Moses, "I am the LORD; tell Pharaoh king of Egypt all that I say to you." But Moses said to the LORD, "Behold, I am of uncircumcised lips; how then shall Pharaoh listen to me?"

(Ch. 7) [P] And the LORD said to Moses, "See, I make you as God to Pharaoh; and Aaron your brother shall be your prophet. You shall speak all that I command you; and Aaron your brother shall tell Pharaoh to let the people of Israel go out of his land. But I will harden Pharaoh's heart, and though I multiply my signs and wonders in the land of Egypt, Pharaoh will not listen to you; then I will lay my hand upon Egypt and bring forth my hosts, my people the sons of Israel, out of the land of Egypt by great acts of judgment. And the Egyptians shall know that I am the LORD, when I stretch forth my hand upon Egypt and bring out the people of Israel from among them." And Moses and Aaron did so; they did as the LORD commanded them. Now Moses was eighty years old, and Aaron eighty-three years old, when they spoke to Pharaoh.

And the LORD said to Moses and Aaron, "When Pharaoh says to you, 'Prove yourselves by working a miracle,' then you shall say to Aaron, 'Take your rod and cast it down before Pharaoh, that it may become a serpent.'" So Moses and Aaron went to Pharaoh and did as the LORD commanded; Aaron cast down his rod before Pharaoh and his servants, and it became a serpent. Then Pharaoh summoned the wise men and the sorcerers; and they also, the magicians of Egypt, did the same by their secret arts. For every man cast down his rod, and they became serpents. But Aaron's rod swallowed up their rods. Still Pharaoh's heart was hardened, and he would not listen to them; as the LORD had said.

[Here follows (7:14–11:9) the story of the plagues (blood, frogs, gnats, flies, etc.) and God's word that all of the Egyptian first-born would be killed, but that the Israelites would be saved.]

(Ch. 11) [R^{JE}] Moses and Aaron did all these wonders before Pharaoh; and the LORD hardened Pharaoh's heart, and he did not let the people of Israel go out of his land.

(Ch. 12) [P] The LORD said to Moses and Aaron in the land of Egypt, "This month shall be for you the beginning of months; it shall be the first month of the year for you. Tell all the congregation of Israel that on the tenth day of this month they shall take every man a lamb according to their fathers' houses, a lamb for a household; and if the household is too small for a lamb, then a man and his neighbor next to his house shall take according to the number of persons; according to what each can eat you shall make your count for the lamb. Your lamb shall be without blemish, a male a year old; you shall take it from the sheep or from the goats; and you shall keep it until the fourteenth day of this month, when the whole assembly of the congregation of Israel shall kill their lambs in the evening. Then they shall take some of the blood, and put it on the two doorposts and the lintel of the houses in which they eat them. They shall eat the flesh that night, roasted; with unleavened bread and bitter herbs they shall eat it. Do not eat any of it raw or boiled with water, but roasted, its head with its legs and its inner parts. And you shall let none of it remain until the morning, anything that remains until the morning you shall burn. In this manner you shall eat it: your loins girded, your sandals on your feet, and your staff in your hand; and you shall eat it in haste. It is the LORD's passover. For I will pass through the land of Egypt that night, and I will smite all the first-born in the land of Egypt, both man and beast; and on all the gods of Egypt I will execute judgments: I am the LORD. The blood shall be a sign for you, upon the houses where you are; and when I see the blood, I will pass over you, and no plague shall fall upon you to destroy you, when I smite the land of Egypt.

"This day shall be for you a memorial day, and you shall keep it as a feast to the LORD; throughout your generations you shall observe it as an ordinance for ever. Seven days you shall eat unleavened bread; on the first day you shall put away leaven out of your houses, for if any one eats what is leavened, from the first day until the seventh day, that person shall be cut off from Israel. On the first day you shall hold a holy assembly, and on the seventh day a holy assembly; no work shall be done on those days; but what every one must eat, that only may be prepared by you. And you shall observe the feast of unleavened bread, for on this very day I brought your hosts out of the land of Egypt: therefore you shall observe this day, throughout your generations, as an ordinance for ever. In the first month, on the fourteenth day of the month at evening, you shall eat unleavened bread, and so until the twenty-first day of the month at evening. For seven days no leaven shall be found in your houses; for if any one eats what is leavened, that person shall be cut off from the congregation of Israel, whether he is a sojourner or a native of the land. You shall eat nothing leavened; in all your dwellings you shall eat unleavened bread."

[J] Then Moses called all the elders of Israel, and said to them, "Select lambs for yourselves according to your families, and kill the passover lamb. Take a bunch of hyssop and dip it in the blood which is in the basin, and touch the lintel and the two doorposts with the blood which is in the basin; and none of you shall go out of the door of his house until the morning. For the LORD will pass through to slay the Egyptians; and when he sees the blood on the lintel and on the two doorposts, the LORD will pass over the door, and will not allow the destroyer to enter your houses to slay you. [P] You shall observe this rite as an ordinance for you and for your sons for ever. [R^D] And when you come to the land which the LORD will give you, as he has promised, you shall keep this service. And when your children say to you, 'What do you mean by this service?' you shall say, 'It is the sacrifice of the LORD's passover, for he passed over the houses of the people of Israel in Egypt, when he slew the Egyptians but spared our houses.' " [J] And the people bowed their heads and worshiped.

[P] Then the people of Israel went and did so; as the LORD had commanded Moses and Aaron, so they did.

[J] At midnight the LORD smote all the first-born of Egypt, from the first-born of Pharaoh who sat on his throne to the first-born of the captive who was in the dungeon, and all the first-born of the cattle. And Pharaoh rose up in the night, he, and all his servants, and all the Egyptians; and there was a great cry in Egypt, for there was not a house where one was not dead. And he summoned Moses and Aaron by night, and said, "Rise up, go forth from among my people, both you and the people of Israel; and go, serve the LORD, as you have said. Take your flocks and your herds, as you have said, and be gone; and bless me also!"

And the Egyptians were urgent with the people, to send them out of the land in haste; for they said, "We are all dead men." So the people took their dough before it was leavened, their kneading bowls being bound up in their mantles on their shoulders. [E] The people of Israel had also done as Moses told them, for they had asked of the Egyptians jewelry of silver and of gold, and clothing; and the LORD had given the people favor in the sight of the Egyptians, so that they let them have what they asked. Thus they despoiled the Egyptians.

[J] And the people of Israel journeyed from Rameses to Succoth, about six hundred thousand men on foot, besides women and children. A mixed multitude also went up with them, and very many cattle, both flocks and herds. And they baked unleavened cakes of the dough which they had brought out of Egypt, for it was not leavened, because they were thrust out of Egypt and could not tarry, neither had they prepared for themselves any provisions.

[R^P] The time that the people of Israel dwelt in Egypt was four hundred and thirty years. And at the end of four hundred and thirty years, on that very day, all the hosts of the LORD went out from the land of Egypt. It was a night of watching by the LORD, to bring them out of the land of Egypt; so this same night is a night of watching kept to the LORD by all the people of Israel throughout their generations.

[P] And the LORD said to Moses and Aaron, "This is the ordinance of the passover: no foreigner shall eat of it; but every slave that is bought for money may eat of it after you have circumcised him. No sojourner or hired servant may eat of it. In one house shall it be eaten; you shall not carry forth any of the flesh outside the house; and you shall not break a bone of it. All the congregation of Israel shall keep it. And when a stranger shall sojourn with you and would keep the passover to the LORD, let all his males be circumcised, then he may come near and keep it; he shall be as a native of the land. But no uncircumcised person shall eat of it. There shall be one law for the native and for the stranger who sojourns among you."

Thus did all the people of Israel; as the LORD commanded Moses and Aaron, so they did. [R^P] And on that very day the LORD brought the people of Israel out of the land of Egypt by their hosts.

(Ch. 13) [P] The LORD said to Moses, "Consecrate to me all the first-born; whatever is the first to open the womb among the people of Israel, both of man and of beast, is mine."

[J] And Moses said to the people, [R^D] "Remember this day, in which you came out from Egypt, out of the house of bondage, for by strength of hand the LORD brought you out from this place; no leavened bread shall be eaten. [J] This day you are to go forth, in the month of Abib. [R^D] And when the LORD brings you into the land of the Canaanites, the Hittites, the Amorites, the Hivites, and the Jebusites, which he swore to your fathers to give you, a land flowing with milk and honey, you shall keep this service in this month. [J] Seven days you shall eat unleavened bread, and on the seventh day there shall be a feast to the LORD. Unleavened bread shall be eaten for seven days; no leavened bread shall be seen with you, and no leaven shall be seen with you in all your territory. [R^D] And you shall tell your son on that day, 'It is because of what the LORD did for me when I came out of Egypt.' And it shall be to you as a sign on your hand and as a memorial between your eyes, that the law of the LORD may be in your mouth; for with a strong hand the LORD has brought you out of Egypt. [J] You shall therefore keep this ordinance at its appointed time from year to year.

"And when the LORD brings you into the land of the Canaanites, as he swore to you and your fathers, and shall give it to you, you shall set apart to the LORD all that first opens the womb. All the firstlings of your cattle that are males shall be the LORD's. Every firstling of an ass you shall redeem with a lamb, or if you will not redeem it you shall break its neck. Every first-born of man among sons you shall redeem. [R^D] And when in time to come your son asks you, 'What does this mean?' you shall say to him, 'By strength of hand the LORD brought us out of Egypt, from the house of bondage. For when Pharaoh stubbornly refused to let us go, the LORD slew all the first-born in the land of Egypt, both the first-born of man and the first-born of cattle. Therefore I sacrifice to the LORD all the males that first open the womb; but all the first-born of my sons I redeem.' It shall be as a mark on your hand or frontlets between your eyes; for by a strong hand the LORD brought us out of Egypt."

[E] When Pharaoh let the people go, God did not lead them by way of the land of the Philistines, although that was near; for God said, "Lest the people repent when they see war, and return to Egypt." But God led the people round by the way of the wilderness toward the Red Sea. And the people of Israel went up out of the land of Egypt equipped for battle. And Moses took the bones of Joseph with him; for Joseph had solemnly sworn the people of Israel, saying, "God will visit you; then you must carry my bones with you from here." [P] And they moved on from Succoth, and encamped at Etham, on the edge of the wilderness. [J] And the LORD went before them by day in a pillar of cloud to lead them along the way, and by night in a pillar of fire to give them light, that they might travel by day and by night; the pillar of cloud by day and the pillar of fire by night did not depart from before the people.

(Ch. 14) [P] Then the LORD said to Moses, "Tell the people of Israel to turn back and encamp in front of Pihahiroth, between Migdol and the sea, in front of Baal-zephon; you shall encamp over against it, by the sea. For Pharaoh will say of the people of Israel, 'They are entangled in the land; the wilderness has shut them in.' And I will harden Pharaoh's heart, and he will pursue them and I will get glory over Pharaoh and all his host; and the Egyptians shall know that I am the LORD." And they did so.

When the king of Egypt was told that the people had fled, the mind of Pharaoh and his servants was changed toward the people, and they said, "What is this we have done, that we have let Israel go from serving us?" So he made ready his chariot and took his army with him, [E] and took six hundred picked chariots [J] and all the other chariots of Egypt [E] with officers over all of them. [P] And the LORD hardened the heart of Pharaoh king of Egypt and he pursued the people of Israel as they went forth defiantly. The Egyptians pursued them, [R^P] all Pharaoh's horses and chariots and his horsemen and his army, [P] and overtook them encamped at the sea, by Pihahiroth, in front of Baal-zephon.

[JE] When Pharaoh drew near, the people of Israel lifted up their eyes, and behold, the Egyptians were marching after them; and they were in great fear. [E] And the people of Israel cried out to the LORD; [J] and they said to Moses, "Is it because there are no graves in Egypt that you have taken us away to die in the wilderness? What have you done to us, in bringing us out of Egypt? Is not this what we said to you in Egypt, 'Let us alone and let us serve the Egyptians'? For it would have been better for us to serve the Egyptians than to die in the wilderness." And Moses said to the people, "Fear not, stand firm, and see the salvation of the LORD, which he will work for you today; for the Egyptians whom you see today, you shall never see again. The LORD will fight for you, and you have only to be still." [E] The LORD said to Moses, "Why do you cry to me? [P] Tell the people of Israel to go forward. [E] Lift up your rod, and stretch out your hand over the sea and divide it, [P] that the people of Israel may go on dry ground through the sea. And I will harden the hearts of the Egyptians, so that they shall go in after them and I will get glory over Pharaoh and all his host, his chariots, and his horsemen. And the Egyptians shall know that I am the LORD, when I have gotten glory over Pharaoh, his chariots, and his horsemen."

[E] Then the angel of God who went before the host of Israel moved and went behind them; [J] and the pillar of cloud moved from before them and stood behind them, [JE] coming between the host of Egypt and the host of Israel. And there was the cloud and the darkness; and the night passed without one coming near the other all night.

[P] Then Moses stretched out his hand over the sea; [J] and the LORD drove the sea back by a strong east wind all night, and made the sea dry land, [P] and the waters were divided. And the people of Israel went into the midst of the sea on dry ground, the waters being a wall to them on their right hand and on their left. The Egyptians pursued, and went in after them into the midst of the sea, all Pharaoh's horses, his chariots, and his horsemen. [J] And in the morning watch the LORD in the pillar of fire and of cloud looked down upon the host of the Egyptians, and discomfited the host of the Egyptians, clogging their chariot wheels so that they drove heavily; and the Egyptians said, "Let us flee from before Israel; for the LORD fights for them against the Egyptians."

[P] Then the LORD said to Moses, "Stretch out your hand over the sea, that the water may come back upon the Egyptians, upon their chariots, and upon their horsemen." So Moses stretched forth his hand over the sea, [J] and the sea returned to its wonted flow when the morning appeared; and the Egyptians fled into it, and the LORD routed the Egyptians in the midst of the sea. [P] The waters returned and covered the chariots and the horsemen and all the host of Pharaoh that had followed them into the sea; [J] not so much as one of them remained. [R^{P}] But the people of Israel walked on dry ground through the sea, the waters being a wall to them on their right hand and on their left.

[J] Thus the LORD saved Israel that day from the hand of the Egyptians; and Israel saw the Egyptians dead upon the seashore. [R^{D}] And Israel saw the great work which the LORD did against the Egyptians, and the people feared the LORD; and they believed in the LORD and in his servant Moses.

(Ch. 15) [J] Then Moses and the people of Israel sang this song to the LORD, saying,

"I will sing to the LORD, for he has triumphed gloriously;
the horse and his rider he has thrown into the sea.
The LORD is my strength and my song,
and he has become my salvation;
this is my God, and I will praise him,
my father's God, and I will exalt him.
The LORD is a man of war;
the LORD is his name.
"Pharaoh's chariots and his host he cast into the sea;
and his picked officers are sunk in the Red Sea.
The floods cover them;
they went down into the depths like a stone.
Thy right hand, O LORD, glorious in power,
thy right hand, O LORD, shatters the enemy.
In the greatness of thy majesty thou overthrowest thy adversaries;
thou sendest forth thy fury, it consumes them like stubble.
At the blast of thy nostrils the waters piled up,
the floods stood up in a heap;
the deeps congealed in the heart of the sea.
The enemy said, 'I will pursue, I will overtake,
I will divide the spoil, my desire shall have its fill of them.
I will draw my sword, my hand shall destroy them.'
Thou didst blow with thy wind, the sea covered them;
they sank as lead in the mighty waters.
"Who is like thee, O LORD, among the gods?
Who is like thee, majestic in holiness,
terrible in glorious deeds, doing wonders?
Thou didst stretch out thy right hand,
the earth swallowed them.
"Thou hast led in thy steadfast love the people whom thou hast redeemed,
thou hast guided them by thy strength to thy holy abode.
The peoples have heard, they tremble;
pangs have seized on the inhabitants of Philistia.
Now are the chiefs of Edom dismayed;
the leaders of Moab, trembling seizes them;
all the inhabitants of Canaan have melted away.
Terror and dread fall upon them;
because of the greatness of thy arm, they are as still as a stone,
till thy people, O LORD, pass by,
till the people pass by whom thou hast purchased.
Thou wilt bring them in, and plant them on thy own mountain,
the place, O LORD, which thou hast made for thy abode,
the sanctuary, O LORD, which thy hands have established.
The LORD will reign for ever and ever."

[R^{P}] For when the horses of Pharaoh with his chariots and his horsemen went into the sea, the LORD brought back the waters of the sea upon them; but the people of Israel walked on dry ground in the midst of the sea. [E] Then Miriam, the prophetess, the sister of Aaron, took a timbrel in her hand; and all the women went out after her with timbrels and dancing. And Miriam sang to them:

"Sing to the LORD, for he has triumphed
gloriously;
the horse and his rider he has thrown into the
sea."

[J] Then Moses led Israel onward from the Red Sea, and they went into the wilderness of Shur; they went three days in the wilderness and found no water. When they came to Marah, they could not drink the water of Marah because it was bitter; therefore it was named Marah. And the people murmured against Moses, saying, "What shall we drink?" And he cried to the LORD; and the LORD showed him a tree, and he threw it into the water, and the water became sweet.

[E] There the LORD made for them a statute and an ordinance and there he proved them, [R^D] saying, "If you will diligently hearken to the voice of the LORD your God, and do that which is right in his eyes, and give heed to his commandments and keep all his statutes, I will put none of the diseases upon you which I put upon the Egyptians; for I am the LORD, your healer."

[J] Then they came to Elim, where there were twelve springs of water and seventy palm trees; and they encamped there by the water.

(Ch. 16) [P] They set out from Elim, and all the congregation of the people of Israel came to the wilderness of Sin, which is between Elim and Sinai, on the fifteenth day of the second month after they had departed from the land of Egypt. And the whole congregation of the people of Israel murmured against Moses and Aaron in the wilderness, and said to them, "Would that we had died by the hand of the LORD in the land of Egypt, when we sat by the fleshpots and ate bread to the full; for you have brought us out into this wilderness to kill this whole assembly with hunger."

[E] Then the LORD said to Moses, "Behold, I will rain bread from heaven for you; and the people shall go out and gather a day's portion every day, that I may prove them, whether they will walk in my law or not. [P] On the sixth day, when they prepare what they bring in, it will be twice as much as they gather daily." So Moses and Aaron said to all the people of Israel, "At evening you shall know that it was the LORD who brought you out of the land of Egypt, and in the morning you shall see the glory of the LORD, because he has heard your murmurings against the LORD. For what are we, that you murmur against us?" [R^P] And Moses said, "When the LORD gives you in the evening flesh to eat and in the morning bread to the full, because the LORD has heard your murmurings which you murmur against him—what are we? Your murmurings are not against us but against the LORD."

[P] And Moses said to Aaron, "Say to the whole congregation of the people of Israel, 'Come near before the LORD, for he has heard your murmurings.' " And as Aaron spoke to the whole congregation of the people of Israel, they looked toward the wilderness, and behold, the glory of the LORD appeared in the cloud. And the LORD said to Moses, "I have heard the murmurings of the people of Israel; say to them, 'At twilight you shall eat flesh, and in the morning you shall be filled with bread; then you shall know that I am the LORD your God.' "

In the evening quails came up and covered the camp; and in the morning dew lay round about the camp. And when the dew had gone up, there was on the face of the wilderness a fine, flake-like thing, fine as hoarfrost on the ground. [E] When the people of Israel saw it, they said to one another, "What is it?" For they did not know what it was. And Moses said to them, "It is the bread which the LORD has given you to eat. [P] This is what the LORD has commanded: 'Gather of it, every man of you, as much as he can eat; you shall take an omer apiece, according to the number of the persons whom each of you has in his tent.' " And the people of Israel did so; they gathered, some more, some less. But when they measured it with an omer, he that gathered much had nothing over, and he that gathered little had no lack; each gathered according to what he could eat. And Moses said to them, "Let no man leave any of it till the morning." But they did not listen to Moses; some left part of it till the morning, and it bred worms and became foul; and Moses was angry with them. Morning by morning they gathered it, each as much as he could eat; but when the sun grew hot, it melted.

[R^P] On the sixth day they gathered twice as much bread, two omers apiece; and when all the leaders of the congregation came and told Moses, he said to them, "This is what the LORD has commanded: 'Tomorrow is a day of solemn rest, a holy sabbath to the LORD; bake what you will bake and boil what you will boil, and all that is left over lay by to be kept till the morning.' " So they laid it by till the morning, as Moses bade them; and it did not become foul, and there were no worms in it. Moses said, "Eat it today, for today is a sabbath to the LORD; today you will not find it in the field. Six days you shall gather it; but on the seventh day, which is a sabbath, there will be none." On the seventh day some of the people went out to gather, and they found none. And the LORD said to Moses, "How long do you refuse to keep my commandments and my laws? See! The LORD has given you the sabbath, therefore on the sixth day he gives you bread for two days; remain every man of you in his place on the seventh day." So the people rested on the seventh day.

[P] Now the house of Israel called its name manna; it was like coriander seed, white, and the taste of it was like wafers made with honey. And Moses said, "This is what the LORD has commanded: 'Let an omer of it be kept throughout your generations, that they may see the bread with which I fed you in the wilderness, when I brought you out of the land of Egypt.' " And Moses said to Aaron, "Take a jar, and put an omer of manna in it, and place it before the LORD, to be kept throughout your generations." As the LORD commanded Moses, so Aaron placed it before the Testimony, to be kept. And the people of Israel ate the manna forty years, till they came to a habitable land; they ate the manna, till they came to the border of the land of Canaan. (An omer is the tenth part of an ephah.)

(Ch. 17) All the congregation of the people of Israel moved on from the wilderness of Sin by stages, according to the commandment of the LORD, and camped at Rephidim; [E] but there was no water for the people to drink. Therefore the people found fault with Moses, and said, "Give us water to drink." And Moses said to them, "Why do you find fault with me? [J] Why do you put the LORD to the proof?" But the people thirsted there for water, and the people murmured against Moses, and said, "Why did you bring us up out of Egypt, to kill us and our children and our cattle with thirst?" [E] So Moses cried to the LORD, "What shall I do with this people? They are almost ready to stone me." And the LORD said to Moses, "Pass on before the people, taking with you some of the elders of Israel; and take in your hand the rod with which you struck the Nile, and go. Behold, I will stand before you there on the rock at Horeb; and you shall strike the rock, and water shall come out of it, that the people may drink." And Moses did so, in the sight of the elders of Israel. [J] And he called the name of the place Massah [E] and Meribah, because of the fault finding of the children of Israel, [J] and because they put the LORD to the proof by saying, "Is the LORD among us or not?"

[E] Then came Amalek and fought with Israel at Rephidim. And Moses said to Joshua, "Choose for us men, and go out, fight with Amalek; tomorrow I will stand on the top of the hill with the rod of God in my hand." So Joshua did as Moses told him, and fought with Amalek; and Moses, Aaron, and Hur went up to the top of the hill. Whenever Moses held up his hand, Israel prevailed; and whenever he lowered his hand, Amalek prevailed. But Moses' hands grew weary; so they took a stone and put it under him, and he sat upon it, and Aaron and Hur held up his hands, one on one side, and the other on the other side; so his hands were steady until the going down of the sun. And Joshua mowed down Amalek and his people with the edge of the sword.

And the LORD said to Moses, "Write this as a memorial in a book and recite it in the ears of Joshua, that I will utterly blot out the remembrance of Amalek from under heaven." And Moses built an altar and called the name of it, The LORD is my banner, saying, "A hand upon the banner of the LORD! The LORD will have war with Amalek from generation to generation."

(Ch. 18) Jethro, the priest of Midian,

Moses' father-in-law, heard of all that God had done for Moses and for Israel his people, [R^{JE}] how the LORD had brought Israel out of Egypt. Now Jethro, Moses' father-in-law, had taken Zipporah, Moses' wife, after he had sent her away, and her two sons, of whom the name of the one was Gershom (for he said, "I have been a sojourner in a foreign land"), and the name of the other, Eliezer (for he said, "The God of my father was my help, and delivered me from the sword of Pharaoh"). [E] And Jethro, Moses' father-in-law, came with his sons and his wife to Moses in the wilderness where he was encamped at the mountain of God. And when one told Moses, "Lo, your father-in-law Jethro is coming to you with your wife and her two sons with her," [JE] Moses went out to meet his father-in-law, and did obeisance and kissed him; and they asked each other of their welfare, and went into the tent. Then Moses told his father-in-law all that the LORD had done to Pharaoh and to the Egyptians for Israel's sake, all the hardship that had come upon them in the way, and how the LORD had delivered them. And Jethro rejoiced for all the good which the LORD had done to Israel, in that he had delivered them out of the hand of the Egyptians.

And Jethro said, "Blessed be the LORD, who has delivered you out of the hands of the Egyptians and out of the hand of Pharaoh. Now I know that the LORD is greater than all gods, [R] because he delivered the people from under the hand of the Egyptians, [JE] when they dealt arrogantly with them." [E] And Jethro, Moses' father-in-law, offered a burnt offering and sacrifices to God; and Aaron came with all the elders of Israel to eat bread with Moses' father-in-law before God.

On the morrow Moses sat to judge the people, and the people stood about Moses from morning till evening. When Moses' father-in-law saw all that he was doing for the people, he said, "What is this that you are doing for the people? Why do you sit alone, and all the people stand about you from morning till evening?" And Moses said to his father-in-law, "Because the people come to me to inquire of God; when they have a dispute, they come to me and I decide between a man and his neighbor, and I make them know the statutes of God and his decisions." Moses' father-in-law said to him, "What you are doing is not good. You and the people with you will wear yourselves out, for the thing is too heavy for you; you are not able to perform it alone. Listen now to my voice; I will give you counsel, and God be with you! You shall represent the people before God, and bring their cases to God; and you shall teach them the statutes and the decisions, and make them know the way in which they must walk and what they must do. Moreover choose able men from all the people, such as fear God, men who are trustworthy and who hate a bribe; and place such men over the people as rulers of thousands, of hundreds, of fifties, and of tens. And let them judge the people at all times; every great matter they shall bring to you, but any small matter they shall decide themselves; so it will be easier for you, and they will bear the burden with you. If you do this, and God so commands you, then you will be able to endure, and all this people also will go to their place in peace."

So Moses gave heed to the voice of his father-in-law and did all that he had said. Moses chose able men out of all Israel, and made them heads over the people, rulers of thousands, of hundreds, of fifties, and of tens. And they judged the people at all times; hard cases they brought to Moses, but any small matter they decided themselves. Then Moses let his father-in-law depart, and he went his way to his own country.

(Ch. 19) [P] On the third new moon after the people of Israel had gone forth out of the land of Egypt, on that day they came into the wilderness of Sinai. And when they set out from Rephidim and came into the wilderness of Sinai, they encamped in the wilderness; [E] and there Israel encamped before the mountain. And Moses went up to God, [R^{D}] and the LORD called him out of the mountain, saying, "Thus you shall say to the house of Jacob, and tell the people of Israel: You have seen what I did to the Egyptians, and how I bore you on eagles' wings and brought you to myself. Now therefore, if you will obey my voice and keep my covenant, you shall be my own possession among all peoples; for all the earth is mine, and you shall be to me a kingdom of priests and a holy nation. These are the words which you shall speak to the children of Israel."

[E] So Moses came and called the elders of the people, and set before them all these words which the LORD had commanded him. And all the people answered together and said, "All that the LORD has spoken we will do." And Moses reported the words of the people to the LORD. And the LORD said to Moses, "Lo, I am coming to you in a thick cloud, that the people may hear when I speak with you, and may also believe you for ever."

[R^{JE}] Then Moses told the words of the people to the LORD. [E] And the LORD said to Moses, "Go to the people and consecrate them today and tomorrow, and let them wash their garments, and be ready by the third day; [J] for on the third day the LORD will come down upon Mount Sinai in the sight of all the people. And you shall set bounds for the people round about, saying, 'Take heed that you do not go up into the mountain or touch the border of it; whoever touches the mountain shall be put to death; no hand shall touch him but he shall be stoned or shot; whether beast or man, he shall not live.' When the trumpet sounds a long blast, they shall come up to the mountain." [E] So Moses went down from the mountain to the people, and consecrated the people; and they washed their garments. And he said to the people, "Be ready by the third day; do not go near a woman."

On the morning of the third day there were thunders and lightnings, and a thick cloud upon the mountain, and a very loud trumpet blast, so that all the people who were in the camp trembled. Then Moses brought the people out of the camp to meet God; and they took their stand at the foot of the mountain. [J] And Mount Sinai was wrapped in smoke, because the LORD descended upon it in fire; and the smoke of it went up like the smoke of a kiln, and the whole mountain quaked greatly. [E] And as the sound of the trumpet grew louder and louder, Moses spoke, and God answered him in thunder. [J] And the LORD came down upon Mount Sinai, to the top of the mountain; and the LORD called Moses to the top of the mountain, and Moses went up. And the LORD said to Moses, "Go down and warn the people, lest they break through to the LORD to gaze and many of them perish. And also let the priests who come near to the LORD consecrate themselves, lest the LORD break out upon them." [R^{JE}] And Moses said to the LORD, "The people cannot come up to Mount Sinai; for thou thyself didst charge us, saying, 'Set bounds about the mountain, and consecrate it.' " [J] And the LORD said to him, "Go down, and come up bringing Aaron with you; but do not let the priests and the people break through to come up to the LORD, lest he break out against them." So Moses went down to the people and told them.

[Chapters 20–23 are omitted here, since most of the material is found below under "Law." Most scholars think these chapters were arranged in their present form by the Elohist.]

(Ch. 24) [J] And [the LORD] said to Moses, "Come up to the LORD, you and Aaron, Nadab, and Abihu, and seventy of the elders of Israel, and worship afar off. Moses alone shall come near to the LORD; but the others shall not come near, and the people shall not come up with him."

[E] Moses came and told the people all the words of the LORD and all the ordinances; and all the people answered with one voice, and said, "All the words which the LORD has spoken we will do." And Moses wrote all the words of the LORD. And he rose early in the morning, and built an altar at the foot of the mountain, and twelve pillars, according to the twelve tribes of Israel. And he sent young men of the people of Israel, who offered burnt offerings and sacrificed peace offerings of oxen to the LORD. And Moses took half of the blood and put it in basins, and half of the blood he threw against the altar. Then he took the book of the covenant, and read it in the hearing of the people; and they said, "All that the LORD has spoken we will do, and we will be obedient." And Moses took the blood and threw it upon the people, and said, "Behold the blood of the covenant which the LORD has made with you in accordance with all these words."

[J] Then Moses and Aaron, Nadab, and Abihu, and seventy of the elders of Israel went up, and they saw the God of Israel; and there was under his feet as it were a pavement of sapphire stone, like the very heaven for clearness. And he did not lay his hand on the chief men of the people of Israel; they beheld God, and ate and drank.

[E] The LORD said to Moses, "Come up to me on the mountain, and wait there; and I will give you the tables of stone, [R^JE] with the law and the commandment, [E] which I have written for their instruction." So Moses rose with his servant Joshua, and Moses went up into the mountain of God. And he said to the elders, "Tarry here for us, until we come to you again; and, behold, Aaron and Hur are with you; whoever has a cause, let him go to them."

Then Moses went up on the mountain, [P] and the cloud covered the mountain. The glory of the LORD settled on Mount Sinai, and the cloud covered it six days; and on the seventh day he called to Moses out of the midst of the cloud. Now the appearance of the glory of the LORD was like a devouring fire on the top of the mountain in the sight of the people of Israel. And Moses entered the cloud, and went up on the mountain. And Moses was on the mountain forty days and forty nights.

B. The Law

Whereas the biblical tradition, followed by many Christians and Jews, is that the whole of the Torah ("law" or "instruction") was given to Israel on Mount Sinai and then repeated and expanded on the eve of the conquest of Palestine (in Deuteronomy), many scholars find several strata or layers of legal material. The oldest of these is "apodictic" or "unconditional" law; it is characterized by the imperatives, "You shall" and "You shall not." Much of this material may be traced back to the time of Moses himself. The Decalogue or "Ten Commandments," printed below, may be taken as typical. The second type, exemplified by the following material from Exodus 20:23—23:19, also contains demands, but usually speaks of conditions and special cases; since this type of law is similar to legal codes found elsewhere in the ancient Near East it is possible that it was taken over by the Israelites upon their entrance into Canaan. A third body of law is found in the Book of Deuteronomy from which one chapter is included below. It is quite probable that the law-book discovered in the temple during the reign of King Josiah (621 B. C.) consisted of the major part of Deuteronomy; here we have the older laws provided with theological reasons for obeying them. Last in point of time is the priestly legislation, probably drawn up in its present form during the Babylonian Exile. In the passage from Leviticus 19, the reader will note the great emphasis placed upon ritual and cultic action alongside the ethical imperatives.

1. *Unconditional Law*

[EXODUS 20:1–17]

And God spoke all these words, saying, "I am the LORD your God, who brought you out of the land of Egypt, out of the house of bondage.

"You shall have no other gods before me.

"You shall not make yourself a graven image, or any likeness of anything that is in heaven above, or that is in the earth beneath, or that is in the water under the earth; you shall not bow down to them or serve them; for I the LORD your God am a jealous God, visiting the iniquity of the fathers upon the children to the third and the fourth generation of those who hate me, but showing steadfast love to thousands of those who love me and keep my commandments.

"You shall not take the name of the LORD your God in vain; for the LORD will not hold him guiltless who takes his name in vain.

"Remember the sabbath day, to keep it holy. Six days you shall labor, and do all your work; but the seventh day is a sabbath to the LORD your God; in it you shall not do any work, you, or your son, or your daughter, your manservant, or your maidservant, or your cattle, or the sojourner who is within your gates; for in six days the LORD made heaven and earth, the sea, and all that is in them, and rested the seventh day; therefore the LORD blessed the sabbath day and hallowed it.

"Honor your father and your mother, that your days may be long in the land which the LORD your God gives you.

"You shall not kill.

"You shall not commit adultery.

"You shall not steal.

"You shall not bear false witness against your neighbor.

"You shall not covet your neighbor's house; you shall not covet your neighbor's wife, or his manservant, or his maidservant, or his ox, or his ass, or anything that is your neighbor's."

2. *Conditional Law*

[EXODUS 20:23–23:19]

(Ch. 20) "You shall not make gods of silver to be with me, nor shall you make for yourselves gods of gold. An altar of earth you shall make for me and sacrifice on it your burnt offerings and your peace offerings, your sheep and your oxen; in every place where I cause my name to be remembered I will come to you and bless you. And if you make me an altar of stone, you shall not build it of hewn stones; for if you wield your tool upon it you profane it. And you shall not go up by steps to my altar, that your nakedness be not exposed on it.

(Ch. 21) "Now these are the ordinances which you shall set before them. When you buy a Hebrew slave, he shall serve six years, and in the seventh he shall go out free, for nothing. If he comes in single, he shall go out single; if he comes in married, then his wife shall go out with him. If his master gives him a wife and she bears him sons or daughters, the wife and her children shall be her master's and he shall go out alone. But if the slave plainly says, 'I love my master, my wife, and my children; I will not go out free,' then his master shall bring him to God, and he shall bring him to the door or the doorpost; and his master shall bore his ear through with an awl; and he shall serve him for life.

"When a man sells his daughter as a slave, she shall not go out as the male slaves do. If she does not please her master, who has designated her for himself, then he shall let her be redeemed; he shall have no right to sell her to a foreign people, since he has dealt faithlessly with her. If he designates her for his son, he shall deal with her as with a daughter. If he takes another wife to himself, he shall not diminish her food, her clothing, or her marital rights. And if he does not do these three things for her, she shall go out for nothing, without payment of money.

"Whoever strikes a man so that he dies shall be put to death. But if he did not lie in wait for him, but God let him fall into his hand, then I will appoint for you a place to which he may flee. But if a man willfully attacks another to kill him treacherously, you shall take him from my altar, that he may die.

"Whoever strikes his father or his mother shall be put to death.

"Whoever steals a man, whether he sells him or is found in possession of him, shall be put to death.

"Whoever curses his father or his mother shall be put to death.

"When men quarrel and one strikes the other with a stone or with his fist and the man does not die but keeps his bed, then if the man rises again and walks abroad with his staff, he that struck him shall be clear; only he shall pay for the loss of his time, and shall have him thoroughly healed.

"When a man strikes his slave, male or female, with a rod and the slave dies under his hand, he shall be punished. But if the slave survives a day or two, he is not to be punished; for the slave is his money.

"When men strive together, and hurt a woman with child, so that there is a miscarriage, and yet no harm follows, the one who hurt her shall be fined, according as the woman's husband shall lay upon him; and he shall pay as the judges determine. If any harm follows, then you shall give life for life, eye for eye, tooth for tooth, hand for hand, foot for foot, burn for burn, wound for wound, stripe for stripe.

"When a man strikes the eye of his slave, male or female, and destroys it, he shall let the slave go free for the eye's sake. If he knocks out the tooth of his slave, male or female, he shall let the slave go free for the tooth's sake.

"When an ox gores a man or a woman to death, the ox shall be stoned, and its flesh shall not be eaten; but the owner of the ox shall be clear. But if the ox has been accustomed to gore in the past, and its owner has been warned but has not kept it in, and it kills a man or a woman, the ox shall be stoned, and its owner also shall be put to death. If a ransom is laid on him, then he shall give for the redemption of his life whatever is laid upon him. If it gores a man's son or daughter, he shall be dealt with according to this same rule. If the ox gores a slave, male or female, the owner shall give to their master thirty shekels of silver, and the ox shall be stoned.

"When a man leaves a pit open, or when a man digs a pit and does not cover it, and an ox or an ass falls into it, the owner of the pit shall make it good; he shall give money to its owner, and the dead beast shall be his.

"When one man's ox hurts another's, so that it dies, then they shall sell the live ox and divide the price of it; and the dead beast also they shall divide. Or if it is known that the ox has been accustomed to gore in the past, and its owner has not kept it in, he shall pay ox for ox, and the dead beast shall be his.

(Ch. 22) "If a man steals an ox or a sheep, and kills it or sells it, he shall pay five oxen for an ox, and four sheep for a sheep. He shall make restitution; if he has nothing, then he shall be sold for his theft. If the stolen beast is found alive in his possession, whether it is an ox or an ass or a sheep, he shall pay double.

"If a thief is found breaking in, and is struck so that he dies, there shall be no bloodguilt for him; but if the sun has risen upon him, there shall be bloodguilt for him.

"When a man causes a field or vineyard to be grazed over, or lets his beast loose and it feeds in another man's fields, he shall make restitution from the best in his own field and in his own vineyard.

"When fire breaks out and catches in thorns so that the stacked grain or the standing grain or the field is consumed, he that kindled the fire shall make full restitution.

"If a man delivers to his neighbor money or goods to keep, and it is stolen out of the man's house, then, if the thief is found, he shall pay double. If the thief is not found, the owner of the house shall come near to God, to show whether or not he has put his hand to his neighbor's goods.

"For every breach of trust, whether it is for ox, for ass, for sheep, for clothing, or for any kind of lost thing, of which one says, 'This is it,' the case of both parties shall come before God; he whom God shall condemn shall pay double to his neighbor.

"If a man delivers to his neighbor an ass or an ox or a sheep of any beast to keep, and it dies or is hurt or is driven away, without any one seeing it, an oath by the LORD shall be between them both to see whether he has not put his hand to his neighbor's property; and the owner shall accept the oath, and he shall not make restitution. But if it is stolen from him, he shall make restitution to its owner. If it is torn by beasts, let him bring it as evidence; he shall not make restitution for what has been torn.

"If a man borrows anything of his neighbor, and it is hurt or dies, the owner not being with it, he shall make full restitution. If the owner was with it, he shall not make restitution; if it was hired, it came for its hire.

"If a man seduces a virgin who is not betrothed, and lies with her, he shall give the marriage present for her, and make her his wife. If her father utterly refuses to give her to him, he shall pay money equivalent to the marriage present for virgins.

"You shall not permit a sorceress to live.

"Whoever lies with a beast shall be put to death.

"Whoever sacrifices to any god save to the LORD only, shall be utterly destroyed.

"You shall not wrong a stranger or oppress him, for you were strangers in the land of Egypt. You shall not afflict any widow or orphan. If you do afflict them, and they cry out to me, I will surely hear their cry; and my wrath will burn, and I will kill you with the sword, and your wives shall become widows and your children fatherless.

"If you lend money to any of my people with you who is poor, you shall not be to him as a creditor, and you shall not exact interest from him. If ever you take your neighbor's garment in pledge, you shall restore it to him before the sun goes down; for that is his only covering, it is his mantle for his body; in what else shall he sleep? And if he cries to me, I will hear, for I am compassionate.

"You shall not revile God, nor curse a ruler of your people.

"You shall not delay to offer from the fulness of your harvest and from the outflow of your presses.

"The first-born of your sons you shall give to me. You shall do likewise with your oxen and with your sheep: seven days it shall be with its dam; on the eighth day you shall give it to me.

"You shall be men consecrated to me; therefore you shall not eat any flesh that is torn by beasts in the field; you shall cast it to the dogs.

(Ch. 23) "You shall not utter a false report. You shall not join hands with a wicked man, to be a malicious witness. You shall not follow a multitude to do evil; nor shall you bear witness in a suit, turning aside after a multitude, so as to pervert justice; nor shall you be partial to a poor man in his suit.

"If you meet your enemy's ox or his ass going astray, you shall bring it back to him. If you see the ass of one who hates you lying under its burden, you shall refrain from leaving him with it, you shall help him to lift it up.

"You shall not pervert the justice due to your poor in his suit. Keep far from a false charge, and do not slay the innocent and righteous, for I will not acquit the wicked. And you shall take no bribe, for a bribe blinds the officials, and subverts the cause of those who are in the right.

"You shall not oppress a stranger; you know the heart of a stranger, for you were strangers in the land of Egypt.

"For six years you shall sow your land and gather in its yield; but the seventh year you shall let it rest and lie fallow, that the poor of your people may eat; and what they leave the wild beasts may eat. You shall do likewise with your vineyard, and with your olive orchard.

"Six days you shall do your work, but on the seventh day you shall rest; that your ox and your ass may have rest, and the son of your bondmaid, and the alien, may be refreshed. Take heed to all that I have said to you; and make no mention of the names of other gods, nor let such be heard out of your mouth.

"Three times in the year you shall keep a feast to me. You shall keep the feast of unleavened bread; as I commanded you, you shall eat unleavened bread for seven days at the appointed time in the month of Abib, for in it you came out of Egypt. None shall appear before me empty-handed. You shall keep the feast of harvest, of the first fruits of your labor, of what you sow in the field. You shall keep the feast of ingathering at the end of the year, when you gather in from the field the fruit of your labor. Three times in the year shall all your males appear before the Lord GOD.

"You shall not offer the blood of my sacrifice with leavened bread, or let the fat of my feast remain until the morning.

"The first of the first fruits of your ground you shall bring into the house of the LORD your God.

"You shall not boil a kid in its mother's milk.

3. *The Deuteronomic Code*

[DEUTERONOMY 24]

"When a man takes a wife and marries her, if then she finds no favor in his eyes because he has found some indecency in her, and he writes her a bill of divorce and puts it in her hand and sends her out of his house, and she departs out of his house, and if she goes and becomes another man's wife, and the latter husband dislikes her and writes her a bill of divorce and puts it in her hand and sends her out of his house or if the latter husband dies, who took her to be his wife, then the former husband, who sent her away, may not take her again to be his wife, after she has been defiled; for that is an abomination before the LORD, and you shall not bring guilt upon the land which the LORD your God gives you for an inheritance.

"When a man is newly married, he shall not go out with the army or be charged with any business; he shall be free at home one year, to be happy with his wife whom he has taken.

"No man shall take a mill or an upper millstone in pledge; for he would be taking a life in pledge.

"If a man is found stealing one of his brethren, the people of Israel, and if he treats him as a slave or sells him, then that thief shall die; so you shall purge the evil from the midst of you.

"Take heed, in an attack of leprosy, to be very careful to do according to all that the Levitical priests shall direct you; as I commanded them, so you shall be careful to do. Remember what the LORD your God did to Miriam on the way as you came forth out of Egypt.

"When you make your neighbor a loan of any sort, you shall not go into his house to fetch his pledge. You shall stand outside, and the man to whom you make the loan shall bring the pledge out to you. And if he is a poor man, you shall not sleep in his pledge; when the sun goes down, you shall restore to him the pledge that he may sleep in his cloak and bless you; and it shall be righteousness to you before the LORD your God.

"You shall not oppress a hired servant who is poor and needy, whether he is one of your brethren or one of the sojourners who are in your land within your towns; you shall give him his hire on the day he earns it, before the sun goes down (for he is poor, and sets his heart upon it); lest he cry against you to the LORD, and it be sin in you.

"The fathers shall not be put to death for the children, nor shall the children be put to death for the fathers; every man shall be put to death for his own sin.

"You shall not pervert the justice due to the sojourner or to the fatherless, or take a widow's garment in pledge; but you shall remember that you were a slave in Egypt and the LORD your God redeemed you from there; therefore I command you to do this.

"When you reap your harvest in your field, and have forgotten a sheaf in the field, you shall not go back to get it; it shall be for the sojourner, the fatherless, and the widow; that the LORD your God may bless you in all the work of your hands. When you beat your olive trees, you shall not go over the boughs again; it shall be for the sojourner, the fatherless, and the widow. When you gather the grapes of your vineyard, you shall not glean it afterward; it shall be for the sojourner, the fatherless, and the widow. You shall remember that you were a slave in the land of Egypt; therefore I command you to do this.

4. *The Priestly Code*

[LEVITICUS 19]

And the LORD said to Moses, "Say to all the congregation of the people of Israel, You shall be holy; for I the LORD your God am holy. Every one of you shall revere his mother and his father, and you shall keep my sabbaths: I am the LORD your God. Do not turn to idols or make for yourselves molten gods: I am the LORD Your God.

"When you offer a sacrifice of peace offerings to the LORD, you shall offer it so that you may be accepted. It shall be eaten the same day you offer it, or on the morrow; and anything left over until the third day shall be burned with fire. If it is eaten at all on the third day, it is an abomination; it will not be accepted, and every one who eats it shall bear his iniquity, because he has profaned a holy thing of the LORD; and that person shall be cut off from his people.

"When you reap the harvest of your land, you shall not reap your field to its very border, neither shall you gather the gleanings after your harvest. And you shall not strip your vineyard bare, neither shall you gather the fallen grapes of your vineyard; you shall leave them for the poor and for the sojourner: I am the LORD your God.

"You shall not steal, nor deal falsely, nor

lie to one another. And you shall not swear by my name falsely, and so profane the name of your God: I am the LORD.

"You shall not oppress your neighbor or rob him. The wages of a hired servant shall not remain with you all night until the morning. You shall not curse the deaf or put a stumbling block before the blind, but you shall fear your God: I am the LORD.

"You shall do no injustice in judgment; you shall not be partial to the poor or defer to the great, but in righteousness shall you judge your neighbor. You shall not go up and down as a slanderer among your people, and you shall not stand forth against the life of your neighbor: I am the LORD.

"You shall not hate your brother in your heart, but you shall reason with your neighbor, lest you bear sin because of him. You shall not take vengeance or bear any grudge against the sons of your own people, but you shall love your neighbor as yourself: I am the LORD.

"You shall keep my statutes. You shall not let your cattle breed with a different kind; you shall not sow your field with two kinds of seed; nor shall there come upon you a garment of cloth made of two kinds of stuff.

"If a man lies carnally with a woman who is a slave, betrothed to another man and not yet ransomed or given her freedom, an inquiry shall be held. They shall not be put to death, because she was not free; but he shall bring a guilt offering for himself to the LORD, to the door of the tent of meeting, a ram for a guilt offering. And the priest shall make atonement for him with the ram of the guilt offering before the LORD for his sin which he has committed; and the sin which he has committed shall be forgiven him.

"When you come into the land and plant all kinds of trees for food, then you shall count their fruit as forbidden; three years it shall be forbidden to you, it must not be eaten. And in the fourth year all their fruit shall be holy, an offering of praise to the LORD. But in the fifth year you may eat of their fruit, that they may yield more richly for you: I am the LORD your God.

"You shall not eat any flesh with the blood in it. You shall not practice augury or witchcraft. You shall not round off the hair on your temples or mar the edges of your beard. You shall not make any cuttings in your flesh on account of the dead or tattoo any marks upon you: I am the LORD.

"Do not profane your daughter by making her a harlot, lest the land fall into harlotry and the land become full of wickedness. You shall keep my sabbaths and reverence my sanctuary: I am the LORD.

"Do not turn to mediums or wizards; do not seek them out, to be defiled by them: I am the LORD your God.

"You shall rise up before the hoary head, and honor the face of an old man, and you shall fear your God: I am the LORD.

"When a stranger sojourns with you in your land, you shall not do him wrong. The stranger who sojourns with you shall be to you as the native among you, and you shall love him as yourself; for you were strangers in the land of Egypt: I am the LORD your God.

"You shall do no wrong in judgment, in measures of length or weight or quantity. You shall have just balances, just weights, a just ephah, and a just hin: I am the LORD your God, who brought you out of the land of Egypt. And you shall observe all my statutes and all my ordinances, and do them: I am the LORD."

C. The Prophets

Old Testament prophecy begins with Samuel in the eleventh century B. C. Aside from Elijah and Elisha in the ninth century, it reaches its highest development after 750 B. C. For the most part the earlier prophets pronounced the Lord's forthcoming judgments upon the sins of Israel; however, all of the prophetic books also speak of Israel's redemption and salvation. In addition we usually have notes concerning the careers of the prophets, in particular the way in which they were called by the Lord to be his spokesmen to the people. The following selections are arranged according to these major emphases in the various books.

1. *The Call of the Prophet*

Jeremiah

Jeremiah, whose call to be a prophet is related in the following passage, was active in Judah between 626 B. C. and the Exile in 586; he may also have continued his work after he was forced to flee to Egypt. His oracles thus span the period of Israel's greatest crisis and the turning point in her history as a nation. However, Jeremiah is not only to "pluck up and . . . break down," but also "to build and to plant."

[JEREMIAH 1]

The words of Jeremiah, the son of Hilkiah, of the priests who were in Anathoth in the land of Benjamin, to whom the word of the LORD came in the days of Josiah the son of Amon, king of Judah, in the thirteenth year of his reign. It came also in the days of Jehoiakim the son of Josiah, king of Judah, and until the end of the eleventh year of Zedekiah, the son of Josiah, king of Judah, until the captivity of Jerusalem in the fifth month.

Now the word of the LORD came to me saying,

"Before I formed you in the womb I knew you,
and before you were born I consecrated you;
I appointed you a prophet to the nations."

Then I said, "Ah, Lord GOD! Behold, I do not know how to speak, for I am only a youth." But the LORD said to me,

"Do not say, 'I am only a youth';
for to all to whom I send you
you shall go,
and whatever I command you
you shall speak.
Be not afraid of them,
for I am with you to deliver you,
says the LORD."

Then the LORD put forth his hand and touched my mouth; and the LORD said to me,

"Behold, I have put my words in
your mouth.
See, I have set you this day over
nations and over kingdoms,
to pluck up and to break down,
to destroy and to overthrow,
to build and to plant."

And the word of the LORD came to me saying, "Jeremiah, what do you see?" And I said, "I see a rod of almond." Then the LORD said to me, "You have seen well, for I am watching over my word to perform it."

The word of the LORD came to me a second time, saying, "What do you see?" And I said, "I see a boiling pot, facing away from the north." Then the LORD said to me, "Out of the north evil shall break forth upon all the inhabitants of the land. For, lo, I am calling all the tribes of the kingdoms of the north, says the LORD; and they shall come and every one shall set his throne at the entrance of the gates of Jerusalem, against all its walls round about, and against all the cities of Judah. And I will utter my judgments against them, for all their wickedness in forsaking me; they have burned incense to other gods, and worshiped the works of their own hands. But you, gird up your loins; arise, and say to them everything that I command you. Do not be dismayed by them, lest I dismay you before them. And I, behold, I make you this day a fortified city, an iron pillar, and bronze walls, against the whole land, against the kings of Judah, its princes, its priests, and the people of the land. They will fight against you; but they shall not prevail against you, for I am with you, says the LORD, to deliver you."

2. *The Lord's Judgment upon Israel*

Hosea

The following passage from Hosea is typical of that prophet's message. He prophesied in the northern kingdom ("Ephraim" or simply "Israel") in the third quarter of the eighth century B. C., and is particularly noted for his emphasis upon both judgment and love.

[Hosea 5:1–6:6]

Hear this, O priests!
Give heed, O house of Israel!
Hearken, O house of the king!
For the judgment pertains to you;
for you have been a snare at Mizpah,
and a net spread upon Tabor.
And they have made deep the pit of Shittim;
but I will chastise all of them.

I know Ephraim,
and Israel is not hid from me;
for now, O Ephraim, you have played the harlot,
Israel is defiled.
Their deeds do not permit them
to return to their God.
For the spirit of harlotry is within them,
and they know not the Lord.
The pride of Israel testifies to his face;
Ephraim shall stumble in his guilt;
Judah also shall stumble with them.
With their flocks and herds they shall go
to seek the Lord,
but they will not find him;
he has withdrawn from them.
They have dealt faithlessly with the Lord;
for they have borne alien children.
Now the new moon shall devour
them with their fields.

Blow the horn in Gibeah,
the trumpet in Ramah.
Sound the alarm at Beth-aven;
tremble, O Benjamin!
Ephraim shall become a desolation
in the day of punishment;
among the tribes of Israel
I declare what is sure.
The princes of Judah have become
like those who remove the landmark;
upon them I will pour out my wrath like water.
Ephraim is oppressed, crushed in judgment,
because he was determined to go after vanity.
Therefore I am like a moth to Ephraim,
and like dry rot to the house of Judah.

When Ephraim saw his sickness,
and Judah his wound,
then Ephraim went to Assyria,
and sent to the great king.
But he is not able to cure you or heal your wound.
For I will be like a lion to Ephraim,
and like a young lion to the house of Judah.
I, even I, will rend and go away,
I will carry off, and none shall rescue.
I will return again to my place,
until they acknowledge their
guilt and seek my face,
and in their distress they seek me, saying,
(Ch. 6)
"Come, let us return to the Lord;
for he has torn, that he may heal us;
he has stricken, and he will bind us up.
After two days he will revive us;
on the third day he will raise us up,
that we may live before him.
Let us know, let us press on to know the Lord;
his going forth is sure as the dawn;
he will come to us as the showers,
as the spring rains that water the earth."

What shall I do with you, O Ephraim?
What shall I do with you, O Judah?
Your love is like a morning cloud,
like the dew that goes early away.
Therefore I have hewn them by the prophets,
I have slain them by the words of my mouth,
and my judgment goes forth as the light.
For I desire steadfast love and not sacrifice,
the knowledge of God,
rather than burnt offerings.

3. *The Lord's Action in History*

Isaiah

All of the prophets speak of the way in which God will intervene in history to carry out his will. The following passage from (First) Isaiah is particularly instructive, for it makes the audacious claim that the hated Assyrians were actually the instruments of the Lord's anger. The prophet had a lengthy career, lasting from 742 B. C. to at least 701; he was an inhabitant of Jerusalem, and possibly a nobleman or even a member of the royal family.

[ISAIAH 10:5–19]

Ah, Assyria, the rod of my anger,
the staff of my fury!
Against a godless nation I send him,
and against the people of my wrath I command him,
to take spoil and seize plunder,
and to tread them down like the mire of the streets.
But he does not so intend,
and his mind does not so think;
But it is in his mind to destroy,
and to cut off nations not a few;
for he says:
"Are not my commanders all kings?
Is not Calno like Carchemish?
Is not Hamath like Arpad?
Is not Samaria like Damascus?
As my hand has reached to the kingdoms of the idols
whose graven images were greater than those of Jerusalem and Samaria,
shall I not do to Jerusalem and her idols
as I have done to Samaria and her images?"

When the LORD has finished all his work on Mount Zion and on Jerusalem he will punish the arrogant boasting of the king of Assyria and his haughty pride. For he says:

"By the strength of my hand I have done it,
and by my wisdom, for I have understanding;
I have removed the boundaries of peoples,
and have plundered their treasures;
like a bull I have brought down
those who sat on thrones.
My hand has found like a nest
the wealth of the peoples;
and as men gather eggs that have been forsaken
so I have gathered all the earth;
and there was none that moved a wing,
or opened the mouth, or chirped."

Shall the ax vaunt itself over him
who hews with it,
or the saw magnify itself against
him who wields it?
As if a rod should wield him who lifts it,
or as if a staff should lift him who is not wood!
Therefore the Lord, the LORD of hosts,
will send wasting sickness among
his stout warriors,
and under his glory a burning will be kindled,
like the burning of fire.
The light of Israel will become a fire,
and his Holy One a flame;
and it will burn and devour
his thorns and briers in one day.
The glory of his forest and of his fruitful land
the LORD will destroy, both soul and body,
and it will be as when a sick man
wastes away.
The remnant of the trees of his
forest will be so few
that a child can write them down.

4. *The Redemption of Israel*

a. Ezekiel

Ezekiel, whose famous vision of the "valley of dry bones" is found below, was taken into Babylon on the occasion of the exile of 597 B. C., and began his prophetic work in 592. Prior to the fall of Jerusalem in 586 his message was one of judgment; after that time, however, he turned to the forthcoming salvation and restoration of the people.

[Ezekiel 37:1–14]

The hand of the Lord was upon me, and he brought me out by the Spirit of the Lord, and set me down in the midst of the valley; it was full of bones. And he led me round among them; and behold, there were very many upon the valley; and lo, they were very dry. And he said to me, "Son of man, can these bones live?" And I answered, "O, Lord God, thou knowest." Again he said to me, "Prophesy to these bones, and say to them, O dry bones, hear the word of the Lord. Thus says the Lord God to these bones: "Behold, I will cause breath to enter you, and you shall live. And I will lay sinews upon you, and will cause flesh to come upon you, and cover you with skin, and put breath in you, and you shall live; and you shall know that I am the Lord."

So I prophesied as I was commanded; and as I prophesied, there was a noise, and behold, a rattling; and the bones came together, bone to its bone. And as I looked, there were sinews on them, and flesh had come upon them, and skin had covered them; but there was no breath in them. Then he said to me, "Prophesy to the breath, prophesy, son of man, and say to the breath, Thus says the Lord God: Come from the four winds, O breath, and breathe upon these slain, that they may live." So I prophesied as he commanded me, and the breath came into them, and they lived, and stood upon their feet, an exceedingly great host.

Then he said to me, "Son of man, these bones are the whole house of Israel. Behold, they say, 'Our bones are dried up, and our hope is lost; we are clean cut off.' Therefore prophesy, and say to them, Thus says the Lord God: "Behold, I will open your graves, and raise you from your graves, O my people; and I will bring you home into the land of Israel. And you shall know that I am the Lord, when I open your graves, and raise you from your graves, O my people. And I will put my Spirit within you, and you shall live, and I will place you in your own land; then you shall know that I, the Lord have spoken, and I have done it, says the Lord."

b. Second Isaiah

"Second Isaiah" is the name given by biblical critics to the anonymous prophet who was active during the Exile just prior to the capture of Babylon by the Persians in 539 B. C.* His poetic oracles are generally regarded as the high-water mark of Old Testament prophecy, and of these the most famous are the following "suffering servant songs." Christianity has seen in these passages an anticipation if not a prediction of the suffering of Christ for the salvation of mankind; Judaism regards them as a prediction of the suffering of Israel.

[Isaiah 42:1–4; 49:1–6; 50:4–9; 52:12–53:13]

(Ch. 42)

Behold my servant, whom I uphold,
 my chosen, in whom my soul delights;
I have put my spirit upon him,
 he will bring forth justice to the nations.
He will not cry or lift up his voice,
 or make it heard in the street;
a bruised reed he will not break,
 and a dimly burning wick he will not quench;
 he will faithfully bring forth justice.
He will not fail or be discouraged
 till he has established justice in the earth;
 and the coastlands wait for his law.

(Ch. 49)

Listen to me, O coastlands,
 and hearken, you peoples from afar.

* For the distinction between "First," "Second," and "Third" Isaiah, see above, p. 12.

The LORD called me from the womb,
from the body of my mother he named my name.
He made my mouth like a sharp sword,
in the shadow of his hand he hid me;
he made me a polished arrow,
in his quiver he hid me away.
And he said to me, "You are my servant,
Israel, in whom I will be glorified."
But I said, "I have labored in vain,
I have spent my strength for
nothing and vanity;
yet surely my right is with the LORD,
and my recompense with my God."

And now the LORD says,
who formed me from the womb
to be his servant,
to bring Jacob back to him,
and that Israel might be gathered to him,
for I am honored in the eyes of the LORD,
and my God has become my strength—
he says:
"It is too light a thing that you
should be my servant
to raise up the tribes of Jacob
and to restore the preserved of Israel;
I will give you as a light to the nations,
that my salvation may reach to
the end of the earth."
(Ch. 50)
The Lord GOD has given me
the tongue of those who are taught.
that I may know how to sustain with a word
him that is weary.
Morning by morning he wakens,
he wakens my ear
to hear as those who are taught.
The Lord GOD has opened my ear,
and I was not rebellious,
I turned not backward.
I gave my back to the smiters,
and my cheeks to those who pulled out the beard;
I hid not my face
from shame and spitting.

For the Lord GOD helps me;
therefore I have not been confounded;
therefore I have set my face like a flint,
and I know that I shall not be put to shame;
he who vindicates me is near.
Who will contend with me?
Let us stand up together.
Who is my adversary?
Let him come near to me.
Behold, the Lord GOD helps me;
who will declare me guilty?
Behold, all of them will wear out like a garment;
the moth will eat them up.

(Ch. 52)
Behold, my servant shall prosper,
he shall be exalted and lifted up,
and shall be very high.
As many were astonished at him—
his appearance was so marred,
beyond human semblance,
and his form beyond that of the sons of men—
so shall he startle many nations;
kings shall shut their mouths because of him;
for that which has not been told
them they shall see,
and that which they have not
heard they shall understand.

(Ch. 53)
Who has believed what we have heard?
And to whom has the arm of the
LORD been revealed?
For he grew up before him like a young plant,
and like a root out of dry ground;
he had no form or comeliness that
we should look at him,
and no beauty that we should desire him.
He was despised and rejected by men;
a man of sorrows, and acquainted with grief;
and as one from whom men hide their faces
he was despised, and we esteemed him not.

Surely he has borne our griefs
and carried our sorrows;
yet we esteemed him stricken,
smitten by God, and afflicted.
But he was wounded for our transgressions,
he was bruised for our iniquities;
upon him was the chastisement
that made us whole,
and with his stripes we are healed.
All we like sheep have gone astray;
we have turned every one to his own way;
and the LORD has laid on him
the iniquity of us all.

He was oppressed, and he was afflicted,
yet he opened not his mouth;
like a lamb that is led to the slaughter,
and like a sheep that before its shearers is dumb,
so he opened not his mouth.
By oppression and judgment he was taken away;
and as for his generation, who considered

that he was cut off out of the land of the living,
stricken for the transgression of my people?
And they made his grave with the wicked
and with a rich man in his death,
although he had done no violence,
and there was no deceit in his mouth.

Yet it was the will of the LORD to bruise him;
he has put him to grief;
when he makes himself an offering for sin,
he shall see his offspring, he shall
prolong his days;
the will of the LORD shall prosper in his hand;
he shall see the fruit of the
travail of his soul and be satisfied;
by his knowledge shall the righteous
one, my servant,
make many to be accounted righteous;
and he shall bear their iniquities.
Therefore I will divide him a portion
with the great,
and he shall divide the spoil with
the strong;
because he poured out his soul to death,
and was numbered with the transgressors;
yet he bore the sin of many,
and made intercession for the transgressors.

D. The Poetry of Israel

Most of the Old Testament books contain at least some poetry, but the Book of Psalms is especially important because it has a cross-section of the prayers and petitions of individuals and groups from various periods of Israel's history. Modern scholarship usually classifies the psalms according to their "situation in life," which is often that of a festival or the offering of sacrifice. Four main types may be considered here.

1. *Psalms of Thanksgiving*

[PSALM 92]

It is good to give thanks to the LORD,
to sing praises to thy name, O Most High;
to declare thy steadfast love in the morning,
and thy faithfulness by night,
to the music of the lute and the harp,
to the melody of the lyre.
For thou, O LORD, hast made me
glad by thy work;
at the works of thy hands I sing for joy.

How great are thy works, O LORD!
Thy thoughts are very deep!
The dull man cannot know,
the stupid cannot understand this:
that, though the wicked sprout like grass
and all evildoers flourish,
they are doomed to destruction for ever,
but thou, O LORD, art on high for ever.
For, lo, thy enemies, O LORD,
for, lo, thy enemies shall perish;
all evidoers shall be scattered.

But thou hast exalted my horn like
that of the wild ox;
thou hast poured over me fresh oil.
My eyes have seen the downfall of my enemies,
my ears have heard the doom of
my evil assailants.
The righteous flourish like the palm tree,
and grow like a cedar in Lebanon.
They are planted in the house of the LORD,
they flourish in the courts of our God.
They still bring forth fruit in old age,
they are ever full of sap and green,
to show that the LORD is upright;
he is my rock, and there is no
unrighteousness in him.

[PSALM 100]

Make a joyful noise to the LORD, all the lands!
Serve the LORD with gladness!
Come into his presence with singing!

Know that the LORD is God!

It is he that made us, and we are his;
we are his people, and the sheep of his pasture.

Enter his gates with thanksgiving,
and his courts with praise!

Give thanks to him, bless his name!

For the LORD is good;
his steadfast love endures for ever,
and his faithfulness to all generations.

2. *Psalms of Lament*

[PSALM 32]

Blessed is he whose transgression is forgiven,
whose sin is covered.
Blessed is the man to whom the LORD imputes no iniquity,
and in whose spirit there is no deceit.
When I declared not my sin, my body wasted away
through my groaning all day long.
For day and night thy hand was heavy upon me;
my strength was dried up as by the heat of summer. *Selah.*
I acknowledged my sin to thee,
and I did not hide my iniquity;
I said, "I will confess my transgressions to the LORD":
then thou didst forgive the guilt of my sin. *Selah.*
Therefore let every one who is godly
offer prayer to thee;
at a time of distress, in the rush of great waters,
they shall not reach him.
Thou art a hiding place for me,
thou preservest me from trouble;
thou dost encompass me with deliverance. *Selah.*
I will instruct you and teach you
the way you should go;
I will counsel you with my eye upon you.
Be not like the horse or a mule, without understanding,
which must be curbed with bit and bridle,
else it will not keep with you.
Many are the pangs of the wicked;
but steadfast love surrounds him who trusts in the LORD.
Be glad in the LORD, and rejoice, O righteous,
and shout for joy all you upright in heart!

[PSALM 51]

Have mercy on me, O God,
according to thy steadfast love;
according to thy abundant mercy
blot out my transgressions.
Wash me thoroughly from my iniquity,
and cleanse me from my sin!

For I know my transgressions,
and my sin is ever before me.
Against thee, thee only, have I sinned,
and done that which is evil in thy sight,
so that thou art justified in thy sentence
and blameless in thy judgment.
Behold, I was brought forth in iniquity,
and in sin did my mother conceive me.

Behold, thou desirest truth in the inward being;
therefore teach me wisdom in my secret heart.
Purge me with hyssop, and I shall be clean;
wash me, and I shall be whiter than snow.
Fill me with joy and gladness;
let the bones which thou hast broken rejoice.
Hide thy face from my sins,
and blot out all my iniquities.

Create in me a clean heart, O God,
and put a new and right spirit within me.
Cast me not away from thy presence;
and take not thy holy Spirit from me.
Restore to me the joy of thy salvation,
and uphold me with a willing spirit.

Then I will teach transgressors thy ways,
and sinners will return to thee.
Deliver me from bloodguiltiness, O God,
thou God of my salvation,
and my tongue will sing aloud of thy deliverance.

O LORD, open thou my lips,
and my mouth shall show forth thy praise.
For thou hast no delight in sacrifice;
were I to give a burnt offering,
thou wouldst not be pleased.
The sacrifice acceptable to God is a broken spirit;
a broken and contrite heart, O God, thou wilt not despise.
Do good to Zion in thy good pleasure;
rebuild the walls of Jerusalem,
then wilt thou delight in right sacrifices,
in burnt offerings and whole burnt offerings;
then bulls will be offered on thy altar.

3. *Psalms for the King*

[Psalm 2]

Why do the nations conspire
and the people plot in vain?
The kings of the earth set themselves,
and the rulers take counsel together,
against the Lord and his anointed, saying,
"Let us burst their bonds asunder,
and cast their cords from us."
He who sits in the heavens laughs;
the Lord has them in derision.
Then he will speak to them in his wrath,
and terrify them in his fury, saying,
"I have set my king
on Zion, my holy hill."

I will tell of the decree of the Lord:
He said to me, "You are my son,
today I have begotten you.
Ask of me, and I will make the nations your heritage,
and the ends of the earth your possession.
You shall break them with a rod of iron,
and dash them in pieces like a potter's vessel."

Now therefore, O kings, be wise;
be warned, O rulers of the earth.
Serve the Lord with fear,
with trembling kiss his feet,
lest he be angry, and you perish in the way;
for his wrath is quickly kindled.

Blessed are all who take refuge in him.

[Psalm 110]

The Lord says to my lord:
"Sit at my right hand,
till I make your enemies your footstool."

The Lord sends forth from Zion
your mighty scepter.
Rule in the midst of your foes!
Your people will offer themselves freely
on the day you lead your host
upon the holy mountains.
From the womb of the morning
like dew your youth will come to you.
The Lord has sworn
and will not change his mind,
"You are a priest for ever
after the order of Melchizedek."
The Lord is at your right hand;
he will shatter kings on the day of his wrath.
He will execute judgment among the nations,
filling them with corpses;
he will shatter chiefs
over the wide earth.
He will drink from the brook by the way;
therefore he will lift up his head.

4. *Psalms Celebrating the Kingship of God*

[Psalm 47]

Clap your hands, all peoples!
Shout to God with loud songs of joy!
For the Lord, the Most High, is terrible,
a great king over all the earth.
He subdued peoples under us,
and nations under our feet.
He chose our heritage for us,
the pride of Jacob whom he loves. *Selah.*

God has gone up with a shout,
the Lord with the sound of a trumpet.
Sing praises to God, sing praises!
Sing praises to our King, sing praises!
For God is the king of all the earth;
sing praises with a psalm!

God reigns over the nations;
God sits on his holy throne.
The princes of the peoples gather
as the people of the God of Abraham.
For the shields of the earth belong to God;
he is highly exalted!

[Psalm 93]

The Lord reigns; he is robed in majesty;
the Lord is robed, he is girded with strength.
Yea, the world is established; it shall never be moved;
thy throne is established from old;
thou art from everlasting.

The floods have lifted up, O Lord,
the floods have lifted up their voice,
the floods lift up their roaring.
Mightier than the thunders of many waters,

mightier than the waves of the sea,
the LORD on high is mighty!
Thy decrees are very sure;
holiness befits thy house,
O LORD, for evermore.

[PSALM 96]

O sing to the LORD a new song;
sing to the LORD, all the earth!
Sing to the LORD, bless his name;
tell of his salvation from day to day.
Declare his glory among the nations,
his marvelous works among all the peoples!
For great is the LORD, and greatly to be praised;
he is to be feared above all gods.
For all the gods of the peoples are idols;
but the LORD made the heavens.
Honor and majesty are before him;
strength and beauty are in his sanctuary.

Ascribe to the LORD, O families of the peoples,
ascribe to the LORD glory and strength!
Ascribe to the LORD the glory due his name;
bring an offering, and come into his courts!
Worship the LORD in holy array;
tremble before him, all the earth!

Say among the nations, "The LORD reigns!
Yea, the world is established, it
shall never be moved;
he will judge the peoples with equity."
Let the heavens be glad, and let the earth rejoice;
let the sea roar, and all that fills it;
let the field exult, and everything in it!
Then shall all the trees of the wood sing for joy
before the LORD, for he comes,
for he comes to judge the earth.
He will judge the world with righteousness,
and the peoples with his truth.

E. Sayings of the Wise Men

The Book of Proverbs

One of the most common literary forms in the ancient Near East was that of the proverb or instruction from "father" (teacher) to "son" (pupil). The subject matter was usually that of practical advice, warning, and encouragement. The Book of Proverbs is the Old Testament counterpart of this international literature. It shows many parallels with Egyptian and Babylonian examples. At the same time the proverbs are firmly grounded in the faith of Israel: "The fear of the Lord is the beginning of knowledge . . . . (Prov. 1:7)."

[PROVERBS 6]

My son, if you have become
surety for your neighbor,
have given your pledge for a stranger;
if you are snared in the utterance of your lips,
caught in the words of your mouth;
then do this, my son, and save yourself,
for you have come into your neighbor's power:
go, hasten, and importune your neighbor.
Give your eyes no sleep
and your eyelids no slumber;
save yourself like a gazelle from the hunter,
like a bird from the hand of the fowler.

Go to the ant, O sluggard;
consider her ways, and be wise.
Without having any chief,
officer or ruler,
she prepares her food in summer,
and gathers her sustenance in harvest.
How long will you lie there, O sluggard?
When will you arise from your sleep?
A little sleep, a little slumber,
a little folding of the hands to rest,
and poverty will come upon you like a vagabond,
and want like an armed man.

A worthless person, a wicked man,
goes about with crooked speech,
winks with his eyes, scrapes with his feet,
points with his finger,
with perverted heart devises evil,
continually sowing discord;
therefore calamity will come upon him suddenly;
in a moment he will be broken beyond healing.

There are six things which the LORD hates,
seven which are an abomination to him:
haughty eyes, a lying tongue,
and hands that shed innocent blood,
a heart that devises wicked plans,
feet that make haste to run to evil,
a false witness who breathes out lies,
and a man who sows discord among brothers.

My son, keep your father's commandment,
and forsake not your mother's teaching.
Bind them upon your heart always;
tie them about your neck.
When you walk, they will lead you;
when you lie down, they will watch over you;
and when you awake, they will talk with you.
For the commandment is a lamp
and the teaching a light,
and the reproofs or discipline are the way of life,
to preserve you from the evil woman,
from the smooth tongue of the adventuress.
Do not desire her beauty in your heart,
and do not let her capture you with her eyelashes;
for a harlot may be hired for a loaf of bread,
but an adulteress stalks a man's very life.
Can a man carry fire in his bosom
and his clothes not be burned?
Or can one walk upon hot coals
and his feet not be scorched?
So is he who goes in to his neighbor's wife;
none who touches her will go unpunished.
Do not men despise a thief if he steals
to satisfy his appetite when he is hungry?
And if he is caught, he will pay sevenfold;
he will give all the goods of his house.
He who commits adultery has no sense;
he who does it destroys himself.
Wounds and dishonor will he get,
and his disgrace will not be wiped away.
For jealousy makes a man furious,
and he will not spare when he takes revenge.
He will accept no compensation,
nor be appeased though you multiply gifts.

F. A Dialogue on the Problem of Faith

The Book of Job

The Book of Job has many counterparts in the literature of Israel's neighbors. But as an expression of the problem of faith in spite of suffering it is really without parallel in world literature. Most scholars assume that the author of the poetic portions of the book, who probably lived in the sixth century B. C., used a folk tale from an earlier period as the occasion for his own thought. The first part of this tale, immediately preceding Job's lament, tells of the way in which the Lord permits Satan to afflict Job, and of the arrival of Job's friends; the remarks of one of these are to be found in Chapter 4 below.

[JOB 3]

After this Job opened his mouth and cursed the day of his birth. And Job said:

"Let the day perish wherein I was born,
and the night which said,
'A man-child is conceived.'
Let that day be darkness!
May God above not seek it,
nor light shine upon it.
Let gloom and deep darkness claim it.
Let clouds dwell upon it;
let the blackness of the day terrify it.
That night—let thick darkness seize it!
let it not rejoice among the days of the year,
let it not come into the number of the months.
Yea, let that night be barren;
let no joyful cry be heard in it.
Let those curse it who curse the day,
who are skilled to rouse up Leviathan.
Let the stars of its dawn be dark;
let it hope for light, but have none,
nor see the eyelids of the morning;
because it did not shut the doors of my mother's womb,
nor hide trouble from my eyes.

"Why did I not die at birth,
come forth from the womb and expire?

Why did the knees receive me?
Or why the breasts, that I should suck?
For then I should have lain down and been quiet;
I should have slept; then I should have been at rest,
with kings and counselors of the earth
who rebuilt ruins for themselves
or with princes who had gold,
who filled their houses with silver.
Or why was I not as a hidden untimely birth,
as infants that never see the light?
There the wicked cease from troubling,
and there the weary are at rest.
There the prisoners are at ease together;
they hear not the voice of the taskmaster.
The small and the great are there,
and the slave is free from his master.

"Why is light given to him that is in misery,
and life to the bitter in soul,
who long for death, but it comes not,
and dig for it more than for hid treasures;
who rejoice exceedingly,
and are glad, when they find the grave?
Why is light given to a man whose way is hid,
whom God has hedged in?
For my sighing comes as my bread,
and my groanings are poured out like water.
For the thing that I fear comes upon me,
and what I dread befalls me.
I am not at ease, nor am I quiet;
I have no rest; but trouble comes."

[Job 4]

Then Eliphaz the Temanite answered:

"If one ventures a word with you,
will you be offended?
Yet who can keep from speaking?
Behold, you have instructed many,
and you have strengthened the weak hands.
Your words have upheld him who was stumbling,
and you have made firm the feeble knees.
But now it has come to you,
and you are impatient;
it touches you, and you are dismayed.
Is not your fear of God your confidence,
and the integrity of your ways your hope?

"Think now, who that was innocent ever perished?
Or where were the upright cut off?
As I have seen, those who plow iniquity
and sow trouble reap the same.
By the breath of God they perish,
and by the blast of his anger they are consumed.
The roar of the lion, the voice of the fierce lion,
the teeth of the young lions, are broken.
The strong lion perishes for lack of prey,
and the whelps of the lioness are scattered.
Now a word was brought to me stealthily,
my ear received the whisper of it.
Amid thoughts from visions of the night,
when deep sleep falls on men,
dread came upon me, and trembling,
which made all my bones shake.
A spirit glided past my face;
the hair of my flesh stood up.
It stood still,
but I could not discern its appearance.
A form was before my eyes;
there was silence, then I heard a voice:
'Can mortal man be righteous before God?
can a man be pure before his Maker?
Even in his servants he puts no trust,
and his angels he charges with error;
how much more those who dwell in houses of clay,
whose foundation is in the dust,
who are crushed before the moth.
Between morning and evening they are destroyed;
they perish for ever without any regarding it.
If their tent-cord is plucked up within them,
do they not die, and that without wisdom?' "

[The chapters which follow continue the dialogue between Job and his friends. We then have a monologue from Job (Chapters 28–32), some harsh remarks from a certain Elihu (Chapters 32–37), and the beginning of the Lord's reply, the conclusion of which follows here.]

[Job 40:1–14; 42:1–6]

(Ch. 40)
And the Lord said to Job:

"Shall a faultfinder contend with the Almighty?
He who argues with God, let him answer it."

Then Job answered the Lord:

"Behold, I am of small account;
what shall I answer thee?
I lay my hand on my mouth.
I have spoken once, and I will not answer;
twice, but I will proceed no further."

Then God answered Job out of the whirlwind:

"Gird up your loins like a man;
I will question you, and you declare to me.
Will you even put me in the wrong?
Will you condemn me that you may be justified?

Have you an arm like God,
and can you thunder with a voice like his?

"Deck yourself with majesty and dignity;
clothe yourself with glory and splendor.
Pour forth the overflowings of your anger,
and look on every one that is proud, and abase him.
Look on every one that is proud,
and bring him low;
and tread down the wicked where they stand.
Hide them all in the dust together;
bind their faces in the world below.
Then will I also acknowledge to you,
that your own right hand can give you victory.

(Ch. 42)
Then Job answered the LORD:

"I know that thou canst do all things,
and that no purpose of thine can be thwarted.
'Who is this that hides counsel without knowledge?'
Therefore I have uttered what I did not understand,
things too wonderful for me,
which I did not know.
'Hear, and I will speak;
I will question you, and you declare to me.'
I had heard of thee by the hearing of the ear,
but now my eye sees thee;
therefore I despise myself,
and repent in dust and ashes."

[The second half of the folk tale follows Job's remarks, telling of the restoration of his fortunes.]

G. Apocalyptic Literature

"Apocalyptic" writings (from the Greek word meaning "revelation") are relatively rare in the Old Testament, but are of increasing importance in the intertestamental period and are represented by the Book of Revelation in the New Testament. They arose when Israel began to despair of the possibility that peace and justice would come without direct and miraculous intervention by God. Frequently in these writings the history of the world is divided into periods; up until the time of the author, history has been full of evil and rebellion, but the near future will bring a new world of vindication and salvation for the righteous.

The Book of Daniel

The Book of Daniel is considered by many to be a combination of stories concerning Daniel and his friends (Chapters 1–6) and Daniel's mysterious visions (Chapters 7–12). It was actually written just prior to the rededication of the Temple at the end of the first Maccabean war in 165 B. C., but was cast into the form of a historical novel with the Babylonian Exile as its background.

[DANIEL 7:1–18; 12]

(Ch. 7) In the first year of Belshazzar king of Babylon, Daniel had a dream and visions of his head as he lay in his bed. Then he wrote down the dream, and told the sum of the matter. Daniel said, "I saw in my vision by night, and behold, the four winds of heaven were stirring up the great sea. And four great beasts came up out of the sea, different from one another. The first was like a lion and had eagles' wings. Then as I looked its wings were plucked off, and it was lifted up from the ground and made to stand upon two feet like a man; and the mind of a man was given to it. And behold, another beast, a second one, like a bear. It was raised up on one side; it had three ribs in its mouth between its teeth; and it was told, 'Arise, devour much flesh.' After this I looked, and lo, another, like a leopard, with four wings of a bird on its back; and the beast had four heads; and dominion was given to it. After this I saw in the night visions, and behold, a fourth beast, terrible and dreadful and exceedingly strong; and it had great iron teeth; it devoured and broke in pieces, and stamped the residue with its feet. It was different from all the beasts that were before it; and it had ten horns. I considered the horns, and behold, there came up among them another horn, a little one, before which three of the first horns were plucked up by the roots; and behold, in this horn were eyes like the eyes of a man, and a mouth speaking great things. As I looked,

> thrones were placed
> and one that was ancient of days
> took his seat;
> his raiment was white as snow,
> and the hair of his head like pure wool;
> his throne was fiery flames,
> its wheels were burning fire.
> A stream of fire issued
> and came forth from before him;
> a thousand thousands served him,
> and ten thousand times ten thousand
> stood before him;
> the court sat in judgment,
> and the books were opened.

I looked then because of the sound of the great words which the horn was speaking. And as I looked, the beast was slain, and its body destroyed and given over to be burned with fire. As for the rest of the beasts, their dominion was taken away, but their lives were prolonged for a season and a time. I saw in the night visions,

> and behold, with the clouds of heaven
> there came one like a son of man,
> and he came to the Ancient of Days
> and was presented before him.
> And to him was given dominion
> and glory and kingdom,
> that all peoples, nations, and languages
> should serve him;
> his dominion is an everlasting dominion,
> which shall not pass away,
> and his kingdom one
> that shall not be destroyed.

"As for me, Daniel, my spirit within me was anxious and the visions of my head alarmed me. I approached one of those who stood there and asked him the truth concerning all this. So he told me, and made known to me the interpretation of the things. 'These four great beasts are four kings who shall arise out of the earth. But the saints of the Most High shall receive the kingdom, and possess the kingdom for ever, for ever and ever.' . . ."

(Ch. 12) "At that time shall arise Michael, the great prince who has charge of your people. And there shall be a time of trouble, such as never has been since there was a nation till that time; but at that time your people shall be delivered, every one whose name shall be found written in the book. And many of those who sleep in the dust of the earth shall awake, some to everlasting life and some to shame and everlasting contempt. And those who are wise shall shine like the brightness of the firmament; and those who turn many to righteousness, like the stars for ever and ever. But you, Daniel, shut up the words, and seal the book, until the time of the end. Many shall run to and fro, and knowledge shall increase."

Then I Daniel looked, and behold, two others stood, one on this bank of the stream and one on that bank of the stream. And I said to the man clothed in linen, who was above the waters of the stream, "How long shall it be till the end of these wonders?" The man clothed in linen, who was above the waters of the stream, raised his right hand and his left hand toward heaven; and I heard him swear by him who lives for ever that it would be for a time, two times, and half a time; and that when the shattering of the power of the holy people comes to an end all these things would be accomplished. I heard, but I did not understand. Then I said, "O my lord, what shall be the issue of these things?" He said, "Go your way, Daniel, for the words are shut up and sealed until the time of the end. Many shall purify themselves, and make themselves white, and be refined; but the wicked shall do wickedly; and none of the wicked shall understand; but those who are wise shall understand. And from the time that the continual burnt offering is taken away, and the abomination that makes desolate is set up, there shall be a thousand two hundred and ninety days. Blessed is he who waits and comes to the thousand three hundred and thirty-five days. But go your way till the end; and you shall rest, and shall stand in your allotted place at the end of the days."

Introduction to the New Testament

As compared with the Old Testament the New Testament is much more contemporaneous with the events to which it refers. Furthermore the time span of the New Testament is, of course, much shorter than that of the Old Testament. All of the books were produced within approximately one hundred years, the first being the Thessalonian correspondence (early 50's) and the last, according to most scholars, being II Peter (about 150 A. D.). However, there was a considerable body of oral tradition (stories and sayings passed on by word of mouth) prior to the actual writing of the first book.

By far the most important critical problem in the New Testament is that of the relationship of the four gospels to each other and the related question of the reliability of the gospels as records of the life and ministry of Jesus. Every reader has noted the marked differences between the first three gospels (usually called the "Synoptics," from a Greek word meaning "seeing together") and the Gospel of John. In Matthew, Mark, and Luke, Jesus' sayings are relatively short and often deal with the nature of the coming Kingdom of God; in John, however, Jesus delivers lengthy discourses, often beginning, "I am . . ." Furthermore, the chronology of Jesus' ministry found in John is considerably different from that of the Synoptics.

The first three gospels, taken by themselves, contain a great many parallels; for example, almost the whole of the Gospel of Mark is to be found in either Matthew or Luke or both. However, the serious student will discover that Matthew and Luke have a great deal of material in common which is not to be found in Mark; this consists mostly of sayings of Jesus. Furthermore, both Matthew and Luke include stories and sayings not to be found in any other gospel.

On the basis of this evidence modern New Testament scholars have constructed the "Four-Source Theory" on the relation of the Synoptics to each other. There is some disagreement in matters of detail, but it is generally held that Mark is the earliest of the gospels and that both Matthew and Luke used Mark and another source (now lost), written or oral, containing sayings of Jesus. This source is usually called "Q" (from the German, *Quelle*, meaning "source"). In addition to Mark and "Q," Matthew and Luke each had access to written or oral traditions apparently unknown to the others. The author of John, on the other hand, although he was probably familiar with the Synoptics, began afresh and wrote what has been called a theological tract organized in terms of events in Jesus' life.

The question of the "reliability" of the gospels is really independent of the "Synoptic Problem" discussed above. The issue is whether the gospels or their sources accurately report the actions and words of Jesus and the disciples, or whether interpretations have been added to the words, even going so far as to construct new sayings of Jesus. It has been pointed out that many passages seem to reflect the situation of the early church rather than the teaching of Jesus. At the same time it must be recognized that the gospels are not and were not intended to be biographies in the modern sense of the word. They are the faithful response of the church to the Incarnation of God in Christ, and have as their purpose the spreading and confirming of that faith. The "event" of revelation includes not only the words and deeds of Jesus, but also the way in which these were apprehended and interpreted by the earliest Christians. Thus, for many the question of "historical reliability" is less important than it once seemed to be.

The criticism of the other New Testament books has dealt largely with questions of date and authorship. For example, most critics attribute the epistles of John to the author of the fourth gospel, although they separate the gospel and the Book of Revelation on the basis of differing style and theology. Furthermore, it is doubtful that Paul is the author of I and II Timothy and Titus in their present form; these were probably written toward the end of the first century. Some regard Ephesians as a letter written in the spirit of Paul by one of his disciples. And it is extremely doubtful, say the critics, that the letters of Peter were actually written by the disciple himself. They are couched in excellent Greek, and Peter was a simple Galilean fisherman; furthermore, I Peter reflects the condition of the church toward the beginning of the second century and II Peter, the struggles of an even later period. Other questions of New Testament criticism will be discussed in the prefaces to the individual readings.

A. The Gospels

Modern theories concerning the composition and significance of the gospels have been outlined in the Introduction of the New Testament. The following passages are representative of the unique character of each of the gospels and are presented in their approximate order in the life of Jesus; the Prologue to John interrupts the chronological order but it has seemed advisable to present it along with other material from the fourth gospel.

1. *The Gospel According to Luke*

Luke is traditionally identified as the physician who was a companion of Paul. However, the internal evidence of the gospel seems to point to a date toward the end of the first century. Of special interest are the birth stories. Mark and John have none of these, and Matthew relatively few; the following passages are thus said to be from Luke's special source.

[LUKE 1:5–2:52]

In the days of Herod, king of Judea, there was a priest named Zechariah, of the division of Abijah; and he had a wife of the daughters of Aaron, and her name was Elizabeth. And they were both righteous before God, walking in all the commandments and ordinances of the Lord blameless. But they had no child, because Elizabeth was barren, and both were advanced in years.

Now while he was serving as priest before God when his division was on duty, according to the custom of the priesthood, it fell to him by lot to enter the Temple of the Lord and burn incense. And the whole multitude of the people were praying outside at the hour of incense. And there appeared to him an angel of the Lord standing on the right side of the altar of incense. And Zechariah was troubled when he saw him, and fear fell upon him. But the angel said to him, "Do not be afraid, Zechariah, for your prayer is heard, and your wife Elizabeth will bear you a son, and you shall call his name John.

And you will have joy and gladness,
and many will rejoice at his birth;
for he will be great before the Lord,
and he shall drink no wine nor strong drink,
and he will be filled with the Holy Spirit,
even from his mother's womb.
And he will turn many of the sons
of Israel to the Lord their God,
and he will go before him in the
spirit and power of Elijah,
to turn the hearts of the fathers to the children,
and the disobedient to the wisdom of the just,
to make ready for the Lord a people prepared."

And Zechariah said to the angel, "How shall I know this? For I am an old man, and my wife is advanced in years." And the angel answered him, "I am Gabriel, who stand in the presence of God; and I was sent to speak to you, and to bring you this good news. And behold, you will be silent and unable to speak until the day that these things come to pass, because you did not believe my words, which will be fulfilled in their time." And the people were waiting for Zechariah, and they wondered at his delay in the temple. And when he came out, he could not speak to them, and they perceived that he had seen a vision in the temple;

and he made signs to them and remained dumb. And when his time of service was ended, he went to his home.

After these days his wife Elizabeth conceived, and for five months she hid herself, saying, "Thus the Lord has done to me in the days when he looked on me, to take away my reproach among men."

In the sixth month the angel Gabriel was sent from God to a city of Galilee named Nazareth, to a virgin betrothed to a man whose name was Joseph, of the house of David; and the virgin's name was Mary. And he came to her and said, "Hail, O favored one, the Lord is with you!" But she was greatly troubled at the saying, and considered in her mind what sort of greeting this might be. And the angel said to her, "Do not be afraid, Mary, for you have found favor with God. And behold, you will conceive in your womb and bear a son, and you shall call his name Jesus.

He will be great, and will be called
the Son of the Most High;
and the Lord God will give to him
the throne of his father David,
and he will reign over the house of
Jacob for ever;
and of his kingdom there will be no end."

And Mary said to the angel, "How can this be, since I have no husband?" And the angel said to her,

"The Holy Spirit will come upon you,
and the power of the Most High
will overshadow you;
therefore the child to be born
will be called holy,
the Son of God.

And behold, your kinswoman Elizabeth in her old age has also conceived a son; and this is the sixth month with her who was called barren. For with God nothing will be impossible." And Mary said, "Behold I am the handmaid of the Lord; let it be to me according to your word." And the angel departed from her.

In those days Mary arose and went with haste into the hill country, to a city of Judah, and she entered the house of Zechariah and greeted Elizabeth. And when Elizabeth heard the greeting of Mary, the babe leaped in her womb; and Elizabeth was filled with the Holy Spirit and she exclaimed with a loud cry, "Blessed are you among women, and blessed is the fruit of your womb! And why is this granted me, that the mother of my Lord should come to me? For behold, when the voice of your greeting came to my ears, the babe in my womb leaped for joy. And blessed is she who believed that there would be a fulfillment of what was spoken to her from the Lord." And Mary said,

"My soul magnifies the Lord,
and my spirit rejoices in God my Savior,
for he has regarded the low estate
of his handmaiden.
For behold, henceforth all generations
will call me blessed;
for he who is mighty has done great things for me,
and holy is his name.
And his mercy is on those who fear him
from generation to generation.
He has shown strength with his arm,
he has scattered the proud in the
imagination of their hearts,
he has put down the mighty from their thrones,
and exalted those of low degree;
he has filled the hungry with good things,
and the rich he has sent empty away.
He has helped his servant Israel,
in remembrance of his mercy,
as he spoke to our fathers,
to Abraham and to his posterity for ever."

And Mary remained with her about three months, and returned to her home.

Now the time came for Elizabeth to be delivered, and she gave birth to a son. And her neighbors and kinsfolk heard that the Lord had shown great mercy to her, and they rejoiced with her. And on the eighth day they came to circumcise the child; and they would have named him Zechariah after his father, but his mother said, "Not so; he shall be called John." And they said to her, "None of your kindred is called by this name." And they made signs to his father, inquiring what he would have him called. And he asked for a writing tablet, and wrote, "His name is John." And they all marveled. And immediately his mouth was opened and his tongue loosed, and he spoke, blessing God. And fear came on all their neighbors. And all these things were talked about through all the hill country of Judea; and all who heard them laid them up in their hearts, saying, "What then will this child be?" For the hand of the Lord was with him.

And his father Zechariah was filled with the Holy Spirit, and prophesied, saying,

"Blessed be the Lord God of Israel,
for he has visited and redeemed his people,
and has raised up a horn of salvation for us
in the house of his servant David,
as he spoke by the mouth of his
holy prophets from of old,
that we should be saved from our enemies,
and from the hand of all who hate us;
to perform the mercy promised to our fathers,
and to remember his holy covenant,
the oath which he swore to our father Abraham,
to grant us
that we, being delivered from the hand of our enemies,
might serve him without fear,
in holiness and righteousness before him
all the days of our life.
And you, child, will be called the
prophet of the Most High;
for you will go before the Lord to
prepare his ways,
to give knowledge of salvation to his people
in the forgiveness of their sins,
through the tender mercy of our God,
when the day shall dawn upon us from on high
to give light to those who sit in darkness and in the shadow of death
to guide our feet into the way of peace."

And the child grew and became strong in spirit, and he was in the wilderness till the day of his manifestation to Israel.

(Ch. 2) In those days a decree went out from Caesar Augustus that all the world should be enrolled. This was the first enrollment, when Quirinius was governor of Syria. And all went to be enrolled, each to his own city. And Joseph also went up from Galilee, from the city of Nazareth, to Judea, to the city of David, which is called Bethlehem, because he was of the house and lineage of David, to be enrolled with Mary, his betrothed, who was with child. And while they were there, the time came for her to be delivered. And she gave birth to her first-born son and wrapped him in swaddling cloths, and laid him in a manger, because there was no place for them in the inn.

And in that region there were shepherds out in the field, keeping watch over their flock by night. And an angel of the Lord appeared to them, and the glory of the Lord shone around them, and they were filled with fear. And the angel said to them, "Be not afraid; for behold, I bring you good news of a great joy which will come to all the people; for to you is born this day in the city of David a Savior, who is Christ the Lord. And this will be a sign for you: you will find a babe wrapped in swaddling cloths and lying in a manger." And suddenly there was with the angel a multitude of the heavenly host praising God and saying,

"Glory to God in the highest,
and on earth peace among men
with whom he is pleased!"

When the angels went away from them into heaven, the shepherds said to one another, "Let us go over to Bethlehem and see this thing that has happened, which the Lord has made known to us." And they went with haste, and found Mary and Joseph, and the babe lying in a manger. And when they saw it they made known the saying which had been told them concerning this child; and all who heard it wondered at what the shepherds told them. But Mary kept all these things, pondering them in her heart. And the shepherds returned, glorifying and praising God for all they had heard and seen, as it had been told them.

And at the end of eight days, when he was circumcised, he was called Jesus, the name given by the angel before he was conceived in the womb.

And when the time came for their purification according to the law of Moses, they brought him up to Jerusalem to present him to the Lord (as it is written in the law of the Lord, "Every male that opens the womb shall be called holy to the Lord") and to offer a sacrifice according to what is said in the law of the Lord, "a pair of turtledoves, or two young pigeons." Now there was a man in Jerusalem, whose name was Simeon, and this man was righteous and devout, looking for the consolation of Israel, and the Holy Spirit was upon him. And it had been revealed to him by the Holy Spirit that he should not see death before he had seen the Lord's Christ. And inspired by the Spirit he came into the temple;

and when the parents brought in the child Jesus, to do for him according to the custom of the law, he took him up in his arms and blessed God and said,

"Lord, now lettest thou they servant
depart in peace,
according to thy word;
for mine eyes have seen thy salvation
which thou hast prepared in the presence
of all peoples,
a light for revelation to the Gentiles,
and for glory to thy people Israel."

And his father and his mother marveled at what was said about him; and Simeon blessed them and said to Mary his mother,

"Behold, this child is set for the fall
and rising of many in Israel,
and for a sign that is spoken against
(and a sword will pierce through
your own soul also),
that thoughts out of many hearts
may be revealed."

And there was a prophetess, Anna, the daughter of Phanuel, of the tribe of Asher; she was of a great age, having lived with her husband seven years from her virginity, and as a widow till she was eighty-four. She did not depart from the temple, worshiping with fasting and prayer night and day. And coming up at that very hour she gave thanks to God, and spoke of him to all who were looking for the redemption of Jerusalem.

And when they had performed everything according to the law of the Lord, they returned into Galilee, to their own city, Nazareth. And the child grew and became strong, filled with wisdom; and the favor of God was upon him.

Now his parents went to Jerusalem every year at the feast of the Passover. And when he was twelve years old, they went up according to custom; and when the feast was ended, as they were returning, the boy Jesus stayed behind in Jerusalem. His parents did not know it, but supposing him to be in the company they went a day's journey, and they sought him among their kinsfolk and acquaintances; and when they did not find him, they returned to Jerusalem, seeking him. After three days they found him in the temple, sitting among the teachers, listening to them and asking them questions; and all who heard him were amazed at his understanding and his answers. And when they saw him they were astonished; and his mother said to him, "Son, why have you treated us so? Behold, your father and I have been looking for you anxiously." And he said to them, "How is it that you sought me? Did you not know that I must be in my Father's house?" And they did not understand the saying which he spoke to them. And he went down with them and came to Nazareth and was obedient to them; and his mother kept all these things in her heart.

And Jesus increased in wisdom and in stature, and in favor with God and man.

2. *The Gospel According to Mark*

Mark, the earliest gospel, was probably written in the period just before or just after the first Jewish revolt against the Romans in 66–70 A. D. An ancient tradition states that the gospel transmits the reminiscences of Peter. In general the author concentrates on the things Jesus did, rather than on what he said, and Mark's chronology has been followed faithfully by both Matthew and Luke. The following passage is typical of the way in which Mark presents Jesus as a teacher and healer.

[MARK 2–4]

(Ch. 2) And when he returned to Capernaum after some days, it was reported that he was at home. And many were gathered together, so that there was no longer room for them, not even about the door; and he was preaching the word to them. And they came, bringing to him a paralytic carried by four men. And when they could not get near him because of the crowd, they removed the roof above him; and when they had made an opening, they let down the pallet on which the paralytic lay. And when Jesus saw their faith, he said to the paralytic, "My son, your sins are forgiven." Now some of the scribes were sitting there, questioning in their hearts, "Why does this man speak thus? It is blasphemy! Who can forgive sins but God alone?" And immediately Jesus, perceiving in his spirit that they thus questioned within themselves, said to them, "Why do you question thus in your hearts? Which is easier, to say to the paralytic, 'Your sins are forgiven,' or to say, 'Rise, take up your pallet and walk'? But that you may know that the Son of man has authority on earth to forgive sins"—he said to the paralytic —"I say to you, rise, take up your pallet and go home." And he rose, and immediately took up the pallet and went out before them all; so that they were all amazed and glorified God, saying, "We never saw anything like this!"

He went out again beside the sea; and all the crowd gathered about him, and he taught them. And as he passed on, he saw Levi the son of Alphaeus sitting at the tax office, and he said to him, "Follow me." And he rose and followed him.

And as he sat at table in his house, many tax collectors and sinners were sitting with Jesus and his disciples; for there were many who followed him. And the scribes of the Pharisees, when they saw that he was eating with sinners and tax collectors, said to his disciples, "Why does he eat with tax collectors and sinners?" And when Jesus heard it, he said to them, "Those who are well have no need of a physician, but those who are sick; I came not to call the righteous, but sinners."

Now John's disciples and the Pharisees were fasting; and people came and said to him, "Why do John's disciples and the disciples of the Pharisees fast, but your disciples do not fast?" And Jesus said to them, "Can the wedding guests fast while the bridegroom is with them? As long as they have the bridegroom with them, they cannot fast. The days will come, when the bridegroom is taken away from them, and then they will fast in that day. No one sews a piece of unshrunk cloth on an old garment; if he does, the patch tears away from it, the new from the old, and a worse tear is made. And no one puts new wine into old wine-skins; if he does, the wine will burst the skins, and the wine is lost, and so are the skins; but new wine is for fresh skins."

One sabbath he was going through the grainfields; and as they made their way his disciples began to pluck ears of grain. And the Pharisees said to him, "Look, why are they doing what is not lawful on the sabbath?" And he said to them, "Have you never read what David did, when he was in need and was hungry, he and those who were with him: how he entered the house of God, when Abiathar was high priest, and ate the bread of the Presence, which it is not lawful for any but the priests to eat, and also gave it to those who were with him?" And he said to them, "The sabbath was made for man, not man for the sabbath; so the Son of man is lord even of the sabbath."

(Ch. 3) Again he entered the synagogue, and a man was there who had a withered hand. And they watched him, to see whether he would heal him on the sabbath, so that they might accuse him. And he said to the man who had the withered hand, "Come here." And he said to them, "Is it lawful on the sabbath to do good or to do harm, to save life or to kill?" But they were silent. And he looked around at them with anger, grieved at their hardness of heart, and said to the man, "Stretch out your hand." He stretched it out, and his hand was restored. The Pharisees went out, and immediately held counsel with the Herodians against him, how to destroy him.

Jesus withdrew with his disciples to the sea, and a great multitude from Galilee followed; also from Judea and Jerusalem and Idumea and from beyond the Jordan and from about Tyre and Sidon a great multitude, hearing all that he did, came to him. And he told his disciples to have a boat ready for him because of the crowd, lest they should crush him; for he had healed many, so that all who had diseases pressed upon him to touch him. And whenever the unclean spirits beheld him, they fell down before him and cried out, "You are the Son of God." And he strictly ordered them not to make him known.

And he went up into the hills, and called to him those whom he desired; and they came to him. And he appointed twelve, to be with him, and to be sent out to preach and have authority to cast out demons: Simon whom he surnamed Peter; James the son of Zebedee and John the brother of James, whom he surnamed Boanerges, that is, sons of thunder; Andrew, and Philip, and Bartholomew, and Matthew, and Thomas, and James the son of Alphaeus, and Thaddaeus, and Simon the Cananaean, and Judas Iscariot, who betrayed him.

Then he went home; and the crowd came together again, so that they could not even eat. And when his friends heard it, they went out to seize him, for they said, "He is beside himself." And the scribes who came down from Jerusalem said, "He is possessed by Beelzebub, and by the prince of demons he casts out the demons." And he called them to him, and said to them in parables, "How can Satan cast out Satan? If a kingdom is divided against itself, that kingdom cannot stand. And if a house is divided against itself, that house will not be able to stand. And if Satan has risen up against himself and is divided, he cannot stand, but is coming to an end. But no one can enter a strong man's house and plunder his goods, unless he first binds the strong man; then indeed he may plunder his house.

"Truly, I say to you, all sins will be forgiven the sons of men, and whatever blasphemies they utter; but whoever blasphemes against the Holy Spirit never has forgiveness, but is guilty of an eternal sin"—for they had said, "He has an unclean spirit."

And his mother and his brothers came; and standing outside they sent to him and called him. And a crowd was sitting about him; and they said to him, "Your mother and your brothers are outside, asking for you." And he replied, "Who are my mother and my brothers?" And looking around on those who sat about him, he said, "Here are my mother and my brothers! Whoever does the will of God is my brother, and sister, and mother."

(Ch. 4) Again he began to teach beside the sea. And a very large crowd gathered about him, so that he got into a boat and sat in it on the sea; and the whole crowd was beside the sea on the land. And he taught them many things in parables, and in his teaching he said to them: "Listen! A sower went out to sow. And as he sowed, some seed fell along the path, and the birds came and devoured it. Other seed fell on rocky ground, where it had not much soil and immediately it sprang up, since it had no depth of soil; and when the sun rose it was scorched, and since it had no root it withered away. Other seed fell among thorns and the thorns grew up and choked it, and it yielded no grain. And other seeds fell into good soil and brought forth grain, growing up and increasing and yielding thirtyfold and sixtyfold and a hundredfold." And he said, "He who has ears to hear, let him hear."

And when he was alone, those who were about him with the twelve asked him concerning the parables. And he said to them, "To you has been given the secret of the kingdom of God, but for those outside everything is in parables; so that they may indeed see but not perceive, and may indeed hear but not understand; lest they should turn again, and be forgiven." And he said to them, "Do you not understand this parable? How then will you understand all the parables? The sower sows the word. And these are the ones along the path, where the word is sown; when they hear, Satan immediately comes and takes away the word which is sown in them. And these in like manner are the ones sown upon rocky ground, who, when they hear the word, immediately receive it with joy; and they have no root in themselves, but endure for a while; then, when tribulation or persecution arises on account of the word, immediately they fall away. And others are the ones sown among thorns; they are those who hear the word, but the cares of the world, and the delight in riches, and the desire for other things, enter in and choke the word, and it proves unfruitful. But those that were sown upon the good soil are the ones who hear the word and accept it and bear fruit, thirtyfold and sixtyfold and a hundredfold."

And he said to them, "Is a lamp brought in to be put under a bushel, or under a bed, and not on a stand? For there is nothing hid, except to be made manifest; nor is anything secret, except to come to light. If any man has ears to hear, let him hear." And he said to them, "Take heed what you hear; the measure you give will be the measure you get, and still more will be given you. For to him who has will more be given; and from him who has not, even what he has will be taken away."

And he said, "The kingdom of God is as if a man should scatter seed upon the ground, and should sleep and rise night and day, and the seed should sprout and grow, he knows not how. The earth produces of itself, first the blade, then the ear, then the full grain in the ear. But when the grain is ripe, at once he puts in the sickle, because the harvest has come."

And he said, "With what can we compare the kingdom of God, or what parable shall we use for it? It is like a grain of mustard seed, which, when sown upon the ground, is the smallest of all the seeds on earth; yet when it is sown it grows up and becomes the greatest of all shrubs, and puts forth large branches, so that the birds of the air can make nests in its shade."

With many such parables he spoke the word to them, as they were able to hear it; he did not speak to them without a parable, but privately to his own disciples he explained everything.

On that day, when evening had come, he said to them, "Let us go across to the other side." And leaving the crowd, they took him with them, just as he was, in the boat. And other boats were with him. And a great storm of wind arose, and the waves beat into the boat, so that the boat was already filling. But he was in the stern, asleep on the cushion; and they awoke him and said to him, "Teacher, do you not care if we perish?" And he awoke and rebuked the wind, and said to the sea, "Peace! Be still!" And the wind ceased, and there was a great calm. He said to them, "Why are you afraid? Have you no faith?" And they were filled with awe, and said to one another, "Who then is this, that even wind and sea obey him?"

3. *Sayings of Jesus ("Q")*

The evidence used by scholars in the reconstruction of the hypothetical source "Q" has been outlined in the Introduction to the New Testament. In point of time it originates in the teachings of Jesus himself and was used by the early church in the instruction of its members. Matthew and Luke vary in their use of "Q"; the order of the material is somewhat different in the two gospels, and there are cases where the evangelists independently altered the wording of the common source. The following passage is traditionally known as the "Sermon on the Mount"; it is presented here in its Matthean form, omitting the material not to be found in Luke.

[MATTHEW 5–7, OMITTING 5:17–20, 21–24, 27–30, 31–32, 33–37; 6:1–8; 6:13b, 14–18; 7:6, 28–29]

(Ch. 5) Seeing the crowds, he went up on the mountain, and when he sat down his disciples came to him. And he opened his mouth and taught them, saying:

"Blessed are the poor in spirit, for theirs is the kingdom of heaven.

"Blessed are those who mourn, for they shall be comforted.

"Blessed are the meek, for they shall inherit the earth.

"Blessed are those who hunger and thirst for righteousness, for they shall be satisfied.

"Blessed are the merciful, for they shall obtain mercy.

"Blessed are the pure in heart, for they shall see God.

"Blessed are the peacemakers, for they shall be called sons of God.

"Blessed are those who are persecuted for righteousness' sake, for theirs is the kingdom of heaven.

"Blessed are you when men revile you and persecute you and utter all kinds of evil against you falsely on my account. Rejoice and be glad, for your reward is great in heaven, for so men persecuted the prophets who were before you.

"You are the salt of the earth; but if salt has lost its taste, how shall its saltness be restored? It is no longer good for anything except to be thrown out and trodden under foot by men.

"You are the light of the world. A city set on a hill cannot be hid. Nor do men light a lamp and put it under a bushel, but on a stand, and it gives light to all in the house. Let your light so shine before men, that they may see your good works and give glory to your Father who is in heaven. . . .

"Make friends quickly with your accuser, while you are going with him to court, lest your accuser hand you over to the judge, and the judge to the guard, and you be put in prison; truly, I say to you, you will never get out till you have paid the last penny. . . .

"You have heard that it was said, 'An eye for an eye and a tooth for a tooth.' But I say to you, Do not resist one who is evil. But if any one strikes you on the right cheek, turn to him the other also; and if any one would sue you and take your coat let him have your cloak as well; and if any one forces you to go one mile, go with him two miles. Give to him who begs from you, and do not refuse him who would borrow from you.

"You have heard that it was said, 'You shall love your neighbor and hate your enemy.' But I say to you, Love your enemies and pray for those who persecute you so that you may be sons of your Father who is in heaven; for he makes his sun rise on the evil and on the good, and sends rain on the just and on the unjust. For if you love those who love you, what reward have you? Do not even the tax collectors do the same? And if you salute only your brethren, what more are you doing than others? Do not even the Gentiles do the same? You, therefore, must be perfect, as your heavenly Father is perfect. . . .

(Ch. 6)
Pray then like this:

Our Father who art in heaven,
Hallowed be thy name.
Thy kingdom come,
Thy will be done,
On earth as it is in heaven.
Give us this day our daily bread;
And forgive us our debts,
As we also have forgiven our debtors;
And lead us not into temptation. . . .

"Do not lay up for yourselves treasures on earth, where moth and rust consume and where thieves break in and steal, but lay up for yourselves treasures in heaven, where neither moth nor rust consumes and where thieves do not break in and steal. For where your treasure is, there will your heart be also.

"The eye is the lamp of the body. So, if your eye is sound, your whole body will be full of light; but if your eye is not sound, your whole body will be full of darkness. If then the light in you is darkness, how great is the darkness!

"No one can serve two masters; for either he will hate the one and love the other, or he will be devoted to the one and despise the other. You cannot serve God and mammon.

"Therefore I tell you, do not be anxious about your life, what you shall eat or what you shall drink, nor about your body, what you shall put on. Is not life more than food, and the body more than clothing? Look at the birds of the air: they neither sow nor reap nor gather into barns, and yet your heavenly Father feeds them. Are you not of more value than they? And which of you by being anxious can add one cubit to his span of life? And why are you anxious about clothing? Consider the lilies of the field, how they grow; they neither toil nor spin; yet I tell you, even Solomon in all his glory was not arrayed like one of these. But if God so clothes the grass of the field, which today is alive and tomorrow is thrown into the oven, will he not much more clothe you, O men of little faith? Therefore do not be anxious, saying, 'What shall we eat?' or 'What shall we drink?' or 'What shall we wear?' For the Gentiles seek all these things; and your heavenly Father knows that you need them all. But seek first his kingdom and his righteousness, and all these things shall be yours as well.

"Therefore do not be anxious about tomorrow, for tomorrow will be anxious for itself. Let the day's own trouble be sufficient for the day.

(Ch. 7) "Judge not, that you be not judged. For with the judgment you pronounce you will be judged, and the measure you give will be the measure you get. Why do you see the speck that is in your brother's eye, but do not notice the log that is in your own eye? Or how can you say to your brother, 'Let me take the speck out of your eye,' when there is the log in your own eye? You hypocrite, first take the log out of your own eye, and then you will see clearly to take the speck out of your brother's eye. . . .

"Ask, and it will be given you; seek and you will find; knock, and it will be opened to you. For every one who asks receives, and he who seeks finds, and to him who knocks it will be opened. Or what man of you, if his son asks him for a loaf, will give him a stone? Or if he asks for a fish, will give him a serpent?

If you then, who are evil, know how to give good gifts to your children, how much more will your Father who is in heaven give good things to those who ask him? So whatever you wish that men would do to you, do so to them; for this is the law and the prophets.

"Enter by the narrow gate; for the gate is wide and the way is easy, that leads to destruction, and those who enter by it are many. For the gate is narrow and the way is hard, that leads to life, and those who find it are few.

"Beware of false prophets, who come to you in sheep's clothing but inwardly are ravenous wolves. You will know them by their fruits. Are grapes gathered from thorns, or figs from thistles? So, every sound tree bears good fruit, but the bad tree bears evil fruit. A sound tree cannot bear evil fruit, nor can a bad tree bear good fruit. Every tree that does not bear good fruit is cut down and thrown into the fire. Thus you will know them by their fruits.

"Not every one who says to me, 'Lord, Lord,' shall enter the kingdom of heaven, but he who does the will of my Father who is in heaven. On that day many will say to me, 'Lord, Lord, did we not prophesy in your name, and cast out demons in your name, and do many mighty works in your name?' And then will I declare to them, 'I never knew you; depart from me, you evildoers.'

"Every one then who hears these words of mine and does them will be like a wise man who built his house upon the rock; and the rain fell, and the floods came, and the winds blew and beat upon that house, but it did not fall, because it had been founded on the rock. And every one who hears these words of mine and does not do them will be like a foolish man who built his house upon the sand; and the rain fell, and the floods came, and the winds blew and beat against that house, and it fell; and great was the fall of it."

4. *The Gospel According to Matthew*

The author of Matthew was almost contemporary with the author of Luke and, as has been seen, used Mark, "Q," and a special source in the preparation of his gospel. Matthew is especially noted for his quotations from the Old Testament in connection with the work of Jesus, for instructions on church order and discipline, and for a number of parables not to be found elsewhere. Examples of each of these types are given below, along with Matthew's version of Peter's confession of faith in Jesus as the Messiah.

[MATTHEW 2:13–23; 5:17–20, 27–30, 33–37; 6:1–8; 18:15–20; 13:34–52; 18:23–35; 20:1–16; 16:13–23]

(Ch. 2) Now when [the wise men] had departed, behold, an angel of the Lord appeared to Joseph in a dream and said, "Rise, take the child and his mother, and flee to Egypt, and remain there till I tell you; for Herod is about to search for the child, to destroy him." And he rose and took the child and his mother by night, and departed to Egypt, and remained there until the death of Herod. This was to fulfil what the Lord has spoken by the prophet, "Out of Egypt have I called my son."

Then Herod, when he saw that he had been tricked by the wise men, was in a furious rage, and he sent and killed all the male children in Bethlehem and in all that region who were two years old or under, according to the time which he had ascertained from the wise men. Then was fulfilled what was spoken by the prophet Jeremiah:

"A voice was heard in Ramah,
wailing and loud lamentation,
Rachel weeping for her children;
she refused to be consoled,
because they were no more."

But when Herod died, behold, an angel of the Lord appeared in a dream to Joseph in Egypt, saying, "Rise, take the child and his mother, and go to the land of Israel, for those who sought the child's life are dead." And he rose and took the child and his mother, and went to the land of Israel. But when he heard that Archelaus reigned over Judea in place of his father Herod, he was afraid to go there, and being warned in a dream he withdrew to the district of Galilee. And he went and dwelt in a city called Nazareth, that what was spoken by the prophets might be fulfilled, "He shall be called a Nazarene." . . .

(Ch. 5) "Think not that I have come to abolish the law and the prophets; I have come not to abolish them but to fulfil them. For truly, I say to you, till heaven and earth pass away, not an iota, not a dot, will pass from the law until all is accomplished. Whoever then relaxes one of the least of these commandments and teaches men so, shall be called least in the kingdom of heaven; but he who does them and teaches them shall be called great in the kingdom of heaven. For I tell you, unless your righteousness exceeds that of the scribes and Pharisees, you will never enter the kingdom of heaven. . . .

"You have heard that it was said, 'You shall not commit adultery.' But I say to you that every one who looks at a woman lustfully has already committed adultery with her in his heart. If your right eye causes you to sin, pluck it out and throw it away; it is better that you lose one of your members than that your whole body be thrown into hell. And if your right hand causes you to sin, cut it off and throw it away; it is better that you lose one of your members than that your whole body go into hell. . . .

"Again you have heard that it was said to the men of old, 'You shall not swear falsely, but shall perform to the Lord what you have sworn.' But I say to you, Do not swear at all, either by heaven, for it is the throne of God, or by the earth, for it is his footstool, or by Jerusalem, for it is the city of the great King. And do not swear by your head, for you cannot make one hair white or black. Let what you say be simply 'Yes' or 'No'; anything more than this comes from evil. . . .

(Ch. 6) "Beware of practicing your piety before men in order to be seen by them; for then you will have no reward from your Father who is in heaven.

"Thus, when you give alms, sound no trumpet before you, as the hypocrites do in the synagogues and in the streets, that they may be praised by men. Truly, I say to you, they have their reward. But when you give alms, do not let your left hand know what your right hand is doing, so that your alms may be in secret; and your Father who sees in secret will reward you.

"And when you pray, you must not be like the hypocrites; for they love to stand and pray in the synagogues and at the street corners, that they may be seen by men. Truly, I say to you, they have their reward. But when you pray, go into your room and shut the door and pray to your Father who is in secret; and your Father who sees in secret will reward you.

"And in praying do not heap up empty phrases as the Gentiles do; for they think that they will be heard for their many words. Do not be like them, for your Father knows what you need before you ask him. . . .

(Ch. 18) "If your brother sins against you, go and tell him his fault, between you and him alone. If he listens to you, you have gained your brother. But if he does not listen, take one or two others along with you, that every word may be confirmed by the evidence of two or three witnesses. If he refuses to listen to them, tell it to the church; and if he refuses to listen even to the church, let him be to you as a Gentile and a tax collector. Truly, I say to you, whatever you bind on earth shall be bound in heaven, and whatever you loose on earth shall be loosed in heaven. Again I say to you, if two of you agree on earth about anything they ask, it will be done for them by my Father in heaven. For where two or three are gathered in my name, there am I in the midst of them." . . .

(Ch. 13) All this Jesus said to the crowds in parables; indeed he said nothing to them without a parable. This was to fulfil what was spoken by the prophet:

"I will open my mouth in parables,
I will utter what has been hidden
since the foundation of the world."

Then he left the crowds and went into the house. And his disciples came to him, saying, "Explain to us the parable of the weeds of the field." He answered, "He who sows the good seed is the Son of man; the field is the world, and the good seed means the sons of the kingdom; the weeds are the sons of the evil one, and the enemy who sowed them is the devil; the harvest is the close of the age, and the reapers are angels. Just as the weeds are gathered and burned with fire, so will it be at the close of the age. The Son of man will send his angels and they will gather out of his kingdom all causes of sin and all evildoers, and throw them into the furnace of fire; there men will weep and gnash their teeth. Then the righteous will shine like the sun in the kingdom of their Father. He who has ears, let him hear.

"The kingdom of heaven is like treasure hidden in a field, which a man found and covered up; then in his joy he goes and sells all that he has and buys that field.

"Again, the kingdom of heaven is like a merchant in search of fine pearls, who, on finding one pearl of great value, went and sold all that he had and bought it.

"Again, the kingdom of heaven is like a net which was thrown into the sea and gathered fish of every kind; when it was full, men drew it ashore and sat down and sorted the good into vessels but threw away the bad. So it will be at the close of the age. The angels will come out and separate the evil from the righteous, and throw them into the furnace of fire; there men will weep and gnash their teeth.

"Have you understood all this?" They said to him, "Yes." And he said to them, "Therefore every scribe who has been trained for the kingdom of heaven is like a householder who brings out of his treasure what is new and what is old." . . .

(Ch. 18) "Therefore the kingdom of heaven may be compared to a king who wished to settle accounts with his servants. When he began the reckoning, one was brought to him who owed him ten thousand talents; and as he could not pay, his lord ordered him to be sold, with his wife and children and all that he had, and payment to be made. So the servant fell on his knees, imploring him, 'Lord, have patience with me, and I will pay you everything.' And out of pity for him the lord of that servant released him and forgave him the debt. But that same servant, as he went out came upon one of his fellow servants who owed him a hundred denarii; and seizing him by the throat he said, 'Pay what you owe.' So his fellow servant fell down and besought him, 'Have patience with me, and I will pay you.' He refused and went and put him in prison till he should pay the debt. When his fellow servants saw what had taken place, they were greatly distressed, and they went and reported to their lord all that had taken place. Then his lord summoned him and said to him, 'You wicked servant! I forgave you all that debt because you besought me; and should not you have had mercy on your fellow servant, as I had mercy on you?' And in anger his lord delivered him to the jailers, till he should pay all his debt. So also my heavenly Father will do to every one of you, if you do not forgive your brothers from your heart." . . .

(Ch. 20) "For the kingdom of heaven is like a householder who went out early in the morning to hire laborers for his vineyard. After agreeing with the laborers for a denarius a day, he sent them into his vineyard. And going out about the third hour he saw others standing idle in the market place; and to them he said, 'You go into the vineyard too, and whatever is right I will give you.' So they went. Going out again about the sixth hour and the ninth hour, he did the same. And about the eleventh hour he went out and found others standing; and he said to them, 'Why do you stand here idle all day?' They said to him, 'Because no one has hired us.' He said to them, 'You go into the vineyard too.' And when evening came, the owner of the vineyard said to his steward, 'Call the laborers and pay them their wages, beginning with the last, up to the first.' And when those hired about the eleventh hour came, each of them received a denarius. Now when the first came, they thought they would receive more; but each of them also received a denarius. And on receiving it they grumbled at the householder, saying, 'These last worked only one hour, and you have made them equal to us who have borne the burden of the day and the scorching heat.' But he replied to one of them, 'Friend, I am doing you no wrong; did you not agree with me for a denarius? Take what belongs to you, and go; I choose to give to this last as I give to you. Am I not allowed to do what I choose with what belongs to me? Or do you begrudge my generosity? So the last will be first, and the first last.' . . .

(Ch. 16) Now when Jesus came into the district of Caesarea Philippi, he asked his disciples, "Who do men say that the Son of man is?" And they said, "Some say John the Baptist, others say Elijah, and others Jeremiah or one of the prophets." He said to them, "But who do you say that I am?" Simon Peter replied, "You are the Christ, the Son of the living God." And Jesus answered him, "Blessed are you, Simon Bar-Jona! For flesh and blood has not revealed this to you, but my Father who is in heaven. And I tell you, you are Peter, and on this rock I will build my church, and the powers of death shall not prevail against it. I will give you the keys of the kingdom of heaven, and whatever you bind on earth shall be bound in heaven, and whatever you loose on earth shall be loosed in heaven." Then he strictly charged the disciples to tell no one that he was the Christ.

From that time Jesus began to show his disciples that he must go to Jerusalem and suffer many things from the elders and chief priests and scribes, and be killed, and on the third day be raised. And Peter took him and began to rebuke him, saying, "God forbid, Lord! This shall never happen to you." But he turned and said to Peter, "Get behind me, Satan! You are a hindrance to me; for you are not on the side of God, but of men."

5. The Gospel According to John

The Gospel of John, although written in the same general period as Matthew and Luke, represents a different perspective of the life and teachings of Jesus than do the Synoptic gospels. Like the other gospels John is vitally concerned with the spread and confirmation of faith in Jesus as the Christ (20:31); however, the manner of presentation is peculiar to this gospel. We begin, not with the birth of Jesus, but with the Christ who is co-eternal with God; in his earthly ministry this Christ performs seven mighty "signs" around which the gospel is organized; there are extensive passages in which the relationship between Christ and God is presented. The following passages are typical of John's style and theology.

[John 1:1–18; 13–14; 18–20]

(Ch. 1) In the beginning was the Word, and the Word was with God, and the Word was God. He was in the beginning with God; all things were made through him, and without him was not anything made that was made. In him was life, and the life was the light of men. The light shines in the darkness, and the darkness has not overcome it.

There was a man sent from God, whose name was John. He came for testimony, to bear witness to the light, that all might believe through him. He was not the light, but came to bear witness to the light.

The true light that enlightens every man was coming into the world. He was in the world, and the world was made through him, yet the world knew him not. He came to his own home, and his own people received him not. But to all who received him, who believed in his name, he gave power to become children of God; who were born, not of blood nor of the will of the flesh nor of the will of man, but of God.

And the Word became flesh and dwelt among us, full of grace and truth; we have beheld his glory, glory as of the only Son from the Father. (John bore witness to him, and cried, "This was he of whom I said, 'He who comes after me ranks before me, for he was before me.' ") And from his fullness have we all received, grace upon grace. For the law was given through Moses; grace and truth came through Jesus Christ. No one has ever seen God; the only Son, who is in the bosom of the Father, he has made him known.

(Ch. 13) Now before the feast of the Passover, when Jesus knew that his hour had come to depart out of this world to the Father, having loved his own who were in the world, he loved them to the end. And during supper, when the devil had already put it into the heart of Judas Iscariot, Simon's son, to betray him, Jesus, knowing that the Father had given all things into his hands, and that he had come from God and was going to God, rose from supper, laid aside his garments, and girded himself with a towel. Then he poured water into a basin, and began to wash the disciples' feet, and to wipe them with the towel with which he was girded. He came to Simon Peter; and Peter said to him, "Lord do you wash my feet?" Jesus answered him, "What I am doing you do not know now, but afterward you will understand." Peter said to him, "You shall never wash my feet." Jesus answered him, "If I do not wash you, you have no part in me." Simon Peter said to him, "Lord, not my feet only but also my hands and my head!" Jesus said to him, "He who has bathed does not need to wash, except for his feet, but he is clean all over; and you are clean, but not all of you." For he knew who was to betray him; that was why he said, "You are not all clean."

When he had washed their feet, and taken his garments, and resumed his place, he said to them, "Do you know what I have done to you? You call me Teacher and Lord; and you are right, for so I am. If I then, your Lord and Teacher, have washed your feet, you also ought to wash one another's feet. For I have given you an example, that you also should do as I have done to you. Truly, truly, I say to you, a servant is not greater than his master; nor is he who is sent greater than he who sent him. If you know these things, blessed are you if you do them. I am not speaking of you all; I know whom I have chosen; it is that the scripture may be fulfilled, 'He who ate my bread has lifted his heel against me.' I tell you this now, before it takes place that when it does take place you may believe that I am he. Truly, truly, I say to you, he who receives any one whom I send receives me; and he who receives me receives him who sent me."

When Jesus had thus spoken, he was troubled in spirit, and testified, "Truly, truly, I say to you, one of you will betray me." The disciples looked at one another, uncertain of whom he spoke. One of his disciples, whom Jesus loved, was lying close to the breast of Jesus; so Simon Peter beckoned to him and said, "Tell us who it is of whom he speaks." So lying thus, close to the breast of Jesus, he said to him, "Lord, who is it?" Jesus answered, "It is he to whom I shall give this morsel when I have dipped it." So when he had dipped the morsel, he gave it to Judas, the son of Simon Iscariot. Then after the morsel, Satan entered into him. Jesus said to him, "What you are going to do, do quickly." Now no one at the table knew why he said this to him. Some thought that because Judas had the money box, Jesus was telling him, "Buy what we need for the feast"; or, that he should give something to the poor. So, after receiving the morsel, he immediately went out; and it was night.

When he had gone out, Jesus said, "Now is the Son of man glorified, and in him God is glorified; if God is glorified in him, God will also glorify him in himself, and glorify him at once. Little children, yet a little while I am with you. You will seek me; and as I said to the Jews so now I say to you, 'Where I am going you cannot come.' A new commandment I give to you, that you love one another; even as I have loved you, that you also love one another. By this all men will know that you are my disciples, if you have love for one another."

Simon Peter said to him, "Lord, where are you going?" Jesus answered, "Where I am going you cannot follow me now; but you shall follow afterward." Peter said to him, "Lord, why cannot I follow you now? I will lay down my life for you." Jesus answered, "Will you lay down your life for me? Truly, truly, I say to you, the cock will not crow, till you have denied me three times."

(Ch. 14) "Let not your hearts be troubled; believe in God, believe also in me. In my Father's house are many rooms; if it were not so, would I have told you that I go to prepare a place for you? And when I go and prepare a place for you, I will come again and will take you to myself, that where I am you may be also. And you know the way where I am going." Thomas said to him, "Lord, we do not know where you are going; how can we know the way?" Jesus said to him, "I am the way, and the truth, and the life; no one comes to the Father, but by me. If you had known me, you would have known my Father also; henceforth you know him and have seen him."

Philip said to him, "Lord, show us the Father, and we shall be satisfied." Jesus said to him, "Have I been with you so long, and yet you do not know me, Philip? He who has seen me has seen the Father; how can you say, 'Show us the Father'? Do you not believe that I am in the Father and the Father in me? The words that I say to you I do not speak on my own authority; but the Father who dwells in me does his works. Believe me that I am in the Father and the Father in me; or else believe me for the sake of the works themselves.

"Truly, truly, I say to you, he who believes in me will also do the works that I do; and greater works than these will he do, because I go to the Father. Whatever you ask in my name, I will do it, that the Father may be glorified in the Son; if you ask anything in my name, I will do it.

"If you love me, you will keep my commandments. And I will pray the Father, and he will give you another Counselor, to be with you for ever, even the Spirit of truth, whom the world cannot receive, because it neither sees him nor knows him; you know him, for he dwells with you, and will be in you.

"I will not leave you desolate; I will come to you. Yet a little while, and the world will see me no more, but you will see me; because I live, you will live also. In that day you will know that I am in my Father, and you in me, and I in you. He who has my commandments and keeps them, he it is who loves me; and he who loves me will be loved by my Father, and I will love him and manifest myself to him." Judas (not Iscariot) said to him, "Lord, how is it that you will manifest yourself to us, and not to the world?" Jesus answered him, "If a man loves me, he will keep my word, and my Father will love him, and we will come to him and make our home with him. He who does not love me does not keep my words; and the word which you hear is not mine but the Father's who sent me.

"These things I have spoken to you, while I am still with you. But the Counselor, the Holy Spirit, whom the Father will send in my name, he will teach you all things, and bring to your remembrance all that I have said to you. Peace I leave with you; my peace I give to you; not as the world gives do I give to you. Let not your hearts be troubled, neither let them be afraid. You heard me say to you, 'I go away, and I will come to you.' If you loved me, you would have rejoiced, because I go to the Father; for the Father is greater than I. And now I have told you before it takes place, so that when it does take place, you may believe. I will no longer talk much with you, for the ruler of this world is coming. He has no power over me; but I do as the Father has commanded me, so that the world may know that I love the Father. Rise, let us go hence."

(Ch. 18) When Jesus had spoken these words, he went forth with his disciples across the Kidron valley, where there was a garden, which he and his disciples entered. Now Judas, who betrayed him, also knew the place; for Jesus often met there with his disciples. So Judas, procuring a band of soldiers and some officers from the chief priests and the Pharisees, went there with lanterns and torches and weapons. Then Jesus, knowing all that was to befall him, came forward and said to them, "Whom do you seek?" They answered him, "Jesus of Nazareth." Jesus said to them, "I am he." Judas, who betrayed him, was standing with them. When he said to them, "I am he," they drew back and fell to the ground. Again he asked them, "Whom do you seek?" And they said, "Jesus of Nazareth." Jesus answered, "I told you that I am he; so, if you seek me, let these men go." This was to fulfil the word which he had spoken, "Of those whom thou gavest me I lost not one." Then Simon Peter, having a sword drew it and struck the high priest's slave and cut off his right ear. The slave's name was Malchus. Jesus said to Peter, "Put your sword into its sheath; shall I not drink the cup which the Father has given me?"

So the band of soldiers and their captain and the officers of the Jews seized Jesus and bound him. First they led him to Annas; for he was the father-in-law of Caiaphas, who was high priest that year. It was Caiaphas who had given counsel to the Jews that it was expedient that one man should die for the people.

Simon Peter followed Jesus, and so did another disciple. As this disciple was known to the high priest, he entered the court of the high priest along with Jesus, while Peter stood outside at the door. So the other disciple, who was known to the high priest, went out and spoke to the maid who kept the door, and brought Peter in. The maid who kept the door said to Peter, "Are not you also one of this man's disciples?" He said, "I am not." Now the servants and officers had made a charcoal fire, because it was cold, and they were standing and warming themselves; Peter also was with them, standing and warming himself.

The high priest then questioned Jesus about his disciples and his teaching. Jesus answered him, "I have spoken openly to the world; I have always taught in synagogues and in the temple, where all Jews come together; I have said nothing secretly. Why do you ask me? Ask those who have heard me, what I said to them; they know what I said." When he had said this, one of the officers standing by struck Jesus with his hand, saying, "Is that how you answer the high priest?" Jesus answered him, "If I have spoken wrongly, bear witness to the wrong; but if I have spoken rightly, why do you strike me?" Annas then sent him bound to Caiaphas the high priest.

Now Simon Peter was standing and warming himself. They said to him, "Are not you also one of his disciples?" He denied it and said, "I am not." One of the servants of the high priest, a kinsman of the man whose ear Peter had cut off, asked, "Did I not see you in the garden with him?" Peter again denied it; and at once the cock crowed.

Then they led Jesus from the house of Caiaphas to the praetorium. It was early. They themselves did not enter the praetorium, so that they might not be defiled, but might eat the passover. So Pilate went out to them and said, "What accusation do you bring against this man?" They answered him, "If this man were not an evildoer, we would not have handed him over." Pilate said to them, "Take him yourselves and judge him by your own law." The Jews said to him, "It is not lawful for us to put any man to death." This was to fulfil the word which Jesus had spoken to show by what death he was to die.

Pilate entered the praetorium again and called Jesus, and said to him, "Are you the King of the Jews?" Jesus answered, "Do you say this of your own accord, or did others say it to you about me?" Pilate answered, "Am I a Jew? Your own nation and the chief priests have handed you over to me; what have you done?" Jesus answered, "My kingship is not of this world; if my kingship were of this world, my servants would fight, that I might not be handed over to the Jews; but my kingship is not from the world." Pilate said to him, "So you are a king?" Jesus answered, "You say that I am a king. For this I was born, and for this I have come into the world, to bear witness to the truth. Every one who is of the truth hears my voice." Pilate said to him, "What is truth?"

After he had said this, he went out to the Jews again, and told them, "I find no crime in him. But you have a custom that I should release one man for you at the Passover; will you have me release for you the King of the Jews?" They cried out again, "Not this man, but Barabbas!" Now Barabbas was a robber.

(Ch. 19) Then Pilate took Jesus and scourged him. And the soldiers plaited a crown of thorns, and put it on his head, and arrayed him in a purple robe; they came up to him, saying, "Hail, King of the Jews!" and struck him with their hands. Pilate went out again, and said to them, "Behold, I am bringing him out to you, that you may know that I find no crime in him." So Jesus came out, wearing the crown of thorns and the purple robe. Pilate said to them, "Here is the man!" When the chief priests and the officers saw him, they cried out, "Crucify him, crucify him!" Pilate said to them, "Take him yourselves and crucify him, for I find no crime in him." The Jews answered him, "We have a law, and by that law he ought to die, because he has made himself the Son of God." When Pilate heard these words, he was the more afraid; he entered the praetorium again and said to Jesus, "Where are you from?" But Jesus gave no answer. Pilate therefore said to him, "You will not speak to me? Do you not know that I have power to release you, and power to crucify you?" Jesus answered him, "You would have no power over me unless it had been given you from above; therefore he who delivered me to you has the greater sin."

Upon this Pilate sought to release him, but the Jews cried out, "If you release this man, you are not Caesar's friend; every one who makes himself a king sets himself against Caesar." When Pilate heard these words, he brought Jesus out and sat down on the judgment seat at a place called The Pavement, and in Hebrew, Gabbatha. Now it was the day of Preparation for the Passover; it was about the sixth hour. He said to the Jews, "Here is your king!" They cried out, "Away with him, away with him, crucify him!" Pilate said to them, "Shall I crucify your King?" The chief priests answered, "We have no king but Caesar." Then he handed him over to them to be crucified.

So they took Jesus, and he went out, bearing his own cross, to the place called the place of a skull, which is called in Hebrew Golgotha. There they crucified him, and with him two others, one on either side, and Jesus between them. Pilate also wrote a title and put it on the cross; it read, "Jesus of Nazareth, the King of the Jews." Many of the Jews read this title, for the place where Jesus was crucified was near the city; and it was written in Hebrew, in Latin, and in Greek. The chief priests of the Jews then said to Pilate, "Do not write, 'The King of the Jews,' but, 'This man said, I am King of the Jews.'" Pilate answered, "What I have written I have written."

When the soldiers had crucified Jesus they took his garments and made four parts, one for each soldier. But his tunic was without seam, woven from top to bottom; so they said to one another, "Let us not tear it, but cast lots for it to see whose it shall be." This was to fulfil the scripture.

"They parted my garments among them,
and for my clothing they cast lots."

So the soldiers did this; but standing by the cross of Jesus were his mother, and his mother's sister, Mary the wife of Clopas, and Mary Magdalene. When Jesus saw his mother, and the disciple whom he loved standing near, he said to his mother, "Woman, behold your son!" Then he said to the disciple, "Behold your mother!" And from that hour the disciple took her to his own home.

After this Jesus, knowing that all was not finished, said (to fulfil the scripture), "I thirst." A bowl full of vinegar stood there; so they put a sponge full of the vinegar on hyssop and held it to his mouth. When Jesus had received the vinegar, he said, "It is finished"; and he bowed his head and gave up his spirit.

Since it was the day of Preparation, in order to prevent the bodies from remaining on the cross on the sabbath (for that sabbath was a high day), the Jews asked Pilate that their legs might be broken, and that they might be taken away. So the soldiers came and broke the legs of the first, and of the other who had been crucified with him; but when they came to Jesus and saw that he was already dead, they did not break his legs. But one of the soldiers pierced his side with a spear, and at once there came out blood and water. He who saw it has borne witness—his testimony is true, and he knows that he tells the truth—that you also may believe. For these things took place that the scripture might be fulfilled, "Not a bone of him shall be broken." And again another scripture says, "They shall look on him whom they have pierced."

After this Joseph of Arimathea, who was a disciple of Jesus, but secretly, for fear of the Jews, asked Pilate that he might take away the body of Jesus, and Pilate gave him leave. So he came and took away his body. Nicodemus also, who had at first come to him by night, came bringing a mixture of myrrh and aloes, about a hundred pounds' weight. They took the body of Jesus, and bound it in linen cloths with the spices, as is the burial custom of the Jews. Now in the place where he was crucified there was a garden, and in the garden a new tomb where no one had ever been laid. So because of the Jewish day of Preparation, as the tomb was close at hand, they laid Jesus there.

(Ch. 20) Now on the first day of the week Mary Magdalene came to the tomb early, while it was still dark, and saw that the stone had been taken away from the tomb. So she ran, and went to Simon Peter and the other disciple, the one whom Jesus loved, and said to them, "They have taken the Lord out of the tomb, and we do not know where they have laid him." Peter then came out with the other disciple, and they went toward the tomb. They both ran, but the other disciple outran Peter and reached the tomb first; and stooping to look in, he saw the linen cloths lying there, but he did not go in. Then Simon Peter came following him, and he went into the tomb; he saw the linen cloths lying, and the napkin, which had been on his head, not lying with the linen cloths but rolled up in a place by itself. Then the other disciple, who reached the tomb first, also went in, and he saw and believed; for as yet they did not know the scripture, that he must rise from the dead. Then the disciples went back to their homes.

But Mary stood weeping outside the tomb, and as she wept she stooped to look into the tomb; and she saw two angels in white, sitting where the body of Jesus had lain, one at the head and one at the feet. They said to her, "Woman, why are you weeping?" She said to them, "Because they have taken away my Lord, and I do not know where they have laid him." Saying this, she turned round and saw Jesus standing, but she did not know that it was Jesus. Jesus said to her, "Woman, why are you weeping? Whom do you seek?" Supposing him to be the gardener, she said to him, "Sir, if you have carried him away, tell me where you have laid him, and I will take him away." Jesus said to her, "Mary." She turned and said to him in Hebrew, "Rabboni!" (which means Teacher). Jesus said to her, "Do not hold me, for I have not yet ascended to the Father; but go to my brethren and say to them, I am ascending to my Father and your Father, to my God and your God." Mary Magdalene went and said to the disciples, "I have seen the Lord"; and she told them that he had said these things to her.

On the evening of that day, the first day of the week, the doors being shut where the disciples were, for fear of the Jews, Jesus came and stood among them and said to them, "Peace be with you." When he had said this, he showed them his hands and his side. Then the disciples were glad when they saw the Lord. Jesus said to them again, "Peace be with you. As the Father has sent me, even so I send you." And when he had said this, he breathed on them, and said to them, "Receive the Holy Spirit. If you forgive the sins of any, they are forgiven; if you retain the sins of any they are retained."

Now Thomas, one of the twelve, called the Twin, was not with them when Jesus came. So the other disciples told him, "We have seen the Lord." But he said to them, "Unless I see in his hands the print of the nails, and place my finger in the mark of the nails, and place my hand in his side, I will not believe."

Eight days later, his disciples were again in the house, and Thomas was with them. The doors were shut, but Jesus came and stood among them, and said, "Peace be with you." Then he said to Thomas, "Put your finger here, and see my hands; and put out your hand, and place it in my side; do not be faithless, but believing." Thomas answered him, "My Lord and my God!" Jesus said to him "Have you believed because you have seen me? Blessed are those who have not seen and yet believe."

Now Jesus did many other signs in the presence of the disciples, which are not written in this book; but these are written that you may believe that Jesus is the Christ, the Son of God, and that believing you may have life in his name.

B. The Acts of the Apostles

The Book of Acts

Acts was written by the author of the Gospel of Luke; both books are addressed to a certain Theophilus. The main concern of the work is to show the gradual and inevitable expansion of the church both in Palestine and in the Mediterranean world. The first passage reproduced here tells of the fulfillment of Jesus' promise that he would send the Holy Spirit to his followers, and of Peter's sermon upon that occasion; the second passage is the story of Paul's first missionary journey to the Gentile world.

[ACTS 2]

When the day of Pentecost had come, they were all together in one place. And suddenly a sound came from heaven like the rush of a mighty wind, and it filled all the house where they were sitting. And there appeared to them tongues as of fire, distributed and resting on each one of them. And they were all filled with the Holy Spirit and began to speak in other tongues, as the Spirit gave them utterance.

Now there were dwelling in Jerusalem Jews, devout men from every nation under heaven. And at this sound the multitude came together, and they were bewildered, because each one heard them speaking in his own language. And they were amazed and wondered, saying, "Are not all these who are speaking Galileans? And how is it that we hear, each of us in his own native language? Parthians and Medes and Elamites and residents of Mesopotamia, Judea and Cappadocia, Pontus and Asia, Phrygia and Pamphylia, Egypt and the parts of Libya belonging to Cyrene, and visitors from Rome, both Jews and proselytes, Cretans and Arabians, we hear them telling in our own tongues the mighty works of God." And all were amazed and perplexed, saying to one another, "What does this mean?" But others mocking said, "They are filled with new wine."

But Peter, standing with the eleven, lifted up his voice and addressed them, "Men of Judea and all who dwell in Jerusalem, let this be known to you, and give ear to my words. For these men are not drunk, as you suppose, since it is only the third hour of the day; but this is what was spoken by the prophet Joel:

'And in the last days it shall be, God declares,
that I will pour out my Spirit upon all flesh,
and your sons and your daughters shall prophesy,
and your young men shall see visions,
and your old men shall dream dreams;
yea, and on my menservants and
my maidservants in those days
I will pour out my Spirit; and they
shall prophesy.
And I will show wonders in the heaven above
and signs on the earth beneath,
blood, and fire, and vapor of smoke;
the sun shall be turned into darkness
and the moon into blood,
before the day of the Lord comes,
the great and manifest day.
And it shall be that whoever calls
on the name of the Lord shall be saved.'

"Men of Israel, hear these words: Jesus of Nazareth, a man attested to you by God with mighty works and wonders and signs which God did through him in your midst, as you yourselves know—this Jesus, delivered up according to the definite plan and foreknowledge of God, you crucified and killed by the hands of lawless men. But God raised him up, having loosed the pangs of death, because it was not possible for him to be held by it. For David says concerning him,

'I saw the Lord always before me,
for he is at my right hand that I
may not be shaken;
therefore my heart was glad, and
my tongue rejoiced;
moreover my flesh will dwell in hope.
For thou wilt not abandon my soul to Hades,
nor let thy Holy One see corruption.
Thou hast made known to me the ways of life;
thou wilt make me full of gladness
with thy presence.'

"Brethren, I may say to you confidently of the patriarch David that he both died and was buried, and his tomb is with us to this day. Being therefore a prophet, and knowing that God had sworn with an oath to him that he would set one of his descendants upon his throne, he foresaw and spoke of the resurrection of the Christ, that he was not abandoned to Hades, nor did his flesh see corruption. This Jesus God raised up, and of that we all are witnesses. Being therefore exalted at the right hand of God, and having received from the Father the promise of the Holy Spirit, he has poured out this which you see and hear. For David did not ascend into the heavens; but he himself says,

'The Lord said to my Lord, Sit at my right hand,
till I make thy enemies a stool for thy feet.'

Let all the house of Israel therefore know assuredly that God has made him both Lord and Christ, this Jesus whom you crucified."

Now when they heard this they were cut to the heart, and said to Peter and the rest of the apostles, "Brethren, what shall we do?" And Peter said to them, "Repent, and be baptized every one of you in the name of Jesus Christ for the forgiveness of your sins; and you shall receive the gift of the Holy Spirit. For the promise is to you and to your children and to all that are far off, every one whom the Lord our God calls to him." And he testified with many other words and exhorted them, saying, "Save yourselves from this crooked generation." So those who received his word were baptized, and there were added that day about three thousand souls. And they devoted themselves to the apostles' teaching and fellowship, to the breaking of bread and the prayers.

And fear came upon every soul; and many wonders and signs were done through the apostles. And all who believed were together and had all things in common; and they sold their possessions and goods and distributed them to all, as any had need. And day by day, attending the temple together and breaking bread in their homes, they partook of food with glad and generous hearts, praising God and having favor with all the people. And the Lord added to their number day by day those who were being saved.

[ACTS 13–14]

(Ch. 13) Now in the church at Antioch there were prophets and teachers, Barnabas, Symeon who was called Niger, Lucius of Cyrene, Manaen a member of the court of Herod the tetrarch, and Saul [the earlier name of Paul]. While they were worshiping the Lord and fasting, the Holy Spirit said, "Set apart for me Barnabas and Saul for the work to which I have called them." Then after fasting and praying they laid their hands on them and sent them off.

So, being sent out by the Holy Spirit, they went down to Seleucia; and from there they sailed to Cyprus. When they arrived at Salamis, they proclaimed the word of God in the synagogues of the Jews. And they had John to assist them. When they had gone through the whole island as far as Paphos, they came upon a certain magician, a Jewish false prophet, named Bar-Jesus. He was with the proconsul, Sergius Paulus, a man of intelligence, who summoned Barnabas and Saul and sought to hear the word of God. But Elymas the magician (for that is the meaning of his name) withstood them, seeking to turn away the proconsul from the faith. But Saul, who is also called Paul, filled with the Holy Spirit looked intently at him and said, "You son of the devil, you enemy of all righteousness, full of all deceit and villainy, will you not stop making crooked the straight paths of the Lord? And now, behold, the hand of the Lord is upon you, and you shall be blind and unable to see the sun for a time." Immediately mist and darkness fell upon him and he went about seeking people to lead him by the hand. Then the proconsul believed, when he saw what had occurred, for he was astonished at the teaching of the Lord.

Now Paul and his company set sail from Paphos, and came to Perga in Pamphylia. And John left them and returned to Jerusalem; but they passed on from Perga and came to Antioch of Pisidia. And on the sabbath day they went into the synagogue and sat down. After the reading of the law and the prophets, the rulers of the synagogue sent to them, saying, "Brethren, if you have any word of exhortation for the people, say it." So Paul stood up, and motioning with his hand said:

"Men of Israel, and you that fear God, listen. The God of this people Israel chose our fathers and made the people great during their stay in the land of Egypt, and with uplifted arm he led them out of it. And for about forty years he bore with them in the wilderness. And when he had destroyed seven nations in the land of Canaan, he gave them their land as an inheritance, for about four hundred and fifty years. And after that he gave them judges until Samuel the prophet. Then they asked for a king; and God gave them Saul the son of Kish, a man of the tribe of Benjamin, for forty years. And when he had removed him, he raised up David to be their king; of whom he testified and said, 'I have found in David the son of Jesse a man after my heart, who will do all my will.' Of this man's posterity God has brought to Israel a Savior, Jesus, as he promised. Before his coming John had preached a baptism of repentance to all the people of Israel. And as John was finishing his course, he said, 'What do you suppose that I am? I am not he. No, but after me one is coming, the sandals of whose feet I am not worthy to untie.'

"Brethren, sons of the family of Abraham, and those among you that fear God, to us has been sent the message of this salvation. For those who live in Jerusalem and their rulers, because they did not recognize him nor understand the utterances of the prophets which are read every sabbath, fulfilled these by condemning him. Though they could charge him with nothing deserving death, yet they asked Pilate to have him killed. And when they had fulfilled all that was written of him, they took him down from the tree, and laid him in a tomb. But God raised him from the dead; and for many days he appeared to those who came up with him from Galilee to Jerusalem, who are now his witnesses to the people. And we bring you the good news that what God promised to the fathers, this he has fulfilled to us their children by raising Jesus; as also it is written in the second psalm,

'Thou art my Son,
today I have begotten thee.'

"And as for the fact that he raised him from the dead, no more to return to corruption, he spoke in this way,

'I will give you the holy and sure
blessings of David.'

"Therefore he says also in another psalm,

'Thou wilt not let thy Holy One see corruption.'

"For David, after he had served the counsel of God in his own generation, fell asleep, and was laid with his fathers, and saw corruption; but he whom God raised up saw no corruption. Let it be known to you therefore, brethren, that through this man forgiveness of sins is proclaimed to you, and by him every one that believes is freed from everything from which you could not be freed by the law of Moses. Beware, therefore, lest there come upon you what is said in the prophets:

'Behold, you scoffers, and wonder, and perish;
for I do a deed in your days,
a deed you will never believe, if one
declares it to you.' "

As they went out, the people begged that these things might be told them the next sabbath. And when the meeting of the synagogue broke up, many Jews and devout converts to Judaism followed Paul and Barnabas, who spoke to them and urged them to continue in the grace of God.

The next sabbath almost the whole city gathered together to hear the word of God. But when the Jews saw the multitudes, they were filled with jealousy, and contradicted what was spoken by Paul, and reviled him. And Paul and Barnabas spoke out boldly, saying, "It was necessary that the word of God should be spoken first to you. Since you thrust it from you, and judge yourselves unworthy of eternal life, behold, we turn to the Gentiles. For so the Lord has commanded us, saying,

'I have set you to be a light for the Gentiles,
that you may bring salvation to the
uttermost parts of the earth.' "

And when the Gentiles heard this, they were glad and glorified the word of God; and as many as were ordained to eternal life believed. And the word of the Lord spread throughout all the region. But the Jews incited the devout women of high standing and the leading men of the city, and stirred up persecution against Paul and Barnabas, and drove them out of their district. But they shook off the dust from their feet against them, and went to Iconium. And the disciples were filled with joy and with the Holy Spirit.

(Ch. 14) Now at Iconium they entered together into the Jewish synagogue, and so spoke that a great company believed, both of Jews and of Greeks. But the unbelieving Jews stirred up the Gentiles and poisoned their minds against the brethren. So they remained for a long time, speaking boldly for the Lord, who bore witness to the word of his grace, granting signs and wonders to be done by their hands. But the people of the city were divided; some sided with the Jews, and some with the apostles. When an attempt was made by both Gentiles and Jews, with their rulers, to molest them and to stone them, they learned of it and fled to Lystra and Derbe, cities of Lycaonia, and to the surrounding country; and there they preached the gospel.

Now at Lystra there was a man sitting, who could not use his feet; he was a cripple from birth, who had never walked. He listened to Paul speaking; and Paul, looking intently at him and seeing that he had faith to be made well, said in a loud voice, "Stand upright on your feet." And he sprang up and walked. And when the crowds saw what Paul had done, they lifted up their voices, saying in Lycaonian, "The gods have come down to us in the likeness of men!" Barnabas they called Zeus, and Paul, because he was the chief speaker, they called Hermes. And the priest of Zeus, whose temple was in front of the city, brought oxen and garlands to the gates and wanted to offer sacrifice with the people. But when the apostles

Barnabas and Paul heard of it, they tore their garments and rushed out among the multitude, crying, "Men, why are you doing this? We also are men, of like nature with you, and bring you good news, that you should turn from these vain things to a living God who made the heaven and the earth and the sea and all that is in them. In past generations he allowed all the nations to walk in their own ways; yet he did not leave himself without witness, for he did good and gave you from heaven rains and fruitful seasons, satisfying your hearts with food and gladness." With these words they scarcely restrained the people from offering sacrifice to them.

But the Jews came there from Antioch and Iconium; and having persuaded the people, they stoned Paul and dragged him out of the city, supposing that he was dead. But when the disciples gathered about him, he rose up and entered the city; and on the next day he went on with Barnabas to Derbe. When they had preached the gospel to that city and had made many disciples, they returned to Lystra and to Iconium and to Antioch, strengthening the souls of the disciples, exhorting them to continue in the faith, and saying that through many tribulations we must enter the kingdom of God. And when they had appointed elders for them in every church, with prayer and fasting, they committed them to the Lord in whom they believed.

Then they passed through Pisidia, and came to Pamphylia. And when they had spoken the word in Perga, they went down to Attalia; and from there they sailed to Antioch, where they had been commended to the grace of God for the work which they had fulfilled. And when they arrived, they gathered the church together and declared all that God had done with them, and how he had opened a door of faith to the Gentiles. And they remained no little time with the disciples.

C. The Letters of Paul

1. *The First Letter of Paul to the Corinthians*

Although the letters of Paul follow the gospels and Acts in the order of the New Testament books, they were probably all written before the first gospel was composed in its present form. Paul was a convert from Judaism to Christianity and became the leading missionary to the Gentile world; the account of one of his journeys is found above. However, he was not content merely to found new churches; he continually sent them letters of encouragement and warning in which he dealt with the religious problems faced by the new converts. The following passage from the first letter to Corinth, written about 54 A. D., deals with the proper observance of the Lord's Supper, the nature of "spiritual gifts," and the significance of the Resurrection.

[I Corinthians 11:17–13:13; 15]

(Ch. 11) But in the following instructions I do not commend you, because when you come together it is not for the better but for the worse. For, in the first place, when you assemble as a church, I hear that there are divisions among you; and I partly believe it, for there must be factions among you in order that those who are genuine among you may be recognized. When you meet together, it is not the Lord's supper that you eat. For in eating, each one goes ahead with his own meal, and one is hungry and another is drunk. What! Do you not have houses to eat and drink in? Or do you despise the church of God and humiliate those who have nothing? What shall I say to you? Shall I commend you in this? No, I will not.

For I received from the Lord what I also delivered to you, that the Lord Jesus on the night when he was betrayed took bread, and when he had given thanks, he broke it, and said, "This is my body which is for you. Do this in remembrance of me." In the same way also the cup, after supper, saying, "This cup is the new covenant in my blood. Do this, as often as you drink it, in remembrance of me." For as often as you eat this bread and drink the cup, you proclaim the Lord's death until he comes.

Whoever, therefore, eats the bread or drinks the cup of the Lord in an unworthy manner will be guilty of profaning the body and blood of the Lord. Let a man examine himself, and so eat of the bread and drink of the cup. For any one who eats and drinks without discerning the body eats and drinks judgment upon himself. That is why many of you are weak and ill, and some have died. But if we judged ourselves truly, we should not be judged. But when we are judged by the Lord, we are chastened so that we may not be condemned along with the world.

So then, my brethren, when you come together to eat, wait for one another—if any one is hungry, let him eat at home—lest you come together to be condemned. About the other things I will give directions when I come.

(Ch. 12) Now concerning spiritual gifts, brethren, I do not want you to be uninformed. You know that when you were heathen, you were led astray to dumb idols, however you may have been moved. Therefore I want you to understand that no one speaking by the Spirit of God ever says "Jesus be cursed!" and no one can say "Jesus is Lord" except by the Holy Spirit.

Now there are varieties of gifts, but the same Spirit; and there are varieties of service, but the same Lord; and there are varieties of working, but it is the same God who inspires them all in every one. To each is given the manifestation of the Spirit for the common good. To one is given through the Spirit the utterance of wisdom, and to another the utterance of knowledge according to the same Spirit, to another faith by the same Spirit, to another gifts of healing by the one Spirit, to another the working of miracles, to another prophecy, to another the ability to distinguish between spirits, to another various kinds of tongues, to another the interpretation of tongues. All these are inspired by one and the same Spirit, who apportions to each one individually as he wills.

For just as the body is one and has many members, and all the members of the body, though many, are one body, so it is with Christ. For by one Spirit we were all baptized into one body—Jews or Greeks, slaves or free—and all were made to drink of one Spirit.

For the body does not consist of one member but of many. If the foot should say, "Because I am not a hand, I do not belong to the body," that would not make it any less a part of the body. And if the ear should say, "Because I am not an eye, I do not belong to the body" that would not make it any less a part of the body. If the whole body were an eye, where would be the hearing? If the whole body were an ear, where would be the sense of smell? But as it is, God arranged the organs in the body, each one of them, as he chose. If all were a single organ, where would the body be? As it is, there are many parts, yet one body. The eye cannot say to the hand, "I have no need of you," nor again the head to the feet, "I have no need of you." On the contrary, the parts of the body which seem to be weaker are indispensable, and those parts of the body which we think less honorable we invest with the greater honor, and our unpresentable parts are treated with greater modesty, which our more presentable parts do not require. But God has so adjusted the body, giving the greater honor to the inferior part, that there may be no discord in the body, but that the members may have the same care for one another. If one member suffers, all suffer together; if one member is honored, all rejoice together.

Now you are the body of Christ and individually members of it. And God has appointed in the church first apostles, second prophets, third teachers, then workers of miracles, then healers, helpers, administrators, speakers in various kinds of tongues. Are all apostles? Are all prophets? Are all teachers? Do all work miracles? Do all possess gifts of healing? Do all speak with tongues? Do all interpret? But earnestly desire the higher gifts.

And I will show you a still more excellent way.

(Ch. 13) If I speak in the tongues of men and of angels, but have not love, I am a noisy gong or a clanging cymbal. And if I have prophetic powers, and understand all mysteries and all knowledge, and if I have all faith, so as to remove mountains, but have not love, I am nothing. If I give away all I have, and if I deliver my body to be burned, but have not love, I gain nothing.

Love is patient and kind; love is not jealous or boastful; it is not arrogant or rude. Love does not insist on its own way; it is not irritable or resentful; it does not rejoice at wrong but rejoices in the right. Love bears all things, believes all things, hopes all things, endures all things.

Love never ends; as for prophecy, it will pass away; as for tongues, they will cease; as for knowledge, it will pass away. For our knowledge is imperfect and our prophecy is imperfect; but when the perfect comes, the imperfect will pass away. When I was a child, I spoke like a child, I thought like a child, I reasoned like a child; when I became a man, I gave up childish ways. For now we see in a mirror dimly, but then face to face. Now I know in part; then I shall understand fully, even as I have been fully understood. So faith, hope, love abide, these three; but the greatest of these is love.

(Ch. 15) Now I would remind you, brethren, in what terms I preached to you the gospel, which you received, in which you stand, by which you are saved, if you hold it fast—unless you believed in vain.

For I delivered to you as of first importance what I also received, that Christ died for our sins in accordance with the scriptures, that he was buried, that he was raised on the third day in accordance with the scriptures, and that he appeared to Cephas [Peter], then to the twelve. Then he appeared to more than five hundred brethren at one time, most of whom are still alive, though some have fallen asleep. Then he appeared to James, then to all the apostles. Last of all as to one untimely born, he appeared also to me. For I am the least of the apostles, unfit to be called an apostle, because I persecuted the church of God. But by the grace of God I am what I am, and his grace toward me was not in vain. On the contrary, I worked harder than any of them, though it was not I, but the grace of God which is with me. Whether then it was I or they, so we preach and so you believed.

Now if Christ is preached as raised from the dead, how can some of you say that there is no resurrection of the dead? But if there is no resurrection of the dead, then Christ has not been raised; if Christ has not been raised, then our preaching is in vain and your faith is in vain. We are even found to be misrepresenting God, because we testified of God that he raised Christ, whom he did not raise if it is true that the dead are not raised. For if the dead are not raised, then Christ has not been raised. If Christ has not been raised, your faith is futile and you are still in your sins. Then those also who have fallen asleep in Christ have perished. If in this life we who are in Christ have only hope, we are of all men most to be pitied.

But in fact Christ has been raised from the dead, the first fruits of those who have fallen asleep. For as by a man came death, by a man has come also the resurrection of the dead. For as in Adam all die, so also in Christ shall all be made alive. But each in his own order: Christ the first fruits, then at his coming those who belong to Christ. Then comes the end, when he delivers the kingdom of God the Father after destroying every rule and every authority and power. For he must reign until he has put all his enemies under his feet. The last enemy to be destroyed is death. "For God has put all things in subjection under his feet." But when it says, "All things are put in subjection under him," it is plain that he is excepted who put all things under him. When all things are subjected to him, then the Son himself will also be subjected to him who put all things under him, that God may be everything to every one.

Otherwise, what do people mean by being baptized on behalf of the dead? If the dead are not raised at all, why are people baptized on their behalf? Why am I in peril every hour? I protest, brethren, by my pride in you which I have in Christ Jesus our Lord, I die every day! What do I gain if, humanly speaking, I fought with beasts at Ephesus? If the dead are not raised, "Let us eat and drink, for tomorrow we die." Do not be deceived: "Bad company ruins good morals." Come to your right mind, and sin no more. For some have no knowledge of God. I say this to your shame.

But some one will ask, "How are the dead raised? With what kind of body do they come?" You foolish man! What you sow does not come to life unless it dies. And what you sow is not the body which is to be, but a bare kernel, perhaps of wheat or of some other grain. But God gives it a body as he has chosen, and to each kind of seed its own body. For not all flesh is alike, but there is one kind for men, another for animals, another for birds, and another for fish. There are celestial bodies and there are terrestrial bodies; but the glory of the celestial is one, and the glory of the terrestrial is another. There is one glory of the sun, and another glory of the moon, and another glory of the stars; for star differs from star in glory.

So is it with the resurrection of the dead. What is sown is perishable, what is raised is imperishable. It is sown in dishonor, it is raised in glory. It is sown in weakness, it is raised in power. It is sown a physical body, it is raised a spiritual body. If there is a physical body, there is also a spiritual body. Thus it is written, "The first man Adam became a living being"; the last Adam became a life-giving spirit. But it is not the spiritual which is first but the physical, and then the spiritual. The first man was from the earth, a man of dust; the second man is from heaven. As was the man of dust, so are those who are of the dust; and as is the man of heaven, so are those who are of heaven. Just as we have borne the image of the man of dust, we shall also bear the image of the man of heaven. I tell you this, brethren: flesh and blood cannot inherit the kingdom of God, nor does the perishable inherit the imperishable.

Lo! I tell you a mystery. We shall not all sleep, but we shall all be changed, in a moment, in the twinkling of an eye, at the last trumpet. For the trumpet will sound, and the dead will be raised imperishable, and we shall be changed. For this perishable nature must put on the imperishable, and this mortal nature must put on immortality. When the perishable puts on the imperishable, and the mortal puts on immortality, then shall come to pass the saying that is written:

"Death is swallowed up in victory."
"O death, where is thy victory?
O death, where is thy sting?"

The sting of death is sin, and the power of sin is the law. But thanks be to God, who gives us the victory through our Lord Jesus Christ.

Therefore, my beloved brethren, be steadfast, immovable, always abounding in the work of the Lord, knowing that in the Lord your labor is not in vain.

2. *The Letter of Paul to the Romans*

The letter to the church in Rome, the first half of which is found below, was probably written two or three years after I Corinthians. Paul had never been to Rome but was looking forward to visiting the church in the near future; he writes this letter to acquaint the Romans with the main tenets of his theology.

[Romans 1–8]

(Ch. 1) Paul, a servant of Jesus Christ, called to be an apostle, set apart for the gospel of God which he promised beforehand through his prophets in the holy scriptures, the gospel concerning his Son, who was descended from David according to the flesh and designated Son of God in power according to the Spirit of holiness by his resurrection from the dead, Jesus Christ our Lord, through whom we have received grace and apostleship to bring about obedience to the faith for the sake of his name among all the nations, including yourselves who are called to belong to Jesus Christ.

To all God's beloved in Rome, who are called to be saints:

Grace to you and peace from God our Father and the Lord Jesus Christ.

First, I thank my God through Jesus Christ for all of you, because your faith is proclaimed in all the world. For God is my witness, whom I serve with my spirit in the gospel of his Son, that without ceasing I mention you always in my prayers, asking that somehow by God's will I may now at last succeed in coming to you. For I long to see you, that I may impart to you some spiritual gift to strengthen you, that is, that we may be mutually encouraged by each other's faith, both yours and mine. I want you to know, brethren, that I have often intended to come to you (but thus far have been prevented), in order that I may reap some harvest among you as well as among the rest of the Gentiles. I am under obligation both to Greeks and to barbarians, both to the wise and to the foolish: so I am eager to preach the gospel to you also who are in Rome.

For I am not ashamed of the gospel: it is the power of God for salvation to every one who has faith, to the Jew first and also to the Greek. For in it the righteousness of God is revealed through faith for faith; as it is written, "He who through faith is righteous shall live."

For the wrath of God is revealed from heaven against all ungodliness and wickedness of men who by their wickedness suppress the truth. For what can be known about God is plain to them, because God has shown it to them. Ever since the creation of the world his invisible nature, namely, his eternal power and deity, has been clearly perceived in the things that have been made. So they are without excuse; for although they knew God they did not honor him as God or give thanks to him, but they became futile in their thinking and their senseless minds were darkened. Claiming to be wise, they became fools, and exchanged the glory of the immortal God for images resembling mortal man or birds or animals or reptiles.

Therefore God gave them up in the lusts of their hearts to impurity, to the dishonoring of their bodies among themselves, because they exchanged the truth about God for a lie and worshiped and served the creature rather than the Creator, who is blessed forever! Amen.

For this reason God gave them up to dishonorable passions. Their women exchanged natural relations for unnatural, and the men likewise gave up natural relations with women and were consumed with passion for one another, men committing shameless acts with men and receiving in their own persons the due penalty for their error.

And since they did not see fit to acknowledge God, God gave them up to a base mind and to improper conduct. They were filled with all manner of wickedness, evil, covetousness, malice. Full of envy, murder, strife, deceit, malignity, they are gossips, slanderers, haters of God, insolent, haughty, boastful, inventors of evil, disobedient to parents, foolish, faithless, heartless, ruthless. Though they know God's decree that those who do such things deserve to die, they not only do them but approve those who practice them.

(Ch. 2) Therefore you have no excuse, O man, whoever you are, when you judge another; for in passing judgment upon him you condemn yourself, because you, the judge, are doing the very same things. We know that the judgment of God rightly falls upon those who do such things. Do you suppose, O man, that when you judge those who do such things and yet do them yourself, you will escape the judgment of God? Or do you presume upon the riches of his kindness and forbearance and patience? Do you not know that God's kindness is meant to lead you to repentance? But by your hard and impenitent heart you are storing up wrath for yourself on the day of wrath when God's righteous judgment will be revealed. For he will render to every man according to his works: to those who by patience in well-doing seek for glory and honor and immortality, he will give eternal life; but for those who are factious and do not obey the truth, but obey wickedness, there will be wrath and fury. There will be tribulation and distress for every human being who does evil, the Jew first and also the Greek, but glory and honor and peace for every one who does good, the Jew first and also the Greek. For God shows no partiality.

All who have sinned without the law will also perish without the law, and all who have sinned under the law will be judged by the law.

For it is not the hearers of the law who are righteous before God, but the doers of the law who will be justified. When Gentiles who have not the law do by nature what the law requires, they are a law to themselves, even though they do not have the law. They show that what the law requires is written on their hearts, while their conscience also bears witness and their conflicting thoughts accuse or perhaps excuse them on that day when, according to my gospel, God judges the secrets of men by Christ Jesus.

But if you call yourself a Jew and rely upon the law and boast of your relation to God and know his will and approve what is excellent, because you are instructed in the law, and if you are sure that you are a guide to the blind, a light to those who are in darkness, a corrector of the foolish, a teacher of children, having in the law the embodiment of knowledge and truth—you then who teach others, will you not teach yourself? While you preach against stealing, do you steal? You who say that one must not commit adultery, do you commit adultery? You who abhor idols, do you rob temples? You who boast in the law, do you dishonor God by breaking the law? For, as it is written, "The name of God is blasphemed among the Gentiles because of you."

Circumcision indeed is of value if you obey the law; but if you break the law, your circumcision becomes uncircumcision. So, if a man who is uncircumcised keeps the precepts of the law, will not his uncircumcision be regarded as circumcision? Then those who are physically uncircumcised but keep the law will condemn you who have the written code and circumcision but break the law. For he is not a real Jew who is one outwardly, nor is true circumcision something external and physical. He is a Jew who is one inwardly, and real circumcision is a matter of the heart, spiritual and not literal. His praise is not from men but from God.

(Ch. 3) Then what advantage has the Jew? Or what is the value of circumcision? Much in every way. To begin with, the Jews are entrusted with the oracles of God. What if some were unfaithful? Does their faithlessness nullify the faithfulness of God? By no means! Let God be true though every man be false, as it is written,

"That thou mayest be justified in thy words,
and prevail when thou art judged."

But if our wickedness serves to show the justice of God, what shall we say? That God is unjust to inflict wrath on us? (I speak in a human way.) By no means! For then how could God judge the world? But if through my falsehood God's truthfulness abounds to his glory, why am I still being condemned as a sinner? And why not do evil that good may come?—as some people slanderously charge us with saying. Their condemnation is just.

What then? Are we Jews any better off? No, not at all; for I have already charged that all men, both Jews and Greeks, are under the power of sin, as it is written:

"None is righteous, no, not one;
no one understands, no one seeks for God.
All have turned aside, together they
have gone wrong;
no one does good, not even one."
"Their throat is an open grave,
they use their tongues to deceive."
"The venom of asps is under their lips."
"Their mouth is full of curses and bitterness."
"Their feet are swift to shed blood,
in their paths are ruin and misery,
and the way of peace they do not know."
"There is no fear of God before their eyes."

Now we know that whatever the law says it speaks to those who are under the law, so that every mouth may be stopped, and the whole world may be held accountable to God. For no human being will be justified in his sight by works of the law since through the law comes knowledge of sin.

But now the righteousness of God has been manifested apart from law, although the law and the prophets bear witness to it, the righteousness of God through faith in Jesus Christ for all who believe. For there is no distinction; since all have sinned and fall short of the glory of God, they are justified by his grace as a gift, through the redemption which is in Christ Jesus, whom God put forward as an expiation by his blood, to be received by faith. This was to show God's righteousness, because in his divine forbearance he had passed over former sins; it was to prove at the present time that he himself is righteous and that he justifies him who has faith in Jesus.

Then what becomes of our boasting? It is excluded. On what principle? On the principle of works? No, but on the principle of faith. For we hold that a man is justified by faith apart from works of law. Or is God the God of Jews only? Is he not the God of Gentiles also? Yes, of Gentiles also, since God is one; and he will justify the circumcised on the ground of their faith and the uncircumcised because of their faith. Do we then overthrow the law by this faith? By no means! On the contrary, we uphold the law.

(Ch. 4) What then shall we say about Abraham, our forefather according to the flesh? For if Abraham was justified by works, he has something to boast about, but not before God. For what does the scripture say? "Abraham believed God, and it was reckoned to him as righteousness." Now to one who works, his wages are not reckoned as a gift but as his due. And to one who does not work but trusts him who justifies the ungodly, his faith is reckoned as righteousness. So also David pronounces a blessing upon the man to whom God reckons righteousness apart from works:

"Blessed are those whose iniquities are forgiven,
and whose sins are covered;
blessed is the man against whom
the Lord will not reckon his sin,"

Is this blessing pronounced only upon the circumcised, or also upon the uncircumcised? We say that faith was reckoned to Abraham as righteousness. How then was it reckoned to him? Was it before or after he had been circumcised? It was not after, but before he was circumcised. He received circumcision as a sign or seal of the righteousness which he had by faith while he was still uncircumcised. The purpose was to make him the father of all who believe without being circumcised and who thus have righteousness reckoned to them, and likewise the father of the circumcised who are not merely circumcised but also follow the example of the faith which our father Abraham had before he was circumcised.

The promise to Abraham and his descendants, that they should inherit the world, did not come through the law but through the righteousness of faith. If it is the adherents of the law who are to be the heirs, faith is null and the promise is void. For the law brings wrath, but where there is no law there is no transgression.

That is why it depends on faith, in order that the promise may rest on grace and be guaranteed to all his descendants—not only to the adherents of the law but also to those who share the faith of Abraham, for he is the father of us all, as it is written, "I have made you the father of many nations"—in the presence of the God in whom he believed, who gives life to the dead and calls into existence the things that do not exist. In hope he believed against hope, that he should become the father of many nations; as he had been told, "So shall your descendants be." He did not weaken in faith when he considered his own body, which was as good as dead because he was about a hundred years old, or when he considered the barrenness of Sarah's womb. No distrust made him waver concerning the promise of God, but he grew strong in his faith as he gave glory to God, fully convinced that God was able to do what he had promised. That is why his faith was "reckoned to him as righteousness." But the words, "it was reckoned to him," were written not for his sake alone, but for ours also. It will be reckoned to us who believe in him that raised from the dead Jesus our Lord, who was put to death for our trespasses and raised for our justification.

(Ch. 5) Therefore, since we are justified by faith, we have peace with God through our Lord Jesus Christ. Through him we have obtained access to this grace in which we stand, and we rejoice in our hope of sharing the glory of God. More than that, we rejoice in our sufferings, knowing that suffering produces endurance, and endurance produces character, and character produces hope, and hope does not disappoint us, because God's love has been poured into our hearts through the Holy Spirit which has been given to us.

While we were yet helpless, at the right time Christ died for the ungodly. Why, one will hardly die for a righteous man—though perhaps for a good man one will dare even to die. But God shows his love for us in that while we were yet sinners Christ died for us. Since, therefore, we are now justified by his blood, much more shall we be saved by him from the wrath of God. For if while we were enemies we were reconciled to God by the death of his Son, much more, now that we are reconciled, shall we be saved by his life. Not only so, but we also rejoice in God through our Lord Jesus Christ, through whom we have now received our reconciliation.

Therefore as sin came into the world through one man and death through sin, and so death spread to all men because all men sinned—sin indeed was in the world before the law was given, but sin is not counted where there is no law. Yet death reigned from Adam to Moses, even over those whose sins were not like the transgression of Adam, who was a type of the one who was to come.

But the free gift is not like the trespass. For if many died through one man's trespass, much more have the grace of God and the free gift in the grace of that one man Jesus Christ abounded for many. And the free gift is not like the effect of that one man's sin. For the judgment following one trespass brought condemnation, but the free gift following many trespasses brings justification. If, because of one man's trespass, death reigned through that one man, much more will those who receive the abundance of grace and the free gift of righteousness reign in life through the one man Jesus Christ.

Then as one man's trespass led to condemnation for all men, so one man's act of righteousness leads to acquittal and life for all men. For as by one man's disobedience many were made sinners, so by one man's obedience many will be made righteous. Law came in, to increase the trespass; but where sin increased, grace abounded all the more, so that, as sin reigned in death, grace also might reign through righteousness to eternal life through Jesus Christ our Lord.

(Ch. 6) What shall we say then? Are we to continue in sin that grace may abound? By no means! How can we who died to sin still live in it? Do you not know that all of us who have been baptized into Christ Jesus were baptized into his death? We were buried therefore with him by baptism into death, so that as Christ was raised from the dead by the glory of the Father, we too might walk in newness of life.

For if we have been united with him in a death like his, we shall certainly be united with him in a resurrection like his. We know that our old self was crucified with him so that the sinful body might be destroyed, and we might no longer be enslaved to sin. But if we have died with Christ, we believe that we shall also live with him. For we know that Christ being raised from the dead will never die again; death no longer has dominion over him. The death he died he died to sin, once for all, but the life he lives he lives to God. So you also must consider yourselves dead to sin and alive to God in Christ Jesus.

Let not sin therefore reign in your mortal bodies, to make you obey their passions. Do not yield your members to sin as instruments of wickedness, but yield yourselves to God as men who have been brought from death to life, and your members to God as instruments of righteousness. For sin will have no dominion over you, since you are not under law but under grace.

What then? Are we to sin because we are not under law but under grace? By no means! Do you not know that if you yield yourselves to any one as obedient slaves, you are slaves of the one whom you obey, either of sin, which leads to death, or of obedience, which leads to righteousness? But thanks be to God, that you who were once slaves of sin have become obedient from the heart to the standard of teaching to which you were committed, and, having been set free from sin, have become slaves of righteousness. I am speaking in human terms, because of your natural limitations. For just as you once yielded your members to impurity and to greater and greater iniquity, so now yield your members to righteousness for sanctification.

When you were slaves of sin, you were free in regard to righteousness. But then what return did you get from the things of which you are now ashamed? The end of those things is death. But now that you have been set free from sin and have become slaves of God, the return you get is sanctification and its end, eternal life. For the wages of sin is death, but the free gift of God is eternal life in Christ Jesus our Lord.

(Ch. 7) Do you not know, brethren—for I am speaking to those who know the law—that the law is binding on a person only during his life? Thus a married woman is bound by law to her husband as long as he lives; but if her husband dies she is discharged from the law concerning the husband. Accordingly, she will be called an adulteress if she lives with another man while her husband is alive. But if her husband dies she is free from that law, and if she marries another man she is not an adulteress.

Likewise, my brethren, you have died to the law through the body of Christ, so that you may belong to another, to him who has been raised from the dead in order that we may bear fruit for God. While we were living in the flesh, our sinful passions, aroused by the law, were at work in our members to bear fruit for death. But now we are discharged from the law, dead to that which held us captive, so that we serve not under the old written code but in the new life of the Spirit.

What then shall we say? That the law is sin? By no means! Yet, if it had not been for the law, I should not have known sin. I should not have known what it is to covet if the law had not said, "You shall not covet." But sin, finding opportunity in the commandment, wrought in me all kinds of covetousness. Apart from the law sin lies dead. I was once alive apart from the law, but when the commandment came, sin revived and I died; the very commandment which promised life proved to be death to me. For sin, finding opportunity in the commandment, deceived me and by it killed me. So the law is holy, and the commandment is holy and just and good.

Did that which is good, then, bring death to me? By no means! It was sin, working death in me through what is good, in order that sin might be shown to be sin, and through the commandment might become sinful beyond measure. We know that the law is spiritual; but I am carnal, sold under sin. I do not understand my own actions. For I do not do what I want, but I do the very thing I hate. Now if I do what I do not want, I agree that the law is good. So then it is no longer I that do it, but sin which dwells within me. For I know that nothing good dwells within me, that is, in my flesh. I can will what is right, but I cannot do it. For I do not do the good I want, but the evil I do not want is what I do. Now if I do what I do not want, it is no longer I that do it, but sin which dwells within me.

So I find it to be a law that when I want to do right, evil lies close at hand. For I delight in the law of God, in my inmost self, but I see in my members another law at war with the law of my mind and making me captive to the law of sin which dwells in my members. Wretched man that I am! Who will deliver me from this body of death? Thanks be to God through Jesus Christ our Lord! So then, I of myself serve the law of God with my mind, but with my flesh I serve the law of sin.

(Ch. 8) There is therefore now no condemnation for those who are in Christ Jesus. For the law of the Spirit of life in Christ Jesus has set me free from the law of sin and death. For God has done what the law, weakened by the flesh, could not do: sending his own Son in the likeness of sinful flesh and for sin, he condemned sin in the flesh, in order that the just requirement of the law might be fulfilled in us, who walk not according to the flesh but according to the Spirit. For those who live according to the flesh set their minds on the things of the flesh, but those who live according to the Spirit set their minds on the things of the Spirit. To set the mind on the flesh is death, but to set the mind on the Spirit is life and peace. For the mind that is set on the flesh is hostile to God; it does not submit to God's law, indeed it cannot; and those who are in the flesh cannot please God.

But you are not in the flesh, you are in the Spirit, if the Spirit of God really dwells in you. Any one who does not have the Spirit of Christ does not belong to him. But if Christ is in you, although your bodies are dead because of sin, your spirits are alive because of righteousness.

If the Spirit of him who raised Jesus from the dead dwells in you, he who raised Christ Jesus from the dead will give life to your mortal bodies also through his Spirit which dwells in you.

So then, brethren, we are debtors, not to the flesh, to live according to the flesh—for if you live according to the flesh you will die, but if by the Spirit you put to death the deeds of the body you will live. For all who are led by the Spirit of God are sons of God. For you did not receive the spirit of slavery to fall back into fear, but you have received the spirit of sonship. When we cry, "Abba! Father!" it is the Spirit himself bearing witness with our spirit that we are children of God, and if children, then heirs, heirs of God and fellow heirs with Christ, provided we suffer with him in order that we may also be glorified with him.

I consider that the sufferings of this present time are not worth comparing with the glory that is to be revealed to us. For the creation waits with eager longing for the revealing of the sons of God; for the creation was subjected to futility, not of its own will but by the will of him who subjected it in hope; because the creation itself will be set free from its bondage to decay and obtain the glorious liberty of the children of God. We know that the whole creation has been groaning in travail together until now; and not only the creation, but we ourselves, who have the first fruits of the Spirit, groan inwardly as we wait for adoption as sons, the redemption of our bodies. For in this hope we were saved. Now hope that is seen is not hope. For who hopes for what he sees? But if we hope for what we do not see, we wait for it with patience.

Likewise the Spirit helps us in our weakness; for we do not know how to pray as we ought, but the Spirit himself intercedes for us with sighs too deep for words. And he who searches the hearts of men knows what is the mind of the Spirit, because the Spirit intercedes for the saints according to the will of God.

We know that in everything God works for good with those who love him, who are called according to his purpose. For those whom he foreknew he also predestined to be conformed to the image of his Son, in order that he might be the first-born among many brethren. And those whom he predestined he also called; and those whom he called he also justified; and those whom he justified he also glorified.

What then shall we say to this? If God is for us, who is against us? He who did not spare his own Son but gave him up for us all, will he not also give us all things with him? Who shall bring any charge against God's elect? It is God who justifies; who is to condemn? Is it Christ Jesus, who died, yes, who was raised from the dead, who is at the right hand of God, who indeed intercedes for us? Who shall separate us from the love of Christ? Shall tribulation, or distress, or persecution, or famine, or nakedness, or peril, or sword? As it is written,

"For thy sake we are being killed
all the day long;
we are regarded as sheep to be slaughtered."

No, in all these things we are more than conquerors through him who loved us. For I am sure that neither death, nor life, nor angels, nor principalities, nor things present, nor things to come, nor powers, nor height, nor depth, nor anything else in all creation, will be able to separate us from the love of God in Christ Jesus our Lord.

D. Crisis and Consolidation

In the waning years of the first century the Christian church faced a series of critical problems which threatened to destroy the new religion. First, the Roman Empire began a series of extensive persecutions of all those who refused to worship the emperor as a god. Second, the church was infiltrated by some who, although calling themselves Christians, denied that Jesus was a real man and claimed that only those who possessed a secret knowledge available to the small inner circle could be true believers.* In response

* See pp. 123f.

to these challenges the following letter, probably written from Rome in the name of Peter, emphasizes true doctrine and encourages obedience to Rome because the end of the world is near. The second passage, from the Book of Revelation, is even more explicit on the nature of the coming Kingdom of God; earlier in the book Rome, under the symbolic name "Babylon," is severely attacked. For the literary form of the Book of Revelation the reader is referred to the discussion of apocalyptic literature on p. 52.

1. *The First Letter of Peter*

[I PETER 1:1–21; 2:4–3:9; 4:7–19; 5:6–14]

(Ch. 1) Peter, an apostle of Jesus Christ, To the exiles of the dispersion in Pontus, Galatia, Cappadocia, Asia, and Bithynia, chosen and destined by God the Father and sanctified by the Spirit for obedience to Jesus Christ and for sprinkling with his blood:

May grace and peace be multiplied to you.

Blessed be the God and Father of our Lord Jesus Christ! By his great mercy we have been born anew to a living hope through the resurrection of Jesus Christ from the dead, and to an inheritance which is imperishable, undefiled, and unfading, kept in heaven for you, who by God's power are guarded through faith for a salvation ready to be revealed in the last time. In this you rejoice, though now for a little while you may have to suffer various trials, so that the genuineness of your faith, more precious than gold which though perishable is tested by fire, may redound to praise and glory and honor at the revelation of Jesus Christ. Without having seen him you love him; though you do not now see him you believe in him and rejoice with unutterable and exalted joy. As the outcome of your faith you obtain the salvation of your souls.

The prophets who prophesied of the grace that was to be yours searched and inquired what person or time was indicated by the Spirit of Christ within them when predicting the sufferings of Christ and the subsequent glory. It was revealed to them that they were serving not themselves but you, in the things which have now been announced to you by those who preached the good news to you through the Holy Spirit sent from heaven, things into which angels long to look.

Therefore gird up your minds, be sober, set your hope fully upon the grace that is coming to you at the revelation of Jesus Christ. As obedient children, do not be conformed to the passions of your former ignorance, but as he who called you is holy, be holy yourselves in all your conduct; since it is written, "You shall be holy, for I am holy." And if you invoke as Father him who judges each one impartially according to his deeds, conduct yourselves with fear throughout the time of your exile. You know that you were ransomed from the futile ways inherited from your fathers, not with perishable things such as silver or gold, but with the precious blood of Christ, like that of a lamb without blemish or spot. He was destined before the foundation of the world but was made manifest at the end of the times for your sake. Through him you have confidence in God, who raised him from the dead and gave him glory, so that your faith and hope are in God. . . .

(Ch. 2) Come to him, to that living stone, rejected by men but in God's sight chosen and precious; and like living stones be yourselves built into a spiritual house, to be a holy priesthood, to offer spiritual sacrifices acceptable to God through Jesus Christ. For it stands in scripture:

"Behold, I am laying in Zion a stone,
a cornerstone chosen and precious,
and he who believes in him will not
be put to shame."

To you therefore who believe, he is precious, but for those who do not believe,

"The very stone which the builders rejected
has become the head of the corner,"

and

"A stone that will make men stumble,
a rock that will make them fall";

for they stumble because they disobey the word, as they were destined to do.

But you are a chosen race, a royal priesthood, a holy nation, God's own people, that you may declare the wonderful deeds of him who called you out of darkness into his marvelous light. Once you were no people but now you are God's people; once you had not received mercy but now you have received mercy.

Beloved, I beseech you as aliens and exiles to abstain from the passions of the flesh that wage war against your soul. Maintain good conduct among the Gentiles, so that in case they speak against you as wrongdoers, they may see your good deeds and glorify God on the day of visitation.

Be subject for the Lord's sake to every human institution, whether it be to the emperor as supreme, or to governors as sent by him to punish those who do wrong and to praise those who do right. For it is God's will that by doing right you should put to silence the ignorance of foolish men. Live as free men, yet without using your freedom as a pretext for evil; but live as servants of God. Honor all men. Love the brotherhood. Fear God. Honor the emperor.

Servants, be submissive to your masters with all respect, not only to the kind and gentle but also to the overbearing. For one is approved if, mindful of God, he endures pain while suffering unjustly. For what credit is it, if when you do wrong and are beaten for it you take it patiently? But if when you do right and suffer for it you take it patiently, you have God's approval. For to this you have been called, because Christ also suffered for you, leaving you an example, that you should follow in his steps. He committed no sin; no guile was found on his lips. When he was reviled, he did not revile in return; when he suffered, he did not threaten; but he trusted to him who judges justly. He himself bore our sins in his body on the tree, that we might die to sin and live to righteousness. By his wounds you have been healed. For you were straying like sheep, but have now returned to the Shepherd and Guardian of your souls.

(Ch. 3) Likewise you wives, be submissive to your husbands, so that some, though they do not obey the word, may be won without a word by the behavior of their wives, when they see your reverent and chaste behavior. Let not yours be the outward adorning with braiding of hair, decoration of gold, and wearing of robes, but let it be the hidden person of the heart with the imperishable jewel of a gentle and quiet spirit, which in God's sight is very precious. So once the holy women who hoped in God used to adorn themselves and were submissive to their husbands, as Sarah obeyed Abraham, calling him lord. And you are now her children if you do right and let nothing terrify you.

Likewise you husbands, live considerately with your wives, bestowing honor on the woman as the weaker sex, since you are joint heirs of the grace of life, in order that your prayers may not be hindered.

Finally, all of you, have unity of spirit, sympathy, love of the brethren, a tender heart and a humble mind. Do not return evil for evil or reviling for reviling; but on the contrary bless, for to this you have been called, that you may obtain a blessing. . . .

(Ch. 4) The end of all things is at hand; therefore keep sane and sober for your prayers. Above all hold unfailing your love for one another, since love covers a multitude of sins. Practice hospitality ungrudgingly to one another. As each has received a gift, employ it for one another, as good stewards of God's varied grace: whoever speaks, as one who utters oracles of God; whoever renders service, as one who renders it by the strength which God supplies; in order that in everything God may be glorified through Jesus Christ. To him belong glory and dominion for ever and ever. Amen.

Beloved, do not be surprised at the fiery ordeal which comes upon you to prove you, as though something strange were happening to you. But rejoice in so far as you share Christ's sufferings, that you may also rejoice and be glad when his glory is revealed. If you are reproached for the name of Christ, you are blessed, because the spirit of glory and of God rests upon you. But let none of you suffer as a murderer, or a thief, or a wrongdoer, or a mischief-maker; yet if one suffers as a Christian, let him not be ashamed, but under that name let him glorify God. For the time has come for judgment to begin with the household of God; and if it begins with us, what will be the end of those who do not obey the gospel of God? And

"If the righteous man is scarcely saved,
where will the impious and sinner appear?"

Therefore let those who suffer according to God's will do right and entrust their souls to a faithful creator.

(Ch. 5) Humble yourselves therefore under the mighty hand of God, that in due time he may exalt you. Cast all your anxieties on him, for he cares about you. Be sober, be watchful. Your adversary the devil prowls around like a roaring lion, seeking some one to devour. Resist him, firm in your faith, knowing that the same experience of suffering is required of your brotherhood throughout the world. And after you have suffered a little while, the God of all grace, who has called you to his eternal glory in Christ, will himself restore, establish, and strengthen you. To him be the dominion for ever and ever. Amen.

By Silvanus, a faithful brother as I regard him, I have written briefly to you, exhorting and declaring that this is the true grace of God; stand fast in it. She who is at Babylon, who is likewise chosen, sends you greetings; and so does my son Mark. Greet one another with the kiss of love.

Peace to all of you that are in Christ.

2. *The Revelation to John*

[REVELATION 18; 21–22]

(Ch. 18) After this I saw another angel coming down from heaven, having great authority; and the earth was made bright with his splendor. And he called out with a mighty voice,

"Fallen, fallen is Babylon the great!
It has become a dwelling place of demons,
a haunt of every foul spirit,
a haunt of every foul and hateful bird;
for all nations have drunk the wine of
her impure passion,
and the kings of the earth have committed
fornication with her,
and the merchants of the earth have grown
rich with the wealth of her wantonness."

Then I heard another voice from heaven saying,

"Come out of her, my people,
lest you take part in her sins,
lest you share in her plagues;
for her sins are heaped high as heaven,
and God has remembered her iniquities.
Render to her as she herself has rendered,
and repay her double for her deeds;
mix a double draught for her in the cup
she mixed.
As she glorified herself and played the wanton,
so give her a like measure of torment and
mourning.
Since in her heart she says, 'A queen I sit,
I am no widow, mourning I shall never see,'
so shall her plagues come in a single day,
pestilence and mourning and famine,
and she shall be burned with fire;
for mighty is the Lord God who judges her."

And the kings of the earth, who committed fornication and were wanton with her, will weep and wail over her when they see the smoke of her burning; they will stand far off, in fear of her torment, and say,

"Alas! alas! thou great city,
thou mighty city, Babylon!
In one hour has thy judgment come."

And the merchants of the earth weep and mourn for her, since no one buys their cargo any more, cargo of gold, silver, jewels and pearls, fine linen, purple, silk and scarlet, all kinds of scented wood, all articles of ivory, all articles of costly wood, bronze, iron and marble, cinnamon, spice, incense, myrrh, frankincense, wine, oil, fine flour and wheat, cattle and sheep, horses and chariots, and slaves, that is, human souls.

"The fruit for which thy soul longed
has gone from thee,
and all thy dainties and thy splendor
are lost to thee, never to be found again!"

The merchants of these wares, who gained wealth from her, will stand far off, in fear of her torment, weeping and mourning aloud,

"Alas, alas, for the great city

that was clothed in fine linen, in
purple and scarlet,
bedecked with gold, with jewels, and with pearls!
In one hour all this wealth has been laid waste."

And all shipmasters and seafaring men, sailors and all whose trade is on the sea, stood far off and cried out as they saw the smoke of her burning,

"What city was like the great city?"

And they threw dust on their heads, as they wept and mourned, crying out,

"Alas, alas, for the great city
where all who had ships at sea grew rich
by her wealth!
In one hour she has been laid waste.
Rejoice over her, O heaven,
O saints and apostles and prophets,
for God has given judgment for you against her!"

Then a mighty angel took up a stone like a great millstone and threw it into the sea, saying,

"So shall Babylon the great city be
thrown down with violence,
and shall be found no more;
and the sound of harpers and minstrels,
of flute players and trumpeters
shall be heard in thee no more;
and a craftsman of any craft
shall be found in thee no more;
and the sound of the millstone
shall be heard in thee no more;
and the light of a lamp
shall shine in thee no more;
and the voice of bridegroom and bride
shall be heard in thee no more;
for thy merchants were the great
men of the earth,
and all nations were deceived by thy sorcery.
And in her was found the blood of
prophets and of saints,
and of all who have been slain on earth."

(Ch. 21) Then I saw a new heaven and a new earth; for the first heaven and the first earth had passed away, and the sea was no more. And I saw the holy city, new Jerusalem, coming down out of heaven from God, prepared as a bride adorned for her husband; and I heard a great voice from the throne saying, "Behold, the dwelling of God is with men. He will dwell with them, and they shall be his people, and God himself will be with them; he will wipe away every tear from their eyes, and death shall be no more, neither shall there be mourning nor crying nor pain any more, for the former things have passed away."

And he who sat upon the throne said, "Behold, I make all things new." Also he said, "Write this, for these words are trustworthy and true." And he said to me, "It is done! I am the Alpha and the Omega, the beginning and the end. To the thirsty I will give water without price from the fountain of the water of life. He who conquers shall have this heritage, and I will be his God and he shall be my son. But as for the cowardly, the faithless, the polluted, as for murderers, fornicators, sorcerers, idolaters, and all liars, their lot shall be in the lake that burns with fire and brimstone, which is the second death."

Then came one of the seven angels who had the seven bowls full of the seven last plagues, and spoke to me, saying, "Come, I will show you the Bride, the wife of the Lamb." And in the Spirit he carried me away to a great, high mountain, and showed me the holy city Jerusalem coming down out of heaven from God, having the glory of God, its radiance like a most rare jewel, like a jasper, clear as crystal. It had a great, high wall, with twelve gates, and at the gates twelve angels, and on the gates the names of the twelve tribes of the sons of Israel were inscribed; on the east three gates, on the north three gates, on the south three gates, and on the west three gates. And the wall of the city had twelve foundations and on them the twelve names of the twelve apostles of the Lamb.

And he who talked to me had a measuring rod of gold to measure the city and its gates and walls. The city lies foursquare, its length the same as its breadth; and he measured the city with his rod, twelve thousand stadia; its length and breadth and height are equal. He also measured its wall, a hundred and forty-four cubits by a man's measure, that is, an angel's. The wall was built of jasper, while the city was pure gold, clear as glass. The foundations of the wall of the city were adorned with every jewel; the first was jasper, the second sapphire, the third agate, the fourth emerald, the fifth onyx, the sixth carnelian, the seventh chrysolite, the eighth beryl, the ninth topaz, the tenth chrysoprase, the eleventh jacinth, the twelfth amethyst. And the twelve gates were twelve pearls, each of the gates made of a single pearl, and the street of the city was pure gold, transparent as glass.

And I saw no temple in the city, for its temple is the Lord God the Almighty and the Lamb. And the city has no need of sun or moon to shine upon it, for the glory of God is its light, and its lamp is the Lamb. By its light shall the nations walk; and the kings of the earth shall bring their glory into it, and its gates shall never be shut by day—and there shall be no night there; they shall bring into it the glory and the honor of the nations. But nothing unclean shall enter it, nor any one who practices abomination or falsehood, but only those who are written in the Lamb's book of life.

(Ch. *22*) Then he showed me the river of the water of life, bright as crystal, flowing from the throne of God and of the Lamb through the middle of the street of the city; also, on either side of the river, the tree of life with its twelve kinds of fruit, yielding its fruit each month; and the leaves of the tree were for the healing of the nations. There shall no more be anything accursed, but the throne of God and of the Lamb shall be in it, and his servants shall worship him; they shall see his face, and his name shall be on their foreheads. And night shall be no more; they need no light of lamp or sun, for the Lord God will be their light, and they shall reign for ever and ever.

And he said to me, "These words are trustworthy and true. And the Lord, the God of the spirits of the prophets, has sent his angel to show his servants what must soon take place. And behold, I am coming soon." Blessed is he who keeps the words of the prophecy of this book.

I John am he who heard and saw these things. And when I heard and saw them, I fell down to worship at the feet of the angel who showed them to me; but he said to me, "You must not do that! I am a fellow servant with you and your brethren the prophets, and with those who keep the words of this book. Worship God."

And he said to me, "Do not seal up the words of the prophecy of this book, for the time is near. Let the evildoer still do evil, and the filthy still be filthy, and the righteous still do right, and the holy still be holy."

"Behold, I am coming soon, bringing my recompense, to repay every one for what he has done. I am the Alpha and the Omega, the first and the last, the beginning and the end."

Blessed are those who wash their robes, that they may have the right to the tree of life and that they may enter the city by the gates. Outside are the dogs and sorcerers and fornicators and murderers and idolaters, and every one who loves and practices falsehood.

"I Jesus have sent my angel to you with this testimony for the churches. I am the root and the offspring of David, the bright morning star."

The Spirit and the Bride say, "Come." And let him who hears say, "Come." And let him who is thirsty come, let him who desires take the water of life without price.

I warn every one who hears the words of the prophecy of this book: if any one adds to them, God will add to him the plagues described in this book, and if any one takes away from the words of the book of this prophecy, God will take away his share in the tree of life and in the holy city, which are described in this book.

He who testifies to these things says, "Surely I am coming soon." Amen. Come, Lord Jesus!

The grace of the Lord Jesus be with all the saints. Amen.

The Emergence of Rabbinic Judaism

In the post-Biblical period Judaism split into various sects; the Sadducees, the Pharisees, the Zealots, and the Essenes are the most important of these. Of course all of these groups produced their own distinctive literature; much has been preserved, although many works have perished over the centuries. The Apocrypha (see above, p. 8) consists of such writings, and even more are to be found in the Pseudepigrapha ("false writings"), a collection of documents from the same period but enjoying no canonical status. But by far the largest body of literature is to be found in the Talmud, excerpts from which are found below, and the Midrashim, expositions of Old Testament books; these are the classic works of Pharisaism. However, in order to indicate the diversity of Judaism at the turn of the era we have also included one of the Dead Sea Scrolls, a work of the anti-Pharisaic Essenes.

A. The Dead Sea Scrolls

The Dead Sea Scrolls were first discovered in 1947 by two Arab boys in a cave at the northwest side of the Dead Sea. Seven relatively complete manuscripts, six in Hebrew and one in Aramaic, were found at that time: two manuscripts of Isaiah, a series of "Thanksgiving psalms," a commentary on the first two chapters of Habakkuk, a description of the great war to take place at the end of history, an Aramaic paraphrase and expansion of parts of Genesis, and the document which follows, the "Manual of Discipline," which is, in effect, the constitution of the sect. Subsequently thousands of scroll fragments were discovered in this cave and elsewhere in the vicinity. It is now apparent that these materials were either written or passed on by the sect referred to as the Essenes by ancient historians; they flourished at least from the middle of the second century B. C. to the time of the first Jewish revolt against the Romans in 66–70 A. D. Presumably they hid their library in the caves near their buildings (excavated from 1951 to 1956) in order to protect it from the Romans, and fled, never to return.

The Manual of Discipline*

(*I—Entering the Covenant*)

. . . the order of the community; to seek God . . .; to do what is good and upright before him as he commanded through Moses and through all his servants the prophets; to love all that he has chosen and hate all that he has rejected; to be far from all evil and cleave to all good works; to do truth and righteousness and justice in the land; to walk no longer in the stubbornness of a guilty heart and eyes of fornication, doing all evil; to bring all those who have offered themselves to do God's statutes into a covenant of steadfast love; to be united in the counsel of God and to walk before him perfectly with regard to all the things that have been revealed for the appointed times of their testimonies; to love all the sons of light, each according to his lot in the counsel of God, and to hate all the sons of darkness, each according to his guilt in vengeance of God.

And all who have offered themselves for his truth shall bring all their knowledge and strength and wealth into the community of God, to purify their knowledge in the truth of God's statutes, and to distribute their strength according to the perfection of his ways and all their property according to his righteous counsel; not to transgress in any one of all the words of God in their periods; not to advance their times or postpone any of their appointed festivals; not to turn aside from his true statutes, going to the right or to the left. . . .

Everyone who refuses to enter God's covenant, walking in the stubbornness of his heart, shall not attain to his true community. For his soul has abhorred the discipline of knowledge, the judgments of righteousness he has not confirmed because of his apostasies; and with the upright he will not be reckoned. His knowledge and his strength and his wealth shall not come into the council of community, because in the traffic of wickedness is his devising, and there is pollution in his plans. He will not be justified while giving free rein to the stubbornness of his heart. In darkness he looks at the ways of light, and with the perfect he will not be reckoned. He will not be purified by atonement offerings, and he will not be made clean with the water for impurity; he will not sanctify himself with seas and rivers or be made clean with any water for washing. Unclean, unclean he will be all the days that he rejects the ordinances of God, not being instructed in the community of his counsel.

But in a spirit of true counsel for the ways of a man all his iniquities will be atoned, so that he will look at the light of life, and in a holy spirit he will be united in his truth; and he will be cleansed from all his iniquities; and in an upright and humble spirit his sin will be atoned, and in the submission of his soul to all the statutes of God his flesh will be cleansed, that he may be sprinkled with water for impurity and sanctify himself with water of cleanness. And he will establish his steps, to walk perfectly in all the ways of God, as he commanded for the appointed times of his testimonies, and not to turn aside to right or left, and not to transgress against one of all his words. Then he will be accepted by pleasing atonements before God; and this will be for him a covenant of eternal community.

(II—The Two Spirits in Man)

The instructor's duty is to make all the sons of light understand and to teach them in the history of all the sons of man as to all their kinds of spirits with their signs, as to their works in their generations, and as to the visitation of their afflictions together with the periods of their recompense. From the God of knowledge is all that is and that is to be; and before they came into being he established all their designing. And when they come into being for their testimony according to his glorious design, they fulfill their work; and nothing is to be changed. In his hand are the ordinances of all; and he provides for them in all their affairs.

He created man to have dominion over the world and made for him two spirits, that he might walk by them until the appointed time of his visitation; they are the spirits of truth and of error. In the abode of light are the origins of truth, and from the source of darkness are the origins of error. In the hand of the prince of lights is dominion over all sons of righteousness; in the ways of light they walk. And in the hand of the angel of darkness is all dominion over the sons of error; and in the ways of darkness they walk. And by the angel of darkness is the straying of all the sons of righteousness, and all their sin and their iniquities and their guilt, and the transgressions of their works in his dominion, according to the mysteries of God, until his time, and all their afflictions and the appointed times of their distress in the dominion of his enmity. And all the spirits of his lot try to make the sons of light stumble; but the God of Israel and his angel of truth have helped all the sons of light. For he created the spirits of light and of darkness, and upon them he founded every work and upon their ways every service. One of the spirits God loves for all the ages of eternity, and with all its deeds he is pleased forever; as for the other, he abhors its company, and all its ways he hates forever.

And these are their ways in the world: to shine in the heart of man, and to make straight before him all the ways of true righteousness, and to make his heart be in dread of the judgments of God, and to induce a spirit of humility, and slowness to anger, and great compassion, and eternal goodness, and understanding and insight, and mighty wisdom, which is supported by all the works of God and leans upon the abundance of his steadfast love, and a spirit of knowledge in every thought of action, and zeal for righteous judgments, and holy thought with sustained purpose, and abundance of steadfast love for all the sons of truth, and glorious purity, abhorring all unclean idols, and walking humbly with prudence in all things, and concealing the truth of the mysteries of knowledge.

These are the counsels of the Spirit for the sons of the truth of the world and the visitation of all who walk by it, for healing and abundance of peace in length of days, and bringing forth seed, with all eternal blessings and everlasting joy in the life of eternity, and a crown of glory with raiment of majesty in everlasting light.

But to the spirit of error belong greediness, slackness of hands in the service of righteousness, wickedness and falsehood, pride and haughtiness, lying and deceit, cruelty and great impiety, quickness to anger and abundance of folly and proud jealousy, abominable works in a spirit of fornication and ways of defilement in the service of uncleanness, and a blasphemous tongue, blindness of eyes and dullness of ears, stiffness of neck and hardness of heart, walking in all the ways of darkness and evil cunning. And the visitation of all who walk by it is for abundance of afflictions by all destroying angels, to eternal perdition in the fury of the God of vengeance, to eternal trembling and everlasting dishonor, with destroying disgrace in the fire of dark places. And all their periods to their generations will be in sorrowful mourning and bitter calamity, in dark disasters until they are destroyed, having no remnant or any that escape.

In these two spirits are the origins of all the sons of man, and in their divisions all the hosts of men have their inheritance in their generations. In the ways of the two spirits men walk. And all the performance of their works is in their two divisions, according to each man's inheritance, whether much or little, for all the periods of eternity. For God has established the two spirits in equal measure until the last period, and has put eternal enmity between their divisions. An abomination to truth are deeds of error, and an abomination to error are all ways of truth. And contentious jealousy is on all their judgments, for they do not walk together.

But God in the mysteries of his understanding and in his glorious wisdom has ordained a period for the ruin of error, and in the appointed time of punishment he will destroy it forever. And then shall come out forever the truth of the world, for it has wallowed in the ways of wickedness in the dominion of error until the appointed time of judgment which has been decreed. And then God will refine in his truth all the deeds of a man, and will purify for himself the frame of man, consuming every spirit of error hidden in his flesh, and cleansing him with a holy spirit from all wicked deeds. And he will sprinkle upon him a spirit of truth, like water for impurity, from all abominations of falsehood and wallowing in a spirit of impurity, to make the upright perceive the knowledge of the Most High and the wisdom of the sons of heaven, to instruct those whose conduct is blameless. For God has chosen them for an eternal covenant, and theirs is all the glory of man; and there shall be no error, to the shame of all works of deceit.

Thus far the spirits of truth and of error struggle in the heart of a man; they walk in wisdom and folly; and according to each man's inheritance in truth he does right, and so he hates error; but according to his possession in the lot of error he does wickedly in it, and so he abhors truth. For in equal measure God has established the two spirits until the period which has been decreed and the making new; and he knows the performance of their works for all the periods of eternity. And he causes the sons of men to inherit them, that they may know good and evil, making the lots fall for every living man according to his spirit in the world until the time of visitation.

(III—Rules of the Order)

And this is the order for the men of the community who have offered themselves to turn from all evil and to lay hold of all that he commanded according to his will, to be separated from the congregation of the men of error, to become a community in law and in wealth, answering when asked by the sons of Zadok, the priests who keep the covenant, and when asked by the majority of the men of the community, who lay hold of the covenant. At their direction the regulation of the lot shall be decided for every case regarding law, wealth, or justice, to practice truth, unity, and humility, righteousness and justice and loyal love, and to walk humbly in all their ways, that each may not walk in the rebelliousness of his heart or go astray after his heart and his eyes and the thought of his guilty impulse; to circumcise in unity the uncircumcision of impulse and the stiff neck, to lay a foundation of truth for Israel for the community of an eternal covenant, to atone for all who offer themselves for holiness in Aaron and for a house of truth in Israel, and those who joined with them for community and for controversy and for judgment, to condemn all who transgress the statute. . . .

When he enters the covenant to do according to all these statutes, to be united for a holy congregation, they shall investigate his spirit in the community, between a man and his neighbor, according to his understanding and his works in the law, as directed by the majority of Israel, who have offered themselves to turn in unity to his covenant. They shall be registered in order, each before his neighbor, according to his understanding and his works, so that every one of them shall obey his neighbor, the lesser obeying the greater; and so that they shall have an investigation of their spirits and their works year by year, so as to elevate each one according to his understanding and the perfection of his way or put him back according to his perversions, so that each one may reprove his neighbor in truth and humility and loyal love for each one.

One shall not speak to his brother in anger or in resentment, or with a stiff neck or a hard heart or a wicked spirit; one shall not hate him in the folly of his heart. In his days he shall reprove him and shall not bring upon him iniquity; and also a man shall not bring against his neighbor a word before the masters without having rebuked him before witnesses.

In these ways they shall walk in all their dwellings, every living man, each with his neighbor. The lesser shall obey the greater with regard to wages and property. Together they shall eat, and together they shall worship, and together they shall counsel.

In every place where there are ten men of the council of the community there shall not be absent from them a priest. Each according to his position, they shall sit before him; and thus they shall be asked for their counsel regarding everything. And when they set the table to eat, or the wine to drink, the priest shall stretch out his hand first to pronounce a blessing with the first portion of the bread and the wine. And from the place where the ten are there shall never be absent a man who searches the law day and night, by turns, one after another. And the masters shall keep watch together a third of all the nights of the year, reading the book and searching for justice, and worshiping together. . . .

Everyone who has offered himself from Israel to be added to the council of the community shall be examined by the man appointed at the head of the masters as to his understanding and his works. If he comprehends instruction, he shall bring him into the covenant, to turn to the truth and to turn away from all error; and he shall explain to him all the ordinances of the community. Then later, when he comes in to stand before the masters, they shall all be questioned about his affairs; and as the lot determines, according to the counsel of the masters, he shall be admitted or depart. On being admitted to the council of the community, he shall not touch the sacred food of the masters until they examine him as to his spirit and his deeds when he has completed a whole year; moreover he shall not participate in the wealth of the masters.

When he has completed a year within the community, the masters shall be questioned about his affairs, as to his understanding and his deeds in the law; and if the lot determines that he shall be admitted to the assembly of the community, as directed by the priests and the majority of the men of their covenant, his wealth and his wages shall be put at the disposal of the man who has supervision over the wages of the masters, and he shall enter it in the account at his disposal, but shall not spend it for the masters.

The new member shall not touch the sacred drink of the masters until he has completed a second year among the men of the community; but when he has completed a second year, he shall be examined with questioning by the masters. If the lot determines that he is to be admitted to the community, he shall be registered in the order of his position among his brethren, for law and for judgment and for the sacred food and for the sharing of his property; and the community shall have his counsel and his judgment.

These are the ordinances by which they shall judge when investigating together concerning cases. If there is found among them a man who lies about his wealth, and knows it, he shall be excluded from the sacred food of the masters for a year, and shall be deprived of a fourth of his food ration. One who answers his neighbor with a stiff neck, or speaks with impatience, breaking the foundation of his fellowship by disobeying his neighbor who is registered before him, his own hand has delivered him; therefore he shall be punished for a year. Any man who mentions anything by the Name which is honored above all shall be set apart. If one has cursed, either when frightened by trouble or for any reason he may have, he shall be set apart and shall not return again to the council of the community. If he spoke in wrath against one of the priests registered in the book, he shall be punished for a year and set apart by himself from the sacred food of the masters. But if he spoke unintentionally, he shall be punished six months.

One who lies about what he knows shall be punished six months. A man who without justification knowingly denounces his neighbor shall be punished for a year and set apart. One who speaks craftily with his neighbors, or knowingly perpetrates a fraud, shall be punished six months. If he commits a fraud against his neighbor, he shall be punished three months; if he commits a fraud against the wealth of the community, causing its loss, he shall repay it in full. If he is not able to pay it, he shall be punished sixty days.

One who bears a grudge against his neighbor without justification shall be punished six months [*inserted above this line:* a year]; so also he who takes vengeance for himself for anything. One who speaks with his mouth the word of a fool shall be punished three months. For one who speaks while his neighbor is speaking the punishment shall be ten days. One who lies down and goes to sleep during a session of the masters, thirty days. So also a man who leaves during a session of the masters unadvisedly and without cause as many as three times at one session shall be punished ten days; but if they object and he leaves, he shall be punished thirty days.

One who walks before his neighbor naked when he does not have to do so shall be punished six months. A man who spits into the midst of the session of the masters shall be punished thirty days. One who brings his hand out from beneath his robe when it is torn, so that his nakedness is seen, shall be punished thirty days. One who laughs foolishly, making his voice heard, shall be punished thirty days. One who brings out his left hand to gesticulate with it shall be punished ten days.

A man who gossips about his neighbor shall be separated for a year from the sacred food of the masters, and he shall be punished; and a man who gossips about the masters is to be dismissed from among them and shall not come back again. A man who murmurs against the institution of the community shall be dismissed and shall not come back; but if he murmurs against his neighbor without justification he shall be punished six months.

If a man's spirit wavers from the institution of the community, so that he becomes a traitor to the truth and walks in the stubbornness of his heart; if he repents he shall be punished two years. During the first he shall not touch the sacred food of the masters, and during the second he shall not touch the drink of the masters; and he shall be seated after all the men of the community. When his two years are completed, the masters shall be asked about his case. If they admit him, he shall be registered in his position; and after that he shall be asked for judgment. If any man is in the council of the community for ten full years, and his spirit turns back so that he becomes a traitor to the community and goes out from before the masters to walk in the stubbornness of his heart, he shall not come back again to the council of the community. If any man of the men of the community partakes with him of his sacred food, or of his wealth which he has delivered to the masters, his sentence shall be like his; he shall be dismissed.

There shall be in the council of the community twelve men, and there shall be three priests who are perfect in all that has been revealed of the whole law, to practice truth and righteousness and justice and loyal love and walking humbly each with his neighbor, to preserve faithfulness in the land with sustained purpose and a broken spirit, and to make amends for iniquity by the practice of justice and the distress of tribulation, and to walk with all by the standard of truth and by the regulation of the time. . . .

Only the sons of Aaron shall administer judgment and wealth, and as they direct the lot shall determine for every regulation of the men of the community. As for the wealth of the holy men, who conduct themselves blamelessly, their wealth shall not be combined with the wealth of the men of deceit, who have not purified their conduct by separating themselves from error and conducting themselves blamelessly. They shall not depart from any counsel of the law, walking in all the stubbornness of their hearts; but they shall judge by the first judgments by which the men of the community began to be disciplined, until there shall come a prophet and the Messiahs of Aaron and Israel.

These are the statutes for the wise man, that he may walk in them with every living being, according to the regulation of one time and another and the weight of one man and another; to do the will of God according to all that has been revealed for each time at that time; and to learn all the wisdom that has been found, according to the times, and the statute of the time; and to set apart and weigh the sons of Zadok according to their spirit; and to hold firmly to the elect of the time according to his will, as he commanded. According to each man's spirit he is to be given his due; according to the cleanness of each man's hands he is to be admitted; and according to his understanding he is to be accepted; so too his love together with his hate.

There must be no admonitions or contention with the men of the pit, for the counsel of the law must be concealed among the men of error; but there must be admonition of true knowledge and righteous judgment for those who choose the way; each according to his spirit, according to the regulation of the time, to guide them in knowledge and so to give them understanding in the marvelous mysteries and truth among the men of the community, that they may conduct themselves blamelessly, each with his neighbor, in all that has been revealed to them—that is the time of clearing the way to the wilderness—to give them understanding of all that has been found to be done at this time; and to be separated from every man, and not to pervert his way because of any error.

These are the regulations of the way for the wise man in these times, for his love together with his hate, eternal hate for the men of the pit in a spirit of concealment, leaving to them wealth and manual labor like a slave for the man who rules over him, and humility before the man who has the mastery over him. Each one must be zealous for the statute and its time, for the day of vengeance, to do what is acceptable in everything he puts his hands to, and in all his dominion as he commanded; and everything done in it will be accepted freely. . . .

B. The Talmud

The word *Talmud* comes from the Hebrew verb meaning "to study," and the very word expresses the Jewish belief that the study of the Torah represents an important aspect of worship. After the destruction of the Temple in 70 A. D., when sacrificial worship was no longer possible, this emphasis on study was further heightened. As a body of literature the Talmud consists of (1) the *Mishnah* (literally "repetition" [of the Torah]), a compilation of oral tradition made by Judah the Prince in about 200 A. D., and (2) the subsequent discussions of the Mishnah in the Jewish academies from about 200 A. D. to about 500 A. D.; this latter is called the *Gemara,* literally, "completion." The Talmud exists in two versions, one from Palestine and one from Babylonia; both are divided into six "orders" and then subdivided into sixty-three "tractates."

According to Orthodox Judaism the Talmud is merely the writing down of traditional material which had existed since the time of Moses only in oral tradition; indeed it is said that when God gave Moses the written Torah on Sinai he also whispered its (oral) interpretation into his ear. This belief accounts for the high authority ascribed to the Talmud, and the legal codes derived from it, by Orthodox Jews. Others regard it as a highly significant body of rabbinic interpretation, but without binding authority upon modern Jews.

The following selections are from Tractate Aboth (Fathers), which contains some of the most ancient material in the Talmud, and from Tractates Shabbath and Ḥullin (Profane Things). Aboth consists entirely of Mishnah; along with twenty-five other tractates of the Babylonian Talmud, it has no Gemara. Shabbath and Ḥullin do have Gemara, and are somewhat more typical of the Talmud in that they deal largely with legal questions.

1. Aboth*

Moses received Torah from Sinai and handed it on to Joshua, and Joshua to the elders, and the elders to the prophets, and the prophets handed it on to the men of the Great Assembly.

They said three things: Be deliberate in judgment, raise many disciples, and make a hedge about the Torah.

Simeon the Righteous was one of the last members of the Great Assembly.

He used to say: On three things the age stands—on the Torah, on the temple service, and on acts of piety.

Antigonus of Soko took over from Simeon the Righteous.

He used to say: Be not like slaves who serve their master for the sake of their allowance; be rather like slaves who serve their master with no thought of an allowance—and let the fear of heaven be upon you.

Yose ben Joezer of Zeredah and Yose ben Johanan of Jerusalem took over from them.

Yose ben Joezer says: Let thy house be a meeting-place for the sages, and sit in the very dust at their feet, and thirstily drink in their words.

Yose ben Johanan of Jerusalem says: Let thy house be opened wide, and let the poor be members of thy household; and talk not overmuch with women—even with one's own wife, the sages said, all the more then with his fellow's wife! Hence the sages said: So long as a man talks overmuch with women he brings evil upon himself, neglects the study of Torah, and in the end Gehenna is his portion.

Joshua ben Perahyah and Nittai the Arbelite took over from them.

Joshua ben Perahyah says: Provide thyself with a teacher, get thee a comrade, and judge

* From *The Living Talmud,* selected and translated by Judah Goldin. Copyright 1957 by Judah Goldin. Reprinted by permission of the author and The New American Library of World Literature, Inc., New York.

everyone with the scale weighted in his favor.

Nittai the Arbelite says: Keep far away from an evil neighbor, do not associate with the wicked, and do not shrug off all thought of calamity.

Judah ben Tabbai and Simeon ben Shetah took over from them.

Judah ben Tabbai says: Do not play the part of chief justice; and when there are litigants standing before thee, look upon them as likely to be guilty; but when they depart from thy presence look upon them as likely to be innocent, as soon as they have accepted the sentence.

Simeon ben Shetah says: Again and again examine the witnesses; and be guarded in thy speech lest from it they learn to lie.

Shemaiah and Abtalyon took over from them.

Shemaiah says: Love work, hate lordship, and seek no intimacy with the ruling powers.

Abtalyon says: Sages, watch your words lest you incur the penalty of exile and be carried off to a place of evil waters, and your disciples who come after you drink thereof and die—and thus the name of heaven be profaned.

Hillel and Shammai took over from them.

Hillel says: Be of the disciples of Aaron, loving peace and pursuing peace, loving mankind and drawing them to the Torah.

He used to say: A name made great is a name destroyed; he that does not increase shall cease; he that does not learn deserves to die; and he that puts the crown to his own use shall perish.

He used to say: If not I for myself, who then? And being for myself, what am I? And if not now, when?

Shammai says: Make of thy study of the Torah a fixed practice; say little and do much; and receive all men with a cheerful countenance.

Rabban Gamaliel says: Provide thyself with a teacher, and eschew doubtful matters, and tithe not overmuch by guesswork.

Simeon his son says: All my life I grew up among the sages and have found nothing better for anybody than silence; not study is the chief thing, but action; and he who is verbose brings on sin.

Rabban Simeon ben Gamaliel says: By three things is the world sustained: by justice, by truth, and by peace, as it is said, "Truth and justice and peace judge ye in your gates" (Zechariah 8:16).

Rabbi says: Which is the right course that a man ought to choose for himself? Whatever is deemed praiseworthy by the one who adopts it and [for which] he is also deemed praiseworthy by men.

Be as attentive to a minor commandment as to a major one, for thou knowest not what is the reward to be given for the commandments. Take into account the loss incurred by fulfilling a commandment against the reward for it, and the profit gained by transgression against the loss it entails.

Mark well three things and thou wilt not fall into the clutches of sin: know what is above thee—an eye that sees, an ear that hears, and all thine actions recorded in the book.

Rabban Gamaliel, the son of Rabbi Judah the Prince, says: Splendid is the study of Torah when combined with a worldly occupation, for toil in them both puts sin out of mind; but study [Torah] which is not combined with work, falls into neglect in the end, and becomes the cause of sin.

Let all those who labor in behalf of the community, labor in their behalf for the sake of heaven—for the merit of their fathers upholds them and their grace endures forever. And as for you, I lay up to your credit a rich reward as though yourselves had accomplished it.

Beware of the ruling powers! For they do not befriend a person except for their own needs: they seem like friends when it is to their advantage, but they do not stand by a man when he is hard-pressed.

He used to say: Do His will as though it were thy will so that He may do thy will as though it were His will; undo thy will for the sake of His will so that He may undo the will of others for the sake of thy will.

Hillel says:

Do not withdraw from the community.

Put no trust in thyself until the day of thy death.

Do not judge thy comrade until thou hast stood in his place.

Say not of a thing which cannot be understood that in the end it will be understood.

And say not "When I have leisure I will study"—perchance thou shalt have no leisure.

He used to say: The boor is no fearer of sin, the *am ha-arez* cannot be a saint, the timid cannot learn, the short tempered cannot teach; he who is mostly in trade will not grow wise; and where there are no men, strive to be a man.

Moreover he saw a skull floating on the face of the water. He said to it: "For drowning others thou wast drowned; and in the end they that drowned thee shall be drowned."

He used to say:

The more flesh, the more worms.

The more possessions, the more worry.

The more wives, the more witchcraft.

The more maidservants, the more unchastity.

The more slaves, the more robbery.

The more Torah, the more life.

The more the company of scholars, the more wisdom.

The more counsel, the more understanding.

The more charity, the more peace.

If one acquires a good name he acquires something for himself.

If one acquires for himself knowledge of the Torah he acquires for himself life in the world to come.

Rabban Johanan ben Zakkai took over from Hillel and Shammai. He used to say: If thou hast wrought much in the study of Torah take no credit to thyself, for to this end wast thou created.

Rabban Johanan ben Zakkai had five disciples, to wit: Rabbi Eliezer ben Hyrcanus, Rabbi Joshua ben Hananiah, Rabbi Yose the priest, Rabbi Simeon ben Nathanel, and Rabbi Eleazar ben Arak.

He used to list their outstanding virtues:

Rabbi Eliezer ben Hyrcanus—a plastered cistern which loses not a drop.

Rabbi Joshua—happy is she who bore him!

Rabbi Yose—a saint.

Rabbi Simeon ben Nathanel—fears sin.

Rabbi Eleazar ben Arak—ever-flowing stream.

He used to say: If all the sages of Israel were in one scale of the balance and Eliezer ben Hyrcanus were in the other scale, he would outweigh them all.

Abba Saul says in his name: If all the sages of Israel were in one scale of the balance, and even if Rabbi Eliezer ben Hyrcanus were with them, and Rabbi Eleazar were in the other scale, he would outweigh them all.

Rabban Johanan said to them: Go out and see which is the right way to which a man should cleave.

Rabbi Eliezer replied: A liberal eye.

Rabbi Joshua replied: A good companion.

Rabbi Yose replied: A good neighbor.

Rabbi Simeon replied: Foresight.

Rabbi Eleazar replied: Goodheartedness.

Said Rabban Johanan ben Zakkai to them: I prefer the answer of Eleazar ben Arak, for in his words your words are included.

Rabban Johanan said to them: Go out and see which is the evil way which a man should shun.

Rabbi Eliezer replied: A grudging eye.

Rabbi Joshua replied: An evil companion.

Rabbi Yose replied: An evil neighbor.

Rabbi Simeon replied: Borrowing and not repaying; for he that borrows from man is as one who borrows from God, blessed be He, as it is said, "The wicked borroweth, and payeth not; but the righteous dealeth graciously, and giveth" (Psalm 37:21).

Rabbi Eleazar replied: Meanheartedness.

Rabban Johanan said to them: I prefer the answer of Eleazar ben Arak, for in his words your words are included.

Each of them said three things.

Rabbi Eliezer says: Let the honor of thy fellow be as dear to thee as thine own. Be not easily angered. Repent one day before thy death.

And keep warm at the fire of the sages, but beware of their glowing coal lest thou be scorched: for their bite is the bite of a jackal, and their sting the sting of a scorpion, and their hiss the hiss of a serpent—moreover all their words are like coals of fire.

Rabbi Joshua says: A grudging eye, evil impulse, and hatred of mankind put a man out of the world.

Rabbi Yose says: Let thy fellow's property be as dear to thee as thine own. Make thyself fit for the study of Torah, for it will not be thine by inheritance. Let all thine actions be for the sake of heaven.

Rabbi Simeon says: Be alert in reciting the *shema* and the prayer. When thou prayest, do not make of thy prayer something automatic, but a plea for compassion, a supplication before God, blessed be He, for it is said, "For He is a God gracious and compassionate, long-suffering and abundant in mercy, and repenteth Him of the evil" (Joel 2:13). And be not wicked in thine own sight.

Rabbi Eleazar says: Be diligent in the study of Torah, and know how to answer an *epicuros*. Know in whose presence thou art toiling; and faithful is thy taskmaster to pay thee the reward of thy labor.

Rabbi Tarfon says: The day is short, the work is plentiful, the laborers are sluggish, and the reward is abundant, and the master of the house presses.

He used to say: It is not thy duty to finish the work, but thou art not at liberty to neglect it. If thou hast studied much Torah, thou shalt be given much reward: faithful is thy taskmaster to pay thee the reward of thy labor. And know that the rewarding of the righteous is in the age to come.

Akabya ben Mahalalel says: Mark well three things, and thou wilt not fall into the clutches of sin. Know whence thou art come, whither thou art going, and before whom thou art destined to give an account and reckoning.

"Whence thou art come?" From a putrid drop.

"Whence thou art going?" To a place of dust, worm, and maggot.

"And before whom thou art desined to give an account and reckoning?" Before the King of kings of kings, the Holy One, blessed be He.

Rabbi Hananiah, prefect of the priests, says: Do thou pray for the welfare of the empire, because were it not for the fear it inspires, every man would swallow his neighbor alive.

Rabbi Hananiah ben Teradyon says: If two sit together and the words between them are not of Torah, then that is a session of scorners, as it is said, "Nor hath sat in the seat of the scornful" (Psalm 1:1). But if two sit together and the words between them are of Torah, then the *Shekinah* is in their midst, as it is said, "Then they that feared the Lord spoke one with another; and the Lord hearkened, and heard, and a book of remembrance was written before Him, for them that feared the Lord and that thought upon His name" (Malachi 3:16). Now I know it is so of two; how do we know that even when one sits studying the Torah, the Holy One, blessed be He, fixes a reward for him? For it is said, "Though he sit alone and quietly he has surely received his [reward]" (Lamentations 3:28).

Rabbi Simeon says: When three eat at one table and do not speak words of Torah there, it is as though they had eaten of the sacrifices of the dead, as it is said, "For all tables are full of filthy vomit, when God is absent" (Isaiah 28:8). But when three eat at one table and do speak words of Torah there, it is as though they have eaten from the table of God, blessed be He, as it is said, "And He said unto me, this is the table that is before the Lord" (Ezekiel 41:22).

Rabbi Hananiah ben Hakinai says: If one wakes in the night, or walks by himself on the highway, and turns his heart to idle matters, he is mortally guilty.

Rabbi Nehunya ben Ha-Kana says: He who takes upon himself the yoke of Torah will be relieved of the yoke of the government and the yoke of mundane matters; but he who removes from himself the yoke of Torah will have imposed upon him the yoke of the government and the yoke of mundane matters.

Rabbi Halafta of Kefar Hananiah says: When ten sit studying the Torah, the *Shekina* resides in their midst, as it is said, "God standeth in the congregation of God" (Psalm 82:1). How do we know that the same is true of five? For it is said, "This band of His He hath established on the earth" (Amos 9:6). How do we know that the same is true of three? For it is said, "In the midst of the judges He judgeth" (Psalm 82:1). How do we know that the same is true of two? For it is said, "Then they that feared the Lord spoke one with another; and the Lord hearkened, and heard" (Malachi 3:16). How do we know that the same is true of one? For it is said, "In every place where I cause My name to be mentioned I will come unto thee and bless thee" (Exodus 20:21).

Rabbi Eleazar of Bartota says: Give to Him of His own, for thou and thine are His. And so too of David it says, "For everything is from Thee and of Thine own we have given to Thee" (I Chronicles 29:14).

Rabbi Simeon says: If one is studying as he walks along the highway, and he interrupts his study and exclaims, "How handsome is this tree, how handsome this field!", scripture (Deuteronomy 4:9) accounts it to him as though he were mortally guilty.

Rabbi Dostai bar Yannai says in the name of Rabbi Meir: If one forgets any thing of his studies, scripture accounts it to him as though he were mortally guilty, for it is said, "Only take heed to thyself, and keep thy soul diligently, lest thou forget the things which thine eyes saw" (Deuteronomy 4:9). Is this true even of one whose studies proved too difficult for him? The verse says, "And lest they depart from thy heart all the days of thy life" (*ibid.*): lo, one is not mortally guilty until he deliberately removes them from his heart.

Rabbi Hanina ben Dosa says: He whose fear of sin takes precedence over his wisdom, his wisdom will endure; but he whose wisdom takes precedence over his fear of sin, his wisdom will not endure.

He used to say: He whose works exceed his wisdom, his wisdom will endure; but he whose wisdom exceeds his works, his wisdom will not endure.

He used to say: One with whom men are pleased, God is pleased; and one with whom men are displeased, God is displeased.

Rabbi Dosa ben Harkinas says: Morning sleep, midday wine, children's prattle and sitting in the gathering places of the *am ha-arez* put a man out of the world.

Rabbi Eleazar of Modaim says: He who profanes the sacred things, and despises the festivals, and publicly disgraces his fellow, and annuls the covenant of Abraham our father, may he rest in peace, and is contemptuous towards the Torah—even though he have Torah and good works to his credit, has no share in the world to come.

Rabbi Ishmael says: Be suppliant to a superior, submissive under compulsory service (*Tishhoret*), and receive every man happily.

Rabbi Akiba says:

Merriment and frivolity accustom one to unchastity.

Tradition is a hedge about the Torah.

Tithes are a hedge about riches.

Vows are a hedge about abstinence.

A hedge about wisdom—silence.

He used to say: Beloved is man for he was created in the image. Extraordinary is the love made known to him that he was created in the image, as it is said, "For in the image of God made He man" (Genesis 9:6).

Beloved are Israel for they were called children of God. Extraordinary is the love made known to them that they were called children of God, as it is said, "Ye are the children of the Lord, your God" (Deuteronomy 14:1).

Beloved are Israel for to them was given a precious implement. Extraordinary is the love made known to them that they were given the precious implement with which the world was created, as it is said, "For I give you good doctrine, forsake ye not My Torah" (Proverbs 4:2).

Everything is foreseen, yet freedom of choice is granted; in mercy is the world judged; and everything is according to the preponderance of works.

He used to say: Everything is given against a pledge and a net is cast over all the living: the shop is open, the shopkeeper extends credit, the ledger lies open, the hand writes, and whoever wishes to borrow may come and borrow; and the collectors make the rounds continually, every day, and exact payment of man with his consent or without it. They have what to base their claims on. And the judgment is a judgment of truth. And everything is prepared for the feast.

Rabbi Eleazar ben Azariah says: Where there is no Torah, there's no right conduct, where there is no right conduct, there's no Torah; where there is no wisdom, there's no piety, where there is no piety, there's no wisdom; where there is no perception, there's no knowledge, where there is no knowledge, there's no perception; where there is no bread, there's no Torah, where there is no Torah, there's no bread.

He used to say: He whose wisdom exceeds his works, to what may he be likened? To a tree whose branches are numerous but whose roots are few. The wind comes along and uproots it and sweeps it down, as it is said, "For he shall be like a tamarisk in the desert, and shall not see when good cometh; but shall inhabit the parched places in the wilderness, a salt land and not inhabited" (Jeremiah 17:6). But he whose works exceed his wisdom, to what may he be likened? To a tree whose branches are few but whose roots are numerous. Then even if all the winds of the world come along and blow against it they cannot stir it from its place, as it is said, "For he shall be as a tree planted by the waters, and that spreadeth out its roots by the river, and shall not see when heat cometh, but its foliage shall be luxuriant; and shall not be anxious in the year of drought, neither shall cease from yielding fruit" (Jeremiah 17:8).

Rabbi Eleazar [ben] Hisma says: The laws of mixed bird offerings and the key to the calculations of menstruation days—these, these are the body of the Halakah. Equinoxes and Gematria are the desserts of wisdom.

Ben Zoma says: Who is a wise man? He that learns from all men, as it is said, "From all my teachers have I got understanding" (Psalm 119:99).

Who is a mighty man? He that subdues his evil impulse, as it is said, "He that is slow to anger is better than the mighty, and he that ruleth his spirit than him that taketh a city" (Proverbs 16:32).

Who is a rich man? He that is content with his portion, as it is said, "When thou eatest the labor of thy hands happy shalt thou be and it shall be well with thee" (Psalm 128:2): "Happy shalt thou be in this world, and it shall be well with thee in the world to come."

Who is an honorable man? He that honors mankind, as it is said, "For them that honor me I will honor and they that despise me shall be lightly esteemed" (I Samuel 2:30).

Ben Azzai says: Be quick in carrying out a minor commandment as in the case of a major one, and flee from transgression: for one good deed leads to another good deed and one transgression leads to another transgression; for the reward for a good deed is another good deed and the reward for a transgression is another transgression.

He used to say: Despise no man and consider nothing impossible, for there is no man who does not have his hour and there is no thing that does not have its place.

Rabbi Levitas of Yavneh says: Be of an exceedingly humble spirit, for the end of man is the worm.

Rabbi Johanan ben Baroka says: If one profanes the name of heaven in secret he shall be punished in broad daylight: unwittingly or wittingly, it is all one in profaning the name.

Rabbi Ishmael his son says: If one studies in order to teach, it is granted to him to study and to teach; but if one studies in order to practice, it is granted to him to study and to teach, to observe and to practice.

Rabbi Zadok says: Do not make them a crown for self-exaltation nor a spade to dig with. So too Hillel used to say: "And he that puts the crown to his own use shall perish." Thus thou dost learn: he that puts the words of Torah to personal profit removes his life from the world.

Rabbi Yose says: He who honors the Torah will himself be honored by men; he who dishonors the Torah will himself be dishonored by men.

Rabbi Ishmael his son says: He who refrains from judgment rids himself of enmity, robbery, and false swearing. But he who is presumptuous in rendering decision is a fool, wicked, and arrogant.

He used to say: Do not act the judge's part by thyself alone, for none may act the judge's part by himself alone—save one. And say not: "Adopt my view"—for they may say it, but not thou.

Rabbi Jonathan says: He who fulfills the Torah in poverty will in the end fulfill it in riches; but he who neglects the Torah in riches will in the end neglect it in poverty.

Rabbi Meir says: Engage but little in business, and be busy with the Torah; be of humble spirit before all men. If thou hast neglected the Torah, thou shalt have many who bring thee to neglect it; but if thou hast toiled away at the study of Torah, there is a rich reward to be given thee.

Rabbi Eliezer ben Jacob says: He who carries out one good deed acquires one advocate in his own behalf, and he who commits one transgression acquires one accuser against himself. Repentance and good works are like a shield against calamity.

Rabbi Johanan Ha-Sandelar says: Every assembly which is for the sake of heaven will in the end endure; but one which is not for the sake of heaven will not endure in the end.

Rabbi Eleazar ben Shammua says: Let the

honor of thy disciple be as dear to thee as thine own, and the honor of thy comrade as fear of thy master, and fear of thy master as fear of heaven.

Rabbi Judah says: Study with care, for error in the course of study is accounted deliberate sin.

Rabbi Simeon says: There are three crowns: the crown of Torah, the crown of priesthood, and the crown of royalty; but the crown of a good name must accompany them all.

Rabbi Nehorai says: Betake thyself to a place of Torah and say not that it will come after thee, that thy companions will set it up for thee to master; "And lean not upon thine own understanding" (Proverbs 3:5).

Rabbi Yannai says: Within our reach is neither the tranquillity of the wicked nor even the suffering of the righteous.

Rabbi Mattiah ben Heresh says: On meeting any man be the first to extend greetings; and be a tail to lions rather than a head to jackals.

Rabbi Jacob says: This world is like a foyer leading into the world to come—prepare thyself in the foyer so that thou mayest enter into the inner chamber.

He used to say: Richer is one hour of repentance and good works in this world than all of life of the world to come; and richer is one hour's calm of spirit in the world to come than all of life of this world.

Rabbi Simeon ben Eleazar says: Do not appease thy fellow in his hour of anger; do not comfort him while the dead is still laid out before him; do not question him in the hour of his vow; and do not strive to see him in his hour of misfortune.

Samuel "The Little" says: "Rejoice not when thine enemy falleth, and let not thy heart be glad when he stumbleth; lest the Lord see it, and it displease Him and He turn away His wrath from him" (Proverbs 24:17–17).

Elisha ben Abuyah says: He that studies as a child, to what may he be likened? To ink written on fresh paper. But he that studies as an old man, to what may he be likened? To ink written on wornout paper.

Rabbi Yose Bar Judah of Kefar Ha-Babli says: He who learns from the young, to what may he be likened? To one that eats unripe grapes and drinks wine from the vat. But he who learns from the old, to what may he be likened? To one that eats ripe grapes and drinks wine that's aged.

Rabbi says: Do not look at the jug but at its contents—there are new jugs filled with old wine, and old ones in which there is not even new wine!

He used to say: The ones who were born are to die, and the ones who have died are to be brought to life again, and the ones who are brought to life are to be summoned to judgment—so that one may know, make known, and have the knowledge that He is God, He is the designer, He is the creator, He is the discerner, He is the judge, He the witness, He the plaintiff, and He will summon to judgment: blessed be He, in whose presence is neither iniquity, nor forgetfulness, nor respect of persons, nor taking of bribes—for everything is His. Know thou that everything is according to the reckoning.

And let not thine impulse give thee reassurances that the nether world will prove a refuge to thee—for against thy will art thou formed, against thy will art thou born, against thy will dost thou live, against thy will die, and against thy will shalt thou give account and reckoning before the King of kings of kings, the Holy One, blessed be He.

By ten utterances was the world created. And what does this teach? Surely it could have been created by one utterance! But this was so that the wicked be punished, for they destroy a world created by ten utterances; and that the righteous be richly rewarded, for they sustain a world created by ten utterances.

Ten generations from Adam to Noah—to make known what long-suffering was His: for all these generations kept on provoking Him until He brought upon them the waters of the flood.

Ten generations from Noah to Abraham—to make known what long-suffering was His: for all the generations kept on provoking Him until Abraham appeared, and he received the reward of all of them.

With ten trials was Abraham our father (may he rest in peace) tried, and he withstood them all—to make known how great was the love of Abraham our father, may he rest in peace.

Ten miracles were wrought for our ancestors in Egypt and ten at the sea.

Ten plagues the Holy One, blessed be He, visited on the Egyptians in Egypt, and ten at the sea.

With ten trials our ancestors tried God, blessed be He, in the wilderness, as it is said, "They have put Me to proof these ten times, and have not hearkened to My voice" (Numbers 14:22).

Ten miracles were wrought for our ancestors in the Temple:

No woman ever miscarried because of the smell of the sacred flesh;

The sacred flesh never went bad;

Never was a fly seen in the slaughterhouse;

Never did the high priest suffer uncleanness on the day of atonement;

Never did the rains extinguish the fire of the woodpile [on the altar];

No wind prevailed over the pillar of smoke;

Never was a defect found in the omer or in the two loaves or in the showbread;

The people stood pressed together yet bowed down and had room enough;

Never did a serpent or scorpion harm anyone in Jerusalem;

No man ever said to his fellow: "Too congested is the place for me that I should lodge in Jerusalem."

Ten things were created on the [first] Sabbath eve at twilight, to wit: the mouth of the earth, the mouth of the well [in the wilderness], the ass's power of speech, the rainbow, the manna, the rod [of Moses], the *shamir,* the letters, the writing, and the tables of the commandments.

Some say: Also the demons, the burial place of Moses, and the ram offered up by Abraham our father.

And some say: Also the tongs made with tongs.

Seven qualities characterize the clod and seven the wise man: the wise man does not speak before him that is greater than he in wisdom; he does not break into his fellow's speech; he is not in a rush to reply; he asks what is relevant and replies to the point; he speaks of first things first and of last things last; of what he has not heard he says: "I have not heard;" and he acknowledges what is true.

And the opposites apply to the clod.

Seven kinds of calamity come upon the world for seven classes of transgression:

If some tithe and some do not, famine as a result of drought comes—some go hungry and [only] some have enough to eat;

If [all] determine not to tithe, a famine as a result of tumult and of drought comes;

And if [they resolved] not to set aside the dough-offering, an all-consuming famine comes.

Pestilence comes upon the world for crimes punishable by death according to the Torah which have not been turned over to the court, and for neglect of the law regarding the earth's fruits in the sabbatical year.

The sword comes upon the world for the delay of justice, for the perversion of justice, and because of those that teach the Torah not in accordance with the Halakah.

Evil beasts come upon the world for the taking of false oaths and for profaning the name.

Exile comes upon the world for idolatrous worship, for unchastity, for bloodshed, and for neglect of the year of release of the land.

At four periods pestilence is on the increase: in the fourth year, in the seventh, at the departure of the seventh, and annually at the departure of the feast—

"In the fourth," for neglecting the poor man's tithe in the third; "in the seventh," for neglecting the poor man's tithe in the sixth year; "at the departure of the seventh year," for neglecting the commandment to release the fruits of the earth in the seventh year; "annually, at the departure of the feast," for robbing the poor of their gifts.

There are four types of men:

One who says, "Mine is mine and thine is thine"—this is the commonplace type. Some say: That is the Sodom type.

"Mine is thine and thine is mine"—the *am ha-arez.*

"Mine is thine and thine is thine"—the saint.

"Mine is mine and thine is mine"—the wicked.

There are four kinds of temperament:

Easily angered and easily appeased—his gain is canceled by his loss.

Hard to anger and hard to appease—his loss is canceled by his gain.

Hard to anger and easy to appease—the saint.

Easily angered but hard to appease—the wicked.

There are four types of disciples:

Quick to understand but quick to forget—his gain is canceled by his loss.

Understands with difficulty but forgets with difficulty—his loss is canceled by his gain.

Quick to understand and forgets with difficulty—the wise.

Understands with difficulty and quick to forget—this is an evil lot!

There are four types of charity givers:

He who wishes to give but that others should not give—begrudges what belongs to others.

That others should give but not he—begrudges what belongs to himself.

That he should give and others too—the saint.

That neither he nor others give—the wicked.

There are four types among those that frequent the study-house: there is one who attends but does not put to practice—he receives the reward for attendance.

There is one who puts to practice but does not attend—he receives the reward for practice.

There is one who attends and puts to practice—the saint.

Neither attends nor puts to practice—the wicked.

There are four types among those that sit in the presence of the sages: the sponge, the funnel, the strainer, and the sifter.

The sponge soaks up everything.

The funnel takes in at one ear and lets out at the other.

The strainer lets pass the wine and retains the lees.

The sifter holds back the coarse and collects the fine flour.

If love depends on some selfish end, when the end fails, love fails; but if it does not depend on a selfish end, it will never fail. An example of love which depended on a selfish end? That was the love of Amnon for Tamar. An example of love which did not depend on a selfish end? That was the love of David and Jonathan.

Every controversy which is for the sake of heaven will in the end endure; but one which is not for the sake of heaven will not endure in the end. A controversy for the sake of heaven? Such was the controversy of Hillel and Shammai. And one which was not for the sake of heaven? Such was the controversy of Korah and all his company.

If one leads the multitudes to virtue, through him shall no sin come; but one who causes the multitudes to sin shall be given no opportunity to repent. Moses was himself virtuous and led the multitudes to virtue; therefore the merit of the many is linked to him, as it is said, "He achieved the righteousness of the Lord, and his ordinances are with Israel" (Deuteronomy 33:21). Jeroboam himself sinned and caused the multitudes to sin; therefore the sin of the many is linked to him, as it is said, "For the sins of Jeroboam which he sinned, and wherewith he made Israel to sin" (I Kings 15:30).

He who has to his credit the following three things is of the disciples of Abraham our father; but if three other things, is of the disciples of the wicked Balaam:

A liberal outlook, a humble spirit, and a modest appetite—of the disciples of Abraham our father.

A grudging eye, and arrogant spirit, and limitless appetite—of the disciples of the wicked Balaam.

What distinguishes the disciples of Abraham our father from the disciples of the wicked Balaam? The disciples of Abraham our father enjoy this world and inherit the world to come, as it is said, "That I may cause those that love me to inherit substance and that I may fill their treasuries" (Proverbs 8:21). But as to the disciples of the wicked Balaam, their portion is Gehenna and they go down to the pit of destruction, as it is said, "But thou, O God, wilt bring them down into the nethermost pit; men of blood and deceit shall not live out half their days; but as for me, I will trust in Thee" (Psalm 55:24).

Judah ben Tema says: Be strong as the

leopard, swift as the eagle, fleet as the gazelle, and brave as the lion, to do the will of thy father who is in heaven.

He used to say: The arrogant is headed for Gehenna, the blushing for the Garden of Eden.

May it be Thy will, O Lord our God, to rebuild Thy city speedily in our days, and set our portion in the studying of Thy Torah.

He used to say:

At five years of age the study of scripture;
At ten, the study of Mishna;
At thirteen, subject to the commandments;
At fifteen, the study of Talmud;
At eighteen, marriage;
At twenty, pursuit [of livelihood];
At thirty, the peak of strength;
At forty, wisdom;
At fifty, able to give counsel;
At sixty, old age creeping on;
At seventy, fullness of years;
At eighty, the age of "strength";
At ninety, body bent;
At one hundred, as good as dead and gone completely out of the world.

Ben Bag Bag says: Turn it this way, turn it that way, everything is in it; keep thine eye on it, grow old and aged over it, and from it do not stir—for thou hast no better portion than it.

Ben He He says: According to the painstaking, the reward.

The sages have taught in the idiom of the Mishna: blessed be he who chose them and their Mishna.

Rabbi Meir says: He who studies the Torah for its own sake merits many things; not only that, but he is worth the whole world, all of it. He is called beloved friend; he loves God, he loves mankind, he is a joy to God and a joy to man. And the Torah clothes him with humility and reverence, equips him to be righteous and saintly and upright and trustworthy; it keeps him far from sin and draws him to virtue; and men profit from his counsel and wisdom, understanding and strength; as it is said, "Counsel is Mine, and sound wisdom; I am understanding, power is Mine" (Proverbs 8:14). And it bestows upon him royalty and dominion and acuteness of judgment. To him are revealed the secrets of Torah, and he becomes as it were an everflowing spring, a river of unceasing streams; he becomes modest, long-suffering, forgiving of insult; and it magnifies him and exalts him over everything.

Rabbi Joshua ben Levi said: Every single day a *Bat Kol* goes forth from Mount Horeb, proclaiming as follows: "Woe to mankind for their contempt of the Torah!" For he who does not study the Torah is called *Nazuf* (reprobate), as it is said, "As a ring of gold in a swine's snout, so is a fair woman that turneth aside from discretion" (Proverbs 11:22). And it says, "And the tables were the work of God, and the writing was the writing of God, graven upon the tables" (Exodus 32:16). Read not *"harut"* (graven) but *"herut"* (freedom), for thou wilt find no free man save him who is engaged in the study of Torah. But he who is always preoccupied with the Torah is surely exalted, as it is said, "And from the gift, his heritage is God, and from the heritage of God, he is raised to high places" (Numbers 21:19).

He who learns from his fellow one chapter, or one law, or one verse, or one word, even one letter—is obliged to treat him with honor. For thus we find concerning David, king of Israel. He learned from Ahitophel no more than two things, yet he addressed him as his master, his guide, his beloved, as it is said, "But it was thou, a man mine equal, my guide, my beloved" (Psalm 55:14). Now is there not an inference to be drawn from this? If David, king of Israel, who learned from Ahitophel no more than two things, addressed him as his master, his guide, and his beloved, all the more must he who learns from his fellow one chapter or one law or one verse or one word, even one letter, treat him with honor! And honor applies to naught save Torah, as it is said, "It is honor that sages inherit" (Proverbs 3:35); "and the wholehearted shall inherit good" (Proverbs 28:10): And the good is naught but Torah, as it is said, "For I give you good doctrine, forsake ye not My Torah" (Proverbs 4:2).

This is the highway to the Torah—a salty crust for food, water in ration for drink, the ground thy bed, thy life a life of privation, and thy labors in the Torah. If thou doest thus, "Happy shalt thou be and it shall be well with thee" (Psalm 128:2): Happy shalt thou be in this world; and it shall be well with thee in the world to come.

Seek not greatness for thyself, covet not honor; practice more than thou learnest. And yearn not for the table of kings, for thy table is greater than their table, and thy crown greater than their crown. "And faithful is thy task-master to pay thee the reward of thy labor."

Greater is learning [Torah] than priesthood and than royalty, for royalty is acquired by thirty stages, priesthood by twenty-four: but the Torah is acquired by forty-eight things—by study, by diligent attention, by proper speech, by an understanding heart, by a perceptive heart, by awe, by fear, by humility, by joy, by attendance upon sages, by critical give and take with fellows, by acute exchanges among disciples, by clear thinking, by study of scripture, by study of Mishna, by a minimum of sleep, by a minimum of chatter, by a minimum pursuit of pleasure, by a minimum of frivolity, by a minimum preoccupation with worldly matters, by long-suffering, by generosity, by faith in the sages, by acceptance of suffering.

[Learning is acquired also by him] who knows his place, who is content with his portion, who makes a hedge about his words, who takes no credit to himself, who is beloved, who loves God, loves mankind, loves acts of charity, loves reproof, loves rectitude, keeps far from honors, is not puffed up with his learning, does not delight in handing down decisions, bears the yoke along with his fellow, judges him with the scales weighted in his favor, leads him on to the truth, leads him on to peace, concentrates on his study, is capable of intellectual give and take, is capable of adding to what he has learned, studies in order to teach, and studies in order to practice, makes his teacher wiser, is exact in what he has learned, and quotes his source. Thus thou dost learn that whoever quotes his source brings deliverance to the world, as it is said, "And Esther told the King thereof in Mordecai's name" (Esther 2:22).

How grand is Torah, for to those who engage in it, it gives life in this world and the world to come! As it is said, "For they are life unto those that find them, and health to all their flesh" (Proverbs 4:22). And it says, "It shall be health to thy navel, and marrow to thy bones" (Proverbs 3:8). And it says, "She is a tree of life to them that lay hold upon it, and happy is everyone that holdeth her fast" (Proverbs 3:18). And it says, "For they shall be a chaplet of grace unto thy head, and chains about thy neck" (Proverbs 1:9). And it says, "She will give to thy head a chaplet of grace: a crown of glory will she bestow on thee" (Proverbs 4:9). And it says, "Length of days is in her right hand; in her left hand are riches and honor" (Proverbs 3:16). And it says, "For length of days, and years of life, and peace, will they add to thee" (Proverbs 3:2).

Rabbi Simeon ben Menasia says in the name of Rabbi Simeon ben Yohai: Beauty, strength, riches, honor, wisdom, old age, fullness of years, and children are becoming to the righteous and becoming to the world. As it is said, "The hoary head is a crown of glory, it is found in the way of righteousness" (Proverbs 16:31). And it says: "The crown of the wise is their riches" (Proverbs 14:24). And it says, "Children's children are the crown of old men; and the glory of children are their fathers" (Proverbs 17:6). And it says, "The glory of young men is their strength; and the beauty of old men is the hoary head" (Proverbs 20:29). And it says, "Then the moon shall be confounded and the sun ashamed; for the Lord of Hosts will reign in Mount Zion and in Jerusalem, and before His elders shall be glory" (Isaiah 24:23).

Rabbi Simeon ben Menasia says: These seven items which the sages listed for the righteous, were all of them fulfilled in Rabbi and his sons.

Said Rabbi Yose ben Kisma: One time as I was walking on the highway a certain man met me and greeted me. I returned his greeting.

He said to me: "Rabbi, from what place art thou?"

I said to him: "From a great city of sages and teachers am I."

He said to me: "Rabbi, wouldst thou like to dwell with us in our place? I would give thee one thousand thousand *denar* and precious stones and pearls."

I said to him: "My son, even if thou wert to give me all the silver and gold and precious stones and pearls in the world, I would dwell nowhere save in a place of Torah—for in the hour of a man's departure, neither silver nor gold nor precious stones and pearls accompany the man, only Torah and good works, as it is said, "When thou walkest it shall lead thee, when thou liest down, it shall watch over thee: and when thou awakest, it shall talk with thee" (Proverbs 6:22): When thou walkest, it shall lead thee, in this world; When thou liest down, it shall watch over thee, in the grave; And when thou awakest, it shall talk with thee, in the world to come. And so too it is written in the Book of Psalms by David, King of Israel, "The law of Thy mouth is better unto me than thousands of gold and silver" (Psalm 119:72). And it says, "Mine is the silver, and Mine the gold, saith the Lord of Hosts" (Haggai 2:8).

Five possessions did the Holy One, blessed be He, set aside for Himself in this world, to wit: Torah, one possession; the heavens and the earth, another possession; Abraham, another possession; Israel, another possession; the Temple, another possession.

How do we know that Torah is one possession? For it is written, "The Lord made me as the beginning of His way, the first of His works of old" (Proverbs 8:22).

How do we know that the heavens and the earth are one of His possessions? For it is said, "Thus saith the Lord: The heaven is My throne, and the earth is My footstool; where is the house that ye may build unto me? And where is the place that may be My resting-place" (Isaiah 66:1)? And it says, "How manifold are Thy works, O Lord! In wisdom hast Thou made them all; the earth is full of Thy possessions" (Psalm 104:24).

How do we know that Abraham is one of his possessions? For it is written, "And He blessed him, and said: Blessed be Abram of God most high, possessor of heaven and earth" (Genesis 14:19).

How do we know that Israel is one of his possessions? For it is written, "Till Thy people pass over, O Lord, till the people pass over that Thou hast gotten" (Exodus 15:16). And it says, "As for the holy that are in the earth, they are excellent in whom is all My delight" (Psalm 16:3).

How do we know that the Temple is one of his possessions? For it is said, "The sanctuary, O Lord, which Thy hands have established" (Exodus 15:17). And it says, "And He brought them to His holy border, to the mountain, which His right hand had gotten" (Psalm 78:54).

Whatsoever the Holy One, blessed be He, created in His world, He created for His own glory only, as it is said, "Every one that is called by My name, him I created for My glory, I have formed him, yea, I have made him" (Isaiah 43:7). It says also, "The Lord shall reign for ever and ever" (Exodus 15:18).

Said Rabbi Hananiah ben Akashya: It pleased the Holy One, blessed be He, to grant merit to Israel; that is why He gave them Torah and commandments in abundance, as it is said, "The Lord was pleased for His righteousness' sake, to make Torah great and glorious" (Isaiah 42:21).

2. Shabbath*

MISHNAH. *The primary labours are forty less one,* [Viz.:] *sowing, ploughing, reaping, binding sheaves, threshing, winnowing, selecting, grinding, sifting, kneading, baking, shearing wool, bleaching, hackling, dyeing, spinning, stretching the threads, the making of two meshes, weaving two threads, dividing two threads, tying* [knotting] *and untying, sewing two stitches, tearing in order to sew two stitches, capturing a deer, slaughtering or flaying, or salting it, curing its hide, scraping it* [of its hair], *cutting it up, writing two letters, erasing in order to write two letters* [over the erasure], *building, pulling down, extinguishing, kindling, striking with a hammer,* [and] *carrying out from one domain to another: these are the forty primary labours less one.*

GEMARA. Why state the number?—Said R.

* The text consists of Chapter VII, paragraph 2 of the Mishnah, and pages 73b–75b of the Gemara. The translation is that of Rabbi Dr. H. Freedman in *The Babylonian Talmud,* I. Epstein, ed., Part II, Volume I, London: The Soncino Press, 1938, pp. 348–59. The footnotes are those of the present editors.

Joḥanan: [to teach] that if one performs them all in one state of unawareness, he is liable on account of each separately.

Sowing and ploughing. Let us see: ploughing is done first, then let him [the Tanna][1] state *ploughing* first and then *sowing?*—The Tanna treats of Palestine, where they first sow and then plough.

A Tanna taught: Sowing, pruning, planting, bending, and grafting are all one labour. What does this inform us?—This: that if one performs many labours of the same nature, he is liable only to one [sacrifice]. R. Abba said in the name of R. Ḥiyya b. Ashi in R. Ammi's name: He who prunes is culpable on account of planting, while he who plants, bends [the vine], or grafts is culpable on account of sowing. On account of sowing only but not on account of planting?—Say: on account of planting too.

R. Kahana said: If one prunes and needs the wood [too], he is liable to two [penalties], one on account of reaping and one on account of planting. R. Joseph said: He who cuts hay is liable to two [penalties], one on account of reaping and the other on account of planting. Abaye said: He who trims beets [in the ground] is liable to two [penalties], one on account of reaping and one on account of planting.

Ploughing. A Tanna taught: Ploughing, digging, and trenching are all one [form of] work. R. Shesheth said: If one has a mound [of earth] and removes it, in the house, he is liable on the score of building; if in the field, he is liable on the score of ploughing. Raba said: If one has a depression and fills it up: if in the house, he is liable on account of building; if in the field, he is liable on account of ploughing.

R. Abba said: If one digs a pit on the Sabbath, needing only the earth thereof, he is not culpable on its account. And even according to R. Judah, who ruled: One is liable on account of a labour which is not required on its own account: that is only when he effects an improvement, but this man causes damage.

Reaping: A Tanna taught: Reaping, vintaging, gathering [dates], collecting [olives], and gathering [figs] are all one [form of] labour. R. Papa said: He who throws a clod of earth at a palm tree and dislodges dates is liable to two [penalties], one on account of detaching and one on account of stripping. R. Ashi said: This is not the mode of detaching, nor is it the mode of stripping.

Binding sheaves. Raba said: He who collects salt out of a salina[2] is liable on the score of binding sheaves. Abaye said: Binding sheaves applies only to products of the soil.

Threshing. It was taught: Threshing, beating [flax in their stalks], and beating [cotton] are all the same form of work.

Winnowing, selecting, grinding and sifting. But winnowing, selecting, and sifting are identical?—Abaye and Raba both said: Whatever was performed in [connection with the erection of] the Tabernacle, even if there are [labours] similar thereto, is counted [separately]. Then let him also enumerate pounding [wheat]?—Said Abaye: Because a poor man eats his bread without pounding. Raba said: This agrees with Rabbi, who said: The primary labours are forty less one; but if pounding were enumerated, there would be forty. Then let one of these be omitted and pounding be inserted? Hence it is clear [that it must be explained] as Abaye [does].

Our Rabbis taught: If various kinds of food lie before one, he may select and eat, select and put aside; but he must not select, and if he does, he incurs a sin-offering. What does this mean?—Said 'Ulla, This is its meaning: He may select to eat on the same day, and he may select and put aside for the same day; but he must not select for [use on] the morrow, and if he does, he incurs a sin-offering. R. Ḥisda demurred: Is it then permitted to bake for [use on] the same day, or is it permitted to cook for the same day? Rather said R. Ḥisda: He may select and eat less than the standard quantity, and he may select and put aside less than the standard quantity; but he must not select as much as the standard quantity, and if he does, he incurs a sin-offering. R. Joseph demurred: Is it then permitted to bake less than the standard quantity? Rather said R. Joseph: He may select by hand and eat, or

[1] One who passes on a Mishnaic statement.

[2] A salt deposit.

select by hand and put aside; but he may not select with a reed-basket or a dish; and if he does, he is not culpable, nevertheless it is forbidden. He may not select with a sieve or a basket-sieve, and if he does he incurs a sin-offering. R. Hamnuna demurred: Are then a reed-basket and a dish mentioned?—Rather said R. Hamnuna: He may select and eat, [taking the] eatable from the non-eatable, and he may select and put aside, [taking] the eatable from the non-eatable. But he must not select the non-eatable out of the eatable, and if he does, he incurs a sin-offering. Abaye demurred: Is it then taught, "the eatable from the non-eatable"? Rather said Abaye: He may select and eat immediately, and he may select and put aside for immediate use; but he may not select for [later consumption on] the same day, and if he does, it is regarded as though he were selecting for [making] a store, and he incurs a sin-offering. The Rabbis reported this to Raba. Said he to them, Naḥmani has said well.

If two kinds of food lie before a person, and he selects and eats or selects and puts aside,[3]—R. Ashi learnt: He is not culpable: R. Jeremiah of Difti learnt: He is culpable, "R. Ashi learnt: He is not culpable"! but it was taught: "He is culpable"?—There is no difficulty: the one treats of a reed-basket and a plate; the other refers to a sieve and a basket-seive.

When R. Dimi came, he related: It was R. Bibi's Sabbath, and R. Ammi and R. Assi chanced to be there. He cast a basket of fruit before them, and I do not know whether it was because he held that it is forbidden to pick out the eatable from the non-eatable, or whether he wished to be generous.

Hezekiah said: One who picks lupines [after boiling] out of their husks is culpable. Shall we say that Hezekiah holds that it is forbidden to select the eatable from the non-eatable? [No.] Lupines are different, because they are boiled seven times, and if one does not remove it [the edible portion], it goes rancid, hence it is like [picking] the non-edible out of the edible.

Grinding. R. Papa said: He who cuts up beets very fine is liable on account of grinding. R. Manasseh said: He who cuts chips [for fuel] is liable on account of grinding. Said R. Ashi: If he is particular about their size, he is liable on account of cutting.

Kneading and baking. R. Papa said: Our Tanna omits the boiling of ingredients [for dyes], which took place in [connection with] the Tabernacle, and treats of baking!—Our Tanna takes the order of [making] bread.

R. Aḥa son of R. Awira said: He who throws a tent peg into a stove is liable on account of cooking. But that is obvious?—You might say, His intention is to strengthen [harden] the article, therefore we are informed that it [first] softens and then hardens.

Rabbah son of R. Huna said: He who boils pitch is liable on account of cooking. But that is obvious?—You might argue, Since it hardens again, I might say [that he is] not [liable]. Hence he informs us [otherwise].

Raba said: He who makes an [earthenware] barrel is culpable on account of seven sin-offerings. [He who makes] an oven is liable on account of eight sin-offerings. Abaye said: He who makes a wicker work is liable to eleven sin-offerings, and if he sews round the mouth thereof, he is liable to thirteen sin offerings.

Shearing wool and bleaching. Rabbah b. Bar Ḥanah said in R. Joḥanan's name: He who spins wool from off the animal's back on the Sabbath incurs three sin-offerings, one on account of shearing, another on account of hackling, and the third on account of spinning. R. Kahana said: Neither shearing, hackling, nor spinning is [done] in this manner. But is it not so? Surely it was taught in the name of R. Nehemiah: It was washed [direct] on the goats and spun on the goats: which proves that spinning direct from the animal is designated spinning?—Superior skill is different.

Our Rabbis taught: He who plucks the wing [of a bird], trims it [the feather], and plucks it [the down], is liable to three sin-offerings. Said R. Simeon b. Laḳish: For plucking [the wing] one is liable on account of shearing; for trimming [the feather] he is liable on the score of cutting; and for plucking [the down] he is liable under the head of smoothing.

Tying and untying. Where was there tying in the Tabernacle?—Said Raba: The tent-pegs were tied. But that was tying with the intention of [subsequent] untying? But said Abaye:

[3] For someone else.

The weavers of the curtains, when a thread broke, tied it up. Said Raba to him: You have explained tying; but what can be said about untying? And should you answer that when two knots [in the material] chanced to come together, one untied one and left the other knotted: [it may be asked], seeing that one would not do thus before a king of flesh and blood, how much more so before the Supreme King of kings, the Holy One, blessed be He? Rather said Raba—others state, R. Elai: Those who caught the *ḥillazon*[4] tied and untied.

Sewing two stitches. But it cannot endure?—Said Rabbah b. Bar Ḥanah in R. Joḥanan's name: Providing that he knots them.

Tearing in order to sew two stitches. Was there any tearing in the Tabernacle?—Rabbah and R. Zera both say: A curtain which was attacked by a moth was torn [round the moth hole] and resewn.

R. Zuṭra b. Ṭobiah said in Rab's name: He who pulls the thread of a seam on the Sabbath is liable to a sin-offering; and he who learns a single thing from a Magian[5] is worthy of death; and he who is able to calculate the cycles and planetary courses but does not, one may hold no conversation with him.

As to magianism, Rab and Samuel [differ thereon]: one maintains that it is sorcery; the other, blasphemy. It may be proved that it is Rab who maintains that it is blasphemy. For R. Zuṭra b. Ṭobiah said in Rab's name: He who learns a single thing from a magian is worthy of death. Now should you think that it is a sorcerer, surely it is written, *thou shalt not learn to do [after the abominations of those nations]*,[6] [implying], but you may learn in order to understand and instruct! This proves it.

R. Simeon b. Pazzi said in the name of R. Joshua b. Levi on the authority of Bar Kappara: He who knows how to calculate the cycles and planetary courses, but does not, of him Scripture saith, *but they regard not the work of the Lord, neither have they considered the operation of his hands.*[7]

R. Samuel b. Naḥmani said in R. Joḥanan's name: How do we know that it is one's duty to calculate the cycles and planetary courses? Because it is written, *for this is your wisdom and understanding in the sight of the peoples:*[8] what wisdom and understanding is in the sight of the peoples? Say, that it is the science of cycles and planets.

Capturing a deer, etc. Our Rabbis taught: He who captures a purple-fish and crushes it is liable to one [sin-offering]; R. Judah said: He is liable to two, for R. Judah maintained: Crushing comes under the head of threshing. Said they to him: Crushing does not come under the head of threshing. Raba observed: What is the Rabbis' reason? They hold that threshing is applicable only to produce from the soil. But let him be culpable too on the score of taking life?—Said R. Joḥanan: This means that he crushed it when [already] dead. Raba said: You may even explain that he crushed it whilst alive: in respect to the taking of life he is but incidentally occupied. But Abaye and Raba both maintain: R. Simeon admits in a case of "cut off his head but let him not die!" Here it is different, because he is more pleased that it should be alive, so that the dye should be clearer.

And slaughtering it. As for him who slaughters, on what score is he culpable?—Rab said: On the score of dyeing; while Samuel said: On the score of taking life. On the score of dyeing but not on the score of taking life! Say, on the score of dyeing too. Rab said: As to this dictum of mine, I will make an observation thereon so that later generations should not come and deride me. Wherein is one pleased with the dyeing? One is pleased that the throat should be stained with blood, so the people may see it and come and buy from him.

Salting and curing it. But salting and tanning are identical?—R. Joḥanan and Resh Laḳish both said: Omit one of these and insert the tracing of lines. Rabbah son of R. Huna said: He who salts meat is liable on account of tanning [dressing]. Raba said: Curing does not apply to foodstuffs. R. Ashi observed: And even Rabbah son of R. Huna ruled thus only when he requires it for a journey; but [when

[4] A shellfish the blood of which is used for dye.

[5] A Persian priest.

[6] Deut. 18:9.

[7] Isa. 5:12.

[8] Deut. 4:6.

he needs it] for his house, one does not turn his food into wood.

Scraping and cutting it up. R. Aḥa b. Ḥanina said: He who rubs [smooths skins] between columns on the Sabbath is liable on the score of scraping. R. Ḥiyya b. Abba said, R. Ammi told me three things in the name of R. Joshua b. Levi: He who planes the tops of beams on the Sabbath is culpable on account of cutting. He who spreads a poultice [evenly over a sore] on the Sabbath is culpable on the grounds of scraping. And he who chisels round a stone on the Sabbath is liable on the score of striking with the hammer. R. Simeon b. Bisna said in the name of R. Simeon b. Laḳish: He who describes a figure on a utensil, and he who blows in glassware, is liable on the score of striking with a hammer. Rab Judah said: He who removes threads from garments on the Sabbath is liable on the score of striking with the hammer; but that is only when he objects to them.[9]

Writing two letters. Our Rabbis taught: If one writes one large letter in the place of which there is room for writing two, he is not culpable. If he erases one large letter and there is room in its place for writing two, he is culpable. Said R. Menaḥem son of R. Jose: And this is the greater stringency of erasing over writing.

Building, pulling down, extinguishing, kindling, and striking with a hammer. Rabbah and R. Zera both say: Whatever comprises the finishing of the work imposes liability on the score of striking with a hammer.

These are the primary labours. These is to reject R. Eleazar's view, who imposes liability on account of a derivative labour [when performed concurrently] with a primary labour.

Less one. This is to reject R. Judah's view. For it was taught: R. Judah adds the closing up of the web and the beating of the woof. Said they to him: Closing up of the web is included in stretching the threads, and beating [the woof] is included in weaving.

3. Ḥullin*

MISHNAH. *Every kind of flesh is forbidden to be cooked in milk,*[1] *excepting the flesh of fish and of locusts; and it is also forbidden to place upon the table* [flesh] *with cheese, excepting the flesh of fish and of locusts. If a person vowed to abstain from flesh, he may partake of the flesh of fish and of locusts.*

GEMARA. It follows [from our Mishnah] that the flesh of fowls is prohibited by the law of the Torah; now in accordance with whose view would this be? It surely is not in accordance with R. Akiba's view, for R. Akiba maintains that the flesh of wild animals and of fowls is not prohibited by the law of the Torah. Consider now the final clause, *if a person vowed to abstain from flesh, he may partake of the flesh of fish and of locusts.* It follows however that he is forbidden the flesh of fowl, which is in accordance with R. Akiba's view, namely, that any variation concerning which the agent would ask for special instructions is deemed to be of the same species. For we have learnt: If a person vowed to abstain from vegetables, he is permitted gourds; R. Akiba forbids them. They said to R. Akiba, Is it not a fact that when a man says to his agent, "Bring me vegetables," the other might [come back and] say, "I can only obtain gourds"? He replied, Exactly so; for he surely would not come back and say, "I can only obtain pulse." This proves that gourds are included among vegetables and pulse is not included among vegetables. [Must it then be that] the first clause of our Mishnah is in accordance with the view of the Rabbis, and the second clause is in accordance with R. Akiba's view?—R. Joseph said, The author [of our Mishnah] is Rabbi[2] who incorporated the views of various Tannaim: with regard to vows he adopted the view of R. Akiba, and with regard to flesh [cooked] in milk he adopted the view of the Rabbis. R. Ashi said, The whole of our Mishnah is in accordance

[9] That is, the threads.

[1] Ex. 23:19; 34:26; Deut. 14:21.

[2] Judah the Prince, who originally compiled the Mishnah.

* The text consists of Chapter VIII, paragraph 1 of the Mishnah, and pages 104a–104b of the Gemara. The translation is that of Eli Cashdan in *The Babylonian Talmud,* I. Epstein, ed., Part I, Volume 4, London: The Soncino Press, 1948, pp. 576–79. The footnotes are those of the present editors.

with R. Akiba's view, for this is what it means, *every kind of flesh is forbidden to be cooked in milk:* some being forbidden by the law of the Torah and others by the enactment of the Scribes, *excepting the flesh of fish and of locusts,* which are neither prohibited by the law of the Torah nor by the enactment of the Scribes.

And it is also forbidden to place, etc. R. Joseph said, You can infer from this that the flesh of fowl [cooked] in milk is prohibited by the law of the Torah, for were it only [prohibited by the enactment] of the Rabbis, seeing that the actual eating thereof is [prohibited only as] a precautionary measure, would we forbid the placing [of them together upon the table] as a safeguard against the eating thereof? And whence do you derive the rule that we do not impose a precautionary measure upon a precautionary measure?—From the following [Mishnah] which we have learnt: The dough-offering [of produce grown] outside the Land [of Israel] may be eaten [by a priest] in company with a non-priest at the table, and may be given to any priest one likes. Said Abaye to him, I grant you, if we were told that the dough-offering [of produce grown] outside the Land [may be eaten] in the Land [in company with a non-priest at the table], in which case there would be good cause to enact a precautionary measure on account of the dough-offering [of produce grown] in the Land which is ordained by the Torah, and yet we do not take this precaution, that the inference can be made. But outside the Land of Israel [it is allowed] surely because there is no reason to take any precautionary measure. In the case [of our Mishnah], however, if you permit one to place [upon the table] fowl and cheese, one might even place [upon the table] flesh and cheese, and so come to eat flesh with milk which is prohibited by the law of the Torah.

R. Shesheth demurred saying, Yet after all it is but cold [food] with cold [food]!—Abaye answered, It is prohibited lest it be placed upon the table in a boiling pot. But even in that case it is only in a "second vessel"[3] and a second vessel cannot bring anything to the boil!—It is only prohibited lest it be placed upon the table in the "first vessel."

[3] That is, a vessel into which boiled food has been poured; the "first vessel" is that placed on the fire itself.

Selected Readings on the Biblical Period

I. THE BIBLE

A. Old Testament

Anderson, Bernhard W., *Understanding the Old Testament*. Englewood Cliffs, N. J.: Prentice-Hall, Inc., 1957.

Bright, John, *A History of Israel*. Philadelphia: Westminster Press, 1959.

Driver, S. R., *Introduction to the Literature of the Old Testament*, 9th ed. New York: Charles Scribner's Sons, 1913.

Gottwald, Norman K., *A Light to the Nations: An Introduction to the Old Testament*. New York: Harper & Brothers, 1959.

Jacob, Edmond, *Theology of the Old Testament*. New York: Harper & Brothers, 1958.

James, Fleming, *Personalities of the Old Testament*. New York: Charles Scribner's Sons, 1939.

Pfeiffer, Robert H., *The Books of the Old Testament*. New York: Harper & Brothers, 1957.

Robinson, H. Wheeler, *Inspiration and Revelation in the Old Testament*. New York: Oxford University Press, 1946.

Rowley, H. H., *The Faith of Israel: Aspects of Old Testament Thought*. Philadelphia: Westminster Press, 1956.

———, *The Growth of the Old Testament*. New York: Hillary House Publishers, Ltd., 1950.

Vriezen, Th. C., *An Outline of Old Testament Theology*. Oxford: Basil Blackwell, 1958.

Wright, G. Ernest, *God Who Acts: Biblical Theology as Recital*. Chicago: Henry Regnery Co., Publishers, 1952.

Wright, G. Ernest, and Floyd V. Filson, *The Westminster Historical Atlas to the Bible*, rev. ed. Philadelphia: Westminster Press, 1956.

B. New Testament

Bornkamm, Gunter, *Jesus of Nazareth*. New York: Harper & Brothers, 1960.

Bultmann, Rudolph, *Theology of the New Testament*. 2 vols. New York: Charles Scribner's Sons, 1951 and 1955.

———, *Primitive Christianity*. New York: Meridian Books, Inc., 1956.

Craig, Clarence T., *The Beginning of Christianity*. New York and Nashville: Abingdon-Cokesbury Press, 1943.

Cullmann, Oscar, *The State in the New Testament*. New York: Charles Scribner's Sons, 1956.

Dibelius, Martin, *Jesus*. Philadelphia: Westminster Press, 1949.

Dibelius, Martin, and Werner Kümmel, *Paul*. Philadelphia: Westminster Press, 1953.

Dodd, C. H., *The Meaning of Paul for Today*. London: George Allen & Unwin, Ltd., 1920.

Fuller, Reginald H., *The Mission and Achievement of Jesus*. Naperville, Ill.: Alec R. Allenson, Inc., 1956.

Goodspeed, Edgar J., *An Introduction to the New Testament*. Chicago: University of Chicago Press, 1937.

Goguel, Maurice, *The Life of Jesus*. New York: Macmillan Company, 1933.

Grant, Frederick C., *An Introduction to New Testament Thought*. New York and Nashville: Abingdon-Cokesbury Press, 1950.

Heard, Richard, *An Introduction to the New Testament*. New York: Harper & Brothers, 1950.

Knox, John, *Chapters in a Life of Paul*. New York and Nashville: Abingdon-Cokesbury Press, 1950.

———, *Christ the Lord*. Chicago and New York: Willett, Clark & Co., 1945.

———, *The Man Christ Jesus*. New York: Willett, Clark & Co., 1942.

———, *On the Meaning of Christ*. New York: Charles Scribner's Sons, 1947.

Lietzmann, Hans, *The Beginnings of the Christian Church*. London: Lutterworth Press, 1952.

Manson, T. W., *The Teaching of Jesus*, 2nd ed. Cambridge: Cambridge University Press, 1939.

Pfeiffer, Robert H. *History of New Testament Times*. New York: Harper & Brothers, 1949.

Riddle, Donald W., *Paul, Man of Conflict*. Nashville: Cokesbury Press, 1940.

Stauffer, E., *New Testament Theology*. London: S. C. M. Press, 1955.

Taylor, Vincent, *The Life and Ministry of Jesus*. New York and Nashville: Abingdon Press, 1955.

Weiss, Johannes, *Earliest Christianity: A History of the Period A. D. 30–150*. 2 vols. New York: Harper & Brothers, 1959.

Wilder, Amos, *New Testament Faith for Today*. New York: Harper & Brothers, 1955.

In addition to the above, the volumes of the *Interpreter's Bible*, 12 volumes, New York and Nashville, 1951–57, will be found useful; in particular, the student will wish to consult the introductory articles in Volumes I and VII.

II. THE EMERGENCE OF RABBINIC JUDAISM

Baron, Salo W., *A Social and Religious History of the Jews*. 3 vols. New York: Columbia University Press, 1937.

Birnbaum, Philip, ed., *Daily Prayer Book*. New York: Hebrew Publishing Co., 1949.

Burrows, Millar, *The Dead Sea Scrolls*. New York: Viking Press, 1955.

———, *More Light on the Dead Sea Scrolls*. New York: Viking Press, 1958.

Cohen, Abraham, *Everyman's Talmud*. London: J. M. Dent & Sons Ltd., 1932.

Cross, Frank M., Jr., *The Ancient Library of Qumran and Modern Biblical Studies*. New York: Doubleday & Co., Inc., 1958.

Danby, Herbert, *The Mishnah*. Oxford: Oxford University Press, 1933.

Finkelstein, Louis, *The Pharisees*. 2 vols. Philadelphia: Jewish Publication Society of America, 1938.

Finkelstein, Louis, ed., *The Jews: Their History, Culture, and Religion*. 3rd ed. 2 vols. Philadelphia: Jewish Publication Society of America, 1955.

Gaster, T. H., *The Dead Sea Scriptures in English Translation*. Garden City, N. Y.: Doubleday & Co., Inc., 1956.

Ginzberg, Louis, *On Jewish Law and Lore*. Philadelphia: Jewish Publication Society of America, 1955.

———, *Students, Scholars and Saints*. Philadelphia: Jewish Publication Society of America, 1928.

Goldin, Judah, ed., *The Living Talmud*. New Haven: Yale University Press, 1955.

Kadushin, Max, *The Rabbinic Mind*. New York: The Jewish Theological Seminary of America, 1952.

Moore, George Foot, *Judaism in the First Centuries of the Christian Era: The Age of the Tannaim*. 3 vols. Cambridge, Mass.: Harvard University Press, 1927 and 1930.

Margolis, Max L., and Alexander Marx, *A History of the Jewish People*. Philadelphia: Jewish Publication Society of America, 1927.

Schechter, Solomon, *Some Aspects of Rabbinic Theology*. New York: The Macmillan Company, 1909.

Schwartz, Leo, ed., *Great Ages and Ideas of the Jewish People*. New York: Random House, 1956.

Strack, Hermann L., *Introduction to the Talmud and Midrash*. Philadelphia: Jewish Publication Society of America, 1931.

An annotated bibliography on Judaism will be found in Schwartz; see above.

PART TWO

THE EARLY AND MEDIEVAL PERIODS

The spire of the Gothic cathedral pointing heavenward symbolized the unity of medieval culture.

Chartres Cathedral—Northern Portal—An example of the finest of medieval sculpture.

Basilica Euphrasiana—A church of the early Christian period.

The Emergence and Growth of the Christian Church

Half a century ago a renowned French theologian and biblical scholar passed the following judgment on the Christian Church: "Jesus proclaimed the Kingdom of God, but it was the Church that came." By this A. Loisy meant to emphasize the disparity that has often existed between the ideal community of love as preached by Jesus and the actual historical organization of the Church which arose in the centuries following his death.

Despite the resurgence of interest in religion today, there are many who still feel that the Church as we know it—in any of its many forms—has no warrant in the teachings of Jesus; that Jesus never intended, either explicitly or implicitly, to found an institution such as the Christian Church. Representatives of this view contend that Jesus taught a spiritual way of life, a life of love and faith, and that external forms, ordinances, or institutions only encumber and impede such spirituality. The fact that even a cursory reading of Christian history discloses many unsavory epochs in the Church's life seems to the advocates of these views to corroborate their position.

The majority of Christian scholars today believe that the words of Jesus either expressly state or at least imply that he intended to found a visible institution that would perpetuate the work which he had begun and which was prematurely cut short by his death at the age of thirty years. While there is a paucity of original sources, certain things seem to stand out clearly in support of the traditional view that Jesus did intend the Church. Even beyond this lack of certainty as to Jesus' own intentions, however, stands the incontestable fact that an institution did arise immediately after his death which was composed of his disciples and friends, and which continued to flourish and grow in an amazingly vigorous fashion despite efforts by the Imperial authorities to destroy it. There is the further significant fact that for nearly twenty centuries this Church—in all of its forms—has been the conveyor of Christian teaching as well as the preserver of much that was best in the culture of antiquity and of the Middle Ages.

Just as the synagogue of Judaism was a product of the development of Hebrew history rather than a consciously formulated institution brought into actuality at some specific point of time, so also the many forms of the Christian Church must be viewed in their historical development. The central question is thus one of *existence* rather than one of *origin.* As Judaism cannot be studied—or lived, for that matter—apart from the fact of the synagogue, so also Christianity cannot be disassociated from the visible institution which is so much a part of her existence. In one sense it is almost impossible to believe that the "spiritual" teachings of Jesus could have ever been preserved for posterity without the Church.

The question of the origin of the Church is important, and despite the meager records of that origin it is possible to form some tentative judgment on this question. It seems reasonably clear from the Gospels that the mission of Jesus—both as he envisaged it himself, and as others understood it—was to be the Messiah sent by God in fulfillment of the prophecies of the Old Testament. The whole framework of the messianic idea implied an "Anointed One" and an eschatological people who were to be led by this Messiah into a golden age of God's kingdom. Thus implicit in the messianic idea itself was the fact of a *king* and a *people.* Further, as Jesus, at least, interpreted the messianic role, the Messiah and his people were not only to enjoy the fruits of the kingdom of God but were also to assume the great responsibility of bringing others to this kingdom. This *responsible action* on the part of the disciples is a self-evident feature of all of Jesus' teaching. Most significant of all, perhaps, is the indelible impression one receives upon reading the Gospels that this movement begun by Jesus was not intended to cease with his death. There is an unmistakable note of urgency in all of Jesus' teaching. *His work must be completed:* it must not end prematurely. In certain parts of the Gospels there are express commands of Jesus to the effect that his disciples and followers are to finish the work which he has begun.

It would seem, then, that Jesus intended some kind of a visible fellowship which would live on after him and continue his work of bringing men and women into the kingdom of God. It cannot be said that he ever intended any specific form of the Church as we know it today. That is the fruit of the evolutionary spirit in history and in Christianity itself. But that Jesus did intend some kind of a visible fellowship of believers which would represent him on earth, after his death, seems certain. The Apostle Paul meant to convey this idea when he called the Church "The Body of Christ."*

If it can be said that Jesus *founded* (established) a church, it can also be said that in a sense he *found* (discovered) a church already existing. Jesus and his disciples were Jews, and as Jews they were deeply influenced by the worship and forms of the synagogue. During his public ministry Jesus preached in the synagogue and visited the Temple. It is not surprising, then, that when the Church arose as the result of the new ferment introduced into Judaism by the life and death of Jesus, it should resemble and, indeed, be dependent upon, the synagogue and its forms of worship. The Church was thus both new and old: *new* in the sense that the uniqueness of Jesus' teaching demanded departures from traditional beliefs and forms; *old* in the sense that it had continuity with the life and history of Israel.

The earliest Church is witness to this combination of the old and new. Established formally on the day of Pentecost (fifty days after Passover—the same Passover period during which Jesus was killed), it had nonetheless existed in fact since the time of Jesus' public ministry. The first Easter had corroborated for the disciples the fact of Jesus' messiahship. From that time on they were conscious of being a visible fellowship of believers committed to the cause of the Kingdom preached by Jesus. On the day of Pentecost itself they received what they believed to be a supernatural attestation of their visible community of faith, and numerous conversions as a result of this experience increased their number.

But it was a Jewish community which first believed that Jesus was the Christ (Messiah) sent by God; its life, belief, and adherence to the Law fell generally within the framework of Judaism. Although at first they attended the Temple daily, rising opposition from the Pharisees and Sadducees forced them more and more to meet in homes.

In this earliest period of the Church the followers of Jesus the Christ were almost wholly confined to Palestine and within Palestine primarily to Jerusalem. The movement seems to have attracted a sizable number of adherents from Judaism, although the great mass of Jews rejected it just as they had rejected the new teaching of Jesus himself. After the first year, Jewish authorities began a systematic effort to stamp out what they believed to be a serious heresy.

But this was a movement marked by great fervor and determination. Its leaders were Peter and James, the brother of Jesus. The government of the

* Roman Catholic scholars interpret Matt. 16:13–20 as Jesus' express commission to Peter for the establishment of the Church with Peter as head. Protesant scholars generally reject the Roman Catholic exegesis of this passage and incline to the "evolutionary" view stated above. There are, however, some scholars who take the very radical position that Jesus did not intend any kind of Church.

infant Church followed the pattern of the synagogue where elders (*presbyters*) were the ruling body. Corporate worship also followed the form used in the synagogue, and the scriptures were those of the Old Testament. In several significant aspects, however, this "Jewish-Christian" worship service differed from the traditional service; namely, in the fact that Jesus was worshipped as the Christ of God, and in the use of a common meal together which was a re-enactment of the Last Supper.

Further, this earliest Christian Church had a profound sense of its corporate solidarity. They had "all things in common" and provisions were made to care for widows, orphans, and the sick. The origin of the office of "deacon" is traced to this early period when the apostles and elders assumed the primary function of leadership in worship and seven deacons were elected to care for the distribution of alms to the needy. This task had also been one of the duties of the Apostles and elders, but due to the increasing demands of the growing Church it was relinquished to the new deacons.

Thus we see the earliest Church take form and grow. This initial phase of the Christian movement, which is best described as Jewish-Christian, lasted for only about two or three decades. By mid-century a prominent and energetic Pharisee by the name of Saul of Tarsus (later called Paul) had been converted to Christianity, and due largely to his efforts, Jewish-Christianity was eclipsed by a form of Christianity universal in its scope and appeal and which denied the need to maintain distinctively Jewish elements of the law such as dietary regulations.

Paul and certain like-minded companions opposed the more narrow Jewish-Christianity of Peter and James and the Jerusalem Church, and out of this conflict came the first great missionary appeal to the pagan, non-Jewish world. Paul, although a Jew, had been influenced by the Hellenistic culture of his time. Greek language, Greek philosophy, Greek ways of viewing things were henceforth all to have their influence on subsequent Christian belief and practice.

That period of Christian history which is usually designated as the "Apostolic" period began with the missionary career of Paul (ca. 48 A. D.), and lasted through the first quarter of the second century. During that time the Christian faith moved out of its birthplace in Palestine to touch all the major cultural centers of the Roman Empire. By the turn of the first century Christian churches existed in Rome, Corinth, Ephesus, Antioch, and Alexandria, as well as in the areas of Asia Minor, Africa, and Spain. This remarkable growth can be attributed in large measure to the indefatigable efforts of Paul, who travelled thousands of miles in three long trips which lasted nearly 13 years. At the conclusion of this momentous undertaking the die was cast for the future development of Christendom. Henceforth the Church was to be a "Gentile" church rather than a "Jewish-Christian" church. That is, the Christian Gospel found its greatest appeal and made its deepest inroads in the gentile, pagan world of Graeco-Roman culture rather than in the Jewish environment of its birthplace. By the end of the first century "Jewish-Christianity" as such had nearly disappeared.

The major reason for this triumph of a more "universal" type of Christianity lay with the elaboration by Paul of a more detailed and refined theological reflection on the person and work of Christ. In Paul's teaching the Christ is the pre-existent Son of God who becomes incarnate in the man Jesus. This incarnation of God in the Christ culminates in the death and resurrection of Jesus. By the death and resurrection of Jesus atonement is made for man's sin and rebellion against God; the powers of evil and death are overcome and the way is made clear for man's acceptance by God. This total work of Christ is the salvation which is henceforth available to mankind through faith in the Christ.

From this standpoint, then, salvation does not come by doing the works of the law (as Judaism held), but rather through faith in the Christ (Messiah) of God. Hence, adherence to Jewish law is not a necessary prerequisite for salvation. The Gospel, in Paul's mind, is for both Jew and Greek. Accordingly, the Christian does not need circumcision nor does he need to observe Jewish ceremonial law. Faith in the Incarnate Christ brings salvation.

The translation of Christianity out of its Jewish-Christian framework into that larger framework of the gentile, pagan world thus brought about the final establishment of the Church as a religious organization distinct from the Judaism which gave it birth. During this "Apostolic" period (50–125 A. D.) the basic documents of a new body of scriptures (a New Covenant or New Testament) which would be a fulfilment and completion of the Old Testament were written and assembled. They consisted of four Gospels (narratives and accounts of Jesus' life and teaching), a book of Acts (a history of the Apostolic Church), and many letters written by Paul and other leaders in the early Church.

Christian worship in this period incorporated the reading of not only the Old Testament but also the New Testament in this early and rudimentary form. The celebration of the Lord's Supper (or Last Supper) became a fixed part of worship and the earlier common meal with which it had been linked was divorced from the worship service proper and relegated to what would be called today a church "pot-luck supper." This modified form of the Lord's Supper was known as the "Eucharist" because of the Greek word used in the liturgy to render the idea of thanksgiving (*eucharisteîn*). The Eucharist thus embraced several meanings: it was, first, a giving of thanks to God for creation and redemption in Christ, and second, a mystical participation in the fruits of Christ's sacrificial death and his resurrection by God. Bread and wine were the sole symbols of this sacrament and the earlier custom of the common meal was reserved for other less sacred occasions.

Toward the close of this "Apostolic" period a significant change took place in the government of the Church. As we have seen in the first years of the

Church's history, it was governed after the pattern of the Synagogue; that is, by a group of *presbyters* (Greek word for "elder"). Soon, however, for purposes of leadership, one elder or *presbyter* was elected (or recognized) as a sort of chairman or president of the group. The name given to this elder was *episcopos,* a Greek term meaning *overseer* or *superintendent;* the English word *bishop* is derived from this Greek word, *episcopos.*

At first the *episcopos* or *bishop* was one among equals.* He, too, was a *presbyter* (or elder), but also a *bishop* by virtue of his presidency of the group. Scholars have called this early form of the episcopate the "collegiate" episcopate. This form of episcopal government continued well into the second century. However, parallel with this development of the episcopate, there was another form which developed and gradually became dominant in the Church. This was the "monarchical" episcopate where the office of *episcopos* or bishop was considered to be a distinct office and one standing above that of the *presbyter* or elder. Examples of this type of the episcopate are to be found in Syria as early as 115 A. D. The office of *bishop,* like that of *elder,* was soon considered to be divinely given in the Church.

Finally, the close of the "Apostolic" period of the Church (ca. 125 A. D.) witnesses to the growing importance of the church at Rome and of her bishop. The influence of this church had greatly increased because of the importance of Rome as the capital city of the empire, but probably also because of the early connection between the Roman church and the Apostles Paul and Peter.

After 125 A. D. the growth and expansion of the Christian Church can be traced in a much more accurate way. Contrasted with the paucity of documents that have survived from the first century of the Church's life, there is an abundance of original sources from the middle of the second century onwards. In such a brief introduction as this, the full picture of the subsequent history of the Church cannot possibly be drawn in any detail. Instead, several brief sketches of the Church at certain significant points in her history will be drawn.

The Holy Catholic Church (ca. 200 A. D.)

During the second century, significant events took place which decisively affected the Christian faith. Christianity had been declared an "illicit religion" by the empire. Severe persecutions were aimed both at the Church and at individual Christians. Much of this persecution resulted from the Christian refusal to worship the emperor or Caesar.

Also, certain heresies had arisen within the Church which tended to corrupt and alter its basic faith. Such heresies were Docetism (denial of the reality of Christ's human life), Marcionism (denial of any Hebraic or Old Testament

* On this point Roman Catholic scholars hold that Peter's primacy was given from the very first in Jesus' words in Matt. 16:13–20.

elements in Christianity), Gnosticism (belief in a secret, esoteric knowledge that brings salvation), and Montanism (an ecstatic, prophetic movement that claimed to have special revelations beyond those possessed by the Church). In meeting these challenges the Church developed in polity and theology.

The organization of the Church was unified around the concept of the monarchical bishop. The regular clergy of the Church became that of bishop, presbyter (priest), and deacon. This centralization of Church authority was a necessary development in view of the threats of persecution and heresy. To consolidate against these threats, the Church claimed to be able to trace her teaching and doctrine back to the Apostles themselves. The true Church stood in this "apostolic succession," of which the church in Rome was pre-eminent because of her position in the imperial city.* Further, the Church developed a "canon" of her scriptures; that is, a list of authoritative scriptures wherein the truths of the faith could be preserved against all efforts to alter or change them. By 200 A. D. this "canon" was nearly like our own New Testament.

The Church, in meeting the threat of heresy, had also drawn together a "summary" of Apostolic teaching which became a rudimentary creed. In this creed the doctrine of the Trinity, together with other doctrines about the Church and the future life, were stated in a concise way.

The Church now called herself the "Holy Catholic" Church (Catholic being from a Greek word meaning "universal") to distinguish herself from the partial and fragmentary groupings of the heretical sects. Finally, a more formal set of specifically Christian ritual practices resulted: baptism, catechetical training, confirmation, rudimentary forms of penitential discipline, and the liturgy of Holy Communion or Eucharist.

The Imperial State Church (ca. 450 A. D.)

In 312 A. D. the Emperor Constantine accepted Christianity and the beginnings of the Imperial State Church were laid. After his death in 337 A. D., the empire entered upon the century of its "death-throes." The empire was largely divided between two parts, the West with its capital in Rome, and the East with its capital in Constantinople. The Church tended to assume the colorations of this geographical division.

In the fourth and fifth centuries the Imperial State Church held a series of important church-wide (or *ecumenical*) councils, during which the theological beliefs of the Church were defined. Resulting from this were the Nicene (325 A. D.) and the Chalcedon (451 A. D.) Creeds. This was the age also of the great theological writers such as Athanasius and Augustine.

In 410 A. D. barbarian tribes from the North and East invaded Italy and sacked Rome. In this upheaval the Bishop of Rome became the dominant

* Roman Catholic scholars would hold that the pre-eminence of the Church in Rome was due to the primacy of Peter (Matt. 16:13–20).

figure in the West, inheriting, to a great extent, the former imperial power. The Church emerged from this tempestuous period with the characteristics that were to be her hallmark for the next one thousand years.

The Western (Latin-speaking) Church acknowledged the supremacy of Rome, although some of the Eastern Churches denied this supremacy. The Bishop of Rome was now the Pope (father) of the Church. The Church was everywhere episcopally governed by bishop, priest, and deacon, and she had a highly developed creed and theology based upon the great councils and theologians. Furthermore, she now had an authoritative and final "canon" of scripture to which no additions or from which no subtractions could be made. The worship of the Church was centered around the Eucharist which was conceived also as a sacrifice which the Church "re-presented" to God. Ritual, customs, and vestments were added to the Church to portray vividly the central moment of worship.

Monasticism had now become an accepted feature of the Church. Christian monasticism had its origin in the third century and received its amazing growth in the fourth century. The first monks were hermits, the most famous being Anthony who lived an austere life in the upper region of the Nile in Egypt. This early type of monasticism was a protest against the worldliness of the average Christian. Particularly after the recognition of Christianity as the religion of the empire, the quality of Christian life deteriorated. When Christianity began to be a prerequisite for "good citizenship," secularization of the faith became pronounced. Bishops were high officials of the state. Great sums of money and great land holdings were put at the disposal of the Churches. They administered the hospitals, the charitable institutions, and other relief agencies. When it became easy to be a Christian, an understandable lack of stringent and rigorous Christian practice set in.

This general state of affairs repelled many ardent Christians, and their reaction to it was a flight to the desert and to the hermit's cave. There, in their caves, living alone, they practiced a rigorous asceticism and spent long periods in devotion and prayer.

Another factor which contributed to the rise of monasticism lay in the very nature of the faith itself. Many sayings of Jesus could be properly interpreted in an ascetical light, and his commands to "be perfect" and "to sell all that you have and give to the poor" were understood by many to mean that the monastic life was the ideal Christian life. In the fifth century monasticism, having spread to the Western parts of the empire, was organized into communities of monks and the older hermit-type monk gave way to the coenobite monk (a monk living in community). Probably the most famous of the early coenobite monks was Benedict, whose famous "rule" became the standard for all monastic discipline (see p. 176).

The Church had thus become the continuation of the empire. Through the Church Roman culture, Roman language and literature, and Roman ideals were passed on to the Middle Ages. By the time of Pope Gregory the Great (ca. 600 A.D .), the Roman Catholic Church had received the form and the content which it was to pass on to succeeding centuries. In Pope Gregory can be seen the sole ecclesiastical ruler of the Western (Latin-speaking) Church. In his person he was the embodiment of the spirit of both the Roman Empire and the new Holy Roman Empire which was to replace the old secular regime. He was both bishop and civil servant. He undertook to guide the secular affairs of Rome through one of its dark periods, combining in himself the offices of mayor, city treasurer, ambassador, and father or Pope of the Church. Gregory was an intensely practical man and had a gift for bringing together the practical religion of the multitudes with the newly won orthodoxy that came from the great councils and from theologians such as Augustine. He contributed to the liturgical development of the Church and its worship. All of the theological, liturgical, and hierarchical concepts and forms which denote the essence of Roman Catholicism can be seen in the person and heritage of this great pope. He stood as head of the Holy Roman Church on the watershed which separated the age of classical antiquity from the medieval period. In the West he was the leader of what remained of the ancient empire, which had officially "declined" in 476, but in reality continued to exist under the aegis of the various barbarian kings. At the time of his pontificate, which closed out the sixth century, the great majority of the barbarian tribes had been won over to Christianity and it could be said that Western Europe was nominally Christian.

The Middle Ages (800–1400)

The centuries intervening between Alaric's sack of Rome in 410 A. D. and the beginning of the reign of Charlemagne (800 A. D.), witness the tremendous change that came over the Latin world. The Goths and the Vandals had been subjugated finally by the Franks. The Frankish state then began to draw together the disordered threads of Western society and was finally able to produce a somewhat orderly society. Indeed they attempted to recreate a new society. During the several centuries of barbarian occupation learning had all but been extinguished. Now, however, during the reign of Charlemagne (768–814 A. D.), the basis for Western society was laid. Charlemagne's rule extended over the majority of Europe and he instituted a great number of missionary enterprises to Christianize those areas that were still pagan. He set up educational and ecclesiastical reforms which were to have the greatest influence on subsequent medieval life. There was a new interest in learning which was exemplified by new scholarship and by the attempt to educate the heretofore illiterate clergy and ecclesiastical leaders. Liturgical developments were carried through; attempts to reform the monastic communities were zealously carried out. All in all the reign of Charlemagne produced a renaissance in both secular and religious life and may be said to have stemmed the inroads of barbarism.

Perhaps the most important feature of the long reign of Charlemagne was the alliance between the Frankish kingdom and the Holy Roman Church which was sealed at Rome on Christmas Day, 800 A. D., by Pope Leo III. In this alliance can be seen the model for the conception of the Holy Roman Empire which was to be the ideal of subsequent centuries. Although this ideal of a homogeneous religious culture was never fully realized, even during the reign of Charlemagne, nonetheless it dominated the thinking of the great popes throughout the Middle Ages.

In a sense Europe *was* a homogeneous religious culture. The fabric of culture was largely overlaid with Christian mythology, Christian ideas, and Christian practices. The daily life of the peasant centered around the parish church and his only knowledge came to him through the parish priest and the cathedral schools. His calendar year was the religious year with the lives of the saints denoting his "holy days." Everyone was born a Christian and persecutions and repressive measures were carried out against the Jews, the infidels, and other non-European, non-Christian groups. Public morality, although never "Christian" in any truly ethical sense, was nonetheless informed by Christian idealism, however badly and feebly understood. The beginnings of social justice funneled out of the Church and her charitable institutions. The average peasant looked to the Church not only for his future passport to heaven but also for guarantees of whatever justice might be accorded him on earth. The ironic thing about this unity of Church and culture was that force came to be the weapon used by the state to secure the proper ends of the Church. Crusades against unbelievers as well as crusades against heretical and deviationist Christian groups became the order of the day. One exterminated heretical Christians and infidels for their own good. However barbarous in practice, the crusades, the inquisitions, the use of force to extract Christian confessions, were all motivated by a pious, though credulous, desire for the greater glory of God.

The proper relations between the church and the state were never clearly understood, even in the time of St. Paul. St. Augustine, who was a bishop in the Church at the very time when the empire was disintegrating, had tried to understand this vexing question. His answer in the monumental *City of God* gave rise in later centuries to as much misunderstanding as understanding of this question. For the most part the history of medieval Europe is the history of the struggle between Pope and king, between papacy and empire. In different centuries popes or kings dominated the political scene. At one time it might be the great and powerful Gregory VII (1073 A. D.), who brought the emperor Henry IV to his knees in the snow at Canossa. Or again it might be Innocent III (1198–1216 A. D.), who wielded greater power over the secular state than any other pope. But just as often it was a king or an emperor who refused a pope fealty; at the close of the Middle Ages the papacy itself was subjected to the state and the popes made virtual prisoners in Avignon, where a new papacy was established by the French kings.

The issues at stake between Church and empire were centered in the dispute over episcopal appointments and of course, episcopal revenues. The Church had always demanded and asserted her right to make episcopal appointments and to govern religious affairs in the empire. When the emperor or his vassal kings usurped the right of investiture and appointment, conflict inevitably arose between Church and state. The great medieval ideal of one homogeneous culture infused by and informed by Christian idealism finally was utterly destroyed in the Renaissance and in the rise of the national states of Europe.

Largely speaking, the Middle Ages can be described as a time of great piety, but a piety without great learning. The typical peasant was abysmally ignorant and he lived a parochial and sheltered life, unaware of the activities of statecraft and world events which took place more than a parish boundary from his home. Affairs of state were largely settled by violence. The peasant worked long hours in the field, attended Mass in the village Church and suffered greatly at the hands of a predatory feudalism. Even among the clergy ignorance was the rule rather than the exception. Illiteracy was almost universal. Centers of learning such as the universities and the cathedral schools were few.

The monasteries, which in the early Church had been the stronghold of deep and sincere piety, were very often the very opposite of that piety in the Middle Ages. As a result of this laxity in the monasteries a movement took place which sought to reform and recreate the monastic ideal. Generally, these monastic reforms were in a very stringent direction, and such new monastic groups as the Cistercians, with all of their rigorous discipline and austerity of life, came to dominate the scene. The friar movements also won widespread recognition. Men such as Francis of Assisi (died 1226) and Dominic of Osma (died 1221) were unusual men whose idealism and asceticism bequeathed to the orders which now bear their names a new vision of social justice in the world. Very often the orders of friars were in conflict with the Church because they gave great importance to the laity. More and more lay movements arose in the closing years of the Middle Ages. That of John Wyclif (died 1384), for example, was in many ways a prelude to the age of the Reformation shortly to follow.

The Christian world and Western society as a whole owe an incalculable debt to the monastic communities of the Middle Ages, because within these communities the treasure of learning was guarded and passed on to succeeding generations. In a time of general darkness the Church, nonetheless, maintained the light of learning, and although there was little that might be called creative learning in the Middle Ages, yet the Church guarded the tradition, enlarged it, and passed it on. This was the very nature of the intellectual effort of the medieval Church. Her thought was not so much a new creation as a new formulation of the ancient tradition. The theologians and philosophers of the Middle Ages understood their task to lie in a detailed examination and discussion of the "faith once delivered." The vast theological and philosophical system of Thomas Aquinas was the high point of medieval scholasticism. St. Thomas was able to take the philosophy of Aristotle and use it as the vehicle for preserving the theological ideas and doctrines defined by the great councils in the early Church. But he also incorporated in his system all of the growing piety and tradition that belonged to the Church during the Middle Ages. We see in "Thomism" the culmination of twelve centuries of Christian thought and practice.

The development of the intricate liturgical life of the Church must also be understood in the same way. The liturgical forms, customs, and usages which one sees in the late medieval Church were the end product also of a millennium and a half of Christian life. This reverent attitude toward tradition, toward the past, was to be severely criticised by many of the Protestant reformers. The final end of scholasticism and the Catholic determination to maintain the tradition in all its breadth and scope was to come at the Council of Trent in the sixteenth century. At this time the Church sought to draw together—with a view toward meeting inroads of the new Protestant reformation —all of the life and thought of fifteen centuries. This Tridentine (that is, the result of the Council of Trent) formulation became the official statement of the doctrine and teaching of the Roman Church. Even this formulation, however, was not static but was to be enlarged and redefined in the successive centuries.

The Catholic "reformation," culminating in the Council of Trent, was actually the end-point of several centuries of "reform" activity. The demands for celibacy among the clergy, for an end to simony (sale of ecclesiastical offices), for reforms within the *curia,* and for recourse to ecumenical councils, were not raised only in opposition to the Protestant reformation. They had their origins in the monastic reforms of earlier centuries and in the mystical movements of the late Middle Ages. The Catholic reformation was not as cataclysmic in its effects as that of the Protestants but it was no less a reformation for all that.

Thus, the great venture of Western society—the Holy Roman Empire—which had its origin in the fall of the Western Roman Empire in 476 A. D., when the prerogatives and power of the *old empire* passed on to the *new Church,* came to an end in the fifteenth century. The Holy Roman Empire had never been a reality. At times strong and extensive in its power, at other times weak and divided, it had now entered the century of its death-throes. Throughout Europe national states were asserting their autonomy and their independence from Rome. The Papacy itself had just emerged from a "Babylonian Captivity" in Avignon where powerful French kings had made the popes virtual prisoners. Its release from Avignon and return to Italy had been marked by the scandal of rival claimants for St. Peter's throne. This, coupled with the aggressive military operations of the French in Italy, had made the power of the popes more apparent than real. The attempts to hold the Holy Empire together were based largely on "balances of power" between the strengths of the rising national states who, within themselves, sought release from papal taxation and land holdings. The Empire was bound together by delicate threads and was in constant danger of disruption. Coupled with this were the facts of the obvious corruption and worldliness of the Church in high places and low. In Alexander VI (1492–1503) the world saw a pope whose personal life was more lax than that of the most untutored and immoral parish priest.

Thus the corporate ideal of the one Christian society, of one empire under the inspiration of the one Church, which had so characterized the Middle Ages, was fast disappearing under the impact of the new trend toward nationalism and individualism. Certainly the dominant feature of the medieval period had been the feudal system. This system was predicated upon the conception of "divine right" of rule and of obedience to that rule. The lord or ruler gave out land tenure and authority to lesser nobles who in turn, then, owed obedience and support to their "liege lord" as the condition of their "fiefdom" or holding. This conception of society was corporate and cohesive to the greatest possible extent. Its gradations of authority and obedience ran throughout every class of society, from the peasant who owed his very existence to his immediate "lord" all the way to the great noble who was dependent upon the king for his largesse. In turn the very stability of a kingdom rested on the quality of the obedience and fealty of the fief-holders. The army to fight his battles and the money to finance those battles were the king's only by reason of the loyalty of his barons.

At the turn of the sixteenth century this "feudal" organization of society was fast giving way to a rising new class of "bourgeoisie" or merchants and bankers. The medieval guilds, so much a part of feudal society, gave way to the needs of larger production and the greater capital needed for large production. Money, rather than exchange of goods, became the new economic basis for society. The new class of merchants and bankers replaced the older feudal lords, and kings became dependent on this new class of capitalists.

Thus was bred a new individualism which shattered the weakened remnants of the older feudal system. The alliance of individualism and nationalism paved the way for the transition from the medieval age to the modern age. By 1500 A. D., therefore, German states, or a France or an England existed in which were visible seeds of rebellion and reaction to the ideal of the Holy Empire. Discontent with and suspicion of "foreign princes," feelings such as those giving voice to "Germany for the Germans," were in evidence everywhere.

If all of this were not enough to break down the old order, there were even more decisive events to come. Europe was breaking out of its shell. In the last quarter of the fifteenth century the geographical horizons of Western man were expanded to a degree undreamed of. In 1488 Bartholomew Dias rounded the Cape of Good Hope (Africa). In 1492 Christopher Columbus discovered the Western Hemisphere. In 1498 Vasco da Gama reached India by way of the tip of South Africa. After this epic period of exploration came Magellan's circumnavigation of the world in 1522. Literally a new world had been discovered.

And not only a new terrestrial world had been discovered but a new celestial world as well. The findings of Copernicus that the sun and not the earth was the center of man's universe became the basis for a totally new conception of the world in relation to the limitless reaches of space.

Another world opened up for man was the world of knowledge. Hitherto learning was the luxury of a privileged few. The great masses of the people together with a preponderance of their rulers lived in ignorance. Illiterate and lacking in any real knowledge of their culture past or present, they were prisoners of a shallow and parochial society. There was a lack of adequate means of knowledge. To be sure there were the universities with their meagre libraries of handwritten manuscripts, but at best these served but a small percentage of the population. Education was costly and scarce because the means of education, books, were so expensive.

All of this was changed by the invention of the printing press with its movable type. By 1454 the first book to be "printed" was available in quantities and at costs never thought possible. Suddenly the knowledge of the ages became available for the wider reaches of society. The success of Luther's reforming activity depended to a great extent on the fact that his many writings were immediately published and that they were read by the populace in general.

Yet another different world was disclosed to the men and women of this extraordinary age. This was the world of classical antiquity, the world of ancient Greece and Rome, with all of its splendor and opulence, its literature and art, its epic history and myth. The disclosure of this world came about by reason of the alliance of two intellectual movements which in subsequent history and in our own day have figured so largely. These were the movements of science and humanism. Science provided the techniques for the discovery and dissemination of the ancient world and humanism provided the interest and the moving spirit for the venture. Renaissance humanism with its interest in "man as the measure of all things," with its devotion to the classical ideals of human virtue, beauty, and truth, would never have achieved its purposes without the aid of the new sciences of philology, archaeology, and historical research. This, coupled with scientific discoveries such as the printing press, which made the results of humanist studies available to a wide public, explains the tremendous impact which the Renaissance or "new learning" had upon the sixteenth century. Of direct consequence to the Reformation were the efforts of humanist scholars such as Reuchlin and Erasmus who produced critical editions of the Old and New Testaments in the original Hebrew and Greek language. It was from such a work that Martin Luther made his famous translation of the Bible.

The interests of the humanist scholars and artists were "earthly" instead of "heavenly." They sought to direct man's hopes and aspirations away from heaven and back to that very real realm of heroic human achievement. They gloried in man and his works. They saw in the literature and art of ancient Greece and Rome a model of perfection. The ancient Socratic maxim, "Know thyself," was more meaningful to them than all of the obscure and complicated theology of the medieval Church. Therefore, Renaissance thought, art, and architecture all bear the stamp of the classical ideal of the human search for goodness, beauty, and truth.

From the standpoint of their freedom from intellectual obedience to medieval philosophy and theology the humanists were very often severe critics of the Church. Books like Erasmus' *Praise of Folly* were witty yet caustic denunciations of the worldliness, pretension, and immorality of pope and priest and Church. There were no greater critics of the papacy than the learned spirits of renaissance humanism.

It would be wrong, however, to characterize this momentous period as one of scientific and humanist progress and religious retrogression. It was undoubtedly a low-water mark in Christian history, with need for reform within the Church manifest to all. And yet there were heartening signs. In addition to the formal and often credulous piety in Christian society there was a growing movement of "mystical" piety which produced many earnest Christian believers. Such a view of the Christian life circulated in Germany in a little book entitled, *German Theology*. The point of view of this mystical Christianity was simplicity and genuineness. Abstract theology and obscure doctrine only impede faith, it said. The Christian should seek to live a simple life of goodness, abstaining from worldly pursuits, using Christ's life as his own example of humility and love. The Church and sacraments with all of their splendor are too often impediments to true faith. God is within man and man need only look within himself to find his true life. Christian faith is mystical and individual in its highest moment. This mystical movement laid the stress on life rather than doctrine, on Christian acts of love rather than creeds.

Yet it was still an age of violence for all the gentle thoughts and noble ideals of the renaissance humanists and the Christian mystics. It was still an age that could force men to accept Christian creeds and burn or bury alive those that would not. It was an age that still witnessed to a drastic discrepancy between the "haves" and "have-nots," between the rich and the poor. It was still an age of superstition and ignorance despite the inroads which the new learning and the new science had made into these areas of darkness. Thus the Middle Ages came to their end and the world entered into a new age in which the Christian faith would meet challenges hitherto unknown.

The Early Period

IRENAEUS

Irenaeus, Bishop of Lugdunum (modern Lyons, France) was born ca. 130 A. D. in Smyrna, Asia Minor. Although he came from the Greek East, Irenaeus made his greatest contribution in the Latin West. He represents the watershed between the "speculative" theology of the East and the "practical" theology of the West. After Irenaeus, theology takes on either a "Western" or "'Eastern" color depending on the place of its origin. For this reason alone Irenaeus is the most important early witness to an "ecumenical" theology.

Again, Irenaeus was a practical churchman, interested in the welfare of his diocese. He saw Gnosticism, Montanism and the other heretical forms of Christendom as primal forces bent upon the destruction of the "faith once delivered." His writings abound, therefore, in attacks upon these heresies. As a matter of fact, the title of his monumental five-volume work was *Against Heresies.*

Finally, his writings disclose an early and important witness to the development of credal formulations. Irenaeus gives a wealth of theological standards by which the orthodoxy or heterodoxy of any theological system can be measured. Probably no other figure in the early Church is so significant as the "Bishop of Lugdunum." He died during the persecution of Severus in 202 A. D. After Irenaeus the Church enters the age of theological conflict and the ever-widening rift between East and West.

Against the Heresies*

The church, though dispersed throughout the whole world, even to the ends of the earth, has received from the apostles and their disciples this faith: (She believes) in one God, the Father Almighty, Maker of heaven, and earth, and the sea, and all things that are in them; and in one Christ Jesus, the Son of God, who became incarnate for our salvation; and in the Holy Spirit, who proclaimed through the prophets the dispensations of God, and the advents, and the birth from a virgin, and the passion, and the resurrection from the dead, and the ascension into heaven in the flesh of the beloved Christ Jesus, our Lord, and His (future) manifestation from heaven in the glory of the Father "to gather all things in one," and to raise up anew all flesh of the whole human race, in order that to Christ Jesus, our Lord, and God, and Saviour, and King, according to the will of the invisible Father, "every knee should bow, of things in heaven, and things in earth, and things under the earth,

* From Irenaeus, *Writings,* translated by Alexander Roberts and W. H. Rambaut, *Ante-Nicene Library.* Edinburgh: T. and T. Clark, 1868, Vol. I, pp. 42–45 and 258–268; Vol. II, pp. 54–61.

and that every tongue should confess" to Him, and that He should execute just judgment towards all; that He may send "spiritual wickednesses," and the angels who transgressed and became apostates, together with the ungodly, and unrighteous, and wicked, and profane among men, into everlasting fire; but may, in the exercise of His grace, confer immortality on the righteous, and holy, and those who have kept His commandments, and have persevered in His love, some from the beginning (of their Christian course), and others from (the date of) their repentance, and may surround them with everlasting glory.

As I have already observed, the church, having received this preaching and this faith, although scattered throughout the whole world, yet, as if occupying but one house, carefully preserves it. She also believes these points (of doctrine) just as if she had but one soul, and one and the same heart, and she proclaims them, and teaches them, and hands them down, with perfect harmony, as if she possessed only one mouth. For, although the languages of the world are dissimilar, yet the import of the tradition is one and the same. For the churches which have been planted in Germany do not believe or hand down anything different, nor do those in Spain, nor those in Gaul, nor those in the East, nor those in Egypt, nor those in Libya, nor those which have been established in the central regions of the world. But as the sun, that creature of God, is one and the same throughout the whole world, so also the preaching of the truth shineth everywhere, and enlightens all men that are willing to come to a knowledge of the truth. Nor will any one of the rulers in the churches, however highly gifted he may be in point of eloquence, teach doctrines different from these (for no one is greater than the Master): nor, on the other hand, will he who is deficient in power of expression inflict injury on the tradition. For the faith being ever one and the same, neither does one who is able at great length to discourse regarding it, make any addition to it, nor does one, who can say but little, diminish it.

It does not follow because men are endowed with greater and less degrees of intelligence, that they should therefore change the subject-matter (of the faith) itself, and should conceive of some other God besides Him who is the Framer, Maker, and Preserver of this universe, (as if He were not sufficient for them), or of another Christ, or another Only-begotten. But the fact referred to simply implies this, that one may (more accurately than another) bring out the meaning of those things which have been spoken in parables, and accommodate them to the general scheme of the faith; and explain (with special clearness) the operation and dispensation of God connected with human salvation; and show that God manifested longsuffering in regard to the apostasy of the angels who transgressed, as also with respect to the disobedience of men; and set forth why it is that one and the same God has made some things temporal and some eternal, some heavenly and others earthly; and understand for what reason God, though invisible, manifested Himself to the prophets not under one form, but differently to different individuals; and show why it was that more covenants than one were given to mankind; and teach what was the special character of each of these covenants; and search out for what reason "God hath concluded every man in unbelief, that He may have mercy upon all; and gratefully describe on what account the Word of God became flesh and suffered; and relate why the advent of the Son of God took place in these last times, that is, in the end, rather than in the beginning (of the world); and unfold what is contained in the Scriptures concerning the end (itself), and things to come; and not be silent as to how it is that God has made the Gentiles, whose salvation was despaired of, fellow-heirs, and of the same body, and partakers with the saints; and discourse how it is that "this mortal body shall put on immortality, and this corruptible shall put on incorruption;" and proclaim in what sense (God) says, "That is a people who was not a people; and she is beloved who was not beloved;" and in what sense He says that "more are the children of her that was desolate, than of her who possessed a husband." For in reference to these points, and others of a like nature, the apostle exclaims: "Oh! the depth of the riches both of the wisdom and knowledge of God; how unsearchable are His judgments, and His ways past finding out!" But (the superior skill spoken of) is not found in this, that any one should, beyond the Creator and Framer (of the world), conceive of the Enthymesis of an erring AEon, their mother and his, and should thus proceed to such a pitch of blasphemy; nor does it consist in this, that he should again falsely imagine, as being above this (fancied being), a Pleroma at one time supposed to contain thirty, and at another time an innumerable tribe of AEons, as these teachers who are destitute of truly divine wisdom maintain; while the Catholic church possesses one and the same faith throughout the whole world, as we have already said. . . .

We have learned from none others the plan of our salvation, than from these through whom the gospel has come down to us, which they did at one time proclaim in public, and, at a later period, by the will of God, handed down to us in the Scriptures, to be the ground and pillar of our faith. For it is unlawful to assert that they preached before they possessed "perfect knowledge," as some do even venture to say, boasting themselves as improvers of the apostles. For, after our Lord rose from the dead, (the apostles) were invested with power from on high when the Holy Spirit came down (upon them), were filled from all (His gifts), and had perfect knowledge: they departed to the ends of the earth, preaching the glad tidings of the good things (sent) from God to us, and proclaiming the peace of heaven to men, who indeed do all equally and individually possess the gospel of God. Matthew also issued a written gospel among the Hebrews in their own dialect, while Peter and Paul were preaching at Rome, and laying the foundations of the church. After their departure, Mark, the disciple and interpreter of Peter, did also hand down to us in writing what had been preached by Peter. Luke also the companion of Paul, recorded in a book the gospel preached by him. Afterwards, John, the disciple of the Lord, who also had leaned upon His breast, did himself publish a gospel during his residence at Ephesus in Asia.

These have all declared to us that there is one God, Creator of heaven and earth, announced by the law and the prophets; and one Christ, the Son of God. If any one do not agree to these truths, he despises the companions of the Lord; nay more, he despises Christ Himself the Lord; yea, he despises the Father also, and stands self-condemned, resisting and opposing his own salvation, as is the case with all heretics.

When, however, they are confuted from the Scriptures, they turn round and accuse these same Scriptures, as if they were not correct, nor of authority, and (assert) that they are ambiguous, and that the truth cannot be extracted from them by those who are ignorant of tradition. For (they allege) that the truth was not delivered by means of written documents, but *viva voce:* wherefore also Paul declared, "But we speak wisdom among those that are perfect, but not the wisdom of this world." And this wisdom each one of them alleges to be the fiction of his own inventing, forsooth; so that, according to their idea, the truth properly resides at one time in Valentinus, at another in Marcion, at another in Cerinthus, then afterwards in Basilides, or has even been indifferently in any other opponent, who could speak nothing pertaining to salvation. For every one of these men, being altogether of a perverse disposition, depraving the system of truth, is not ashamed to preach himself.

But, again, when we refer them to that tradition which originates from the apostles, (and) which is preserved by means of the successions of presbyters in the churches, they object to tradition, saying that they themselves are wiser not merely than the presbyters, but even than the apostles, because they have discovered the unadulterated truth. For (they maintain) that the apostles intermingled the things of the law with the words of the Saviour; and that not the apostles alone, but even the Lord Himself, spoke as at one time from the Demiurge, at another from the intermediate place, and yet again from the Pleroma, but that they themselves, indubitably, unsulliedly, and purely, have knowledge of the hidden mystery: this is, indeed, to blaspheme their Creator after a most impudent manner! It comes to this, therefore, that these men do now consent neither to Scripture nor to tradition.

Such are the adversaries with whom we have to deal, my very dear friend, endeavouring like slippery serpents to escape at all points. Wherefore they must be opposed at all points, if perchance, by cutting off their retreat, we may succeed in turning them back to the truth. For, though it is not an easy thing for a soul under the influence of error to repent, yet, on the other hand, it is not altogether impossible to escape from error when the truth is brought alongside it.

It is within the power of all, therefore, in every church, who may wish to see the truth, to contemplate clearly the tradition of the apostles manifested throughout the whole world; and we are in a position to reckon up those who were by the apostles instituted bishops in the churches, and (to demonstrate) the successions of these men to our own times; those who neither taught nor knew of anything like what these (heretics) rave about. For if the apostles had known hidden mysteries, which they were in the habit of imparting to "the perfect" apart and privily from the rest, they would have delivered them especially to those to whom they were also committing the churches themselves. For they were desirous that these men should be very perfect and blameless in all things, whom also they were leaving behind as their successors, delivering up their own place of government to these men; which men, if they discharged their functions honestly, would be a great boon (to the church), but if they should fall away, the direst calamity.

Since, however, it would be very tedious, in such a volume as this, to reckon up the successions of all the churches, we do put to confusion all those who, in whatever manner, whether by an evil self-pleasing, by vainglory, or by blindness and perverse opinion, assemble in unauthorized meetings; (we do this, I say,) by indicating that tradition derived from the apostles, of the very great, the very ancient, and universally known church founded and organized at Rome by the two most glorious apostles, Peter and Paul; as also (by pointing out) the faith preached to men, which comes down to our time by means of the successions of the bishops. For it is a matter of necessity that every church should agree with this church, on account of its pre-eminent authority, that is, the faithful everywhere inasmuch as the apostolical tradition has been preserved continuously by those (faithful men) who exist everywhere.

The blessed apostles, then, having founded and built up the church, committed into the hands of Linus the office of the episcopate. Of this Linus, Paul makes mention in the Epistles to Timothy. To him succeeded Anacletus; and after him, in the third place from the apostles, Clement was allotted the bishopric. This man, as he had seen the blessed apostles, and had been conversant with them, might be said to have the preaching of the apostles still echoing (in his ears), and their traditions before his eyes. Nor was he alone (in this), for there were many still remaining who had received instructions from the apostles. In the time of this Clement, no small dissension having occurred among the brethren at Corinth, the church in Rome despatched a most powerful letter to the Corinthians exhorting them to peace, renewing their faith, and declaring the tradition which it had lately received from the apostles, proclaiming the one God, omnipotent, the Maker of heaven and earth, the Creator of man, who brought on the deluge, and called Abraham, who led the people from the land of Egypt, spake with Moses, set forth the law, sent the prophets, and who has prepared fire for the devil and his angels. From this document, whosoever chooses to do so, may learn that He, the Father of our Lord Jesus Christ, was preached by the churches, and may also understand the apostolical tradition of the church, since this epistle is of older date than these men who are now propagating falsehood, and who conjure into existence another god beyond the Creator and the Maker of all existing things. To this Clement there succeeded Evaristus. Alexander followed Evaristus; then, sixth from the apostles, Sixtus was appointed; after him Telesphorus, who was gloriously martyred; then Hyginus; after him, Pius; then after him, Anicetus. Soter having succeeded Anicetus, Eleutherius does now, in the twelfth place from the apostles, hold the inheritance of the episcopate. In this order, and by this succession the ecclesiastical tradition from the apostles, and the preaching of the truth, have come down to us. And this is most abundant proof that there is one and the same vivifying faith, which has been preserved in the church from the apostles until now, and handed down in truth.

But Polycarp also was not only instructed by apostles, and conversed with many who had seen Christ, but was also, by apostles in Asia, appointed bishop of the church in Smyrna, whom I also saw in my early youth, for he tarried (on earth) a very long time, and, when a very old man, gloriously and most nobly suffering martydom, departed this life, having always taught the things which he had learned from the apostles, and which the church has handed down, and which alone are true. To these things all the Asiatic churches testify, as do also those men who have succeeded Polycarp down to the present time,—a man who was of much greater weight, and a more stedfast witness of truth, than Valentinus, and Marcion, and the rest of the heretics. He it was who, coming to Rome in the time of Anicetus, caused many to turn away from the aforesaid heretics to the church of God, proclaiming that he had received this one and sole truth from the apostles,—that, namely, which is handed down by the church. There are also those who heard from him that John, the disciple of the Lord, going to bathe at Ephesus, and perceiving Cerinthus within, rushed out of the bath-house without bathing, exclaiming, "Let us fly, lest even the bath-house fall down, because Cerinthus, the enemy of the truth, is within." And Polycarp himself replied to Marcion, who met him on one occasion, and said, "Dost thou know me?" "I do know thee, the firstborn of Satan." Such was the horror which the apostles and their disciples had against holding even a verbal communication with any corrupters of the truth; as Paul also says, "A man that is an heretic, after the first and second admonition, reject; knowing that he that is such is subverted, and sinneth, being condemned of himself." There is also a very powerful epistle of Polycarp written to the Philippians, from which those who choose to do so, and are anxious about their salvation, can learn the character of his faith, and the preaching of the truth. Then, again, the church in Ephesus, founded by Paul, and having John remaining among them permanently until the times of Trajan, is a true witness of the tradition of the apostles.

Since therefore we have such proofs, it is not necessary to seek the truth among others which it is easy to obtain from the church; since the apostles, like a rich man (depositing his money) in a bank, lodged in her hands most copiously all things pertaining to the truth: so that every man, whosoever will, can draw from her the water of life. For she is the entrance to life; all others are thieves and robbers. On this account are we bound to avoid them, but to make choice of the things pertaining to the church with the utmost diligence, and to lay hold of the tradition of the truth. For how stands the case? Suppose there arise a dispute relative to some important question among us, should we not have recourse to the most ancient churches with which the apostles held constant intercourse, and learn from them what is certain and clear in regard to the present question? For how should it be if the apostles themselves had not left us writings? Would it not be necessary, (in that case,) to follow the course of the tradition which they handed down to those to whom they did commit the churches?

To which course many nations of those barbarians who believe in Christ do assent, having salvation written in their hearts by the spirit, without paper or ink, and, carefully preserving the ancient tradition, believing in one God, the Creator of heaven and earth, and all things therein, by means of Christ Jesus, the Son of God; who, because of His surpassing love towards His creation, condescended to be born of the virgin, He Himself uniting man through Himself to God, and having suffered under Pontius Pilate, and rising again, and having been received up in splendour, shall come in glory, the Saviour of those who are saved, and the Judge of those who are judged, and sending into eternal fire those who transform the truth, and despise His Father and His advent. Those who, in the absence of written documents, have believed this faith, are barbarians, so far as regards our language; but as regards doctrine, manner, and tenor of life, they are, because of faith, very wise indeed; and they do please God, ordering their conversation in all righteousness, chastity, and wisdom. If any one were to preach to these men the inventions of the heretics, speaking to them in their own language, they would at once stop their ears, and flee as far off as possible, not enduring even to listen to the blasphemous address. Thus, by means of that ancient tradition of the apostles, they do not suffer their mind to conceive anything of the (doctrines suggested by the) portentous language of these teachers, among whom neither church nor doctrine has ever been established.

For, prior to Valentinus, those who follow Valentinus had no existence; nor did those from Marcion exist before Marcion; nor, in short, had any of those malignant-minded people, whom I have above enumerated, any being previous to the initiators and inventors of their perversity. For Valentinus came to Rome in the time of Hyginus, flourished under Pius, and remained until Anicetus. Cerdon, too, Marcion's predecessor, himself arrived in time of Hyginus, who was the ninth bishop. Coming frequently into the church, and making public confession, he thus remained, one time teaching in secret, and then again making public confession; but at last, having been denounced for corrupt teaching, he was excommunicated from the assembly of the brethren. Marcion, then, succeeding him, flourished under Anicetus, who held the tenth place of the episcopate. But the rest, who are called Gnostics, take rise from Menander, Simon's disciple, as I have shown; and each one of them appeared to be both the father and the high priest of that doctrine into which he has been initiated. But all these (the Marcosians) broke out into their apostasy much later, even during the intermediate period of the church.

Since, therefore, the tradition from the apostles does thus exist in the church, and is permanent among us, let us revert to the scriptural proof furnished by those apostles who did also write the Gospel, in which they recorded the doctrine regarding God, pointing out that our Lord Jesus Christ is the truth, and that no lie is in Him. As also David says, prophesying His birth from a virgin, and the resurrection from the dead, "Truth has sprung out of the earth." The apostles, likewise, being disciples of the truth, are above all falsehood; for a lie has no fellowship with the truth, just as darkness has none with light, but the presence of the one shuts out that of the other. Our Lord, therefore, being the truth, did not speak lies; and whom He knew to have taken origin from a defect, He never would have acknowledged as God, even the God of all, the Supreme King, too, and His own Father, an imperfect being as a perfect one, an animal one as a spiritual, Him who was without the Plēroma as Him who was within it. Neither did His disciples make mention of any other God, or term any other Lord, except Him, who was truly the God and Lord of all, as these most vain sophists affirm that the apostles did with hypocrisy frame their doctrine according to the capacity of their hearers, and gave answers after the opinions of their questions,—fabling blind things for the blind, according to their blindness; for the dull according to their dulness; for those in error according to their error. And to those who imagined that the Demiurge alone was God, they preached him; but to those who are capable of comprehending the unnameable Father, they did declare the unspeakable mystery through parables and enigmas: so that the Lord and the apostles exercised the office of teacher not to further the cause of truth, but even in hypocrisy, and as each individual was able to receive it.

Such (a line of conduct) belongs not to those who heal, or who give life: it is rather that of those bringing on diseases, and increasing ignorance; and much more true than these men shall the law be found, which pronounces every one accursed who sends the blind man astray in the way. For the apostles, who were commissioned to find out the wanderers, and to be for sight to those who saw not, and medicine to the weak, certainly did not address them in accordance with their opinion at the time, but according to revealed truth. For no persons of any kind would act properly, if they should advise blind men, just about to fall over a precipice, to continue their most dangerous path, as if it were the right one, and as if they might go on in safety. Or what medical man, anxious to heal a sick person, would prescribe in accordance with the patient's whims, and not according to the requisite medicine? But that the Lord came as the physician of the sick, He does Himself declare, saying, "They that are whole need not a physician, but they that are sick; I came not to call the righteous, but sinners to repentance." How then shall the sick be strengthened, or how shall sinners come to repentance? Is it by persevering in the very same courses? or, on the contrary, is it by undergoing a great change and reversal of their former mode of living, by which they have brought upon themselves no slight amount of sickness, and many sins? But ignorance, the mother of all these, is driven out by knowledge. Wherefore the Lord used to impart knowledge to His Disciples, by which also it was His practice to heal those who were suffering, and to keep back sinners from sin. He therefore did not address them in accordance with their pristine notions, nor did He reply to them in harmony with the opinion of His questioners, but according to the doctrine leading to salvation, without hypocrisy or respect of person.

This is also made clear from the words of the Lord, who did truly reveal the Son of God to those of the circumcision—Him who had been foretold as Christ by the prophets; that is, He set Himself forth, who had restored liberty to men, and bestowed on them the inheritance of incorruption. And again, the apostles taught the Gentiles that they should leave vain stocks and stones, which they imagined to be gods, and worship the true God, who had created and made all the human family, and, by means of His creation, did nourish, increase, strengthen, and preserve them in being; and that they might look for His Son Jesus Christ, who redeemed us from apostasy with His own blood, so that we should also be a sanctified people,—who shall also descend from heaven in His Father's power, and pass judgment upon all, and who shall freely give the good things of God to those who shall have kept His commandments. He, appearing in these last times, the chief corner-stone, has gathered into one, and united those that were far off and those that were near; that is, the circumcision and the uncircumcision, enlarging Japhet, and placing him in the dwelling of Shem. . . .

In the four preceding books, my very dear friend, which I put forth to thee, all the heretics have been exposed, and their doctrines brought to light, and these men refuted who have devised irreligious opinions. (I have accomplished this by adducing) something from the doctrine peculiar to each of these men, which they have left in their writings, as well as by using arguments of a more general nature, and applicable to them all. Then I have pointed out the truth, and shown the preaching of the church, which the prophets proclaimed (as I have already demonstrated), but which Christ brought to perfection, and the apostles have handed down, from whom the church, receiving (these truths), and throughout all the world alone preserving them in their integrity (bene), has transmitted them to her sons. Then also—having disposed of all questions which the heretics propose to us, and having explained the doctrine of the apostles, and clearly set forth many of those things which were said and done by the Lord in parables—I shall endeavour, in this the fifth book of the entire work which treats of the exposure and refutation of knowledge falsely so called, to exhibit proofs from the rest of the Lord's doctrine and the apostolical epistles: (thus) complying with thy demand, as thou didst request of me (since indeed I have been assigned a place in the ministry of the word); and, labouring by every means in my power to furnish thee with large assistance against the contradictions of the heretics, as also to reclaim the wanderers and convert them to the church of God, to confirm at the same time the minds of the neophytes, that they may preserve steadfast the faith which they have received, guarded by the church in its integrity, in order that they be in no way perverted by those who endeavour to teach them false doctrines, and lead them away from the truth. It will be incumbent upon thee, however, and all who may happen to read this writing, to peruse with great attention what I have already said, that thou mayest obtain a knowledge of the subjects against which I am contending. For it is thus that thou wilt both controvert them in a legitimate manner, and wilt be prepared to receive the proofs brought forward against them, casting away their doctrines as filth by means of the celestial faith; but following the only true and steadfast teacher, the Word of God, our Lord Jesus Christ, who did, through His transcendent love, become what we are, that He might bring us to be even what He is Himself.

For in no other way could we have learned

the things of God, unless our Master, existing as the Word, had become man. For no other being had the power of revealing to us the things of the Father, except His own proper Word. For what other person "knew the mind of the Lord," or who else "has become His counsellor?" Again, we could have learned in no other way than by seeing our Teacher, and hearing His voice with our own ears, that, having become imitators of His works as well as doers of His words, we may have communion with Him, receiving increase from the perfect One, and from Him who is prior to all creation. We—who were but lately created by the only best and good Being, by Him also who has the gift of immortality, having been formed after His likeness (predestinated, according to the prescience of the Father, that we, who had as yet no existence, might come into being), and made the first-fruits of creation—have received, in the times known beforehand, (the blessings of salvation) according to the ministration of the Word, who is perfect in all things, as the mighty Word, and very man, who redeeming us by His own blood in a manner consonant to reason, gave Himself as a redemption for those who had been led into captivity. And since the apostasy tyrannized over us unjustly, and, though we were by nature the property of the omnipotent God, alienated us contrary to nature, rendering us its own disciples, the Word of God, powerful in all things, and not defective with regard to His own justice, did righteously turn against that apostasy, and redeem from it His own property, not by violent means, as the (apostasy) had obtained dominion over us at the beginning, when it insatiably snatched away what was not its own, but by means of persuasion, as became a God of counsel, who does not use violent means to obtain what He desires; so that neither should justice be infringed upon, nor the ancient handiwork of God go to destruction. Since the Lord thus has redeemed us through His own blood, giving His soul for our souls, and His flesh for our flesh, and has also poured out the Spirit of the Father for the union and communion of God and man, imparting indeed God to men by means of the Spirit, and, on the other hand, attaching man to God by His own incarnation, and bestowing upon us at His coming immortality durably and truly, by means of communion with God,—all the doctrines of the heretics fall to ruin.

Vain indeed are those who allege that He appeared in mere seeming. For these things were not done in appearance only, but in actual reality. But if He did appear as a man, when He was not a man, neither could the Holy Spirit have rested upon Him,—an occurrence which did actually take place—as the Spirit is invisible; nor, (in that case), was there any degree of truth in Him, for He was not that which He seemed to be. But I have already remarked that Abraham and the other prophets beheld Him after a prophetical manner, foretelling in vision what should come to pass. If, then, such a being has now appeared in outward semblance different from what he was in reality, there has been a certain prophetical vision made to men; and another advent of His must be looked forward to, in which He shall be such as He has now been seen in a prophetic manner. And I have proved already, that it is the same thing to say that He appeared merely to outward seeming, and (to affirm) that He received nothing from Mary. For He would not have been one truly possessing flesh and blood, by which He redeemed us, unless He had summed up in Himself the ancient formation of Adam. Vain therefore are the disciples of Valentinus who put forth this opinion, in order that they may exclude the flesh from salvation, and cast aside what God has fashioned.

Vain also are the Ebionites, who do not receive by faith into their soul the union of God and man, but who remain in the old leaven of (the natural) birth, and who do not choose to understand that the Holy Ghost came upon Mary, and the power of the Most High did overshadow her: wherefore also what was generated is a holy thing, and the Son of the Most High God the Father of all, who effected the incarnation of this being, and showed forth a new (kind of) generation; that as by the former generation we inherited death, so by this new generation we might inherit life. Therefore do these men reject the commixture of the heavenly wine, and wish it to be water of the world only, not receiving God so as to have union with Him, but they remain in that Adam who had been conquered and was expelled from Paradise: not considering that as at the beginning of our formation in Adam, that breath of life which proceeded from God, having been united to what had been fashioned, animated the man, and manifested him as a being endowed with reason: so also, in (the times of) the end, the Word of the Father and the Spirit of God, having become united with the ancient substance of Adam's formation, rendered man living and perfect, receptive of the perfect Father, in order that as in the natural (Adam) we all were dead, so in the spiritual we may all be made alive. For never at any time did Adam escape the hands of God, to whom the Father speaking, said, "Let us make man in our image, after our likeness." And for this reason in the last times (*fine*), not by the will of the flesh, nor by the will of man, but by the good pleasure of the Father, His hands formed a living man, in order that Adam might be created (again) after the image and likeness of God.

And vain likewise are those who say that God came to those things which did not belong to Him, as if covetous of another's property; in order that He might deliver up that man who had been created by another, to that God who had neither made nor formed anything, but who also was deprived from the beginning of His own proper formation of men. The advent, therefore, of Him whom these men represent as coming to the things of others, was not righteous; nor did He truly redeem us by His own blood, if He did not really become man, restoring to His own handiwork what was said (of it) in the beginning, that man was made after the image and likeness of God; not snatching away by stratagem the property of another, but taking possession of His own in a righteous and gracious manner. As far as concerned the apostasy, indeed, He redeems us righteously from it by His own blood; but as regards us who have been redeemed, (He does this) graciously. For we have given nothing to Him previously, nor does He desire anything from us, as if He stood in need of it; but we do stand in need of fellowship with Him. And for this reason it was that He graciously poured Himself out, that He might gather us into the bosom of the Father.

But vain in every respect are they who despise the entire dispensation of God, and disallow the salvation of the flesh, and treat with contempt its regeneration, maintaining that it is not capable of incorruption. But if this indeed do not attain salvation, then neither did the Lord redeem us with His blood, nor is the cup of the Eucharist the communion of His blood, nor the bread which we break the communion of His body. For blood can only come from veins and flesh, and whatsoever else makes up the substance of man, such as the Word of God was actually made. By His own blood He redeemed us, as also His apostle declares, "In whom we have redemption through His blood, even the remission of sins." And as we are His members, we are also nourished by means of the creation (and He Himself grants the creation to us, for He causes His sun to rise, and sends rain when He wills). He has acknowledged the cup (which is a part of the creation) as His own blood, from which He bedews our blood; and the bread (also a part of the creation) He has established as His own body, from which He gives increase to our bodies.

When, therefore, the mingled cup and the manufactured bread receives the Word of God, and the Eucharist of the blood and the body of Christ is made, from which things the substance of our flesh is increased and supported, how can they affirm that the flesh is incapable of receiving the gift of God, which is life eternal, which (flesh) is nourished from the body and blood of the Lord, and is a member of Him?—even as the blessed Paul declares in his Epistle to the Ephesians, that "we are members of His body, of His flesh, and of His bones." He does not speak these words of some spiritual and invisible man, for a spirit has not bones nor flesh: but (he refers to) that dispensation (by which the Lord became) an actual man, consisting of flesh, and nerves, and bones,—that (flesh) which is nourished by the cup which is His blood, and receives increase from the bread which is His body. And just as a cutting from the vine planted in the ground fructifies in its season, or as a corn of wheat falling into the earth and becoming decomposed, rises with manifold increase by the Spirit of God, who contains all things, and then, through the wisdom of God, serves for the use of men, and having received the Word of God, becomes the Eucharist, which is the body and blood of Christ; so also our bodies, being nourished by it, and deposited in the earth, and suffering decomposition there, shall rise at their appointed time, the Word of God granting them resurrection to the glory of God, even the Father, who freely gives to this mortal immortality, and to this corruptible incorruption, because the strength of God is made perfect in weakness, in order that we may never become puffed up, as if we had life from ourselves, and exalted against God, our minds becoming ungrateful; but learning by experience that we possess eternal duration from the excelling power of this Being, not from our own nature, we may neither undervalue that glory which surrounds God as He is, nor be ignorant of our own nature, but that we may know what God can effect, and what benefits man receives, and thus never wander from the true comprehension of things as they are, that is, both with regard to God and with regard to man. And might it not be the case, perhaps, as I have already observed, that for this purpose God permitted our resolution into the common dust of mortality, that we, being instructed by every mode, may be accurate in all things for the future, being ignorant neither of God nor of ourselves?

CYPRIAN (d. 258)

Thascius Caecilianus Cyprianus was, before his conversion to Christianity in 246 A. D., a pagan rhetorician of some note. Little is known of his early life, but after 246 A. D. we have a rather adequate knowledge of him and his teaching. Within two years of his conversion, Cyprian was elected Bishop of Carthage and served the Church faithfully and energetically until his martyrdom in 258 A. D. during the Decian persecution.

Cyprian was an able student of the Bible and a zealous theologian of the orthodox faith. He engaged in several major disputes in the early Church over the questions of the readmission of the "lapsed" (those who fell away from Christianity under duress of persecution) and the "rebaptism" of schismatics. He is an important early witness of the growth of the episcopacy and the primacy of the Roman Church. He discussed the doctrine of the Church and Sacraments in ways that directly anticipated later fully developed Catholic theology.

In the following treatise on the *Unity of the Catholic Church,* there are two variant readings in the manuscripts. The "primacy" passage is generally considered to be the original reading which Cyprian himself later changed to the alternative reading because of his dispute with the Bishop of Rome.

The Unity of the Catholic Church*

"Ye are the salt of the earth." These words of the Lord convey a warning. Since he bids us be simple and innocent, yet prudent in our simplicity, is it not proper, my dear brothers, that we should show foresight, uncovering the snares of our wily enemy and taking precau-

* From Cyprian, "The Unity of the Catholic Church," *Library of Christian Classics,* Volume V, translated and edited by S. L. Greenslade. Pages 124–128, 129–131, 132–134, 136–140 and 140–142 reproduced by permission of the publisher, The Westminster Press.

tions against them by our anxious thought and watchful care? We who have put on Christ, the Wisdom of God the Father, must not lack the wisdom to safeguard our salvation. It is not only persecution that we have to fear, and the attack which advances openly to subvert and overthrow the servants of God. Caution is not difficult where the danger is obvious. When the adversary reveals himself, our minds are prepared for the encounter. There is more to fear, more care to be taken, with an enemy who creeps upon us secretly, tricks us with a show of peace, and hides his approach by serpentine deviations, true to his name of serpent. Cleverness of that kind, dark lurking deceit, has always been his way of circumventing us. That is how he has tricked us and deceived us from the very beginning of the world, his lies wheedling the inexperienced soul in its reckless confidence. That is how he tried to tempt the Lord himself, approaching him secretly as if to steal upon him again and trick him. But he was understood, turned back and laid low, because he was recognized and unmasked.

So we were taught by example to shun the way of the old man and tread in the footsteps of the victorious Christ, so that we may not be caught again in the snare of death through our heedlessness, but rather, being awake to our danger, take possession of the immortality we have received. And how can we possess immortality unless we keep the commandments of Christ by which death is conquered and defeated, as he warns us: "If thou wouldest enter into life, keep the commandments," and again: "If ye do the things which I command you, henceforth I call you not servants, but friends"? Mark what sort of men he calls strong and steadfast, founded securely upon a rock, established in unmoveable and unshakable solidity against every storm and tempest of the world. He says: "He that heareth my words and doeth them, I will liken him unto a wise man, which built his house upon a rock; and the rain descended, and the floods came, and the winds blew and beat upon that house; and it fell not; for it was founded upon a rock."

It is our duty to stand upon his words, to learn and do all that he taught and did. How can anyone profess faith in Christ without doing what Christ commanded? How can he come to the reward of faith without keeping faith with the commandments? He cannot but totter and wander, snatched up by the spirit of error and whirled about like dust scattered by the wind. One who leaves the true way of salvation will never find his own road to it.

We must guard against wily trickery and subtle deceit no less than open and obvious perils. And could anything more subtle and wily have been devised than this? The enemy had been exposed and laid low by the coming of Christ, light came to the nations, the sun of salvation shined to save mankind, so that the deaf received the hearing of spiritual grace, the blind opened their eyes to the Lord, the weak recovered strength in eternal health, the lame ran to church, the dumb prayed aloud. Yet, when he saw the idols abandoned and his seats and temples deserted through the host of believers, our enemy thought of a new trick, to deceive the unwary under cover of the name Christian. He invented heresies and schisms to undermine faith, pervert truth, and break unity. Unable to keep us in the dark ways of former error, he draws us into a new maze of deceit. He snatches men away from the Church itself and, just when they think they have drawn near to the light and escaped the night of the world, he plunges them unaware into a new darkness. Though they do not stand by the gospel and discipline and law of Christ, they call themselves Christians. Though they are walking in darkness, they think they are in the light, through the deceitful flattery of the adversary who, as the Apostle said, transforms himself into an angel of light and adorns his ministers as ministers of righteousness who call night day, death salvation, despair hope, perfidy faith, antichrist Christ, cunningly to frustrate truth by their lying show of truth. That is what happens, my brothers, when we do not return to the fount of truth, when we are not looking to the head and keeping the doctrine taught from heaven.

Due consideration of these points renders lengthy discussion and argument unnecessary. Faith finds ready proof when the truth is stated succinctly. The Lord says to Peter: "I say unto thee that thou art Peter, and upon this rock I will build my Church; and the gates of hell shall not prevail against it. I will give unto thee the keys of the kingdom of heaven: and whatsoever thou shalt bind on earth shall be bound in heaven; and whatsoever thou shalt loose on earth shall be loosed also in heaven." He builds the Church upon one man. True, after the resurrection he assigned the like power to all the apostles, saying: "As the Father hath sent me, even so send I you. Receive ye the Holy Ghost: whose soever sins ye remit, they shall be remitted unto him; whose soever ye retain, they shall be retained." Despite that, in order to make unity manifest, he arranged by his own authority that this unity should, from the start, take its beginning from one man. Certainly the rest of the apostles were exactly what Peter was; they were endowed with an equal share of office and power. But there was unity at the beginning before any development, to demonstrate that the Church of Christ is one. This one Church is also intended in the Song of Songs, when the Holy Spirit says, in the person of the Lord: "My dove, my perfect one, is but one; she is the only one of her mother, the choice one of her that bare her." Can one who does not keep this unity of the Church believe that he keeps the faith? Can one who resists and struggles against the Church be sure that he is in the Church? For the blessed apostle Paul gives the same teaching and declares the same mystery of unity when he says: "There is one body and one Spirit, one hope of your calling, one Lord, one faith, one baptism, one God."

It is particularly incumbent upon those of us who preside over the Church as bishops to uphold this unity firmly and to be its champions, so that we may prove the episcopate also to be itself one and undivided. Let no one deceive the brotherhood with lies or corrupt the true faith with faithless treachery. (And after his resurrection he also says to him, Feed my sheep. On him he builds the Church, and to him he entrusts the sheep to be fed. And although he gives equal power to all the apostles, yet he established one chair [cathedram] and arranged by his own authority the origin and principle [rationem] of unity. Certainly the rest of the apostles were exactly what Peter was, but primacy is given to Peter [primatus Petro datur] and one Church and one chair is demonstrated. And they are all shepherds but the flock is shown to be one, which is to be fed by all the apostles in unanimous agreement. He who does not hold this unity of Peter, does he believe he holds the faith? He who deserts the chair of Peter on whom the Church was founded, does he trust that he is in the Church?) The episcopate is a single whole, in which each bishop's share gives him a right to, and a responsibility for, the whole. So is the Church a single whole, though she spreads far and wide into a multitude of churches as her fertility increases. We may compare the sun, many rays but one light, or a tree, many branches but one firmly rooted trunk. When many streams flow from one spring, although the bountiful supply of water welling out has the appearance of plurality, unity is preserved in the source. Pluck a ray from the body of the sun, and its unity allows no division of the light. Break a branch from the tree, and when it is broken off it will not bud. Cut a stream off from its spring, and when it is cut off it dries up. In the same way the Church, bathed in the light of the Lord, spreads her rays throughout the world, yet the light everywhere diffused is one light and the unity of the body is not broken. In the abundance of her plenty she stretches her branches over the whole earth, far and wide she pours her generously flowing streams. Yet there is one head, one source, one mother boundlessly fruitful. Of her womb are we born, by her milk we are nourished, by her breath we are quickened.

The bride of Christ cannot be made an adulteress. She is undefiled and chaste. She knows but one home, she guards with virtuous chastity the sanctity of one bed-chamber. It is she who keeps us for God and seals for the kingdom the sons she has borne. If you abandon the Church and join yourself to an adulteress, you are cut off from the promises of the Church. If you leave the Church of Christ you will not come to Christ's rewards, you will be an alien, an outcast, an enemy. You cannot have God for your father unless you have the Church for your mother. If you could escape outside Noah's ark, you could escape outside the Church. The Lord warns us, saying: "He that is not with me is against me; and he that gathereth not with me scattereth." To break the peace and concord of Christ is to go against Christ. To gather somewhere outside the Church is to scatter Christ's Church. The Lord says: "I and the Father are one," and again, of Father, Son, and Holy Spirit it is written: "And the three are one." Can you believe that this unity, which originates in the immutability of God and coheres in heavenly mysteries, can be broken in the Church and split by the divorce of clashing wills? He who does not keep this unity does not keep the law of God, not the faith of the Father and the Son—nor life and salvation.

Who then is so wicked and perfidious, so mad with the fury of discord as to believe that the unity of God, the garment of the Lord, the Church of Christ, can be rent—as to dare to rend it? He himself instructs us in his Gospel with words of warning: "And there shall be one flock and one shepherd." A number of shepherds or of flocks in one place is unthinkable. Teaching us the same unity the apostle Paul exhorts us: "I beseech you, brethren, by the name of our Lord Jesus Christ, that ye all speak the same thing, and that there be no divisions among you; but that ye be perfected together in the same mind and in the same judgment." Again: "Sustaining one another in love, endeavouring to keep the unity of the Spirit in the bond of peace." Do you think a man can abandon the Church, set up for himself another house and home, and yet stay alive, despite the words spoken to Rahab, the type of the Church: "Thou shalt gather unto thee into thy house thy father, and thy mother, and thy brethren, and all thy father's household. And it shall be that whosoever shall go out of the doors of thy house into the street, his blood shall be upon his head" and despite the express requirement of the law of Exodus touching the Passover rite, that the lamb (whose killing prefigures Christ) should be eaten in one house? God says: "In one house shall it be eaten; ye shall not cast the flesh abroad out of the house." The flesh of Christ and the holy thing of the Lord cannot be cast out. The faithful have no home but the one Church. This home, this house of unanimity, the Holy Spirit announces unmistakably in the Psalms: "God who maketh men to dwell together of one mind in a house." In the house of God, in the Church of Christ, they indeed live with one mind, they indeed persist in harmony and singleness of heart.

So also the Holy Spirit came as a dove, an innocent and happy creature, not bitter with gall, with no savage bite or lacerating claws. It loves human company and knows the fellowship of a single home. When they breed, they bring up their young together; when they go out, they fly close to each other. They pass their lives in mutual intercourse, marking their peace and concord with a kiss and fulfilling in every point the law of unanimity. The Church should exhibit their innocence and practice their affection. We should be like doves in brotherly love, like lambs and sheep in kindness and gentleness. What room is there in a Christian's breast for the fierceness of wolves, for the madness of dogs, the deadly poison of snakes, the bloody savagery of beasts? We may well congratulate ourselves when men like that are removed from the Church and Christ's doves and sheep are no longer the prey of their savage and poisonous contagion. There can be no fellowship between sweet and bitter, light and darkness, rain and sunshine, between war and peace, famine and plenty, drought and waters, calm and storm. Believe me, good men cannot leave the Church. The wind does not carry off the grain, the storm does not bring down the tree with strong roots. It is the empty husks that are tossed away by the tempest, the feeble trees that are thrown down by the hurricane. And it is such men that John the Apostle upbraids and smites when he says: "They went out from us, but they were not of us; for if they had been of us, they would have continued with us."

From such men have heresies often come, and still come. The twisted mind knows no peace and warring perfidy cannot keep unity. But the Lord allows such things out of respect for the freedom of the will, so that, when our hearts and minds are probed by the test of truth, the undamaged faith of such as are approved may shine out in manifest light. The Holy Spirit warns us through the Apostle: "There must be also heresies among you, that they which are approved may be made manifest among you." In this way the faithful are approved and the faithless detected. Here and now, even before the Day of Judgment, the souls of the just and the unjust are parted and the chaff is separated from the wheat.

From such men come those who, without divine appointment, set themselves over their rash associates, make themselves prelates without any lawful ordination and call themselves bishops though no one gives them a bishopric. The Holy Spirit portrays them in the Psalms "sitting in the seat of pestilence," plagues and blights to faith, snake-mouthed traitors, scheming to pervert truth, spewing deadly poisons from their pestiferous tongues. Their words "spread like a canker," their teaching pours fatal venom into men's hearts and breasts . . .

Some deceive themselves with a vain interpretation of the words of the Lord: "Wheresoever two or three are gathered together in my name, I am with them." Corrupters and false interpreters of the Gospel, they set down the last words and omit what precedes them, remembering one part and craftily suppressing the other. Themselves cut off from the Church, they cut up the sense of a passage which must be taken as a whole. The Lord was urging peace and unanimity upon his disciples. "I say unto you, that if two of you shall agree on earth as touching anything that ye shall ask, it shall be done for you of my Father which is in heaven. For wheresoever two or three are gathered together in my name, I am with them." These words prove that much is given not to the mere number but to the unanimity of those who pray. "If two of you shall agree on earth," he says, putting unanimity and peaceful concord first, teaching us to agree firmly and loyally. But how can one man agree with another when he disagrees with the body of the Church itself, with the whole brotherhood? How can two or three be gathered together in the name of Christ when they are known to be separated from Christ and his Gospel? For we did not go out from them, but they from us. Heresies and schisms were born after the Church, as men set up separate conventicles to suit themselves. It is they who have abandoned the head and fount of truth.

The Lord's words were spoken about his own Church and addressed to members of the Church. If they are agreed, if, as he commanded, but two or three are gathered together and pray with one mind, then, although they are but two or three, they can obtain from the divine majesty what they ask. "Wheresoever two or three are gathered, I (he said) am with them." That means, of course, with the single-hearted and peaceable, with those who fear God and keep his commandments. With these, though but two or three, he declared his presence, as he was present also with the Three Children in the fiery furnace, and, because they continued single-hearted and of one mind, refreshed them with the breath of dew as the flames surrounded them; or as he was present with the two apostles in prison, because they were single-hearted and of one mind, and himself opened the prison gates and set them again in the market-place to deliver to the crowds the word which they had been faithfully preaching.

So when he lays down with authority: "Where two or three are gathered, I am with them," he is not separating men from the Church which he founded and created. Rebuking the faithless for their discord and with his own voice commending peace to the faithful, he shows that he is present with two or three praying with one mind rather than with a large number of dissidents, and that more can be obtained by the united prayer of a few than by the discordant petition of many.

So when he gave the rule of prayer he added: "And when ye stand praying, forgive, if you have aught against any one: that your Father also which is in heaven may forgive you your trespasses." He calls back from the altar one going to the sacrifice with angry feelings and tells him first to be reconciled to his brother and then to come back and offer his gift to God. For God had no respect to Cain's gifts, nor could he have God at peace with him when by his envious hate he had no peace with his brother. What peace can the enemies of their own brothers promise themselves? What sacrifices do the rivals of the priests think they celebrate? Do those who gather themselves outside the Church fancy that Christ is with them when they are gathered together?

Suppose such men are put to death confessing the Name. Their blood cannot wash away that stain, their suffering cannot purge the grievous and inexpiable guilt of discord.

You cannot be a martyr if you are not in the Church. You cannot come into the kingdom if you desert her who is to reign there. Christ gave us peace, ordered us to be of one heart and mind, commanded us to keep the bonds of love and charity unharmed and inviolate. You cannot prove yourself a martyr if you have not kept brotherly charity. Witness the words of the apostle Paul: "Though I have faith, so that I could remove mountains, and have not charity, I am nothing. And though I bestow all my goods to feed the poor, and though I give my body to be burned, and have not charity, it profiteth me nothing. Charity suffereth long, and is kind; charity envieth not, is not puffed up, is not provoked, doth not behave itself unseemly, thinketh no evil, loveth all things, believeth all things, hopeth all things, endureth all things. Charity will never fail." Never, he says, will charity fail. There will always be charity in the kingdom, it will abide for ever in the unity of a harmonious brotherhood. Discord cannot enter the kingdom of heaven. One who has violated the love of Christ by faithless dissension cannot attain to the reward of a Christ who said: "This is my commandment, that ye love one another, even as I have loved you." He who has not charity, has not God. It was the blessed apostle John who said: "God is love; and he that abideth in love abideth in God, and God abideth in him." Those who have refused to be of one mind in the Church of God cannot abide with God. Though they give their bodies to be burned in flame and fire, though they expose themselves to wild beasts and lay down their lives, they shall have no crown of faith, but the penalty of perfidy, no glorious end of pious virtue, but the death of despair. Such a man may be killed; he cannot be crowned. He professes himself a Christian only as the devil not seldom feigns himself to be Christ. Of this the Lord himself warned us, saying: "Many shall come in my name, saying, I am Christ; and shall deceive many." As the devil is not Christ; though he deceives in his name, so he who does not stand fast in Christ's Gospel and the true faith cannot be reckoned a Christian. . . .

One who separates himself from the Church is to be avoided and fled from. He is perverted, sinful, self-condemned. Can any one believe he is with Christ when he works against Christ's priests and withdraws himself from the fellowship of his clergy and people? He is bearing arms against the Church, fighting against the providence of God. An enemy of the altar, a rebel against Christ's sacrifice, a traitor to his faith, a blasphemous renegade, a disobedient servant, an undutiful son, a hostile brother, he scorns the bishops, turns his back on God's priests, and dares to set up another altar, to offer another prayer in unlawful words, to profane the true offering of the Lord with false sacrifices. Does he not know that the presumption which strives against the ordinance of God is punished by the chastisement of God?

Of this Korah, Dathan, and Abiram are an example. When they tried to claim for themselves the right to sacrifice, in opposition to Moses and Aaron, they at once paid the penalty for their attempt. Bursting its bonds, the earth gaped deep asunder, and as the ground parted, the gulf swallowed them up alive where they stood. And it was not only the originators of this insane venture who were struck by the wrath of God's indignation. With speedy vengeance fire issuing from the Lord consumed the two hundred and fifty more who share in it, their partners in audacity, clear proof that all wicked efforts to destroy the ordinance of God by human wills are rebellion against God himself. Similarly, when King Uzziah carried a censer and violently took upon himself to sacrifice, against the law of God, and refused to submit or give place, despite the opposition of Azariah the priest, he was confounded by God's indignation and defiled with the markings of leprosy on his forehead, branded by the Lord's anger upon that part of the body on which those who win the Lord's favour are sealed. The sons of Aaron also, who set upon the altar a strange fire not commanded by the Lord, were at once blotted out in the sight of the avenging Lord.

These examples, you will see, are being followed wherever the tradition which comes from God is despised by lovers of strange doctrine and replaced by teaching of merely human authority. The Lord rebukes and castigates them in his Gospel: "Ye reject the commandment of God that ye may establish your own tradition." This is a worse offence than to fall before persecution, for the lapsed at least do penance for their offence and ask God's mercy with works of full satisfaction. The lapsed seek the Church and plead with it, the schismatic fights against the Church. In the one case there may have been constraint, in the other the will is guilty. The lapsed has harmed himself alone, the author of heresy or schism has deceived many, dragging them with him. With the former only one soul is lost, with the latter many are imperilled. The one knows his sin and laments it with tears, the other, puffed up by his sin and delighting in his offences, separates the sons from their mother, wheedles the sheep from their shepherd, and upsets the mysteries of God. While the lapsed sinned but once, he sins every day. Finally, it is possible for the lapsed, by undergoing martyrdom afterwards, to receive the promises of the kingdom, but if the schismatic is put to death outside the Church, he cannot attain to the rewards which belong to the Church.

Do not be surprised, dear brothers, that even some of the confessors go to such lengths and sin, some or them, so wickedly and grievously. Confession does not guarantee immunity from the snares of the devil nor provide lasting security against the temptations, the perils, the attacks and assaults of the world, as long as you are in the world. Otherwise we should never see fraud and fornication and adultery in confessors after their confession, as we are now seeing in some of them, to our grief and pain. No matter who he is, the confessor is not greater or better or dearer to God than Solomon. And Solomon kept the grace which the Lord had given him as long as he walked in his ways, but lost the Lord's grace after he left the Lord's way. Therefore it is written: "Hold fast that which thou hast, that no other take thy crown." Surely God would not threaten that the crown of righteousness might be taken away, if it were not necessary that when justice goes, the crown should go also.

Confession is the beginning of glory, it does not earn the crown at once. It does not perfect praise, but initiates honour. Scripture says: "He that endureth to the end shall be saved." Therefore anything before the end can be no more than a step by which we climb to the summit of salvation, and not the goal where the mountain-top is already gained. He is a confessor—but after the confession the danger is greater, since the adversary is more provoked. He is a confessor—then, having obtained glory of the Lord through the Gospel, he is all the more bound to stand firmly by the Lord's Gospel. "To whom much is given, of him is much required: and to whom more honour is ascribed, of him more service is demanded." Let no one perish through the example of a confessor, let no one learn unrighteousness or insolence or perfidy from a confessor's behaviour. He is a confessor—then let him be humble and peaceable, modest and disciplined in his conduct. One who is called a confessor of Christ should imitate the Christ whom he confesses. He says: "Every one that exalteth himself shall be humbled, and he that humbleth himself shall be exalted;" and he was himself exalted by his Father because on earth he, the word and power and wisdom of God, humbled himself. How then can he love self-exaltation when his own law enjoins humility upon us and when he himself received from his Father the name above every name as the reward of humility? He is a confessor of Christ—but only if afterwards the majesty and dignity of Christ is not blasphemed through him. Let not the tongue which has confessed Christ be evil-speaking or turbulent, noisily abusive and quarrelsome, changing from words of praise to envenomed darts against the brethren and the priests of God. If a confessor afterwards becomes culpable and obnoxious, wasting his confession by evil living and staining his life with base filthiness, if, to conclude, he abandons the Church in which he became a confessor, rends the bond of unity and exchanges his first faith for faithlessness, he cannot flatter himself, on the strength of his confession, that he is elect to the reward of glory, when for that very reason he deserves all the more punishment.

The Lord chose Judas among the apostles, and yet Judas afterwards betrayed the Lord. Even so, the defection of the traitor Judas from their company did not make the apostles fall from their own strong faith. Similarly, in the present case, the sanctity and worth of the confessors was not at once shattered because the faith of some few was broken. The blessed Apostle says in his epistle: "What if some of them fell from the faith? has their unfaithfulness made the faith of God of none effect? God forbid: for God is true, but every man a liar." The larger and better part of the confessors stand firm in the strength of their faith and in the truth of the Lord's law and discipline. Mindful that, by the favour of God, they obtained grace in the Church, they do not secede from the peace of the Church. Their faith wins an ampler praise in that they have separated themselves from the perfidy of their fellow-confessors and escaped the infection of their crime. Illumined by the true light of the Gospel and bathed in the pure, bright radiance of the Lord, they are as praiseworthy in keeping the peace of Christ as they were victorious in their encounter with the devil.

Dearest brothers, my desire, my counsel, my exhortation to you is that, if it be possible, not one of the brethren perish, that our mother may joyfully gather into her bosom the one body of the People of God in full accord. But if some leaders of schism, some authors of faction, persist in their blind and stubborn madness, and cannot be recalled by wholesome counsel to the way of salvation, the rest of you, who were caught through your simplicity or led on by error or deceived by some clever trick, must set yourselves free from the snares of deceit. Free your wayward steps from wandering, mark the straight path to heaven. The Apostle bears witness: "We command you in the name of the Lord Jesus Christ, that ye withdraw yourselves from every brother that walketh disorderly, and not after the tradition which they received from us." And again: "Let no man deceive you with vain words: for because of these things cometh the wrath of God upon the sons of disobedience. Be not ye therefore partakers with them." You must withdraw, you must fly from sinners. To join those who walk wickedly, to journey with them on the roads of error and crime, straying from the true path, involves you in the same crime. There is one God and one Christ and one Church and one faith and one people, fastened together into a solid corporate unity by the glue of concord. The unity cannot be rent, nor can the one body be divided by breaking up its structure; it cannot be broken into fragments by tearing and mangling the flesh. Whatever leaves the womb cannot live and breathe apart. It loses the substance of health. . . .

This unanimity prevailed once, in the time of the apostles. The new company of believers, keeping the Lord's commandments, preserved its charity. There is scriptural proof of this in the words: "And the multitude of them that believed were of one soul and of one mind." And again: "And they all continued of one mind in prayer, with the women and Mary, the mother of Jesus, and his brethren." That is why their prayer was effectual, that is why they could be confident of obtaining whatever they asked of God's mercy.

In us, however, unanimity has diminished in proportion as liberality in good works has decayed. In those days they used to sell their houses and farms. Laying up for themselves treasure in heaven, they would offer the price to the apostles to be shared out among the poor. Now we do not even give a tithe of our patrimony, and though the Lord bids us sell, we prefer to buy and enlarge our estate. With us the vigour of faith has withered, the strength of belief has grown faint. And so, reviewing our times, the Lord says in his Gospel: "When the Son of man cometh, think you he shall find faith on the earth?" We are seeing his prediction fulfilled. In the fear of God, in the law of righteousness, in love, in good works, our faith is nothing. No one meditates on the fear of things to come, no one takes to heart the day of the Lord and the wrath of God, the punishment in store for the unbeliever, the eternal torment appointed for the apostate. What our conscience would fear if it believed, it does not fear at all because it does not believe. If it believed, it would take care; if it took care, it would escape.

Dearest brothers, let us rouse ourselves to the full, let us break off the slumber of our former sloth and awake to observe and fulfill the Lord's commands. Behave as he taught us to behave when he said: "Let your loins be girded about and your lights burning; and ye yourselves like unto men that wait for their Lord, when he will return from the wedding; that when he cometh and knocketh, they may open unto him. Blessed are those servants, whom the lord when he cometh shall find watching."

We must gird ourselves, lest when the day of expedition comes, he find us impeded and encumbered. Let our light so shine and gleam in good works that it may lead us from the night of this world into the light of eternal day. Let us await the sudden advent of the Lord with ever-watchful care, that when he knocks our faith may be found awake to receive of him the reward of vigilance. If we keep these commandments, if we hold by these precepts and monitions, we cannot be overtaken in sleep by the wiles of the devil. As watchful servants, we shall reign with Christ in his kingdom.

AUGUSTINE (354–430)

In Augustine, Bishop of Hippo (in Africa), we see one of the truly great figures of Christian history. His voluminous writings are a treasure upon which not only the Christian Church but the world as a whole still draws. His influence as an intellectual of great power, as a student of the passing Roman culture, and as a Christian theologian can hardly be measured.

Born into a pagan-Christian home where his early education was largely under Christian auspices, Augustine nevertheless deserted the faith and lived as a pagan during his early manhood. After experience in Manichaeism, and deeply influenced by Neo-platonism, Augustine finally found peace in the Christian faith. He was baptized in 387 A. D. and ordained a priest in 391 A. D.

During his later life Augustine wrote constantly on a great number of Christian themes. His most important works deal with the definition of certain doctrines which were under dispute in his own day. The great philosophy of history, *The City of God,* as well as the autobiographical *Confessions,* are considered classics in the world's literature.

The following treatise on *Faith, Hope, and Love* was written toward the close of his life. It represents, in summary, the fruit of Augustine's mature theology.

Enchiridion On Faith, Hope, and Love*

Chapter I

The Occasion and Purpose of This "Manual"

I cannot say, my dearest son Laurence, how much your learning pleases me, and how much I desire that you should be wise—though not one of those of whom it is said: "Where is the wise? Where is the scribe? Where is the disputant of this world? Hath not God made foolish the wisdom of this world?"[1] Rather, you should be one of those of whom it is written, "The multitude of the wise is the health of the world"[2]; and also you should be the kind of man the apostle wishes those men to be to whom he said,[3] "I would have you be wise in goodness and simple in evil."[4]

Human wisdom consists in piety. This you have in the book of the saintly Job, for there

* From Albert C. Outler, ed., *Augustine: Confessions and Enchiridion,* Volume VII, Library of Christian Classics. Philadelphia: The Westminster Press, 1955, pages 337-345, 353-378, 401-407 and 409-412 are reproduced by permission of the publisher.

[1] I Cor. 1:20.

[2] Wis. 6:26 (Vulgate).

[3] Rom. 16:19.

[4] A later interpolation, not found in the best MSS., adds, "As no one can exist from himself, so also no one can be wise in himself save only as he is enlightened by Him of whom it is written, 'All wisdom is from God' [Eccls. 1:1]."

he writes that Wisdom herself said to man, "Behold, piety is wisdom."[5] If, then, you ask what kind of piety she was speaking of, you will find it more distinctly designated by the Greek term *θεοσέβεια*, literally, "the service of God." The Greek has still another word for "piety," *εὐσέβεια*, which also signifies "proper service." This too refers chiefly to the service of God. But no term is better that *θεοσέβεια*, which clearly expresses the idea of the man's service of God as the source of human wisdom.

When you ask me to be brief, you do not expect me to speak of great issues in a few sentences, do you? Is not this rather what you desire: a brief summary or a short treatise on the proper mode of worshiping [serving] God?

If I should answer, "God should be worshiped in faith, hope, love," you would doubtless reply that this was shorter than you wished, and might then beg for a brief explication of what each of these three means: What should be believed, what should be hoped for, and what should be loved? If I should answer these questions, you would then have everything you asked for in your letter. If you have kept a copy of it, you can easily refer to it. If not, recall your questions as I discuss them.

It is your desire, as you wrote, to have from me a book, a sort of *enchiridion*,[6] as it might be called—something to have "at hand"—that deals with your questions. What is to be sought after above all else? What, in view of the divers heresies, is to be avoided above all else? How far does reason support religion; or what happens to reason when the issues involved concern faith alone; what is the beginning and end of our endeavor? What is the most comprehensive of all explanation? What is the certain and distinctive foundation of the catholic faith? You would have the answers to all these questions if you really understood what a man should believe, what he should hope for, and what he ought to love. For these are the chief things—indeed, the only things—to seek for in religion. He who turns away from them is either a complete stranger to the name of Christ or else he is a heretic. Things that arise in sensory experience, or that are analyzed by the intellect, may be demonstrated by the reason. But in matters that pass beyond the scope of the physical senses, which we have not settled by our own understanding, and cannot—here we must believe, without hesitation, the witness of those men by whom the Scriptures (rightly called divine) were composed, men who were divinely aided in their senses and their minds to see and even to foresee the things about which they testify.

But, as this faith, which works by love,[7] begins to penetrate the soul, it tends, through the vital power of goodness, to change into sight, so that the holy and perfect in heart catch glimpses of that ineffable beauty whose full vision is our highest happiness. Here, then, surely, is the answer to your question about the beginning and the end of our endeavor. We begin in faith, we are perfected in sight.[8] This likewise is the most comprehensive of all explanations. As for the certain and distinctive foundation of the catholic faith, it is Christ. "For other foundation," said the apostle, "can no man lay save that which has been laid, which is Christ Jesus."[9] Nor should it be denied that this is the distinctive basis of the catholic faith, just because it appears that it is common to us and to certain heretics as well. For if we think carefully about the meaning of Christ, we shall see that among some of the heretics who wish to be called Christians, the *name* of Christ is held in honor, but the reality itself is not among them. To make all this plain would take too long—because we would then have to review all the heresies that have been, the ones that now exist, and those which could exist under the label "Christian," and we would have to show that what we have said of all is true of each of them. Such a discussion would take so many volumes as to make it seem endless.[10]

You have asked for an *enchiridion*, something you could carry around, not just baggage for your bookshelf. Therefore we may return

[5] Job 28:28.

[6] A transliteration of the Greek *ἐγχειρίδιον*, literally, a handbook or manual.

[7] Cf. Gal. 5:6.

[8] Cf. I Cor. 13:10, 11.

[9] I Cor. 3:11.

[10] Already, very early in his ministry (397), Augustine had written *De agone Christiano*, in which he had reviewed and refuted a full score of heresies threatening the orthodox faith.

to these three ways in which, as we said, God should be served: faith, hope, love. It is easy to *say* what one ought to believe, what to hope for, and what to love. But to defend our doctrines against the calumnies of those who think differently is a more difficult and detailed task. If one is to have this wisdom, it is not enough just to put an *enchiridion* in the hand. It is also necessary that a great zeal be kindled in the heart.

Chapter II

The Creed and the Lord's Prayer as Guides to the Interpretation of the Theological Virtues of Faith, Hope, and Love

Let us begin, for example, with the Symbol[11] and the Lord's Prayer. What is shorter to hear or to read? What is more easily memorized? Since through sin the human race stood grievously burdened by great misery and in deep need of mercy, a prophet, preaching of the time of God's grace, said, "And it shall be that all who invoke the Lord's name will be saved."[12] Thus, we have the Lord's Prayer. Later, the apostle, when he wished to commend this same grace, remembered this prophetic testimony and promptly added, "But how shall they invoke him in whom they have not believed?"[13] Thus, we have the Symbol. In these two we have the three theological virtues working together: faith believes; hope and love pray. Yet without faith nothing else is possible; thus faith prays too. This, then, is the meaning of the saying, "How shall they invoke him in whom they have not believed?"

Now, is it possible to hope for what we do not believe in? We can, of course, believe in something that we do not hope for. Who among the faithful does not believe in the punishment of the impious? Yet he does not hope for it, and who ever believes that such a punishment is threatening him and draws back in horror from it is more rightly said to fear than to hope. A poet, distinguishing between these two feelings, said,

> "Let those who dread be allowed to hope,"[14]

but another poet, and a better one, did not put it rightly:

> "Here, if I could have hoped for [i.e., foreseen]
> such a grievous blow . . ."[15]

Indeed, some grammarians use this as an example of inaccurate language and comment, "He said 'to hope' when he should have said 'to fear.' "

Therefore faith may refer to evil things as well as to good, since we believe in both the good and evil. Yet faith is good, not evil. Moreover, faith refers to things past and present and future. For we believe that Christ died; this is a past event. We believe that he sitteth at the Father's right hand; this is present. We believe that he will come as our judge; this is future. Again, faith has to do with our own affairs and with those of others. For everyone believes, both about himself and other persons—and about things as well—that at some time he began to exist and that he has not existed forever. Thus, not only about men, but even about angels, we believe many things that have a bearing on religion.

But hope deals only with good things, and only with those which lie in the future, and which pertain to the man who cherishes the hope. Since this is so, faith must be distinguished from hope: they are different terms and likewise different concepts. Yet faith and hope have this in common: they refer to what is not seen, whether this unseen is believed in or hoped for. Thus in the Epistle to the Hebrews, which is used by the enlightened defenders of the catholic rule of faith, faith is said to be "the conviction of things not seen."[16] However, when a man maintains that neither words nor witnesses nor even arguments, but only the evidence of present experience, determine his faith, he still ought not to be called absurd or told, "You have seen; therefore you have not believed." For it does not follow that unless a thing is not seen it cannot be believed. Still it is better for us to use the term "faith," as we

[11] The Apostles' Creed. Cf. Augustine's early essay *On Faith and the Creed.*

[12] Joel 2:32.

[13] Rom. 10:14.

[14] Lucan, *Pharsalia,* II, 15.

[15] Virgil, *Aeneid,* IV, 419. The context of this quotation is Dido's lament over Aeneas' prospective abandonment of her. She is saying that if she could have foreseen such a disaster, she would have been able to bear it. Augustine's criticism here is a literalistic quibble.

[16] Heb. 11:1.

are taught in "the sacred eloquence,"[17] to refer to things not seen. And as for hope, the apostle says: "Hope that is seen is not hope. For if a man sees a thing, why does he hope for it? If, however, we hope for what we do not see, we then wait for it in patience."[18] When, therefore, our good is believed to be future, this is the same thing as hoping for it.

What, then, shall I say of love, without which faith can do nothing? There can be no true hope without love. Indeed, as the apostle James says, "Even the demons believe and tremble."[19] Yet they neither hope nor love. Instead, believing as we do that what we hope for and love is coming to pass, they tremble. Therefore, the apostle Paul approves and commends the faith that works by love and that cannot exist without hope. Thus it is that love is not without hope, hope is not without love, and neither hope nor love are without faith.

Chapter III

God the Creator of All; and the Goodness of All Creation

Wherefore, when it is asked what we ought to believe in matters of religion, the answer is not to be sought in the exploration of the nature of things [*rerum natura*], after the manner of those whom the Greeks called "physicists."[20] Nor should we be dismayed if Christians are ignorant about the properties and the number of the basic elements of nature, or about the motion, order, and deviations of the stars, the map of the heavens, the kinds and nature of animals, plants, stones, springs, rivers, and mountains; about the divisions of space and time, about the signs of impending storms, and the myriad other things which these "physicists" have come to understand, or think they have. For even these men, gifted with such superior insight, with their ardor in study and their abundant leisure, exploring some of these matters by human conjecture and others through historical inquiry, have not yet learned everything there is to know. For that matter, many of the things they are so proud to have discovered are more often matters of opinion than of verified knowledge.

For the Christian, it is enough to believe that the cause of all created things, whether in heaven or on earth, whether visible or invisible, is nothing other than the goodness of the Creator, who is the one and the true God.[21] Further, the Christian believes that nothing exists save God himself and what comes from him; and he believes that God is triune, i.e., the Father, and the Son begotten of the Father, and the Holy Spirit proceeding from the same Father, but one and the same Spirit of the Father and the Son.

By this Trinity, supremely and equally and immutably good, were all things created. But they were not created supremely, equally, nor immutably good. Still, each single created thing is good, and taken as a whole they are very good, because together they constitute a universe of admirable beauty.

In this universe, even what is called evil, when it is rightly ordered and kept in its place, commends the good more eminently, since good things yield greater pleasure and praise when compared to the bad things. For the Omnipotent God, whom even the heathen acknowledge as the Supreme Power over all, would not allow any evil in his works, unless in his omnipotence and goodness, as the Supreme Good, he is able to bring forth good out of evil. What, after all, is anything we call evil except the privation of good? In animal bodies, for instance, sickness and wounds are nothing but the privation of health. When a cure is effected, the evils which were present (i.e., the sickness and the wounds) do not retreat and go elsewhere. Rather, they simply do not exist any more. For such evil is not a substance; the wound or the disease is a defect of the bodily substance which, as a substance, is good. Evil, then, is an accident, i.e., a privation of that good which is called health. Thus, whatever defects there are in a

[17] *Sacre eloquia*—a favorite phrase of Augustine's for the Bible.

[18] Rom. 8:24, 25 (Old Latin).

[19] James 2:19.

[20] One of the standard titles of early Greek philosophical treatises was περὶ φύσεως, which would translate into Latin as *De rerum natura*. This is, in fact, the title of Lucretius' famous poem, the greatest philosophical work written in classical Latin.

[21] This basic motif appears everywhere in Augustine's thought as the very foundation of his whole system.

soul are privations of a natural good. When a cure takes place, they are not transferred elsewhere but, since they are no longer present in the state of health, they no longer exist at all.[22]

Chapter IV

The Problem of Evil

All of nature, therefore, is good, since the Creator of all nature is supremely good. But nature is not supremely and immutably good as is the Creator of it. Thus the good in created things can be diminished and augmented. For good to be diminished is evil; still, however much it is diminished, something must remain of its original nature as long as it exists at all. For no matter what kind or however insignificant a thing may be, the good which is its "nature" cannot be destroyed without the thing itself being destroyed. There is good reason, therefore, to praise an uncorrupted thing, and if it were indeed an incorruptible thing which could not be destroyed, it would doubtless be all the more worthy of praise. When, however, a thing is corrupted, its corruption is an evil because it is, by just so much, a privation of the good. Where there is no privation of the good, there is no evil. Where there is evil, there is a corresponding diminution of the good. As long, then, as a thing is being corrupted, there is good in it of which it is being deprived; and in this process, if something of its being remains that cannot be further corrupted, this will then be an incorruptible entity [*natura incorruptibilis*], and to this great good it will have come through the process of corruption. But even if the corruption is not arrested, it still does not cease having some good of which it cannot be further deprived. If, however, the corruption comes to be total and entire, there is no good left either, because it is no longer an entity at all. Wherefore corruption cannot consume the good without also consuming the thing itself. Every actual entity [*natura*] is therefore good; a greater good if it cannot be corrupted, a lesser good if it can be. Yet only the foolish and unknowing can deny that it is still good even when corrupted. Whenever a thing is consumed by corruption, not even the corruption remains, for it is nothing in itself, having no subsistent being in which to exist.

From this it follows that there is nothing to be called evil if there is nothing good. A good that wholly lacks an evil aspect is entirely good. Where there is some evil in a thing, its good is defective or defectible. Thus there can be no evil where there is no good. This leads us to a surprising conclusion: that, since every being, in so far as it is a being, is good, if we then say that a defective thing is bad, it would seem to mean that we are saying that what is evil is good, that only what is good is ever evil and that there is no evil apart from something good. This is because every actual entity is good [*omnis natura bonum est.*] Nothing evil exists *in itself,* but only as an evil aspect of some actual entity. Therefore, there can be nothing evil except something good. Absurd as this sounds, nevertheless the logical connections of the argument compel us to it as inevitable. At the same time, we must take warning lest we incur the prophetic judgment which reads: "Woe to those who call evil good and good evil: who call darkness light and light darkness; who call the bitter sweet and the sweet bitter."[23] Moreover the Lord himself saith: "An evil man brings forth evil out of the evil treasure of his heart."[24] What, then, is an evil man but an evil entity [*natura mala*], since man is an entity? Now, if a man is something good because he is an entity, what, then, is a bad man except an evil good? When, however, we distinguish between these two concepts, we find that the bad man is not bad because he is a man, nor is he good because he is wicked. Rather, he is a good entity in so far as he is a man, evil in so far as he is wicked. Therefore, if anyone says that simply to be a man

[22] This section (Chs. III and IV) is the most explicit statement of a major motif which pervades the whole of Augustinian metaphysics. We see it in his earliest writings, *Soliloquies,* I, 2, and *De ordine,* II, 7. It is obviously a part of the Neoplatonic heritage which Augustine appropriated for his Christian philosophy. The good is positive, constructive, essential; evil is privative, destructive, parasitic on the good. It has its origin, not in nature, but in the will. Cf. *Confessions,* Bk. VII, Chs. III, V, XII–XVI; *On Continence,* 14–16; *On the Gospel of John,* Tractate XCVIII, 7; *City of God,* XI, 17; XII, 7–9.

[23] Isa. 5:20.

[24] Matt. 12:35.

is evil, or that to be a wicked man is good, he rightly falls under the prophetic judgment: "Woe to him who calls evil good and good evil." For this amounts to finding fault with God's work, because man is an entity of God's creation. It also means that we are praising the defects in this particular man *because* he is a wicked person. Thus, every entity, even if it is a defective one, in so far as it is an entity, is good. In so far as it is defective it is evil.

CHAPTER VIII

The Plight of Man After the Fall

With this much said, within the necessary brevity of this kind of treatise, as to what we need to know about the causes of good and evil—enough to lead us in the way toward the Kingdom, where there will be life without death, truth without error, happiness without anxiety—we ought not to doubt in any way that the cause of everything pertaining to our good is nothing other than the bountiful goodness of God himself. The cause of evil is the defection of the will of a being who is mutably good from the Good which is immutable. This happened first in the case of the angels and, afterward, that of man.

This was the primal lapse of the rational creature, that is, his first privation of the good. In train of this there crept in, even without his willing it, ignorance of the right things to do and also an appetite for noxious things. And these brought along with them, as their companions, error and misery. When these two evils are felt to be imminent, the soul's motion in flight from them is called fear. Moreover, as the soul's appetites are satisfied by things harmful or at least inane—and as it fails to recognize the error of its ways—it falls victim to unwholesome pleasures or may even be exhilarated by vain joys. From these tainted springs of action—moved by the lash of appetite rather than a feeling of plenty—there flows out every kind of misery which is now the lot of rational natures.

Yet such a nature, even in its evil state, could not lose its appetite for blessedness. There are the evils that both men and angels have in common, for whose wickedness God hath condemned them in simple justice. But man has a unique penalty as well: he is also punished by the death of the body. God had indeed threatened man with death as penalty if he should sin. He endowed him with freedom of the will in order that he might rule him by rational command and deter him by the threat of death. He even placed him in the happiness of paradise in a sheltered nook of life [*in umbra vitae*] where, by being a good steward of righteousness, he would rise to better things.

From this state, after he had sinned, man was banished, and through his sin he subjected his descendants to the punishment of sin and damnation, for he had radically corrupted them, in himself, by his sinning. As a consequence of this, all those descended from him and his wife (who had prompted him to sin and who was condemned along with him at the same time)—all those born through carnal lust, on whom the same penalty is visited as for disobedience—all these entered into the inheritance of original sin. Through this involvement they were led, through divers errors and sufferings (along with the rebel angels, their corruptors and possessors and companions), to that final stage of punishment without end. "Thus by one man, sin entered into the world and death through sin; and thus death came upon all men, since all men have sinned."[25] By "the world" in this passage the apostle is, of course, referring to the whole human race.

This, then, was the situation: the whole mass of the human race stood condemned, lying ruined and wallowing in evil, being plunged from evil into evil and, having joined causes with the angels who had sinned, it was paying the fully deserved penalty for impious desertion. Certainly the anger of God rests, in full justice, on the deeds that the wicked do freely in blind and unbridled lust; and it is manifest in whatever penalties they are called on to suffer, both openly and secretly. Yet the Creator's goodness does not cease to sustain life and vitality even in the evil angels, for were *this* sustenance withdrawn, they would simply cease to exist. As for mankind, although born of a corrupted and condemned stock, he still retains the power to form and animate his seed, to direct his members in their temporal order, to enliven his senses in their spatial relations,

[25] Rom. 5:12.

and to provide bodily nourishment. For God judged it better to bring good out of evil than not to permit any evil to exist. And if he had willed that there should be no reformation in the case of men, as there is none for the wicked angels, would it not have been just if the nature that deserted God and, through the evil use of his powers, trampled and transgressed the precepts of his Creator, which could have been easily kept—the same creature who stubbornly turned away from His Light and violated the image of the Creator in himself, who had in the evil use of his free will broken away from the wholesome discipline of God's law—would it not have been just if such a being had been abandoned by God wholly and forever and laid under the everlasting punishment which he deserved? Clearly God would have done this if he were only just and not also merciful and if he had not willed to show far more striking evidence of his mercy by pardoning some who were unworthy of it.

Chapter IX

The Replacement of the Fallen Angels by Elect Men; The Necessity of Grace

While some of the angels deserted God in impious pride and were cast into the lowest darkness from the brightness of their heavenly home, the remaining number of the angels persevered in eternal bliss and holiness with God. For these faithful angels were not descended from a single angel, lapsed and damned. Hence, the original evil did not bind them in the fetters of inherited guilt, nor did it hand the whole company over to a deserved punishment, as is the human lot. Instead, when he who became the devil first rose in rebellion with his impious company and was then with them prostrated, the rest of the angels stood fast in pious obedience to the Lord and so received what the others had not had—a sure knowledge of their everlasting security in his unfailing steadfastness.

Thus it pleased God, Creator and Governor of the universe, that since the whole multitude of the angels had not perished in this desertion of him, those who had perished would remain forever in perdition, but those who had remained loyal through the revolt should go on rejoicing in the certain knowledge of the bliss forever theirs. From the other part of the rational creation—that is, mankind—although it had perished as a whole through sins and punishments, both original and personal, God had determined that a portion of it would be restored and would fill up the loss which that diabolical disaster had caused in the angelic society. For this is the promise to the saints at the resurrection, that they shall be equal to the angels of God.[26]

Thus the heavenly Jerusalem, our mother and the commonwealth of God, shall not be defrauded of her full quota of citizens, but perhaps will rule over an even larger number. We know neither the number of holy men nor of the filthy demons, whose places are to be filled by the sons of the holy mother, who seemed barren in the earth, but whose sons will abide time without end in the peace the demons lost. But the number of those citizens, whether those who now belong or those who will in the future, is known to the mind of the Maker, "who calleth into existence things which are not, as though they were,"[27] and "ordereth all things in measure and number and weight."[28]

But now, can that part of the human race to whom God hath promised deliverance and a place in the eternal Kingdom be restored through the merits of their own works? Of course not! For what good works could a lost soul do except as he had been rescued from his lostness? Could he do this by the determination of his free will? Of course not! For it was in the evil use of his free will that man destroyed himself and his will at the same time. For as a man who kills himself is still alive when he kills himself, but having killed himself is then no longer alive and cannot resuscitate himself after he has destroyed his own life—so also sin which arises from the action of the free will turns out to be victor over the will and the free will is destroyed. "By whom a man is overcome, to this one he then is bound as slave."[29] This is clearly the judgment of the apostle Peter. And since it is true, I ask you what kind of liberty can one have who is bound

[26] Cf. Luke 20:36.
[27] Rom. 4:17.
[28] Wis. 11:20.
[29] II Peter 2:19.

as a slave except the liberty that loves to sin?

He serves freely who freely does the will of his master. Accordingly he who is slave to sin is free to sin. But thereafter he will not be free to do right unless he is delivered from the bondage of sin and begins to be the servant of righteousness. This, then, is true liberty: the joy that comes in doing what is right. At the same time, it is also devoted service in obedience to righteous precept.

But how would a man, bound and sold, get back his liberty to do good, unless he could regain it from Him whose voice saith, "If the Son shall make you free, then you will be free indeed"?[30] But before this process begins in man, could anyone glory in his good works as if they were acts of his free will, when he is not yet free to act rightly? He could do this only if, puffed up in proud vanity, he were merely boasting. This attitude is what the apostle was reproving when he said, "By grace you have been saved by faith."[31]

And lest men should arrogate to themselves saving faith as their own work and not understand it as a divine gift, the same apostle who says somewhere else that he had "obtained mercy of the Lord to be trustworthy"[32] makes here an additional comment: "And this is not of yourselves; rather it is a gift of God—not because of works either, lest any man should boast."[33] But then, lest it be supposed that the faithful are lacking in good works, he added further, "For we are his workmanship, created in Christ Jesus to good works, which God hath prepared beforehand for us to walk in them."[34]

We are then truly free when God ordereth our lives, that is, formeth and createth us not as men—this he hath already done—but also as good men, which he is now doing by his grace, that we may indeed be new creatures in Christ Jesus.[35] Accordingly, the prayer: "Create in me a clean heart, O God."[36] This does not mean, as far as the natural human heart is concerned, that God hath not already created this.

Once again, lest anyone glory, if not in his own works, at least in the determination of his free will, as if some merit had originated from him and as if the freedom to do good works had been bestowed on him as a kind of reward, let him hear the same herald of grace, announcing: "For it is God who is at work in you both to will and to do according to his good will."[37] And, in another place: "It is not therefore a matter of man's willing, or of his running, but of God's showing mercy."[38] Still, it is obvious that a man who is old enough to exercise his reason cannot believe, hope, or love unless he wills it, nor could he run for the prize of his high calling in God without a decision of his will. In what sense, therefore, is it "not a matter of human willing or running but of God's showing mercy," unless it be that "the will itself is prepared by the Lord," even as it is written?[39] This saying, therefore, that "it is not a matter of human willing or running but of God's showing mercy," means that the action is from both, that is to say, from the will of man and from the mercy of God. Thus we accept the dictum, "It is not a matter of human willing or running but of God's showing mercy," as if it meant, "The will of man is not sufficient by itself unless there is also the mercy of God." By the same token, the mercy of God is not sufficient by itself unless there is also the will of man. But if we say rightly that "it is not a matter of human willing or running but of God's showing mercy," because the will of man alone is not enough, why, then, is not the contrary rightly said, "It is not a matter of God's showing mercy but of a man's willing," since the mercy of God by itself alone is not enough? Now, actually, no Christian would dare to say, "It is not a matter of God's showing mercy but of man's willing," lest he explicitly contradict the apostle. The conclusion remains, therefore, that this saying: "Not man's willing or running but God's showing mercy," is to be understood to mean that the whole process is credited to God, who both prepareth the will to receive divine aid and

[30] John 8:36.
[31] Eph. 2:8.
[32] I Cor. 7:25.
[33] Eph. 2:8, 9.
[34] Eph. 2:10.
[35] Cf. Gal. 6:15; II Cor. 5:17.
[36] Ps. 51:10.
[37] Phil. 2:13.
[38] Rom. 9:16.
[39] Prov. 8:35 (LXX).

aideth the will which has been thus prepared.[40]

For a man's good will comes before many other gifts from God, but not all of them. One of the gifts it does not antedate is—just itself! Thus in the Sacred Eloquence we read both, "His mercy goes before me,"[41] and also, "His mercy shall follow me."[42] It predisposes a man before he wills, to prompt his willing. It follows the act of willing, lest one's will be frustrated. Otherwise, why are we admonished to pray for our enemies,[43] who are plainly not now willing to live piously, unless it be that God is even now at work in them and in their wills?[44] Or again, why are we admonished to ask in order to receive, unless it be that He who grants us what we will is he through whom it comes to pass that we will? We pray for enemies, therefore, that the mercy of God should go before them, as it goes before us; we pray for ourselves that his mercy shall follow us.

Chapter X

Jesus Christ the Mediator

Thus it was that the human race was bound in a just doom and all men were children of wrath. Of this wrath it is written: "For all our days are wasted; we are ruined in thy wrath; our years seem like a spider's web."[45] Likewise Job spoke of this wrath: "Man born of woman is of few days and full of trouble."[46] And even the Lord Jesus said of it: "He that believes in the Son has life everlasting, but he that believes not does not have life. Instead, the wrath of God abides in him."[47] He does not say, "It will come," but, "It now abides." Indeed every man is born into this state. Wherefore the apostle says, "For we too were by nature children of wrath even as the others."[48] Since men are in this state of wrath through original sin—a condition made still graver and more pernicious as they compounded more and worse sins with it—a Mediator was required; that is to say, a Reconciler who by offering a unique sacrifice, of which all the sacrifices of the Law and the Prophets were shadows, should allay that wrath. Thus the apostle says, "For if, when we were enemies, we were reconciled to God by the death of his Son, even more now being reconciled by his blood we shall be saved from wrath through him."[49] However, when God is said to be wrathful, this does not signify any such perturbation in him as there is in the soul of a wrathful man. His verdict, which is always just, takes the name "wrath" as a term borrowed from the language of human feelings. This, then, is the grace of God through Jesus Christ our Lord—that we are reconciled to God through the Mediator and receive the Holy Spirit so that we may be changed from enemies into sons, "for as many as are led by the Spirit of God, they are the sons of God."[50]

It would take too long to say all that would be truly worthy of this Mediator. Indeed, men cannot speak properly of such matters. For who can unfold in cogent enough fashion this statement, that "the Word became flesh and

[40] From the days at Cassiciacum till the very end, Augustine toiled with the mystery of the primacy of God's grace and the reality of human freedom. Of two things he was unwaveringly sure, even though they involved him in a paradox and the appearance of confusion. The first is that God's grace is not only primary but also sufficient as the ground and source of human willing. And against the Pelagians and other detractors from grace, he did not hesitate to insist that grace is irresistible and inviolable. Cf. *On Grace and Free Will,* 29, 41–43; *On the Predestination of the Saints,* 19:10; *On the Gift of Perseverance,* 41; *On the Soul and Its Origin,* 16; and even the *Enchiridion,* XXIV, 97.

But he never drew from this deterministic emphasis the conclusion that man is unfree and everywhere roundly rejects the not illogical corollary of his theonomism, that man's will counts for little or nothing except as passive agent of God's will. He insists on responsibility on man's part in responding to the initiatives of grace. For this emphasis, which is characteristically directed to the faithful themselves, see *On the Psalms,* LXVIII, 7–8; *On the Gospel of John,* Tractate, 53:6–8; and even his severest anti-Pelagian tracts: *On Grace and Free Will,* 6–8, 10, 31 and *On Admonition and Grace,* 2–8.

[41] Ps. 58:11 (Vulgate).

[42] Ps. 23:6.

[43] Cf. Matt. 5:44.

[44] The theme that he had explored in *Confessions,* Bks. I–IX. See especially Bk. V, Chs. X, XIII; Bk. VII, Ch. VIII; Bk. IX, Ch. I.

[45] Cf. Ps. 90:9.

[46] Job 14:1.

[47] John 3:36.

[48] Eph. 2:3.

[49] Rom. 5:9, 10.

[50] Rom. 8:14.

dwelt among us,"[51] so that we should then believe in "the only Son of God the Father Almighty, born of the Holy Spirit and Mary the Virgin." Yet it is indeed true that the Word was made flesh, the flesh being assumed by the Divinity, not the Divinity being changed into flesh. Of course, by the term "flesh" we ought here to understand "man," an expression in which the part signifies the whole, just as it is said, "Since by the works of the law no flesh shall be justified,"[52] which is to say, no *man* shall be justified. Yet certainly we must say that in that assumption nothing was lacking that belongs to human nature.

But it was a nature entirely free from the bonds of all sin. It was not a nature born of both sexes with fleshly desires, with the burden of sin, the guilt of which is washed away in regeneration. Instead, it was the kind of nature that would be fittingly born of a virgin, conceived by His mother's faith and not her fleshly desires. Now if in his being born, her virginity had been destroyed, he would not then have been born of a virgin. It would then be false (which is unthinkable) for the whole Church to confess him "born of the Virgin Mary." This is the Church which, imitating his mother, daily gives birth to his members yet remains virgin. Read, if you please, my letter on the virginity of Saint Mary written to that illustrious man, Volusianus, whom I name with honor and affection.[53]

Christ Jesus, Son of God, is thus both God and man. He was God before all ages; he is man in this age of ours. He is God because he is the Word of God, for "the Word was God."[54] Yet he is man also, since in the unity of his Person a rational soul and body is joined to the Word.

Accordingly, in so far as he is God, he and the Father are one. Yet in so far as he is man, the Father is greater than he. Since he was God's only Son—not by grace but by nature—to the end that he might indeed be the fullness of all grace, he was also made Son of Man—and yet he was in the one nature as well as in the other, one Christ. "For being in the form of God, he judged it not a violation to be what he was by nature, the equal of God. Yet he emptied himself, taking on the form of a servant,"[55] yet neither losing nor diminishing the form of God.[56] Thus he was made less and remained equal, and both these in a unity as we said before. But he is one of these because he is the Word; the other, because he was a man. As the Word, he is the equal of the Father; as a man, he is less. He is the one Son of God, and at the same time Son of Man; the one Son of Man, and at the same time God's Son. These are not two sons of God, one God and the other man, but *one* Son of God—God without origin, man with a definite origin—our Lord Jesus Christ.

Chapter XI

The Incarnation as Prime Example of the Action of God's Grace

In this the grace of God is supremely manifest, commended in grand and visible fashion; for what had the human nature in the man Christ merited, that it, and no other, should be assumed into the unity of the Person of the only Son of God? What good will, what zealous strivings, what good works preceded this assumption by which that particular man deserved to become one Person with God? Was he a man before the union, and was this singular grace given him as to one particularly deserving before God? Of course not! For, from the moment he began to be a man, that man began to be nothing other than God's Son, the only Son, and this because the Word of God assuming him became flesh, yet still assuredly remained God. Just as every man is a personal unity—that is, a unity of rational soul and flesh—so also is Christ a personal unity: Word and man.

Why should there be such great glory to a human nature—and this undoubtedly an act of

[51] John 1:14.

[52] Rom. 3:20.

[53] *Epistle* CXXXVII, written in 412 in reply to a list of queries sent to Augustine by the proconsul of Africa.

[54] John 1:1.

[55] Phil. 2:6, 7.

[56] These metaphors for contrasting the "two natures" of Jesus Christ were favorite figures of speech in Augustine's Christological thought. Cf. *On the Gospel of John,* Tractate 78; *On the Trinity,* I, 7; II, 2; IV, 19–20; VII, 3; *New Testament Sermons,* 76, 14.

grace, no merit preceding it—unless it be that those who consider such a question faithfully and soberly might have here a clear manifestation of God's great and sole grace, and this in order that they might understand how they themselves are justified from their sins by the selfsame grace which made it so that the man Christ had no power to sin? Thus indeed the angel hailed his mother when announcing to her the future birth: "Hail," he said, "full of grace." And shortly thereafter, "You have found favor with God."[57] And this was said of her, that she was full of grace, since she was to be mother of her Lord, indeed the Lord of all. Yet, concerning Christ himself, when the Evangelist John said, "And the Word became flesh and dwelt among us," he added, "and we beheld his glory, a glory as of the only Son of the Father, full of grace and truth."[58] When he said, "The Word was made flesh," this means, "Full of grace." When he also said, "The glory of the only begotten of the Father," this means, "Full of truth." Indeed it was Truth himself, God's only-begotten Son—and, again, this not by grace but by nature—who, by grace, assumed human nature into such a personal unity that he himself became the Son of Man as well.

This same Jesus Christ, God's one and only Son our Lord, was born of the Holy Spirit and the Virgin Mary. Now obviously the Holy Spirit is God's gift, a gift that is itself equal to the Giver; wherefore the Holy Spirit is God also, not inferior to the Father and the Son. Now what does this mean, that Christ's birth in respect to his human nature was of the Holy Spirit, save that this was itself also a work of grace?

For when the Virgin asked of the angel the manner by which what he announced would come to pass (since she had known no man), the angel answered: "The Holy Spirit shall come upon you and the power of the Most High shall overshadow you; therefore the Holy One which shall be born of you shall be called the Son of God."[59] And when Joseph wished to put her away, suspecting adultery (since he knew she was not pregnant by him), he received a similar answer from the angel: "Do not fear to take Mary as your wife; for that which is conceived in her is of the Holy Spirit"[60]—that is, "What you suspect is from another man is of the Holy Spirit."

Chapter XII

The Role of the Holy Spirit

Are we, then, to say that the Holy Spirit is the Father of Christ's human nature, so that as God the Father generated the Word, so the Holy Spirit generated the human nature, and that from both natures Christ came to be one, Son of God the Father as the Word, Son of the Holy Spirit as man? Do we suppose that the Holy Spirit is his Father through begetting him of the Virgin Mary? Who would dare to say such a thing? There is no need to show by argument how many absurd consequences such a notion has, when it is so absurd in itself that no believer's ear can bear to hear it. Actually, then, as we confess our Lord Jesus Christ, who is God from God yet born as man of the Holy Spirit and the Virgin Mary, there is in each nature (in both the divine and the human) the only Son of God the Father Almighty, from whom proceeds the Holy Spirit.

How, then, do we say that Christ is born of the Holy Spirit, if the Holy Spirit did not beget him? Is it because he made him? This might be, since through our Lord Jesus Christ—in the form of God—all things were made. Yet in so far as he is man, he himself was made, even as the apostle says: "He was made of the seed of David according to the flesh."[61] But since that creature which the Virgin conceived and bore, though it was related to the Person of the Son alone, was made by the whole Trinity—for the works of the Trinity are not separable—why is the Holy Spirit named as the One who made it? Is it, perhaps, that when any One of the Three is named in connection with some divine action, the whole Trinity is to be understood as involved in that action? This is true and can be shown by examples, but we should not dwell too long on this kind of solution.

[57] Luke 1:28–30.
[58] John 1:14.
[59] Luke 1:35.
[60] Matt. 1:20.
[61] Rom. 1:3.

For what still concerns us is how it can be said, "Born of the Holy Spirit," when he is in no wise the Son of the Holy Spirit? Now, just because God made [*fecit*] this world, one could not say that the world is the son of God, or that it is "born" of God. Rather, one says it was "made" or "created" or "founded" or "established" by him, or however else one might like to speak of it. So, then, when we confess, "Born of the Holy Spirit and the Virgin Mary," the sense in which he is not the Son of the Holy Spirit and yet is the son of the Virgin Mary, when he was born both of him and of her, is difficult to explain. But there is no doubt as to the fact that he was not born from him as Father as he was born of her as mother.

Consequently we should not grant that whatever is born of something should therefore be called the son of that thing. Let us pass over the fact that a son is "born" of a man in a different sense than a hair is, or a louse, or a maw worm—none of these is a son. Let us pass over these things, since they are an unfitting analogy in so great a matter. Yet it is certain that those who are born of water and of the Holy Spirit would not properly be called sons of the water by anyone. But it does make sense to call them sons of God the Father and of Mother Church. Thus, therefore, the one born of the Holy Spirit is the son of God the Father, not of the Holy Spirit.

What we said about the hair and the other things has this much relevance, that it reminds us that not everything which is "born" of something is said to be "son" to him from which it is "born." Likewise, it does not follow that those who are called sons of someone are always said to have been born of him, since there are some who are adopted. Even those who are called "sons of Gehenna" are not born *of* it, but have been destined *for* it, just as the sons of the Kingdom are destined for that.

Wherefore, since a thing may be "born" of something else, yet not in the fashion of a "son," and conversely, since not everyone who is called son is born of him whose son he is called—this is the very mode in which Christ was "born" of the Holy Spirit (yet not as a son), and of the Virgin Mary as a son—this suggests to us the grace of God by which a certain human person, no merit whatever preceding, at the very outset of his existence, was joined to the Word of God in such a unity of person that the selfsame one who is Son of Man should be Son of God, and the one who is Son of God should be Son of Man. Thus, in his assumption of human nature, grace came to be natural to that nature, allowing no power to sin. This is why grace is signified by the Holy Spirit, because he himself is so perfectly God that he is also called God's Gift. Still, to speak adequately of this—even if one could—would call for a very long discussion.

Chapter XIII

Baptism and Original Sin

Since he was begotten and conceived in no pleasure of carnal appetite—and therefore bore no trace of original sin—he was, by the grace of God (operating in a marvelous and an ineffable manner), joined and united in a personal unity with the only-begotten Word of the Father, a Son not by grace but by nature. And although he himself committed no sin, yet because of "the likeness of sinful flesh"[62] in which he came, he was himself called sin and was made a sacrifice for the washing away of sins.

Indeed, under the old law, sacrifices for sins were often called sins.[63] Yet he of whom those sacrifices were mere shadows was himself actually made sin. Thus, when the apostle said, "For Christ's sake, we beseech you to be reconciled to God," he straightway added, "Him, who knew no sin, he made to be sin for us that we might be made to be the righteousness of God in him."[64] He does not say, as we read in some defective copies, "He who knew no sin did sin for us," as if Christ himself committed sin for our sake. Rather, he says, "He [Christ] who knew no sin, he [God] made to be sin for us." The God to whom we are to be reconciled hath thus made him the sacrifice for sin by which we may be reconciled.

He himself is therefore sin as we ourselves are righteousness—not our own but God's, not in ourselves but in him. Just as he was sin—not his own but ours, rooted not in himself but

[62] Rom. 8:3.
[63] Cf. Hos. 4:8.
[64] II Cor. 5:20, 21.

in us—so he showed forth through the likeness of sinful flesh, in which he was crucified, that since sin was not in him he could then, so to say, die to sin by dying in the flesh, which was "the likeness of sin." And since he had never lived in the old manner of sinning, he might, in his resurrection, signify the new life which is ours, which is springing to life anew from the old death in which we had been dead to sin.

This is the meaning of the great sacrament of baptism, which is celebrated among us. All who attain to this grace die thereby to sin—as he himself is said to have died to sin because he died in the flesh, that is, "in the likeness of sin"—and they are thereby alive by being reborn in the baptismal font, just as he rose again from the sepulcher. This is the case no matter what the age of the body.

For whether it be a newborn infant or a decrepit old man—since no one should be barred from baptism—just so, there is no one who does not die to sin in baptism. Infants die to original sin only; adults, to all those sins which they have added, through their evil living, to the burden they brought with them at birth.

But even these are frequently said to die to sin, when without doubt they die not to one but to many sins, and to all the sins which they have themselves already committed by thought, word, and deed. Actually, by the use of the singular number the plural number is often signified, as the poet said,

> "And they fill the belly with the armed warrior,"[65]

although they did this with many warriors. And in our own Scriptures we read: "Pray therefore to the Lord that he may take from us the serpent."[66] It does not say "serpents," as it might, for they were suffering from many serpents. There are, moreover, innumerable other such examples.

Yet, when the original sin is signified by the use of the plural number, as we say when infants are baptized "unto the remission of sins," instead of saying "unto the remission of sin," then we have the converse expression in which the singular is expressed by the plural number. Thus in the Gospel, it is said of Herod's death, "For they are dead who sought the child's life";[67] it does not say, "He is dead." And in Exodus: "They made," [Moses] says, "to themselves gods of gold," when they had made one calf. And of this calf, they said: "These are thy gods, O Israel, which brought you out of the land of Egypt,"[68] here also putting the plural for the singular.

Still, even in that one sin—which "entered into the world by one man and so spread to all men,"[69] and on account of which infants are baptized—one can recognize a plurality of sins, if that single sin is divided, so to say, into its separate elements. For there is pride in it, since man preferred to be under his own rule rather than the rule of God; and sacrilege too, for man did not acknowledge God; and murder, since he cast himself down to death; and spiritual fornication, for the integrity of the human mind was corrupted by the seduction of the serpent; and theft, since the forbidden fruit was snatched; and avarice, since he hungered for more than should have sufficed for him—and whatever other sins that could be discovered in the diligent analysis of that one sin.

It is also said—and not without support—that infants are involved in the sins of their parents, not only of the first pair, but even of their own, of whom they were born. Indeed, that divine judgment, "I shall visit the sins of the fathers on their children,"[70] definitely applies to them before they come into the New Covenant by regeneration. This Covenant was foretold by Ezekiel when he said that the sons should not bear their fathers' sins, nor the proverb any longer apply in Israel, "Our fathers have eaten sour grapes and the children's teeth are set on edge."[71]

This is why each one of them must be born again, so that he may thereby be absolved of whatever sin was in him at the time of birth. For the sins committed by evil-doing after birth can be healed by repentance—as, indeed, we see it happen even after baptism. For the new birth [*regeneratio*] would not have been

[65] Virgil, *Aeneid,* II, 1, 20.
[66] Num. 21:7 (LXX).
[67] Matt. 2:20.
[68] Ex. 32:4.
[69] Rom. 5:12.
[70] Deut. 5:9.
[71] Ezek. 18:2.

instituted except for the fact that the first birth [*generatio*] was tainted—and to such a degree that one born of even a lawful wedlock said, "I was conceived in iniquities; and in sins did my mother nourish me in her womb."[72] Nor did he say "in iniquity" or "in sin," as he might have quite correctly; rather, he preferred to say "iniquities" and "sins," because, as I explained above, there are so many sins in that one sin—which has passed into all men, and which was so great that human nature was changed and by it brought under the necessity of death—and also because there are other sins, such as those of parents, which, even if they cannot change our nature in the same way, still involve the children in guilt, unless the gracious grace and mercy of God interpose.

But, in the matter of the sins of one's other parents, those who stand as one's forebears from Adam down to one's own parents, a question might well be raised: whether a man at birth is involved in the evil deeds of all his forebears, and their multiplied original sins, so that the later in time he is born, the worse estate he is born in; or whether, on this very account, God threatens to visit the sins of the parents as far as—but no farther than—the third and fourth generations, because in his mercy he will not continue his wrath beyond that. It is not his purpose that those not given the grace of regeneration be crushed under too heavy a burden in their eternal damnation, as they would be if they were bound to bear, as original guilt, all the sins of their ancestors from the beginning of the human race, and to pay the due penalty for them. Whether yet another solution to so difficult a problem might or might not be found by a more diligent search and interpretation of Holy Scripture, I dare not rashly affirm.

Chapter XIV

The Mysteries of Christ's Mediatorial Work and Justification

That one sin, however, committed in a setting of such great happiness, was itself so great that by it, in one man, the whole human race was originally and, so to say, radically condemned. It cannot be pardoned and washed away except through "the one mediator between God and men, the man Christ Jesus,"[73] who alone could be born in such a way as not to need to be reborn.

They were not reborn, those who were baptized by John's baptism, by which Christ himself was baptized.[74] Rather, they were *prepared* by the ministry of this forerunner, who said, "Prepare a way for the Lord,"[75] for Him in whom alone they could be reborn.

For his baptism is not with water alone, as John's was, but with the Holy Spirit as well. Thus, whoever believes in Christ is reborn by that same Spirit, of whom Christ also was born, needing not to be reborn. This is the reason for the Voice of the Father spoken over him at his baptism, "Today have I begotten thee,"[76] which pointed not to that particular day on which he was baptized, but to that "day" of changeless eternity, in order to show us that this Man belonged to the personal Unity of the Only Begotten. For a day that neither begins with the close of yesterday nor ends with the beginning of tomorrow is indeed an eternal "today."

Therefore, he chose to be baptized in water by John, not thereby to wash away any sin of his own, but to manifest his great humility. Indeed, baptism found nothing in him to wash away, just as death found nothing to punish. Hence, it was in authentic justice, and not by violent power, that the devil was overcome and conquered: for, as he had most unjustly slain Him who was in no way deserving of death, he also did most justly lose those whom he had justly held in bondage as punishment for their sins. Wherefore, He took upon himself both baptism and death, not out of a piteous necessity but through his own free act of showing mercy—as part of a definite plan whereby One might take away the sin of the world, just as one man had brought sin into the world, that is, the whole human race.

There is a difference, however. The first man brought sin into the world, whereas this One took away not only that one sin but also all the

[72] Ps. 51:5.
[73] I Tim. 2:5.
[74] Matt. 3:13.
[75] Luke 3:4; Isa. 40:3.
[76] Ps. 2:7; Heb. 5:5; cf. Mark 1:9–11.

others which he found added to it. Hence, the apostle says, "And the gift [of grace] is not like the effect of the one that sinned: for the judgment on that one trespass was condemnation; but the gift of grace is for many offenses, and brings justification."[77] Now it is clear that the one sin originally inherited, even if it were the only one involved, makes men liable to condemnation. Yet grace justifies a man for many offenses, both the sin which he originally inherited in common with all the others and also the multitude of sins which he has committed on his own.

However, when he [the apostle] says, shortly after, "Therefore, as the offense of one man led all men to condemnation, so also the righteousness of one man leads all men to the life of justification,"[78] he indicates sufficiently that everyone born of Adam is subject to damnation, and no one, unless reborn of Christ, is free from such a damnation.

And after this discussion of punishment through one man and grace through the Other, as he deemed sufficient for that part of the epistle, the apostle passes on to speak of the great mystery of holy baptism in the cross of Christ, and to do this so that we may understand nothing other in the baptism of Christ than the likeness of the death of Christ. The death of Christ crucified is nothing other than the likeness of the forgiveness of sins—so that in the very same sense in which the death is real, so also is the forgiveness of our sins real, and in the same sense in which his resurrection is real, so also in us is there authentic justification.

He asks: "What, then, shall we say? Shall we continue in sin, that grace may abound?"[79] —for he had previously said, "But where sin abounded, grace did much more abound."[80] And therefore he himself raised the question whether, because of the abundance of grace that follows sin, one should then continue in sin. But he answers, "God forbid!" and adds, "How shall we, who are dead to sin, live any longer therein?"[81] Then, to show that we are dead to sin, "Do you not know that all we who were baptized in Christ Jesus were baptized into his death?"[82]

If, therefore, the fact that we are baptized into the death of Christ shows that we are dead to sin, then certainly infants who are baptized in Christ die to sin, since they are baptized into his own death. For there is no exception in the saying, "All we who are baptized into Christ Jesus are baptized into his death." And the effect of this is to show that we are dead to sin.

Yet what sin do infants die to in being reborn except that which they inherit in being born? What follows in the epistle also pertains to this: "Therefore we were buried with him by baptism into death; that, as Christ was raised up from the dead by the glory of the Father, even so we also should walk in the newness of life. For if we have been united with him in the likeness of his death, we shall be also united with him in the likeness of his resurrection, knowing this, that our old man is crucified with him, that the body of sin might be destroyed, that henceforth we should not serve sin. For he that is dead is freed from sin. Now if we are dead with Christ, we believe that we shall also live with him: knowing that Christ, being raised from the dead, dies no more; death has no more dominion over him. For the death he died, he died to sin, once for all; but the life he lives, he lives unto God. So also, reckon yourselves also to be dead to sin, but alive unto God through Christ Jesus."[83]

Now, he had set out to prove that we should not go on sinning, in order that thereby grace might abound, and had said, "If we have died to sin, how, then, shall we go on living in it?" And then to show that we were dead to sin, he had added, "Know you not, that as many of us as were baptized into Jesus Christ were baptized into his death?" Thus he concludes the passage as he began it. Indeed, he introduced the death of Christ in order to say that even he died to sin. To what sin, save that of the flesh in which he existed, not as sinner, but in "the likeness of sin" and which was, therefore, called by the name of sin? Thus, to those

[77] Rom. 5:16.
[78] Rom. 5:18.
[79] Rom. 6:1.
[80] Rom. 5:20.
[81] Rom. 6:2.
[82] Rom. 6:3.
[83] Rom. 6:4–11.

baptized into the death of Christ—into which not only adults but infants as well are baptized —he says, "So also you should reckon yourselves to be dead to sin, but alive to God in Christ Jesus."

Whatever was done, therefore, in the crucifixion of Christ, his burial, his resurrection on the third day, his ascension into heaven, his being seated at the Father's right hand—all these things were done thus, that they might not only signify their mystical meanings but also serve as a model for the Christian life which we lead here on the earth. Thus, of his crucifixion it was said, "And they that are Jesus Christ's have crucified their own flesh, with the passions and lusts thereof";[84] and of his burial, "For we are buried with Christ by baptism into death"; of his resurrection, "Since Christ is raised from the dead through the glory of the Father, so we also should walk with him in newness of life"; of his ascension and session at the Father's right hand: "But if you have risen again with Christ, seek the things which are above, where Christ is sitting at the right hand of God. Set your affection on things above, not on things on the earth. For you are dead, and your life is hid with Christ in God."[85]

Now what we believe concerning Christ's future actions, since we confess that he will come again from heaven to judge the living and the dead, does not pertain to this life of ours as we live it here on earth, because it belongs not to his deeds already done, but to what he will do at the close of the age. To this the apostle refers and goes on to add, "When Christ, who is your life, shall appear, you shall then also appear with him in glory."[86]

There are two ways to interpret the affirmation that he "shall judge the living and the dead." On the one hand, we may understand by "the living" those who are not yet dead but who will be found living in the flesh when he comes; and we may understand by "the dead" those who have left the body, or who shall have left it before his coming. Or, on the other hand, "the living" may signify "the righteous," and "the dead" may signify "the unrighteous" —since the righteous are to be judged as well as the unrighteous. For sometimes the judgment of God is passed upon the evil, as in the word, "But they who have done evil [shall come forth] to the resurrection of judgment."[87] And sometimes it is passed upon the good, as in the word, "Save me, O God, by thy name, and judge me in thy strength."[88] Indeed, it is by the judgment of God that the distinction between good and evil is made, to the end that, being freed from evil and not destroyed with the evildoers, the good may be set apart at his right hand.[89] This is why the psalmist cried, "Judge me, O God," and, as if to explain what he had said, "and defend my cause against an unholy nation."[90]

Chapter XV

The Holy Spirit and the Church

Now, when we have spoken of Jesus Christ, the only Son of God our Lord, in the brevity befitting our confession of faith, we go on to affirm that we believe also in the Holy Spirit, as completing the Trinity which is God; and after that we call to mind our faith "in holy Church." By this we are given to understand that the rational creation belonging to the free Jerusalem ought to be mentioned in a subordinate order to the Creator, that is, the supreme Trinity. For, of course, all that has been said about the man Christ Jesus refers to the unity of the Person of the Only Begotten.

Thus, the right order of the Creed demanded[91] that the Church be made subordinate to the Trinity, as a house is subordinate to him who dwells in it, the temple to God, and the city to its founder. By the Church here we are to understand the whole Church, not just the part that journeys here on earth from rising of the sun to its setting, praising the name of the Lord[92] and singing a new song of deliverance from its old captivity, but also that part which, in heaven, has always, from creation, held fast

[84] Gal. 5:24.
[85] Col. 3:1–3.
[86] Col. 3:4.
[87] John 5:29.
[88] Ps. 54:1.
[89] Cf. Matt. 25:32, 33.
[90] Ps. 43:1.
[91] Reading the classical Latin form *poscebat* (as in Scheel and *PL*) for the late form *poxebat* (as in Rivière and many old MSS.).
[92] Cf. Ps. 113:3.

to God, and which never experienced the evils of a fall. This part, composed of the holy angels, remains in blessedness, and it gives help, even as it ought, to the other part still on pilgrimage. For both parts together will make one eternal consort, as even now they are one in the bond of love—the whole instituted for the proper worship of the one God.[93] Wherefore, neither the whole Church nor any part of it wishes to be worshiped as God nor to be God to anyone belonging to the temple of God—the temple that is being built up of "the gods" whom the uncreated God created.[94] Consequently, if the Holy Spirit were creature and not Creator, he would obviously be a rational creature, for this is the highest of the levels of creation. But in this case he would not be set in the rule of faith *before* the Church, since he would then belong *to* the Church, in that part of it which is in heaven. He would not have a temple, for he himself would be a temple. Yet, in fact, he hath a temple of which the apostle speaks, "Know you not that your body is the temple of the Holy Spirit, who is in you, whom you have from God?"[95] In another place, he says of this body, "Know you not that your bodies are members of Christ?"[96] How, then, is he not God who has a temple? Or how can he be less than Christ whose members are his temple? It is not that he has one temple and God another temple, since the same apostle says: "Know you not that you are the temple of God," and then, as if to prove his point, added, "and that the Spirit of God dwelleth in you?"

God therefore dwelleth in his temple, not the Holy Spirit only, but also Father and Son, who saith of his body—in which he standeth as Head of the Church on earth "that in all things he may be pre-eminent"[97]—"Destroy this temple and in three days I will raise it up again."[98] Therefore, the temple of God—that is, of the supreme Trinity as a whole—is holy Church, the Universal Church in heaven and on the earth.

But what can we affirm about that part of the Church in heaven, save that in it no evil is to be found, nor any apostates, nor will there be again, since that time when "God did not spare the sinning angels"—as the apostle Peter writes—"but casting them out, he delivered them into the prisons of darkness in hell, to be reserved for the sentence in the Day of Judgment"?[99]

Still, how is life ordered in that most blessed and supernal society? What differences are there in rank among the angels, so that while all are called by the general title "angels"—as we read in the Epistle to the Hebrews, "But to which of the angels said he at any time, 'Sit at my right hand'?";[1] this expression clearly signifies that all are angels without exception—yet there are archangels there as well? Again, should these archangels be called "powers" [*virtutes*], so that the verse, "Praise him, all his angels; praise him, all his powers,"[2] would mean the same thing as, "Praise him, all his angels; praise him, all his archangels"? Or, what distinctions are implied by the four designations by which the apostle seems to encompass the entire heavenly society, "Be they thrones or dominions, principalities, or powers"?[3] Let them answer these questions who can, if they can indeed prove their answers. For myself, I confess to ignorance of such matters. I am not even certain about another question: whether the sun and moon and all the stars belong to that same heavenly society—although they seem to be nothing more than luminous bodies, with neither perception nor understanding.

Furthermore, who can explain the kind of bodies in which the angels appeared to men, so that they were not only visible, but tangible as well? And, again, how do they, not by impact of physical stimulus but by spiritual force,

[93] Here reading *unum deum* (with Rivière and *PL*) against *deum* (in Scheel).

[94] A hyperbolic expression referring to "the saints." Augustine's Scriptural backing for such an unusual phrase is Ps. 82:6 and John 10:34f. But note the firm distinction between *ex diis quos facit* and *non factus Deus*.

[95] I Cor. 6:19.

[96] I Cor. 6:15.

[97] Col. 1:18.

[98] John 2:19.

[99] II Peter 2:4 (Old Latin).

[1] Heb. 1:13.

[2] Ps. 148:2 (LXX).

[3] Col. 1:16.

bring certain visions, not to the physical eyes but to the spiritual eyes of the mind, or speak something, not to the ears, as from outside us, but actually from within the human soul, since they are present within it too? For, as it is written in the book of the Prophets: "And the angel that spoke in me, said to me . . ."[4] He does not say, "Spoke *to* me" but "Spoke *in* me." How do they appear to men in sleep, and communicate through dreams, as we read in the Gospel: "Behold, the angel of the Lord appeared to him in his sleep, saying . . ."?[5] By these various modes of presentation, the angels seem to indicate that they do not have tangible bodies. Yet this raises a very difficult question: How, then, did the patriarchs wash the angels' feet?[6] How, also, did Jacob wrestle with the angel in such a tangible fashion?[7]

To ask such questions as these, and to guess at the answers as one can, is not a useless exercise in speculation, so long as the discussion is moderate and one avoids the mistake of those who think they know what they do not know.

Chapter XVI

Problems About Heavenly and Earthly Divisions of the Church

It is more important to be able to discern and tell when Satan transforms himself as an angel of light, lest by this deception he should seduce us into harmful acts. For, when he deceives the corporeal senses, and does not thereby turn the mind from that true and right judgment by which one leads the life of faith, there is no danger to religion. Or if, feigning himself to be good, he does or says things that would fit the character of the good angels, even if then we believe him good, the error is neither dangerous nor fatal to the Christian faith. But when, by these alien wiles, he begins to lead us into his own ways, then great vigilance is required to recognize him and not follow after. But how few men are there who are able to avoid his deadly stratagems, unless God guides and preserves them! Yet the very difficulty of this business is useful in this respect: it shows that no man should rest his hopes in himself, nor one man in another, but all who are God's should cast their hopes on him. And that this latter is obviously the best course for us no pious man would deny.

This part of the Church, therefore, which is composed of the holy angels and powers of God will become known to us as it really is only when, at the end of the age, we are joined to it, to possess, together with it, eternal bliss. But the other part which, separated from this heavenly company, wanders through the earth is better known to us because we are in it, and because it is composed of men like ourselves. This is the part that has been redeemed from all sin by the blood of the sinless Mediator, and its cry is: "If God be for us, who is against us? He that spared not his own Son, but delivered him up for us all. . . ."[8] Now Christ did not die for the angels. But still, what was done for man by his death for man's redemption and his deliverance from evil was done for the angels also, because by it the enmity caused by sin between men and the angels is removed and friendship restored. Moreover, this redemption of mankind serves to repair the ruins left by the angelic apostasy.

Of course, the holy angels, taught by God—in the eternal contemplation of whose truth they are blessed—know how many of the human race are required to fill up the full census of that commonwealth. This is why the apostle says "that all things are restored to unity in Christ, both those in heaven and those on the earth in him."[9] The part in heaven is indeed restored when the number lost from the angelic apostasy are replaced from the ranks of mankind. The part on earth is restored when those men predestined to eternal life are redeemed from the old state of corruption.

Thus by the single sacrifice, of which the many victims of the law were only shadows, the heavenly part is set at peace with the earthly part and the earthly reconciled to the heavenly. Wherefore, as the same apostle says: "For it pleased God that all plenitude of being should dwell in him and by him to reconcile

[4] Zech. 1:9.
[5] Matt. 1:20.
[6] Gen. 18:4; 19:2.
[7] Gen. 32:24.
[8] Rom. 8:31, 32.
[9] Cf. Eph. 1:10.

all things to himself, making peace with them by the blood of his cross, whether those things on earth or those in heaven."[10]

This peace, as it is written, "passes all understanding." It cannot be known by us until we have entered into it. For how is the heavenly realm set at peace, save together with us; that is, by concord with us? For in that realm there is always peace, both among the whole company of rational creatures and between them and their Creator. This is the peace that, as it is said, "passes all understanding." But obviously this means *our* understanding, not that of those who always see the Father's face. For no matter how great our understanding may be, "we know in part, and we see in a glass darkly."[11] But when we shall have become "equal to God's angels,"[12] then, even as they do, "we shall see face to face."[13] And we shall then have as great amity toward them as they have toward us; for we shall come to love them as much as we are loved by them.

In this way their peace will become known to us, since ours will be like theirs in kind and measure—nor will it then surpass our understanding. But the peace of God, which is there, will still doubtless surpass our understanding and theirs as well. For, of course, in so far as a rational creature is blessed, this blessedness comes, not from himself, but from God. Hence, it follows that it is better to interpret the passage, "The peace of God which passes all understanding," so that from the word "all" not even the understanding of the holy angels should be excepted. Only God's understanding is excepted; for, of course, his peace does not surpass his own understanding.

Chapter XVII

Forgiveness of Sins in the Church

The angels are in concord with us even now, when our sins are forgiven. Therefore, in the order of the Creed, after the reference to "holy Church" is placed the reference to "forgiveness of sins." For it is by this that the part of the Church on earth stands; it is by this that "what was lost and is found again"[14] is not lost again. Of course, the gift of baptism is an exception. It is an antidote given us against original sin, so that what is contracted by birth is removed by the new birth—though it also takes away actual sins as well, whether of heart, word, or deed. But except for this great remission—the beginning point of a man's renewal, in which all guilt, inherited and acquired, is washed away—the rest of life, from the age of accountability (and no matter how vigorously we progress in righteousness), is not without the need for the forgiveness of sins. This is the case because the sons of God, as long as they live this mortal life, are in a conflict with death. And although it is truly said of them, "As many as are led by the Spirit of God, they are the sons of God,"[15] yet even as they are being led by the Spirit of God and, as sons of God, advance toward God, they are also being led by their own spirits so that, weighed down by the corruptible body and influenced by certain human feelings, they thus fall away from themselves and commit sin. But it matters *how much*. Although every crime is a sin, not every sin is a crime. Thus we can say of the life of holy men even while they live in this mortality, that they are found without crime. "But if we say that we have no sin," as the great apostle says, "we deceive even ourselves, and the truth is not in us."[16]

Nevertheless, no matter how great our crimes, their forgiveness should never be despaired of in holy Church for those who truly repent, each according to the measure of his sin. And, in the act of repentance,[17] where a crime has been committed of such gravity as also to cut off the sinner from the body of Christ, we should not consider the measure of time as much as the measure of sorrow. For, "a contrite and humbled heart God will not despise."[18]

Still, since the sorrow of one heart is mostly hid from another, and does not come to notice through words and other such signs—even

[10] Col. 1:19, 20.
[11] Cf. I Cor. 13:9, 12.
[12] Cf. Luke 20:36.
[13] I Cor. 13:12.
[14] Cf. Luke 15:24.
[15] Rom. 8:14.
[16] I John 1:8.
[17] In *actione poenitentiae;* cf. Luther's similar conception of *poenitentiam agite* in the *95 Theses* and in *De poenitentia.*
[18] Ps. 51:17.

when it is plain to Him of whom it is said, "My groaning is not hid from thee"[19]—times of repentance have been rightly established by those set over the churches, that satisfaction may also be made in the Church, in which the sins are forgiven. For, of course, outside her they are not forgiven. For she alone has received the pledge of the Holy Spirit,[20] without whom there is no forgiveness of sins. Those forgiven thus obtain life everlasting.

Now the remission of sins has chiefly to do with the future judgment. In this life the Scripture saying holds true: "A heavy yoke is on the sons of Adam, from the day they come forth from their mother's womb till the day of their burial in the mother of us all."[21] Thus we see even infants, after the washing of regeneration, tortured by divers evil afflictions. This helps us to understand that the whole import of the sacraments of salvation has to do more with the hope of future goods than with the retaining or attaining of present goods.

Indeed, many sins seem to be ignored and go unpunished; but their punishment is reserved for the future. It is not in vain that the day when the Judge of the living and the dead shall come is rightly called the Day of Judgment. Just so, on the other hand, some sins are punished here, and, if they are forgiven, will certainly bring no harm upon us in the future age. Hence, referring to certain temporal punishments, which are visited upon sinners in this life, the apostle, speaking to those whose sins are blotted out and not reserved to the end, says: "For if we judge ourselves truly we should not be judged by the Lord. But when we are judged, we are chastised by the Lord, that we may not be condemned along with this world."[22]

Chapter XXVII

Limits of God's Plan for Human Salvation

When we hear and read in sacred Scripture that God "willeth that all men should be saved,"[23] although we know well enough that not all men are saved, we are not on that account to underrate the fully omnipotent will of God. Rather, we must understand the Scripture, "Who will have all men to be saved," as meaning that no man is saved unless God willeth his salvation: not that there is no man whose salvation he doth not will, but that no one is saved unless He willeth it. Moreover, his will should be sought in prayer, because if he willeth, then what he willeth must necessarily be. And, indeed, it was of prayer to God that the apostle was speaking when he made that statement. Thus, we are also to understand what is written in the Gospel about Him "who enlighteneth every man."[24] This means that there is no man who is enlightened except by God.

In any case, the word concerning God, "who will have all men to be saved," does not mean that there is no one whose salvation he doth not will—he who was unwilling to work miracles among those who, he said, would have repented if he had wrought them—but by "all men" we are to understand the whole of mankind, in every single group into which it can be divided: kings and subjects; nobility and plebeians; the high and the low; the learned and unlearned; the healthy and the sick; the bright, the dull, and the stupid; the rich, the poor, and the middle class; males, females, infants, children, the adolescent, young adults and middle-aged and very old; of every tongue and fashion, of all the arts, of all professions, with the countless variety of wills and minds and all the other things that differentiate people. For from which of these groups doth not God will that some men from every nation should be saved through his only-begotten Son our Lord? Therefore, he doth save them since the Omnipotent cannot will in vain, whatsoever he willeth.

Now, the apostle had enjoined that prayers should be offered "for all men"[25] and especially "for kings and all those of exalted station,"[26] whose worldly pomp and pride could be supposed to be a sufficient cause for them to despise the humility of the Christian faith. Then, continuing his argument, "for this is good and

[19] Ps. 38:9.
[20] II Cor. 1:22.
[21] Ecclus. 40:1 (Vulgate).
[22] I Cor. 11:31, 32.

[23] I Tim. 2:4.
[24] John 1:9.
[25] I Tim. 2:1.
[26] I Tim. 2:2.

acceptable in the sight of God our Saviour"[27] —that is, to pray even for such as these [kings]—the apostle, to remove any warrant for despair, added, "Who willeth that all men be saved and come to the knowledge of the truth."[28] Truly, then, God hath judged it good that through the prayers of the lowly he would deign to grant salvation to the exalted—a paradox we have already seen exemplified. Our Lord also useth the same manner of speech in the Gospel, where he saith to the Pharisees, "You tithe mint and rue and every herb."[29] Obviously, the Pharisees did not tithe what belonged to others, nor all the herbs of all the people of other lands. Therefore, just as we should interpret "every herb" to mean "every kind of herb," so also we can interpret "all men" to mean "all kinds of men." We could interpret it in any other fashion, as long as we are not compelled to believe that the Omnipotent hath willed anything to be done which was not done. "He hath done all things in heaven and earth, whatsoever he willed,"[30] as Truth sings of him, and surely he hath not willed to do anything that he hath not done. There must be no equivocation on this point.

Chapter XXVIII

The Destiny of Man

Consequently, God would have willed to preserve even the first man in that state of salvation in which he was created and would have brought him in due season, after the begetting of children, to a better state without the intervention of death—where he not only would have been unable to sin, but would not have had even the will to sin—if he had foreknown that man would have had a steadfast will to continue without sin, as he had been created to do. But since he did foreknow that man would make bad use of his free will—that is, that he would sin—God prearranged his own purpose so that he could do good to man, even in man's doing evil, and so that the good will of the Omnipotent should be nullified by the bad will of men, but should nonetheless be fulfilled.

Thus it was fitting that man should be created, in the first place, so that he could will both good and evil—not without reward, if he willed the good; not without punishment, if he willed the evil. But in the future life he will not have the power to will evil; and yet this will not thereby restrict his free will. Indeed, his will will be much freer, because he will then have no power whatever to serve sin. For we surely ought not to find fault with such a will, nor say it is no will, or that it is not rightly called free, when we so desire happiness that we not only are unwilling to be miserable, but have no power whatsoever to will it.

And, just as in our present state, our soul is unable to will unhappiness for ourselves, so then it will be forever unable to will iniquity. But the ordered course of God's plan was not to be passed by, wherein he willed to show how good the rational creature is that is able not to sin, although one unable to sin is better.[31] So, too, it was an inferior order of immortality —but yet it was immortality—in which man was capable of not dying, even if the higher order which is to be is one in which man will be incapable of dying.[32]

Human nature lost the former kind of immortality through the misuse of free will. It is to receive the latter through grace—though it was to have obtained it through merit, if it had not sinned. Not even then, however, could there have been any merit without grace. For although sin had its origin in free will alone, still free will would not have been sufficient to maintain justice, save as divine aid had been afforded man, in the gift of participation in the immutable good. Thus, for example, the power to die when he wills it is in a man's own hands

[27] I Tim. 2:3.
[28] I Tim. 2:4.
[29] Luke 11:42.
[30] Ps. 135:6.
[31] Another example of Augustine's wordplay. Man's original capacities included both the power not to sin and the power to sin (*passe non peccare et posse peccare*). In Adam's original sin, man lost the *posse non peccare* (the power not to sin) and retained the *posse peccare* (the power to sin)—which he continues to exercise. In the fulfillment of grace, man will have the *posse peccare* taken away and receive the highest of all, the power not to be able to sin, *non posse peccare*. Cf. *On Correction and Grace* XXXIII.
[32] Again, a wordplay between *posset non mori* and *non possit mori*.

—since there is no one who could not kill himself by not eating (not to mention other means). But the bare will is not sufficient for maintaining life, if the aids of food and other means of preservation are lacking.

Similarly, man in paradise was capable of self-destruction by abandoning justice by an act of will; yet if the life of justice was to be maintained, his will alone would not have sufficed, unless He who made him had given him aid. But, after the Fall, God's mercy was even more abundant, for then the will itself had to be freed from the bondage in which sin and death are the masters. There is no way at all by which it can be freed by itself, but only through God's grace, which is made effectual in the faith of Christ. Thus, as it is written, even the will by which "the will itself is prepared by the Lord"[33] so that we may receive the other gifts of God through which we come to the Gift eternal—this too comes from God.

Accordingly, even the life eternal, which is surely the wages of good works, is called a *gift* of God by the apostle. "For the wages of sin," he says, "is death; but the gift of God is eternal life in Christ Jesus our Lord."[34] Now, wages for military service are paid as a just debit, not as a gift. Hence, he said "the wages of sin is death," to show that death was not an unmerited punishment for sin but a just debit. But a gift, unless it be gratuitous, is not grace. We are, therefore, to understand that even man's merited goods are gifts from God, and when life eternal is given through them, what else do we have but "grace upon grace returned"?[35]

Man was, therefore, made upright, and in such a fashion that he could either continue in that uprightness—though not without divine aid—or become perverted by his own choice. Whichever of these two man had chosen, God's will would be done, either by man or at least *concerning* him. Wherefore, since man chose to do his own will instead of God's, God's will *concerning* him was done; for, from the same mass of perdition that flowed out of that common source, God maketh "one vessel for honorable, another for ignoble use";[36] the ones for honorable use through his mercy, the ones for ignoble use through his judgment; lest anyone glory in man, or—what is the same thing—in himself.

Now, we could not be redeemed, even through "the one Mediator between God and man, Man himself, Christ Jesus,"[37] if he were not also God. For when Adam was made—being made an upright man—there was no need for a mediator. Once sin, however, had widely separated the human race from God, it was necessary for a mediator, who alone was born, lived, and was put to death without sin, to reconcile us to God, and provide even for our bodies a resurrection to life eternal—and all this in order that man's pride might be exposed and healed through God's humility. Thus it might be shown man how far he had departed from God, when by the incarnate God he is recalled to God; that man in his contumacy might be furnished an example of obedience by the God-Man; that the fount of grace might be opened up; that even the resurrection of the body—itself promised to the redeemed—might be previewed in the resurrection of the Redeemer himself; that the devil might be vanquished by that very nature he was rejoicing over having deceived—all this, however, without giving man ground for glory in himself, lest pride spring up anew. And if there are other advantages accruing from so great a mystery of the Mediator, which those who profit from them can see or testify—even if they cannot be described—let them be added to this list.

CHAPTER XXIX

"The Last Things"

Now, for the time that intervenes between man's death and the final resurrection, there is a secret shelter for his soul, as each is worthy of rest or affliction according to what it has merited while it lived in the body.

There is no denying that the souls of the dead are benefited by the piety of their living friends, when the sacrifice of the Mediator is offered for the dead, or alms are given in the

[33] Prov. 8:35 (LXX).
[34] Rom. 6:23.
[35] Cf. John 1:16.
[36] Rom. 9:21.
[37] I Tim. 2:5 (mixed text).

church. But these means benefit only those who, when they were living, have merited that such services could be of help to them. For there is a mode of life that is neither so good as not to need such helps after death nor so bad as not to gain benefit from them after death. There is, however, a good mode of life that does not need such helps, and, again, one so thoroughly bad that, when such a man departs this life, such helps avail him nothing. It is here, then, in this life, that all merit or demerit is acquired whereby a man's condition in the life hereafter is improved or worsened. Therefore, let no one hope to obtain any merit with God after he is dead that he has neglected to obtain here in this life.

So, then, those means which the Church constantly uses in interceding for the dead are not opposed to that statement of the apostle when he said, "For all of us shall stand before the tribunal of Christ, so that each may receive according to what he has done in the body, whether good or evil."[38] For each man has for himself while living in the body earned the merit whereby these means can benefit him [after death]. For they do not benefit all. And yet why should they not benefit all, unless it be because of the different kinds of lives men lead in the body?

Accordingly, when sacrifices, whether of the altar or of alms, are offered for the baptized dead, they are thank offerings for the very good, propitiations for the not-so-very-bad [*non valde malis*], and, as for the very bad—even if they are of no help to the dead—they are at least a sort of consolation to the living. Where they are of value, their benefit consists either in obtaining a full forgiveness or, at least, in making damnation more tolerable.

After the resurrection, however, when the general judgment has been held and finished, the boundary lines will be set for the two cities: the one of Christ, the other of the devil; one for the good, the other for the bad—both including angels and men. In the one group, there will be no will to sin, in the other, no power to sin, nor any further possibility of dying. The citizens of the first commonwealth will go on living truly and happily in life eternal. The second will go on, miserable in death eternal, with no power to die to it. The condition of both societies will then be fixed and endless. But in the first city, some will outrank others in bliss, and in the second, some will have a more tolerable burden of misery than others.

It is quite in vain, then, that some—indeed very many—yield to merely human feelings and deplore the notion of the eternal punishment of the damned and their interminable and perpetual misery. They do not believe that such things will be. Not that they would go counter to divine Scripture—but, yielding to their own human feelings, they soften what seems harsh and give a milder emphasis to statements they believe are meant more to terrify than to express the literal truth. "God will not forget," they say, "to show mercy, nor in his anger will he shut up his mercy." This is, in fact, the text of a holy psalm.[39] But there is no doubt that it is to be interpreted to refer to those who are called "vessels of mercy,"[40] those who are freed from misery not by their own merits but through God's mercy. Even so, if they suppose that the text applies to all men, there is no ground for them further to suppose that there can be an end for those of whom it is said, "Thus these shall go into everlasting punishment."[41] Otherwise, it can as well be thought that there will also be an end to the happiness of those of whom the antithesis was said: "But the righteous into life eternal."

But let them suppose, if it pleases them, that, for certain intervals of time, the punishments of the damned are somewhat mitigated. Even so, the wrath of God must be understood as still resting on them. And this is damnation—for this anger, which is not a violent passion in the divine mind, is called "wrath" in God. Yet even in his wrath—his wrath resting on them—he does not "shut up his mercy." This is not to put an end to their eternal afflictions, but rather to apply or interpose some little respite in their torments. For the psalm does not say, "To put an end to his wrath," or, "*After* his wrath," but, "*In* his wrath." Now, if this wrath were all there is [in man's dam-

[38] Rom. 14:10; II Cor. 5:10.
[39] Cf. Ps. 77:9.
[40] Rom. 9:23.
[41] Matt. 25:46.

nation], and even if it were present only in the slightest degree conceivable—still, to be lost out of the Kingdom of God, to be an exile from the City of God, to be estranged from the life of God, to suffer loss of the great abundance of God's blessings which he has hidden for those who fear him and prepared for those who hope in him[42]—this would be a punishment so great that, if it be eternal, no torments that we know could be compared to it, no matter how many ages they continued.

The eternal death of the damned—that is, their estrangement from the life of God—will therefore abide without end, and it will be common to them all, no matter what some people, moved by their human feelings, may wish to think about gradations of punishment, or the relief or intermission of their misery. In the same way, the eternal life of the saints will abide forever, and also be common to all of them no matter how different the grades of rank and honor in which they shine forth in their effulgent harmony.

Chapter XXXI

Love

And now regarding *love,* which the apostle says is greater than the other two—that is, faith and hope—for the more richly it dwells in a man, the better the man in whom it dwells. For when we ask whether someone is a good man, we are not asking what he believes, or hopes, but what he loves. Now, beyond all doubt, he who loves aright believes and hopes rightly. Likewise, he who does not love believes in vain, even if what he believes is true; he hopes in vain, even if what he hopes for is generally agreed to pertain to true happiness, unless he believes and hopes for this: that he may through prayer obtain the gift of love. For, although it is true that he cannot hope without love, it may be that there is something without which, if he does not love it, he cannot realize the object of his hopes. An example of this would be if a man hopes for life eternal—and who is there who does not love that?—and yet does not love *righteousness,* without which no one comes to it.

Now this is the true faith of Christ which the apostle commends: faith that works through love. And what it yet lacks in love it asks that it may receive, it seeks that it may find, and knocks that it may be opened unto it.[43] For faith achieves what the law commands [*fides namque impetrat quod lex imperat*]. And, without the gift of God—that is, without the Holy Spirit, through whom love is shed abroad in our hearts—the law may bid but it cannot aid [*jubere lex poterit, non juvare*]. Moreover, it can make of man a transgressor, who cannot then excuse himself by pleading ignorance. For appetite reigns where the love of God does not.[44]

When, in the deepest shadows of ignorance, he lives according to the flesh with no restraint of reason—this is the primal state of man.[45] Afterward, when "through the law the knowledge of sin"[46] has come to man, and the Holy Spirit has not yet come to his aid—so that even if he wishes to live according to the law, he is vanquished—man sins knowingly and is brought under the spell and made the slave of sin, "for by whatever a man is vanquished, of this master he is the slave."[47] The effect of the knowledge of the law is that sin works in man the whole round of concupiscence, which adds to the guilt of the first transgression. And thus it is that what was written is fulfilled: "The law entered in, that the offense might abound."[48] This is the *second* state of man.[49]

But if God regards a man with solicitude so that he then believes in God's help in fulfilling His commands, and if a man begins to be led by the Spirit of God, then the mightier power of love struggles against the power of the flesh.[50] And although there is still in man a power that fights against him—his infirmity being not yet fully healed—yet he [the righteous man] lives by faith and lives righteously

[42] Cf. Ps. 31:19.

[43] Matt. 7:7.

[44] Another wordplay on *cupiditas* and *caritas.*

[45] An interesting resemblance here to Freud's description of the Id, the primal core of our unconscious life.

[46] Rom. 3:20.

[47] II Peter 2:19.

[48] Rom. 5:20.

[49] Compare the psychological notion of the effect of external moral pressures and their power to arouse guilt feelings, as in Freud's notion of "superego."

[50] Gal. 5:17.

in so far as he does not yield to evil desires, conquering them by his love of righteousness. This is the *third* stage of the man of good hope.

A final peace is in store for him who continues to go forward in this course toward perfection through steadfast piety. This will be perfected beyond this life in the repose of the spirit, and, at the last, in the resurrection of the body.

Of these four different stages of man, the first is before the law, the second is under the law, the third is under grace, and the fourth is in full and perfect peace. Thus, also, the history of God's people has been ordered by successive temporal epochs, as it pleased God, who "ordered all things in measure and number and weight."[51] The first period was before the law; the second under the law, which was given through Moses; the next, under grace which was revealed through the first Advent of of the Mediator.[52] This grace was not previously absent from those to whom it was to be imparted, although, in conformity to the temporal dispensations, it was veiled and hidden. For none of the righteous men of antiquity could find salvation apart from the faith of Christ. And, unless Christ had also been known to them, he could not have been prophesied to us—sometimes openly and sometimes obscurely—through their ministry.

Now, in whichever of these four "ages"—if one can call them that—the grace of regeneration finds a man, then and there all his past sins are forgiven him and the guilt he contracted in being born is removed by his being reborn. And so true is it that "the Spirit breatheth where he willeth"[53] that some men have never known the second "age" of slavery under the law, but begin to have divine aid directly under the new commandment.

Yet, before a man can receive the commandment, he must, of course, live according to the flesh. But, once he has been imbued with the sacrament of rebirth, no harm will come to him even if he then immediately depart this life—"Wherefore on this account Christ died and rose again, that he might be the Lord of both the living and the dead."[54] Nor will the kingdom of death have dominion over him for whom He, who was "free among the dead,"[55] died.

Chapter XXXII

The End of All the Law

All the divine precepts are, therefore, referred back to *love,* of which the apostle says, "Now the end of the commandment is love, out of a pure heart, and a good conscience and a faith unfeigned."[56] Thus every commandment harks back to love. For whatever one does either in fear of punishment or from some carnal impulse, so that it does not measure up to the standard of love which the Holy Spirit sheds abroad in our hearts—whatever it is, it is not yet done as it should be, although it may seem to be. Love, in this context, of course includes both the love of God and the love of our neighbor and, indeed, "on these two commandments hang all the Law and the Prophets"[57]—and, we may add, the gospel and the apostles, for from nowhere else comes the voice, "The end of the commandment is love,"[58] and, "God is love."[59]

Therefore, whatsoever things God commands (and one of these is, "Thou shalt not commit adultery")[60] and whatsoever things are not positively ordered but are strongly advised as good spiritual counsel (and one of these is, "It is a good thing for a man not to touch a woman")[61]—all of these imperatives are rightly obeyed only when they are measured by the standard of our love of God and our love of our neighbor in God [*propter Deum*]. This applies both in the present age and in the world to come. Now we love God in faith; then, at sight. For, though mortal men ourselves, we do not know the hearts of mortal men. But then "the Lord will illuminate the hidden things in the darkness and will make manifest the cogitations of the heart; and then shall each one have his praise from God"[62]—

[51] Wis. 11:21 (Vulgate).
[52] Cf. John 1:17.
[53] John 3:8.
[54] Rom. 14:9.
[55] Cf. Ps. 88:5.
[56] I Tim. 1:5.
[57] Matt. 22:40.
[58] I Tim. 1:5.
[59] I John 4:16.
[60] Ex. 20:14; Matt. 5:27; etc.
[61] I Cor. 7:1.
[62] I Cor. 4:5.

for what will be praised and loved in a neighbor by his neighbor is just that which, lest it remain hidden, God himself will bring to light. Moreover, passion decreases as love increases[63] until love comes at last to that fullness which cannot be surpassed, "for greater love than this no one has, that a man lay down his life for his friends."[64] Who, then, can explain how great the power of love will be, when there will be no passion [*cupiditas*] for it to restrain or overcome? For, then, the supreme state of true health [*summa sanitas*] will have been reached, when the struggle with death shall be no more.

THE EARLY CREEDS OF CHRISTENDOM

The following creeds represent the efforts of the early Christian Church to summarize its essential beliefs. With the exception of the Apostles' Creed (which is predominantly a Western, Latin creed), they were adopted by ecumenical councils (Church-wide or universal councils) as the authoritative statement of the Christian faith.

Both the Nicene-Constantinopolitan Creed and the Creed of Chalcedon were the end products of serious theological controversies within the Church. The Nicene Creed (in our present form the Nicene-Constantinopolitan Creed) was formed as an answer to the Arian heresy, which, in effect, denied the concept of the Trinity. The Creed of Chalcdon was formulated in order to define more carefully the relations of the two natures of Christ (the human and divine natures in Christ).

The Apostles' Creed was the end development of some very early baptismal formulae. Its earliest forms go back to the second century, and these forms in turn reflect credal statements that were current in the first century. The Apostles' Creed has always been a creed of the Western Church and today is affirmed by all Roman Catholics and by a majority of Protestants.

The Apostles' Creed

I believe in God the Father Almighty; Maker of heaven and earth.

And in Jesus Christ his only (begotten) Son our Lord; who was conceived by the Holy Ghost, born of the Virgin Mary; suffered under Pontius Pilate, was crucified, dead, and buried; he descended into Hell (Hades, spirit-world); the third day he rose from the dead; he ascended into heaven; and sitteth at the right hand of God the Father Almighty; from thence he shall come to judge the quick and the dead.

I believe in the Holy Ghost; the holy catholic Church; the communion of saints; the forgiveness of sins; the resurrection of the body (flesh); and the life everlasting. Amen.

The Nicene-Constantinopolitan Creed (325 A. D.-381 A. D.)

I believe in one God the Father Almighty; Maker of heaven and earth, and of all things visible and invisible.

And in one Lord Jesus Christ, the only-begotten Son of God, begotten of the Father before all worlds (God of God), Light of Light,

[63] *Minuitur autem cupiditas caritate crescente.*

[64] John 15:13.

very God of very God, begotten, not made, being of one substance (essence) with the Father; by whom all things were made; who, for us men and for our salvation, came down from heaven, and was incarnate by the Holy Ghost of the Virgin Mary, and was made man; and was crucified also for us under Pontius Pilate; he suffered and was buried; and the third day he rose again, according to the Scriptures; and ascended into heaven, and sitteth on the right hand of the Father; and he shall come again, with glory, to judge both the quick and the dead; whose kingdom shall have no end.

And (I believe) in the Holy Ghost, the Lord and Giver of Life; who proceedeth from the Father (and the Son); who with the Father and the Son together is worshiped and glorified; who spake by the Prophets. And (I believe) one Holy Catholic and Apostolic Church. I acknowledge one Baptism for the remission of sins; and I look for the resurrection of the dead, and the life of the world to come. Amen.

The Creed of Chalcedon (451 A. D.)

We, then, following the holy Fathers, all with one consent, teach men to confess one and the same Son, our Lord Jesus Christ, the same perfect in Godhead and also perfect in manhood; truly God and truly man, of a reasonable (rational) soul and body; consubstantial (coessential) with the Father according to the Godhead, and consubstantial with us according to the Manhood; in all things like unto us, without sin; begotten before all ages of the Father according to the Godhead, and in these latter days, for us and for our salvation, born of the Virgin Mary, the Mother of God, according to the Manhood; one and the same Christ, Son, Lord, Only-begotten, to be acknowledged in two natures, inconfusedly, unchangeably, indivisibly, inseparably; the distinction of natures being by no means taken away by the union, but rather the property of each nature being preserved, and concurring in one Person and one Subsistence, not parted or divided into two persons, but one and the same Son, the only begotten, God the Word, the Lord Jesus Christ; as the prophets from the beginning (have declared) concerning him, and the Lord Jesus Christ himself has taught us, and the Creed of the holy Father has handed down to us.

The Medieval Period

BENEDICT OF NURSIA (CA. 480–CA. 550)

The extracts which follow have been taken from what was undoubtedly the first systematic rule for the monastic life. This rule was composed by Benedict for his small group of fellow monks from which the later Benedictine order has stemmed. In 500 A. D. Benedict withdrew from the world to live as a hermit in a cave at Subiaco. After a period of some years in this anchorite existence he drew to himself followers which he eventually formed into twelve monasteries of twelve monks each with an abbot for each monastery. After the year 525 A. D. he moved his monks to Monte Cassino where a permanent monastery was established.

It was during this period that the famous "Rule of Benedict" was composed and laid down for the members of his order.

Essentially, monasticism was a movement of reproach against the worldliness of the Church. It began in the fourth century in Egypt after the adoption of Christianity as the state religion of the Empire. Clergy and laity alike were responsible for the obvious lowering of the stringent moral standards that had existed when the Church was still under persecution. Sensitive Christians, repelled by this laxity, sought the isolation of the desert where they could fulfill the "counsels of perfection" which they believed best exemplified the Gospel. Others, deeply influenced by Greek ways of thought, looked upon the monastic life as the necessary ascetical training for the purification of the soul.

This anchorite or "hermit-type" monasticism penetrated early into Western Christendom where it was enthusiastically received by many ardent believers. However, in the transition from the East to the West, monasticism took on new forms. Henceforth the hermit-type monk gave way to groups of monks who lived together. The monastic experiment of Benedict and its resulting "rule" witness to this important change.

The Rule of Saint Benedict*

Listen, my son, and turn the ear of thine heart to the precepts of thy Master. Receive readily, and faithfully carry out the advice of a loving Father, so that by the work of obedience you may return to Him, whom you have left by the sloth of disobedience. For thee, therefore, whosoever thou be, my words are intended, who, giving up thy own will, dost take the all-powerful and excellent arms of obedience to fight under the Lord Christ, the true King.

First, beg of Him with most earnest prayer to finish the good work begun; that He who now hath deigned to count us among His children may never be grieved by our evil deeds. For at all times we must so serve Him with the good things He has given us, that He may not, as an angry Father, disinherit His children, nor as a dread Lord, provoked by our evil deeds, deliver us to everlasting punishment as wicked servants who refuse to follow Him to glory.

Let us, therefore, arise at one, the Scripture stirring us up, saying, "It is now the hour for us to rise from sleep. And, our eyes now open to the divine light, let us with wondering ears hearken to the divine voice, daily calling to us and warning us, "To-day if you shall hear His voice, harden not your hearts;" and again, "He that hath ears, let him hear what the Spirit saith to the Churches." And what does He say? "Come, ye children, and hearken unto Me: I will teach you the fear of the Lord. Run while ye have the light of life, that the darkness of death overtake ye not."

And our Lord, seeking His workman among the multitude of those to whom He thus speaks, says again, "Who is the man that will have life, and desireth to see good days?" And if thou, hearing this, reply, "I am he": God says to you, If thou desirest to possess true and everlasting life, "restrain thy tongue from evil, and thy lips that they speak no guile. Decline from evil and do good; seek after peace and pursue it." And when you have done this My eyes shall be on you, and My ears shall be open to your prayers. And before you can call upon Me, I will say to you, "Behold, I am present." What can be more agreeable, dearest brethren, than this voice of our Lord inviting us? Behold how in His loving kindness He shows us the way of life!

Therefore, with our loins girt by faith, and by the practice of good works under the guid-

* *The Rule of Saint Benedict,* translated by Cardinal Gasquet. London: Chatto and Windus, 1925. Pages 1–7, 7–9, and 17–22 are reproduced by permission of Chatto and Windus.

ance of His Gospel, let us walk in the path He has marked out for us, that we may deserve to see Him who has called us in His kingdom.

If we would live in the shelter of this kingdom, we can reach it only by speeding on the way of good works (by this path alone is it to be attained). But let us, with the prophet, ask our Lord, and say to Him, "Lord, who shall dwell in Thy tabernacle? or who shall rest on Thy holy hill?" And when we have so asked, let us hear our Lord's answer, pointing out to us the way to this His dwelling, and saying "He that walketh without spot and worketh justice: he that speaketh truth in his heart: that hath not forged guile with his tongue: he that hath not done evil to his neighbour, and hath not taken up reproach against him." He that, casting out of the inmost thoughts of his heart the suggestions of the evil-minded devil trying to lead him astray, has brought them all to naught: he that taking hold of his thoughts whilst in their birth hath dashed them against the rock, which is Christ. They who, fearing the Lord, are not lifted up by their good observance, but knowing that all that is good in them comes not from themselves but from the Lord, extol His work in them, saying with the prophet, "Not to us, O Lord, not to us, but to Thy Name give glory. Thus the Apostle Paul imputed nothing of his preaching to himself, saying, "By the grace of God I am what I am." And again he saith, "He that glorieth, let him glory in the Lord."

Hence also our Lord in the Gospel says, "He that heareth these My words and doth them, I will liken him to a wise man that hath built his house upon a rock. The floods came, the winds blew and beat against that house, and it fell not, because it was founded upon a rock." In fulfilment whereof our Lord daily looketh for deeds in us complying with His holy admonitions. Therefore are the days of this our life lengthened for awhile for the mending of our evil deeds, according to the words of the apostle, "Knowest thou not that the patience of God leadeth thee to repentance?" For our loving Lord says, "I will not the death of the sinner, but that he be converted and live."

So questioning the Lord, brethren, we have heard on what conditions we may dwell in His temple; and if we fulfil these we shall be heirs of the kingdom of heaven. Therefore must our hearts and bodies be prepared to fight under the holy obedience of His commands, and we must beg our Lord to supply by the help of His grace what by nature is not possible to us. And if, fleeing from the pains of hell, we will to attain to life everlasting, we must, whilst time yet serves and whilst we live in the flesh and the light is still on our path, hasten to do now what will profit us for all eternity.

We are therefore now about to institute a school for the service of God, in which we hope nothing harsh nor burdensome will be ordained. But if we proceed in certain things with some little severity, sound reason so advising for the amendment of vices or the preserving of charity, do not for fear of this forthwith flee from the way of salvation, which is always narrow in the beginning. In living our life, however, and by the growth of faith, when the heart has been enlarged, the path of God's commandments is run with unspeakable loving sweetness; so that never leaving His school but persevering in the monastery until death in His teaching, we share by our patience in the sufferings of Christ, and so merit to be partakers of His kingdom.

It is recognized that there are four kinds of monks. The first are the Cenobites: that is, those who live in a monastery under a Rule or an abbot. The second kind is that of Anchorites, or Hermits, who not in the first fervour of conversion, but after long trial in the monastery, and already taught by the example of many others, have learnt to fight against the devil, are well prepared to go forth from the ranks of the brotherhood to the single combat of the desert. They can now, by God's help, safely fight against the vices of their flesh and against evil thoughts singly, with their own hand and arm and without the encouragement of a companion. The third and worst kind of monks is that of the Sarabites, who have not been tried under any Rule nor schooled by an experienced master, as gold is proved in the furnace, but soft as is lead and still in their works cleaving to the world, are known to lie to God by their tonsure.

These in twos or threes, or more frequently singly, are shut up, without a shepherd; not in our Lord's fold, but in their own. The pleasure or carrying out their particular desires is their law, and whatever they dream of or choose this they call holy; but what they like not, that they account unlawful.

The fourth class of monks is called Gyrovagi (or Wanderers). These move about all their lives through various countries, staying as guests for three or four days at different monasteries. They are always on the move and never settle down, and are slaves to their own wills and to the enticements of gluttony. In every way they are worse than the Sarabites, and of their wretched way of life it is better to be silent than to speak.

Leaving these therefore aside, let us by God's help set down a Rule for Cenobites, who are the best kind of monks.

First of all, to love the Lord God with all our heart, with all our soul, with all our strength.

2. Then, to love our neighbour as ourself.
3. Then, not to kill.
4. Not to commit adultery.
5. Not to steal.
6. Not to be covetous.
7. Not to bear false witness.
8. To respect all men.
9. Not to do to another what one would not have done to oneself.
10. To deny oneself in order to follow Christ.
11. To chastise the body.
12. Not to be fond of pleasures.
13. To love fasting.
14. To give refreshment to the poor.
15. To clothe the naked.
16. To visit the sick.
17. To bury the dead.
18. To come to the help of those in trouble.
19. To comfort those in sadness.
20. To become a stranger to the ways of the world.
21. To prefer nothing to the love of Christ.
22. Not to give way to wrath.
23. Not to harbour anger for any time.
24. Not to foster deceit in the heart.
25. Not to make a false peace.
26. Not to depart from charity.
27. Not to swear at all, lest one forswears.
28. To speak the truth with heart and lips.
29. Not to return evil for evil.
30. Not to do an injury, but patiently to suffer one when done.
31. To love one's enemies.
32. Not to speak ill of those who speak ill of one, but rather to speak well of them.
33. To suffer persecution for justice sake.
34. Not to be proud.
35. Not to be a winebibber.
36. Not to be a great eater.
37. Not to be given to sleep.
38. Not to be slothful.
39. Not to be a murmurer.
40. Not to be a detractor.
41. To put one's trust in God.
42. When one sees any good in oneself to attribute it to God, not to oneself.
43. That a man recognize that it is he who does evil, and so let him attribute it to himself.
44. To fear the day of judgment.
45. To be afraid of hell.
46. To desire life everlasting with entire spiritual longing.
47. To have the vision of death before one's eyes daily.
48. To watch over the actions of one's life every hour of the day.
49. To know for certain that God sees one everywhere.
50. To dash at once against Christ (as against a rock) evil thoughts which rise up in the mind.
51. And to reveal all such to one's spiritual Father.
52. To guard one's lips from uttering evil or wicked words.
53. Not to be fond of much talking.
54. Not to speak idle words, or such as move to laughter.
55. Not to love much or boisterous laughter.
56. Willingly to hear holy reading.
57. Often to devote oneself to prayer.
58. Daily with tears and sighs to confess to God in prayer one's past offences, and to avoid them for the future.
59. Not to give way to the desires of the flesh: and to hate one's own will.
60. In all things to obey the abbot's commands, even though he himself (which God forbid) should act otherwise, remembering our Lord's precept, "What

they say, do ye, but what they do, do ye not."

61. Not to wish to be called holy before one is so; but to be holy first so as to be called such with truth.
62. Daily in one's acts to keep God's commandments.
63. To love chastity.
64. To hate no man.
65. Not to be jealous or envious.
66. Not to love wrangling.
67. To show no arrogant spirit.
68. To reverence the old.
69. To love the young.
70. To pray for one's enemies for the love of Christ.
71. To make peace with an adversary before the sun sets.
72. And, never to despair of God's mercy.

Behold these are the tools of our spiritual craft; when we shall have made use of them constantly day and night, and shall have proved them at the day of judgment, that reward shall be given us by our Lord, which He has promised, "Which eye hath not seen, nor ear heard, nor hath it entered into the heart of man to conceive what God hath prepared for those that love Him." Steadfastly abiding in the community, the workshop where all these instruments are made use of is the cloister of the monastery.

THOMAS À KEMPIS (CA. 1380–1471 A. D.)

Thomas Hemerken, born at Kempen near Cologne, was, according to the usual and most probable tradition, the author of *The Imitation of Christ.* This devotional masterpiece has had a vast influence and has been much beloved by Christians ever since it was written.

The author was educated in one of the schools of the Brethren of the Common Life, and the spirit of this movement is to be found on every page of Thomas's work. These Brethren represent a mystical tradition, but they were also very much concerned to reform the late medieval Church of its rather worldly attachments and, as it seemed to them, its pomp. This movement left its stamp upon German mysticism, of which indeed it is one expression, and this in turn had a good deal of influence upon later Reformers, especially Luther. It is clear, however, that Thomas has no thought of breaking from the Church of Rome. He wishes only for a new purity and discipleship within that Church.

The Imitation of Christ*

Of The Imitation Of Christ, And Contempt Of All The Vanities Of The World

[First Book]

CHAPTER I

Whoso followeth Me, walketh not in darkness: saith the Lord. These are the words of Christ by which we are admonished, to imitate His life and manners: if we will be truly enlightened, and delivered from all blindness of heart. Be it therefore our chief pursuit: to meditate upon the life of Jesus Christ.

The doctrine of Christ excels all doctrines of holy men; and whoso had the Spirit: would find therein the hidden manna. But it happens that from often hearing many have but small desire for the Gospel: because they have not

* From Thomas à Kempis, *The Imitation of Christ,* translated and edited by C. Bigg. London: Methuen and Company, 1898.

the Spirit of Christ. But whoso would fully and feelingly understand the words of Christ: must endeavour to conform his whole life to Him. What doth it profit thee to lecture profoundly on the Trinity; if thou be void of humility and thereby displeasing to the Trinity? Truly profound words do not make a man holy and just: but a virtuous life makes him dear to God. I had rather feel compunction: than know its definition. If thou knewest the whole Bible in the letter and the sayings of all philosophers; what would all that profit thee without the love of God and grace?

Vanity of vanities and all is vanity: except to love God and to serve Him only. This is the highest wisdom: through contempt of the world to journey towards the Kingdom of Heaven. Vanity therefore it is to seek after perishing riches: and to trust in them. Vanity is it also to solicit honours: and climb to high degree. Vanity it is to follow the desires of the flesh: and to desire that for which thou must afterwards be heavily punished. Vanity it is to covet a long life: and neglect a good life. Vanity it is to mind only the present life: and not foresee those things which are to come. Vanity it is to set thy heart on that which speedily passes away: and not hasten thither where everlasting joy abides.

Call often to mind the proverb; The eye is not satisfied with seeing: nor the ear filled with hearing. Study therefore to withdraw thy heart from the love of the visible: and to give thyself over to the invisible. For they that follow their appetites stain their conscience: and forfeit the grace of God.

Chapter III

He to whom the Eternal Word speaks: is freed from many opinions. From one Word are all things; and all speak that one: and this is the Beginning, which also speaks to us. No man without that Word understands, or judges aright. He to whom all things are one, he who draws all things to one, and sees all things in one; may be stablished in heart: and rest as a peacemaker in God. O God who art Truth: make me one with Thee in everlasting charity. It wearies me often to read and hear many things: in Thee is all that I want and desire. Let all doctors hold their peace, let all creatures keep silence in Thy sight: speak Thou alone to me.

II

The more a man is made one with himself and simplified inwardly; the more and higher things he understands without labour: for he receives the light of intelligence from above. A pure simple and stable spirit does not waste its force on many occupations; for it does all to the honour of God: and strives to be at peace within itself from every selfish aim. Who hinders and troubles thee more; than the unmortified affection of thine own heart? A good and devout man first plans within himself: those things which he is to do outwardly. Neither do they warp him to the desires of a vicious inclination: but he bends them himself to fit the prescript of right reason. Who hath a harder battle; than he that strives to overcome himself? And this should be our business, to conquer ourselves; and daily wax stronger than ourselves: and make some growth in holiness.

III

All perfection in this life, has some imperfection cleaving to it: and no speculation of ours is without some darkness. An humble knowledge of thyself, is a surer way to God: than a deep search after learning. Learning is not to be blamed, nor any simple knowledge of things, for considered in itself it is good and ordained by God: but a good conscience and a virtuous life is always to be preferred. But because many are more anxious to know than to live well; therefore they are often deceived: and bear little fruit or next to none.

Chapter IX

OF OBEDIENCE AND SUBJECTION

It is a great matter to stand in obedience; to live under a prelate: and not to be our own masters. It is much safer to stand in subjection: than in office. Many are under obedience rather for necessity than for charity; and they have their punishment: and do easily repine. Neither will they attain to freedom of mind: unless with their whole heart they obey for the love of God. Run hither and thither: thou shalt find no rest but in humble subjection, under the rule of a prelate. Fancifulness and change of place, have deceived many.

True it is that every one cheerfully does what he likes: and inclines to those who agree with him. But if God be amongst us: we must sometimes give up our own opinion for the good of peace. Who is so wise; that he can fully know all things? Be not therefore too confident in thine own opinion: but be even glad to listen to the thought of others. If that which thou thinkest be good; and yet thou renounce it for God's sake and follow another: thou shalt make more profit thereby.

Chapter XV

OF WORKS DONE IN CHARITY

For no worldly thing, nor for the love of any man is any evil to be done; yet for the profit of one that is in need, a good work is sometimes to be broken off without any scruple: or say rather changed for a better. For by doing this a good work is not lost: but changed into a better.

Without charity the outward work profits not at all; but whatever is done of charity be it never so little and despised: becomes wholly fruitful. For God weighs rather the means of the worker: than the work that he does. He does much: that loves much. He does much: that does a thing well. He does well: that serves the community rather than his own will.

Oftentimes it seems to be charity, and is rather carnality: because natural inclination, self-will, hope of requital, desire of gain, will seldom be away. He that has true and perfect charity seeks himself in nothing: but only desires in all things that God alone should be glorified. He also envieth none, because he loves no private joy; neither will he rejoice in himself: but wishes above all blessings to be made happy in God. To no man does he attribute anything that is good; but refers it all unto God, from whom as Fountain all things flow: in whom as End all the saints do rest in fruition.

O he that had but a spark of true charity: would certainly feel that all earthly things are full of vanity.

Chapter XX

OF THE LOVE OF SOLITUDE AND SILENCE

Seek a fit time to retire into thyself: and meditate often upon God's loving-kindnesses. Throw aside subtleties; read thoroughly such books: as rather stir compunction, than furnish occupation. If thou wilt withdraw from needless talk, and idle gadding about, as also from listening to news and rumours: thou shalt find leisure enough and suitable for meditation on good things. The greatest Saints avoided the society of men when they could: and rather chose to serve God in secret.

One said: As oft as I have gone among men: I returned home less a man. This we often find: when we talk long together. It is easier not to speak a word at all: than not to speak a word too much. It is easier to hide at home: than to be guarded abroad. He therefore that intends to attain to the inward and spiritual: must with Jesus withdraw from the press. No man goes out securely: but he who loves to hide. No man speaks securely: but he who loves to hold his peace. No man rules securely: but he that loves to be beneath. No man commands securely: but he that has learned loyally to obey. No man rejoices securely: unless he has within him the testimony of a good conscience.

Chapter XXIII

OF MEDITATION ON DEATH

Very soon there will be an end of thee here: change thy view of thy condition. To-day man is: to-morrow he is no more seen. And when he is out of sight: quickly also is he out of mind.

O the stupidity and hardness of man's heart: which thinks only of the present, and does not rather provide for the future. Thou oughtest so to order thyself in all thy deeds and thoughts: as if to-day thou wert doomed to die.

If thou hadst a good conscience: thou wouldst not greatly fear death. Better to guard against sins: than fly from death. If to-day thou art not ready; how wilt thou be so to-morrow? To-morrow is uncertain; and how knowest thou that thou wilt have a morrow? What avails it to live long; when there is so small amendment? Ah length of days does not always amend: but often adds to our sins. O that we had spent but one day in this world well. Many count the years of their conversion: yet scanty oftentimes is the fruit of amendment.

If to die be dreadful: to live long may perhaps prove more dangerous. Happy is he that has always the hour of his death before his eyes: and daily prepares himself to die. If thou hast ever seen a man die: think that thou also must travel the same road. When it is morning: think thou mayest not live till evening. And when evening comes: dare not to promise thyself the morning. Be thou therefore always ready: and so live, that death may never take thee unprepared. Many die suddenly and when they look not for it: for at an hour when we think not, the Son of Man will come.

When that last hour shall come; thou wilt begin to think far differently of thy whole past life: and be exceeding sorry that thou hast been so careless and remiss. How happy and wise is he, that now strives so to live: as he would be found at his death. For a perfect contempt of the world; a fervent desire for growth in virtue; the love of discipline the toil of penance; the readiness of obedience; the denying of ourselves; and the bearing of all afflictions for the love of Christ: will give us great assurance of a happy death.

. . .

Trust not on friends and kindred; neither do thou put off thy salvation till hereafter: for men will forget thee sooner than thou thinkest. It is better to make provision betimes, and send some good before thee: than to trust to other men's help. If thou be not careful for thyself now: who will be careful for thee hereafter? The time that is now is very precious: now are the days of salvation: now is the acceptable time. But alas that thou shouldest spend so idly: the time in which thou mightest earn the means for eternal life. The time will come, when thou shalt desire one day or hour to amend in: and I know not that it will be granted thee.

Come beloved, from what danger mightest thou deliver thyself, from what fear save thyself: if thou wouldst be ever fearful and mindful of death. Study now so to live: that at the hour of death thou mayest rather rejoice than fear. Learn now to die to the world: that thou mayest then begin to live with Christ. Learn now to despise all things: that thou mayest then freely go to Christ. Chastise thy body now by penance: that thou mayest then have assured confidence.

. . .

Who will remember thee when thou art dead; and who will pray for thee? Do do now my beloved whatsoever thou canst do; for thou knowest not when they shalt die: nor yet what shall befall thee after death. Whilst thou hast time: heap unto thyself everlasting riches. Think on nothing but thy salvation: care for nothing but the things of God. Make now friends to thyself by venerating the Saints of God, and imitating their actions; that when thou failest in this life: they may receive thee into everlasting habitations. Keep thyself as a pilgrim and stranger upon the earth: to whom the affairs of this world do nothing appertain. Keep thy heart free and uplifted to God: because thou hast here no abiding city. Thither send daily thy prayers and sighs with tears: that after death thy spirit may be found worthy to pass happily to the Lord. Amen.

[Second Book]

Chapter I

OF THE INNER LIFE

The Kingdom of God is within you saith the Lord. Turn thee with thy whole heart unto the Lord; and forsake this wretched world: and thy soul shall find rest. Learn to despise the outward and to give thyself to the inward: and thou shalt see the Kingdom of God come into thee. For the Kingdom of God is peace and joy in the Holy Ghost: which is not given to the unholy. Christ will come unto thee and shew thee His own consolation: if thou prepare for Him a worthy abode within.

All His glory and beauty is within: and there He delights Himself. Frequent are His visits to the inward man; sweet His discourse, pleasant His solace: great His peace, exceeding wonderful His familiarity.

Come faithful soul make ready thy heart for this Bridegroom: that He may deign to come unto thee, and dwell within thee. For thus saith He. If any love Me he will keep My words; and We will come unto him: and will make our abode with him. Make therefore room for Christ: and deny entrance to all others.

Chapter XI

OF THE FEWNESS OF THE LOVERS OF THE CROSS OF JESUS

Jesus has now many lovers of His heavenly kingdom: but few bearers of His Cross. He has many that long for consolation: but few that long for tribulation. He finds many companions of His table: but few of His fast. All desire to rejoice with Him: few are willing to suffer any thing for Him.

Many follow Jesus unto the breaking of bread: but few to the drinking of the cup of His Passion. Many reverence His miracles: few follow the ignominy of His Cross. Many love Jesus: so long as no adversities befall. Many praise and bless Him: so long as they receive consolations from Him. But if Jesus hide Himself and leave them but a little while: they fall either into complaining or into great dejection.

But they who love Jesus for the sake of Jesus and not for some special comfort of their own: bless Him in all tribulation and distress of heart as well as in the dearest comfort. Yea though He should never choose to give them comfort; yet would they ever praise Him: and wish to be always giving thanks.

O how strong is the pure love of Jesus: which is alloyed with no self-interest or self-love. Are not all those to be called hirelings; who are ever seeking consolations? Do they not shew themselves lovers of themselves rather than of Christ; who are always scheming their own profit and advantage? Where shall one be found; who will serve God for nought? Seldom is any so spiritual: as to be stripped of all. For who can find one that is truly poor in spirit, and bared of all created things?

Chapter XII

OF THE KING'S WAY OF THE HOLY CROSS

The Cross will be the sign in Heaven: when the Lord shall come to judgment. Then all the servants of the Cross who in their lifetime conformed themselves to the Crucified: shall draw near to Christ the Judge with great confidence.

Why then fear to take up the Cross; through which lies the road to the kingdom? In the Cross is salvation, in the Cross is life; in the Cross is protection from enemies: in the Cross is infusion of heavenly sweetness; in the Cross is strength of mind, in the Cross joy of Spirit: in the Cross the sum of virtue, in the Cross perfection of sanctity. There is no salvation for the soul nor hope of eternal life: but in the Cross. Take up therefore thy Cross and follow Jesus: and thou shalt go into life eternal. He went before bearing His Cross, and died for thee on the Cross; that thou also mayest bear thy Cross: and desire to die on the Cross. For if thou be dead with Him: thou shalt also live with Him. And if thou be partaker of His punishment: thou shalt be also of His glory.

Lo in the Cross is all, and in dying is all; and there is no other way to life and true inward peace: but the way of the holy Cross and of daily mortification. Walk where thou wilt, seek what thou wilt; thou wilt find no higher way above, nor safer way below: than the way of the holy Cross. Dispose and order all things as thou wilt and seest; yet shalt thou only learn that thou must always suffer, willingly or unwillingly: and so shalt thou always find the Cross.

[Third Book]

Chapter I

WITH WHAT REVERENCE CHRIST OUGHT TO BE RECEIVED

These are Thy words O Christ eternal Truth; though not uttered at one time: nor written in one place. Because therefore they are Thine and true: they are all thankfully and faithfully to be received by me. They are Thine and Thou hast uttered them; and they are mine also: because Thou hast spoken them for my salvation. I receive them gladly from Thy mouth: that they may be the closer grafted in my heart. Those most gracious words embolden me: full as they are of sweetness and of love. But mine own offences make me afraid: and an unclean conscience drives me back from receiving so great Mysteries. The sweetness of Thy words invites me: but the multitude of my sins doth weigh me down.

Thou commandest me to come confidently unto Thee, if I would have part with Thee; and to receive the food of immortality, if I would obtain eternal life and glory. Come unto Me sayest Thou all ye that labour and are heavy laden: and I will refresh you. O word sweet and friendly in a sinner's ear: that Thou O Lord my God shouldest invite the poor and needy to the Communion of Thy most holy Body.

But who am I Lord; that I should dare to approach Thee? Behold the Heaven of Heavens cannot contain Thee; and Thou sayest Come ye all unto Me. What means this most gracious condescension; and this so friendly invitation? How shall I dare to come; who know not any good in myself whereon I may presume? How shall I bring Thee into my house; who have so often offended Thy most benign countenance? Angels and Archangels stand in awe of Thee, holy and righteous men do fear Thee; and sayest Thou Come ye all unto Me?

. . .

Many run to divers places to visit the relics of Saints: and hear with wonder of their deeds, gaze upon the spacious buildings of their temples; and kiss their sacred bones wrapped up in silk and gold: and behold Thou art present with me here upon the altar my God Holy of Holies, Creator of men and Lord of Angels.

Often in such spectacles men are moved by curiosity and the novelty of strange sights; and little fruit of amendment is carried home: particularly when they so heedlessly wander about without true contrition. But here in the Sacrament of the Altar Thou art wholly present my God the Man Christ Jesus; here too a rich harvest of eternal salvation is reaped: as oft as thou art worthily and devoutly received. But to this we are drawn not by frivolity or curiosity or sensuality: but by firm devout hope and sincere charity.

That The Devout Soul Ought With The Whole Heart To Seek Union With Christ In The Sacrament

Chapter XIII

THE VOICE OF THE DISCIPLE

O that it were granted me Lord, to find Thee alone and open unto Thee my whole heart; and enjoy Thee as my soul desires: and that henceforth none may despise me, nor any creature attract nor regard me; but that Thou alone mayest speak unto me and I to Thee: as the beloved is wont to speak to his beloved, and friend to feast with friend.

This I pray this I long for; that I may be wholly united unto Thee, and withdraw my heart from all created things: and by means of sacred Communion and frequent celebration may learn more and more to taste things heavenly and eternal. Ah Lord God, when shall I be wholly united to Thee and absorbed by Thee: and altogether forgetful of myself. Thou in me and I in Thee: so also grant that we may both continue together in one.

THOMAS AQUINAS (1225–1274)

Born in Aquino in the province of Naples in 1225 A. D., Thomas entered the Dominican Order, studied at the University of Paris under Albert the Great, and eventually taught at Paris, Rome and Naples. In Thomas' own day, the Church had been agitated by the rediscovery of the works of Aristotle. Many feared that the influence of this great Greek thinker would threaten orthodoxy. However, the achievement of St. Thomas was to show not only that Aristotle could be harmonized with the Christian faith but that he could also provide a sound philosophical basis for it.

In his encyclical *Aeterni Patris* (see p. 370), Pope Leo XIII exhorted the faithful to study St. Thomas, the "Angelic Doctor," because of "his solidity and excellence above the other authors." It is not too much to say that the influence of St. Thomas has towered above that of all others in the development of modern Roman Catholic philosophy.

Essentially the "Thomistic" system is the correlation of philosophy and theology. Thomas asserted that reason (that is, philosophy) can discern "natural" (scientific) truths but that it is incapable of uncovering "supernatural" (theological) truths. Such truth comes only by way of revelation from God through Scripture and Tradition. Revelation, then, completes reason. Theology fulfills philosophy.

The net result of Thomas' effort was to bring together in a grand summary (*Summa Theologica*) the intellectual history of the Middle Ages. His system became the basis for the definitions of the Council of Trent, often called the "Counter-Reformation" (see p. 219).

Summa Theologica*

Question One

What Sacred Doctrine Is, and What It Concerns

In order to confine our purpose within definite limits, we must first inquire into sacred doctrine itself, what it is and what it concerns. Ten questions are asked: 1. Whether sacred doctrine is necessary. 2. Whether it is a science. 3. Whether it is one science, or several. 4. Whether it is speculative or practical. 5. How it is related to other sciences. 6. Whether it is wisdom. 7. What is its subject-matter. 8. Whether it proceeds by argument. 9. Whether it ought to make use of metaphors or figures of speech. 10. Whether the sacred Scriptures of this doctrine should be expounded in several ways.

ARTICLE ONE

WHETHER ANOTHER DOCTRINE IS NECESSARY, BESIDES THE PHILISOPHICAL SCIENCES

We proceed to the first article thus:

1. It seems that there is no need for any other doctrine besides the philosophical sciences. Man should not strive to know what is above reason, since it is said in Ecclesiasticus 3:22: "seek not to know what is higher than thyself." Now what is within the reach of reason is adequately dealt with in the philosophical sciences. It seems superfluous, therefore, that there should be another doctrine besides the philosophical sciences.

2. Again, a doctrine can be concerned only with "what is," since only what is true can be known, and whatever is true, is. Now all things which "are" are dealt with in the philosophical sciences, which treat even of God, wherefore one part of philosophy is called theology, or the science of divine things, as the philosopher[1] says in 6 *Metaph.* (Commentary II). There was therefore no need for another doctrine, besides the philosophical sciences.

On the other hand: it is said in II Tim. 3:16: "All scripture is given by inspiration of God, and is profitable for doctrine, for reproof,

* From A. M. Fairweather, ed., *Aquinas on Nature and Grace,* Volume XI, Library of Christian Classics. Philadelphia: Westminster Press, 1954. Pages 35–41, 50–56, 92–98, 101–103, 105f, 119–125, 137–148, 156–162, 174–177, 202–206, 208–211, 240–242, and 285–287 are reproduced by permission of the publisher.

[1] I.e., Aristotle, Bekker's pages are quoted in the index for all references to Aristotle's works except the *Ethics,* to which references in the text should be sufficiently clear.

for correction, for instruction in righteousness. . . ."[2] Now the divinely inspired Scriptures are quite distinct from the philosophical sciences, which are devised by human reason. It is therefore expedient that there should be another science which is divinely inspired, besides the philosophical sciences.

I answer: it was necessary for man's salvation that there should be a doctrine founded on revelation, as well as the philosophical sciences discovered by human reason. It was necessary, in the first place, because man is ordained to God as his end, who surpasses the comprehension of reason, according to Isa. 64:4: "neither hath the eye seen, O God, besides thee, what he hath prepared for him that waiteth for him." Men must have some foreknowledge of the end to which they ought to direct their intentions and actions. It was therefore necessary that some things which transcend human reason should be made known through divine revelation. It was necessary also that man should be instructed by divine revelation even in such things concerning God as human reason could discover. For such truth about God as could be discovered by reason would be known only by the few, and that after a long time, and mixed with many errors. Now the whole salvation of man, which lies in God, depends on the knowledge of this truth. It was therefore necessary that men should be instructed in divine things through divine revelation, in order that their salvation might come to pass the more fittingly and certainly. It was necessary, therefore, that there should be a sacred doctrine given through revelation, as well as the philosophical sciences discovered by reason.

On the first point: although things which are beyond human knowledge are not to be sought by man through reason, such things are revealed by God, and are to be accepted by faith. Hence Ecclesiasticus adds in the same passage: "many things beyond human understanding have been revealed unto thee" (3:25).

On the second point: sciences are distinguished by their different ways of knowing. The astronomer and the naturalist prove the same thing, for example, that the world is round. But the astronomer proves it by mathematics, without reference to matter, whereas the naturalist proves it by examining the physical. There is no reason, then, why the same things, which the philosophical sciences teach as they can be known by the light of natural reason, should not also be taught by another science as they are known through divine revelation. The theology which depends on sacred Scripture is thus generically different from the theology which is a part of philosophy.

ARTICLE TWO

WHETHER SACRED DOCTRINE IS A SCIENCE

We proceed to the second article thus:

1. It seems that sacred doctrine is not a science. For every science depends on principles which are self-evident, whereas sacred doctrine depends on articles of faith which are not self-evident, since they are not conceded by everybody. As is said in II Thess. 3:2: "all men have not faith." Hence sacred doctrine is not a science.

2. Again, there is no science of particulars.[1] But sacred doctrine is concerned with particulars, such as the deeds of Abraham, Isaac, Jacob, and others. It is not therefore a science.

On the other hand: Augustine says (14 *De Trin.* 1): "by this science only is faith begun, nourished, defended, and strengthened." Now this is true of no science except sacred doctrine. Sacred doctrine is therefore a science.

I answer: sacred doctrine is a science. But we must realize that there are two kinds of sciences. Some of them, such as arithmetic, geometry, and the like, depend on principles known by the natural light of reason. Others depend on principles known through a higher science. Thus the science of perspective depends on principles known through geometry, and music on principles known through arith-

[2] Scriptural passages are quoted from the Authorized Version, any significant divergences in the text being indicated by footnotes.

[1] Aristotle held that the sheer individuality of a particular, its "primary substance," could never be an object of science because it could never be a predicate. Only the "secondary substance," or essence, comprising the universals which must apply to a particular of a certain kind, could be known scientifically. Cf. *Categories V*.

metic. Sacred doctrine is a science of the latter kind, depending on principles known through a higher science, namely the science of God and the blessed. Just as music accepts the principles given to it by arithmetic, so does sacred doctrine accept the principles revealed to it by God.

On the first point: the principles of any science are either self-evident, or derived from what is known through a higher science. The principles of sacred doctrine are so derived, as we have said.

On the second point: sacred doctrine does not narrate particular things because it is principally concerned with them. It introduces them as examples to follow, as do the moral sciences; and also as proofs of the authority of those through whom the divine revelation, on which sacred Scripture and sacred doctrine are founded, reaches us.

ARTICLE THREE

WHETHER SACRED DOCTRINE IS A SINGLE SCIENCE

We proceed to the third article thus:

1. It seems that sacred doctrine is not a single science. As the philosopher says: "one science treats of one kind of subject only" (I *Post. An.*, Text 43). Now sacred doctrine treats of the Creator and also of creatures, and these do not belong to one kind of subject. Hence it is not a single science.

2. Again, sacred doctrine treats of angels, of creatures with bodies, and of the customs of men. These belong to different philosophical sciences. Hence sacred doctrine is not a single science.

On the other hand: sacred Scripture speaks of these things as of a single science, for it is said in Wisdom 10:10: "She hath given him the science of holy things."

I answer: sacred doctrine is a single science. The unity of a power or habit[1] is indeed to be judged by its object, but by the formal nature of its object, not by the material nature of it. For example, man, ass, and stone agree in possessing the formal nature of "the coloured," which is the object of sight. Now since sacred doctrine treats of things as divinely revealed, as we said in the previous article, all things which are divinely revealed agree in the one formal nature which is the object of this science. They are therefore comprehended under sacred doctrine as a single science.

On the first point: sacred doctrine is not concerned with God and with creatures equally. It is concerned with God fundamentally, and with creatures in so far as they relate to God as their beginning or end. Thus the unity of the science is not destroyed.

On the second point: there is nothing to prevent lower powers or habits being differentiated in their relation to matters which yet go together for a higher power or habit, because a higher power or habit comprehends its object under a more universal aspect. Thus the object of the common sense is "the sensible," which includes both the "visible" and the "audible." Common sense is a single power which comprehends all objects of the five senses. Similarly, sacred doctrine remains a single science while it treats under one aspect, in so far as they are all revealed by God, matters which are dealt with by separate philosophical sciences. Sacred doctrine is thus like an imprint of God's knowledge, which is one and undivided, yet is knowledge of all things.

ARTICLE FOUR

WHETHER SACRED DOCTRINE IS A PRACTICAL SCIENCE

We proceed to the fourth article thus:

1. It seems that sacred doctrine is a practical science. For "the end of practical knowledge is action," according to the philosopher (2 *Metaph.*, Text 3), and sacred doctrine is concerned with action, according to James 1:22: "Be ye doers of the word, and not hearers only." Sacred doctrine is therefore a practical science.

2. Again, sacred doctrine is divided into the Old and the New Law, and the Law has to do with the science of morals, which is practical. Sacred doctrine is therefore a practical science.

On the other hand: every practical science is concerned with the works of men. Ethics is concerned with their actions, and architecture

[1] See note to 12ae, Q. 82, Art. 1.

with their buildings. But sacred doctrine is concerned principally with God, whose works men are. Hence it is not a practical science. Rather is it speculative.

I answer: as was said in the preceding article, sacred doctrine embraces matters dealt with by separate philosophical sciences while it itself remains one, because the formal nature to which it attends in diverse things is their being made known by the divine light. Hence even though some matters in the philosophical sciences are speculative and some practical, sacred doctrine includes them all within itself, just as God knows both himself and his works by the same knowledge. But sacred doctrine is more speculative than practical, since it is concerned with divine things more fundamentally than with the actions of men, in which it is interested in so far as through them men are brought to the perfect knowledge of God in which their eternal happiness consists. The answer to the objections is then obvious.

ARTICLE FIVE

WHETHER SACRED DOCTRINE IS NOBLER THAN OTHER SCIENCES

We proceed to the fifth article thus:

1. It seems that sacred doctrine is not nobler than other sciences. For the dignity of a science is indicated by its certainty, and other sciences whose principles cannot be doubted appear to be more certain than sacred doctrine, whose principles, i.e., the articles of faith, are the subject of debate. Thus it seems that other sciences are nobler.

2. Again, a lower science depends on a higher, as music depends on arithmetic. Now sacred doctrine derives something from the philosophical sciences. Hieronymus, indeed, says that "the ancient teachers filled their books with so many philosophical doctrines and opinions that one does not know which to admire the more, their secular learning or their knowledge of the scriptures" (*Epist.* 84 to Magnus the Roman orator). Sacred doctrine is therefore lower than other sciences.

On the other hand: other sciences are said to be subsidiary to this doctrine in Prov. 9:3: "She hath sent forth her maidens: she crieth upon the highest places of the city."

I answer: since sacred doctrine is speculative in some things and practical in others, it transcends all other sciences, whether speculative or practical. One speculative science is said to be nobler than another either because it is more certain, or because it treats of a nobler subject. Sacred doctrine surpasses other speculative sciences in both respects. It is more certain, since the certainty of other sciences depends on the natural light of human reason, which is liable to err, whereas its own certainty is founded on the light of divine knowledge, which cannot be deceived. Its subject is also nobler, since it is concerned principally with things above reason, whereas other sciences deal with things within the reach of reason. Finally, one practical science is nobler than another if it serves a more ultimate end. Politics is nobler than military science, because the good of an army is subsidiary to the good of the state. Now in so far as sacred doctrine is practical, its end is eternal happiness, and all other ends of the practical sciences are subsidiary to this as their ultimate end. It is plain, then, that it is nobler than the others in every way.

On the first point: there is nothing to prevent what is in itself the more certain from appearing to us to be the less certain, owing to the weakness of the intellect, "which is to the things most manifest to nature like the eyes of a bat to the light of the sun," as is said in *Metaph.* 2. The doubt felt by some in respect of the articles of faith is not due to any uncertainty in the thing itself. It is due to the weakness of human understanding. Nevertheless, the least knowledge which one can have of higher things is worth more than the most certain knowledge of lesser things, as is said in the *De Partibus Animalium* (bk. 1, ch. 5).

On the second point: this science can make use of the philosophical sciences in order to make what it teaches more obvious, not because it stands in need of them. It does not take its principles from other sciences, but receives them directly from God through revelation. It thus derives nothing from other sciences as from superiors, but uses them as ancillary inferiors, as the master sciences use subsidiary sciences, or as politics uses military science. Its use of them is not due to any defect or inadequacy in itself. It is due to the limitation of our understanding. We are more easily led from what is known by natural reason, on which other sciences depend, to the things above reason which this science teaches us.

Question Two

The Existence of God

Three questions are asked concerning the existence of God.

1. Whether it is self-evident that God exists. 2. Whether the existence of God can be demonstrated. 3. Whether God exists.

ARTICLE ONE

WHETHER IT IS SELF-EVIDENT THAT GOD EXISTS

We proceed to the first article thus:

1. It seems to be self-evident that God exists. Things are said to be self-evident when the knowledge of them is naturally in us, as is obviously the case with first principles. Now the Damascene* says that "the knowledge that God exists is naturally inborn in all men" (1 *De Fid. Orth.* 1, 3). It is therefore self-evident that God exists.

2. Again, as the philosopher says of the first principles of demonstration, whatever is known as soon as the terms are known is self-evident (1 *Post. An.*, ch. 2). Thus we know that any whole is greater than its part as soon as we know what a whole is, and what a part is. Now when it is understood what the term "God" signifies, it is at once understood that God exists. For the term "God" means that than which nothing greater can be signified, and that which exists in reality is greater than that which exists only in the intellect. Hence since "God" exists in the intellect as soon as the term is understood, it follows that God exists also in reality. It is therefore self-evident that God exists.

3. Again, it is self-evident that truth exists. For truth exists if anything at all is true, and if anyone denies that truth exists, he concedes that it is true that it does not exist, since if truth does not exist it is then true that it does exist. Now God is truth itself, according to John 14:6: "I am the way, and the truth, and the life." It is therefore self-evident that God exists.

On the other hand: no one can conceive the opposite of what is self-evident, as the philosopher explains in dealing with the first principles of demonstration (4 *Metaph.*, text 9; 1 *Post. An.*, texts 5 and *ult.*). Now the opposite of "God exists" can be conceived, according to Ps. 53:1: "The fool hath said in his heart, There is no God." It follows that it is not self-evident that God exists.

I answer: there are two ways in which a thing may be self-evident. It may be self-evident in itself, but not self-evident to us. It may also be self-evident both in itself and to us. A proposition is self-evident when its predicate is contained in the meaning of its subject. For example, the proposition "man is an animal" is self-evident, because "animal" is contained in the meaning of "man." Hence if the predicate and the subject are known to everyone, the proposition will be self-evident to everyone. This is obviously the case with regard to the first principles of demonstration, whose terms are universals known to everyone, such as being and not-being, whole, part, and the like. But when there are some to whom the predicate and the subject are unknown, the proposition will not be self-evident to them, however self-evident it may be in itself. Thus Boethius says (*Lib. de Hebd.*—Whether all Existence is Good): "it happens that some universal concepts of mind are self-evident only to the wise, e.g., that the incorporeal is not in space." I say, then, that this proposition "God exists" is self-evident in itself, since its predicate is the same with its subject. For God is his existence, as we shall show in Q. 3, Art. 4. But since we do not know what God is, it is not self-evident to us, but must be proved by means of what is better known to us though less well known to nature,[1] i.e., by means of the effects of God.

* St. John of Damascus, 700–754.

[1] According to 1 *Post. An.*, chs. 2, 3, the ultimate grounds of scientific proof must be self-evident principles which are "better known to nature," i.e., first in the order of nature, and thus naturally prior to the conclusions drawn from them. The order of our knowing is then the same as the order of being, so that we understand things through their causes.

On the first point: the knowledge that God exists is inborn in us in a general and somewhat confused manner. For God is the final beatitude of man, and a man desires beatitude naturally, and is also naturally aware of what he desires. But this is not absolute knowledge that God exists, any more than to know that someone is coming is to know that Peter is coming, even though it should actually be Peter who comes. Many indeed think that riches are man's perfect good, and constitute his beatitude. Others think that pleasures are his perfect good, and others again something else.

On the second point: he who hears the term "God" may not understand it to mean that than which nothing greater can be conceived, since some have believed that God is a body. But given that one understands the term to mean this, it does not follow that he understands that that which the term signifies exists in the nature of things, but only that it exists in the intellect. Neither can it be argued that God exists in reality, unless it is granted that that than which nothing greater can be conceived exists in reality, which is not granted by those who suppose that God does not exist.

On the third point: it is self-evident that truth in general exists. But it is not self-evident to us that the first truth exists.

ARTICLE TWO

WHETHER GOD'S EXISTENCE CAN BE DEMONSTRATED

We proceed to the second article thus:

1. It seems that God's existence cannot be demonstrated. God's existence is an article of faith. But matters of faith cannot be demonstrated, since demonstration makes a thing to be known, whereas the apostle makes it clear that faith is of things not seen (Heb., ch. 11). It follows that God's existence cannot be demonstrated.

2. Again the medium of demonstration is the essence. But as the Damascene says (1 *De. Fid. Orth.* 4), we cannot know what God is, but only what he is not. It follows that we cannot demonstrate that God exists.

This is obviously impossible in the present instance. Cf. Art. 2.

3. Again, God's existence could be demonstrated only from his effects. But his effects are not proportionate to God himself, since God is infinite while they are finite, and the finite is not proportionate to the infinite. Now a cause cannot be demonstrated from an effect which is not proportionate to itself. It follows that God's existence cannot be demonstrated.

On the other hand: the apostle says in Rom. 1:20: "the invisible things of him . . . are clearly seen, being understood by the things that are made." Now this is possible only if God's existence can be demonstrated from the things that are made. For the first thing that is understood about anything is its existence.

I answer: there are two kinds of demonstration. There is demonstration through the cause, or, as we say, "from grounds," which argues from what comes first in nature. There is also demonstration by means of effects, or "proof by means of appearances," which argues from what comes first for ourselves. Now when an effect is more apparent to us than its cause, we reach a knowledge of the cause through its effect. Even though the effect should be better known to us, we can demonstrate from any effect that its cause exists, because effects always depend on some cause, and a cause must exist if its effect exists. We can demonstrate God's existence in this way, from his effects which are known to us, even though we do not know his essence.

On the first point: the existence of God, and similar things which can be known by natural reason as Rom., ch. 1, affirms, are not articles of faith, but preambles to the articles. Faith presupposes natural knowledge as grace presupposes nature, and as perfection presupposes what can be perfected. There is no reason, however, why what is in itself demonstrable and knowable should not be accepted in faith by one who cannot understand the demonstration of it.

On the second point: when a cause is demonstrated by means of its effect, we are bound to use the effect in place of a definition of the cause in proving the existence of the cause. This is especially the case with regard to God. For in proving that something exists, we are bound to accept the meaning of the name as the medium of demonstration, instead of the essence, since the question of what a thing is must follow the question of its existence. Since the names applied to God are derived from his effects, as we shall show in Q. 13, Art. 1,[1] we may use the name "God" as the medium in demonstrating God's existence from his effect.

On the third point: effects which are not proportionate to their cause do not give us perfect knowledge of their cause. Nevertheless, it can be clearly demonstrated from any effect whatever that its cause exists, as we have said. In this way we can prove God's existence from his effects, even though we cannot know his essence perfectly by means of them.

ARTICLE THREE

WHETHER GOD EXISTS

We proceed to the third article thus:

1. It seems that God does not exist. If one of two contraries were to be infinite, the other would be wholly excluded. Now the name "God" means that he is infinite good. There would therefore be no evil if God were to exist. But there is evil in the world. It follows that God does not exist.

2. Again, what can be explained by comparatively few principles is not the consequence of a greater number of principles. Now if we suppose that God does not exist, it appears that we can still account for all that we see in the world by other principles, attributing all natural things to nature as their principle, and all that is purposive to human reason or will. There is therefore no need to suppose that God exists.

On the other hand: in Ex. 3:14 God says in person: "I AM THAT I AM."

I answer: God's existence can be proved in five ways. The first and clearest proof is the argument from motion.[1] It is certain, and in accordance with sense experience, that some things in this world are moved. Now everything that is moved is moved by something else, since nothing is moved unless it is potentially that to which it is moved, whereas that which moves is actual. To move is nothing other than to bring something from potentiality to actuality, and a thing can be brought from potentiality to actuality only by something which is actual. Thus a fire, which is actually hot, makes wood, which is potentially hot, to be actually hot, so moving and altering it. Now it is impossible for the same thing to be both actual and potential in the same respect, although it may be so in different respects. What is actually hot cannot at the same time be potentially hot, although it is potentially cold. It is therefore impossible that, in the same respect and in the same way, anything should be both mover and moved, or that it should move itself. Whatever is moved must therefore be moved by something else. If, then, that by which it is moved is itself moved, this also must be moved by something else, and this in turn by something else again. But this cannot go on for ever, since there would then be no first mover, and consequently no other mover, because secondary movers cannot move unless moved by a first mover, as a staff cannot move unless it is moved by the hand. We are therefore bound to arrive at a first mover which is not moved by anything, and all men understand that this is God.

The second way is from the nature of an efficient cause. We find that there is a sequence of efficient causes in sensible things. But we do not find that anything is the efficient cause of itself. Nor is this possible, for the thing would then be prior to itself, which is impossible. But neither can the sequence of efficient causes be infinite, for in every sequence the first efficient cause is the cause of an intermediate cause, and an intermediate cause is the cause of the ultimate cause, whether the intermediate causes be many, or only one. Now if a cause is removed, its effect is removed. Hence if there were no first efficient cause, there would be no ultimate cause, and no intermediate cause. But if the regress of efficient causes were infinite, there would be no first efficient cause. There would consequently be no ultimate effect, and no intermediate causes. But this is plainly false. We are therefore bound to suppose that

[1] See appendix to Q. 4, Art. 3.

[1] This paragraph may be compared with Aristotle's *Physics*, bk. 7, ch. 1, 242a; bk. 8, ch. 4, 254b, ch. 5, 256a. Cf. also *S. Contra Gentiles* I, ch. 13, which contains all except the third way. The third way is contained with slight variations in *ibid.* I, ch. 15, II, ch. 15.

there is a first efficient cause. And all men call this God.

The third way is from the nature of possibility and necessity. There are some things which may either exist or not exist, since some things come to be and pass away, and may therefore be or not be. Now it is impossible that all of these should exist at all times, because there is at least some time when that which may possibly not exist does not exist. Hence if all things were such that they might not exist, at some time or other there would be nothing. But if this were true there would be nothing existing now, since what does not exist cannot begin to exist, unless through something which does exist. If there had been nothing existing, it would have been impossible for anything to begin to exist, and there would now be nothing at all. But this is plainly false, and hence not all existence is merely possible. Something in things must be necessary. Now everything which is necessary either derives its necessity from elsewhere, or does not. But we cannot go on to infinity with necessary things which have a cause of their necessity, any more than with efficient causes, as we proved. We are therefore bound to suppose something necessary in itself, which does not owe its necessity to anything else, but which is the cause of the necessity of other things. And all men call this God.

The fourth way is from the degrees that occur in things, which are found to be more and less good, true, noble, and so on. Things are said to be more and less because they approximate in different degrees to that which is greatest. A thing is the more hot the more it approximates to that which is hottest. There is therefore something which is the truest, the best, and the noblest, and which is consequently the greatest in being, since that which has the greatest truth is also greatest in being, as is said in 2 *Metaph.*, text 4. Now that which most thoroughly possesses the nature of any genus is the cause of all that the genus contains. Thus fire, which is most perfectly hot, is the cause of all hot things, as is said in the same passage. There is therefore something which is the cause of the being of all things that are, as well as of their goodness and their every perfection. This we call God.

The fifth way is from the governance of things. We see how some things, like natural bodies, work for an end even though they have no knowledge. The fact that they nearly always operate in the same way, and so as to achieve the maximum good, makes this obvious, and shows that they attain their end by design, not by chance. Now things which have no knowledge tend towards an end only through the agency of something which knows and also understands, as an arrow through an archer. There is therefore an intelligent being by whom all natural things are directed to their end. This we call God.

On the first point: as Augustine says (*Enchirid.* 11): "since God is supremely good, he would not allow any evil thing to exist in his works, were he not able by his omnipotence and goodness to bring good out of evil." God's infinite goodness is such that he permits evil things to exist, and brings good out of them.

On the second point: everything that can be attributed to nature must depend on God as its first cause, since nature works for a predetermined end through the direction of a higher agent. Similarly, whatever is due to purpose must depend on a cause higher than the reason or will of man, since these are subject to change and defect. Anything which is changeable and subject to defect must depend on some first principle which is immovable and necessary in itself, as we have shown.

Question Twenty-Two

Of Divine Providence

Four questions are asked concerning divine providence. 1. Whether providence is appropriately ascribed to God. 2. Whether all things are under divine providence. 3. Whether divine providence affects all things directly. 4. Whether divine providence imposes a necessity on all that it provides.

ARTICLE ONE

WHETHER PROVIDENCE IS APPROPRIATELY ASCRIBED TO GOD

We proceed to the first article thus:

1. It seems that providence is not appropriately ascribed to God. For Tullius says that

"providence is part of prudence" (2 *De Invent.*), and prudence cannot be ascribed to God. Prudence, according to the philosopher (6 *Ethics* 5, 8, 18), gives good counsel, whereas God is not subject to any doubt which could require good counsel. Hence providence is not appropriately ascribed to God.

2. Again, whatever is in God is eternal. But providence is not eternal, since it is concerned with existing things, which are not eternal, as the Damascene says (1 *De Fid. Orth.* 3). Hence providence is not in God.

3. Again, there is nothing composite in God. But providence seems to be composite, since it involves both intellect and will. Hence providence is not in God.

On the other hand: it is said in Wisdom 14:3: "Thou, O Father, rulest all things by providence."

I answer: we are bound to say that there is providence in God, since God has created every good that exists in things, as we said in Q. 6, Art. 4. Now there is good not only in the substance of things, but also in their ordination to an end, especially to the ultimate end, which is a divine good, as we said in Q. 21, Art. 4. God is therefore the source of the good which exists in the order which relates created things to their end. Further, since God is the cause of things through his intellect, the reason for every one of his effects must pre-exist in his intellect, as we explained in Q. 21, Art. 4, also. Hence the reason why things are ordained to their end must pre-exist in the mind of God. But the reason why things are ordained to their end is, properly speaking, providence, because it is the principal part of prudence. The other two parts of prudence, memory of the past and understanding of the present, are subordinate to it, helping us to decide how to provide for the future. As the philosopher says in 6 *Ethics* 12, prudence directs other capacities to an end, whether it be for one's own sake or for the sake of one's dependents in a family, state, or kingdom. Thus we say that a man is prudent when he directs his actions well in view of the end of life, and Matt. 24:45 speaks of "a faithful and wise servant, whom his lord hath made ruler over his household." Prudence or providence of this kind is appropriately ascribed to God. There is indeed nothing in God which needs to be directed to its end, since God is himself the ultimate end. But what we mean by "providence" in God is the reason for the ordination of things to their end. Thus Boethius says (4 *De Consol.* 6): "Providence is the divine reason which resides in the highest principle of all things, and which disposes all things." We may add that this disposition is the reason for the ordination of things to their end, as well as for the ordering of parts in a whole.

On the first point: as the philosopher says in 6 *Ethics* 9 and 10, "prudence properly directs us in what good deliberation rightly advises, and in what sound judgment rightly judges." God does not indeed take counsel, for this means to inquire into what is doubtful. But he does decree the ordering of things to their end, since the true idea of things lies in him. As Ps. 148:6 says: "he hath made a decree which shall not pass." Prudence and providence in this sense are appropriately ascribed to God. The reason for doing things may be called "counsel" in God, not because it involves inquiry, but because of the certainty of the knowledge of it, to which those who take counsel can attain only by means of inquiry. Thus it is said in Eph. 1:11: ". . . who worketh all things after the counsel of his own will."

On the second point: there are two aspects of providential care. There is the reason for the order in things, which is called providence, and there is the disposition and execution of this order. The former is eternal, the latter temporal.

On the third point: providence does belong to the intellect, and also presupposes an end which is willed, since no one determines the means to an end unless he wills the end. Prudence likewise presupposes the moral virtues through which desires are related to the good, as is said in 6 *Ethics* 12. But even though providence should relate both to the will and to the intellect of God, this would not destroy the simple nature of God, since in God will and intellect are the same, as we said in Q. 19, Arts. 2 and 4.

ARTICLE TWO

WHETHER ALL THINGS ARE UNDER DIVINE PROVIDENCE

We proceed to the second article thus:

1. It seems that not all things are under divine providence. For nothing that is ordained happens contingently, and if all things were provided by God, nothing would happen contingently. There would then be no such thing as chance or fortune. But this is contrary to common opinion.

2. Again, every wise provider, so far as he is able, preserves those in his care from defect and from evil. But we see many evils in things. Hence either God cannot prevent evil, and is not omnipotent, or not all things are under his care.

3. Again, that which happens by necessity does not require providence, or prudence. As the philosopher says (6 *Ethics* 4, 9, 11): "prudence is right reason applied to contingencies, which demand deliberation and choice." Now many things happen by necessity. Not all things, therefore, are ruled by providence.

4. Again, he who is left to himself is not under the providence of any governor. Now God leaves men to themselves, according to Ecclesiasticus 15:14: "God made man from the beginning, and left him in the hands of his own counsel," especially so the wicked, according to Ps. 81:12: "So I gave them up unto their own hearts' lust." Not all things, therefore, are under divine providence.

5. Again, the apostle says in 1 Cor. 9:9: "Doth God take care for oxen?"—or, we may say, for any irrational creature. Not all things, therefore, are under divine providence.

On the other hand: Wisdom 8:1 says of the wisdom of God: "It extends from end to end with power, and disposes all things sweetly."

I answer: Democritus and the Epicureans, and others also, denied any such thing as providence, maintaining that the world was made by chance. Others again have held that incorruptible things are under the care of providence, but that only the incorruptible species of corruptible things are so, not the corruptible individuals. The voice in Job 22:14 speaks their views: "Thick clouds are a covering to him, that he seeth not; and he walketh in the circuit of heaven." Rabbi Moses, also, excluded men from the class of corruptible things on account of their surpassing intelligence, but followed the opinion of the others concerning things which pass away.

But we are bound to say that all things are under divine providence, individually as well as collectively. We prove this as follows. Every agent acts for the sake of an end. The effects of a first agent will therefore serve his end to the extent to which his causality extends. This means that the works of an agent may contain something which results from some cause other than his own intention, and which does not serve his end. But God's causality extends to all being, since God is the first of all agents. It extends to the principles of individuals as well as of species, and to the principles of corruptibles as well as of incorruptibles. Everything which has any kind of being is therefore bound to be ordained by God to some end. As the apostle says in Rom. 13:1: "the powers that be are ordained of God."[1] Now we said in the previous article that God's providence is nothing other than the reason why things are ordained to an end. It follows that all things which have any kind of being must be under the rule of divine providence. We also said that God knows all things, whether universal or particular, and that his knowledge is related to things as the knowledge of an art to the things which it makes (Q. 14, Arts. 6, 11). It follows from this that all things are under the ordinance of God, just as the creations of an art are under the ordinance of the art.

On the first point: there is a difference between a universal cause and a particular cause. A thing may avoid being determined by a particular cause, but it cannot avoid being determined by a universal cause. It can avoid determination by one particular cause only through the intervention of another, as wood is prevented from burning by the action of water. It is therefore impossible for any effect to escape determination by the universal cause to which all particular causes are subordinate. Now in so far as an effect escapes determination by one particular cause, it is said to occur by chance, or to be contingent so far as that

[1] Migne: "The things which are of God are ordained."

particular cause is concerned. But it is still said to be provided by the universal cause whose ordinance it cannot escape. For example, the meeting of two slaves may be due to chance so far as they are concerned, but it has nevertheless been arranged by the master who wittingly sent them to the same place, without either of them knowing about the other.

On the second point: there is a difference between a universal provider and one who cares for a particular thing. One who is entrusted with the care of a particular thing guards it from defect so far as he can. But a universal provider allows some defect to occur in some things, lest the good of the whole should be impaired. Corruptions and defects in natural things are said to be contrary to their particular natures, but to be nevertheless in harmony with universal nature, in as much as the defect of one issues in the good of another, even of the whole universe. The passing away of one individual is the generation of another, and the species is preserved by means of it. Now God is the universal provider of all that is. It is therefore fitting that his providence should permit certain defects in particular things, lest the perfect good of the universe should be impaired. The universe would lack many good things, if all evils were excluded. There would not be the life of a lion, if there were no slaying of animals. There would not be the endurance of martyrs, if there were no persecution by tyrants. Thus Augustine says: "God omnipotent would not allow any evil thing to exist in his works, were he not able by his omnipotence and goodness to bring good out of evil" (*Enchirid.* 2). Those who have believed that corruptible things subject to chance and to evil are outside the care of divine providence seem to have been influenced by these two objections which we have answered.

On the third point: man uses nature when he practises the arts and the virtues. But he did not make nature, and for this reason man's providence does not extend to what nature determines by necessity. But God's providence does so extend, since God is the author of nature. It was, apparently, this objection that induced Democritus and other ancient naturalists to think that the course of natural things was outside the scope of divine providence, and due to a material necessity.

On the fourth point: the saying that man is left to himself does not mean that he is altogether cut off from God's providence. It means that the power which works determinately towards a single end is not extended to him as it is even to natural things, which act for an end only through the direction of something else, and do not direct themselves to it like rational creatures, who deliberate and choose by free will. The words "in the hands of his own counsel" are therefore significant. Yet the activity of man's free will still derives from God as its cause, so that whatever he does by means of it is still under the rule of God's providence. Even man's own providence remains under God's providence, as a particular cause under a universal cause. Nevertheless, God's providence cares for the just in a more excellent way than it cares for the ungodly, since he allows nothing to happen to the just which might finally prevent their salvation. As Rom. 8:28 says: "all things work together for good to them that love God." When it is said that God leaves the ungodly to themselves, this means that he does not restrain them from the evil of guilt, not that they are altogether excluded from his providence. They would indeed fall away into nothing, if his providence did not preserve them in being. When Tullius said that the matters concerning which men take counsel were outside the scope of divine providence, he seems to have been influenced by this objection.

On the fifth point: as we said in Q. 19, Art. 10, a rational creature is master of its own actions, since it possesses a free-will. But it is under divine providence in a special way as the recipient of blame or praise, and of punishment or reward. It is this aspect of God's care which the apostle denies to oxen. He does not say that God's providence has no regard for irrational creatures, as Rabbi Moses thought.

Question Twenty-Three

Of Predestination

After divine providence, we must consider predestination. There are eight questions on predestination. 1. Whether God predestines. 2. What predestination is, and whether it implies anything in one who is predestined. 3. Whether God rejects some men. 4. How predestination relates to election, or, whether the predestined are chosen. 5. Whether merits are the ground or cause of predestination or reprobation, or of election. 6. Of the certainty of predestination, or, whether the predestined are bound to be saved. 7. Whether the number of the predestined is certain. 8. Whether predestination can be furthered by the prayers of the saints.

ARTICLE ONE

WHETHER MEN ARE PREDESTINED BY GOD

We proceed to the first article thus:

1. It seems that men are not predestined by God. For the Damascene says: "We ought to know that God foreknows all things, but does not predetermine all things. He has foreknowledge of all that is in us, but does not predetermine it" (*2 De Fid. Orth.* 30). Now human merits and demerits are in us, since free will makes us master of our actions. It follows that whatever has to do with merit or demerit is not predestined by God. But this makes the predestination of men impossible.

2. Again, it was said in Q. 22, Arts. 1 and 2 that all creatures are directed to their end by divine providence. Yet other creatures are not said to be predestined by God. Neither, then, are men.

3. Again, angels are capable of blessedness no less than men. But predestination does not apply to angels, apparently because they have never known misery and because predestination is the decision to have mercy, as Augustine says (*De Praed. Sanct.* 17). Neither, therefore, does it apply to men.

4. Again, the benefits which God bestows on men are revealed to the saints by the Holy Spirit, according to I Cor. 2:12: "Now we have received, not the spirit of the world, but the spirit which is of God; that we might know the things that are freely given to us of God." Hence if men were predestined by God, their predestination would be known to those who were predestined, since predestination is a benefit which God bestows. But this is obviously untrue.

On the other hand: it is said in Rom. 8:30: "whom he did predestinate, them he also called."

I answer: it is rightly said that God predestines men. We have shown that all things are ruled by divine providence (Q. 22, Art. 4), and that providence ordains things to their end (Q. 22, Arts. 1 and 2). Now the end to which God ordains creatures is twofold. There is, first, the end which exceeds the proportion and the capacity of created nature. This is eternal life, which consists in the vision of the divine essence, which is beyond the nature of any creature, as we said in Q. 12, Art. 4. There is, secondly, the end which is proportionate to created nature, which a created thing may attain by means of its own natural power. Now when a thing cannot attain something by its own natural power, it must be directed to it by another, as an arrow is directed to its mark by an archer. Properly speaking, then, although a rational creature is capable of eternal life, he is brought to this life by God. The reason why he is brought to eternal life must therefore pre-exist in God, since the reason why anything is ordained to its end lies in God, and we have said that this is providence. The reason which exists in the mind of an agent is, as it were, a pre-existence in him of the thing which he intends to do. We give the name of "predestination" to the reason why a rational creature is brought to eternal life, because to destine means to bring. It is plain, then, that predestination is a part of providence, if we consider it in relation to its objects.

On the first point: by predetermination the Damascene means the imposition of a necessity such as occurs in natural things predetermined to a single end. His next words make this clear —"God does not will malice, nor compel virtue." This does not make predestination impossible.

On the second point: irrational creatures are not capable of the end which exceeds the capacity of human nature. Hence they are not properly said to be predestined, although we do speak loosely of predestination in relation to other ends.

On the third point: predestination applies to angels as well as to men, even though they have never known misery. A movement is defined by its *terminus ad quem,* not by its *terminus a quo.* To be made white means the same thing whether one who is made white was formerly black, pale, or red. Predestination also means the same thing whether or not one is predestined to eternal life from a state of misery.

On the fourth point: their predestination is revealed to some by special privilege. But to reveal it in every case would be improvident. Those who are not predestined would despair, and security would engender negligence in those who are.

ARTICLE THREE

WHETHER GOD REJECTS ANY MAN

We proceed to the third article thus:

1. God, it seems, rejects no man. Nobody rejects one whom he loves, and God loves every man, according to Wisdom 11:24: "Thou lovest all things that are, and hatest nothing that thou hast made." It follows that God rejects no man.

2. Again, if God does reject anyone, rejection must be related to the rejected as predestination is related to the predestined. Rejection must then be the cause of the perdition of the rejected, as predestination is the cause of the salvation of the predestined. But this is not true, since it is said in Hos. 13:9: "O Israel, thou hast destroyed thyself; but in me is thine help." It follows that God does not reject anyone.

3. Again, no one can be held responsible for what he cannot avoid. But no one could avoid destruction if God were to reject him. As Ecclesiastes says (7:13): "Consider the work of God: for who can make that straight which he hath made crooked."[1] Men would not then be responsible for their own destruction. But this is false. It follows that God does not reject any man.

On the other hand: it is said in Mal. 1:2–3: "I loved Jacob. And I hated Esau."

I answer: God does reject some men. We have said that predestination is a part of providence (Art. 1), and that providence permits a measure of defect in the things over which it rules (Q. 22, Art. 2). Now although providence ordains men to eternal life, it permits some of them to fail to attain this end. This is what is called rejection. Rejection is the part of providence which relates to those who fail to attain eternal life, just as predestination is the part of providence which relates to those who are ordained to it. Rejection therefore means more than foreknowledge, just as we agreed with Augustine (1 *Ad Simplician* 3) that providence means more than this (Q. 22, Art. 1). While predestination includes the will to bestow grace and glory, rejection includes the will to allow some to incur guilt, and to impose the penalty of damnation on account of guilt.

On the first point: God loves every man, and every creature also, in that he wills some good for every one of them. But he does not will every good for every one, and is said to hate some in so far as he does not will for them the good of eternal life.

On the second point: predestination is the cause of the glory which the predestined expect to receive in the life to come, and also of the grace which they receive in this present life. Rejection is the cause of desertion by God, but not of present guilt. It is the cause of eternal punishment to come, but guilt is due to the free will of him who is rejected and deserted by grace. What the prophet says is therefore true—"O Israel, thou hast destroyed thyself."

On the third point: rejection by God does not deprive the rejected one of any power. When it is said that a rejected man cannot receive grace, this does not mean that it is absolutely impossible for him to do so. It means that this is conditionally impossible. The salvation of a predestined man is ensured by a necessity which is likewise conditional, in that it permits freedom of choice. Thus even though one who is rejected by God cannot receive grace, it lies with his free will whether he falls into one sin or another, and his sin is deservedly imputed to him as guilt.

Question Eighty-Two

The Essence of Original Sin

We must now consider the essence of original

[1] Migne: "whom he hath despised."

sin. There are four questions asked concerning it. 1. Whether original sin is a habit. 2. Whether original sin is one only, in any one man. 3. Whether original sin is desire. 4. Whether original sin is equally in all men.

ARTICLE ONE

WHETHER ORIGINAL SIN IS A HABIT

We proceed to the first article thus:

1. It seems that original sin is not a habit. As Anselm says (*De Conceptu Virginali* 2, 3, 26), original sin is the lack of original justice. It is therefore a kind of privation. But a privation is opposed to a habit. Hence original sin is not a habit.

2. Again, the character of guilt attaches to actual sin more than to original sin, since actual sin has more of the nature of the voluntary. But there is no guilt in the habit of actual sin. If there were, a man would sin guiltily while he slept. There cannot then be any guilt in a habit which is original.

3. Again, an act of sin always precedes the habit of it, because sinful habits are always acquired, never infused. But there is no act which precedes original sin. Hence original sin is not a habit.

On the other hand: Augustine says (*De Baptismo Puer; De Peccat. Mer. et Remis.* I, ch. 39; *De Tempt., Sermo* 45): "because of original sin infants have a tendency to desire, even though they do not actually desire." Now we speak of a tendency where there is a habit. Original sin is therefore a habit.

I answer: as we said in Q. 50, Art. 1, there are two kinds of habit. There is the habit which inclines a power to act, of the kind which enables us to say that sciences and virtues are habits. Original sin is not a habit of this kind. But we also give the name of habit to the disposition by which a composite nature is well or ill disposed in a certain way, especially when such a disposition has become almost second nature, as in the case of sickness or of health. Original sin is such a habit. It is the disordered disposition which has resulted from the dissolution of the harmony which was once the essence of original justice, just as bodily sickness is the disordered disposition of a body which has lost the equilibrium which is the essence of health. Original sin is accordingly called the languor of nature.

On the first point: just as sickness of the body involves positive disorder in the disposition of the humours, as well as privation of the equilibrium of health, so original sin involves disorder in the disposition of the parts of the soul, as well as the privation of original justice. It is more than mere privation. It is a corrupt habit.

On the second point: actual sin is the disorder of an act. But original sin is the disordered disposition of nature itself, since it is the sin of nature. Now this disordered disposition has the character of guilt in so far as it is inherited from our first parent, as we said in Q. 81, Art. 1. It also has the character of a habit, which the disordered disposition of an act has not. Original sin can therefore be a habit, though actual sin cannot be a habit.

On the third point: this objection argues about the kind of habit which inclines a power to act. Original sin is not a habit of this kind, although it does result in an inclination to disordered actions. It results in such inclination not directly but indirectly, through depriving us of the original justice which would have prevented disorderly actions, and once did prevent them. The inclination to disordered bodily functions results from sickness in this same indirect way. But we should not say that original sin is an infused habit, nor that it is acquired through action (unless the action of our first parent, but not that of any present person). It is inborn by reason of our corrupt origin.

ARTICLE FOUR

WHETHER ORIGINAL SIN IS IN ALL MEN EQUALLY

We proceed to the fourth article thus:

1. It seems that original sin is not in all men equally. It was said in the preceding article that original sin is inordinate desire. But all men are not equally subject to desire. It follows that original sin is not in all men equally.

2. Again, original sin is the disordered disposition of the soul, as sickness is the disor-

dered disposition of the body. Now sickness admits of more or less. Therefore original sin also admits of more and less.

3. Again, Augustine says: "lust transmits original sin to posterity." (1 *De Nup. et Concup.* 23–24.) But the lust in generation may be greater in one than in another. Original sin may therefore be greater in one than in another.

On the other hand: it was said in the preceding article that original sin is the sin of nature. But nature is in all men equally. Original sin is therefore also in all men equally.

I answer: there are two things in original sin. One is the lack of original justice. The other is the relation of this lack to the sin of our first parent, from whom it is inherited through our corrupt origin. Now original sin cannot be greater or less in respect of the lack of original justice, since the whole gift of original justice has been taken away. Privations do not admit of more and less when they deprive us of something altogether, as we said of death and darkness in Q. 73, Art. 2. Nor can original sin be greater or less in respect of its relation to its origin. Everyone bears the same relation to the first beginning of the corrupt origin from which sin derives its guilt, and relations do not admit of greater and less. It is plain, then, that original sin cannot be greater in one man than in another.

On the first point: since man has lost the control of original justice which once kept all the powers of his soul in order, each power tends to follow its own natural movement, and to follow it more vehemently the stronger it is. Now some powers of the soul may be stronger in one man than in another, because bodily characteristics vary. That one man should be more subject to desire than another is not therefore the consequence of original sin, since all are equally deprived of the control of original justice, and the lower parts of the soul are equally left to themselves in all men. It is due to the different dispositions of their powers, as we have said.

On the second point: sickness of the body does not have an equal cause in all cases, even if it is of the same kind. For example, fever which results from putrefaction of the bile may be due to a greater or lesser putrefaction, or to one which is more or less removed from a vital principle. But the cause of original sin is equal in respect of everyone. There is therefore no comparison.

On the third point: it is not actual lust that transmits original sin to posterity, for one would still transmit original sin even if it were divinely granted that one should feel no lust in generation. We must understand it to be habitual lust, on account of which the sensitive appetite is not subject to reason, now that the control of original justice is lost. Lust of this kind is equally in all.

Question One Hundred and Nine

Concerning the External Principle of Human Actions, That Is, the Grace of God

We must now consider the external principle of human actions, that is, God, in so far as we are helped by him to act rightly through grace. We shall consider first the grace of God, secondly its cause, and thirdly its effects. The first of these inquiries will be threefold, since we shall inquire first into the necessity of grace, second into the essence of grace itself, and third into the divisions of it.

There are ten questions concerning the necessity of grace. 1. Whether without grace a man can know any truth. 2. Whether without grace a man can do or will any good. 3. Whether without grace a man can love God above all things. 4. Whether without grace a man can keep the commandments of the law, by his own natural powers. 5. Whether without grace he can merit eternal life. 6. Whether without grace a man can prepare himself for grace. 7. Whether without grace he can rise from sin. 8. Whether without grace he can avoid sin. 9. Whether, having received grace, a man can do good and avoid sin without further divine help. 10. Whether he can persevere in good by himself.

ARTICLE ONE

WHETHER A MAN CAN KNOW ANY TRUTH WITHOUT GRACE

We proceed to the first article thus:

1. It seems that a man cannot know any truth without grace. The gloss by Ambrose on

I Cor. 12:3, "no man can say that Jesus is the Lord, but by the Holy Ghost," says that "every truth, by whomsoever uttered, is by the Holy Ghost." Now the Holy Ghost dwells in us by grace. Hence we cannot know truth without grace.

2. Again, Augustine says (1 *Soliloq.* 6): "the most certain sciences are like things lit up by the sun so that they may be seen. But it is God who gives the light. Reason is in our minds as sight is in our eyes, and the eyes of the mind are the senses of the soul." Now however pure it be, bodily sense cannot see any visible thing without the light of the sun. Hence however perfect be the human mind, it cannot by reasoning know any truth without the light of God, which belongs to the aid of grace.

3. Again, the human mind cannot understand truth except by thinking, as Augustine explains (14 *De Trin.* 7). Now in II Cor. 3:5 the apostle says: "Not that we are sufficient of ourselves to think anything as of ourselves." Hence a man cannot know truth by himself, without the help of grace.

On the other hand: Augustine says (1 *Retract.* 4): "I do not now approve of having said in a prayer 'O God, who dost will that only the pure shall know truth.' For it may be replied that many who are impure know many truths." Now a man is made pure by grace, according to Ps. 51:10: "Create in me a clean heart, O God, and renew a right spirit within me." It follows that a man can know truth by himself, without the help of grace.

I answer: to know truth is a use or action of the intellectual light, since the apostle says that "whatever doth make manifest is light"[1] (Eph. 5:13), and every use involves movement, in the broad sense in which understanding and will are said to be movements, as the philosopher explains in 3 *De Anima,* text 28. In corporeal things, we see that any movement not only requires a formal principle of the movement or action itself, but also requires a motion of the first mover. Since the first mover in the order of material things is the heavenly body, fire could not cause change otherwise than through the motion of the heavenly body, even though it should possess perfect heat. It is plain, then, that just as every corporeal movement derives from the movement of the heavenly body as the first corporeal mover, so all movements, whether corporeal or spiritual, derive from the absolute prime mover, which is God. Hence no matter how perfect any corporeal or spiritual nature is supposed to be, it cannot issue in its act unless it is moved by God, whose moving is according to the plan of his providence, not necessitated by nature like the moving of the heavenly body. Now not only is every motion derived from God as first mover, but every formal perfection is likewise derived from God, as from the first act. It follows that an action of the intellect, or of any created thing, depends on God in two ways: first, in that it has from him the perfection or the form by means of which it acts, and second, in that it is moved to its act by him. Every power bestowed by God upon created things has the power to achieve some definite action by means of its own properties. But it cannot achieve anything further, unless through a form which is added to it. Water, for example, cannot heat unless it is itself heated by fire. So also the human intellect possesses the form of intellectual light, which by itself is sufficient for the knowledge of such intelligible things as we can learn through sense. But it cannot know intelligible things of a higher order unless it is perfected by a stronger light, such as the light of faith or prophecy, which is called "the light of glory" since it is added to nature.

We must therefore say that, if a man is to know any truth whatsoever, he needs divine help in order that his intellect may be moved to its act by God. But he does not need a new light added to his natural light in order to know the truth in all things, but only in such things as transcend his natural knowledge. Yet God sometimes instructs men miraculously by grace in matters which can be known through natural reasons, just as he sometimes achieves by miracle things which nature can do.

On the first point: "every truth, by whomsoever uttered, is by the Holy Ghost"—but as bestowing the natural light and as moving us to understand and to speak the truth, not as dwelling in us through sanctifying grace, or as bestowing any permanent gift superadded to nature. This is the case only with certain truths

[1] Migne: "All that is made manifest is light."

which must be known and spoken—especially with truths of faith, of which the apostle is speaking.

On the second point: the corporeal sun illumines externally, God internally. The natural light bestowed on the mind is God's light, by which we are enlightened to know such things as belong to natural knowledge. Other light is not required for this, but only for such things as transcend natural knowledge.

On the third point: we always need divine help for any thinking, in so far as God moves the intellect to act. For to think is to understand something actively, as Augustine explains (14 *De Trin.* 7).

ARTICLE TWO

WHETHER A MAN CAN WILL OR DO GOOD WITHOUT GRACE

We proceed to the second article thus:

1. It seems that a man can will and do good without grace. For that of which he is master is within a man's power, and it was said previously that a man is master of his actions, especially of his willing. (Q. 1, Art. 1; Q. 13, Art. 6.) It follows that a man can will and do good by himself, without the help of grace.

2. Again, a man is master of what conforms with his nature more than of what is contrary to it. Now to sin is contrary to nature, as the Damascene says (2 *De Fid. Orth.* 30), whereas the practice of virtue conforms with nature, as was said in Q. 71, Art. 1. It seems, therefore, that since a man can sin by himself, he can much more will and do good by himself.

3. Again, "truth is the good of the intellect," as the philosopher says in 6 *Ethics* 2. Now the intellect can know truth by itself, just as any other thing can perform its natural action by itself. Much more, then, can a man will and do good by himself.

On the other hand: the apostle says in Rom. 9:16: "it is not of him that willeth, nor of him that runneth, but of God that sheweth mercy." Augustine, also, says that "men do absolutely nothing good without grace, whether by thought, will, love, or deed" (*De Corrept. et Grat.* 2).

I answer: man's nature may be considered in two ways, either in its purity, as it was in our first parent before sin, or as corrupt, as it is in ourselves after the sin of our first parent. In either state, human nature needs divine help in order to do or to will any good, since it needs a first mover, as we said in the preceding article. In regard to the sufficiency of his operative power, man in the state of pure nature could will and do, by his own natural power, the good proportionate to his nature, such as the good of acquired virtue, though not surpassing good such as the good of infused virtue. In the state of corrupt nature he falls short of what nature makes possible, so that he cannot by his own power fulfil the whole good that pertains to his nature. Human nature is not so entirely corrupted by sin, however, as to be deprived of natural good altogether. Consequently, even in the state of corrupt nature a man can do some particular good by the power of his own nature, such as build houses, plant vineyards, and things of this kind. But he cannot achieve the whole good natural to him, as if he lacked nothing. One who is infirm, similarly, can make some movements by himself, but cannot move himself naturally like a man in health, unless cured by the help of medicine.

Thus in the state of pure nature man needs a power added to his natural power by grace, for one reason, namely, in order to do and to will supernatural good. But in the state of corrupt nature he needs this for two reasons, in order to be healed, and in order to achieve the meritorious good of supernatural virtue. In both states, moreover, he needs the divine help by which he is moved to act well.

On the first point: it is because of the deliberation of his reason, which can turn to one side or the other, that a man is master of his actions, and of willing and not willing. But although he is thus master, it is only through a previous deliberation that he either deliberates or does not deliberate. Since this regress cannot be infinite, we are finally driven to say that a man's free will is moved by an external principle higher than the mind of man, that is, by God. The philosopher indeed proves this in his chapter on Good Fortune (7 *Mor. Eudem.* 18). Thus even the mind of a healthy man is not so thoroughly master of its actions that it does not need to be moved by God. Much more so the free will of a man weakened by sin and thereby hindered from good by the corruption of nature.

On the second point: to sin is nothing other than to fall short of the good which befits one according to one's nature. Now just as every created thing has its being from another, and considered in itself is nothing, so also it must be preserved by another in the good which befits its nature. It can nevertheless through itself fall short of this good, just as it can through itself cease to exist, if it is not providentially preserved.

On the third point: as we said in Art. 1, a man cannot even know truth without divine help. Now his nature is impaired by sin more in the desire for good than in the knowledge of truth.

ARTICLE THREE

WHETHER A MAN CAN LOVE GOD ABOVE ALL THINGS BY HIS NATURAL POWERS ALONE, WITHOUT GRACE

We proceed to the third article thus:

1. It seems that a man cannot love God above all things by his natural powers alone, without grace. To love God above all things is the proper and principal act of charity, and a man cannot have charity of himself, since "the love of God is shed abroad in our hearts by the Holy Ghost, which is given unto us" (Rom. 5:5). It follows that a man cannot love God above all things by his natural powers alone.

2. Again, no nature can rise above itself. But to love God more than oneself is to tend to what is above oneself. Hence no created nature can love God more than itself, without the help of grace.

3. Again, since God is the greatest good, we ought to give him the greatest love, which is to love him above all things. But without grace a man is not fit to give to God the greatest love, which we ought to give him, since it would be useless to add grace if he were so. It follows that a man cannot love God by his natural powers alone, without grace.

On the other hand: as some maintain, the first man was made with natural powers only, and it is obvious that in this state he loved God to some extent. But he loved God neither equally with himself nor less than himself, since he would have sinned in either case. He therefore loved God more than himself. It follows that man can love God more than himself and above all things by his natural powers alone.

I answer: as we said when we stated the various opinions about the natural love of angels (Pt. I, Q. 60, Art. 5), man in the state of pure nature could do such good as was natural to him by means of his natural power, without any superadded gift of grace, though not without the help of God moving him. To love God above all things is natural to man, and indeed to every creature, irrational as well as rational, and even to inanimate things, according to the manner of love of which each creature is capable. The reason for this is that it is natural for each thing to desire and to love something, according to what it is made fit to love, just as each thing acts as it is made fit to act, as is said in *2 Physics,* text 78. Now it is clear that the good of the part is for the sake of the good of the whole. It follows that every particular thing, by its own natural desire or love, loves its own peculiar good for the sake of the common good of the whole universe, which is God. As Dionysius says, "God directs everything to love himself" (4 *Div. Nom.,* lect. 11). In the state of pure nature, accordingly, man subordinated his love of himself, and of all other things also, to love of God as its end. Thus he loved God more than himself, and above all things. But in the state of corrupt nature he falls short of this in the desire of his rational will, which through corruption seeks its own private good, unless it is healed by the grace of God.

We must say, accordingly, that in the state of pure nature man did not need a gift of grace added to his natural power, in order to love God above all things, although he did need the help of God moving him to do so. But in the state of corrupt nature he needs further help of grace, that his nature may be healed.

On the first point: charity loves God above all things more eminently than does nature. Nature loves God above all things because he is the beginning and the end of the good of nature. Charity loves God because he is the object of beatitude, and because man has spiritual fellowship with him. Moreover, charity adds an immediate willingness and joy to the natural love of God, just as the habit of virtue adds something to a good action which springs solely from the natural reason of a man who lacks the habit of virtue.

On the second point: when it is said that no nature can rise above itself, we must not understand that it cannot be drawn to what is above itself. For it is evident that the intellect can know, by natural knowledge, some things above itself, as it manifestly does in the natural knowledge of God. What we must understand is that a nature cannot be incited to an action which exceeds the proportion of its power. But to love God above all things is not such an action. This is natural to every created nature, as we have said.

On the third point: love is said to be greatest, not only on the ground of the degree of its affection, but also on the ground of the reason for it and the quality of it. On such grounds, the greatest love is the love with which charity loves God as him who leads us to beatitude, as we have said.

ARTICLE FOUR

WHETHER A MAN CAN FULFIL THE COMMANDMENTS OF THE LAW BY HIS NATURAL POWERS, WITHOUT GRACE

We proceed to the fourth article thus:

1. It seems that a man can fulfil the commandments of the law by his own natural powers, without grace. For the apostle says that "the Gentiles, which have not the law, do by nature the things contained in the law" (Rom. 2:14). But what a man does by nature he can do by himself, without grace. He can therefore keep the commandments of the law without grace.

2. Again, Hieronymus (Pelagius) says that "they speak ill who affirm that God has commanded anything impossible for man" (*Expositio Cath. Fidei, Epist. ad Damasc.*). Now what a man cannot fulfil is impossible for him. It follows that he can fulfil all the commandments of the law by himself.

3. Again, it is plain from Matt. 22:37 that the greatest commandment of all is this: "thou shalt love the Lord thy God with all thy heart." Now a man can fulfil this commandment by his natural powers alone, by loving God above all things, which the preceding article affirmed that he can do. He can therefore fulfil all the commandments of the law without grace.

On the other hand: Augustine says (*De Haer.* 88): "to believe that a man can fulfil all the divine commandments without grace is part of the Pelagian heresy."

I answer: there are two ways of fulfilling the commandments of the law. In the first place, one may actually do what the law commands, by performing acts of justice or fortitude, for example, or other acts of virtue. Man could fulfil all the commandments of the law in this way when he was in the state of pure nature, since he would not otherwise have been able to avoid sin, which is nothing other than transgression of the divine commandments. But a man in the state of corrupt nature cannot fulfil all the divine commandments without healing grace. In the second place, the law may be fulfilled not only in respect of what it commands, but also in respect of the manner of action. It is so fulfilled when actions are inspired by charity. A man cannot fulfil the law in this way without grace, whether in the state of pure nature or in the state of corrupt nature. For this reason, when Augustine said that men do absolutely nothing good without grace, he added: "not only do they know by grace what they ought to do, but they do it out of love by the aid of grace" (*De Corrept. et. Grat.*). In both states, moreover, men need the help of God moving them to fulfil his commandments, as we said in Art. 3.

On the first point: as Augustine says (*De Spiritu et Littera,* 27): "It should not disturb us that he said that these do by nature the things contained in the law. For this is wrought by the spirit of grace, to restore within us the image of God in which we were naturally made."

On the second point: what we can do by means of divine help is not absolutely impossible for us. As the philosopher says: "what we can do through our friends we can in a sense do ourselves" (3 *Ethics* 3). Hieronymus (Pelagius) accordingly confesses, in the passage quoted, that "our will is free enough to allow us to say that we always need God's help."

On the third point: it is clear from what was

said in Art. 3 that a man cannot, by his natural powers alone, fulfil the commandment about love to God in the same way as it is fulfilled through charity.

ARTICLE FIVE

WHETHER A MAN CAN MERIT ETERNAL LIFE, WITHOUT GRACE

We proceed to the fifth article thus:

1. It seems that a man can merit eternal life without grace. Our Lord says (Matt. 19: 17): "if thou wilt enter into life, keep the commandments"— whence it appears that whether a man enters into eternal life depends on his own will. Now we can do by ourselves what depends on our own will. It seems, therefore, that a man can merit eternal life by himself.

2. Again, God gives eternal life to men as a meed or reward, according to Matt. 5:12: "great is your reward in heaven," and Ps. 62: 12 says that a meed or reward is rendered by God according to a man's works: "thou renderest to every man according to his work." Hence the attainment of eternal life seems to depend on a man's own power, since a man has control of his own works.

3. Again, eternal life is the ultimate end of human life. Now every natural thing can attain its end by its natural power. Much more then can man, who is of a higher nature, attain eternal life by his natural power, without any grace.

On the other hand: the apostle says: "the gift of God is eternal life" (Rom. 6:23), and the gloss by Augustine says: "this means that God leads us to eternal life for his mercy's sake" (*De Grat. et Lib. Arb.* 9).

I answer: actions which lead to an end must be commensurate with the end. But no action transcends the limits of the principle by which a thing acts. Thus we see that no natural thing can produce, by its own action, an effect which is greater than its own active power, but only an effect commensurate with this power. Now eternal life is an end which exceeds what is commensurate with human nature, as is clear from what we said in Q. 5, Art. 5. It follows that a man cannot, by his natural powers, produce meritorious works commensurate with eternal life. A higher power is needed for this, namely, the power of grace. Hence a man cannot merit eternal life without grace, although he can perform works which lead to such good as is connatural to him, such as labour in the field, eat, drink, have friends, and so on, as is said by Augustine (or by another, in *Contra Pelagianos* 3; *Hypognosticon* 3, cap. 4).

On the first point: a man performs works deserving of eternal life by his own will. But as Augustine says in the same passage, his will must be prepared by God through grace.

On the second point: if one is to fulfil the commandments of the law in the adequate way which is meritorious, grace is indispensable. This agrees with what Augustine's gloss says on Rom. 6:23, "the gift of God is eternal life," namely that "it is certain that eternal life is the reward for good works, but works so rewarded are the result of God's grace" (*De Grat. et Lib. Arb.* 8). It also agrees with what we said in the preceding article.

On the third point: this objection argues from the end which is connatural to man. But the very fact that human nature is nobler than natural things means that it can be raised, at least through the help of grace, to an end higher than this, to which inferior natures can nowise attain. A man who can recover his health through the help of medicine is, similarly, nearer to health than another who can in nowise do so, as the philosopher remarks in 2 *De Coelo,* texts 64, 65.

ARTICLE SIX

WHETHER WITHOUT GRACE A MAN CAN PREPARE HIMSELF FOR GRACE

We proceed to the sixth article thus:

1. It seems that a man can prepare himself for grace by himself, without the external help of grace. For nothing impossible is laid upon man, as was said in Art. 4, and yet it is written in Zech. 1:3: "Turn ye unto me, and I will turn unto you." To prepare oneself for grace is nothing other than to turn unto God. It seems, therefore, that a man can prepare himself for grace by himself, without the help of grace.

2. Again, a man prepares himself for grace

by doing what lies within him. For God will not refuse him grace if he does what lies within him, since Matt., ch. 7, says that "God gives his good spirit to them that ask him." Now what is said to lie within us is within our power. Hence it seems that to prepare ourselves for grace is within our power.

3. Again, if a man needs grace to prepare himself for grace, for the same reason he will need grace to prepare himself for this latter grace, and so on to infinity, which is impossible. It seems to hold good in the first instance, therefore, that without grace a man can prepare himself for grace.

4. Again, Prov. 16:1 says: "The preparations of the heart in man."[1] Now that is said to be of man which he can do by himself. Hence it seems that a man can prepare himself for grace by himself.

On the other hand: it is said in John 6:44: "no man can come to me, except the Father which hath sent me draw him." But a man would not need to be drawn by another if he could prepare himself for grace. Hence a man cannot prepare himself for grace without the help of grace.

I answer: the preparation of the human will for grace is two-fold. In the first place, the will must be prepared for good works, and for the enjoyment of God. Such preparation is impossible without an enduring gift of grace, grace being the principle of meritorious works, as we said in the preceding article. But we may have in mind, in the second place, the preparation of the will so that this enduring gift may follow. We do not need to suppose another enduring gift already in the soul, by means of which a man is enabled to receive this enduring gift, since this would go on to infinity. But we are bound to suppose the gift of God's help in moving the soul inwardly, and inspiring it to aim at good. For we need God's help in these two ways, as we said in Arts. 2 and 3. It is plain that we need the help of God as mover. Every agent acts for some definite end, and every cause is therefore bound to direct its effects to its own end. Since the hierarchy of ends is parallel to the hierarchy of agents, it follows that man must be directed to his ultimate end by the moving of the first mover, and to his penultimate end by the moving of lesser movers, just as a soldier's mind is set on victory by the influence of the army commander, and on following a standard by the influence of a captain. Now since God is the absolute first mover, it is by God's moving that all things are directed to him, in accordance with the universal tendency to good by which each thing strives to resemble God after its own fashion. As Dionysius says: "God turns all things to himself" (4 *Div. Nom.*, lect. 11). But God turns just men to himself as the special end which they seek, and to which they desire to cleave as to their true good, in accordance with Ps. 73:28: "It is good for me to draw near to God." A man cannot therefore turn to God except through God turning him to himself. To turn to God is to prepare oneself for grace, just as one whose eyes are turned away from the light of the sun prepares himself to receive its light by turning his eyes towards the sun. It is clear, then, that a man cannot prepare himself for the light of grace without the gracious help of God, who moves him inwardly.

On the first point: a man turns to God of his own free will. Hence he is bidden to do so. But his free will can turn to God only through God turning it to himself, according to Jer. 31:18: "turn thou me, and I shall be turned; for thou art the Lord my God," and also Lam. 5:21: "Turn thou us unto thee, O Lord, and we shall be turned."

On the second point: a man can do nothing unless he is moved by God, as is said in John 15:5: "without me ye can do nothing." When a man is said to do what lies within him, this is said to be within his power as moved by God.

On the third point: this objection argues from habitual[1] grace, which needs preparation, since every form requires an amenable disposition. But no other previous moving is needed in order that a man may be moved by God, since God is the first mover. There is therefore no infinite regress.

On the fourth point: it is for man to prepare his soul, since he does this by his own free will. Yet he does not do so without God helping

[1] Migne: "It is of man to prepare the soul."

[1] I.e., a habit which is a gift of grace. Cf. Art. 9, *infra*.

him as mover, and drawing him to himself, as we have said.

Question One Hundred and Ten

The Essence of God's Grace

We must now consider the essence of God's grace, concerning which there are four questions. 1. Whether grace denotes something in the soul. 2. Whether grace is a quality. 3. Whether grace differs from infused virtue. 4. Concerning the subject of grace.

ARTICLE ONE

WHETHER GRACE DENOTES SOMETHING IN THE SOUL

We proceed to the first article thus:

1. It seems that grace does not denote anything in the soul. One is said to have the grace[1] of a man as one is said to have the grace of God. Thus it is said in Gen. 39:21: "the Lord gave Joseph favour in the sight of the keeper of the prison." Now to say that one man has the favour of another is not to denote anything in him who has the favour, but to denote acceptance in him whose favour he enjoys. To say that a man has the grace of God, therefore, is not to denote anything in his soul, but merely to affirm that God accepts him.

2. Again, God enlivens the soul in the same way as the soul enlivens the body. Thus it is said Deut. 30:20: "He is thy life." Now the soul enlivens the body immediately. Hence there is nothing which stands as a medium between God and the soul. It follows that grace does not denote anything created in the soul.

3. Again, the gloss on Rom. 1:7, "Grace to you and peace . . .," says: "grace, i.e., the remission of sins." But the remission of sins does not denote anything in the soul. It signifies only that God does not impute sin, in accordance with Ps. 32:2: "Blessed is the man unto whom the Lord imputeth not iniquity." Neither then does grace denote anything in the soul.

On the other hand: light denotes something in what is illumined, and grace is a light of the soul. Thus Augustine says (*De Nat. et Grat.* 22): "The light of truth rightly deserts him who falsifies the law, and he who is thus deserted is left blind." Hence grace denotes something in the soul.

I answer: there are three things commonly meant by grace, as the word is used in ordinary speech. First, it means someone's love, as when we say that a certain soldier has the king's favour, i.e., that the king holds him in favour. Secondly, it means a gift freely given, as when we say: "I do you this favour." Thirdly, it means the response to a gift freely given, as when we are said to give thanks for benefits received. The second of these depends on the first, since it is out of love for another whom one holds in favour that one freely bestows a gift upon him. The third likewise depends on the second, since gratitude is due to gifts freely given.

Now if grace is understood according to either of the two latter meanings, it is obvious that it leaves something in the recipient of grace—the gift freely given, or the acknowledgment of it. But if grace means someone's love, we must observe the difference between the grace of God and the favour of a man. For the good which is in a creature is due to the will of God, and therefore some of the good in a creature is due to the love of God, who wills the good of the creature. The will of a man, on the other hand, is moved by good which already exists in things, so that his approval does not wholly cause the good in a thing, but presupposes it, partially or wholly. It is plain, then, that God's love invariably causes some good to be in the creature at some time, although such good is not co-eternal with his eternal love. God's love to creatures has then two aspects, on account of this special kind of good. It is universal, in so far as God gives to created things their natural being. As it is said in Wisdom, ch. 11: "He loves all things that are." It is also special, in so far as God raises a rational creature above its natural state, to share in divine good. It is in this special sense of love that God is said to love someone absolutely, since it is by this special love that he wills for a creature, absolutely, the eternal good which is himself. To say that

[1] The Latin words for "grace," "favour," "freely," "thanks," "gratitude," all have the same root—*gratia, gratis, gratias, agere, gratiarum actio.*

a man has the grace of God, therefore, is to say that there is something supernatural in him, which God bestows.

Sometimes, however, the grace of God means God's eternal love, as it does when we speak of the grace of predestination, which signifies that God predestines or elects some by grace, and not on account of merit, as according to Eph. 1:5–6: "Having predestined us unto the adoption of children . . . to the praise of the glory of his grace."

On the first point: even when a man is said to have the favour of another man, something is understood to be in him which pleases the other. So also when one is said to have the grace of God, but with this difference, that whereas a man's approval presupposes that which pleases him in another, God's love causes that which pleases him in a man, as we have said.

On the second point: God is the life of the soul as its efficient cause, whereas the soul is the life of the body as its formal cause.[1] There is no medium between a form and its matter, because a form determines the formation of its matter, or subject, by means of itself. But an agent does not determine a subject by means of its own substance. It does so by means of the form which it causes to be in the matter.

On the third point: Augustine says (1 *Retract.* 5): "when I say that grace is for the remission of sins, and peace for reconciliation to God, I do not mean that peace and reconciliation are outside the scope of grace, but that the name of grace signifies the remission of sins especially." There are thus many other gifts of God which pertain to grace, besides the remission of sins. Indeed there is no remission of sin without some effect divinely caused within us, as will be explained in Q. 113, Art. 2.

ARTICLE TWO

WHETHER GRACE IS A QUALITY OF THE SOUL

We proceed to the second article thus:

1. It seems that grace is not a quality of the soul. No quality acts on the subject to which it belongs. If it did, the subject would have to act on itself, since there is no action of a quality without the action of its subject. But grace acts on the soul, in justifying it. It follows that grace is not a quality.

2. Again, a substance is nobler than its quality. But grace is nobler than the soul's nature, since we can do many things by grace which we cannot do by nature, as was said in Q. 109, Arts. 1, 2, and 3. It follows that grace is not a quality.

3. Again, no quality persists after it ceases to be in its subject. But grace persists, since it is not corrupted. If grace were corrupted it would be reduced to nothing, since it is created out of nothing—wherefore it is called a "new creature" in Galatians. It follows that grace is not a quality.

On the other hand: the gloss by Augustine on Ps. 104:15, "Oil to make his face to shine," says that "grace is a beauty of the soul, which wins the divine love." Beauty of soul is a quality, just as comeliness of body is a quality. It follows that grace is a quality.

I answer: as we maintained in the preceding article, to say that a man has the grace of God is to say that there is within him an effect of God's gracious will. Now God's gracious will helps a man in two ways, as we said in Q. 109, Art. 1. In the first place, a man's mind is helped by God to know, to will, or to act. Such an effect of grace is not a quality, but a movement of the soul, since "in the moved, the act of the mover is a movement," as is said in 3 *Physics*, text 18. Secondly, God infuses a habitual gift into the soul, for the reason that it would not be fitting that God should give less to those whom he loves in order that they may attain supernatural good, than he gives to creatures whom he loves in order that they may attain only natural good. Now God provides for natural creatures not only by moving them to their natural actions, but by endowing them with forms and powers which are the principles of actions, so that they may incline to such movements of their own

[1] For the distinction between final, formal, efficient, and material cause, see 22ae, Q. 27, Art. 3; cf. Aristotle's *Physics*, bk. 2, ch. 3 (194b), ch. 7 (198a); also *Metaph. A*, ch. 3 (983a), *D*, ch. 2 (1013a–b).

accord. In this way the movements to which God moves them become natural to creatures, and easy for them, in accordance with Wisdom 8:1: ". . . and disposes all things sweetly." Much more, then, does God infuse certain forms or supernatural qualities into those whom he moves to seek after supernatural and eternal good, that they may be thus moved by him to seek it sweetly and readily. The gift of grace, therefore, is a certain quality.

On the first point: as a quality, grace is said to act on the soul not as an efficient cause, but as a formal cause, as whiteness makes things white, or as justice makes things just.

On the second point: any substance is either the nature of that of which it is the substance, or a part of its nature. In this sense, matter and form are both called "substance." But grace is higher than human nature. It cannot then be its substance, nor yet the form of its substance. Grace is a form accidental to the soul. What exists as substance in God occurs as accident in the soul which shares in divine good, as is obvious in the case of knowledge. But since the soul shares in divine good imperfectly, this participation itself, which is grace, exists in the soul in a less perfect mode than that in which the soul exists in itself. Such grace is nevertheless nobler than the soul's nature, in so far as it is an expression or sharing of the divine goodness, even though it is not nobler than the soul in respect of its mode of being.

On the third point: as Boethius says (*Isagogue Porphyri*): "the being of an accident is to inhere." Thus an accident is said to "be," not as if it existed by itself, but because some subject "is" through possessing it. It is thus affirmed of an existence, rather than affirmed to be an existence, as is said in 7 *Metaph.*, text 2. Now since coming to be and passing away are affirmed of what exists, properly speaking no accident comes to be or passes away. But an accident is said to come to be or to pass away when its subject begins or ceases to be actualized through possession of it. In this sense, grace is said to be created when it is men who are created in grace, i.e., when they are created anew out of nothing, and not on account of merit, according to Eph. 2:10: "created in Christ Jesus unto good works."

ARTICLE THREE

WHETHER GRACE IS THE SAME AS VIRTUE

We proceed to the third article thus:

1. It seems that grace is the same as virtue. For Augustine says "operative grace is faith that works by love" (*De Spiritu et Littera* 14, 32). But faith that works by love is a virtue. Therefore grace is a virtue.

2. Again, whatever a definition fits, fits the thing defined. Now the definitions of virtue fit grace, whether they are given by saints or by philosophers—"it makes him who possesses it good, and his work good," "it is a good quality of mind, whereby one lives rightly," etc. Therefore grace is a virtue.

3. Again, grace is a quality of some kind. But it manifestly does not belong to the fourth species of quality, which comprises "the form or unchanging pattern of things." Neither does it belong to the third species, since it is neither a "passion" nor a "passionate quality." These belong to the sensitive part of the soul, as is proved in 8 *Physics,* text 14, whereas grace is principally in the mind. Nor does it belong to the second species, which includes "natural power and impotence." It must therefore belong to the first species, which is that of "habit" or "disposition." But habits of mind are virtues, since even knowledge is in a sense a virtue. Hence grace is the same as virtue.

On the other hand: if grace is a virtue, it must certainly be one of the three theological virtues. But grace is neither faith nor hope, since these occur without sanctifying grace. Nor is it charity, since "grace precedes charity," as Augustine says (*De Dono Persev.* 16). Hence grace is not a virtue.

I answer: some have held that grace and virtue differ only as different aspects of one identical essence, which we call grace in so far as it is freely given, or makes men pleasing to God, and which we call virtue in so far as it perfects us in well-doing. So indeed the Master[1] seems to have thought, in *2 Sent., Dist.* 26. But this cannot be maintained if one

[1] Peter the Lombard, to whom the title refers throughout this volume; generally known as "Magister Sententiarum," or the "Master of Sentences," from his work *Libri Sententiarum.*

pays due attention to the meaning of virtue. As the philosopher says in 7 *Physics,* text 17: "virtue is the disposition of the perfect, and I call that perfect which is disposed according to nature." This makes it clear that the virtue of any particular thing is determined by a nature which is prior to it, and means the disposition of all its elements according to what is best for its nature. Now the virtues which a man acquires through practice, of which we spoke in Q. 55 ff., are obviously dispositions by which he is disposed in a manner which befits his nature as a man. But the infused virtues dispose men in a higher way to a higher end, and therefore according to a higher nature, indeed according to the divine nature in which he participates. We call this participation "the light of grace," on account of what is said in II Peter 1:4: "Whereby are given unto us exceeding great and precious promises: that by these ye might be partakers of the divine nature." It is in fact as receiving this nature that we are said to be born again as sons of God. Hence just as the natural light of reason is something over and above the acquired virtues, which are called virtues because they are ordered by this light, so the light of grace, which is a partaking of the divine nature, is something over and above the infused virtues, which are derived from it and ordered by it. Thus the apostle says in Eph. 5:8: "For ye were sometimes darkness, but now are ye light in the Lord: walk as children of light." Just as the acquired virtues enable a man to walk by the natural light of reason, so do the infused virtues enable him to walk by the light of grace.

On the first point: Augustine gives the name of grace to "faith that works by love" because the act of faith which works by love is the first act in which sanctifying grace is manifest.

On the second point: the term "good," as used in the definition of virtue, means conformity with a nature which is either prior, essential, or partaken. It is not applied in this sense to grace, but to the root of goodness in man, as we have said.

On the third point: grace belongs to the first species of quality. But it is not the same as virtue. It is the disposition which the infused virtues presuppose as their principle and root.

Question One Hundred and Twelve

The Cause of Grace

We must now consider the cause of grace, concerning which there are five questions. 1. Whether God is the sole efficient cause of grace. 2. Whether any disposition for grace is required on the part of the recipient, by an act of free will. 3. Whether such a disposition can ensure grace. 4. Whether grace is equal in everyone. 5. Whether any man can know that he has grace.

ARTICLE ONE

WHETHER GOD IS THE SOLE CAUSE OF GRACE

We proceed to the first article thus:

1. It seems that God is not the sole cause of grace. For it is said in John 1:17 that "grace and truth came by Jesus Christ," and the name Jesus Christ means the creaturely nature assumed as well as the divine nature which assumed it. It follows that what is creaturely can be the cause of grace.

2. Again, the sacraments of the new law are said to differ from those of the old in this respect, namely that the sacraments of the new law are causes of the grace which those of the old law only signify. Now the sacraments of the new law are visible elements. It follows that God is not the sole cause of grace.

3. Again, according to Dionysius (*Coel. Hier.* 3, 4): "angels purge, enlighten, and perfect both lesser angels and men." But rational creatures are purged, enlightened, and perfected through grace. It follows that God is not the sole cause of grace.

On the other hand: it is said in Ps. 84:11: "the Lord will give grace and glory."

I answer: nothing can act upon what is above its own species, since a cause must always be greater than its effect. Now the gift of grace exceeds every capacity of nature, since it is none other than a participation of the divine nature, which exceeds every other nature. It is therefore impossible for any creature to be a cause of grace. Hence it is just as inevitable that God alone should deify, by communicating a sharing of the divine nature through a participation of likeness, as it is impossible that anything save fire alone should ignite.

On the first point: the humanity of Christ is "an organ of his divinity," as the Damascene says (3 *De Fid. Orth.* 15). Now an instrument carries out the action of a principal agent by the power of the principal agent, not by its own power. Thus the humanity of Christ does not cause grace by its own power, but by the power of the divinity conjoined with it, through which the actions of the humanity of Christ are redemptive.

On the second point: just as in the person of Christ humanity is the cause of our salvation through the divine power which operates as the principal agent, so it is with the sacraments of the new law. Grace is caused instrumentally by the sacraments themselves, yet principally by the power of the Holy Spirit operating in the sacraments.

On the third point: an angel purges, enlightens, and perfects an angel or a man by instruction, not by justification through grace. Wherefore Dionysius says (*Coel. Hier.* 7): "this kind of purging, enlightening, and perfecting is nothing other than the acquisition of divine knowledge."

ARTICLE TWO

WHETHER A PREPARATION OR DISPOSITION FOR GRACE IS REQUIRED ON THE PART OF MAN

We proceed to the second article thus:

1. It seems that no preparation or disposition for grace is required on the part of man. For the apostle says (Rom. 4:4): "Now to him that worketh[1] is the reward not reckoned of grace, but of debt." But a man could not of his own free will prepare himself for grace, unless by an operation. The meaning of grace would then be taken away.

2. Again, a man who walks in sin does not prepare himself for grace. Yet grace is given to some while they walk in sin. This is evident in the case of Paul, who received grace while "breathing out threatenings and slaughter against the disciples of the Lord" (Acts 9:1).

[1] *qui operatur.*

Hence no preparation for grace is required on the part of man.

3. Again, an agent whose power is infinite does not need any disposition of matter, since he does not even need matter itself, as is obvious in creation. Now grace is likened to creation, being called a new creature in Gal. ch. 6, and it was said in the preceding article that God, whose power is infinite, is the sole cause of grace. It follows that no preparation for receiving grace is required on the part of man.

On the other hand: it is said in Amos 4:12: "prepare to meet thy God, O Israel," and in I Sam. 7:3: "prepare your hearts unto the Lord."

I answer: as we said in Q. 111, Art. 2, grace may be understood in two ways. Sometimes it means a habitual gift which God bestows. At other times it means the help of God, who moves the soul to good. Now some preparation is required for grace as a habitual gift, since a form can exist only in matter which is disposed to it. But no previous preparation is required on the part of man if we are speaking of grace as the help of God, by which he moves him to good. Rather is any preparation which can take place within him due to the help of God, who thus moves him. Even the good action of his free will, by which he is made ready to receive the gift of grace, is an action of his free will as moved by God. Hence a man is said to prepare himself. As it is said in Prov. 16:1: "the preparations of the heart in man."[1] But since his free will is moved by God as principal agent, his will is also said to be prepared by God, and his steps guided by the Lord.

On the first point: there is a preparation of oneself for grace which is simultaneous with the infusion of grace. This is indeed a meritorious work. But it merits the glory which a man does not yet possess, not the grace which he now has. There is also an incomplete preparation for grace which sometimes precedes sanctifying grace, though nevertheless due to God as mover. But this last is not sufficient for merit, since there is as yet no justification by grace. As we shall show in Q. 114, Art. 2, there is no merit except by grace.

[1] Migne: "It is of man to prepare the soul."

On the second point: since a man cannot prepare himself for grace unless God first moves him to good, it is immaterial whether one is perfectly prepared all at once, or little by little. As it is said in Ecclesiasticus 11:21: "In the eyes of God, it is easy for a poor man suddenly to become rich." Sometimes God moves a man to good, but not perfectly. This is a preparation which precedes grace. At other times he moves a man to good both instantaneously and perfectly, and such a one then receives grace suddenly, after the manner spoken of in John 6:45: "Every man therefore that hath heard, and hath learned of the Father, cometh unto me." This is what happened to Paul, whose heart was suddenly moved by God to hear, to learn, and to come, even while he yet walked in sin. He thus received grace suddenly.

On the third point: an agent whose power is infinite needs neither matter nor a disposition of matter provided by the action of any other cause. Such an agent is nevertheless bound to cause both the matter in a thing and a disposition favourable to its form, according to the condition of the thing to be made. So likewise when God infuses grace into the soul, no preparation is required which God does not himself achieve.

Question One Hundred and Fourteen

Concerning Merit, Which Is the Effect of Co-operative Grace

We must now consider merit, which is the effect of co-operative grace. There are ten questions concerning merit. 1. Whether a man can merit anything from God. 2. Whether without grace one can merit eternal life. 3. Whether through grace one can merit eternal life condignly. 4. Whether grace is the principle of merit, through charity as the principal medium. 5. Whether a man can merit the grace first given to himself. 6. Whether he can merit it on behalf of another. 7. Whether anyone can merit for himself restoration after a lapse. 8. Whether anyone can merit for himself an increase of grace, or of charity. 9. Whether anyone can merit for himself perseverance to the end. 10. Whether temporal goods can be merited.

ARTICLE ONE

WHETHER A MAN CAN MERIT ANYTHING FROM GOD

We proceed to the first article thus:

1. It seems that a man cannot merit anything from God. No one merits a reward by repaying what he owes to another. But we cannot even fully repay what we owe to God, by all the good that we do. For we always owe him more than this, as the philosopher says in 8 *Ethics* 14. Hence it is said in Luke 17:10: "when ye shall have done all those things which are commanded you, say, We are unprofitable servants: we have done that which was our duty to do." It follows that a man cannot merit anything from God.

2. Again, it seems that a man merits nothing from God if he profits himself, but profits God nothing. Now by good work a man profits himself or another man, but not God. For it is said in Job 35:7: "If thou be righteous, what givest thou him? Or what receiveth he of thine hand?" It follows that a man cannot merit anything from God.

3. Again, whoever merits anything from another makes that other his debtor, since he who owes a reward ought to render it to him who merits it. But God is a debtor to no one, wherefore it is said in Rom. 11:35: "Or who hath first given to him, and it shall be recompensed unto him again?" It follows that no one can merit anything from God.

On the other hand: it is said in Jer. 31:16: "thy work shall be rewarded." Now a reward means something given for merit. Hence it seems that a man can merit something from God.

I answer: merit and reward mean the same thing. We call it a reward when it is given to someone in return for his work or labour, as a price for it. Now to give a reward for work or labour is an act of justice, just as to give a fair price for something received from another is an act of justice, and justice, as the philosopher says in 5 *Ethics* 4, is a kind of equality. Justice obtains absolutely between those between whom equality obtains absolutely. It does not obtain absolutely between those between whom equality does not obtain absolutely, but there may nevertheless be a kind of justice between them, since we speak of the "right" of a father, or of a master, as the philosopher says in ch. 6 of the same book. Merit and reward have accordingly an absolute meaning where justice obtains absolutely. But in so far as the meaning of justice remains where justice obtains relatively and not absolutely, the meaning of merit is relative though not absolute, such as is applicable to a son who deserves something from his father, or to a slave who deserves something from his master.

Now there is obviously a very great inequality between God and man. The gulf betwixt them is indeed infinite. Moreover, all the good that is in a man is due to God. The kind of justice which obtains where there is absolute equality cannot therefore obtain between man and God. There obtains only the justice which is relative to the proportion of what is wrought by each, according to their own mode. But since both the mode and the manner of man's virtue are due to God, it is only by a previous divine ordination that a man can merit anything from God. That is, a man can receive as a reward from God only what God has given him the power to work for by his own effort; just as natural things attain, by their own movements and activities, that to which they are divinely ordained. There is this difference, however. A rational creature moves itself to its action by its free will, and its action is therefore meritorious. This is not the case with other creatures.

On the first point: a man has merit in so far as he does what he ought by his own will. The act of justice whereby one repays a debt would not otherwise be meritorious.

On the second point: God does not seek to gain anything from our good works. He seeks to be glorified by them, i.e., that his goodness should be shown forth. He seeks this by his own works also. Neither does anything accrue to God from our worship of him, but to ourselves. Hence we merit something from God not because our works profit him, but because we work to his glory.

On the third point: our own action is meritorious only by reason of a previous divine ordination. It does not follow, therefore, that God becomes a debtor to ourselves simply. Rather does he become a debtor to himself, in so far as it is right that what he has ordained should be fulfilled.

ARTICLE TWO

WHETHER ONE CAN MERIT ETERNAL LIFE WITHOUT GRACE

We proceed to the second article thus:

1. It seems that one can merit eternal life without grace. It was said in the preceding article that a man merits from God that to which he is divinely ordained. Now it is of the very nature of man that he is ordained to blessedness as his end, which is indeed the reason why he naturally seeks to be blessed. A man can therefore merit blessedness, which is eternal life, by his own natural powers and without grace.

2. Again, a work is the more meritorious the less it is incumbent upon one, and a good work is the less incumbent if it is done by him who has received the fewer benefits. Now a man who has only his own natural good has received less from God than one who has received gifts of grace in addition. His work is therefore the more meritorious in God's sight. Hence if one who has grace can in any wise merit eternal life, much more can one who is without grace.

3. Again, the mercy and liberality of God are infinitely greater than the mercy and liberality of man. Now one man can merit something from another, even though he has never had his grace. Much more, then, does it seem that a man without grace can merit eternal life from God.

On the other hand: the apostle says (Rom. 6:23): "the gift of God is eternal life."

I answer: there are two states of man without grace, as we said in Q. 109, Art. 2. One is the state of pure nature, such as was in Adam before his sin. The other is the state of corrupt nature, such as is in ourselves before restoration through grace. If we are speaking of man in the first of these states, there is one reason why he cannot merit eternal life by his natural powers alone, and that is that his merit depends on a divine preordination. No action of anything whatsoever is divinely ordained to that which exceeds what is commensurate with the power which is its principle of action. It is indeed an ordinance of divine providence that nothing shall act beyond its own power. Now eternal life is a good which exceeds what is commensurate with created nature, since it transcends both natural knowledge and natural desire, according to I Cor. 2:9: "Eye hath not seen, nor ear heard, neither have entered into the heart of man. . . ." No created nature, therefore, can suffice as the principle of an action which merits eternal life, unless there is added to it a supernatural gift, which we call grace. But if we are speaking of man as he exists in sin, there is a second reason why this is so, namely, the impediment of sin. Sin is an offence against God which excludes us from eternal life, as we said in Q. 71, Art. 6, and Q. 113, Art. 2. Hence no one who lives in sin can merit eternal life unless he is first reconciled to God by the remission of sin. Now sin is remitted by grace, since the sinner merits not life but death, according to Rom. 6:23: "the wages of sin is death."

On the first point: God has ordained that human nature shall attain the end of eternal life by the help of grace, not by its own power. Its own action can merit eternal life by the help of grace.

On the second point: a man without grace cannot have it in him to perform a work equal to that which proceeds from grace, since action is the more perfect the more perfect is its principle. This reasoning would be valid, however, if such works were equal in each case.

On the third point: the first reason to which we have referred relates to God and to man in dissimilar ways. For it is from God, and not from man, that a man has every power of welldoing which he possesses. He cannot therefore merit anything from God except by means of God's gift. The apostle expresses this pointedly when he says: "who hath first given to him, and it shall be recompensed unto him again?" (Rom. 11:35). The second reason, on the other hand, which is concerned with the impediment of sin, relates to man and to God in a similar way, since one man cannot merit anything even from another man whom he has offended, unless he first makes retribution, and is reconciled to him.

ARTICLE FOUR

WHETHER GRACE IS THE PRINCIPLE OF MERIT THROUGH CHARITY MORE PRINCIPALLY THAN THROUGH OTHER VIRTUES

We proceed to the fourth article thus:

1. It seems that grace is not the principle of merit through charity more principally than through other virtues. Labour is worthy of its hire, according to Matt. 20:8: "call the labourers, and give them their hire." But every virtue is the principle of some labour, since a virtue is a habit of action, as was said in Q. 55, Art. 2. Every virtue is therefore equally a principle of merit.

2. Again, the apostle says (I Cor. 3:8): "and every man shall receive his own reward, according to his own labour." But charity lightens labour rather than increases it, since "love makes every hard and heavy task easy, and almost as nothing," as Augustine says (*De Verb. Dom., Sermo* 9; *De Tempt., Sermo* 49). Charity is not then the principle of merit more principally than other virtues.

3. Again, the virtue which is most principally the principle of merit would seem to be the virtue whose actions are the most meritorious. Now the most meritorious actions seem to be those of faith and patience, or fortitude. This is apparent from the martyrs, who for their faith remained steadfast unto death with patience and fortitude. Other virtues are therefore the principle of merit more principally than charity.

On the other hand: our Lord says: "he that loveth me shall be loved of my Father, and I will love him, and will manifest myself to him" (John 14:21). Now eternal life consists in the manifest knowledge of God, according to John 17:3: "this is life eternal, that they might know thee the only true God." The meriting of eternal life therefore depends principally on charity.

I answer: there are two sources from which

the meritorious character of a human action is derived, as may be understood from what we said in the first article. First and foremost, there is the divine ordination. This is the ground upon which an action is said to merit the good to which a man is divinely ordained. Secondly, there is the free will of man, which gives him the power to act voluntarily on his own part, more than any other creature. In regard to either source, the principle of merit depends especially on charity. For we must observe in the first place that eternal life consists in the enjoyment of God. The movement of man's mind towards the enjoyment of divine good is the proper action of charity, and it is the action of charity that directs all actions of the other virtues to this end, since charity commands the other virtues. The meriting of eternal life therefore depends primarily on charity, and secondarily on other virtues, in so far as their actions are directed by charity. It is apparent, also, that we do most willingly what we do out of love. Even in respect of the voluntary character essential to its nature, therefore, merit depends principally on charity.

On the first point: since charity has the ultimate end as its object, it moves the other virtues to act. A habit which relates to an end always commands the habits which relate to the means to it, as we explained in Q. 9, Art. 1.

On the second point: there are two ways in which a work may be laborious and difficult. It may be so because of its magnitude, which increases its merit. Charity does not lighten labour in this respect. On the contrary, it causes us to undertake the greatest works. As Gregory says, "charity is such that it does great works" (*Hom. in Evang.* 30). But a work may also be laborious and difficult because of a fault in him who labours. Anything can be hard and difficult if it is not done readily and with a will. Such labour lessens merit, and is removed by charity.

On the third point: an act of faith is not meritorious unless faith works by love, as is said in Gal. 5. Neither is an act of patience and fortitude meritorious unless performed through charity, according to I Cor. 13:3: "though I give my body to be burned, and have not charity, it profiteth me nothing."

ARTICLE FIVE

WHETHER A MAN CAN MERIT THE FIRST GRACE FOR HIMSELF

We proceed to the fifth article thus:

1. It seems that a man can merit the first grace for himself. For Augustine says that "faith merits justification" (*Praef. Ps.* 32), and a man is justified by the grace first given to him. It follows that a man can merit the first grace for himself.

2. Again, God gives grace only to those who are worthy. But we do not say that anyone is worthy of something good unless he has merited it condignly. It follows that one can merit the first grace condignly.

3. Again, with men, one can merit a gift which has already been received. One who has been given a horse by his master, for example, may deserve it through using it well in his master's service. Now God is more generous than a man. Much more, then, can a man merit the first grace which he has already received from God, by reason of his subsequent works.

On the other hand: the very meaning of grace excludes the notion of reward for works, according to Rom. 4:4: "Now to him that worketh is the reward not reckoned of grace, but of debt." But what a man merits is credited to him as a reward for works. Hence he cannot merit the first grace.

I answer: we may think of a gift of grace in two ways. If we are thinking of the gratuitous character of the gift, it is obvious that all merit is opposed to grace, since the apostle says: "and if by grace, then it is no more of works" (Rom. 11:6). If, on the other hand, we are thinking of the nature of what is given, such a gift cannot be merited by one who does not have grace. For not only does grace exceed what is commensurate with nature, but a man in the state of sin before grace is prevented from meriting grace by the impediment of sin. Neither can grace already possessed be merited subsequently, since a reward is the outcome of work, and grace is the principle of all our good works, as we said in Q. 109. Finally, if one should merit another gratuitous gift by virtue of grace already received, this would not be the first grace. It is apparent, then, that no man can merit the first grace for himself.

On the first point: as Augustine says in 1 *Retract.* 23, he was at one time deceived in this matter, when he believed that the beginning of faith lay with ourselves, although its consummation was a gift of God. He retracts this belief, but it is apparently on this assumption that he declares that faith merits justification. But if we suppose that faith is begun in us by God, this being indeed a truth of faith, then even the act of faith follows the first grace. It cannot then merit the first grace. Hence a man is justified by faith not in the sense that he merits justification by believing, but in the sense that he believes while he is being justified. This movement of faith is required for the justification of the ungodly, as we said in Q. 113, Art. 4.

On the second point: the reason why God gives grace only to the worthy is not that they were previously worthy, but that by grace God makes them worthy, who alone "can bring a clean thing out of an unclean" (Job 14:4).

On the third point: every good work which a man does proceeds from the first grace as its principle. But it does not proceed from any gift of man. We cannot therefore argue in the same way about a gift of grace and a gift of man.

Treatise on the Theological Virtues

Question Two

The Act of Faith

We must now consider the act of faith, first the inward act, and second the outward act. There are ten questions concerning the inward act of faith. 1. In what belief consists, which is the inward act of faith. 2. In how many ways one may speak of belief. 3. Whether, for salvation, it is necessary to believe anything which is beyond natural reason. 4. Whether it is necessary to believe such things as are attainable by natural reason. 5. Whether, for salvation, it is necessary to believe anything explicitly. 6. Whether explicit belief is required of all men equally. 7. Whether, for salvation, it is always necessary to have explicit belief concerning Christ. 8. Whether explicit belief in the Trinity is necessary for salvation. 9. Whether the act of faith is meritorious. 10. Whether a human reason diminishes the merit of faith.

Article One

Whether to Believe Is to Think with Assent

We proceed to the first article thus:

1. It seems that to believe is not to think with assent. For "to think" implies inquiry of some kind, the word being a contraction of "to consider together" (*cogitare* = *coagitare* = *simul agitare*). But the Damascene says that "faith is assent without inquiry" (4 *De Fid. Orth.* 1). It follows that the act of faith does not involve thinking.

2. Again, it will be shown in Q. 4, Art. 2, that faith belongs to reason. But it was said in Pt. I, Q. 78, Art. 4, that thinking is an act of the cogitative power, which belongs to the sensitive part of the soul.[1] It follows that faith does not involve thinking.

3. Again, belief is an act of the intellect, since the object of belief is the true. Now it was said in 12ae, Q. 15, Art. 1, ad. 3 that assent is not an act of the intellect, but an act of the will, just as consent is an act of the will. It follows that to believe is not to think with assent.

On the other hand: "to believe" is thus defined by Augustine. (*De Praed. Sanct.* 2.)

I answer: "to think" can mean three things. Firstly, it means any deliberative intellectual act in general. This is what Augustine has in mind in 14 *De Trin.* 7, when he says: "what I now call understanding is that whereby we understand when we think." Secondly, and more precisely, it means the kind of intellectual deliberation which involves a degree of questioning, and which occurs before the intellect reaches perfection through the certainty of vision. This is what Augustine has in mind in

[1] The sensitive power operates through a corporeal organ, through which it perceives things which are actually present. The cogitative power perceives and preserves the "intention" or practical significance of particular things present or absent, by means of collating ideas. It is also called the "particular reason."

15 *De Trin.* 16, where he says: "The Son of God is not called the Thought of God, but the Word of God. When our thought has reached what we know and become formed by it, it becomes our word. The Word of God should therefore be conceived as without the thought of God, since it contains nothing which remains to be formed, and which could be unformed." In this sense, thought properly means the movement of a soul which deliberates, and which is not yet perfected by a full vision of the truth. But since such movement may be either deliberation about universal meanings, which are the concern of the intellect, or deliberation about particular meanings, which are the concern of the sensitive part of the soul, the word "to think" is used in this second sense to mean the intellectual act of deliberation, and in yet a third sense to mean an act of the cogitative power.

Now if "to think" is understood in the first or general sense, "to think with assent" does not express the whole meaning of "to believe." For a man thinks in this way even about what he knows and understands in science, and also gives his assent. But if it is understood in the second sense, then by means of this expression we understand the whole nature of the act of belief. There are some acts of the intellect, such as those whereby one contemplates what one knows and understands in science, in which assent is given with confidence, without any deliberation. There are also others in which thought is unformed, and in which there is no firm assent. One may incline to neither alternative, as one who doubts. Or one may incline to the one rather than to the other on the strength of slight evidence, as does one who suspects. Or, again, one may choose one alternative with misgivings about the other, as does one who holds an opinion. Now the act which is "to believe" holds firmly to the one alternative. In this respect, belief is similar to science and understanding. Yet its thought is not perfected by clear vision, and in this respect belief is similar to doubt, suspicion, and opinion. To think with assent is thus the property of one who believes, and distinguishes the act of "belief" from all other acts of the intellect which are concerned with truth or falsity.

On the first point: faith does not make use of inquiry by natural reason to demonstrate what it believes. But it does inquire into the evidence by which a man is induced to believe, for example, into the circumstance that such things are spoken by God and confirmed by miracles.

On the second point: as we have said above, the word "to think" is here understood as it applies to the intellect, not as meaning an act of the cogitative power.

On the third point: the intellect of the believer is determined by the will, not by reason. Hence assent is here understood to mean the act of the intellect as determined by the will.

Question Six

The Cause of Faith

We must now consider the cause of faith, concerning which there are two questions. 1. Whether faith is infused into man by God. 2. Whether unformed faith is a gift of God.

ARTICLE ONE

WHETHER FAITH IS INFUSED INTO MAN BY GOD

We proceed to the first article thus:

1. It seems that faith is not infused into man by God. For Augustine says (14 *De Trin.* 1): "by knowledge is faith begotten, nourished, defended, and strengthened in us." Now what is begotten in us by knowledge would seem to be acquired, rather than infused. Thus it appears that faith is not in us by divine infusion.

2. Again, what a man attains through hearing and seeing would seem to be acquired. Now a man comes to believe both through seeing miracles and through hearing the doctrine of the faith. Thus it is said in John 4:53: "So the father knew that it was at the same hour in which Jesus said unto him, Thy son liveth: and himself believed, and his whole house," and in Rom. 10:17: "faith cometh by hearing." Hence faith can be acquired.

3. Again, a man can acquire what depends on his will, and Augustine says that "faith depends on the will of those who believe" (*De Praed. Sanct.* 5). It follows that a man can acquire faith.

On the other hand: it is said in Eph. 2:8–9: "by grace are ye saved through faith; and that not of yourselves; it is the gift of God: . . . lest any man should boast."

I answer: for faith, two things are required. In the first place, the things which a man is to believe must be proposed to him. This is necessary if anything is to be believed explicitly. Secondly, the believer must give his assent to what is proposed. Now faith is bound to be from God as regards the first of these conditions. For the things of faith are beyond human reason, so that a man cannot know them unless God reveals them. They are revealed by God immediately to some, such as the apostles and the prophets, and mediately to others, through preachers of the faith who are sent by God according to Rom. 10:15: "And how shall they preach except they be sent?" The cause of the believer's assent to the things of faith is twofold. There is in the first place an external cause which induces him to believe, such as the sight of a miracle, or the persuasion of another who leads him to the faith. But neither of these is a sufficient cause. For of those who see one and the same miracle, or who hear the same prophecy, some will believe and others will not believe. We must therefore recognize that there is also an inward cause, which moves a man from within to assent to the things of faith.

The Pelagians attributed this inward cause solely to a man's own free will, and said accordingly that the beginning of faith lies with ourselves, since we prepare ourselves to assent to the things of faith, although the consummation of faith lies with God, who proposes to us such things as we ought to believe. But this is false. For when a man gives his assent to the things of faith, he is raised above his own nature, and this is possible only through a supernatural principle which moves him from within. This principle is God. The assent of faith, which is the principal act of faith, is therefore due to God, who moves us inwardly through grace.

On the first point: faith is begotten by knowledge, and is nourished by the external persuasion which knowledge provides. But the principal and proper cause of faith is that which inwardly moves us to give our assent.

On the second point: this reasoning argues from the cause whereby the things of faith are externally proposed, or whereby one is persuaded to believe them by means of word or deed.

On the third point: to believe does depend on the will of those who believe. But a man's will must be prepared by God through grace, in order that he may be raised to things which are above nature, as we have said.

THE COUNCIL OF TRENT (1545–1563)

The vigorous spread of Protestantism on the Continent, together with the long-felt need within the Roman Catholic Church for a reform in doctrine and morals, led to the convening of the Council of Trent in 1545. Owing to two lengthy interruptions caused by political events and the rivalry between pope and emperor, the Council did not finish its work until 1563. Although Protestants were at various times invited and some were even in attendance for a short while, the Council's clear intention was, at all times, not to *modify* but to *clarify* and *define* long-held Catholic positions in strict opposition to Protestant beliefs and practices. The resulting body of doctrinal statements was divided into decrees and canons. The decrees contain summaries of those doctrines and practices which the Council felt needed to be defined, while the canons list the views which are to be rejected as heretical by all faithful Catholics.

The following selections deal with the meaning and significance, according to Catholic understanding, of the Bible, Tradition, Justification, the Sacraments, the Mass, Orders, Purgatory, and the Veneration of the Saints. They have been chosen so as to point out some of the more significant doctrines and forms of piety of the Roman Catholic Church which, at the same time, are major areas of difference between that church and Protestantism.

The Canons and Dogmatic Decrees of the Council of Trent*

Decree Touching the Symbol of Faith

In the name of the Holy and Undivided Trinity, Father, and Son, and Holy Ghost. This sacred and holy, oecumenical, and general Synod of Trent,—lawfully assembled in the Holy Ghost, the same three legates of the Apostolic See presiding therein,—considering the magnitude of the matters to be treated of, especially of those comprised under the two heads of the extirpating of heresies, and the reforming of manners, for the sake of which chiefly it is assembled, and recognizing with the apostles, that its "wrestling is not against flesh and blood, but against the spirits of wickedness in the high places," exhorts, with the same apostle, all and each, above all things, to be "strengthened in the Lord, and in the might of his power, in all things taking the shield of faith, wherewith they may be able to extinguish all the fiery darts of the most wicked one, and to take the helmet of salvation, with the sword of the Spirit, which is the word of God." Wherefore, that this its pious solicitude may begin and proceed by the grace of God, it ordains and decrees that, before all other things, a confession of faith is to be set forth; following herein the examples of the Fathers, who have been wont, in the most sacred councils, at the beginning of the Actions thereof, to oppose this shield against heresies; and with this alone, at times, have they drawn the unbelieving to the faith, overthrown heretics, and confirmed the faithful. For which cause, this Council has thought good, that the Symbol of faith which the holy Roman Church makes use of,—as being that principle wherein all who profess the faith of Christ necessarily agree, and that firm and alone foundation "against which the gates of hell shall never prevail,"—be expressed in the very same words in which it is read in all the churches. Which Symbol is as follows:

I believe in one God, the Father Almighty, Maker of heaven and earth, of all things visible and invisible; and in one Lord Jesus Christ, the only-begotten Son of God, and born of the Father before all ages; God of God, light of light, true God of true God; begotten, not made, consubstantial with the Father, by whom all things were made: who for us men, and for our salvation, came down from the heavens, and was incarnate by the Holy Ghost of the Virgin Mary, and was made man: crucified also for us under Pontius Pilate, he suffered and was buried; and he rose again on the third day, according to the Scriptures; and he ascended into heaven, sitteth at the right hand of the Father; and again he will come with glory to judge the living and the dead; of whose kingdom there shall be no end: and in the Holy Ghost, the Lord, and the giver of life, who proceedeth from the Father and the Son; who with the Son; who with the Father and the Son together is adored and glorified; who spoke by the prophets: and one holy Catholic and Apostolic Church. I confess one baptism for the remission of sins; and I look for the resurrection of the dead, and the life of the world to come. Amen.

Decree Concerning the Canonical Scriptures

The sacred and holy, oecumenical, and general Synod of Trent,—lawfully assembled in the Holy Ghost, the same three legates of the Apostolic See presiding therein,—keeping this always in view, that, errors being removed, the

* From Philip Schaff, *Creeds of Christendom,* New York: Harper & Brothers, 1889, Vol. II, pp. 77–80, 82f, 89–100, 103–111, 113–115, 117–121, 126f, 130, 176–181, 186–190, and 198–205.

purity itself of the Gospel be preserved in the Church; which (Gospel), before promised through the prophets in the holy Scriptures, our Lord Jesus Christ, the Son of God, first promulgated with His own mouth, and then commanded to be preached by His Apostles to every creature, as the fountain of all, both saving truth, and moral discipline; and seeing clearly that this truth and discipline are contained in the written books, and the unwritten traditions which, received by the Apostles from the mouth of Christ himself, or from the apostles themselves, the Holy Ghost dictating, have come down even unto us, transmitted as it were from hand to hand: [the Synod] following the examples of the orthodox Fathers, receives and venerates with an equal affection of piety and reverence, all the books both of the Old and of the New Testament—seeing that one God is the author of both—as also the said traditions, as well those appertaining to faith as to morals, as having been dictated, either by Christ's own word of mouth, or by the Holy Ghost, and preserved in the Catholic Church by a continuous succession.

Decree Concerning the Edition, and the Use, of the Sacred Books

Moreover, the same sacred and holy Synod, —considering that no small utility may accrue to the Church of God, if it be made known which out of all the Latin editions, now in circulation, of the sacred books, is to be held as authentic,—ordains and declares, that the said old and vulgate edition, which, by the lengthened usage of so many ages, has been approved of in the Church, be, in public lectures, disputations, sermons, and expositions, held as authentic; and that no one is to dare, or presume to reject it under any pretext whatever.

Furthermore, in order to restrain petulant spirits, it decrees, that no one, relying on his own skill, shall,—in matters of faith, and of morals pertaining to the edification of Christian doctrine,—wresting the sacred Scripture to his own senses, presume to interpret the said sacred Scripture contrary to that sense which holy mother Church,—whose it is to judge of the true sense and interpretation of the holy Scriptures,—hath held and doth hold; or even contrary to the unanimous consent of the Fathers; even though such interpretations were never [intended] to be at any time published. Contraveners shall be made known by their Ordinaries, and be punished with the penalties by law established.

Decree on Justification

ON THE INABILITY OF NATURE AND OF THE LAW TO JUSTIFY MAN

The holy Synod declares first, that, for the correct and sound understanding of the doctrine of Justification, it is necessary that each one recognize and confess, that, whereas all men had lost their innocence in the prevarication of Adam,—having become unclean, and, as the apostle says, "by nature children of wrath," as (this Synod) has set forth in the decree on original sin,—they were so far "the servants of sin," and under the power of the devil and of death, that not the Gentiles only by the force of nature, but not even the Jews by the very letter itself of the law of Moses, were able to be liberated, or to arise, therefrom; although free-will, attenuated as it was in its powers, and bent down, was by no means extinguished in them.

ON THE DISPENSATION AND MYSTERY OF CHRIST'S ADVENT

Whence it came to pass, that the heavenly Father, "the Father of mercies, and the God of all comfort," when that blessed "fullness of the time was come, sent" unto men, Jesus Christ, "his own Son"—who had been, both before the Law, and during the time of the Law, to many of the holy fathers announced and promised—"that he might both redeem the Jews who were under the Law," and that "the Gentiles, who followed not after justice," might attain to justice, and that all men might receive the adoption of sons. Him God hath "proposed" as a propitiator, "through faith in his blood, for our sins, and not for our sins only, but also for those of the whole world."

WHO ARE JUSTIFIED THROUGH CHRIST

But, though "He died for all," yet do not

all receive the benefit of his death, but those only unto whom the merit of his passion is communicated. For as in truth men, if they were not born propagated of the seed of Adam, would not be born unjust,—seeing that, by that propagation, they contract through him, when they are conceived, injustice as their own,—so, if they were not born again in Christ, they never would be justified; seeing that, in that new birth, there is bestowed upon them, through the merit of his passion, the grace whereby they are made just. For this benefit the apostle exhorts us, evermore "to give thanks to the Father, who hath made us worthy to be partakers of the lot of the saints in light, and hath delivered us from the power of darkness, and hath translated us into the Kingdom of the Son of his love, in whom we have redemption, and remission of sins."

A DESCRIPTION IS INTRODUCED OF THE JUSTIFICATION OF THE IMPIOUS, AND OF THE MANNER THEREOF IN THE STATE OF GRACE

By which words, a description of the Justification of the impious is indicated,—as being a translation, from that state wherein man is born a child of the first Adam, to the state of grace, and of "the adoption of the sons of God," through the second Adam, Jesus Christ, our Saviour. And this translation, since the promulgation of the Gospel, can not be effected, without the laver of regeneration, or the desire thereof, as it is written: "unless a man be born again of water and the Holy Ghost, he can not enter into the Kingdom of God."

ON THE NECESSITY, IN ADULTS, OF PREPARATION FOR JUSTIFICATION, AND WHENCE IT PROCEEDS

The Synod furthermore declares, that, in adults, the beginning of the said Justification is to be derived from the prevenient grace of God, through Jesus Christ, that is to say, from his vocation, whereby, without any merits existing on their parts, they are called; that so they, who by sins were alienated from God, may be disposed through his quickening and assisting grace, to convert themselves to their own justification, by freely assenting to and co-operating with that said grace: in such sort that, while God touches the heart of man by the illumination of the Holy Ghost, neither is man himself utterly inactive while he receives that inspiration, forasmuch as he is also able to reject it; yet is he not able, by his own free will, without the grace of God, to move himself unto justice in his sight. Whence, when it is said in the sacred writings: "Turn ye to me, and I will turn to you," we are admonished of our liberty; and when we answer: "Convert us, O Lord, to thee, and we shall be converted," we confess that we are prevented (anticipated) by the grace of God.

THE MANNER OF PREPARATION

Now they [adults] are disposed unto the said justice, when, excited and assisted by divine grace, conceiving "faith by hearing," they are freely moved towards God, believing those things to be true which God has revealed and promised—and this especially, that God justifies the impious "by his grace, through the redemption that is in Christ Jesus;" and when, understanding themselves to be sinners, they, by turning themselves, from the fear of divine justice whereby they are profitably agitated, to consider the mercy of God, are raised unto hope, confiding that God will be propitious to them for Christ's sake; and they begin to love him as the fountain of all justice; and are therefore moved against sins by a certain hatred and detestation, to wit, by that penitence which must be performed before baptism: lastly, when they purpose to receive baptism, to begin a new life, and to "keep the commandments" of God. Concerning this disposition it is written: "He that cometh to God, must believe that he is, and is a rewarder to them that seek him;" and, "Be of good faith, son, thy sins are forgiven thee;" and, "The fear of the Lord driveth out sin;" and, "Do penance, and be baptized every one of you in the name of Jesus Christ, for the remission of your sins, and you shall receive the gift of the Holy Ghost;" and, "Going, therefore, teach ye all nations, baptizing them in the name of the Father, and of the Son, and of the Holy Ghost;" finally, "Prepare your hearts unto the Lord."

WHAT THE JUSTIFICATION OF THE IMPIOUS IS, AND WHAT ARE THE CAUSES THEREOF

This disposition, or preparation, is followed by Justification itself, which is not remission of sins merely, but also the sanctification and renewal of the inward man, through the voluntary reception of the grace, and of the gifts, whereby man of unjust becomes just, and of an enemy a friend, that so he may be "an heir according to hope of life everlasting."

Of this Justification the causes are these: the final cause indeed is the glory of God and of Jesus Christ, and life everlasting; while the efficient cause is a merciful God who "washes and sanctifies" gratuitously, "signing," and anointing with the holy "Spirit of promise, who is the pledge of our inheritance;" but the meritorious cause is his most beloved only-begotten, our Lord Jesus Christ, who, when we were enemies, "for the exceeding charity wherewith he loved us," merited Justification for us by his most holy Passion on the wood of the cross, and made satisfaction for us unto God the Father; the instrumental cause is the sacrament of baptism, which is the sacrament of faith, without which [faith] no man was ever justified; lastly, the alone formal cause is the justice of God, not that whereby he himself is just, but that whereby he maketh us just, that, to wit, with which "we," being endowed by him, "are renewed in the spirit of our mind," and we are not only reputed, but are truly called, and are just, receiving justice within us, each one according to his own measure, "which the Holy Ghost distributes to every one as he wills," and according to each one's proper disposition and co-operation. For, although no one can be just, but he to whom the merits of the Passion of our Lord Jesus Christ are communicated, yet is this done in the said justification of the impious, when by the merit of that same most holy Passion, "the charity of God is poured forth," by the Holy Spirit, "in the hearts" of those that are justified, and is inherent therein: whence, man, through Jesus Christ, in whom he is ingrafted, receives, in the said justification, together with the remission of sins, all these [gifts] infused at once, faith, hope, and charity. For faith, unless hope and charity be added thereto, neither unites man perfectly with Christ, nor makes him a living member of his body. For which reason it is most truly said, that "Faith without works is dead" and profitless; and, "In Christ Jesus neither circumcision availeth any thing nor uncircumcision, but faith which worketh by charity." This faith, Catechumens beg of the Church—agreeably to a tradition of the apostles—previously to the sacrament of Baptism; when they beg for the faith which bestows life everlasting, which, without hope and charity, faith can not bestow: whence also do they immediately hear that word of Christ: "If thou wilt enter into life, keep the commandments." Wherefore, when receiving true and Christian justice, they are bidden, immediately on being born again, to preserve it pure and spotless, as "the first robe" given them through Jesus Christ in lieu of that which Adam, by his disobedience, lost for himself and for us, that so they may bear it before the judgment-seat of our Lord Jesus Christ, and may have life eternal.

IN WHAT MANNER IT IS TO BE UNDERSTOOD, THAT THE IMPIOUS IS JUSTIFIED BY FAITH, AND GRATUITOUSLY

And whereas the Apostle saith, that man is "justified by faith and freely," those words are to be understood in that sense which the perpetual consent of the Catholic Church hath held and expressed; to wit, that we are therefore said to be "justified by faith," because faith is the beginning of human salvation, the foundation, and the root of all Justification; "without which it is impossible to please God," and to come unto the fellowship of his sons: but we are therefore said to be justified "freely," because that none of those things which precede justification—whether faith or works—merit the grace itself of justification. For, "if it be a grace, it is not now by works," otherwise, as the same Apostle says, "grace is no more grace."

AGAINST THE VAIN CONFIDENCE OF HERETICS

But, although it is necessary to believe that sins neither are remitted, nor ever were remitted save gratuitously by the mercy of God for Christ's sake; yet is it not to be said, that sins are forgiven, or have been forgiven, to anyone who boasts of his confidence and certainly of the remission of his sins, and rests on that alone; seeing that it may exist, yea does in our day exist, amongst heretics and schismatics; and with great vehemence is this vain confidence, and one alien from all godliness, preached up in opposition to the Catholic Church. But neither is this to be asserted—that they who are truly justified must needs, without any doubting whatever, settle within themselves that they are justified, and that no one is absolved from sins and justified, but he that believes for certain that he is absolved and justified; and that absolution and justification are effected by this faith alone: as though whoso has not this belief, doubts of the promises of God, and of the efficacy of the death and resurrection of Christ. For even as no pious person ought to doubt of the mercy of God, of the merit of Christ, and of the virtue and efficacy of the sacraments, even so each one, when he regards himself, and his own weakness and indisposition, may have fear and apprehension touching his own grace; seeing that no one can know with a certainty of faith, which can not be subject to error, that he has obtained the grace of God.

ON THE INCREASE OF JUSTIFICATION RECEIVED

Having, therefore, been thus justified, and made the friends and "domestics of God," advancing "from virtue to virtue," they are "renewed," as the Apostle says, "day by day;" that is, "by mortifying the members" of their own flesh, and "by presenting them as instruments of justice unto sanctification," they, through the observance of the commandments of God and of the Church, faith co-operating with good works, increase in that justice which they have received through the grace of Christ, and are still further justified, as it is written: "He that is just, let him be justified still;" and again, "Be not afraid to be justified even to death;" and also, "Do you see that by works a man is justified, and not by faith only." And this increase of justification holy Church begs, when she prays, "Give unto us, O Lord, increase of faith, hope, and charity."

THAT A RASH PRESUMPTUOUSNESS IN THE MATTER OF PREDESTINATION IS TO BE AVOIDED

No one, moreover, so long as he is in this mortal life, ought so far to presume as regards the secret mystery of divine predestination, as to determine for certain that he is assuredly in the number of the predestinate; as if it were true, that he that is justified, either can not sin any more, or, if he do sin, that he ought to promise himself an assured repentance; for except by special revelation, it can not be known whom God hath chosen unto himself.

ON THE GIFT OF PERSEVERANCE

So also as regards the gift of perseverance, of which it is written, "He that shall persevere to the end, he shall be saved;"—which gift can not be derived from any other but Him, who is able to establish him who standeth that he stand perseveringly, and to restore him who falleth:—let no one herein promise himself any thing as certain with an absolute certainty; though all ought to place and repose a most firm hope in God's help. For God, unless men be themselves wanting in his grace, "as he has begun the good work, so will he perfect it, working" (in them) "to will and to accomplish." Nevertheless, let those who "think themselves to stand, take heed lest they fall," and, "with fear and trembling work out their salvation," in labors, in watchings, in almsdeeds, in prayers and oblations, in fastings and chastity: for, knowing that "they are born again unto a hope of glory," but not as yet unto glory, they ought to fear for the combat which yet remains with the flesh, with the world, with the devil, wherein they can not be victorious, unless they be with God's grace, obedient to the Apostle, who says: "We are debtors, not to the flesh, to live according to the flesh; for if you live according to the flesh, you shall die; but if by the spirit you mortify the deeds of the flesh, you shall live."

ON THE FALLEN, AND THEIR RESTORATION

As regards those who, by sin, have fallen from the received grace of Justification, they may be again justified, when, God exciting them, through the sacrament of Penance they shall have attained to the recovery, by the merit of Christ, of the grace lost: for this manner of Justification is of the fallen the reparation: which the holy Fathers have aptly called a second plank after the shipwreck of grace lost. For, on behalf of those who fall into sins after baptism, Christ Jesus instituted the sacrament of Penance, when he said, "Receive ye the Holy Ghost, whose sins you shall forgive, they are forgiven them, and whose sins you shall retain, they are retained." Whence it is to be taught, that the penitence of a Christian, after his fall, is very different from that at (his) baptism; and that therein are included not only a cessation of sins, and a detestation thereof, or, "a contrite and humble heart," but also the sacramental confession of the said sins,—at least in desire, and to be made in its season,—and sacerdotal absolution; and likewise satisfaction by fasts, alms, prayers, and the other pious exercises of a spiritual life; not indeed for the eternal punishment,—which is, together with the guilt, remitted, either by the sacrament, or by the desire of the sacrament,—but for the temporal punishment, which, as the sacred writings teach, is not always wholly remitted, as is done in baptism, to those who, ungrateful to the grace of God which they have received, have "grieved the Holy Spirit," and have not "feared to violate the temple of God." Concerning which penitence it is written: "Be mindful whence thou art fallen; do penance, and do the first works." And again: "The sorrow that is according to God worketh penance steadfast unto salvation." And again: "Do penance," and "bring forth fruits worthy of penance."

ON THE FRUIT OF JUSTIFICATION, THAT IS, ON THE MERIT OF GOOD WORKS, AND ON THE NATURE OF THAT MERIT

Before men, therefore, who have been justified in this manner,—whether they have preserved uninterruptedly the grace received, or whether they have recovered it when lost,—are to be set the words of the Apostle: "Abound in every good work, knowing that your labor is not in vain in the Lord; for God is not unjust, that he should forget your work, and the love which you have shown in his name;" and, "do not lose your confidence, which hath a great reward." And, for this cause, life eternal is to be proposed to those working well "unto the end," and hoping in God, both as a grace mercifully promised to the sons of God through Jesus Christ, and as a reward which is according to the promise of God himself, to be faithfully rendered to their good works and merits. For this is that "crown of justice" which the Apostle declared was, after his "fight" and "course, laid up for him, to be rendered to him by the just Judge, and not only to him, but also to all that love his coming." For, whereas Jesus Christ himself continually infuses his virtue into the said justified,—as the head into the members, and the vine into the branches,—and this virtue always precedes and accompanies and follows their good works, which without it could not in any wise be pleasing and meritorious before God,—we must believe that nothing further is wanting to the justified, to prevent their being accounted to have, by those very works which have been done in God, fully satisfied the divine law according to the state of this life, and to have truly merited eternal life, to be obtained also in its (due) time, if so be, however, that they depart in grace: seeing that Christ, our Saviour, saith: "If any one shall drink of the water that I will give him, he shall not thirst forever; but it shall become in him a fountain of water springing up unto life everlasting." Thus, neither is our own justice "established as our own" as from ourselves; nor is the justice of God ignored or repudiated: for that justice which is called ours, because that we are justified from its being inherent in us, that same is (the justice) of God, because that it is infused into us of God, through the merit of Christ. Neither is this to be omitted,—that although, in the sacred writings, so much is attributed to good works, that Christ promises, that even "he that shall give a drink of cold water to one of his least ones, shall not lose his reward;" and the Apostle testifies that, "That which is at present momentary and light of our tribulation, worketh for us above measure exceedingly an eternal weight of glory;" nevertheless God forbid that a Christian should either trust or glory in himself, and not in the Lord, whose bounty towards all men is so great, that he will have the things which are his own gifts be their merits. And forasmuch as "in many things we all offend," each one ought to have before his eyes, as well the severity and judgment, as the mercy and goodness (of God); neither ought any one "to judge himself, even though he be not conscious to himself of any thing;" because the whole life of man is to be examined and judged, not by the judgment of man, but of God, "who will bring to light the hidden things of darkness, and will make manifest the counsels of the hearts, and then shall every man have praise from God," who, as it is written, "will render to every man according to his works."

After this Catholic doctrine on Justification, which whoso receiveth not faithfully and firmly can not be justified, it hath seemed good to the holy Synod to subjoin these canons, that all may know not only what they ought to hold and follow, but also what to avoid and shun.

Canon I. If any one saith, that man may be justified before God by his own works, whether done through the teaching of human nature, or that of the law, without the grace of God through Jesus Christ: let him be anathema. . . .

Canon IV. If any one saith, that man's free-will moved and excited by God, by assenting to God exciting and calling, nowise co-operates towards disposing and preparing itself for obtaining the grace of Justification; that it can not refuse its consent, if it would, but that, as something inanimate, it does nothing whatever and is merely passive: let him be anathema.

Canon V. If any one saith, that, since Adam's son, the free-will of man is lost and extinguished; or, that it is a thing with only a name, yea a name without a reality, a figment, in fine, introduced into the Church by Satan: let him be anathema. . . .

Canon XVII. If any one saith, that the grace of Justification is only attained to by those who are predestined unto life; but that all others who are called, are called indeed, but receive not grace, as being, by the divine power, predestined unto evil: let him be anathema. . . .

Canon XXIV. If any one saith, that the justice received is not preserved and also increased before God through good works; but that the said works are merely the fruits and signs of Justification obtained, but not a cause of the increase thereof: let him be anathema. . . .

Canon XXX. If any one saith, that, after the grace of Justification has been received, to every penitent sinner the guilt is remitted, and the debt of eternal punishment is blotted out in such wise that there remains not any debt of temporal punishment to be discharged either in this world, or in the next in Purgatory, before the entrance to the kingdom of heaven can be opened [to him]: let him be anathema.

Canon XXXI. If any one saith, that the justified sins when he performs good works with a view to an eternal recompense: let him be anathema.

Canon XXXII. If any one saith, that the good works of one that is justified are in such manner the gifts of God, that they are not also the good merits of him that is justified; or, that the said justified, by the good works which he performs through the grace of God and the merit of Jesus Christ, whose living member he is, does not truly merit increase of grace, eternal life, and the attainment of that eternal life,—if so be, however, that he depart in grace,—and also an increase of glory: let him be anathema. . . .

Decree on the Sacraments

For the completion of the salutary doctrine on Justification, which was promulgated with the unanimous consent of the Fathers in the last preceding Session, it hath seemed suitable to treat of the most holy Sacraments of the Church, through which all true justice either begins, or being begun is increased, or being lost is repaired. With this view, in order to destroy the errors and to extirpate the heresies which have appeared in these our days on the subject of the said most holy sacraments,—as well those have been revived from the heresies condemned of old by our Fathers, as also those newly invented, and which are exceedingly prejudicial to the purity of the Catholic Church, and to the salvation of souls,—the sacred and holy, oecumenical and general Synod of Trent . . . has thought fit that these present canons be established and decreed; intending, the divine Spirit aiding, to publish later the remaining canons which are wanting for the completion of the work which it has begun.

ON THE SACRAMENTS IN GENERAL

Canon I. If any one saith, that the sacraments of the New Law were not all instituted by Jesus Christ, our Lord; or, that they are more, or less, than seven, to wit, Baptism, Confirmation, the Eucharist, Penance, Extreme Unction, Order, and Matrimony; or even that any one of these seven is not truly and properly a sacrament: let him be anathema. . . .

Canon IV. If any one saith, that the sacraments of the New Law are not necessary unto salvation, but superfluous; and that, without them, or without the desire thereof, men obtain of God, through faith alone, the grace of justification;—though all [the sacraments] are not indeed necessary for every individual: let him be anathema. . . .

Canon IX. If any one saith, that, in the three sacraments, to wit, Baptism, Confirmation, and Order, there is not imprinted in the soul a character, that is, a certain spiritual and indelible sign, on account of which they can not be repeated: let him be anathema.

Canon X. If any one saith, that all Christians have power to administer the word, and all the sacraments: let him be anathema. . . .

Decree Concerning the Most Holy Sacrament of the Eucharist

ON THE REAL PRESENCE OF OUR LORD JESUS CHRIST IN THE MOST HOLY SACRAMENT OF THE EUCHARIST

In the first place, the holy Synod teaches, and openly and simply professes, that, in the august sacrament of the holy Eucharist, after the consecration of the bread and wine, our Lord Jesus Christ, true God and man, is truly, really, and substantially contained under the species of those sensible things. For neither are these things mutually repugnant,—that our Saviour himself always sitteth at the right hand of the Father in heaven, according to the natural mode of existing, and that, nevertheless, he be, in many other places, sacramentally present to us in his own substance, by a manner of existing, which, though we can scarcely express it in words, yet can we, by the understanding illuminated by faith, conceive, and we ought most firmly to believe, to be possible unto God: for thus all our forefathers, as many as were in the true Church of Christ, who have treated of this most holy Sacrament, have most openly professed, that our Redeemer instituted this so admirable a sacrament at the last supper, when, after the blessing of the bread and wine, he testified, in express and clear words, that he gave them his own very body, and his own blood, words which,—recorded by the holy Evangelists, and afterwards repeated by Saint Paul, whereas they carry with them that proper and most manifest meaning in which they were understood by the Fathers,—it is indeed a crime the most unworthy that they should be wrested, by certain contentious and wicked men, to fictitious and imaginary tropes, whereby the verity of the flesh and blood of Christ is denied, contrary to the universal sense of the Church, which, as "the pillar and ground of truth," has detested, as satanical, these inventions devised by impious men; she recognizing, with a mind ever grateful and unforgetting, the most excellent benefit of Christ. . . .

ON TRANSUBSTANTIATION

And because that Christ, our Redeemer, declared that which he offered under the species of bread to be truly his own body, therefore has it ever been a firm belief in the Church of God, and this holy Synod doth now declare it anew, that by the consecration of the bread and of the wine, a conversion is made of the whole substance of the bread into the substance of the body of Christ our Lord, and of the whole substance of the wine into the substance of his blood; which conversion is, by the holy Catholic Church, suitably and properly called Transubstantiation. . . .

Doctrine on the Sacrifice of the Mass

ON THE INSTITUTION OF THE MOST HOLY SACRIFICE OF THE MASS

Forasmuch as, under the former Testament,

according to the testimony of the Apostle Paul, there was no perfection, "because of the weakness of the Levitical priesthood;" there was need, God, the Father of mercies, so ordaining, that "another priest should rise, according to the order of Melchisedech," our Lord Jesus Christ, who might consummate, and lead to what is perfect, as many as were to be sanctified. He, therefore, our God and Lord, though he was about to offer himself once on the altar of the cross unto God the Father, "by means of his death," there to operate "an eternal redemption;" nevertheless, because that his priesthood was not to be extinguished by his death, in the Last Supper, on the night in which he was betrayed,—that he might leave, to his own beloved Spouse the Church, a visible sacrifice, such as the nature of man requires, whereby that bloody sacrifice, one to be accomplished on the cross, might be represented, and the memory thereof remain even unto the end of the world, and its salutary virtue be applied to the remission of those sins which we daily commit,—declaring himself constituted "a priest forever, according to the order of Melchisedech," he offered up to God the Father his own body and blood under the species of bread and wine; and, under the symbols of those same things, he delivered (his own body and blood) to be received by his apostles, whom he then constituted priests of the New Testament; and by those words, "Do this in commemoration of me," he commanded them and their successors in the priesthood to offer (them); even as the Catholic Church has always understood and taught. For, having celebrated the ancient Passover, which the multitude of the children of Israel immolated in memory of their going out of Egypt, he instituted the new Passover (to wit), himself to be immolated, under visible signs, by the Church through (the ministry of) priests, in memory of his own passage from this world unto the Father, when by the effusion of his own blood he redeemed us, "and delivered us from the power of darkness, and translated us into his kingdom." And this is indeed that clean oblation, which cannot be defiled by any unworthiness, or malice of those that offer (it); which the Lord foretold by Malachias was to be "offered in every place, clean to his name, which was to be great amongst the Gentiles," and which the Apostle Paul, writing to the Corinthians, has not obscurely indicated, when he says, that they who are defiled by "the participation of the table of devils, cannot be partakers of the table of the Lord"; by the table, meaning in both places the altar. This, in fine, is that oblation which was prefigured by various types of sacrifices, during the period of nature, and of the law; inasmuch as it comprises all the good things signified by those sacrifices, as being the consummation and perfection of them all.

THAT THE SACRIFICE OF THE MASS IS PROPITIATORY, BOTH FOR THE LIVING AND THE DEAD

And forasmuch as, in this divine sacrifice which is celebrated in the mass, that same Christ is contained and immolated in an unbloody manner who once offered himself in a bloody manner on the altar of the cross; the holy Synod teaches, that this sacrifice is truly propitiatory, and that by means thereof this is effected, that we obtain mercy, and find grace "in seasonable aid," if we draw nigh unto God, contrite and penitent, with a sincere heart and upright faith, with fear and reverence. For the Lord, appeased by the oblation thereof, and granting the grace and gift of penitence, forgives even heinous crimes and sins. For the victim is one and the same, the same now offering by the ministry of priests, who then offered himself on the cross, the manner alone of offering being different. The fruits indeed of which oblation of that bloody one to wit, are received most plentifully through this unbloody one; so far is this [latter] from derogating in any way from that [former oblation]. Wherefore, not only for the sins, punishments, satisfactions, and other necessities of the faithful who are living, but also for those who are departed in Christ, and who are not as yet fully purified, is it rightly offered, agreeably to a tradition of the apostles.

ON MASSES IN HONOR OF THE SAINTS

And although the Church has been accustomed at times to celebrate certain masses in honor and memory of the saints; not therefore, however, doth she teach that sacrifice is offered unto them, but unto God alone, who crowned them; whence neither is the priest wont to say, 'I offer sacrifice to thee, Peter or Paul;' but, giving thanks to God for their victories, he implores their patronage, that they may vouchsafe to intercede for us in heaven, whose memory we celebrate upon earth. . . .

ON THE SOLEMN CEREMONIES OF THE SACRIFICE OF THE MASS

And whereas such is the nature of man, that, without external helps, he can not easily be raised to the meditation of divine things; therefore has holy Mother Church instituted certain rites, to wit, that certain things be pronounced in the mass in a low, and others in a louder, tone. She has likewise employed ceremonies, such as mystic benedictions, lights, incense, vestments, and many other things of this kind, derived from an apostolical discipline and tradition, whereby both the majesty of so great a sacrifice might be recommended, and the minds of the faithful be excited, by those visible signs of religion and piety, to the contemplation of those most sublime things which are hidden in this sacrifice. . . .

The True and Catholic Doctrine Concerning the Sacrament of Order

ON THE INSTITUTION OF THE PRIESTHOOD OF THE NEW LAW

Sacrifice and priesthood are, by the ordinance of God, in such wise conjoined, as that both have existed in every law. Whereas, therefore, in the New Testament, the Catholic Church has received, from the institution of Christ, the holy visible sacrifice of the Eucharist; it must needs also be confessed, that there is, in that Church, a new, visible, and external priesthood, into which the old has been "translated." And the sacred Scriptures show, and the tradition of the Catholic Church has always taught, that this priesthood was instituted by the same Lord our Saviour, and that to the Apostles, and their successors in the priesthood, was the power delivered of consecrating, offering, and administering his body and blood, as also of forgiving and of retaining sins. . . .

ON THE ECCLESIASTICAL HIERARCHY, AND ON ORDINATION

But, forasmuch as in the sacrament of Order, as also in Baptism and Confirmation, a character is imprinted which can neither be effaced nor taken away, the holy Synod with reason condemns the opinion of those who assert that the priests of the New Testament have only a temporary power; and that those who have once been rightly ordained can again become laymen, if they do not exercise the ministry of the Word of God. And if any one affirm, that all Christians indiscriminately are priests of the New Testament, or that they are all mutually endowed with an equal spiritual power, he clearly does nothing but confound the ecclesiastical hierarchy, which is "as an army set in array;" as if, contrary to the doctrine of blessed Paul, "all were apostles, all prophets, all evangelists, all pastors, all doctors." Wherefore, the holy Synod declares that, besides the other ecclesiastical degrees, bishops, who have succeeded to the place of the Apostles, principally belong to this hierarchical order; that they are "placed," as the same apostle says, "by the Holy Ghost, to rule the Church of God;" that they are superior to priests; administer the sacrament of Confirmation; ordain the ministers of the Church; and that they can perform very many other things; over which functions others of an inferior order have no power. Furthermore, the sacred and holy Synod teaches, that, in the ordination of bishops, priests, and of the other orders, neither the consent, nor vocation, nor authority, whether of the people, or of any civil power or magistrate whatsoever, is required in such wise as that, without this, the ordination is invalid; yea rather doth it decree, that all those who, being only called and instituted by the people, or by the civil power and magistrate, ascend to the exercise of these ministrations, and those who of their own rashness assume them to themselves, are not ministers of the Church, but are to be looked upon as "thieves and robbers, who have not entered by the door." These are the things which it hath seemed good to the sacred Synod to teach the faithful of Christ, in general terms, touching the sacrament of Order. . . .

DECREE CONCERNING PURGATORY

Whereas the Catholic Church, instructed by the Holy Ghost, has, from the Sacred Writings and the ancient tradition of the Fathers, taught, in sacred Councils, and very recently in this oecumenical Synod, that there is a Purgatory, and that the souls there detained are helped by the suffrages of the faithful, but principally by the acceptable sacrifice of the altar,—the holy Synod enjoins on bishops that they diligently endeavor that the sound doctrine concerning Purgatory, transmitted by the holy Fathers and sacred Councils, be believed, maintained, taught, and everywhere proclaimed by the faithful of Christ. But let the more difficult and subtle questions, and which tend not to edification, and from which for the most part there is no increase of piety, be excluded from popular discourses before the uneducated multitude. In like manner, such things as are uncertain, or which labor under an appearance of error, let them not allow to be made public and treated of. While those things which tend to a certain kind of curiosity or superstition, or which savor of filthy lucre, let them prohibit as scandals and stumbling-blocks of the faithful. But let the bishops take care that the suffrages of the faithful who are living, to wit, the sacrifices of masses, prayers, alms, and other works of piety, which have been wont to be performed by the faithful for the other faithful departed, be piously and devoutly performed, in accordance with the institutes of the Church; and that whatsoever is due on their behalf, from the endowments of testators, or in other way, be discharged, not in a perfunctory manner, but diligently and accurately, by the priests and ministers of the Church, and others who are bound to render this [service].

ON THE INVOCATION, VENERATION, AND RELICS OF SAINTS, AND ON SACRED IMAGES

The holy Synod enjoins on all bishops, and others who sustain the office and charge of teaching, that, agreeably to the usage of the Catholic and Apostolic Church, received from the primitive times of the Christian religion, and agreeably to the consent of the holy Fathers, and to the decrees of sacred Councils, they especially instruct the faithful diligently concerning the intercession and invocation of saints; the honor [paid] to relics; and the legitimate use of images: teaching them, that the saints, who reign together with Christ, offer up their own prayers to God for men; that it is good and useful suppliantly to invoke them, and to have recourse to their prayers, aid, [and] help for obtaining benefits from God, through his Son, Jesus Christ our Lord, who is our alone Redeemer and Saviour; but that they think impiously who deny that the saints, who enjoy eternal happiness in heaven, are to be invocated; or who assert either that they do not pray for me; or that the invocation of them to pray for each of us even in particular is idolatry; or that it is repugnant to the Word of God, and is opposed to the honor of the "one mediator of God and men, Christ Jesus;" or that it is foolish to supplicate, vocally or mentally, those who reign in heaven.

Also, that the holy bodies of holy martyrs, and of others now living with Christ,—which bodies were the living members of Christ, and "the temple of the Holy Ghost," and which are by him to be raised unto eternal life, and to be glorified,—are to be venerated by the faithful; through which [bodies] many benefits are bestowed by God on men; so that they who affirm that veneration and honor are not due to the relics of saints; or that these, and other sacred monuments, are uselessly honored by the faithful; and that the places dedicated to the memories of the saints are in vain visited with the view of obtaining their aid, are wholly to be condemned, as the Church has already long since condemned, and now also condemns them.

Moreover, that the images of Christ, of the Virgin Mother of God, and of the other saints, are to be had and retained particularly in temples, and that due honor and veneration are to be given them; not that any divinity, or virtue, is believed to be in them, on account of which they are to be worshipped; or that anything is to be asked of them; or that trust is to be reposed in images, as was of old done by the Gentiles, who placed their hope in idols;

but because the honor which is shown them is referred to the prototypes which those images represent; in such wise that by the images which we kiss, and before which we uncover the head, and prostrate ourselves, we adore Christ, and we venerate the saints, whose similitude they bear: as, by the decrees of Councils, and especially of the second Synod of Nicaea, has been defined against the opponents of images.

And the bishops shall carefully teach this,—that, by means of the histories of the mysteries of our Redemption, portrayed by paintings or other representations, the people is instructed, and confirmed in [the habit of] remembering, and continually revolving in mind the articles of faith; as also that great profit is derived from all sacred images, not only because the people are thereby admonished of the benefits and gifts bestowed upon them by Christ, but also because the miracles which God has performed by means of the saints, and their salutary examples, are set before the eyes of the faithful; that so they may give God thanks for those things; may order their own lives and manners in imitation of the saints; and may be excited to adore and love God, and to cultivate piety. But if anyone shall teach or entertain sentiments contrary to these decrees: let him be anathema. . . .

Moreover, in the invocation of saints, the veneration of relics, and the sacred use of images, every superstition shall be removed, all filthy lucre be abolished; finally, all lasciviousness be avoided; in such wise that figures shall not be painted or adorned with a beauty exciting to lust; nor the celebration of the saints and the visitation of relics be by any perverted into revelings and drunkenness; as if festivals were celebrated to the honor of the saints by luxury and wantonness.

In fine, let so great care and diligence be used herein by bishops, as that there be nothing seen that is disorderly, or that is unbecomingly or confusedly arranged, nothing that is profane, nothing indecorous, seeing that "holiness becometh the house of God."

Selected Readings in the Early and Medieval Periods

SOURCES IN ENGLISH TRANSLATION

The Ante-Nicene Fathers, Edinburgh ed., rev. by A. Coxe, 10 vols. Buffalo: Christian Literature, 1884–1886.

Ayer, J. C. *A Source Book for Ancient Church History, from the Apostolic Age to the Close of the Conciliar Period.* New York: Charles Scribner's Sons, 1949.

Baillie, J., J. T. McNeill, and H. P. Van Dusen, eds., *The Library of Christian Classics.* Philadelphia: Westminster Press, 1953—.

The Nicene and Post-Nicene Fathers, First Series, 14 vols., Buffalo: Christian Literature, 1886–1894. Second Series, 12 vols., Buffalo: Christian Literature, 1890–1895.

Quasten, J., and J. C. Plumpe, eds., *Ancient Christian Writers.* Westminster, Md.: Newman, 1946—.

Schaff, P., *The Creeds of Christendom,* 4th ed. New York: Harper and Brothers, 1905.

Schopp, L., ed., *The Fathers of the Church*. New York: Christian Heritage, 1947—.

HISTORY OF THOUGHT

Bethune-Baker, J. F., *An Introduction to the Early History of Christian Doctrine*, 9th ed. London: Methuen and Company, 1951.

Cochrane, A. N., *Christianity and Classical Culture*. New York: Oxford University Press, 1944.

Denzinger, H. J. D., *The Sources of Catholic Dogma*, tr. by R. J. Deferrari. St. Louis: Herder, 1957.

De Wulf, M., *A History of Medieval Philosophy*, tr. by E. C. Messenger, 2 vols. New York: Longmans, Green and Company, 1925–1926; rev. ed., 1952, Edinburgh.

Gilson, E., *A History of Christian Philosophy in the Middle Ages*. New York: Random House, 1955.

Harnack, A., *A History of Dogma*, tr. by N. Buchanan, 7 vols. London: Williams and Norgate, 1894ff.

Kelly, J. N. D., *Early Christian Doctrines*. New York: Harper and Brothers, 1958.

Seeberg, R., *Textbook of the History of Doctrines*, tr. by C. E. Hay. Grand Rapids, Michigan: Baker Book House, 1952.

Taylor, H. O., *The Medieval Mind*, 2 vols., 4th ed. Cambridge, Mass. Harvard University Press, 1949.

Troeltsch, E., *The Social Teachings of the Christian Churches*, tr. by O. Wyon, 2 vols. New York: The Macmillan Company, 1949.

HISTORY

Cross, F. L. ed., *Oxford Dictionary of the Christian Church*. New York: Oxford University Press, 1957.

Duchesne, L., *The Early History of the Christian Church*, tr. from 4th French ed., 3 vols. London: John Murray, 1950.

Harnack, A., *The Expansion of Christianity in the First Three Centuries*, tr. by J. Moffatt, 2 vols. New York: G. P. Putnam's Sons, 1908.

Latourette, K. S., *A History of the Expansion of Christianity*, 7 vols. New York: Harper and Brothers, 1937–1945.

Lebreton, J., and Zeiller, J., *The History of the Primitive Church*, tr. by E. C. Messenger, 2 vols. New York: The Macmillan Company, 1949.

Lietzmann, H., *The Beginnings of the Christian Church*, tr. by B. L. Woolf. New York: Charles Scribner's Sons, 1937.

———, *The Era of the Church Fathers*, tr. by B. L. Woolf. New York: Charles Scribner's Sons, 1951.

———, *The Founding of the Church Universal*, tr. by B. L. Woolf. New York: Charles Scribner's Sons, 1938.

———, *From Constantine to Julian*, tr. by B. L. Woolf. New York: Charles Scribner's Sons, 1950.

van der Meer, F., and Mohrmann, C., *Atlas of the Early Christian World*, tr. and ed. by M. F. Hedlund and H. H. Rowley. London: Nelson, 1958.

Walker, W. *A History of the Christian Church.* New York: Charles Scribner's Sons, rev. by C. C. Richardson, W. Pauck and R. T. Handy, 1959.

THE CHURCH

Gore, C., *The Ministry of the Christian Church.* London: Rivington's, 1889.

Kirk, K. E., ed., *The Apostolic Ministry.* London: Hodder and Stoughton, 1946.

Lindsay, T. M., *The Church and the Ministry in the Early Centuries.* London: Hodder and Stoughton, 1910.

Manson, T. W., *The Church's Ministry.* Philadelphia: Westminster Press, 1948.

Streeter, H. B., *The Primitive Church.* New York: The Macmillan Company, 1929.

CREEDS

Kelly, J. N. D., *Early Christian Creeds.* New York: Longmans, Green and Company, 1950.

AUGUSTINE

Battenhouse, R. W., ed., *A Companion to the Study of St. Augustine.* New York: Oxford University Press, 1955.

Burnaby, J., *Amor Dei.* London: Hodder and Stoughton, 1938.

The Confessions of Saint Augustine, tr. by F. J. Sheed. New York: Sheed and Ward, Inc., 1944.

D'Arcy, M. C., and others, *St. Augustine, His Age, His Life and Thought.* New York: Meridian Books, Inc., 1957.

Introduction to Saint Augustine, The City of God, tr. by R. H. Burrow, London: Faber, 1950.

Oates, W. J., ed., *Basic Writings of Saint Augustine,* 2 vols. New York: Random House, 1948.

THE CHURCH IN THE MIDDLE AGES

Deansley, M., *A History of the Medieval Church, 590–1500,* 6th ed. London: Methuen and Company, 1950.

Dawson, C., *Medieval Essays.* New York: Sheed and Ward, Inc., 1954.

Lagarde, A., *The Latin Church in the Middle Ages.* Edinburgh: T. and T. Clark, 1915.

Previte-Orton, C. W., *The Shorter Cambridge Medieval History,* 2 vols. New York: Cambridge University Press, 1952.

RELIGIOUS LIFE AND THOUGHT IN THE MIDDLE AGES

de Jaeger, P., ed., *Anthology of Mysticism,* tr. by D. Attwater. Westminster: Newman, 1950.

Fairweather, E. R., ed., *A Scholastic Miscellany: Anselm to Occam* (Library of Christian Classics, vol. X). Philadelphia: Westminster Press, 1956.

Hannah, I. C., *Christian Monasticism.* New York: The Macmillan Company, 1925.

McCracken, G. E., ed., *Early Medieval Theology* (Library of Christian Classics, Vol. IX). Philadelphia: Westminster Press, 1957.

Pegis, A. C., ed., *The Wisdom of Catholicism.* New York: Modern Library, 1955.

Petry, R. C., ed., *Late Medieval Mysticism* (Library of Christian Classics, vol. XIII). Philadelphia: Westminster Press, 1957.

Underhill, E., *Mysticism,* 12th ed. London: Methuen and Company, 1930.

Workman, H. B., *The Evolution of the Monastic Ideal.* London: The Epworth Press, 1927.

AQUINAS

Copleston, F. C. *Aquinas.* London: Penguin Books, 1955.

Gilson, E., *The Philosophy of St. Thomas Aquinas,* tr. by E. Bullough. Cambridge, England: W. Heffer and Sons, Ltd., 1929.

Grabmann, M., *Thomas Aquinas, His Personality and Thought,* tr. by V. Michel. New York: Longmans, Green and Company, 1928.

Pegis, A. C., ed., *Basic Writings of St. Thomas Aquinas,* 2 vols. New York: Random House, 1944.

RENAISSANCE AND HUMANISM

Cassirer, E., P. O. Kristeller, and J. H. Randall Jr., eds., *The Renaissance Philosophy of Man.* Chicago: University of Chicago Press, 1948.

Flick, A., *The Decline of the Medieval Church,* 2 vols. New York: Alfred A. Knopf, Inc., 1930.

Huizinga, J., *The Waning of the Middle Ages.* London: E. Arnold and Company, 1928.

———, *Erasmus.* New York: Phaidon Publishers, Inc., 1952.

Randall, J. H., Jr., *The Making of the Modern Mind,* rev. ed. Boston: Houghton Mifflin Company, 1940.

Smith, P., *Erasmus.* New York: Harper and Brothers, 1923.

COUNCIL OF TRENT

Jedin, H., *A History of the Council of Trent,* tr. by E. Graf. St. Louis: B. Herder, 1957.

Schaff, P., *The Creeds of Christendom,* 4th ed. New York: Harper and Brothers, 1905, Vol. II.

PART THREE

THE REFORMATION

I·N·R·I

IEAN CALVIN · FIDELLE · MINISTRE · DE·LA·PAROLLE·DE·DIEV · AAGE·DE·50·ANS
Prouerbes j.
La crainte du Seigneur est le commencement de Science.

John Calvin.

Word and Sacrament. Luther, with the open Bible before him, wants to preach nothing but Christ. The congregation is gathered around the altar-table for the Lord's Supper and receives both bread and wine. The papists are being swallowed by hell in the form of a beast.

John Wesley.

Introduction

With the Reformation of the sixteenth century the unity of medieval Christendom disintegrated and Protestantism was born. Future generations would date the beginning of the Reformation movement from the eve of All Saints Day (October 31), 1517, when the Augustinian monk and professor of theology, Martin Luther, nailed ninety-five theses to the door of the Castle Church in Wittenberg. Yet at the time hardly anybody, and least of all Luther himself, could have suspected that the posting of these theses, which was merely the customary way of challenging one's opponents to an academic debate, was the first step in a succession of events which within a few decades would usher in a new era in the history of the Christian Church. That the Reformation movement had this dramatic impact was in part due to the fact that it was related to other movements and events which in this momentous period transformed Western civilization. We cannot understand the Protestant Reformation unless we see it in the larger context of these revolutionary political, social and intellectual changes, of which the Reformation was only one, and which together marked the transition of the western world from the Middle Ages to the modern period (see pp. 129 ff.).

And yet this hardly suffices for a proper understanding of the Reformation. We must recognize that at the heart of this movement was a religious concern, a desire to return to the purity of the Christian faith as found in the Bible and as attested to in the creeds and practices of early Christianity. The reformers made their demands against a church which had become morally lax and which had strayed far from the simple faith and church order of New Testament times. When these demands in due time were rejected by the papal Church, Protestantism was born. The selections from the writings of the various reformers tell the story of Protestantism during its formative years. They will help to make clear that its relationship to the medieval Church must be seen both as a doctrinal and liturgical reformation and as an ecclesiastical revolution. Protestantism reformed the theology and practices of the medieval Church by refocusing the Christian faith in a new understanding of God's relationship to man as revealed by Christ and recorded in the Bible. The reformers stressed Paul's doctrine that salvation comes by faith, and not by "works of the law." Theological reformation was accompanied by a break with papal authority; this in turn opened the door to differing interpretations of Christianity by a variety of groups.

Thus Protestantism did not emerge as a new church which was as unified in its organizational structure and as uniform in its doctrinal beliefs as Roman Catholicism. Rather it emerged as a movement which, although united in its intention to return to the ideal of biblical Christianity, produced a great variety of religious convictions and ecclesiastical organizations. In the sixteenth century we can discern four distinct Reformation patterns. They were distinguished from each other by the way in which they applied their new understanding of the Christian faith to the task of reforming the medieval Church; by different emphases which they placed on questions of theology and church order; by differences between the personalities and the backgrounds of the leading reformers; and by the belief, common to all of them except the Anabaptists, that the organization of the Reformation churches should follow national lines. Thus in the course of time, as the Reformation expanded geographically and grew in strength, the four distinct types of the sixteenth century protest against Rome emerged: Lutheranism, Calvinism, the Anabaptists, and Anglicanism.

From this brief description of some of the essential features of the Protestant movement we now turn to an account of the complex story of Protestantism during its formative years.

Martin Luther

At its beginning stands the towering figure of Martin Luther. It was this son of a Thuringian peasant who became the driving force of the Reformation during its early years, as he worked untiringly and with unfailing courage for a reform of medieval Catholicism.

The break with the medieval Church came over the sale of indulgences. According to Catholic theory, an indulgence provided for the remission of the temporal punishments, including those suffered in Purgatory, which were laid upon the sinner by the church, provided the sin or sins had been forgiven. But in practice some of those selling indulgences made it appear that they not only released one from the temporal punishment for sins committed, but brought about the forgiveness of those sins themselves. This latter understanding apparently was held by the Dominican monk Tetzel who in 1517 was selling indulgences in the neighborhood of Wittenberg. The Ninety-five Theses which Luther posted at the Castle Church in Wittenberg were but a protest against the abuses in the traffic of indulgences. That they became the spark which set the whole structure of medieval Christendom afire was due mainly to Luther's singular personality and, even more important, to a new understanding of the Christian faith which he had gradually developed during the previous years.

This new understanding of the Christian faith had been gained in the course of an intense personal struggle, in the center of which stood Luther's quest for a merciful God. As a law student at the university of Erfurt he had vowed to become a monk after he had been struck down by lightning. He entered the Augustinian order and tried to avail himself of every possible opportunity which the medieval system of sacramental piety provided to gain a merciful God and the salvation of his soul. Yet, confronted with the medieval image of Christ as a stern judge and knowing himself to be under the divine wrath, he felt that he was unable to placate an angry God. The turning point in his struggle for the certainty of salvation came with his appointment to the professorship of Biblical Literature at the newly founded university of Wittenberg, a professorship which he held until his death. Being required to interpret the Bible, and aided by his study of Augustine and the German mystics, he found the answer to his quest for God's mercy. Sometime in 1512 or 1513, while he was meditating on the meaning of St. Paul's reference to the "justice of God" in Romans 1:17, he rediscovered the gospel of God's unmerited mercy. He now understood that the justice of God is that justice by which God forgives and transforms the sinner. It is not the divine justice which man must try to satisfy by doing good works which he is, however, unable to do. Rather God confers his justice upon man for Christ's sake, who through his suffering and death atoned for man's sins once and for all. Man, instead of making futile attempts at earning his own salvation, therefore only has to accept his salvation with childlike trust in God's forgiving love. These were the basic thoughts which were at the heart of Luther's evangelical doctrine of justification by faith alone.

But Luther not only challenged the piety of medieval Catholicism; he was also led to challenge and finally to reject the authority of the papal Church. When in defence of his evangelical doctrines he was confronted with the authority of church councils and the popes, he had no alternative but to insist that the only authority binding on a Christian's conscience is the voice of Christ as found in the Holy Scriptures. Against the traditions of the Catholic Church and the authority of the popes he placed the authority of the Bible.

Thus the two fundamental principles of classical Protestantism had come to the fore: That man is made just through God's grace by faith alone and not by "works of the law"; and that man's sole authority in religious matters is the Bible.

We can see that Luther's protest went hand in hand with a powerful affirmation of evangelical doctrines. Both the protest and the affirmation were bound to have tremendous consequences for the Church. These consequences were already fully visible in Luther's three great Reformation treatises, written in quick succession in the second half of 1520: *An Open Letter to the Christian Nobility of the German Nation* (August), *On the Babylonian Captivity of the Church* (October), and *Treatise on Christian Liberty* (November). In these works he rejected the papal authority, challenged the temporal authorities to cure the body of medieval Christendom of its most glaring ills, reduced the whole elaborate system of medieval piety to the simple principle of faith in Christ, and clearly set forth the evangelical understanding of the relationship between faith and works. From these writings it became clear that, inherent in his evangelical teaching, was the doctrine of the priesthood of all believers.

The depth of Luther's faith, and the courage which it inspired, were soon shown when he openly defied the papacy and the empire. In the fall of 1520, in the presence of the faculty and student body of the university of Wittenberg, he burned the papal bull of excommunication, adding for good measure a copy of the canon law. A year later, before the estates of the empire at the Diet of Worms, he fearlessly refused to recant his doctrines and was placed by Emperor Charles V under the Imperial ban.

Although Luther was now excommunicated and banned, the formidable opposition of the papacy and the emperor did not succeed in crushing him or his movement. This was largely due to popular resentment of the papal church as well as the inefficiency of papal policies in curbing the spread of the Lutheran movement. Also, Luther and his followers benefited from the complexity of the political situation which kept the Emperor Charles V engaged in wars and political quarrels for more than a decade. At the Diet of Speier in 1526, at a time when Charles V needed the support of the Protestant princes and cities, the right was granted to the Protestant party to decide which religion should be followed in their own territories. Three years later, at the second Diet of Speier, having momentarily gained the upper hand over his enemies abroad, the emperor withdrew this privilege, thereby provoking the Protestant members of the Diet to protest against the imperial decision. It is from this occasion that the name *Protestant* is derived.

Thus, favored by the changing fortunes of the political struggle, Luther was able to build the church which, against his will, was named after him. To this church he gave numerous theological tracts, his beautiful translation of the Bible into German, two catechisms, collections of his sermons, and an order of worship purified from what he regarded as Catholic distortions of the Christian faith. But while he had shown himself to be of a revolutionary temperament in his opposition to medieval Catholicism, he became increasingly conservative in his approach to the task of consolidating the forces of the Reform. In the gradual process of establishing the Lutheran Church, its character became more narrowly defined, and it came to stand increasingly apart from most of the other political, cultural, and religious forces of the age. Although he had gained in Melanchthon a brilliant humanist as his closest associate, Luther's book *On the Bondage of the Will* (1525), which was a reply to an earlier treatise by the celebrated Erasmus of Rotterdam, made it clear that the ways of Renaissance humanism and the Lutheran movement were bound to diverge. He alienated the peasants from his cause when he supported the princes and magistrates during the peasant war. And, due to disagreement in the interpretation of the meaning of the Lord's Supper, he found it impossible to extend the hand of fellowship to the Swiss reformer Huldreich Zwingli.

In the further development of the Lutheran Church two facts in particular need to be briefly mentioned. In organizing his followers into a church he relied on the princes and the magistrates as the principal members of the church. Although he considered this only an emergency measure, he nevertheless quite unintentionally made the Lutheran Church dependent upon the political authorities. Again, Luther had insisted that faith alone is the mark of a true Christian and that the preaching of the Word of God and the administration of the two Scriptural sacraments (i.e., baptism and the Lord's supper) alone signify the existence of the Church of Christ. However, in defending the evangelical faith against Roman Catholic critics and other Protestants credal statements became necessary. Increasingly, these came to be regarded by many as an essential mark of the true church. Thus the Lutheran Church gradually developed into a confessional state church and Lutheran theology into strict orthodoxy. This development, however, showed itself clearly only after Luther's death in 1546. The Lutheran Church gained full legal recognition at the Diet of Augsburg in 1555, based on the principle that the religious conviction of the prince or magistrate determines the religious status of their territories. Under this arrangement dissenting groups had the liberty to emigrate.

John Calvin

The Reformed Churches of Switzerland were excluded from the settlement of the religious question which the Diet of Augsburg had achieved. The Swiss Reformation had begun in Zurich under Zwingli and was largely independent from, even at points in opposition to, Luther. But it was John Calvin rather than Zwingli who dominated and determined the course of the Swiss Reformation and the shape of this second Reform pattern. Born in Noyon near Paris in 1509, 25 years younger than Luther, Calvin clearly belonged to the second generation of Protestant reformers and owed his basic insights to Luther. After first preparing for the priesthood and then the law, and after having acquired a brilliant humanistic erudition at various French universities, he experienced, probably in the spring of 1534, a sudden conversion which changed the course of his life. He now joined the Protestant party in France and set himself the task of reforming the French Church according to the biblical pattern. But when the French crown began to persecute the Protestants, Calvin was forced to flee and eventually found refuge in Protestant Basel. The following year, 1536, stands out in Calvin's life and the history of Protestantism for two reasons: Early this year, Calvin's masterpiece *The Institutes of the Christian Religion* had been published. Written by its author at the age of twenty-six, it went through several editions. In the course of these editions it was considerably enlarged until it found its final form in the edition of 1559, but Calvin never changed the basic thoughts which he had first enunciated in 1536. It is above all in the *Institutes* that Calvin's genius as a systematic thinker showed itself most forcefully. He has been called the greatest theologian of the Reformation. Less gifted with creative ability than with a powerful, orderly intellect, he formulated Protestant thought and fashioned it into an impressive structure. In its center stood Calvin's belief that God is the Sovereign from Whom all things come and Whose will they all ultimately must obey.

But Calvin was equally outstanding as a man of action who became the Reformation's greatest ecclesiastical statesman. This he proved through his leadership of the affairs of the city of Geneva where late in 1536, by the powerful admonition of the evangelical preacher Farel, he was persuaded to stay. It is characteristic of Calvin that his two greatest achievements were a book, the *Institutes,* and a city, Geneva.

The city of Geneva, in what is today French Switzerland, had only recently won its independence and accepted the Protestant faith. Here, against much opposition, and constantly harassed until his final triumph in 1553, Calvin established a theocracy in which the church, through a committee of clergy and laymen, sought to regulate the religious and moral life of the entire community. Calvin especially claimed for the church the right of excommunication. In theory, Calvin, like Luther, distinguished between state and church as two different spheres of human life. But prompted by his conviction that all things had to be ordered under God, the church, wherever his influence prevailed, became not only independent of secular control, but dominated the civil community. Nevertheless, it was within this theocracy that institutions of representative government sprang up. These institutions influenced the growth of democratic forms of government, especially in the English-speaking world.

Calvinism was further distinguished by its activism, which, in a way, has always presented a puzzling paradox. In Calvin's theology the contrast between God's all-powerful majesty and sinful man's insignificance is most sharply drawn. From this central tenet of his theology he derived the decree of double predestination which even he called "horrible." With Scriptural passages as his proof and forced by an irresistible logic, he taught that God in his inscrutable wisdom has predestined some to be saved and some to be eternally damned. Yet Calvin's theology, instead of paralyzing human exertions, seemed to give to Calvinists an enthusiasm for becoming the human instruments of God's sovereign will. It was this that filled Calvin's followers with an untiring zeal to shape the world in all its spheres to the will of God. Calvin's influence was spread abroad by Protestant refugees who had come to Geneva from many European countries, by his extensive correspondence, and his numerous writings. It is worth noting that Calvin has been credited with preventing the Catholic Counter-Reformation during the second half of the sixteenth century from overwhelming the emerging Protestant churches. In the long run, Calvin's impact was greatest on the English-speaking world. However, before we turn to the story of the English Reformation, we must consider the third pattern of Reform which had developed besides and in opposition to the Lutheran and Calvinist churches.

The Anabaptists

Already during the early stages of the Reformation there appeared on the European continent groups of Christians who were far more radical in their attempt at reforming the medieval Church than the great reformers. It is neither easy to define this movement nor to name it properly. There was no outstanding leader among them to direct and dominate the thought and life of his followers. Furthermore, this movement produced a great variety of views. In derision, their adversaries named them Anabaptists (Greek for rebaptizers) because of one of their more conspicuous principles, namely, adult or believer's baptism. They have been known by this name ever since. These radical groups held in common certain basic ideas which brought them into open conflict not only with the Roman Catholic Church, but also with the Lutherans and the Swiss reformers. Probably the point of greatest conflict concerned the relationship of the social and political order to the church. According to the medieval understanding, which was retained by the major Protestant reformers, the Christian religion was considered to be the basic unifying force in society. Religious uniformity, it was believed, was essential to political unity and stability and was to be achieved, if necessary, by the use of force. Calvin, for example, felt justified in having Servetus burned at the stake by the city of Geneva because Servetus had denied certain fundamental Christian beliefs. This action was approved by all the major Protestant reformers. The Anabaptist groups, however, rejected the concept of a national or territorial church on Scriptural grounds. They affirmed that the true Church of Christ is a voluntary association of men and women who have had a personal experience of Christ's saving presence and are under the guidance of the Spirit, aspiring to a saintly life. Their refusal to recognize the baptism of infants as it was practiced by all the rest of Christendom was based on the fact that for them the Christian faith was a matter of individual choice and personal decision. Baptism was to follow only upon a conscious consent to the faith of the Church. Again on scriptural grounds, they advocated the withdrawal of the regenerate Christian from a sinful world into the sanctuary of the church. They tried to follow the New Testament precepts of Christ strictly and literally and found it impossible to participate in the ordinary life of society. They refused to render military service, to take an oath, or to become magistrates, and thereby gave the appearance of being enemies of the social and political order. But only small groups among them, caught up in the social unrest of the times, were fanatics and opposed the established order with the sword. In 1534, a group of religious fanatics attempted to establish by force the kingdom of God at Muenster in Westphalia. Under their rule excesses of a grotesque nature occurred. The Muensterites, who were crushed by a combined force of Catholics and Protestants, brought more discredit and renewed persecution to the whole movement. The persecution which the Anabaptists suffered at the hands of both Catholics and Protestants almost exterminated them in the sixteenth century. Hardly any of the early centers of the movement, which had sprung up in Moravia, Switzerland, Southern Germany, along the Rhine, and in the Netherlands, survived for long. The only remaining groups were the Mennonites, gathered under the leadership of Menno Simons, and the Hutterite Church, which was founded by Jacob Hutter in Moravia.

Anglicanism

Besides these three patterns of Reform on the European continent there emerged on English soil a fourth type of the sixteenth century protest against Rome. In common with Anabaptism, the English Reformation produced no great leader or theologian comparable in stature and influence with Luther or Calvin. Furthermore, it was not occasioned by doctrinal questions or disputes. The Church of England, which had long been characterized by a desire for ecclesiastical independence, broke with Rome when the pope denied Henry VIII's demand for an annullment of his marriage to his first wife because she had left him without a male heir. Within a few years the king succeeded by parliamentary action in completely removing papal authority from England. He himself assumed the headship of the English Church. Although at this time the influence of Protestant thought coming from the continent was beginning to be felt in England, the break with Rome under Henry VIII did not mean a rejection of the basic Catholic doctrines and practices. These years of loyalty to the traditional Catholic faith had a lasting influence upon Anglicanism, which still stresses historic continuity with the Catholic past. But it was equally important that, of the two rulers who succeeded Henry VIII, the first, Edward VI, was a Protestant, and the second, Mary I, a Catholic. England was for a time caught between the two religious extremes into which Western Christianity had become divided. Largely due to the experience of seeing such bitter conflict between the two groups, the English nation sought to avoid both extremes by combining what was best in each of them. The Church of England, whose character was finally and definitely decided by the Elizabethan settlement of 1559–63, steered a middle course between Rome and Geneva. It was a national church which retained the inherited structure of the episcopal office. With the traditional liturgical forms it combined a theology which showed Calvin's influence. During Elizabeth's reign the Book of Common Prayer, distinguished not only for its religious spirit but also for its beautiful prose, was accepted in its final form. At the same time an attempt was made to lay down the beliefs of Anglicanism in the so-called Thirty-nine Articles.

Three principles, therefore, can be pointed out as being characteristic of the Anglican communion. The Church of England was first of all a national church. Anglicanism more than any other of the emerging Protestant churches emphasized that the church is an organization which is an integral part of the life of the nation. The second principle, historical continuity, found its clearest expression in the theory and practice of apostolic succession. Anglicans, following the Catholic tradition, believe that the apostolic authority is passed on through history from bishop to bishop. Consequently, they hold that only where the bishop stands in this direct line of succession is the Church of Christ to be found. The third Anglican principle, a comprehensive religious outlook, has certainly been achieved but, as some critics of Anglicanism would maintain, perhaps at the cost of theological unity and even consistency.

Some Major Historical Developments

We cannot even pretend to survey all of the major historical developments which followed upon the establishment of the various Reform patterns in the first half of the sixteenth century. However, we must at least take notice of the emergence within Protestantism of the same critical and reforming spirit which the reformers had applied to the medieval Church. By an inner necessity the Reformation continued within Protestantism itself. For in obedience to the Word of God Protestants wanted to insure that the churches of the Reformation conformed, and continued to conform, to the biblical pattern of faith and church order. Brief mention, therefore, should be made of two movements in particular, the Puritan revolution of the seventeenth century and the revival of the evangelical spirit in the eighteenth century. In these movements the same spirit that animated the great reformers in their struggle with the medieval Church bore its lasting fruit.

The movement in England which became known as Puritanism comprised a wide range of dissenters from the established church. The word "Puritan" meant those who wished to "purify" the English Church from the remnants of Roman Catholicism. After the Elizabethan settlement of 1959–63 an increasing number of Englishmen, many of whom had absorbed the spirit of Calvinism, became determined to recover the pure forms of the Christian life which were solely based on the Bible. But though these groups agreed on the necessity of Protestantizing the Anglican Church, they differed from each other in some important respects. In this movement Calvin's influence is found side by side with the same radical Protestant outlook which had first manifested itself in the Anabaptist movement.

The majority were Presbyterians, loyal followers of Calvin, who desired a reform of the Anglican Church according to the pattern of Geneva. They insisted that the presbytery should take the place of the episcopacy as the ruling body of the church. Others, who were equally strict Calvinists, held that only the Congregational form of church government was in conformity with the New Testament. Still, Presbyterians and Congregationalists agreed that the English Church was to be an all-embracing national church. When the Puritan party under Cromwell succeeded in overthrowing the monarchy and the established church, it insisted like the Anglicans that no religious views and practices dissenting from their own were to be tolerated. But in addition, there was a small band of radical Puritans who became known as "Separatists." They felt that there was little hope for a reform of the English Church from within and wished to sever their connections with the established church altogether. They firmly rejected the notion of a national church. The history of one group of Separatists is well known to us, the group that fled first to Holland and then, in 1620, sailed on the "Mayflower" to New England. Here they were shortly afterwards joined by the more numerous Puritan groups who held to the Congregational ideal and who settled Massachusetts Bay. Together they established Puritanism as a movement in the New World which has influenced American life and thought ever since.

New England Puritanism with its popularly based institutions of church and commonwealth government contributed much to the growth of democratic institutions in this country, but it is a mistake to credit the Puritans with the fully-developed notion of democracy or religious freedom. In fact, guided by the ideal of Calvin's theocracy, they developed also an established church. People were forced to conform to its tenets or, as in the case of Roger Williams, be exiled. Nor was there in any sense a popular vote, either in civil or religious affairs; government in both spheres was, to be sure, representative, but only of the covenant members of the church.

The full notion of religious freedom, and of the separation of church and state, was championed by the Baptists and the Quakers. Both groups developed in England, the Quaker movement dating back to the preaching of the remarkable George Fox (1624–1691). These groups believed, as the Anabaptists had held before them, that religious faith was a matter of personal decision, in response to a personal experience of the Holy Spirit. Therefore, they opposed a church which included everyone in the nation or which brought people into its fold just because they had been born to Christian parents. The church was for them a voluntary association. It is to the Baptists and Quakers, together with men like Madison and Jefferson, who later were influenced by the liberal ideas of the era of Enlightenment, that we must give credit for the really effective struggle for religious liberty in America. In 1636 Roger Williams founded the settlement of Providence and the colony of Rhode Island. Its constitution provided for very broad religious liberties and for a more radical democracy than anything yet known in this country. In 1682 William Penn obtained a charter to found a new colony in America, and in accordance with his Quaker conscience the constitution of Pennsylvania provided for religious liberty to all beliefs compatible with monotheism.

After the short-lived triumph of Puritanism under Cromwell the monarchy was restored in 1660 and the Church of England re-established as the official religion of the country. However, in 1689 an effective Act of Toleration was passed, though even then the Roman Catholics and the Jews were excluded from its benefits, since its real purpose was to unite all Protestants under William III.

Brief reference should be made to the Reformation in Scotland, where the people, under the vigorous leadership of John Knox (died 1572), had embraced an uncompromising Calvinism. In 1560 the Scottish Parliament adopted the Scottish Confession, largely the work of Knox. After long struggles with the English, who sought to impose episcopacy upon Scotland, the Scots finally won the right to their own established church in 1690. It was through the hardy and numerous Scottish immigrants to America that the Presbyterian Church became so prominent in this country.

On the European continent the Peace of Westphalia (1648) had brought to an end the bloody Thirty Years War. Neither Catholicism, backed by the armies of the decaying empire, nor Protestantism, with the help of King Gustavus Adolphus of Sweden, had been successful in imposing its will. A compromise was worked out, according to which each territory would accept the religion of its ruler in accordance with the pattern which had prevailed in 1624. This principle was extended to include the Calvinists as well as the Lutherans and the Roman Catholics. From that time to the present, the religious map of continental Europe has changed little.

By 1700 there was a general exhaustion of the religious life which coincided with the beginning of the era of Enlightenment. It was not long, however, before the evangelical spirit once again asserted itself, and now for the first time in a movement which cut across denominational lines and was world-wide in its influence. It awakened Protestantism, by its insistence on a personal decision for Christ irrespective of denominational affiliation, to a deepened consciousness of the unity of God's people. The main centers of this revival of the evangelical spirit were in Germany, England, and New England. In Germany the movement became known as Pietism. Under the leadership of men like Philipp Spener and August Francke, it was a reaction against the dead Lutheran orthodoxy which had stifled the religious life of German Protestantism. In England it came about as a forceful reaction to the low state of the moral and social life of the nation and to the inroads which rationalism had made into the Church of England. Beyond the Atlantic the revival began with Jonathan Edwards's attempt to revitalize the Calvinist tradition which once had been at the heart of New England Puritanism.

The pattern of thought and action and the ethos which was common to all of these movements can perhaps best be seen in the story of John Wesley and English Methodism. While still a student at Oxford, preparing for the ministry of the Church of England, John Wesley, together with his brother Charles and George Whitefield, had gathered a small group of fellow students who observed a spiritual method in regulating their lives. In derision they were dubbed "Methodists." In 1738, while he was listening to Luther's preface to Paul's letter to the Romans (see p. 78), John Wesley experienced his conversion to Christ. Now began his great career as an evangelical preacher, an indefatigable traveller who claimed the whole world as his parish, and a masterful organizer of his growing following. In his evangelistic campaign he as well as his associates never tired of stressing the necessity of a personal decision for Christ which was to be followed by a morally and religiously perfected life. Wesley's purpose was by no means to found a new church. Yet the Methodist movement became gradually separated from the Church of England and ultimately resulted in the establishment of still another Protestant denomination whose growth has been remarkable. In the United States the Methodists have been in constant contention with the various Baptist groups for the honor of being the largest Protestant body. In Germany, on the other hand, the pietistic movement remained as a powerful leaven within the Lutheran Church. In the New World, revivalism, undergoing in the course of time major changes as to method and theological content, proved to be the most efficient instrument Protestantism had in following the westward movement of the population and in making a major contribution toward winning the whole continent for Christianity.

At the end of this period the denominational pattern of Protestantism had in the main been established in the Old World as well as in the New. These churches now were faced by the challenge of the modern world.

MARTIN LUTHER (1483–1546)

Martin Luther was the acknowledged leader of the Reform movement and the founder of the Lutheran Church. It was only by gradual stages that his deep personal faith and the current of events led him to challenge the whole Catholic system of sacramental piety and papal authority. His appearance before the Emperor Charles V at the Diet of Worms in 1521 stands out as probably the most dramatic event in his career as a reformer. When asked to recant his heretical views he made his famous reply with which our selection begins. Earlier, in *An Open Letter to the Christian Nobility of the German Nation,* which was the first of his three great Reformation treatises of the year 1520, he had attempted to remedy the many ills inflicted upon Germany by the Roman curia by appealing to the temporal authorities for help. The first part of this book contains Luther's most outspoken challenge to papal authority up to this time. Three months later, addressing himself in a conciliatory spirit to Pope Leo X, he wrote his *Treatise on Christian Liberty.* This is one of his most beautiful presentations of the evangelical doctrine of justification by faith alone, the doctrine which was at the heart of his faith and the basis of his life's work. The fundamental convictions underlying his theology and centering on a proper distinction of the "law" and the "gospel" are discussed in a more formal way in his *Preface to St. Paul's Letter to the Romans.* This preface was one of many short introductions which Luther wrote for his German translation of the Bible as an aid to understanding the biblical text. But to understand the depth of Luther's faith and the power of his evangelical message we must also turn to his sermons, one of which is included here, a Christmas sermon based on the familiar Christmas story in the Gospel according to St. Luke. It was Luther's conviction that God through his Word offers sinful man his grace and salvation. Although he did not hesitate to thunder from the pulpit against his many adversaries, what he desired most was to preach Christ and to be a faithful interpreter of the Holy Scriptures to his generation.

Reply at the Diet of Worms*

Most Serene Lord Emperor, Most Illustrious Princess, Most Clement Lords: I now present myself obediently at the time set yesterday evening for my appearance. By the mercy of God, your Most Serene Majesty and your Most Illustrious Lordships, I pray that you will deign to listen leniently to this my cause, which is I hope one of justice and truth. Should I through my inexperience not accord to any one his just titles, or should I err in any way in the matter of customs and courtly manners, may you benignly overlook such mistakes in a man not brought up in palaces, but in monastic seclusion. As concerns myself, I can bear witness to this point only,—that hitherto I have taught and written in simplicity of mind, having in view only the glory of God and the sincere instruction of Christian believers.

Most Serene Emperor, and Most Illustrious Princess: As to the two articles yesterday presented to me by your Most Serene Majesty,—namely, whether I would acknowledge the books edited and published in my name as mine, and whether I wished to persevere in their defense or to revoke them,—I have given my ready and clear response to the first: in that I still per-

* From Charles D. Warner (ed.), *Library of the World's Best Literature.* New York: Warner Library Co., 1913, Vol. XVI, pp. 9328–9332.

sist, and shall persist forever; to wit, that these books are mine, and have been made public by me, in my name—unless meanwhile, haply, any matter in them has been changed, or has been maliciously extracted, through the cunning or the perverse wisdom of my enemies. For clearly, I cannot acknowledge anything as mine, except what has been written of myself and by myself alone, to the exclusion of any explanation which may be the work of some-one else.

To the second point, your Most Serene Majesty and your Lordships, I will reply by asking you to turn your minds condescendingly to this fact,—that my books are not all of the same kind: for there is one group in which I have handled religious faith and conduct in a simple evangelical fashion; moreover, this class has been composd in such a spirit that my very adversaries are forced to recognize the works as useful, harmless, and explicitly worthy of a Christian's perusal. Even the Bull, fierce and cruel as it is, considers my books in part at least as harmless; although it condemns them as a whole, with an altogether unusual severity of judgment. Consider what I would be guilty of, were I to begin any revocation of this class of writings. Should I not be the sole one of all mortals to censure that very truth which is acknowledged by friend and foe equally? Should not I alone be contending against the accordant confession of the rest of the world?

There is another group of my books, which inveighs against the papacy, and the teaching of the papists. This class is directed against those who, by their extremely corrupt doctrine and example, lay waste our entire Christendom, with every evil that spirit and body can invent. For it cannot be denied, nor can any one disguise the fact, attested as it is by the experience of all persons and by the complaints of the entire civilized world, that the consciences of believers are wretchedly entangled, vexed, and tortured, by papal laws and human teachings. Property and substance are devoured by an incredible tyranny, especially in this noble German nation, and will be devoured continuously without end, and by unworthy means. Yet Romanists, by their own edicts, caution us against the papal laws and doctrines which are contrary to the gospel and the opinions of the fathers, and declare that all such variants should be regarded as erroneous and unapproved.

If therefore I should recall these books, I should do nothing else than add to the strength of this tyranny, and should open, not windows only, but doors to this tremendous foe of religion. It would stalk abroad more freely than it has hitherto dared. Yes, from the proof of such a revocation, their wholly lawless and unrestrained kingdom of wickedness would become still more intolerable for the already wretched people; and their rule would be further strengthened and established, especially should it be reported that this evil deed had been done by me in virtue of the authority of your Most Serene Majesty, and of the whole Roman Empire. Good God! what a covert for wickedness and tyranny I should become.

A third series of these books consists of such as I have written against certain private persons, whom people call distinguished; such, namely, as have tried to preserve the Roman tyranny, and to undermine that view of religion which I have inculcated. Toward those individuals I confess that I have been more bitter than befits a churchman and a monk. But then I do not set myself up for a saint; neither am I disputing about my own career, but about the teaching of Christ. It would not then be right for me to recall this class of works, because by such a withdrawal, despotism and irreligion would again obtain sway, and that through my protection. It would rage against the people of Germany more violently than under any previous rule.

Nevertheless, because I am a man and not God, I cannot shield my practices with any other defense than that with which my Lord Jesus Christ himself vindicated his teaching. For when he had been asked about his doctrine before Annas, and had been smitten by the blow of a servant, he said, "If I have spoken evil, bear witness of the evil." If our Lord, who was always conscious of his inability to err, yet did not decline to hear any evidence against his doctrine even from the most contemptible menial,—how much more ought I, who am of the dregs of the people, and powerless in everything save sin, to desire and expect the introduction of testimony against my teaching?

Therefore, your Most Serene Majesty, your Most Illustrious Lordships, I beseech you by the mercy of God, that whoever can, whether high or low, let him bring forward the proof, let him convince me of errors: let the Scriptures of Prophecy and Gospels triumph, for I will be wholly ready to revoke every error, if I can be persuasively taught; yes, I will be the first to cast my books into the fire.

From these considerations it has become manifest that the crisis and danger on the one hand, the zeal and the controversy on the other, which the occasion of my teaching has excited in the world, have been an object of anxious solicitude on my part, and have been thoroughly weighed. It was about this commotion that I was admonished so bravely and forcibly yesterday. Under these agitations, this to me is the most joyous feature of all,—the sight of such zeal and dispute over the Word of God. For the course of that divine Word has just such a fortuity and consequence, in that Christ says: "I came not to send peace, but a sword; for I am come to set a man at variance against his father, and the daughter against her mother, and the daughter-in-law against her mother-in-law."

Moreover, we ought to reflect that since our God is wonderful and terrible in his counsels, he is probably testing us by so large an access of zeal, whether we will begin by condemning the Word of God. If so, we shall afterwards be precipitated into a more unendurable flood of evils. We should particularly avoid making the reign of this youthful and noble Prince Charles, in whom after God we place so much hope, unhappy and inauspicious. I could enforce this point very richly, through the examples furnished by Scripture, in the case of Pharaoh, the king of Babylon, and the kings of Israel, who lost most when they were endeavoring to pacify and establish their kingdoms by seemingly the wisest of counsels. Before they are aware, the Lord takes the crafty in their craftiness, and overturns mountains. Therefore we must fear God. I do not say this because it is necessary for such high authorities as you to be instructed by my teaching or admonition, but because I must not withhold the fealty due to my Germany. With these words I commend myself to your Most Serene Majesty, and to your Lordships; humbly begging you not to suffer me to be rendered odious without cause, by the persecution of my adversaries. I have spoken.

(To these words the same imperial orator replied with harshness that he ought not to have made such a response, nor were the subjects formerly condemned and defined by the councils to be called in question; therefore he sought from him a simple answer, and one without horns: would he revoke or not? Then Luther said:—)

Therefore, your Most Serene Majesty and your Lordships, since they seek a simple reply, I will give one that is without horns or teeth, and in this fashion: I believe in neither pope nor councils alone; for it is perfectly well established that they have frequently erred, as well as contradicted themselves. Unless then I shall be convinced by the testimony of the Scriptures or by clear reason, I must be bound by those Scriptures which have been brought forward by me; yes, my conscience has been taken captive by those words of God. I cannot revoke anything, nor do I wish to; since to go against one's conscience is neither safe nor right: here I stand, I cannot do otherwise. God help me. Amen. . . .

An Open Letter to the Christian Nobility of the German Nation*

The Three Walls of the Romanists

The Romanists, with great adroitness, have built three walls about them, behind which they have hitherto defended themselves in such wise that no one has been able to reform them; and this has been the cause of terrible corruption throughout all Christendom.

First, when pressed by the temporal power, they have made decrees and said that the temporal power has no jurisdiction over them, but, on the other hand, that the spiritual is

* From Martin Luther, "An Open Letter to the Christian Nobility of the German Nation," trans. by C. M. Jacobs, *Works of Martin Luther,* Vol. II. Philadelphia: A. J. Holman Company, 1915. Pages 65–79 are reprinted by permission of the Muhlenberg Press.

above the temporal power. Second, when the attempt is made to reprove them out of the Scriptures, they raise the objection that the interpretation of the Scriptures belongs to no one except the pope. Third, if threatened with a council, they answer with the fable that no one can call a council but the pope.

In this wise they have slyly stolen from us our three rods, that they may go unpunished, and have ensconced themselves within the safe stronghold of these three walls, that they may practise all the knavery and wickedness which we now see. Even when they have been compelled to hold a council they have weakened its power in advance by previously binding the princes with an oath to let them remain as they are. Moreover, they have given the pope full authority over all the decisions of the council, so that it is all one whether there are many councils or no councils,—except that they deceive us with puppet-shows and sham-battles. So terribly do they fear for their skin in a really free council! And they have intimidated kings and princes by making them believe it would be an offence against God not to obey them in all these knavish, crafty deceptions.

Now God help us, and give us one of the trumpets with which the walls of Jericho were overthrown, that we may blow down these walls of straw and paper, and may set free the Christian rods for the punishment of sin, bringing to light the craft and deceit of the devil, to the end that through punishment we may reform ourselves, and once more attain God's favor.

Against the *first wall* we will direct our first attack.

It is pure invention that pope, bishops, priests and monks are to be called the "spiritual estate"; princes, lords, artisans, and farmers the "temporal estate." That is indeed a fine bit of lying and hypocrisy. Yet one should be frightened by it; and for this reason—viz., that all Christians are truly of the "spiritual estate," and there is among them no difference at all but that of office, as Paul says in I Corinthians xii, We are all one body, yet every member has its own work, whereby it serves every other, all because we have one baptism, one Gospel, one faith, and are all alike Christians; for baptism, Gospel and faith alone make us "spiritual" and a Christian people.

But that a pope or a bishop anoints, confers tonsures, ordains, consecrates, or prescribes dress unlike that of the laity,—this may make hypocrites and graven images, but it never makes a Christian or "spiritual" man. Through baptism all of us are consecrated to the priesthood, as St. Peter says in I Peter ii, "Ye are a royal priesthood, a priestly kingdom," and the book of Revelation says, "Thou hast made us by Thy blood to be priests and kings." For if we had no higher consecration than pope or bishop gives, the consecration by pope or bishop would never make a priest, nor might anyone either say mass or preach a sermon or give absolution. Therefore when the bishop consecrates it is the same thing as if he, in the place and stead of the whole congregation, all of whom have like power, were to take one out of their number and charge him to use this power for the others; just as though ten brothers, all king's sons and equal heirs, were to choose one of themselves to rule the inheritance for them all,—they would all be kings and equal in power, though one of them would be charged with the duty of ruling.

To make it still clearer. If a little group of pious Christian laymen were taken captive and set down in a wilderness, and had among them no priest consecrated by a bishop, and if there in the wilderness they were to agree in choosing one of themselves, married or unmarried, and were to charge him with the office of baptising, saying mass, absolving and preaching, such a man would be as truly a priest as though all bishops and popes had consecrated him. That is why in cases of necessity anyone can baptise and give absolution, which would be impossible unless we were all priests. This great grace and power of baptism and of the Christian Estate they have well-nigh destroyed and caused us to forget through the canon law. It was in the manner aforesaid that Christians in olden days chose from their number bishops and priests, who were afterwards confirmed by other bishops, without all the show which now obtains. It was thus that Sts. Augustine, Ambrose and Cyprian became bishops.

Since, then, the temporal authorities are baptised with the same baptism and have the same faith and Gospel as we, we must grant that they are priests and bishops, and count their office one which has a proper and a useful place in the Christian community. For whoever comes out of the water of baptism can boast that he is already consecrated priest, bishop and pope, though it is not seemly that every one should exercise the office. Nay, just because we are all in like manner priests, no one must put himself forward and undertake, without our consent and election, to do what is in the power of all of us. For what is common to all, no one dare take upon himself without the will and the command of the community; and should it happen that one chosen for such an office were deposed for malfeasance, he would then be just what he was before he held office. Therefore a priest of Christendom is nothing else than an office-holder. While he is in office, he has precedence; when deposed, he is a peasant or a townsman like the rest. Beyond all doubt, then, a priest is no longer a priest when he is deposed. But now they have invented *characteres indelebiles* (see p. 228), and prate that a deposed priest is nevertheless something different from a mere layman. They even dream that a priest can never become a layman, or be anything else than a priest. All this is mere talk and man-made law.

From all this it follows that there is really no difference between laymen and priests, princes and bishops, "spirituals" and "temporals," as they call them, except that of office and work, but not of "estate"; for they are all of the same estate,—true priests, bishops and popes,—though they are not all engaged in the same work, just as all priests and monks have not the same work. This is the teaching of St. Paul in Romans xii and I Corinthians xii, and of St. Peter in I Peter ii, as I have said above, viz., that we are all one body of Christ, the Head, all members one of another. Christ has not two different bodies, one "temporal," the other "spiritual." He is one Head, and He has one body.

Therefore, just as those who are now called "spiritual"—priests, bishops or popes—are neither different from other Christians nor superior to them, except that they are charged with the administration of the Word of God and the sacraments, which is their work and office, so it is with the temporal authorities,—they bear sword and rod with which to punish the evil and to protect the good. A cobbler, a smith, a farmer, each has the work and office of his trade, and yet they are all alike consecrated priests and bishops, and every one by means of his own work or office must benefit and serve every other, that in this way many kinds of work may be done for the bodily and spiritual welfare of the community, even as all the members of the body serve one another.

See, now, how Christian is the decree which says that the temporal power is not above the "spiritual estate" and may not punish it. That is as much as to say that the hand shall lend no aid when the eye is suffering. Is it not unnatural, not to say unchristian, that one member should not help another and prevent its destruction? Verily, the more honorable the member, the more should the others help. I say then, since the temporal power is ordained of God to punish evil-doers and to protect them that do well, it should therefore be left free to perform its office without hindrance through the whole body of Christendom without respect of persons, whether it affect pope, bishops, priests, monks, nuns or anybody else. For if the mere fact that the temporal power has a smaller place among the Christian offices than has the office of preachers or confessors, or of the clergy, then the tailors, cobblers, masons, carpenters, pot-boys, tapsters, farmers, and all the secular tradesmen, should also be prevented from providing pope, bishops, priests and monks with shoes, clothing, houses, meat and drink, and from paying them tribute. But if these laymen are allowed to do their work unhindered, what do the Roman scribes mean by their laws, with which they withdraw themselves from the jurisdiction of the temporal Christian power, only so that they may be free to do evil and to fulfil what St. Peter has said: "There shall be false teachers among you, and through covetousness shall they with feigned words make merchandise of you."

On this account the Christian temporal power should exercise its office without let or hindrance, regardless whether it be pope, bishop or priest whom it affects; whoever is guilty, let him suffer. All that the canon law has said to the contrary is sheer invention of Roman presumption. For thus saith St. Paul to all Christians: "Let every soul (I take that to mean the pope's soul also) be subject unto the higher powers; for they bear not the sword in vain, but are the ministers of God for the punishment of evildoers, and for the praise of them that do well." St. Peter also says: "Submit yourselves unto every ordinance of man for the Lord's sake, for so is the will of God." He has also prophesied that such men shall come as will despise the temporal authorities, and this has come to pass through the canon law.

So then, I think this first paper-wall is overthrown, since the temporal power has become a member of the body of Christendom, and is of the "spiritual estate," though its work is of a temporal nature. Therefore its work should extend freely and without hindrance to all the members of the whole body; it should punish and use force whenever guilt deserves or necessity demands, without regard to pope, bishops and priests,—let them hurl threats and bans as much as they will.

This is why guilty priests, if they are surrendered to the temporal law, are first deprived of their priestly dignities, which would not be right unless the temporal sword had previously had authority over them by divine right.

Again, it is intolerable that in the canon law so much importance is attached to the freedom, life and property of the clergy, as though the laity were not also as spiritual and as good Christians as they, or did not belong to the Church. Why are your life and limb, your property and honor so free, and mine not? We are all alike Christians, and have baptism, faith, Spirit and all things alike. If a priest is killed, the land is laid under interdict,—why not when a peasant is killed? Whence comes this great distinction between those who are equally Christians? Only from human laws and inventions!

Moreover, it can be no good spirit who has invented such exceptions and granted to sin such license and impunity. For if we are bound to strive against the works and words of the evil spirit, and to drive him out in whatever way we can, as Christ commands and His Apostles, ought we, then, to suffer it in silence when the pope or his satellites are bent on devilish words and works? Ought we for the sake of men to allow the suppression of divine commandments and truths which we have sworn in baptism to support with life and limb? Of a truth we should then have to answer for all the souls that would thereby be abandoned and led astray.

It must therefore have been the very prince of devils who said what is written in the canon law: "If the pope were so scandalously bad as to lead souls in crowds to the devil, yet he could not be deposed." On this accursed and devilish foundation they build at Rome, and think that we should let all the world go to the devil, rather than resist their knavery. If the fact that one man is set over others were sufficient reason why he should escape punishment, then no Christian could punish another, since Christ commands that every man shall esteem himself the lowliest and the least.

Where sin is, there is no escape from punishment; as St. Gregory also writes that we are indeed all equal, but guilt puts us in subjection one to another. Now we see how they whom God and the Apostles have made subject to the temporal sword deal with Christendom, depriving it of its liberty by their own wickedness, without warrant of Scripture. It is to be feared that this is a game of Antichrist or a sign that he is close at hand.

The *second wall* is still more flimsy and worthless. They wish to be the only Masters of the Holy Scriptures, even though in all their lives they learn nothing from them. They assume for themselves sole authority, and with insolent juggling of words they would persuade us that the pope, whether he be a bad man or a good man, cannot err in matters of faith; and yet they cannot prove a single letter of it. Hence it comes that so many heretical and unchristian, nay, even unnatural ordinances have a place in the canon law, of which, however, there is no present need to speak. For since they think that the Holy Spirit never leaves them, be they never so unlearned and wicked, they make bold to decree whatever they will. And if it were true, where would be the need or use of the Holy Scriptures? Let us burn them, and be satisfied with the unlearned lords at Rome, who are possessed of the Holy Spirit,—although He can possess only pious hearts! Unless I had read it myself, I could not have believed that the devil would make such clumsy pretensions at Rome, and find a following.

But not to fight them with mere words, we will quote the Scriptures. St. Paul says in I Corinthians xiv: "If to anyone something better is revealed, though he be sitting and listening to another in God's Word, then the first, who is speaking, shall hold his peace and give place." What would be the use of this commandment, if we were only to believe him who does the talking or who has the highest seat? Christ also says in John vi, that all Christians shall be taught of God. Thus it may well happen that the pope and his followers are wicked men, and no true Christians, not taught of God, not having true understanding. On the other hand, an ordinary man may have true understanding; why then should we not follow him? Has not the pope erred many times? Who would help Christendom when the pope errs, if we were not to believe another, who had the Scriptures on his side, more than the pope?

Therefore it is a wickedly invented fable, and they cannot produce a letter in defence of it, that the interpretation of Scripture or the confirmation of its interpretation belongs to the pope alone. They have themselves usurped this power; and although they allege that this power was given to Peter when the keys were given to him, it is plain enough that the keys were not given to Peter alone, but to the whole community. Moreover, the keys were not ordained for doctrine or government, but only for the binding and loosing of sin, and whatever further power of the keys they arrogate to themselves is mere invention. But Christ's word to Peter, "I have prayed for thee that thy faith fail not," cannot be applied to the pope, since the majority of the popes have been without faith, as they must themselves confess. Besides, it is not only for Peter that Christ prayed, but also for all Apostles and Christians, as he says in John xvii: "Father, I pray for those whom Thou hast given Me, and not for these only, but for all who believe on Me through their word." Is not this clear enough?

Only think of it yourself! They must confess that there are pious Christians among us, who have the true faith, Spirit, understanding, word and mind of Christ. Why, then, should we reject their word and understanding and follow the pope, who has neither faith nor Spirit? That would be to deny the whole faith and the Christian Church. Moreover, it is not the pope alone who is always in the right, if the article of the Creed is correct: "I believe one holy Christian Church"; otherwise the prayer must run: "I believe in the pope at Rome," and so reduce the Christian Church to one man,—which would be nothing else than a devilish and hellish error.

Besides, if we are all priests, as was said above, and all have one faith, one Gospel, one sacrament, why should we not also have the power to test and judge what is correct or incorrect in matters of faith? What becomes of the words of Paul in I Corinthians ii: "He that is spiritual judgeth all things, yet he himself is judged of no man," and II Corinthians iv: "We have all the same Spirit of faith"? Why, then, should not we perceive what squares with faith and what does not, as well as does an unbelieving pope?

All these and many other texts should make us bold and free, and we should not allow the Spirit of liberty, as Paul calls Him, to be frightened off by the fabrications of the popes, but we ought to go boldly forward to test all that they do or leave undone, according to our interpretation of the Scriptures, which rests on faith, and compel them to follow not their own interpretation, but the one that is better. In the olden days Abraham had to listen to his Sarah, although she was in more complete subjection to him than we are to anyone on earth. Balaam's ass, also, was wiser than the prophet himself. If God then spoke by an ass against a prophet, why should He not be able even now to speak by a righteous man against the pope? In like manner St. Paul rebukes St. Peter as a man in error. Therefore it behooves every Christian to espouse the cause of the faith, to understand and defend it, and to rebuke all errors.

The *third wall* falls of itself when the first two are down. For when the pope acts contrary to the Scriptures, it is our duty to stand by the Scriptures, to reprove him, and to constrain him, according to the word of Christ in Matthew xviii: "If thy brother sin against thee, go and tell it him between thee and him alone; if he hear thee not, then take with thee one or two more; if he hear them not, tell it to the Church; if he hear not the Church, consider him a heathen." Here every member is commanded to care for every other. How much rather should we do this when the member that does evil is a ruling member, and by his evil-doing is the cause of much harm and offence to the rest! But if I am to accuse him before the Church, I must bring the Church together.

They have no basis in Scripture for their contention that it belongs to the pope alone to call a council or confirm its actions; for this is based merely upon their own laws, which are valid only in so far as they are not injurious to Christendom or contrary to the laws of God. When the pope deserves punishment, such laws go out of force, since it is injurious to Christendom not to punish him by means of a council.

Thus we read in Acts xv that it was not St. Peter who called the Apostolic Council, but the Apostles and elders. If, then, that right had belonged to St. Peter alone, the council would not have been a Christian council, but an heretical *conciliabulum* ("a mere gathering of people"). Even the Council of Nicaea—the most famous of all—was neither called nor confirmed by the Bishop of Rome, but by the Emperor Constantine, and many other emperors after him did the like, yet these councils were the most Christian of all. But if the pope alone had the right to call councils, then all these councils must have been heretical. Moreover, if I consider the councils which the pope has created, I find that they have done nothing of special importance.

Therefore, when necessity demands, and the pope is an offence to Christendom, the first man who is able should, as a faithful member of the whole body, do what he can to bring about a truly free council. No one can do this so well as the temporal authorities, especially since now they also are fellow-Christians, fellow-priests, "fellow-spirituals," fellow-lords over all things, and whenever it is needful or profitable, they should give free course to the office and work in which God has put them above every man. Would it not be an unnatural thing, if a fire broke out in a city, and everybody were to stand by and let it burn on and on and consume everything that could burn, for the sole reason that nobody had the authority of the burgomaster, or because, perhaps, the fire broke out in the burgomaster's house? In such case is it not the duty of every citizen to arouse and call the rest? How much more should this be done in the spiritual city of Christ, if a fire of offence breaks out, whether in the papal government, or anywhere else? In the same way, if the enemy attacks a city, he who first rouses the others deserves honor and thanks; why then should he not deserve honor who makes known the presence of the enemy from hell, and awakens the Christians, and calls them together?

But all their boasts of an authority which dare not be opposed amount to nothing after all. No one in Christendom has authority to do injury, or to forbid the resisting of injury. There is no authority in the Church save for edification. Therefore, if the pope were to use his authority to prevent the calling of a free council, and thus became a hindrance to the edification of the Church, we should have regard neither for him nor for his authority; and if he were to hurl his bans and thunderbolts, we should despise his conduct as that of a madman, and relying on God, hurl back the ban on him, and coerce him as best we could. For this presumptuous authority of his is nothing; he has no such authority, and he is quickly overthrown by a text of Scripture; for Paul says to the Corinthians, "God has given us authority not for the destruction, but for the edification of Christendom." Who is ready to overleap this text? It is only the power of the devil and of Antichrist which resists the things that serve for the edification of Christendom; it is, therefore, in no wise to be obeyed, but is to be opposed with life and goods and all our strength.

Even though a miracle were to be done in the pope's behalf against the temporal powers, or though someone were to be stricken with a plague—which they boast has sometimes happened—it should be considered only the work of the devil, because of the weakness of our faith in God. Christ Himself prophesied in Matthew xxiv: "There shall come in My Name false Christs and false prophets, and do signs and wonders, so as to deceive even the elect," and Paul says in II Thessalonians ii, that Antichrist shall, through the power of Satan, be mighty in lying wonders.

Let us, therefore, hold fast to this: No Christian authority can do anything against Christ; as St. Paul says, "We can do nothing against Christ, but for Christ." Whatever does aught against Christ is the power of Antichrist and of the devil, even though it were to rain and hail wonders and plagues. Wonders and plagues prove nothing, especially in these last evil times, for which all the Scriptures prophesy false wonders. Therefore we must cling with firm faith to the words of God, and then the devil will cease from wonders.

Thus I hope that the false, lying terror with which the Romans have this long time made our conscience timid and stupid, has been allayed. They, like all of us, are subject to the temporal sword; they have no power to interpret the Scriptures by mere authority, without learning; they have no authority to prevent a council or, in sheer wantonness, to pledge it, bind it, or take away its liberty; but if they do this, they are in truth the communion of Antichrist and of the devil, and have nothing at all of Christ except the name. . . .

A Treatise on Christian Liberty*

Many have thought Christian faith to be an easy thing, and not a few have given it a place among the virtues. This they do because they have had no experience of it, and have never tasted what great virtue there is in faith. For it is impossible that any one should write well for it or well understand what is correctly written of it, unless he has at some time tasted the courage faith gives a man when trials oppress him. But he who has had even a faint taste of it can never write, speak, meditate or hear enough concerning it. For it is a living fountain springing up into life everlasting, as Christ calls it in John iv. For my part, although I have no wealth of faith to boast of and know how scant my store it, yet I hope that, driven about by great and various temptations, I have attained to a little faith, and that I can speak of it, if not more elegantly, certainly more to the point, than those literalists and all too subtile disputants have hitherto done, who have not even understood what they have written.

That I may make the way easier for the unlearned—for only such do I serve—I set down first these two propositions concerning the liberty and bondage of the spirit:

A Christian man is a perfectly free lord of all, subject to none.

A Christian man is a perfectly dutiful servant of all, subject to all.

Although these two theses seem to contradict each other, yet, if they should be found to fit together they would serve our purpose beautifully. For they are both Paul's own, who says, in I Cor. ix, "Whereas I was free, I made myself the servant of all," and, Rom. xiii, "Owe no man anything, but to love one another." Now love by its very nature is ready to serve and to be subject to him who is loved. So Christ, although Lord of all, was made of a woman, made under the law, and hence was at the same time free and a servant, at the same time in the form of God and in the form of a servant.

Let us start, however, with something more remote from our subject, but more obvious. Man has a twofold nature, a spiritual and a bodily. According to the spiritual nature, which men call the soul, he is called a spiritual, or inner, or new man; according to the bodily nature, which men call the flesh, he is called a carnal, or outward, or old man, of whom the Apostle writes, in II Cor. iv, "Though our outward man is corrupted, yet the inward man is renewed day by day." Because of this diversity of nature the Scriptures assert contradictory things of the same man, since the flesh lusteth against the spirit and the spirit against the flesh (Gal. v).

First, let us contemplate the inward man, to see how a righteous, free and truly Christian man, that is, a new, spiritual, inward man, comes into being. It is evident that no external thing, whatsoever it be, has any influence whatever in producing Christian righteousness or liberty, nor in producing unrighteousness or bondage. A simple argument will furnish the proof. What can it profit the soul if the body fare well, be free and active, eat, drink and do as it pleases? For in these things even the most godless slaves of all the vices fare well. On the other hand, how will ill health or imprisonment or hunger or thirst or any other external misfortune hurt the soul? With these things even the most godly men are afflicted,

* From Martin Luther, "A Treatise on Christian Liberty," trans. by W. A. Lambert, *Works of Martin Luther,* Vol. II. Philadelphia: A. J. Holman Company, 1915. Pages 312–321, 323–336, 338, and 342–344 are reprinted by permission of the Muhlenberg Press.

and those who because of a clear conscience are most free. None of these things touch either the liberty or the bondage of the soul. The soul receives no benefit if the body is adorned with the sacred robes of the priesthood, or dwells in sacred places, or is occupied with sacred duties, or prays, fasts, abstains from certain kinds of food or does any work whatsoever that can be done by the body and in the body. The righteousness and the freedom of the soul demand something far different, since the things which have been mentioned could be done by any wicked man, and such works produce nothing but hypocrites. On the other hand, it will not hurt the soul if the body is clothed in secular dress, dwells in unconsecrated places, eats and drinks as others do, does not pray aloud, and neglects to do all the things mentioned above, which hypocrites can do.

Further, to put aside all manner of works, even contemplation, meditation, and all that the soul can do, avail nothing. One thing and one only is necessary for Christian life, righteousness and liberty. That one thing is the most holy Word of God, the Gospel of Christ, as he says, John xi, "I am the resurrection and the life: he that believeth in me, shall not die forever"; and John viii, "If the Son shall make you free, you shall be free indeed"; and Matthew iv, "Not in bread alone doth man live; but in every word that proceedeth from the mouth of God." Let us then consider it certain and conclusively established that the soul can do without all things except the Word of God, and that where this is not there is no help for the soul in anything else whatever. But if it has the Word it is rich and lacks nothing, since this Word is the Word of life, of truth, of light, of peace, of righteousness, of salvation, of joy, of liberty, of wisdom, of power, of grace, of glory and of every blessing beyond our power to estimate. This is why the prophet in the entire cxix Psalm, and in many other places of Scripture, with so many sighs yearns after the Word of God and applies so many names to it. On the other hand, there is no more terrible plague with which the wrath of God can smite men than a famine of the hearing of His Word, as He says in Amos, just as there is no greater mercy than when He sends forth His Word, as we read in Psalm cvii, "He sent His word and healed them, and delivered them from their destructions." Nor was Christ sent into the world for any other ministry but that of the Word, and the whole spiritual estate, apostles, bishops and all the priests, has been called and instituted only for the ministry of the Word.

You ask, "What then is this Word of God, and how shall it be used, since there are so many words of God?" I answer, The Apostle explains that in Romans i. The Word is the Gospel of God concerning His Son, Who was made flesh, suffered, rose from the dead, and was glorified through the Spirit Who sanctifies. For to preach Christ means to feed the soul, to make it righteous, to set it free and to save it, if it believe the preaching. For faith alone is the saving and efficacious use of the Word of God, Romans x, "If thou confess with thy mouth that Jesus is Lord, and believe with thy heart that God hath raised Him up from the dead, thou shalt be saved"; and again, "The end of the law is Christ, unto righteousness to every one that believeth"; and, Romans i, "The just shall live by his faith." The Word of God cannot be received and cherished by any works whatever, but only by faith. Hence it is clear that, as the soul needs only the Word for its life and righteousness, so it is justified by faith alone and not by any works; for if it could be justified by anything else, it would not need the Word, and therefore it would not need faith. But this faith cannot at all exist in connection with works, that is to say, if you at the same time claim to be justified by works, whatever their character; for that would be to halt between two sides, to worship Baal and to kiss the hand, which, as Job says, is a very great iniquity. Therefore the moment you begin to believe, you learn that all things in you are altogether blameworthy, sinful and damnable, as Romans iii says, "For all have sinned and lack the glory of God"; and again, "There is none just, there is none that doeth good, all have turned out of the way: they are become unprofitable together." When you have learned this, you will know that you need Christ, Who suffered and rose again for you, that, believing in Him, you may through this faith become a new man, in that all your sins are forgiven, and you are justified by the merits of another, namely, of Christ alone.

Since, therefore, this faith can rule only in the

inward man, as Romans x says, "With the heart we believe unto righteousness"; and since faith alone justifies, it is clear that the inward man cannot be justified, made free and be saved by any outward work or dealing whatsoever, and that works, whatever their character, have nothing to do with this inward man. On the other hand, only ungodliness and unbelief of heart, and no outward work, make him guilty and a damnable servant of sin. Wherefore it ought to be the first concern of every Christian to lay aside all trust in works, and more and more to strengthen faith alone, and through faith to grow in the knowledge, not of works, but of Christ Jesus, Who suffered and rose for him, as Peter teaches, in the last chapter of his first Epistle; since no other work makes a Christian. Thus when the Jews asked Christ, John vi, what they should do that they might work the works of God, He brushed aside the multitude of works in which He saw that they abounded, and enjoined upon them a single work, saying, "This is the work of God, that you believe in Him Whom He hath sent. For Him hath God the Father sealed." . . .

(Another) benefit of faith is this, that it unites the soul with Christ as a bride is united with her bridegroom. And by this mystery, as the Apostle teaches, Christ and the soul become one flesh. And if they are one flesh and there is between them a true marriage, nay, by far the most perfect of all marriages, since human marriages are but frail types of this one true marriage, it follows that all they have they have in common, the good as well as the evil, so that the believing soul can boast of and glory in whatever Christ has as if it were its own, and whatever the soul has Christ claims as His own. Let us compare these and we shall see things that cannot be estimated. Christ is full of grace, life and salvation; the soul is full of sins, death and condemnation. Now let faith come between them, and it shall come to pass that sins, death and hell are Christ's, and grace, life and salvation are the soul's. For it behooves Him, if He is a bridegroom, to take upon Himself the things which are His bride's, and to bestow upon her the things that are His. For if He gives her His body and His very self, how shall He not give her all that is His? And if He takes the body of the bride, how shall He not take all that is hers?

Lo! here we have a pleasant vision not only of communion, but of a blessed strife and victory and salvation and redemption. For Christ is God and man in one person, Who has neither sinned nor died, and is not condemned, and Who cannot sin, die or be condemned; His righteousness, life and salvation are unconquerable, eternal, omnipotent; and He by the wedding-ring of faith shares in the sins, death and pains of hell which are His bride's, nay, makes them His own, and acts as if they were His own, and as if He Himself had sinned; He suffered, died and descended into hell that He might overcome them all. Now since it was such a one who did all this, and death and hell could not swallow Him up, they were of necessity swallowed up of Him in a mighty duel. For His righteousness is greater than the sins of all men, His life stronger than death, His salvation more invincible than hell. Thus the believing soul by the pledge of its faith is free in Christ, its Bridegroom, from all sins, secure against death and against hell, and is endowed with the eternal righteousness, life and salvation of Christ, its Bridegroom. So He presents to Himself a glorious bride, without spot or wrinkle, cleansing her with the washing in the Word of life, that is, by faith in the Word of life, of righteousness, and of salvation. Thus He marries her to Himself in faith, in loving kindness, and in mercies, in righteousness and in judgment, as Hosea ii says. . . .

Hence we are all priests and kings in Christ, as many as believe on Christ, as I Pet. ii says, "Ye are a chosen generation, a peculiar people, a royal priesthood and priestly kingdom, that ye should show forth the virtues of Him Who hath called you out of darkness into His marvelous light."

This priesthood and kingship we explain as follows: First, as to the kingship, every Christian is by faith so exalted above all things that by a spiritual power he is lord of all things without exception, so that nothing can do him any harm whatever, nay, all things are made subject to him and compelled to serve him to his salvation. Thus Paul says in Rom. viii, "All things work together for good to them who are called." And, in I Cor. iii, "All things are yours, whether life or death, or things present or things to come, and ye are Christ's." Not as if every Christian were set over all things, to possess and control them by physical power,—a madness with which some churchmen are afflicted,—for such power belongs to kings, princes and men on earth. Our ordinary experience in life shows us that we are subjected to all, suffer many things and even die; nay, the more Christian a man is, the more evils, sufferings and deaths is he made subject to, as we see in Christ the first-born Prince Himself, and in all His brethren, the saints. The power of which we speak is spiritual; it rules in the midst of enemies, and is mighty in the midst of oppression, which means nothing else than that strength is made perfect in weakness, and that in all things I can find profit unto salvation, so that the cross and death itself are compelled to serve me and to work together with me for my salvation. This is a splendid prerogative and hard to attain, and a true omnipotent power, a spiritual dominion, in which there is nothing so good and nothing so evil, but that it shall work together for good to me, if only I believe. And yet, since faith alone suffices for salvation, I have need of nothing, except that faith exercise the power and dominion of its own liberty. Lo, this is the inestimable power and liberty of Christians.

Not only are we the freest of kings, we are also priests forever, which is far more excellent than being kings, because as priests we are worthy to appear before God to pray for others and to teach one another the things of God. For these are the functions of priests, and cannot be granted to any unbeliever. Thus Christ has obtained for us, if we believe on Him, that we are not only His brethren, co-heirs and fellow-kings with Him, but also fellow-priests with Him, who may boldly come into the presence of God in the spirit of faith and cry, "Abba, Father!" pray for one another and do all things which we see done and prefigured in the outward and visible works of priests. But he who does not believe is not served by anything, nor does anything work for good to him, but he himself is a servant of all, and all things become evils to him, because he wickedly uses them to his own profit and not to the glory of God. And so he is no priest, but a profane man, whose prayer becomes sin and never comes into the presence of God, because God does not hear sinners. Who then can comprehend the lofty dignity of the Christian? Through his kingly power he rules over all things, death, life and sin, and through his priestly glory is all powerful with God, because God does the things which he asks and desires, as it is written, "He will fulfil the desire of them that fear Him; He also will hear their cry, and will save them." To this glory a man attains, surely not by any works of his, but by faith alone. . . .

You will ask, "If all who are in the Church are priests, how do those whom we now call priests differ from laymen?" I answer: "Injustice is done those words, 'priest,' 'cleric,' 'spiritual,' 'ecclesiastic,' when they are transferred from all other Christians to those few who are now by a mischievous usage called 'ecclesiastics.' For Holy Scripture makes no distinction between them, except that it gives the name 'ministers,' 'servants,' 'stewards,' to those who are now proudly called popes, bishops, and lords and who should by the ministry of the Word serve others and teach them the faith of Christ and the liberty of believers. For although we are all equally priests, yet we cannot all publicly minister and teach, nor ought we if we could." Thus Paul writes in I Cor. iv, "Let a man so account of us, as of the ministers of Christ, and stewards of the mysteries of God."

But that stewardship has now been developed into so great a pomp of power and so terrible a tyranny, that no heathen empire or earthly power can be compared with it, just as if laymen were not also Christians. Through this perversion the knowledge of Christian grace, faith, liberty and of Christ Himself has altogether perished, and its place has been taken by an unbearable bondage of human words and laws, until we have become, as the Lamentations of Jeremiah say, servants of the vilest men on earth, who abuse our misfortune to serve only their base and shameless will.

To return to our purpose, I believe it has now become clear that it is not enough nor is it Christian, to preach the works, life and words of Christ as historical facts, as if the knowledge of these would suffice for the conduct of life, although this is the fashion of those who must to-day be regarded as our best preachers; and far less is it enough or Christian to say nothing at all about Christ and to teach instead the laws of men and the decrees of the Fathers. And now there are not a few who preach Christ and read about Him that they may move men's affections to sympathy with Christ, to anger against the Jews and such like childish and womanish nonsense. Rather ought Christ to be preached to the end that faith in Him may be established, that He may not only be Christ, but be Christ for thee and for me, and that what is said of Him and what His Name denotes may be effectual in us. And such faith is produced and preserved in us by preaching why Christ came, what He brought and bestowed, what benefit it is to us to accept Him. This is done when that Christian liberty which He bestows is rightly taught, and we are told in what way we who are Christians are all kings and priests and so are lords of all, and may firmly believe that whatever we have done is pleasing and acceptable in the sight of God, as I have said. . . .

Now let us turn to the second part, to the outward man. Here we shall answer all those who, misled by the word "faith" and by all that has been said, now say: "If faith does all things and is alone sufficient unto righteousness, why then are good works commanded? We will take our ease and do no works, and be content with faith." I answer, Not so, ye wicked men, not so. That would indeed be proper, if we were wholly inward and perfectly spiritual men; but such we shall be only at the last day, the day of the resurrection of the dead. As long as we live in the flesh we only begin and make some progress in that which shall be perfected in the future life. For this reason the Apostle, in Romans viii, calls all that we attain in this life "the first fruits" of the spirit, because, forsooth, we shall receive the greater portion, even the fulness of the spirit, in the future. This is the place for that which was said above, that a Christian man is the servant of all and made subject to all. For in so far as he is free he does no works, but in so far as he is a servant he does all manner of works. How this is possible, we shall see.

Although, as I have said, a man is abundantly justified by faith inwardly, in his spirit, and so has all that he ought to have, except in so far as this faith and riches must grow from day to day even unto the future life: yet he remains in this mortal life on earth, and in this life he must needs govern his own body and have dealings with men. Here the works begin; here a man cannot take his ease; here he must, indeed, take care to discipline his body by fastings, watchings, labors and other reasonable discipline, and to make it subject to the spirit so that it will obey and conform to the inward man and to faith, and not revolt against faith and hinder the inward man, as it is the body's nature to do if it be not held in check. For the inward man, who by faith is created in the likeness of God, is both joyful and happy because of Christ in Whom so many benefits are conferred upon him, and therefore it is his one occupation to serve God joyfully and for naught, in love that is not constrained.

While he is doing this, lo, he meets a contrary will in his own flesh, which strives to serve the world and to seek its own advantage. This the spirit of faith cannot tolerate, and with joyful zeal it attempts to put the body under and to hold it in check, as Paul says in Romans vii, "I delight in the law of God after the inward man; but I see another law in my members, warring against the law of my mind, and bringing me into captivity to the law of sin"; and, in another place, "I keep under my body, and bring it into subjection: lest by any means, when I have preached to others, I myself should be a castaway," and in Galatians, "They that are Christ's have crucified the flesh with its lusts."

In doing these works, however, we must not think that a man is jusitfied before God by them: for that erroneous opinion faith, which alone is righteousness before God, cannot endure; but we must think that these works reduce the body to subjection and purify it of its evil lusts, and our whole purpose is to be directed only toward the driving out of lusts. For since by faith the soul is cleansed and made a lover of God, it desires that all things, and especially its own body, shall be as pure as itself, so that all things may join with it in loving and praising God. Hence a man cannot be idle, because the need of his body drives him and he is compelled to do many good works to reduce it to subjection. Nevertheless the works themselves do not justify him before God, but he does the works out of spontaneous love in obedience to God, and considers nothing except the approval of God, Whom he would in all things most scrupulously obey.

In this way every one will easily be able to learn for himself the limit and discretion, as they say of his bodily castigations: for he will fast, watch and labor as much as he finds sufficient to repress the lasciviousness and lust of his body. But they who presume to be justified by works do not regard the mortifying of the lusts, but only the works themselves, and think that if only they have done as many and as great works as are possible, they have done well, and have become righteousness; at times they even addle their brains and destroy, or at least render useless, their natural strength with their works. This is the height of folly, and utter ignorance of Christian life and faith, that a man should seek to be justified and saved by works and without faith. . . .

A bishop, when he consecrates a Church, confirms children or performs any other duty belonging to his office, is not made a bishop by these works, nay, if he had not first been made a bishop none of these works would be valid, they would be foolish, childish and a mere farce. So the Christian, who is consecrated by his faith, does good works, but the works do not make him more holy or more Christian; for that is the work of faith alone, and if a man were not first a believer and a Christian, all his works would amount to nothing at all and would be truly wicked and damnable sins.

These two sayings, therefore, are true: "Good works do not make a good man, but a good man does good works; evil works do not make a wicked man, but a wicked man does evil works"; so that it is always necessary that the "substance" or person itself be good before there can be any good works, and that good works follow and proceed from the good person, as Christ also says, "A corrupt tree does not bring forth good fruit, a good tree does not bring forth evil fruit." It is clear that the fruits do not bear the tree, nor does the tree grow on the fruits, but, on the contrary, the trees bear the fruits and the fruits grow on the trees. As it is necessary, therefore, that the trees must exist before their fruits, and the fruits do not make trees either good or corrupt, but rather as the trees are so are the fruits they bear; so the person of a man must needs first be good or wicked before he does a good or a wicked work, and his works do not make him good or wicked, but he himself makes his works either good or wicked.

Illustrations of the same truth can be seen in all trades. A good or a bad house does not make a good or a bad builder, but a good or a bad builder makes a bad or a good house. And in general, the work never makes the workman like itself, but the workman makes the work like himself. So it is also with the works of man: as the man is, whether believer or unbeliever, so also is his work—good, if it was done in faith; wicked, if it was done in unbelief. But the converse is not true, that the work makes the man either a believer or an unbeliever. For as works do not make a man a believer, so also they do not make him righteous. But as faith makes a man a believer and righteous, so faith also does good works. Since, then, works justify no one, and a man must be righteous before he does a good work, it is very evident that it is faith alone which, because of the pure mercy of God through Christ and in His Word, worthily and sufficiently justifies and saves the person, and a Christian man has no need of any work or of any law in order to be saved, since through faith he is free from every law and does all that he does out of pure liberty and freely, seeking neither benefit nor salvation, since he already abounds in all things and is saved through the grace of God because of his faith, and now seeks only to please God.

Furthermore, no good work helps an unbeliever, so as to justify or save him. And, on the other hand, no evil work makes him wicked or damns him, but the unbelief which makes the person and the tree evil, does the evil and damnable works. Hence when a man is made good or evil, this is effected not by the works, but by faith or unbelief, as the Wise Man says, "This is the beginning of sin, that a man falls away from God," which happens when he does not believe. And Paul, Hebrews xi, says, "He that cometh to God must believe." And Christ says the same: "Either make the tree good and his fruit good; or else make the tree corrupt and his fruit corrupt," as if He would say, "Let him who would have good fruit begin by planting a good tree." So let him who would do good works not begin with the doing of works, but with believing, which makes the person good. For nothing makes a man good except faith, nor evil except unbelief. . . .

From this it is easy to know in how far good works are to be rejected or not, and by what standard all the teachings of men concerning works are to be interpreted. If works are sought after as a means to righteousness, are burdened with this perverse leviathan and are done under the false impression that through them you are justified, they are made necessary and freedom and faith are destroyed; and this addition to them makes them to be no longer good, but truly damnable works. For they are not free, and they blaspheme the grace of God, since to justify and to save by faith belongs to the grace of God alone. What the works have no power to do, they yet, by a godless presumption, through this folly of ours, pretend to do, and thus violently force themselves into the office and the glory of grace. We do not, therefore, reject good works; on the contrary, we cherish and teach them as much as possible. We do not condemn them for their own sake, but because of this godless addition to them and the perverse idea that righteousness is to be sought through them; for that makes them appear good outwardly, when in truth they are not good; they deceive men and lead men to deceive each other, like ravening wolves in sheep's clothing. . . .

Lastly, we will also speak of the things which he does toward his neighbor. A man does not live for himself alone in this mortal body, so as to work for it alone, but he lives also for all men on earth, nay, rather, he lives only for others and not for himself. And to this end he brings his body into subjection, that he may the more sincerely and freely serve others, as Paul says in Romans xiv, "No one lives to himself, and no man dies to himself. For he that liveth, liveth unto the Lord, and he that dieth, dieth unto the Lord." Therefore, it is impossible that he should ever in this life be idle and without works toward his neighbors. For of necessity he will speak, deal with and converse with men, as Christ also, being made in the likeness of men, was found in form as a man, and conversed with men, as Baruch iii says.

But none of these things does a man need for his righteousness and salvation. Therefore, in all his works he should be guided by this thought and look to this one thing alone, that he may serve and benefit others in all that he does, having regard to nothing except the need and the advantage of his neighbor. Thus, the Apostle commands us to work with our hands that we may give to him who is in need, although he might have said that we should work to support ourselves; he says, however, "that he may have to give to him that needeth." And this is what makes it a Christian work to care for the body, that through its health and comfort we may be able to work, to acquire and to lay by funds with which to aid those who are in need, that in this way the strong member may serve the weaker, and we may be sons of God, each caring for and working for the other, bearing one another's burdens, and so fulfilling the law of Christ. Lo, this is a truly Christian life, here faith is truly effectual through love; that is, it issues in works of the freest service cheerfully and lovingly done, with which a man willingly serves another without hope of reward, and for himself is satisfied with the fulness and wealth of his faith.

So Paul after teaching the Philippians how rich they were made through faith in Christ, in which they obtained all things, proceeds immediately to teach them further, saying, "If there be any consolation in Christ, if any comfort of love, if any fellowship of the Spirit, fulfil ye my joy, that ye be likeminded, having the same love, being of one accord, thinking nothing through strife or vainglory, but in lowliness each esteeming the other better than themselves; looking not every man on his own things, but on the things of others." Here we see clearly that the Apostle has prescribed this rule for the life of Christians,—that we should devote all our works to the welfare of others, since each has such abundant riches in his faith, that all his other works and his whole life are a surplus with which he can by voluntary benevolence serve and do good to his neighbor. . . .

Therefore, if we recognize the great and precious things which are given us, as Paul says, there will be shed abroad in our hearts by the Holy Ghost the love which makes us free, joyful, almighty workers and conquerors over all tribulations, servants of our neighbors and yet lords of all. But for those who do not recognize the gifts bestowed upon them through Christ, Christ has been born in vain; they go their way with their works, and shall never come to taste or to feel those things. Just as our neighbor is in need and lacks that in which we abound, so we also have been in need before God and have lacked His mercy. Hence, as our heavenly Father has in Christ freely come to our help, we also ought freely to help our neighbor through our body and its works, and each should become as it were a Christ to the other, that we may be Christs to one another and Christ may be the same in all; that is, that we may be truly Christians. . . .

We conclude, therefore, that a Christian man lives not in himself, but in Christ and in his neighbor. Otherwise he is not a Christian. He lives in Christ through faith, in his neighbor through love; by faith he is caught up beyond himself into God, by love he sinks down beneath himself into his neighbor; yet he always remains in God and in His love, as Christ says in John i, "Verily, I say unto you, Hereafter ye shall see heaven open, and the angels of God ascending and descending upon the Son of man." . . .

Finally, something must be added for the sake of those for whom nothing can be so well said that they will not spoil it by misunderstanding it, though it is a question whether they will understand even what shall here be said. There are very many who, when they hear of this liberty of faith, immediately turn it into an occasion for the flesh, and think that now all things are allowed them. They want to show that they are free men and Christians only by despising and finding fault with ceremonies, traditions and human laws; as if they were Christians because on stated days they do not fast or eat meat when others fast, or because they do not use the accustomed prayers, and with upturned nose scoff at the precepts of men, although they utterly disregard all else that pertains to the Christian religion. The extreme opposite of these are those who rely for their salvation solely on their reverent observance of ceremonies, as if they would be saved because on certain days they fast or abstain from meats, or pray certain prayers; these make a boast of the precepts of the Church and of the Fathers, and care not a fig for the things which are of the essence of our faith. Plainly, both are in error, because they neglect the weightier things which are necessary to salvation, and quarrel so noisily about those trifling and unnecessary matters.

How much better is the teaching of the Apostle Paul, who bids us take a middle course, and condemns both sides when he says, "Let not him that eateth despise him that eateth not; and let not him which eateth not judge him that eateth." Here you see that they who neglect and disparage ceremonies, not out of piety, but out of mere contempt, are reproved, since the Apostle teaches us not to despise them. Such men are puffed up by knowledge. On the other hand, he teaches those who insist on the ceremonies not to judge the others, for neither party acts toward the other according to the love that edifies. Wherefore, we ought here to listen to the Scriptures, which teach that we should not go aside to the right nor to the left, but follow the statutes of the Lord which are right, rejoicing the heart. For as a man is not righteous because he keeps and clings to the works and forms of the ceremonies, so also will a man not be counted righteous merely because he neglects and despises them. . . .

Preface to the Epistle to the Romans*

This Epistle is really the chief part of the New Testament and the very purest Gospel, and it is worthy not only that every Christian should know it word for word, by heart, but occupy himself with it every day, as the daily bread of the soul. It can never be read or pondered too much, and the more it is dealt with the more precious it becomes, and the better it tastes.

Therefore, I, too, will do my best, so far as God has given me power, to open the way into it through this preface, so that it may be the better understood by everyone. For heretofore it has been evilly darkened with commentaries

* From Martin Luther, "Preface to the Epistle to the Romans," trans. by C. M. Jacobs, *Works of Martin Luther,* Vol. VI, Philadelphia: A. J. Holman Company, 1932. Pages 447–452 are reprinted by permission of the Muhlenberg Press.

and all kinds of idle talk, though it is, in itself, a bright light, almost enough to illumine all the Scripture.

To begin with we must have knowledge of its language and know what St. Paul means by the words, law, sin, grace, faith, righteousness, flesh, spirit, etc., otherwise no reading of it has any value.

The little word "law," you must not take here in human fashion, as a teaching about what works are to be done or not done. That is the way it is with human laws,—the law is fulfilled by works, even though there is no heart in them. But God judges according to what is at the bottom of the heart, and for this reason, His law makes its demands on the inmost heart and cannot be satisfied with works, but rather punishes works that are done otherwise than from the bottom of the heart, as hypocrisy and lies. Hence all men are called liars, in Psalm cxvi, for the reason that no one keeps or can keep God's law from the bottom of the heart, for everyone finds in himself displeasure in what is good and pleasure in what is bad. If, then, there is no willing pleasure in the good, then the inmost heart is not set on the law of God, then there is surely sin, and God's wrath is deserved, even though outwardly there seem to be many good works and an honorable life. . . .

For even though you keep the law outwardly, with works, from fear of punishment or love of reward, nevertheless, you do all this without willingness and pleasure, and without love for the law; but rather with unwillingness, under compulsion; and you would rather do otherwise, if the law were not there. The conclusion is that at the bottom of your heart you hate the law. What matter, then, that you teach others not to steal, if you are a thief at heart, and would gladly be one outwardly, if you dared? Though, to be sure, the outward work is not far behind such hypocrites! Thus you teach others, but not yourself; and you yourself know not what you teach, and have never yet rightly understood the law. Nay, the law increases sin, as he says in chapter v, for the reason that the more the law demands what men cannot do, the more they hate the law.

For this reason he says, in chapter vii, "The law is spiritual." What is that? If the law were for the body, it could be satisfied with works; but since it is spiritual, no one can satisfy it, unless all that you do is done from the bottom of the heart. But such a heart is given only by God's Spirit, who makes a man equal to the law, so that he acquires a desire for the law in his heart, and henceforth does nothing out of fear and compulsion, but everything out of a willing heart. That law, then, is spiritual which will be loved and fulfilled with such a spiritual heart, and requires such a spirit. Where that spirit is not in the heart, there sin remains, and displeasure with the law, and enmity toward it; though the law is good and just and holy.

Accustom yourself, then, to this language, and you will find that doing the works of the law and fulfilling the law are two very different things. The work of the law is everything that one does, or can do toward keeping the law of his own free will or by his own powers. But since under all these works and along with them there remains in the heart dislike for the law and the compulsion to keep it, these works are all wasted and have no value. That is what St. Paul means in chapter iii, when he says, "By the works of the law no man becomes righteous before God." Hence you see that the wranglers and sophists are deceivers, when they teach men to prepare themselves for grace by means of works. How can a man prepare himself for good by means of works, if he does no good works without displeasure and unwillingness of heart? How shall a work please God, if it proceeds from a reluctant and resisting heart?

To fulfill the law, however, is to do its works with pleasure and love, and to live a godly and good life of one's own accord, without the compulsion of the law. This pleasure and love for the law is put into the heart by the Holy Ghost, as he says in chapter v. But the Holy Ghost is not given except in, with, and by faith in Jesus Christ, as he says in the introduction; and faith does not come, save only through God's Word or Gospel, which preaches Christ, that He is God's Son and a man, and has died and risen again for our sakes, as he says in chapters iii, iv and x.

Hence it comes that faith alone makes righteous and fulfills the law; for out of Christ's merit, it brings the Spirit, and the Spirit makes the heart glad and free, as the law requires that it shall be. Thus good works come out of faith. That is what he means in chapter iii, after he has rejected the works of the law, so that it sounds as though he would abolish the law by faith; "Nay," he says, "we establish the law by faith," that is, we fulfil it by faith. . . .

Between grace and gift there is this difference. Grace means properly God's favor, or the good-will God bears us, by which He is disposed to give us Christ and to pour into us the Holy Ghost, with His gifts. This is clear from chapter v, where he speaks of "the grace and gift in Christ." The gifts and the Spirit increase in us every day, though they are not yet perfect, and there remain in us the evil lust and sin that war against the Spirit, as he says in Romans vii and Galatians v, and the quarrel between the seed of the woman and the seed of the serpent is foretold in Genesis iii. Nevertheless, grace does so much that we are accounted wholly righteous before God. For His grace is not divided or broken up, as are the gifts, but it takes us entirely into favor, for the sake of Christ our Intercessor and Mediator, and because of that the gifts are begun in us.

In this sense, then, you understand chapter vii, in which St. Paul still calls himself a sinner, and yet says, in chapter viii, that there is nothing condemnable in those who are in Christ on account of the incompleteness of the gifts and of the Spirit. Because the flesh is not yet slain, we still are sinners; but because we believe and have a beginning of the Spirit, God is so favorable and gracious to us that He will not count the sin against us or judge us for it, but will deal with us according to our faith in Christ, until sin is slain.

Faith is not that human notion and dream that some hold for faith. Because they see that no betterment of life and no good works follow it, and yet they can hear and say much about faith, they fall into error, and say, "Faith is not enough; one must do works in order to be righteous and be saved." This is the reason that, when they hear the Gospel, they fall to—and make for themselves, by their own powers, an idea in their hearts, which says, "I believe." This they hold for true faith. But it is a human imagination and idea that never reaches the depths of the heart, and so nothing comes of it and no betterment follows it.

Faith, however, is a divine work in us. It changes us and makes us to be born anew of God (John i); it kills the old Adam and makes altogether different men, in heart and spirit and mind and powers, and it brings with it the Holy Ghost. O, it is a living, busy, active, mighty thing, this faith; and so it is impossible for it not to do good works incessantly. It does not ask whether there are good works to do, but before the question rises it has already done them, and is always at the doing of them. He who does not these works is a faithless man. He gropes and looks about after faith and good works, and knows neither what faith is nor what good works are, though he talks and talks, with many words, about faith and good works.

Faith is a living, daring confidence in God's grace, so sure and certain that a man would stake his life on it a thousand times. This confidence in God's grace and knowledge of it makes men glad and bold and happy in dealing with God and with all His creatures; and this is the work of the Holy Ghost in faith. Hence a man is ready and glad, without compulsion, to do good to everyone, to serve everyone, to suffer everything, in love and praise of God, who has shown him this grace; and thus it is impossible to separate works from faith, quite as impossible as to separate heat and light from fire. Beware, therefore, of your own false notions and of the idle talkers, who would be wise enough to make decisions about faith and good works, and yet are the greatest fools. Pray God to work faith in you; else you will remain forever without faith, whatever you think or do.

Righteousness, then, is such a faith and is called "God's righteousness," or "the righteousness that avails before God," because God gives it and counts it as righteousness for the sake of Christ, our Mediator, and makes a man give to every man what he owes him. For through faith a man becomes sinless and comes to take pleasure in God's commandments; thus he gives to God the honor that is His and pays Him what he owes Him; but he also serves man willingly, by whatever means he can, and thus pays his debt to everyone. Such righteousness nature and free will and all our powers cannot bring into existence. No one can give himself faith, and no more can he take away his own unbelief; how, then, will he take away a single sin, even the very smallest? Therefore, all that is done apart from faith, or in unbelief, is false; it is hypocrisy and sin, no matter how good a show it makes (Romans xiv). . . .

Sermon on the Afternoon of Christmas Day (1530)*

You have heard today the story from the Gospel of St. Luke [Luke 2:1–14] of how it came to pass that our Lord Christ was born and then also the message of the angel, who announced who the boy was who was born. Now we shall go on and take up the message of the angel. So far today you have heard only that the child was born and that he is the Lord and Savior. . . . But for whom was he born and whose Lord and Savior is he? The angels declare that he was born Lord and Savior. The Turks, the pope, and the scholars say the same thing, but only to the extent that it brings in money and honor. But that anyone could say, "to *you* is born," as the angel says, this is the faith which we must preach about. But we cannot preach about it as we would like to do. Indeed, who could ever grasp [the full meaning of] these words of the evangelist: "a Savior, who is the Lord," and, "to you"! I know well enough how to talk about it and what to believe about it, just as others do. So there are many who have this belief and do not doubt this first belief that Christ is the Lord, the Savior, and the virgin's Son. This I too have never doubted. But if these words are planted no higher than in my thoughts, then they have no firm roots. We are certain that this was proclaimed by the angel, but the firm faith does not follow. For the reason does not understand both sides of this faith, first that Christ is a man, but also the Savior and Lord or King. This needs to be revealed from heaven. One who really has the first faith also has the other.

Who, then, are those to whom this joyful news is to be proclaimed? Those who are fainthearted and feel the burden of their sins, like the shepherds, to whom the angels proclaim the message, letting the great lords in Jerusalem, who do not accept it, go on sleeping. Beyond the first faith there must be the second faith, that Christ is not only the virgin's Son, but also the Lord of angels and the Savior of men. The words anyone can understand, anti-sacramentarians, fanatics, sectarians, and Turks; but they do not proceed from the heart, they come only from hearing and go no farther than hearing. This is not faith, however, but only a memory of what has been heard, that one knows that he has heard it. Nobody ventures upon it, so as to stake goods, life, and honor upon it. And yet we must preach it for the sake of those who are in the multitude to whom the angel preached.

This is our theology, which we preach in order that we may understand what the angel wants. Mary bore the child, took it to her breast and nursed it, and the Father in heaven has his Son, lying in the manger and the mother's lap. Why did God do all this? Why does Mary guard the child as a mother should? And reason answers: in order that we may make an idol of her, that honor may be paid to the mother. Mary becomes all this without her knowledge and consent, and all the songs and glory and honor are addressed to the mother. And yet the text does not sound forth the honor of the mother, for the angel says, "I bring to you good news of a great joy; for to you is born this day the Savior" [Luke 2:10–11]. I am to accept the child and his birth and forget the mother, as far as this is possible, although her part cannot be forgotten, for where there is a birth there must also be a mother. Nevertheless, we dare not put our faith in the mother but only in the fact that the child was born. And the angel desired that we should see nothing but the child which is born, just as the angels themselves, as though they were blind, saw nothing but the child born of the virgin, and desired that all created things should be as nothing compared with this child, that we

* From *Luther's Works,* Vol. 51, ed. and trans. by John W. Doberstein. Philadelphia: Muhlenberg Press, 1959. Pages 211–218 are reproduced by permission of the publisher.

should see nothing, be it harps, gold, goods, honor, power, and the like, which we would prefer before their message. For if I receive even the costliest and best in the world, it still does not have the name of Savior. And if the Turk were ten times stronger than he is, he could not for one moment save me from my infirmity, to say nothing of the peril of death, and even less from the smallest sin or from death itself. In my sin, my death, I must take leave of all created things. No, sun, moon, stars, all creatures, physicians, emperors, kings, wise men and potentates cannot help me. When I die I shall see nothing but black darkness, and yet that light, "To you is born this day the Savior" [Luke 2:11], remains in my eyes and fills all heaven and earth. The Savior will help me when all have forsaken me. And when the heavens and the stars and all creatures stare at me with horrible mien, I see nothing in heaven and earth but this child. So great should that light which declares that he is my Savior become in my eyes that I can say: Mary, you did not bear this child for yourself alone. The child is not yours; you did not bring him forth for yourself, but for me, even though you are his mother, even though you held him in your arms and wrapped him in swaddling clothes and picked him up and laid him down. But I have a greater honor than your honor as his mother. For your honor pertains to your motherhood of the body of the child, but my honor is this, that you have my treasure, so that I know none, neither men nor angels, who can help me except this child whom you, O Mary, hold in your arms. If a man could put out of his mind all that he is and has except this child, and if for him everything—money, goods, power, or honor—fades into darkness and he despises everything on earth compared with this child, so that heaven with its stars and earth with all its power and all its treasures becomes as nothing to him, that man would have the true gain and fruit of this message of the angel. And for us the time must come when suddenly all will be darkness and we shall know nothing but this message of the angel: "I bring to you good news of great joy; for to you is born this day the Savior" [Luke 2:10–11]. . . .

Therefore this is the chief article, which separates us from all the heathen, that you, O man, may not only learn that Christ, born of the virgin, is the Lord and Savior, but also accept the fact that he is your Lord and Savior, that you may be able to boast in your heart: I hear the Word that sounds from heaven and says: This child who is born of the virgin is not only his mother's son. I have more than the mother's estate; he is more mine than Mary's, for he was born for me, for the angel said, "To you" is born the Savior. Then ought you to say, Amen, I thank thee, dear Lord.

But then reason says: Who knows? I believe that Christ, born of the virgin, is the Lord and Savior and he may perhaps help Peter and Paul, but for me, a sinner, he was not born. But even if you believed that much, it would still not be enough, unless there were added to it the faith that he was born for you. For he was not born merely in order that I should honor the mother, that she should be praised because he was born of the virgin mother. This honor belongs to none except her and it is not to be despised, for the angel said, "Blessed are you among women!" [Luke 1:28]. But it must be too highly esteemed lest one deny what is written here: "To you is born this day the Savior." He was not merely concerned to be born of a virgin; it was infinitely more than that. It was this, as she herself sings in the Magnificat: "He has helped his servant Israel" [Luke 1:54]; not that he was born of me and my virginity, but born for you and for your benefit, not only for my honor.

Take yourself in hand, examine yourself and see whether you are a Christian! If you can sing: The Son, who is proclaimed to be a Lord and Savior, is my Savior; and if you can confirm the message of the angel and say yes to it and believe it in your heart, then your heart will be filled with assurance and joy and confidence, and you will not worry much about even the costliest and best that this world has to offer. For when I can speak to the virgin from the bottom of my heart and say: O Mary, noble, tender virgin, you have borne a child; this I want more than robes and guldens, yea, more than my body and life; then you are closer to the treasure than everything else in heaven and earth, as Ps. 73 [:25] says, "There is nothing upon earth that I desire besides thee." You see how a person rejoices when he receives a robe or ten guldens. But how many are there who shout and jump for joy when they hear the message of the angel: "To you is born this day the Savior?" Indeed, the majority look upon it as a sermon that must be preached, and when they have heard it, consider it a trifling thing, and go away just as they were before. This shows that we have neither the first nor the second faith. We do not believe that the virgin mother bore a son and that he is the Lord and Savior unless, added to this, I believe the second thing, namely, that he is my Savior and Lord. When I can say: This I accept as my own, because the angel meant it for me, then, if I believe it in my heart, I shall not fail to love the mother Mary, and even more the child, and especially the Father. For, if it is true that the child was born of the virgin and is mine, then I have no angry God and I must know and feel that there is nothing but laughter and joy in the heart of the Father and no sadness in my heart. For if what the angel says is true, that he is our Lord and Savior, what can sin do against us? "If God is for us, who is against us?" [Rom. 8:31]. Greater words than these I cannot speak, nor all the angels and even the Holy Spirit, as is sufficiently testified by the beautiful and devout songs that have been made about it. I do not trust myself to express it. I most gladly hear you sing and speak of it but as long as no joy is there, so long is faith still weak or even nonexistent, and you still do not believe the angel.

You can see what our papists and Junkers, who have chosen innumerable saviors, have felt about this faith. Indeed, the papists still want to retain the mass, the invocation of saints, and their invented works by which we are to be saved. This is as much as to say, I do not believe in the Savior and Lord whom Mary bore; and yet they sing the words of the angel, hold their triple masses [at Christmas] and play their organs. They speak the words with their tongues but their heart has another savior. And the same is true in the monasteries: if you want to be saved, remember to keep the rule and regulations of Francis* and you will have a gracious God! And at the Diet of Augsburg they decided to stick to this. In the name of all the devils, let them stick there! It has been said sufficiently that this Savior lies in the manger. But if there is any other thing that saves me, then I rightly call it my savior. If the sun, moon, and stars save, I can call them saviors. If St. Bartholomew† or St. Anthony** or a pilgrimage to St. James†† or good works save, then they surely are my savior. If St. Francis, then he is my savior. But then what is left of the honor of the child who was born this day, whom the angel calls Lord and Savior, and who wants to keep his name, which is Savior and Christ the Lord. If I set up any savior except this child, no matter who or what it is or is called, then he is not the Savior. But the text says that he is the Savior. And if this is true—and it is the truth—then let everything else go. . . .

What we have said, then, has been about that second faith, which is not only to believe in Mary's Son, but rather that he who lies in the virgin's lap is our Savior, that you accept this and give thanks to God, who so loved you that he gave you a Savior who is yours. And for a sign he sent the angel from heaven to proclaim him, in order that nothing else should be preached except that this child is the Savior and far better than heaven and earth. Him, therefore, we should acknowledge and accept; confess him as our Savior in every need, call upon him, and never doubt that he will save us from all misfortune. Amen.

* Francis of Assisi (1182–1226), founder of the Franciscan Order, who was canonized two years after his death by Pope Gregory IX. (Ed.)

† Bartholomew is one of the twelve apostles. His feast day is usually observed on August 24. (Ed.)

** St. Anthony (born *ca.* 250 A. D.), a hermit who is considered the forerunner of the monastic movement. (Ed.)

†† St. James of Compostella in Spain was the most frequented place of pilgrimage in Europe for many centuries. (Ed.)

JOHN CALVIN (1509–1564)

John Calvin was the father and chief architect of the Reformed or, as it is known in the English-speaking world, the Presbyterian Church. From his numerous writings we have selected his reply to Cardinal Sadolet, which has been called the classic justification of the course and the aims of the Protestant Reformation. When the people of Geneva in 1538 drove Calvin and his associates into exile, the Roman Catholic party entertained hopes of winning the city back to the Catholic faith. Cardinal Sadolet, who was morally beyond reproach and who was known to favor a reform of the church, but not at the price of schism, was commissioned to address the Genevans. Encouraged by friends, Calvin wrote his answer to Sadolet's letter in a few days in the fall of 1539. Two years earlier his small treatise *Instruction in Faith* had appeared, written and published in French, subsequently lost and rediscovered only in 1877. This treatise, most of which is presented here, owed its composition to a suggestion by Farel and was intended to teach the truth of the evangelical faith to the people of Geneva. Written a year after the publication of the first edition of *The Institutes of the Christian Religion,* it presented the essence of his masterpiece in a more popular form.

Outstanding as Calvin was as a systematic theologian, no less remarkable were his achievements as an interpreter of the Holy Scriptures. Calvin, like Luther, considered the Bible to be the only foundation of the Church and of every Christian life. From the wealth of his commentaries we have selected a passage which clearly shows the religious passion which dominated all his life and thought: to render praise to the glory of God's majesty.

Reply to Cardinal Sadolet*

You lately addressed a Letter to the Senate and People of Geneva, in which you tested their mind whether they would submit to have again imposed upon them the yoke of the Roman pontiff which they had once thrown off. In this letter, as it was not expedient to wound the feelings of those whose favour you required to gain your cause, you acted the part of a good pleader. For you tried to soothe them with much flattery, in order that you might gain them over to your views. Anything of abuse and bitterness you directed against those whose exertions had produced the revolt from tyranny. Here, if you please, you bear down full sail upon those who, under pretence of the gospel, have by wicked arts incited the city to what you deplore as the subversion of religion and of the Church. But I, Sadolet, profess to be one of those whom with so much enmity you assail and stigmatize. For though religion was already established and the form of the Church rectified before I was invited to Geneva, yet I not only approved by my assent, but studied as much as in me lay to preserve and confirm what had been done by Farel and Viret; and so I cannot separate my case from theirs. Still, if you had attacked me personally, I could easily have forgiven the attack in consideration of your learning and in honour of letters. But when I see that my ministry, which I feel assured is supported and sanctioned by a call from God, is taken and wounded in the flank, it would be perfidy, not patience, were I have to be silent and disregard what you say. . . .

For though I am for the present relieved of the charge of the Church of Geneva, this cir-

* From *Calvin: Theological Treatises,* translated by J. K. S. Reid, Volume XXII, The Library of Christian Classics. Philadelphia: The Westminster Press, 1954. Pages 221–223, 227–232, 240f, 246–250, and 256 are reproduced by permission of the publisher.

cumstance ought not to prevent me from embracing it with paternal affection; for God, when he charged me with it, bound me to be faithful to it for ever. So, now, when I see the worst snares laid for that Church, whose safety it has pleased the Lord to make my highest care, and grievous peril impending if this be not obviated, who will advise me to await the issue silent and unconcerned? How heartless, I ask, would it be to gape idly and connive at the destruction of something whose life you are bound vigilantly to guard and preserve? . . .

When the Genevans, instructed by our preaching, escaped from the gulf of error in which they were immersed and betook themselves to a purer teaching of the gospel, you call it defection from the truth of God; when they threw off the tyranny of the Roman pontiff, in order that they might establish among themselves a better form of Church, you call it desertion from the Church. Come, then, and let us discuss both points in turn.

As to your preface, which, in proclaiming the excellence of eternal blessedness, occupies about a third of your Letter, it cannot be necessary for me to dwell long in reply. For although commendation of the future and eternal life is a theme worthy to be sounded in our ears by day and by night, kept constantly in remembrance, and made the subject of ceaseless meditation, yet I know not for what reason you have so protracted your discourse upon it here, unless it were to commend yourself by some indication of religious feeling. But whether, in order to remove all doubt about yourself, you wished to testify that a life of glory seriously occupies your thoughts, or whether you supposed that those to whom you wrote required to be excited and spurred on by a long commendation of it (for I am unwilling to probe what your intention may have been), it is not very sound theology to confine a man's thoughts so much to himself, and not to set before him as the prime motive of his existence zeal to show forth the glory of God. For we are born first of all for God, and not for ourselves. As all things flowed from him and subsist in him, as Paul says (Rom. 11:36), they ought to be related to him. I acknowledge indeed that the Lord, to recommend the glory of his name to men the better, has tempered zeal for its advance and extension by uniting it indissolubly with our salvation. But since he has taught that this zeal ought to exceed all thought and care for our own good and advantage, and since natural equity also teaches that God does not receive what is his own unless he be preferred to all things, it certainly is the duty of a Christian man to ascend higher than merely to seek and secure the salvation of his own soul. I therefore believe that there is no man imbued with true piety, who will not regard as in poor taste that long and detailed exhortation to a zeal for heavenly life, which occupies a man entirely concerned with himself, and does not, even by one expression, arouse him to sanctify the name of God. But I readily agree with you that after this sanctification we ought to set ourselves no other object in life than to hasten towards that high calling; for God has set it before us as the constant aim of all our actions, words and thoughts. Indeed there is nothing in which man excels the lower animals, unless it be his spiritual communion with God in the hope of a blessed eternity. In general, all we aim at in our discourses is to arouse men to meditate upon it and aspire to it.

I have also no difficulty in conceding to you that there is nothing more perilous to our salvation than a distorted and perverse worship of God. The primary rudiments by which we are wont to train to piety those whom we wish to win as disciples to Christ, are these: not to frame any new worship of God for themselves at random and their own pleasure, but to know that the only legitimate worship is that which he himself approved from the beginning. For we maintain, what the sacred oracle declared, that obedience is more excellent than any sacrifice (I Sam. 15:22). In short, we train them by every means to keep within the one rule of worship which they have received from his mouth, and bid farewell to all fictitious worship.

Therefore, Sadolet, when you uttered this voluntary confession, you laid the foundation of my defence. For if you admit it to be a fearful destruction to the soul, when by false opinions divine truth is turned into a lie, it now only remains for us to enquire which of the two parties retains that worship of God which is alone legitimate. In order that you may claim it for your side, you assume that the most certain rule of worship is that which is prescribed by the Church, although, as if we here opposed you, you bring the matter to consideration in the manner usually observed in doubtful matters. But, Sadolet, as I see you toiling in vain, I will relieve you from all trouble at this point. You are mistaken in supposing that we desire to lead away the people from the method of worshipping God which the Catholic Church always observed. Either you are deluded about the term Church, or else knowingly and willingly you practice deception. I will immediately show the latter to be the case, though it may also be that you are somewhat in error. First, in defining the term, you omit what would have helped you in no small degree to its right understanding. When you describe it as that which in all past as well as present time, in all regions of the earth, being united and of one mind in Christ, has been always and everywhere directed by the one Spirit of Christ, what becomes of the Word of the Lord, that clearest of all marks, which the Lord himself in designating the Church so often commends to us? For seeing how dangerous it would be to boast of the Spirit without the Word, he declared that the Church is indeed governed by the Holy Spirit; but in order that this government might not be vague and unstable, he bound it to the Word. For this reason Christ exclaims that those who are of God hear the Word of God, that his sheep are those which recognize his voice as that of their Shepherd and any other voice as that of a stranger (John 10:27). For this reason the Spirit by the mouth of Paul declares (Eph. 2:20) that the Church is built upon the foundation of the apostles and prophets; also, that the Church is made holy to the Lord, by the washing of water in the word of life (Eph. 5:26). The same thing is declared still more clearly by the mouth of Peter, when he teaches that people are regenerated to God by that incorrupible seed (I Peter 1:23). In short, why is the preaching of the gospel so often styled the kingdom of God, but because it is the sceptre by which the heavenly King rules his people?

Nor will you find this in the apostolic writings only; whenever the prophets foretell the renewal of the Church or its extension over the whole globe, they always assign the first place to the Word. For they say that from Jerusalem will issue forth living waters, which being divided into four rivers will inundate the whole earth (Zech. 14:8). What these living waters are, they themselves explain when they say: the law will come forth from Zion, and the Word of the Lord from Jerusalem (Isa. 2:3). Chrysostom then rightly admonishes us to reject all who under the pretence of the Spirit lead us away from the simple doctrine of the gospel; for the Spirit was promised, not to reveal a new doctrine, but to impress the truth of the gospel on our minds. We in fact experience in the present day how necessary the admonition was. We are assailed by two sects, which seem to differ most widely from each other. For what similitude is there in appearance between the pope and the Anabaptists? And yet, that you may see that Satan never transforms himself so cunningly as not in some measure to betray himself, the spiritual weapon with which they both assail us is the same. For when they boast extravagantly of the Spirit, they inevitably tend to sink and bury the Word of God, and to make room for their own falsehoods. And you, Sadolet, by stumbling on the very threshold have paid the penalty of the affront you offered the Holy Spirit, when you separated him from the Word. For as if those who seek the way of God stood where two ways meet, destitute of any certain sign, you are forced to present them as hesitating whether it be more expedient to follow the authority of the Church, or to listen to those whom you call the inventors of new dogmas. If you had known or been unwilling to disguise the fact that the Spirit goes before the Church to enlighten her in understanding the Word, while the Word itself is like the Lydian stone by which she tests all doctrines, would you have taken refuge in that most perplexing and thorny question? Learn, then, by your own experience that it is no less unreasonable to boast of the Spirit without the Word, than it would be absurd to bring forward the Word itself without the Spirit. Now if you can bear to receive a truer definition of the Church than your own, say in future that it is the society of all the saints which, spread over the whole world and existing in all ages, yet bound together by the doctrine and the one Spirit of Christ, cultivates and observes unity of faith and brotherly concord. With this Church we deny that we have any disagreement. Rather as we revere her as our mother, so we desire to remain in her bosom.

But here you bring a charge against me. For you teach that all that has been approved for fifteen hundred years or more by the uniform consent of the faithful, is by our rashness torn up and destroyed. Here I will not require you to deal truly and candidly by us (though this should be spontaneously offered by a philosopher, not to say a Christian). I will only ask you not to stoop to a mean indulgence in calumny, which, even though we be silent, must be extremely injurious to your reputation with serious and honest men. You know, Sadolet, and if you venture to deny it, I shall make it plain to all, that you knew but cunningly and craftily disguised the fact, not only that our agreement with antiquity is far closer than yours, but that all we have attempted has been to renew the ancient form of the Church which, at first distorted and stained by illiterate men of indifferent character, was afterwards criminally mangled and almost destroyed by the Roman pontiff and his faction.

I shall not press you so closely as to call you back to that form which the apostles instituted, though in it we have the only model of a true Church, and whosoever deviates from it in the smallest degree is in error. But to indulge you so far, I ask you to place before your eyes the ancient form of the Church as their writings prove it to have been in the ages of Chrysostom and Basil among the Greeks, and of Cyprian, Ambrose and Augustine among the Latins; and after so doing, to contemplate the ruins of that Church which now survive among yourselves. Assuredly the difference will appear as great as that which the prophets describe between the famous Church which flourished under David and Solomon, and that which under Zedekiah and Jehoiakim had lapsed into every kind of superstition and utterly vitiated the purity of divine worship. Will you here declare one an enemy of antiquity who, zealous for ancient piety and holiness and dissatisfied with the corrupt state of matters existing in a dissolute and depraved Church, attempts to ameliorate its condition and restore it to pristine splendour? . . .

That I may altogether disarm you of the authority of the church, which as your shield of Ajax you are always opposing to us, I shall show by some additional examples how widely you differ from holy antiquity. We accuse you of overthrowing the ministry, of which the empty name remains with you without the reality. For as to the office of feeding the people, the very children perceive that bishops and presbyters are dumb statues, while men of all ranks know by experience that they are active only in robbing and devouring. We are indignant that in place of the sacred Supper has been substituted a sacrifice, by which the death of Christ is emptied of its virtue. We exclaim against the execrable traffic in masses, and we complain that one half of the Supper of the Lord has been stolen from Christian people. We combat the scandalous worship of images. We show that the sacraments are vitiated by many profane ideas. We tell how indulgences crept in with fearful dishonour to the cross of Christ. We deplore that by human traditions Christian liberty has been crushed and destroyed. Of these and similar pests we have been careful to purge the churches which the Lord has committed to us. Expostulate with us, if you can, for the injury we inflicted on the Catholic Church by daring to violate its sacred sanctions. The fact is now too notorious for you to gain anything by denying it: in all these points the ancient Church is clearly on our side, and opposes you not less than we ourselves do.

But here we are met by what you say when by way of extenuation you allege that, though your customs be irregular, this is no reason why we should make a schism in the holy Church. It is scarcely possible that the minds of the common people should not be greatly alienated from you by the many examples of cruelty, avarice, intemperance, arrogance, insolence, lust and all sorts of wickedness, which were openly manifested by men of your order; but none of those things have driven us to an attempt which we made under a much stronger necessity. This necessity was that the light of divine truth had been extinguished, the Word of God buried, the virtue of Christ left in profound oblivion, and the pastoral office subverted. Meanwhile impiety so stalked abroad, that almost no religious doctrine was pure from adulteration, no ceremony free from error, no part, however minute, of divine worship untouched by superstition. Do those who contend against such evils declare war against the Church? Do they not rather assist her in extreme distress? Yet you would take credit for your obedience and humility in refraining, through veneration for the Church, from applying your hand to the removal of these abominations. What has a Christian man to do with the prevaricating obedience that boldly despises the Word of God, and yields homage to human vanity? What has he to do with the obstinate and rude humility that disdains the majesty of God and looks up with reverence to men only? Have done with empty names of virtue, employed merely to conceal vice. Let us exhibit the thing in its true colours. Let that humility be ours which, beginning with the lowest and paying respect to each in his degree, yields the highest honour and respect to the Church in subordination, however, to Christ the Church's head; let that obedience be ours which, while it disposes us to listen to our elders and superiors, tests all obedience by the Word of God; in a word, let our Church be one whose supreme concern it is humbly and religiously to venerate the Word of God, and submit in obedience to it. . . .

But since towards the end a person has been introduced to plead our cause, and you have cited us as defenders to the tribunal of God, I have no hesitation in calling upon you to meet me there. For such is our consciousness of the truth of our doctrine, that it has no dread of the heavenly Judge, from whom we do not doubt that it proceeded. But it dwells not on those frivolities with which it has pleased you to amuse yourself, but which are certainly very much out of place. For what could be more inopportune than to come into the presence of God, and to set about devising I know not what follies, and framing for us an absurd defence which must immediately fail? In pious minds, whenever that day is suggested, the impression made is too solemn to leave them at leisure so to amuse themselves. Therefore, frivolity set aside, let us think of that day which the minds of men ought always to expect with suspense. And let us remember that, while desirable to the faithful, it may well be alarming to the ungodly and profane and those who despise God. Let us turn our ears to the sound of that trumpet which even the ashes of the dead will hear in their tombs. Let us direct our thoughts and minds to that Judge who, by the mere brightness of his countenance, will disclose whatever lurks in darkness, lay open all the secrets of the human heart, and crush all the wicked by the mere breath of his mouth. Consider now what serious answer you are to make for yourself and your party; our cause, supported as it is by the truth of God, will be at no loss for a complete defence. I speak not of our persons, whose safety will be found not in defence, but in humble confession and suppliant petition; but in so far as our ministry is concerned, there is none of us who will not be able to speak for himself as follows.

"O Lord, I have indeed experienced how difficult and grievous it is to bear the invidious accusations with which I was harassed on the earth; but with the same confidence with which I then appealed to thy tribunal, I now appear before thee, for I know that in thy judgment truth reigns. Supported by confidence in this truth, I first dared to attempt, and assisted by it I was able to accomplish, whatever was achieved by me in thy Church. They charged me with two of the worst of crimes, heresy and schism. The heresy was that I dared to protest against dogmas received by them. But what could I have done? I heard from thy mouth that there was no other light of truth which could direct our souls into the way of life, than that which was kindled by the Word. I heard that whatever human minds of themselves conceive concerning thy majesty, the worship of thy deity, and the mysteries of thy religion, was vanity. I heard that their introduction into the Church of doctrines sprung from the human brain in place of thy Word was sacrilegious presumption. But when I turned my eyes towards men, I saw very different principles prevailing. Those who were regarded as the leaders of faith neither understood thy Word, nor greatly cared for it. They only drove unhappy people about with stange doctrines, and deluded them with I know not what follies. Among the people themselves, the highest veneration paid to thy Word was to revere it at a distance as something inaccessible, and abstain from all investigation of it. Owing to the supine dullness of the pastors and the stupidity of the people, every place was filled with pernicious errors, falsehoods, and superstition. They indeed called thee the only God, but they did so while transferring to others the glory which thou hast claimed for thy majesty. They imagined for themselves and esteemed as many gods as they had saints to worship. Thy Christ was indeed worshipped as God and retained the name of Saviour; but where he ought to have been honoured, he was left almost destitute of glory. For, spoiled of his own virtue, he passed unnoticed among the crowd of saints, like one of the meanest of them. There was no one who duly considered that one sacrifice which he offered on the cross, and by which he reconciled us to thyself; no one who ever dreamed of thinking of his eternal priesthood, and the intercession depending on it; no one who trusted in his righteousness only. That confident hope of salvation, which is both enjoined by the Word and founded upon it, had almost vanished. Indeed it was received as a kind of oracle; it was foolish arrogance, and, as they said, presumption, for any one to trust in thy goodness and the righteousness of thy Son, and entertain a sure and unfaltering hope of salvation. These were so many profane opinions which, though they were the first principles of that doctrine which thou hast delivered to us in thy Word, they plucked up by the roots. The true meaning of Baptism and the Lord's Supper also was corrupted by numerous falsehoods. And then when everybody, gravely affronting thy mercy, put confidence in good works, when by good works they strove to merit thy favour, to procure justification, to expiate their sins, and make satisfaction to thee (each of these things obliterating and emptying the virtue of Christ's cross), they were yet quite ignorant in what good works consisted. For just as if they were not at all instructed in righteousness by thy law, they had fabricated for themselves many useless trivialities as a means of procuring thy favour, and on these they so prided themselves, that in comparison with them they almost scorned the standard of true righteousness which thy law commended—to such a degree had human desires usurped the ascendancy and derogated, if not from the belief, at least from the authority, of thy precepts contained in it.

"That I might perceive these things, thou, O Lord, didst shine upon me with the brightness of thy Spirit; that I might comprehend how impious and harmful they were, thou didst bear before me the torch of thy Word; that I might abominate them as they deserved, thou didst disturb my soul. But in rendering an account of my doctrine, thou seest, what my own conscience declares, that it was not my intention to stray beyond those limits which I saw had been fixed for all thy servants. Whatever I did not doubt I had learned from thy mouth, I desired to dispense faithfully to the Church. Assuredly the thing at which I chiefly aimed, and for which I most diligently laboured, was that the glory of thy goodness and justice should disperse the mists by which it was formerly obscured, and might shine forth conspicuously, that the virtue and blessings of thy Christ, all disguises being brushed aside, might be fully displayed. For I thought it impious to leave in obscurity things which were born to ponder and mediate. Nor did I think that truths, whose magnitude no language can express, were to be maliciously or falsely declared. I hesitated not to dwell at greater length on topics on which the salvation of my hearers depended. For the oracle could never deceive which declares (John 17:3): 'This is eternal life, to know thee the only true God, and Jesus Christ, whom thou hast sent.'

"As to the charge of forsaking the Church, which they are accustomed to bring against me, there is nothing here of which my conscience accuses me, unless indeed he is to be considered a deserter who, seeing the soldiers routed and scattered and abandoning the ranks, raises the leader's standard, and recalls them to their posts. For thus, O Lord, were all thy servants dispersed, so that they could not by any possibility hear the command, but had almost forgotten their leader, their service, and their military vow. To bring them together when thus scattered, I raised, not a foreign standard, but that noble banner of thine which we must follow, if we would be classed among thy people.

"Then I was assailed by those who, when they ought to have kept others in their ranks, had led them astray, and when I would not at all desist they opposed me with violence. On this grievous tumults arose, and the contest flared up into disruption. Who was to blame it is for thee, O Lord, to decide. Always, both by word and deed, have I protested how eager I was for unity. Mine, however, was a unity of the Church which should begin with thee and end in thee. For whenever thou didst recommend to us peace and concord, thou didst at the same time show thyself to be the only bond for preserving it. But if I desired to be at peace with those who boasted of being the heads of the Church and the pillars of faith, I had to purchase it with the denial of thy truth. I thought that anything was to be endured rather than stoop to such an execrable accommodation. For thy Christ himself declared that, though heaven and earth should be confounded, yet thy Word must endure for ever (Matt. 24:35). Nor did I think that I dissented from thy Church, because I was at war with those leaders. For thou didst forewarn us both by thy Son and by the apostles that into that place there would rise persons to whom I ought by no means to consent. Christ predicted not of strangers, but of men who should pass themselves off as pastors, that they would be ravenous wolves and false prophets, and at the same time warned us to beware of them (Matt. 7:15). Where Christ ordered me to beware, was I to lend my aid? And the apostles declared that there would be no enemies of thy Church more pestilential than those from within, who should conceal themselves under the title of pastors (Acts 20:29; II Pet. 2:1; I John 2:18). Why should I have hesitated to separate myself from persons whom they forewarned me to hold as enemies? I had before my eyes the examples of thy prophets who, I saw, had a similar contest with the priests and prophets of their day, though these were undoubtedly the rulers of the Church among the Israelite people. But thy prophets are not regarded as schismatics because, when they wished to revive religion which had fallen into decay, they did not desist although opposed with the utmost violence. They still remained in the unity of the Church, though they were by wicked priests execrated with awful curses, and thought unworthy of a place among men, not to say saints. Confirmed by their example, I too persisted. Though denounced as a deserter of the Church and threatened, I was in no respect deterred or induced to proceed less firmly and boldly in opposing those who, in the character of pastors, wasted thy Church more than any impious tyranny. My conscience told me how strong the zeal was with which I burned for the unity of thy Church, provided thy truth were made the bond of concord. As the tumults which followed were not excited by me, so there is no ground for imputing them to me.

"Thou, O Lord, knowest, and the fact has testified itself to men, that the only thing I asked was that all controversies should be decided by the Word, that thus both parties might unite with one mind to establish thy kingdom; and I declined not to restore peace to the Church at the expense of my head, if I were found to be the cause of needless disturbance. But what did our opponents do? Did they not forthwith furiously fly to fires, swords, and gibbets? Did they not decide that their only security was in arms and cruelty? Did they not instigate all ranks to the same fury? Did they not spurn all methods of pacification? Thus it happens that a matter, which might at one time have been settled amicably, has blazed up into such a conflict. But although amidst the great confusion the judgments of men were various, I am freed from all fear now that we stand at thy tribunal, where equity combined with truth cannot but decide in favor of innocence." . . .

The Lord grant, Sadolet, that you and all your party may at length perceive that the only true bond of ecclesiastical unity consists in this, that Christ the Lord, who has reconciled us to God the Father, gather us out of our present dispersion into the fellowship of his body, that so, through his one Word and Spirit, we may join together with one heart and one soul.

Instruction in Faith*

All Men Are Born in Order to Know God

As no man is found, however barbarous and even savage he may be, who is not touched by some idea of religion, it is clear that we all are created in order that we may know the

* From John Calvin, *Instruction in Faith (1537),* trans. and ed. by Paul T. Fuhrmann. Philadelphia: The Westminster Press, 1949. Pages 17–24, 32–45, 55–59, and 66–78 are reproduced by permission of the publisher.

majesty of our Creator, that having known it, we may esteem it above all and honor it with all awe, love, and reverence.

But, leaving aside the unbelievers, who seek nothing but to efface from their memory that idea of God which is planted in their hearts, we, who make profession of personal religion, must reflect that this decrepit life of ours, which will soon end, must be nothing else but a meditation of immortality. Now, nowhere can eternal and immortal life be found except in God. It is necessary, therefore, that the principal care and solicitude of our life be to seek God, to aspire to him with all the affection of our heart, and to repose nowhere else but in him alone.

What Difference There is Between True and False Religion

Since it is commonly agreed that if our life is without religion we are most miserable and in no way better than brute animals, no one wishes to be considered as completely alienated from piety and acknowledgment of God. There is, however, a great difference in the way of declaring one's religion, because the majority of men are not truly touched by the awe of God. Yet, willingly or not, they are bound by this thought always coming anew to their minds that there is some divinity by whose power they stand or fall. Hence, being astonished by the thought of such a great power, they revere it in some way in order not to provoke it against themselves by too great a contempt. Yet, living in a disorderly way and rejecting all honesty, they exhibit a great sense of security in despising the judgment of God. Moreover, they turn away from the true God because they estimate God not by his infinite majesty but by the foolish and giddy vanity of their own mind. Hence, although they may afterward strive to serve God with great care, that does not profit them at all, because they do not worship the eternal God, but the dreams and fancies of their own heart in place of God. Now the gist of true piety does not consist in a fear which would gladly flee the judgment of God but, being unable to do so, has horror of it. True piety consists rather in a pure and true zeal which loves God altogether as Father, and reveres him truly as Lord, embraces his justice and dreads to offend him more than to die. All those who possess this zeal do not undertake to forge for themselves a God as their temerity wishes, but they seek the knowledge of the true God from that very God and do not conceive him otherwise than he manifests and declares himself to them.

What We Must Know of God

Now since the majesty of God in itself goes beyond the capacity of human understanding and cannot be comprehended by it, we must adore its loftiness rather than investigate it, so that we do not remain overwhelmed by so great a splendor. Hence, we must seek and consider God in his works, which, for this reason the Scripture calls representations of the invisible things (Rom. 1:20; Heb. 11:1) because these works represent to us that of the Lord which otherwise we cannot see. Now this does not keep our intellect up in the air through frivolous and vain speculations, but is a thing that we must know and that generates, nourishes, and confirms in us a true and solid piety, that is, faith united with reverential fear. We contemplate, therefore, in this universality of things, the immortality of our God, from which immortality have proceeded the beginning and origin of all things; his power which has created such a great system and now sustains it; his wisdom which has composed and rules with such a distinct order such a great and complex variety of beings and things; his goodness which has been the reason in itself why all these things have been created and now subsist; his justice which manifests itself in a marvelous way in the protection of good people and in the retribution of the bad; his mercy which endures our iniquities with such a great kindliness in order to call us to amendment. Certainly all this should abundantly teach us all of such a God as it is necessary to know, if we in our coarseness were not blind to such a great light. Yet here we sin not only by blindness, for our perversity is such that when it estimates the works of God there is nothing that it does not understand in an evil and perverse sense, so that it turns upside down all the heavenly wisdom which otherwise shines so clearly in those works. It is therefore necessary to come to the word [of God] where God is very well described to us through his workings, because in the Scripture these works are estimated not according to the perversity of our judgment, but by the standard of the eternal truth. From God's word, therefore, we learn that our only and eternal God is the spring and fountain of all life, justice, wisdom, virtue, goodness, and clemency. And, as every good without exception comes from him, so also every praise should rightly return to him. And although all these things appear clearly in each part of heaven and earth, yet only then do we at last understand truly that to which they tend, what their value is and at what end we must understand them, when we descend into ourselves and consider in what way the Lord manifests in us his life, wisdom, and power, and exercises toward us his justice, clemency, and goodness.

Man

At first man was formed in the image and resemblance of God in order that man might admire his Author in the adornments with which he had been nobly vested by God and honor him with proper acknowledgment. But, having trusted such a great excellence of his nature and having forgotten from whom it had come and by whom it subsisted, man strove to raise himself up apart from the Lord. Hence man had to be stripped of all God's gifts of which he was foolishly proud, so that, denuded and deprived of all glory, he might know God whom man, after having been enriched by his liberalities, had dared to despise. As a result, this resemblance to God having been effaced in us, we all who descend from the seed of Adam are born flesh from flesh. For, though we are composed of a soul and a body, yet we feel nothing but the flesh, so that to whatever part of man we turn our eyes, it is impossible to see anything that is not impure, profane, and abominable to God. The intellect of man is indeed blinded, wrapped with infinite errors and always contrary to the wisdom of God; the will, bad and full of corrupt affections, hates nothing more than God's justice; and the bodily strength, incapable of all good deeds, tends furiously toward iniquity.

Free Will

The Scripture testifies often that man is a slave of sin. The Scripture means thereby that man's spirit is so alienated from the justice of God that man conceives, covets, and undertakes nothing that is not evil, perverse, iniquitous, and soiled. Because the heart, totally imbued with the poison of sin, can emit nothing but the fruits of sin. Yet one must not infer therefrom that man sins as constrained by violent necessity. For, man sins with the consent of a very prompt and inclined will. But because man, by the corruption of his affections, very strongly keeps hating the whole righteousness of God and, on the other hand, is fervent in all kinds of evil, it is said that he has not the free power of choosing between good and evil —which is called free will.

Sin and Death

Sin means in the Scripture both the perversity of human nature, which is the fountain of all vices, and the evil desires which are born from it and the iniquitous transgressions which spring from these evil desires, such as murders, thefts, adulteries, and other things of this kind. Hence, being sinners from our mothers' wombs, we are all born subject to the wrath and retribution of God. And, having grown up, we pile upon ourselves an ever heavier judgment of God. Finally through all our life we tend ever more toward death. For there is no doubt that all iniquity is execrable to the justice of God. What can we expect in the face of God, we miserable ones who are oppressed by such a great load of sins and soiled by an infinite filth, except a very certain confusion such as his indignation brings? Though it fells man with terror and crushes him with despair, yet this thought is necessary for us in order that, being divested of our own righteousness, having given up faith in our own power, being rejected from all expectation of life, we may learn from the understanding of our poverty, misery, and infamy, to prostrate ourselves before the Lord and, by the acknowledgment of our iniquity, powerlessness, and utter ruin, give him all glory of holiness, might, and deliverance.

How We Are Delivered and Restored to Life

If this knowledge of ourself, which shows us our nothingness, consciously enters into our hearts, an easy access to having the true knowledge of God is made to us. Or rather, God himself has opened to us, as it were, a first door to his kingdom when he has destroyed these two worst pests, which are self-assurance in front of his retribution and false confidence in ourselves. For we begin then to lift our eyes to heaven, those eyes that before were fixed and stopped on earth. And we, who once rested in ourselves, long for the Lord. On the other hand, though our iniquity should deserve something quite different, this merciful Father yet, according to his unspeakable benignity, shows himself voluntarily to us who are thus afflicted and perplexed. And by such means which he knows to be helpful in our weakness, he recalls us from error to the right way, from death to life, from ruin to salvation, from the kingdom of the devil to his own reign. As the Lord had therefore established this first preparation for all those whom he pleases to re-establish as heirs to heavenly life—that is to say, those who distressed by conscience and burdened by the weight of their sins feel themselves stung in the heart and stimulated reverently to fear him—God then first places his Law before us in order that it exercise us in this knowledge. . . .

The Summary of the Law

Now our Lord Jesus Christ has clearly enough declared to us the real purpose of all the commandments of the Law, when he taught that all the Law is comprised in two articles. The first article is that we should love the Lord our God with all our heart, with all our soul, and with all our strength. The second article is that we should love our neighbor as much as ourselves. And this interpretation, our Lord has taken from the Law itself. For the first part is found in Deut. 6:5, and the second is seen in Lev. 19:18.

What Comes to Us from the Law Alone

Behold above, therefore, the standard of a just and holy life and even a very perfect image of justice or righteousness, so that if someone expresses the Law of God in his life, he will lack nothing of the perfection required before the Lord. In order to certify that, God promises to those who shall have fulfilled the Law not only the grand blessings of the present life, which are recited in Lev. 26:3–13 and in Deut. 27:1–14, but also the recompense of eternal life (Lev. 18:5). On the other hand, he pronounces retribution with eternal death against those who shall not have accomplished by deeds that which is commanded in the Law. Moses also, having published the law (Deut. 30:19), took heaven and earth as witnesses that he had proposed to the people good and evil, life and death.

But although the Law shows the way of life, yet we must see what this demonstration can avail us. Certainly if our will be all formed and disposed to obedience toward the divine will, the mere knowledge of the Law would fully suffice for salvation. But as our carnal and corrupt nature altogether wars against the spiritual Law of God and in nothing is mended by the teaching thereof, it results that the very Law (which was given unto salvation if it had found good and capable hearers) becomes on the contrary an occasion of sin and death. For, since we are all convicted of being transgressors of the Law, the more clearly the Law discloses to us the justice of God, the more it uncovers on the other hand our iniquity. And again, as the Law catches us in greater transgression, so it renders us deserving of a heavier judgment of God. And, the promise of eternal life being thus taken away, the curse alone remains for us, which catches us all by means of the Law.

The Law is a Preparation to Come to Christ

The testimony of the Law, however, which convinces us of iniquity and transgression, is not made in order that we should fall into despair, and, having lost courage, stumble into ruin. Certainly the apostles (Rom. 3:19, 20) testifies that by the judgment of the Law we all are condemned, in order that every mouth be closed and the entire world be found guilty before God. Yet that very apostle elsewhere (Rom. 11:32) teaches that God has enclosed all under unbelief, not in order to ruin them or let them perish, but, on the contrary, in order that he may exercise mercy on all.

The Lord, therefore, after reminding us (by means of the Law) of our weakness and impurity, comforts us with the assurance of his power and his mercy. And it is in Christ his son that God shows himself to us benevolent and propitious. For, in the Law he appeared only as remunerator of perfect righteousness (of which we are completely destitute) and, on the other hand, as upright and severe judge of sins. But in Christ his face shines full of grace and kindliness even toward miserable and unworthy sinners; for, he gave this admirable example of his infinite love, when he exposed his own son for us, and in him opened to us all the treasure of his clemency and goodness.

We Apprehend Christ Through Faith

Just as the merciful Father offers us the Son through the word of the Gospel, so we embrace him through faith and acknowledge him as given to us. It is true that the word of the Gospel calls all to participate in Christ, but a number, blinded and hardened by unbelief, despise such a unique grace. Hence, only believers enjoy Christ; they receive him as sent to them; they do not reject him when he is given but follow him when he calls them.

Election and Predestination

Beyond this contrast of attitudes of believers and unbelievers, the great secret of God's counsel must necessarily be considered. For, the seed of the word of *God* takes root and brings forth fruit only in those whom the Lord, by his eternal election, has predestined to be children and heirs of the heavenly kingdom. To all the others (who by the same counsel of God are rejected before the foundation of the world) the clear and evident preaching of truth can be nothing but an odor of death unto death. Now, why does the Lord use his mercy toward some and exercise the rigor of his judgment on the others? We have to leave the reason of this to be known by him alone. For, he, with a certainly excellent intention, has willed to keep it hidden from us all. The crudity of our mind could not indeed bear such a great clarity, nor our smallness comprehend such a great wisdom. And in fact all those who will attempt to rise to such a height and will not repress the temerity of their spirit, shall experience the truth of Solomon's saying (Prov. 25:27) that he who will investigate the majesty shall be oppressed by the glory. Only let us have this resolved in ourselves that the dispensation of the Lord, although hidden from us, is nevertheless holy and just. For, if he willed to ruin all mankind, he has the right to do it, and in those whom he rescues from perdition one can contemplate nothing but his sovereign goodness. We acknowledge, therefore, the elect to be recipients of his mercy (as truly they are) and the rejected to be recipients of his wrath, a wrath, however, which is nothing but just.

Let us take from the lot of both the elect and the others, reasons for extolling his glory. On the other hand, let us not seek (as many do), in order to confirm the certainty of our salvation, to penetrate the very interior of heaven and to investigate what God from his eternity has decided to do with us. That can only worry us with a miserable distress and perturbation. Let us be content, then, with the testimony by which he has sufficiently and amply confirmed to us this certainty. For, as in Christ are elected all those who have been preordained to life before the foundations of the world were laid, so also he is he in whom the pledge of our election is presented to us if we receive him and embrace him through faith. For what do we seek in election except that we be participants in the life eternal? And we have it in Christ, who was the life since the beginning and who is offered as life to us in order that all those who believe in him may not perish but enjoy the life eternal. If, therefore, in possessing Christ through faith we possess in him likewise life, we need no further inquire beyond the eternal counsel of God. For Christ is not only a mirror by which the will of God is presented to us, but he is a pledge by which life is as sealed and confirmed to us.

What True Faith Is

One must not imagine that the Christian faith is a bare and mere knowledge of God or an understanding of the Scripture which flutters in the brain without touching the heart, as it is usually the case with the opinion about things which are confirmed by some probable reason. But faith is a firm and solid confidence of the heart, by means of which we rest surely in the mercy of God which is promised to us through the Gospel. For thus the definition of faith must be taken from the substance of the promise. Faith rests so much on this foundation that, if the latter be taken away, faith would collapse at once, or, rather, vanish away. Hence, when the Lord presents to us his mercy through the promise of the Gospel, if we certainly and without hesitation trust him who made the promise, we are said to apprehend his word through faith. And this definition is not different from that of the apostle (Heb. 11:1) in which he teaches that faith is the certainty of the things to be hoped for and the demonstration of the things not apparent; for he means a sure and secure possession of the things that God promises, and an evidence of the things that are not apparent, that is to say, the life eternal. And this we conceive through confidence in the divine goodness which is offered to us through the Gospel. Now, since all the promises of God are gathered together and confirmed in Christ, and are, so to speak, kept and accomplished in him, it appears without doubt that Christ is the perpetual object of faith. And in that object, faith contemplates all the riches of the divine mercy.

Faith is a Gift of God

If we honestly consider within ourselves how much our thought is blind to the heavenly secrets of God and how greatly our heart distrusts all things, we shall not doubt that faith greatly surpasses all the power of our nature and that faith is a unique and precious gift of God. For, as St. Paul maintains (I Cor. 2:11), if no one can witness the human will, except the spirit of man which is in man, how will man be certain of the divine will? And if the truth of God in us wavers even in things that we see by the eye, how will it be firm and stable where the Lord promises the things that the eye does not see and man's understanding does not comprehend?

Hence there is no doubt that faith is a light of the Holy Spirit through which our understandings are enlightened and our hearts are confirmed in a sure persuasion which is assured that the truth of God is so certain that he can but accomplish that which he has promised through his holy word that he will do. Hence (II Cor. 1:22; Eph. 1:13), the Holy Spirit is called like a guarantee which confirms in our hearts the certainty of the divine truth, and a seal by which our hearts are sealed in the expectation of the day of the Lord. For it is the Spirit indeed who witnesses to our spirit that God is our Father and that similarly we are his children (Rom. 8:16).

We Are Justified in Christ Through Faith

Since it is clear that Christ is the perpetual object of faith, we cannot know what we receive through faith except by looking to him. For truly he has been given to us by the Father in order that we may obtain in him life eternal; as he says (John 17:3), life eternal is to know one God the Father and Jesus Christ whom he has sent. And again (John 11:26), he who comes to believe in me shall never die, and if he has died he shall live. Yet, in order that this might be done, it is necessary that we, who are contaminated by stains of sin, be cleansed in him, because nothing defiled shall enter the kingdom of God. Christ, therefore, makes us thus participants in himself in order that we, who are in ourselves sinners, may be, through Christ's righteousness, considered just before the throne of God. And in this manner being stripped of our own righteousness, we are clothed with the righteousness of Christ; and, being unjust by our own deeds, we are justified through the faith of Christ.

For we are said to be justified through faith, not in the sense, however, that we receive within us any righteousness, but because the righteousness of Christ is credited to us, entirely as if it were really ours, while our iniquity is not charged to us, so that one can truly call this righteousness simply the remission of sins. This the apostle evidently declares when he so often compares the righteousness that some imagine they obtain by means of good deeds with the righteousness that comes to us through faith, and teaches that the latter righteousness destroys the former (Rom. 10:3; Phil. 3:9). Now, we shall see in the Symbol [The Apostles' Creed] in what manner Christ has deserved this righteousness for us and in what this righteousness consists, in which Symbol will indeed be recited in order all the things on which our faith is founded and resting.

We Are Sanctified Through Faith in Order to Obey the Law

Just as Christ by means of his righteousness intercedes for us with the Father in order that (he being as our guarantor) we may be considered as righteous, so by making us participants in his spirit, he sanctifies us unto all purity and innocence. For the spirit of the Lord has reposed on Christ without measure—the spirit (I say) of wisdom, of intelligence, of counsel, of strength, of knowledge and reverential fear of the Lord—in order that we all may draw from his fullness and receive grace through the grace that has been given to Christ. As a result, those who boast of having the faith of Christ and are completely destitute of sanctification by his spirit deceive themselves. For the Scripture teaches that Christ has been made for us not only righteousness but also sanctification. Hence, we cannot receive through faith his righteousness without embracing at the same time that sanctification, because the Lord in one same alliance, which he has made with us in Christ, promises that he will be propitious toward our iniquities and will write his Law in our hearts (Jer. 31:33; Heb. 8:10; 10:16).

Observance of the Law, therefore, is not a work that our power can accomplish, but it is a work of a spiritual power. Through this spiritual power it is brought about that our hearts are cleansed from their corruption and are softened to obey unto righteousness. Now the function of the Law is for Christians quite different from what it may be without faith; for, when and where the Lord has engraved in our hearts the love for his righteousness, the external teaching of the Law (which before was only charging us with weakness and transgression) is now a lamp to guide our feet, to the end that we may not deviate from the right path. It is now our wisdom through which we are formed, instructed, and encouraged to all integrity; it is our discipline which does not suffer us to be dissolute through evil licentiousness.

Repentance and Regeneration

It is now easy from this to understand why repentance is always joined with the faith of Christ, and why the Lord affirms (John 3:3) that no one can enter the kingdom of heaven except he who has been regenerated. For repentance means conversion, turning over to, whereby, having left the perversity of this world, we return to and in the way of the Lord. Now, as Christ is no minister of sin, so, after having purged us from the stains of sin, he does not clothe us with the participation of his righteousness in order that we may afterward profane with new stains so grand a grace, but in order that, being adopted as children of God, we may consecrate our life course and days to come to the glory of our Father.

The effect of this repentance depends upon our regeneration, which has two aspects, that is to say: the mortification of our flesh, that is, a killing of our inborn corruption; and the spiritual vivification through which man's nature is restored to integrity. We must, therefore, meditate during all our life on the fact that, being dead unto sin and unto our former selves, we may live unto Christ and his righteousness. And since this regeneration is never accomplished as long as we are in the prison of this mortal body, it is necessary that the cure of repentance continues until we die.

How the Righteousness through Good Deeds and the Righteousness through Faith Fit and Harmonize Together

There is no doubt that good deeds which proceed from such a purity of conscience—as we have just described—are pleasing to God, for, since he recognizes in us his own righteousness, he can but approve and prize it. Yet, we must very carefully guard ourselves that we be not so carried away by the vain confidence in those good deeds that we forget that we are justified by Christ's faith alone. For before God there is no righteousness through works, except that which may correspond to God's own righteousness. As a result, it is not enough that he (who seeks to be considered just through good works) produces certain good deeds, but it is necessary that he obey the Law perfectly. Now, even those who have progressed above all others in the Law of the Lord are still very far from this perfect obedience demanded by the Law.

Moreover, even supposing that the justice of God would content itself with one good work alone, the Lord would yet not find even one good act in his saints for the merit of which he would praise them as just. For although this may seem astonishing, yet it is very true that no work springs from us that is absolutely perfect and is not infected by some stain. Hence, since we are all sinners and have several residues of sins, it is always necessary that we be justified by something outside of ourselves.

That is to say, we always need Christ, so that his perfection may cover our imperfection, his purity may wash our impurity, his obedience may efface our iniquity; and finally his righteousness may gratuitously credit us with righteousness. And this, without any consideration at all of our acts, which are not of such value as to stand before the judgment of God. But when our stains, which otherwise might before God contaminate our deeds, are thus covered, the Lord no longer observes anything in these acts except an entire purity and holiness. Hence the Lord honors them with grand titles and praises, for, he calls them just, and promises them a very ample remuneration. Finally, we must thus affirm that the company of Jesus has such a value that because of it we are not only received freely as just, but our very deeds are considered just and are recompensed with an eternal reward. . . .

What Hope Is

If Faith (as we have seen) is a sure persuasion of the truth of God which can neither lie nor deceive us and be neither vain nor false, those who have conceived this certainty surely expect likewise that God will accomplish his promises which, according to their conviction, cannot but be true. So that, in sum, Hope is nothing else than the expectation of the things that faith has believed to be truly promised by God. Thus Faith believes God to be truthful: Hope expects that he will show his veracity at the opportune time. Faith believes God to be our Father: Hope expects that he will always act as such toward us. Faith believes the eternal life to be given to us: Hope expects that it shall at some time be revealed. Faith is the foundation on which Hope rests: Hope nourishes and maintains Faith. For, just as no one can expect and hope anything from God, except he who will have first believed his promises, so, on the other hand, it is necessary that our feeble faith (lest it grow weary and fail) be sustained and kept by patient hope and expectation.

Prayer

The man rightly instructed in true faith first of all obviously perceives how indigent and denuded of all goods he is and how much he lacks all help of salvation. Hence, if he seeks some succor to assist him in his poverty, he must go out of himself to seek that succor elsewhere. On the other hand, he contemplates the Lord who liberally and out of his good will offers himself in Jesus Christ and in him opens all the heavenly treasures to the end that the whole faith of that man may stop to look at this beloved Son, all his expectation may depend on him, and all his hope may rest and be fixed in him. Nothing therefore remains but that the man seek unto God and ask him in prayer what he has known to exist in God. Otherwise, to know that God is the Lord and distributor of all goods (who invites us to ask of him what we need), to pray to him and to invoke him profit nothing. This would be as if someone, knowing of a treasure hidden in the ground of the earth, abandoned it there through indifference, being unwilling to take the trouble to unearth it.

What One Must Consider in Prayer

Prayer is similar to a communication between God and us whereby we expound to him our desires, our joys, our sighs, in a word, all the thoughts of our hearts. Hence, each and every time we invoke the Lord, we must diligently strive to descend in the depth of our heart and from there seek him, and not with the throat or the tongue only. For at times the tongue helps in prayer, either in retaining the spirit more attentive in the meditation of God or in occupying this part of our body (which is especially destined to extol the glory of God) along with the heart to meditate the goodness of God. Yet, the Lord declares through his prophet (Isa. 29:13; Matt. 15:8, 9) what prayer avails without the will, when he has pronounced a very heavy punishment on all those who honor him with their lips, while having their hearts far from him. Moreover, if true prayer must be nothing else than a pure affection of our heart when we should thereby approach God, we must dismiss all thought of our own glory, all fancy of our own dignity and all self-confidence. Thus indeed the prophet (Dan. 9:4–19; Baruch 2: 11 ff.) admonishes us to pray, being founded not on our own righteous deeds, but through the great mercies of the Lord, in order that he may answer our prayers out of love for himself, inasmuch as his name is invoked upon us. This knowledge of our misery must not bar our access to God, since prayer has not been instituted in order to raise us arrogantly before God, nor to extol our dignity, but to the end that we confess with sighs our calamities, just as children expound with familiarity their complaints to their fathers. Such a sentiment should rather be like a spur to incite and stimulate us to pray more. Now, there are two things that must marvelously move us to pray. First, the instruction of God by which he commands us to pray. Secondly, the promise whereby he assures us that we shall obtain all that which we will ask. For, those who invoke him, seek him, and depend on him, receive a singular consolation inasmuch as they know that, in doing that, they do a thing pleasing to him. Moreover, being assured of his truth, let them certainly trust that he will answer their prayer. "Ask" (he says: Matt. 7:7) "and it shall be given to you, knock and it will be opened to you; seek and you shall find." And in the psalm (Ps. 50:15): "Call upon me in the day of thy necessity, and I will free thee, and thou wilt glorify me." Here he has comprised or included the two kinds of prayer, which are invocation or request, and thanksgiving. By the former we disclose before God our hearts' desires. By the latter we acknowledge his benefits toward us. We must assiduously use both kinds of prayer, for we are pressed by such poverty and indigence that even the most perfect have sufficient matter to sigh and groan continually, and invoke the Lord with all humility. On the other hand, the liberalities which our Lord by his goodness pours forth upon us are so abundant, and wherever we turn our eyes the miracles of his works appear so great, that we can never lack matter for praise and thanksgiving. . . .

Perseverance in Prayer

Finally we must well observe this: We must not wish to bind God to certain circumstances, because in this very prayer we are taught not to put on him any law, nor to impose upon him any condition. For, before making any prayer for ourselves, before all things, we ask that his will be done; whereby we submit beforehand our will to his, in order that, as if it were caught and retained by a rein, our will may not presume to wish to range and to submit him under our will. If, having the heart formed in this obedience, we permit ourselves to be governed according to the good pleasure of the divine providence, we shall easily learn to persevere in prayer and wait with patience upon the Lord, while deferring the fulfillment of our desires to the hour set by his will; being assured that, although he does not show himself to us, yet he is always present to us and at his own time will reveal that he did not at all have his ears deaf to our prayers, though they seemed to men to be despised by him. And even if at the end, after long waiting, our mind cannot understand the profit of our praying, and our senses feel no fruit thereof, nevertheless our faith will certify unto us what our mind and sense will not be able to perceive, that is, we shall have obtained [from God] all that which was good for us, for he will make us in poverty to possess abundance and in affliction to have consolation. For, even if all things should fail us, yet God will never leave us, inasmuch as he cannot disappoint the expectation and patience of his own. And he alone will be sufficient unto us for all things, inasmuch as he contains in himself all goods, which in the time to come he will fully reveal to us.

The Sacraments

The sacraments are instituted [by God] to this end that they might be exercises of our faith both before God and before men. And certainly before God they exercise our faith when they confirm it in the truth of God. For, the Lord has presented to us the high and heavenly secrets under earthly things, as he knew it to be good for us in the ignorance of our flesh. Not, indeed, that such qualities be inherent in the nature of the things that are offered to us in the sacrament; but because by the word of the Lord they are marked in this significance. For the promise which is contained in the Word always precedes; the sign is added, which sign confirms and seals that promise and renders it unto us as more certified, as the Lord sees that this is adapted to our crude understanding. For our faith is so small and weak that, if it is not upheld from all sides and sustained by all available means, it is immediately shaken on all sides, agitated, and vacillating. Moreover, the sacraments exercise our faith also toward men when faith issues in public acknowledgment and faith is incited to render praises to the Lord.

What the Sacrament Is

The sacrament therefore is an external sign through which the Lord presents and testifies to us his good will toward us in order to sustain us in the weakness of our faith. Or (to speak more briefly and more clearly) the sacrament is a testimony of the grace of God declared by an external sign. The Christian Church uses only two sacraments, which are Baptism and the Lord's Supper.

Baptism

Baptism has been given to us by God, to help, first, our faith in him, and, secondly, our profession of faith before men. Faith looks at the promise through which the merciful Father offers us the communication of his Christ, in order that, being clothed with him, we may be participants in all his goods. Yet baptism represents particularly two things: The first is the purgation which we obtain in the blood of Christ; the second is the mortification of our flesh, which we have had through his death. For the Lord has commanded his own to be baptized in the remission of sins (Matt. 28:19; Acts 2:38). And St. Paul (Eph. 5:26, 27) teaches the Church to be sanctified through her bridegroom, and cleansed through the washing of water unto the word of life. And again (Rom. 6:3–11) St. Paul shows how we are baptized in the death of Christ; that is, we are buried in his death in order that we may walk in newness of life. By these things it is not signified, however, that the water is cause, nor even instrument, of purgation and regeneration, but only that the knowledge of such gifts is received in the sacrament, since we are said to receive, to obtain, and to be appointed to that which we believe to be given by the Lord, be it that then for the first time we know him, or be it that, having known him before, we are more certainly persuaded of it.

Baptism serves likewise as our acknowledgment of faith in the sight of men; because it is a mark by which we publicly declare that we wish to be numbered among the people of God, to the end that we, together with all believers, may serve and honor, with one same religion, one God. Since, therefore, principally through baptism the alliance of the Lord is confirmed with us, we rightly baptize our children, since they are already participants in the eternal covenant through which the Lord promises (Gen. 17:1–14) that he will be God not only of us, but also of our posterity.

The Supper of the Lord

The promise that is added to the mystery of the supper declares clearly to what purpose the supper has been instituted, and whither it tends. That is to say, it confirms to us that the body of the Lord has once for all been given in such a way for us, that it is now ours and will be ours perpetually. It confirms that his blood has once been shed in such a way for us that it [is and] will be always ours. The signs are the bread and the wine, under which the Lord presents to us the true yet spiritual communication of his body and his blood. This communication is content with the bond of his spirit, and does not require at all a presence of the flesh enclosed under the bread, or of the blood under the wine. For, although Christ, being elevated to heaven, has left his abode on earth in which we are still pilgrims, yet no distance can dissolve his power of nourishing his own with himself. He gives us in the supper an instruction concerning this matter so certain and manifest that without any doubt we must be assured that Christ with all his riches is there presented to us, not less than if he could be put in the presence of our eyes and be touched by our hands; and even he is present with so great a power and efficacy that he not only brings there to our spirits assured confidence of eternal life, but also renders us certain of the immortality of our flesh. For our flesh is already vivified by Christ's immortal flesh, and communicates in some way with his immortality.

Hence, under the bread and wine, the body and blood are presented, to the end that we may learn not only that they are ours, but that they are for us life and nourishment. So, when we see the bread set apart as the body of Christ, at once we must think of this simile: Just as the bread nourishes, sustains, and preserves the life of our body, so the body of Christ is the food and preservation of our spiritual life. And when the wine is presented to us as a sign of the blood, we must likewise think that such fruits as he brings to the body we receive spiritually from the blood of Christ.

Now, as this mystery is a teaching of God's liberality which is so great toward us, it must also admonish us not to be ungrateful toward such a generous kindliness, but rather to extol it with fitting praises and to celebrate it with thanksgiving. Moreover, it exhorts us to embrace each other mutually by such a unity as that which binds among themselves and conjoins together the members of one same body. For no harsher or more pricking spur could be given to move and to incite among us a mutual charity than when Christ, giving himself to us, invites us not only by his example to give ourselves and to expose ourselves mutually one for the other, but inasmuch as he makes himself common to all, he makes us also all one in himself.

The Pastors of the Church and Their Power

Since the Lord has willed that both his word and his sacraments be dispensed through the ministry of men, it is necessary that there be pastors ordained to the churches, pastors who teach the people both in public and in private the pure doctrine, administer the sacraments, and by their good example instruct and form all to holiness and purity of life. Those who despise this discipline and this order do injury not only to men, but to God, and even, as heretics, withdraw from the society of the Church, which in no way can stand together without such a ministry. For what the Lord has once (Matt. 10:40) testified is of no little importance: It is that when the pastors whom he sends are welcomed, he himself is welcomed, and likewise he is rejected when they are rejected. And in order that their ministry be not contemptible, pastors are furnished with a notable mandate: to bind and to loose, having the added promise that whatever things they shall have bound or loosed on earth, are bound or loosed in heaven (Matt. 16:19). And Christ himself in another passage (John 20:23) explains that to bind means to retain sins, and to loose means to remit them. Now, the apostle declares what is the mode of loosing when (Rom. 1:16) he teaches the Gospel to be the power of God unto salvation for each believer. And he tells also the way of binding when he declares (II Cor. 10:4–6) the apostles to have retribution ready against any disobedience. For, the sum of the Gospel is that we are slaves of sin and death, and that we are loosed and freed by the redemption which is in Christ Jesus, while those who do not receive him as redeemer are bound as by new bonds of a graver condemnation.

But let us remember that this power (which in the Scripture is attributed to pastors) is wholly contained in and limited to the ministry of the word. For Christ has not given this power properly to these men but to his word, of which he has made these men ministers. Hence, let pastors boldly dare all things by the word of God, of which they have been constituted dispensators; let them constrain all the power, glory, and haughtiness of the world to make room for and to obey the majesty of that word; let them by means of that word command all from the greatest to the smallest; let them edify the house of Christ; let them demolish the reign of Satan; let them feed the sheep, kill the wolves, instruct and exhort the docile; let them rebuke, reprove, reproach, and convince the rebel—but all through and within the word of God. But if pastors turn away from the word to their dreams and to the inventions of their own minds, already they are no longer to be received as pastors, but being seen to be rather pernicious wolves, they are to be chased away. For Christ has commanded us to listen only to those who teach us that which they have taken from his word.

Human Traditions

As we have thus a general thought of St. Paul (that is, that all things in the churches must be done decently and in order) we must not count as human traditions the civic observances by which (as by some bonds of unity) order and honesty stand, and peace and concord are retained in the assemblies of Christians. But rather these observances must be referred to that rule of the apostle, provided that they be not thought necessary for salvation, nor binding consciences through religion, nor related to the service of God, and no piety whatever be put in them. But it is necessary greatly and manfully to resist those rules which, as if they were necessary to serve and to honor God, are made under the name of spiritual laws for binding the consciences, for they not only destroy the liberty which Christ has secured for us, but they obscure also the true religion and they violate the majesty of God, who wishes to reign alone in our consciences through and by means of his word. May this then remain firm and definite: All things are ours provided we belong to Christ (I Cor. 3:21–23); and God is served in vain where are taught doctrines which are merely commandments of men (Matt. 15:1–20).

Excommunication

Excommunication is the act whereby those who are manifestly fornicators, adulterers, thieves, homicides, misers, robbers, iniquitous, pernicious, voracious, drunkards, seditious, and prodigal (if they do not amend themselves after having been admonished) are, according to God's commandments, rejected from the company of believers. The Church does not thereby cast them into perpetual ruin and despair. She simply condemns their ways of life and their manners, and, if they do not correct themselves, she makes them already certain of their condemnation. Now, this discipline is necessary among believers because, as the Church is the body of Christ, she must not be polluted and contaminated by such stinking and rotten members who dishonor the head; moreover, in order that the saints be not (as it is usual to happen) corrupted and spoiled by the company of the bad. This discipline is profitable also to the latter themselves that their malice be thereby thus chastised; while tolerance would render them more obstinate, this disciplinary provision confuses them with shame and teaches them to amend themselves. When this result is obtained, the Church with kindliness will receive them again in her communion and in the participation of that union from which they had been excluded. Now, in order that no one despise obstinately the judgment of the Church, or think it to be of little account to have been condemned by the sentence of believers, the Lord testifies that such judgment of the faithful is nothing else than the pronouncement of his sentence, and that what they shall have done on earth is ratified in heaven (Matt. 18:15–18). For they have the word of God, by which they can condemn the perverse, and they have the word by which they can receive in grace those who amend themselves.

The Magistrate or Civic Officer

The Lord has not only testified that the status of magistrate or civic officer was approved by him and was pleasing to him, but also he has moreover greatly recommended it to us, having honored its dignity with very honorable titles. For the Lord affirms (Prov. 8:15–16) that the fact that kings rule, that counselors order just things, and that the great of the earth are judges, is a work of his wisdom. And elsewhere (Ps. 82:6–7), he calls them gods, because they do his work. In another place also (Deut. 1:17; II Chron. 19:5–7) they are said to exercise judgment for God, and not for man. And Saint Paul (Rom. 12:8) calls the higher offices gifts of God. But (Rom. 13:1–7) where he undertakes a greater discussion of the matter, he teaches very clearly that their power is ordered by God, and that they are ministers of God for praising those who do good and for accomplishing the retribution of God's wrath on the bad. Hence princes and magistrates must think of Him whom they serve in their office, and do nothing unworthy of ministers and lieutenants of God. All their solicitude must be in this: to keep in true purity the public form of religion, to establish and to guide the life of the people by very good laws, and to procure the welfare and the tranquillity of their subjects, both in public and in private. But this cannot be obtained except through justice and judgment, which two things are to them particularly recommended by the prophet (Jer. 22:1–9). Justice is to safeguard the innocent, to maintain, to keep and to free them; judgment is to resist the audacity of evil men, to repress violence and to punish misdeeds.

On the other hand, the mutual duty of subjects and citizens is not only to honor and to revere their superiors, but to recommend by prayers to the Lord their salvation and prosperity, to submit willingly to their rule, to obey their laws and constitutions, and not to refuse the charges imposed by them: be they taxes, tolls, tributes, and other contributions, or be they offices, civic commissions, and all the like. So that we must not only render ourselves obedient to superiors who rightly and dutifully administer their higher office, but also it is fit to endure those who tyrannically abuse their power, until, through legitimate order, we be freed from their yoke. For, just as a good prince is a testimony of the divine beneficence for maintaining the salvation of men, so a bad and evil prince is a plague of God for chastising the sins of the people. Yet, let this generally be held as certain that to both the power is given by God, and we cannot resist them without our resisting the ordinance of God.

But from obedience to superiors we must always except one thing: that it does not draw us away from obedience to Him to whose edicts the commandments of all kings must yield. The Lord, therefore, is the king of kings, and, once he has opened his sacred mouth, he must be listened to by all and above all. Only after that, we are subject to men who are constituted over us, but not otherwise than in him. If men command us to do something against him, we must do nothing, nor keep any account of such an order. On the contrary, let rather this sentence take place: that it is necessary to obey God rather than men (Acts 4:19).

From the Commentary on Genesis 22*

Genesis 22:2. And he said, Take now thy son, thine only son Isaac, whom thou lovest, and get thee into the land of Moriah; and offer him there for a burnt-offering upon one of the mountains which I will tell thee of.

11. And the angel of the Lord called unto him out of heaven, and said, Abraham, Abraham: and he said, Here am I.

12. And he said, Lay not thine hand upon the lad, neither do thou any thing unto him: for now I know that thou fearest God, seeing thou has not withheld thy son, thine only son, from me.

2. *Take now thy son.* Abraham is commanded to immolate his son. If God had said nothing more than that his son should die, even this message would have most grievously wounded his mind because, whatever favour he could hope for from God, was included in this single promise, "In Isaac shall thy seed be called." Whence he necessarily inferred that his own salvation, and that of the whole human race, would perish unless Isaac remained in safety. For he was taught, by that word, that God would not be propitious to man without a Mediator. For although the declaration of Paul that "all the promises of God in Christ are yea and Amen" (2 Cor. i. 20), was not yet written, it was nevertheless engraven on the heart of Abraham. Whence, however, could he have had this hope but from Isaac? The matter had come to this: That God would appear to have done nothing but mock him. Yet not only is the death of his son announced to him, but he is commanded with his own hand to slay him; as if he were required, not only to throw aside, but to cut in pieces, or cast into the fire, the charter of his salvation and to have nothing left for himself but death and hell. But it may be asked, how under the guidance of faith, he could be brought to sacrifice his son, seeing that what was proposed to him was in opposition to that word of God on which it is necessary for faith to rely? To this question the Apostle answers that his confidence in the word of God remained unshaken because he hoped that God would be able to cause the promised benediction to spring up, even out of the dead ashes of his son (Heb. xi. 19). His mind, however, must of necessity have been severely crushed and violently agitated when the command and the promise of God were conflicting within him. But when he had come to the conclusion that the God with whom he knew he had to do, could not be his adversary, although he did not immediately discover how the contradiction might be removed, he nevertheless,

* From *Calvin's Commentaries,* Vol. I. Edinburgh: The Calvin Translation Society, 1844, pages 557 f., 563–565, and 569 f.

by hope, reconciled the command with the promise; because, being indubitably persuaded that God was faithful, he left the unknown issue to Divine Providence. Meanwhile, as with closed eyes, he goes whither he is directed. The truth of God deserves this honour; not only that it should far transcend all human means, or that it alone, even without means, should suffice us, but also that it should surmount all obstacles. Here, then, we perceive more clearly the nature of the temptation which Moses has pointed out. It was difficult and painful to Abraham to forget that he was a father and a husband, to cast off all human affections, and to endure before the world the disgrace of shameful cruelty by becoming the executioner of his son. But the other was a far more severe and horrible thing; namely, that he conceives God to contradict Himself and His own word; and then, that he supposes the hope of the promised blessing to be cut off from him when Isaac is torn away from his embrace. For what more could he have to do with God when the only pledge of grace is taken away? But as before, when he expected seed from his own dead body, he, by hope, rose above what it seemed possible to hope for; so now when, in the death of his son, he apprehends the quickening power of God in such a manner as to promise himself a blessing out of the ashes of his son, he emerges from the labyrinth of temptation; for, in order that he might obey God, it was necessary that he should tenaciously hold the promise which, had it failed, faith must have perished. But with him the promise always flourished because he both firmly retained the love with which God had once embraced him and subjected to the power of God everything which Satan raised up to disturb his mind. But he was unwilling to measure by his own understanding the method of fulfilling the promise which he knew depended on the incomprehensible power of God. It remains for every one of us to apply this example to himself. The Lord, indeed, is so indulgent to our infirmity that he does not thus severely and sharply try our faith; yet he intended, in the father of all the faithful, to propose an example by which he might call us to a general trial of faith. For the faith, which is more precious than gold and silver, ought not to lie idle, without trial; and experience teaches that each will be tried by God according to the measure of his faith. At the same time, also, we may observe that God tempts his servants, not only when he subdues the affections of the flesh, but when he reduces all their senses to nothing, that he may lead them to a complete renunciation of themselves.

Thine only son Isaac, whom thou lovest. As if it were not enough to command in one word the sacrifice of his son, he pierces, as with fresh strokes, the mind of the holy man. By calling him his only son, he again irritates the wound recently inflicted by the banishment of the other son; he then looks forward into futurity because no hope of offspring would remain. If the death of a first-born son is wont to be grievous, what must the mourning of Abraham be? Each word which follows is emphatical, and serves to aggravate his grief. "Slay," he says, "him whom alone thou lovest." And he does not here refer merely to his paternal love, but to that which sprung from faith. Abraham loved his son, not only as nature dictates and as parents commonly do who take delight in their children, but as beholding the paternal love of God in him. Lastly, Isaac was the mirror of eternal life, and the pledge of all good things. Wherefore God seems not so much to assail the paternal love of Abraham as to trample upon His own benevolence. There is equal emphasis in the name Isaac, by which Abraham was taught that nowhere besides did any joy remain for him. Certainly, when he who had been given as the occasion of joy was taken away, it was just as if God should condemn Abraham to eternal torment. We must always remember that Isaac was not a son of the common order, but one in whose person the Mediator was promised. . . .

11. *And the angel of the Lord called unto him.* The inward temptation had been already overcome when Abraham intrepidly raised his hand to slay his son; and it was by the special grace of God that he obtained so signal a victory. But now Moses subjoins that suddenly, beyond all hope, his sorrow was changed into joy. Poets in their fables when affairs are desperate, introduce some god who unexpectedly appears at the critical juncture. It is possible that Satan by figments of this kind has endeavoured to obscure the wonderful and stupendous interpositions of God when he has unexpectedly appeared for the purpose of bring-

ing assistance to his servants. This history ought certainly to be known and celebrated among all people; yet, by the subtlety of Satan, not only has the truth of God been adulterated and turned into a lie, but also distorted into materials for fable, in order to render it the more ridiculous. But it is our business, with earnest minds to consider how wonderfully God, in the very article of death, both recalled Isaac from death to life and restored to Abraham his son, as one who had risen from the tomb. Moses also describes the voice of the angel, as having sounded out of heaven, to give assurance to Abraham that he had come from God in order that he might withdraw his hand under the direction of the same faith by which he had stretched it out. For, in a cause of such magnitude, it was not lawful for him either to undertake or to relinquish anything, except under the authority of God. Let us, therefore, learn from his example by no means to pursue what our carnal sense may declare to be, probably, our right course, but let God by his sole will prescribe to us our manner of acting and of ceasing to act. And truly Abraham does not charge God with inconstancy because he considers that there had been just cause for the exercising of his faith.

12. *Now I know that thou fearest God.* The exposition of Augustine, "I have caused thee to know," is forced. But how can anything become known to God, to whom all things have always been present? Truly, by condescending to the manner of men, God here says that what he has proved by experiment is now made known to himself. And he speaks thus with us, not according to his own infinite wisdom, but according to our infirmity. Moses, however, simply means that Abraham by this very act testified how reverently he feared God. It is however asked whether he had not already on former occasions given many proofs of his piety? I answer that when God had willed him to proceed thus far, he had, at length, completed his true trial; in other persons a much lighter trial might have been sufficient. And as Abraham showed that he feared God by not sparing his own and only begotten son, so a common testimony of the same fear is required from all the pious, in acts of self-denial. Now, since God enjoins upon us a continual warfare, we must take care that none desires his release before the time.

MENNO SIMONS (1496–1561)

The son of a Dutch peasant family, Menno Simons had been ordained to the Catholic priesthood in 1524. Trying to dispel growing doubts concerning the Catholic dogma of transubstantiation and the practice of infant baptism, he turned, under the influence of Luther, to a diligent study of the Bible which subsequently he acknowledged to be the sole authority of the Christian Church. In the course of a long personal struggle he developed his Anabaptist views. He broke publicly with the Catholic Church in 1535 when the disastrous attempt of religious fanatics to establish the kingdom of God at Muenster had brought renewed persecution to the Anabaptists and leadership was sorely needed. He was baptized and ordained a bishop, and in the following years through his courage, untiring labors, and literary fecundity he succeeded in gathering and strengthening the scattered remnants of the Anabaptist movement in Northern Germany and Holland. For this reason the Mennonite Church rightfully bears his name, although it was not founded by him.

The selections which are included here can be considered fairly representative of Anabaptist views. They make clear that Menno Simons, like all the Protestant reformers, rallied his following around a Biblical standard of faith and life. Yet from the Scriptures he derived the distinctive tenets of Anabaptism which were rejected not only by the Roman Catholic Church but by Luther and Calvin as well.

From the Writings of Menno Simons*

[*The Authority of the Scriptures*]

You see, dear reader, I admonish and advise you if you seek God with all your heart, and do not want to be deceived, do not depend upon men and the doctrine of men no matter how venerable, holy, and excellent they may be esteemed. For the experts, ancient as well as modern, are opposed to each other. Put your trust in Christ alone and in His Word, and in the sure instruction and practice of His holy apostles, and by the grace of God you will be safe from all false doctrine and the power of the devil, and will walk with a free and pious mind before God. . . .

For this holy, Christian church has but one doctrine which is fruitful and godly, which is the limpid, pure, and unmixed word of God, the lovely Gospel of the grace of our beloved Lord Jesus Christ. All teachings and decrees which do not accord with the doctrine of Christ are but teachings and commandments of men, be they teachings and opinions of doctors, decrees of popes, councils, or anything else. They are doctrines of man (Matt. 15:9); of the devil (I Tim. 4:11); and anathema (Gal. 1:8). Since we write and teach nothing but the pure, heavenly Word, and the perfect ordinances of the holy Gospel of Jesus Christ and of His apostles, therefore we do not teach and write against the teachings of the holy church, but in favor of them. . . .

Once more, I have no visions nor angelic inspirations. Neither do I desire such lest I be deceived. The Word of Christ alone is sufficient for me. If I do not follow His testimony, then verily all that I do is useless, and even if I had such visions and inspirations, which is not the case, even then it would have to be comformable to the Word and Spirit of Christ, or else it would be mere imagination, deceit, and satanic temptation. . . .

[*The Church*]

Ah, no, the church of Christ is God's elect, His saints and beloved, who have washed their clothes in the blood of the Lamb; who are born of God and driven by the Spirit of Christ; who are in Christ and He in them; who hear and believe His Word; who in their weakness obey His commandments, follow in His footsteps with all patience and humility; who hate evil and love the good; who earnestly desire to apprehend Christ as they are apprehended of Him. For all who are in Christ are new creatures, flesh of His flesh, bone of His bone, and members of His body. . . .

Some of the other parables, as of the net with the good and bad fishes, of the wise and foolish virgins and their lamps, of the royal wedding and of the guests, and of the threshing floor with the wheat and chaff, although the Lord spoke them in allusion to the church, yet they were not spoken for the purpose that the church should knowingly and willingly accept and suffer open transgressors, drunkards, carousers, seducers, avaricious, robbers, gamblers, and usurers in their communion; because then Christ and Paul would differ in doctrine; for Paul says that we should avoid and shun such. But they were spoken because many run along with the Christians in sham, and place themselves under the Word and sacraments, people who in fact are no Christians but hypocrites and make-believers before their God. And these are likened unto the bad fish, unto the foolish virgins who had no oil in their lamps, unto the guest without a wedding garment, and unto the chaff which will be cast out by the angels at the day of Christ. For they pretend that they fear God and seek Christ; they receive baptism and the Lord's Supper and put on an external sham; but faith, repentance, true fear, and love of God, Spirit, power, fruit, and work are not found in them. . . .

In the fourth place, some of them charge that we have our property in common. Answer. This charge is false and without truth. We do not teach and practice community of goods. But we teach and maintain by the Word of the Lord

* From *The Complete Writings of Menno Simons,* tr. by Leonard Verduin and ed. by John Christian Wenger. Scottsdale, Pa.: Herald Press, 1956. Pages 138, 234f, 310, 402, 750f, 558, 962, 453f, 264f, 244, 126, 259, 137, 264, 241f, 135, 241, 44, 777, 198, 922, 924, 521, 605, 779, 550, 599f, 385, 348, and 177 are used by permission of the publisher.

that all truly believing Christians are members of one body and are baptized by one Spirit into one body (I Cor. 12:13); they are partakers of one bread (I Cor. 10:18); they have one Lord and one God (Eph. 4:5, 6).

Inasmuch as then they are one, therefore it is Christian and reasonable that they piously love one another, and that the one member be solicitous for the welfare of the other, for this both the Scripture and nature teach. The whole Scripture speaks of mercifulness and love, and it is the only sign whereby a true Christian may be known. As the Lord says, By this shall all men know that ye are my disciples (that is, that ye are Christians), if ye love one another. (John 13:35).

Beloved reader, it is not customary that an intelligent person clothes and cares for one part of his body and leaves the rest destitute and naked. Oh, no. The intelligent person is solicitous for all his members. Thus it should be with those who are the Lord's church and body. All those who are born of God, who are gifted with the Spirit of the Lord, who are, according to the Scriptures, called into one body and love in Christ Jesus, are prepared by such love to serve their neighbors, not only with money and goods, but also after the example of their Lord and Head, Jesus Christ, in an evangelical manner, with life and blood. They show mercy and love, as much as they can. No one among them is allowed to beg. They take to heart the need of the saints. They entertain those in distress. They take the stranger into their houses. They comfort the afflicted; assist the needy; clothe the naked; feed the hungry; do not turn their face from the poor; do not despise their own flesh (Isa. 58:7, 8) . . .

It is evident that the congregation or church cannot continue in the saving doctrine, in an unblamable and pious life, without the proper use of excommunication. For as a city without walls and gates, or a field without trenches and fences, and a house without walls and doors, so is also a church which has not the true apostolic exclusion or ban. For it stands wide open to every seductive spirit, to all abominations and for proud despisers, to all idolatrous and willfully wicked sinners, yes, to all lewd, unchaste wretches, sodomites, harlots, and knaves, as may be seen in all the large sects of the world (which however pose improperly as the church of Christ). Why talk at length? According to my opinion, it is the distinguished usage, honor, and prosperity of a sincere church if it with Christian discretion teaches the true apostolic separation, and observes it carefuly in solicitous love, according to the ordinance of the holy, sacred Scriptures. . . .

[*Baptism*]

This, in brief, is my position and conviction concerning that which takes place in the Christian church; namely, that before God neither baptism, nor Supper, nor any other outward ordinances avail, if partaken of without Spirit and the new creation. But before God, only faith, love, Spirit, and the new creation or regeneration avail, as Paul plainly shows. (Gal. 5:6.) All those who by the grace of God receive these from above, have themselves baptized according to the commandment of the Lord, and rightly partake of His Supper. Yes, with ardent desire these commit themselves to the ordinance and doctrine of Jesus Christ, and shall nevermore willfully oppose the holy will and plain testimony of God. . . .

For we are not regenerated because we are baptized, . . . but we are baptized because we are regenerated by faith in God's Word. For regeneration is not the result of baptism, but baptism the result of regeneration. This may not be controverted by any man on the basis of Scriptures. . . .

If we ascribe the remission of sins to baptism and not to the blood of Christ, then we mold a golden calf and place it in the stead of Christ. For if we could be washed or cleansed by baptism, then Christ Jesus and His merits would have to abdicate, unless we are prepared to admit that there are two means for the remission of sins, first baptism; and second, the blood of Christ. This can never be. For the most holy and precious blood of our beloved Lord Jesus Christ must and shall have the praise, as has been so clearly declared and testified by all the true prophets and apostles, throughout the Scriptures.

Those who believe receive remission of sins, not through baptism but in baptism, and in this manner. Since they now sincerely believe the blessed Gospel of Jesus Christ which has been preached and taught to them, the glad tidings of grace; namely, of the remission of sin, of grace, of peace, of favor, of mercy, and of eternal life through Jesus Christ our Lord; so they become a new mind, deny themselves, bitterly lament their old corrupted life, and look diligently to the Word of God, who has shown them such great love, to fulfill all that which He has taught and commanded them in His holy Gospel; trusting firmly in the word of grace, in the remission of their sins through the crimson blood and through the merits of our beloved Lord Jesus Christ. They therefore receive the holy baptism as a token of obedience which proceeds from faith, as proof before God and His church that they firmly believe in the remission of their sins through Jesus Christ as it was preached and taught them from the Word of God. . . .

Since we have not a single command in the Scriptures that infants are to be baptized, or that the apostles practiced it, therefore we confess with good sense that infant baptism is nothing but human invention and notion, a perversion of the ordinances of Christ, a manifold abomination standing in the holy place where it ought not to stand. . . .

For they baptize before the thing which is represented by baptism, namely, faith, is found in us. This is as logical as to place the cart before the horse, to sow before we have plowed, to build before we have the lumber at hand, or to seal a letter before it is written. Tell me, would not this be ridiculed by all the world as foolishness? Yes, certainly. . . .

In the last place, they appeal to Origen and Augustine and say that these assert that they have received infant baptism from the apostles. To this we answer asking, Have Origen and Augustine proved this from the Scriptures? If they have, we would like to hear it, and if not, then we must hear and believe Christ and His apostles, not Augustine and Origen. . . .

I repeat, if the advocates of infant baptism assert that . . . infant baptism is not forbidden, and that therefore it is right, then I say it is not expressly forbidden in the holy Scriptures to bless (as they call it) holy water, candles, palms, goblets, and robes; to read mass and other ceremonies. Yet we say decidedly that it is wrong. First, because men put their trust in it. Secondly, because it is done without the ordinance of God, for He has not commanded us a word of all this; and there is no ordinance, is there, in which His holy, blessed Word is not expressed and implied either in spirit or letter. . . .

I know there are a great many who will ask why I, an unlearned man, am not satisfied in regard to this matter with the doctrine of Martin Luther and other renowned doctors, who are versed in the Scriptures and many languages and sciences, who teach, and particularly Luther, that faith lies dormant in a sleeping believer. To this I answer: In the first place, if there were such dormant faith in little children (which, however, is nothing but an invention), then it would not be proper to baptize such children, so long as they would not confess this fruit with their mouth, and show it in their fruits and their deeds. For the holy apostles did not baptize any believers while they were asleep, as we have shown in our former writings. . . .

And although infants have neither faith nor baptism, think not that they are therefore damned. Oh, no! they are saved; for they have the Lord's own promise of the kingdom of God; not through any elements, ceremonies, and external rites, but solely by grace through Christ Jesus. And therefore we do truly believe that they are in a state of grace, pleasing to God, pure, holy, heirs of God and of eternal life. Yes, on account of this promise all sincere Christian believers may assuredly rejoice and comfort themselves in the salvation of their children. . . .

If they die before coming to years of discretion, that is, in childhood, before they have come to years of understanding and before they have faith, then they die under the promise of God, and that by no other means than the generous promise of grace given through Christ Jesus. (Luke 18:16.) And if they come to years of discretion and have faith, then they should be baptized. But if they do not accept or believe the Word when they shall have arrived at the years of discretion, no matter whether they are baptized or not, they will be damned, as Christ Himself teaches. (Mark 16:16.) . . .

[*Nonresistance*]

If Christ fights His enemies with the sword of His mouth, if He smites the earth with the rod of His mouth, and slays the wicked with the breath of His lips; and if we are to be conformed unto His image, how can we, then, oppose our enemies with any other sword? Does not the Apostle Peter say: For even hereto were ye called, because Christ also suffered for us, leaving us an example, that ye should follow his steps, who did no sin, neither was guile found in his mouth: who, when he was reviled, reviled not again; when he suffered he threatened not; but committed himself to him that judgeth righteously [I Pet. 2:21–23; Matt. 16:24]? This agrees with the words of John who says: He that abides in Christ walks as Christ walked [I John 2:6]. Christ Himself says, Whosoever will come after me, let him deny himself, and take up his cross and follow me [Mark 8:34; Luke 9:23]. Again, My sheep hear my voice and follow me [John 10:27]. And this is the voice of Christ: Ye have heard that it hath been said, An eye for an eye, and a tooth for a tooth: but I say unto you, that ye resist not evil: but whosoever shall smite thee on thy right cheek, turn to him the other also [Matt. 5: 38f]. . . .

O reader, beloved reader, if only the poor, ignorant world would sincerely accept this, our hated and despised doctrine, which is not ours but Christ's, and would faithfully obey it, then they might change their deadly swords into plowshares and their spears into pruning hooks; they would level their gates and walls, and dismiss their executioners and hangmen. For all those who accept our doctrine in its power by the grace of God, will not wish evil to anyone upon earth, not even to their most bitter enemies, much less do evil or harm. For they are the children of the most High, who sincerely love all that is good, and in their weakness avoid that which is evil, yes, hate it and loathe it. . . .

Once more, Christ is our fortress; patience our weapon of defense; the Word of God our sword; and our victory a courageous, firm unfeigned faith in Jesus Christ. And iron and metal spears and swords we leave to those who, alas, regard human blood and swine's blood about alike. He that is wise let him judge what I mean. . . .

[*The Swearing of Oaths*]

Christ says, Ye have heard that it hath been said by them of old time, Thou shalt not forswear thyself, but shalt perform unto the Lord thine oaths; but I say unto you, Swear not at all; neither by heaven, for it is God's throne: nor by the earth; for it is his footstool. Matt. 5:33–35. . . .

Tell me, who is wronged because we for conscience' sake (the mouth of the Lord having forbidden it) do not dare to take an oath when we testify the genuine truth when this is called for and do it without guile? The oath serves no other purpose than to make men testify truly. Can the truth not be told without oaths? Do all testify to the truth even when under oath? To the first question you must say yes, and to the last no. Is the oath the truth itself to which one testifies, or does the truth depend upon the man who takes the oath? Why does not the magistracy then accept the testimony confirmed by yea and nay as commanded of God instead of that confirmed by that which is forbidden? For it can punish those who are found false in their yea and nay as well as those who swear falsely. . . .

That yea is Amen with all true Christians is sufficiently shown by those who in our Netherlands are so tyrannically visited with imprisonment, confiscation, and torture; with fire, the stake, and the sword; while with one word they could escape all these if they would but break their yea and nay. But since they are born of the truth, therefore they walk in the truth, and testify to the truth unto death, as may be abundantly seen in Flanders, Brabant, Holland, West Friesland, etc. . . .

[*Religious Toleration*]

Faith, says Paul, is not every man's possession, but it is a gift of God. Now, if it is a gift it may not be thrust upon a man by external force or by the sword; it must put in its appearance only through the pure doctrine of the holy Word and with a humble fervent prayer in God's grace through the Holy Spirit. Moreover, it is not the will of the husbandman that the tares should be rooted up as long as the time of harvest has not yet come, as the evangelical parable shows in great clarity. Now if our persecutors were Christians, as they think, and if they considered the Word of the Lord to be true, why then do they not hear and follow the Word and commandment of Christ? Why do they pluck out before the time? Why are they not afraid lest they pluck up the good wheat and not the tares? Why do they invade the province of the angels, who then will bind the tares in bundles and cast them into the furnace of everlasting fire? . . .

I would say further, If the magistracy rightly understood Christ and His kingdom, they would in my opinion rather choose death than to meddle with their worldly power and sword in spiritual matters which are reserved not to the judgment of man but to the judgment of the great and Almighty God alone. But they are taught by those who have the care of their souls that they may proscribe, imprison, torture, and slay those who are not obedient to their doctrine, as may, alas, be seen in many different cities and countries. . . .

Behold, beloved rulers and judges, if you take to heart these Scriptures and diligently ponder them, then you will observe, first, that your office is not your own but God's, so that you may bend your knees before His majesty; fear His great and adorable name, and rightly and reasonably execute your ordained office. Then you will not so freely with your perishable earthly power invade and transgress against Christ, the Lord of lords in His kingdom, power, and jurisdiction, and with your iron sword adjudicate in that which belongs exclusively to the eternal judgment of the Most High God, such as in faith and matters pertaining to faith. In the same vein Luther and others wrote in the beginning, but after they came to greater and higher estate they forgot it all. . . .

[*Suffering for Christ's Sake*]

For how many pious children of God have we not seen during the space of a few years deprived of their homes and possessions for the testimony of God and their conscience; their poverty and sustenance written off to the emperor's insatisable coffers. How many have they betrayed, driven out of city and country, put to the stocks and torture? How many poor orphans and children have they turned out without a farthing? Some have they hanged, some have they punished with inhuman tyranny and afterward garroted them with cords, tied to a post. Some they have roasted and burned alive. Some, holding their own entrails in their hands, have powerfully confessed the Word of God still. Some they beheaded and gave as food to the fowls of the air. Some have they consigned to the fish. They have torn down the houses of some. Some have they thrust into muddy bogs. They have cut off the feet of some, one of whom I have seen and spoken to. Others wander aimlessly hither and yon in want, misery, and discomfort, in the mountains, in deserts, holes, and clefts of the earth, as Paul says. They must take to their heels and flee away with their wives and little children, from one country to another, from one city to another—hated by all men, abused, slandered, mocked, defamed, trampled upon, styled "heretics." Their names are read from pulpits and town halls; they are kept from their livelihood, driven out into the cold winter, bereft of bread, pointed at with fingers. Yes, whoever can wrong a poor oppressed Christian thinks he has done God a service thereby, even as Christ says. . . .

If a thief is led to the gallows or a murderer is broken upon the wheel, or if a malefactor is punished with death, everyone inquires what he has done. He is not condemned by the judges as long as they have not grasped fully the basis and truth concerning his evil deed. But if an innocent, contrite Christian, whom the merciful Lord has rescued from the evil, ungodly ways of sin, and has placed in the way of peace, is accused by the priests and preachers, and placed before their court, they consider it not worth their time to investigate what reasons or Scriptures move him so that he refuses to hear his priests and preachers, to have his children baptized, to attend their services, to no longer eat and drink to excess with them, and to serve the devil. Nor do they care to know why he reformed his life and received the baptism of Christ, or what drives him so willingly to suffer, or even to die, for his faith. They only ask, Is he baptized? If he answers in the affirmative the sentence is already pronounced that he must die. . . .

If we honor Him, thank Him, serve Him, and walk in His commandments, possessing our souls in patience, no matter how lamentably we are persecuted, oppressed, smitten, robbed, and murdered by the hellish Pharaoh and his fierce, unmerciful servants, burned at the stake or drowned in the water, yet shall the day of our release arrive, and all our tears shall be wiped from our eyes. We shall be gorgeously arrayed in the white silken robes of righteousness and follow the Lamb and sit down in the kingdom of God with Abraham, Isaac, and Jacob, possessing that noble and pleasant land of endless eternal joy. Praise God, ye who suffer for Christ's sake, and lift up your heads, for the time is near when ye shall hear, Come, ye blessed, and ye shall rejoice with Him forever. . . .

For we prefer to endure misery, poverty, tribulation, hunger, thirst, heat, cold, bonds, and death, in our mortal bodies, and continue in the Word of the Lord, rather than to lead secure, easy lives with the world, and for the sake of a short, transitory life ruin our souls. . . .

RICHARD HOOKER (1553?–1600)

The Reformation in England did not produce any outstanding theologian who was comparable in stature and influence to Luther and Calvin. Yet when the Church of England emerged from the Elizabethan settlement of 1559–63 and was confronted by the challenge of Roman Catholicism and the Puritan movement, it found at the right time an able spokesman in Richard Hooker. Hooker had been trained at Corpus Christi College at Oxford, and was later appointed to the mastership of the Temple. There he preached the morning sermon, followed every evening in the same church by a Presbyterian preacher. This and other contemporary events probably made it clear to him that a major literary effort was needed to defend and explain the distinctive features of the Anglican communion. In 1591 Hooker was transferred to a country parish where he wrote his great work *Of the Laws of Ecclesiastical Polity,* which is generally considered the ablest defence of the Anglican position.

The following selections barely touch the rich content of this remarkable work. They deal with several of those issues which were hotly contested between Anglicans and Puritans. In these selections Hooker defends the Anglican understanding of the order of the Church, the office of bishop, and the practice of common prayer which the Puritans in particular were wont to decry as "Popish" and un-Scriptural.

Of the Laws of Ecclesiastical Polity*

Concerning rites and ceremonies there may be fault, either in the kind or in the number and multitude of them. The first thing blamed about the kind of ours is, that in many things we have departed from the ancient simplicity of Christ and his Apostles; we have embraced more outward stateliness, we have those orders in the exercise of religion, which they who best pleased God and served him most devoutly never had. For it is out of doubt that the first state of things was best, that in the prime of Christian religion faith was soundest, the Scriptures of God were then best understood by all men, all parts of godliness did then most abound; and therefore it must needs follow, that customs, laws, and ordinances devised since are not so good for the Church of Christ, but the best way is to cut off later inventions, and to reduce things unto the ancient state wherein at the first they were. Which rule or canon we hold to be either uncertain or at leastwise unsufficient, if not both.

* From *The Works of Richard Hooker,* 7th Edition, edited by John Keble. Oxford: The Clarendon Press, 1888, Vol. I, pp. 421–425 and 428–430, Vol. II, pp. 118 and 121 f., and Vol. III, pp. 143–149.

For in case it be certain, hard it cannot be for them to shew us, where we shall find it so exactly set down, that we may say without all controversy, "these were the orders of the Apostles' times, these wholly and only, neither fewer nor more than these." True it is that many things of this nature be alluded unto, yea many things declared, and many things necessarily collected out of the Apostles' writings. But is it necessary that all the orders of the Church which were then in use should be contained in their books? Surely no. For if the tenor of their writings be well observed, it shall unto any man easily appear, that no more of them are there touched than were needful to be spoken of, sometimes by one occasion and sometimes by another. Will they allow then of any other records besides? Well assured I am they are far enough from acknowledging that the Church ought to keep any thing as apostolical, which is not found in the Apostles' writings, in what other records soever it be found. And therefore whereas St. Augustine affirmeth that those things which the whole Church of Christ doth hold, may well be thought to be apostolical although they be not found written; this his judgment they utterly condemn. I will not here stand in defence of St. Augustine's opinion, which is, that such things are indeed apostolical, but yet with this exception, unless the decree of some general council have haply caused them to be received: for of positive laws and orders received throughout the whole Christian world, St. Augustine could imagine no other fountain save these two. But to let pass St. Augustine; they who condemn him herein must needs confess it a very uncertain thing what the orders of the Church were in the Apostles' times, they tie it to a marvellous uncertain rule; unless they require the observation of no orders but only those which are known to be apostolical by the Apostles' own writings. But then is not this their rule of such sufficiency, that we should use it as a touchstone to try the orders of the Church by for ever.

Our end ought always to be the same; our ways and means thereunto not so. The glory of God and the good of His Church was the thing which the Apostles aimed at, and therefore ought to be the mark whereat we also level. But seeing those rites and orders may be at one time more which at another are less available unto that purpose, what reason is there in these things to urge the state of one only age as a pattern for all to follow? It is not I am right sure their meaning, that we should now assemble our people to serve God in close and secret meetings; or that common brooks or rivers should be used for places of baptism; or that the Eucharist should be ministered after meat; or that the custom of church feasting should be renewed; or that all kind of standing provision for the ministry should be utterly taken away, and their estate made again dependent upon the voluntary devotion of men. In these things they easily perceive how unfit that were for the present, which was for the first age convenient enough. The faith, zeal, and godliness of former times is worthily had in honour; but doth this prove that the orders of the Church of Christ must be still the selfsame with theirs, that nothing may be which was not then, or that nothing which then was may lawfully since have ceased? They who recall the Church unto that which was at the first, must necessarily set bounds and limits unto their speeches. If any thing have been received repugnant unto that which was first delivered, the first things in this case must stand, the last give place unto them. But where difference is without repugnancy, that which hath been can be no prejudice to that which is.

Let the state of the people of God when they were in the house of bondage, and their manner of serving God in a strange land, be compared with that which Canaan and Jerusalem did afford, and who seeth not what huge difference there was between them? In Egypt it may be they were right glad to take some corner of a poor cottage, and there to serve God upon their knees, peradventure covered in dust and straw sometimes. Neither were they therefore the less accepted of God, but he was with them in all their afflictions, and at the length by working their admirable deliverance did testify, that they served him not in vain. Notwithstanding in the very desert they are no sooner possest of some little thing of their own, but a tabernacle is required at their hands. Being planted in the land of Canaan, and having David to be their king, when the Lord had given him rest from all his enemies, it grieved his religious mind to consider the growth of his own estate and dignity, the affairs of religion continuing still in their former manner: "Behold now I dwell in an house of cedar-trees, and the ark of God remaineth still within curtains." What he did purpose it was the pleasure of God that Solomon his son should perform, and perform it in manner suitable unto their present, not their ancient estate and condition. For which cause Solomon writeth unto the king of Tyrus, "The house which I build is great and wonderful, for great is our God above all gods." Whereby it clearly appeareth that the orders of the Church of God may be acceptable unto him, as well being framed suitable to the greatness and dignity of later, as when they keep the reverend simplicity of ancienter times. Such dissimilitude therefore between us and the Apostles of Christ in the order of some outward things is no argument of default.

Yea, but we have framed ourselves to the customs of the church of Rome; our orders and ceremonies are papistical. It is espied that our church founders were not so careful as in this matter they should have been, but contented themselves with such discipline as they took from the church of Rome. Their error we ought to reform by abolishing all popish orders. There must be no communion nor fellowship with Papists, *neither in doctrine, ceremonies, nor government*. It is not enough that we are divided from the church of Rome by the single wall of doctrine, retaining as we do part of their ceremonies and almost their whole government; but government or ceremonies or whatsoever it be which is popish, away with it. This is the thing they require in us, the utter relinquishment of all things popish.

Wherein to the end we may answer them according unto their plain direct meaning, and not take advantage of doubtful speech, whereby controversies grow always endless; their main position being this, that "nothing should be placed in the Church but what God in his word hath commanded," they must of necessity hold all for popish which the church of Rome hath over and besides this. By popish orders, ceremonies, and government, they must therefore mean in every of these so much as the church of Rome hath embraced without commandment of God's word: so that whatsoever such thing we have, if the church of Rome hath it also, it goeth under the name of those things that are popish, yea although it be lawful, although agreeable to the word of God. For so they plainly affirm, saying, "Although the forms and ceremonies which they (the church of Rome) used were not unlawful, and that they contained nothing which is not agreeable to the word of God, yet notwithstanding neither the word of God, nor reason, nor the examples of the eldest churches both Jewish and Christian do permit us to use the same forms and ceremonies, being neither commanded of God, neither such as there may not as good as they, and rather better, be established." The question therefore is, whether we may follow the church of Rome in those orders, rites, and ceremonies, wherein we do not think them blameable, or else ought to devise others, and to have no conformity with them, no not so much as in these things. In this sense and construction therefore as they affirm, so we deny, that whatsoever is popish we ought to abrogate. . . .

Before we answer unto these things, we are to cut off that whereunto they from whom these objections proceed do oftentimes fly for defence and succour, when the force and strength of their arguments is elided. For the ceremonies in use amongst us being in no other respect retained, saving only for that to retain them is to our seeming good and profitable, yea, so profitable and so good, that if we had either simply taken them clean away, or else removed them so as to place in their stead others, we had done worse: the plain and direct way against us herein had been only to prove, that all such ceremonies as they require to be abolished are retained by us to the hurt of the Church, or with less benefit than the abolishment of them would bring. But forasmuch as they saw how hardly they should be able to perform this, they took a more compendious way, traducing the ceremonies of our church under the name of being popish. The cause why this way seemed better unto them was, for that the name of popery is more odious than very paganism amongst divers of the more simple sort, so as whatsoever they hear named popish, they presently conceive deep hatred against it, imagining there can be nothing contained in that name but needs it must be exceeding detestable. The ears of the people they have therefore filled with strong clamour: "The Church of England is fraught with popish ceremonies: they that favour the cause of reformation maintain nothing but the sincerity of the Gospel of Jesus Christ: all such as withstand them, fight for the laws of his sworn enemy, uphold the filthy relics of Antichrist, and are defenders of that which is popish." These are the notes wherewith are drawn from the hearts of the multitude so many sighs; with these tunes their minds are exasperated against the lawful guides and governors of their souls; these are the voices that fill them with general discontentment, as though the bosom of that famous church wherein they live were more noisome than any dungeon. But when the authors of so scandalous incantations are examined, and called to account how can they justify such their dealings; when they are urged directly to answer, whether it be lawful for us to use any such ceremonies as the church of Rome useth, although the same be not commanded in the Word of God; being driven to see that the use of some such ceremonies must of necessity be granted lawful, they go about to make us believe that they are just of the same opinion, and that they only think such ceremonies are not to be used when they are unprofitable, or "when as good or better may be established." Which answer is both idle in regard of us, and also repugnant to themselves.

It is in regard of us very vain to make this answer, because they know that what ceremonies we retain common unto the church of Rome, we therefore retain them, for that we judge them to be profitable, and to be such that others instead of them would be worse. So that when they say that we ought to abrogate such Romish ceremonies as are unprofitable, or else might have other more profitable in their stead, they trifle and they beat the air about nothing which toucheth us; unless they mean that we ought to abrogate all Romish ceremonies which in their judgment have either no use or less use than some other might have. But then must they shew some commission, whereby they are authorized to sit as judges, and we required to take their judgment for good in this case. Otherwise their sentences will not be greatly regarded, when they oppose their *methinketh* unto the orders of the Church of England: as in the question about surplices one of them doth; "If we look to the colour, black methinketh is more decent; if to the form, a garment down to the foot hath a great deal more comeliness in it." If they think that we ought to prove the ceremonies commodious which we have retained, they do in this point very greatly deceive themselves. For in all right and equity, that which the Church hath received and held so long for good, that which public approbation hath ratified, must carry the benefit of presumption with it to be accounted meet and convenient. . . .

A great part of the cause, wherefore religious minds are so inflamed with the love of public devotion, is that virtue, force, and efficacy, which by experience they find that the very form and reverend solemnity of common prayer duly ordered hath, to help that imbecility and weakness in us, by means whereof we are otherwise of ourselves the less apt to perform unto God so heavenly a service, with such affection of heart, and disposition in the powers of our souls as is requisite. To this end therefore all things hereunto appertaining have been ever thought convenient to be done with the most solemnity and majesty that the wisest could devise. It is not with public as with private prayer. In this rather secrecy is commended than outward show, whereas that being the public act of a whole society, requireth accordingly more care to be had of external appearance. The very assembling of men therefore unto this service hath been ever solemn. . . .

But of all helps for due performance of this service the greatest is that very set and standing order itself, which framed with common advice, hath both for matter and form prescribed whatsoever is herein publicly done. No doubt from God it hath proceeded, and by us it must be acknowledged a work of his singular care and providence, that the Church hath evermore held a prescript form of common prayer, although not in all things every where the same, yet for the most part retaining still the same analogy. So that if the liturgies of all ancient churches throughout the world be compared amongst themselves, it may be easily perceived they had all one original mould, and that the public prayers of the people of God in churches thoroughly settled did never use to be voluntary dictates proceeding from any man's extemporal wit.

To him which considereth the grievous and scandalous inconveniences whereto they make themselves daily subject, with whom any blind and secret corner is judged a fit house of common prayer; the manifold confusions which they fall into where every man's private spirit and gift (as they term it) is the only Bishop that ordaineth him to this ministry; the irksome deformities whereby through endless and senseless effusions of indigested prayers they oftentimes disgrace in most unsufferable manner the worthiest part of Christian duty towards God, who herein are subject to no certain order, but pray both what and how they list: to him I say which weigheth duly all these things the reasons cannot be obscure, why God doth in public prayer so much respect the solemnity of places where, the authority and calling of persons by whom, and the precise appointment even with what words or sentences his name should be called on amongst his people.

No man hath hitherto been so impious as plainly and directly to condemn prayer. The best stratagem that Satan hath, who knoweth his kingdom to be no one way more shaken than by the public devout prayers of God's Church, is by traducing the form and manner of them to bring them into contempt, and so to shake the force of all men's devotion towards them. From this and from no other forge hath proceeded a strange conceit, that to serve God with any set form of common prayer is superstitious.

As though God himself did not frame to his Priests the very speech wherewith they were charged to bless the people; or as if our Lord, even of purpose to prevent this fancy of extemporal and voluntary prayers, had not left us of his own framing one, which might both remain as a part of the church liturgy, and serve as a pattern whereby to frame all other prayers with efficacy, yet without superfluity of words. . . .

A thousand five hundred years and upward the Church of Christ hath now continued under the sacred regiment of bishops. Neither for so long hath Christianity been ever planted in any kingdom throughout the world but with this kind of government alone; which to have been ordained of God, I am for mine own part even as resolutely persuaded, as that any other kind of government in the world whatsoever is of God. In this realm of England, before Normans, yea before Saxons, there being Christians, the chief pastors of their souls were bishops. This order from about the first establishment of Christian religion, which was publicly begun through the virtuous disposition of King Lucie not fully two hundred years after Christ, continued till the coming in of the Saxons; by whom Paganism being every where else replanted, only one part of the island, whereinto the ancient natural inhabitants the Britons were driven, retained constantly the faith of Christ, together with the same form of spiritual regiment, which their fathers had before received. Wherefore in the histories of the Church we find very ancient mention made of our own bishops. At the council of Ariminum, about the year three hundred and fifty-nine, Britain had three of her bishops present. At the arrival of Augustine the monk, whom Gregory sent hither to reclaim the Saxons from Gentility about six hundred years after Christ, the Britons he found observers still of the selfsame government by bishops over the rest of the clergy; under this form Christianity took root again, where it had been exiled. Under the selfsame form it remained till the days of the Norman conqueror. By him and his successors thereunto sworn, it hath from that time till now by the space of five hundred years more been upheld. . . .

For whatsoever we bring from antiquity, by way of defence in this cause of bishops, it is cast off as impertinent matter, all is wiped away with an odd kind of shifting answer, "That the bishops which now are, be not like unto them which were." We therefore beseech all indifferent judges to weigh sincerely with themselves how the case doth stand. If it should be at this day a controversy whether kingly regiment were lawful or no, peradventure in defence thereof, the long continuance which it hath had sithence the first beginning might be alleged; mention perhaps might be made what kings there were of old even in Abraham's time, what sovereign princes both before and after. Suppose that herein some man purposely bending his wit against sovereignty, should think to elude all such allegations by making ample discovery through a number of particularities, wherein the kings that are do differ from those that have been, and should therefore in the end conclude, that such ancient examples are no convenient proofs of that royalty which is now in use. Surely for decision of truth in this case there were no remedy, but only to shew the nature of sovereignty, to sever it from accidental properties, make it clear that ancient and present regality are one and the same in substance, how great odds soever otherwise may seem to be between them. In like manner, whereas a question of late hath grown, whether ecclesiastical regiment by bishops be lawful in the Church of Christ or no; in which question, they that hold the negative, being pressed with that general received order, according whereunto the most renowned lights of the Christian world have governed the same in every age as bishops; seeing their manner is to reply, that such bishops as those ancient were, ours are not; there is no remedy but to shew, that to be a bishop is now the selfsame thing which it hath been; that one definition agreeth fully and truly as well to those elder, as to these latter bishops. Sundry dissimilitudes we grant there are, which notwithstanding are not such that they cause any equivocation in the name, whereby we should think a bishop in those times to have had a clean other definition than doth rightly agree unto bishops as they are now. Many things there are in the state of bishops, which the times have changed; many a parsonage at this day is larger than some ancient bishoprics were; many an ancient bishop poorer than at this day sundry under them in degree. The simple hereupon lacking judgment and knowledge to discern between the nature of things which changeth not, and these outward variable accidents, are made believe that a bishop heretofore and now are things in their very nature so distinct that they cannot be judged the same. Yet to men that have any part of skill, what more evident and plain in bishops, than that augmentation or diminution in their precincts, allowances, privileges, and such like, do make a difference indeed, but no essential difference between one bishop and another? As for those things in regard whereof we use properly to term them bishops, those things whereby they essentially differ from other pastors, those things which the natural definition of a bishop must contain; what one of them is there more or less appliable unto bishops now than of old?

The name bishop hath been borrowed from the Grecians, with whom it signifieth one which hath principal charge to guide and oversee others. The same word in ecclesiastical writings being applied unto church governors, at the first unto all and not unto the chiefest only, grew in short time peculiar and proper to signify such episcopal authority alone, as the chiefest governors exercised over the rest. For with all names this is usual, that inasmuch as they are not given till the things whereunto they are given have been sometime first observed, therefore generally things are ancienter than the names whereby they are called. . . .

A bishop is a minister of God, unto whom with permanent continuance there is given not only power of administering the Word and sacraments, which power other presbyters have; but also a further power to ordain ecclesiastical persons, and a power of chiefty in government over presbyters as well as laymen, a power to be by way of jurisdiction a pastor even to pastors themselves. So that this office, as he is a presbyter or pastor, consisteth in those things which are common unto him with other pastors, as in ministering the Word and sacraments: but those things incident unto his office, which do properly make him a bishop, cannot be common unto him with other pastors.

Now even as pastors, so likewise bishops being principal pastors, are either at large or else with restraint: at large, when the subject of their regiment is indefinite, and not tied to any certain place; bishops with restraint are they whose regiment over the Church is contained within some definite, local compass, beyond which compass their jurisdiction reacheth not. Such therefore we always mean when we speak of that regiment by bishops which we hold a thing most lawful, divine and holy in the Church of Christ. . . .

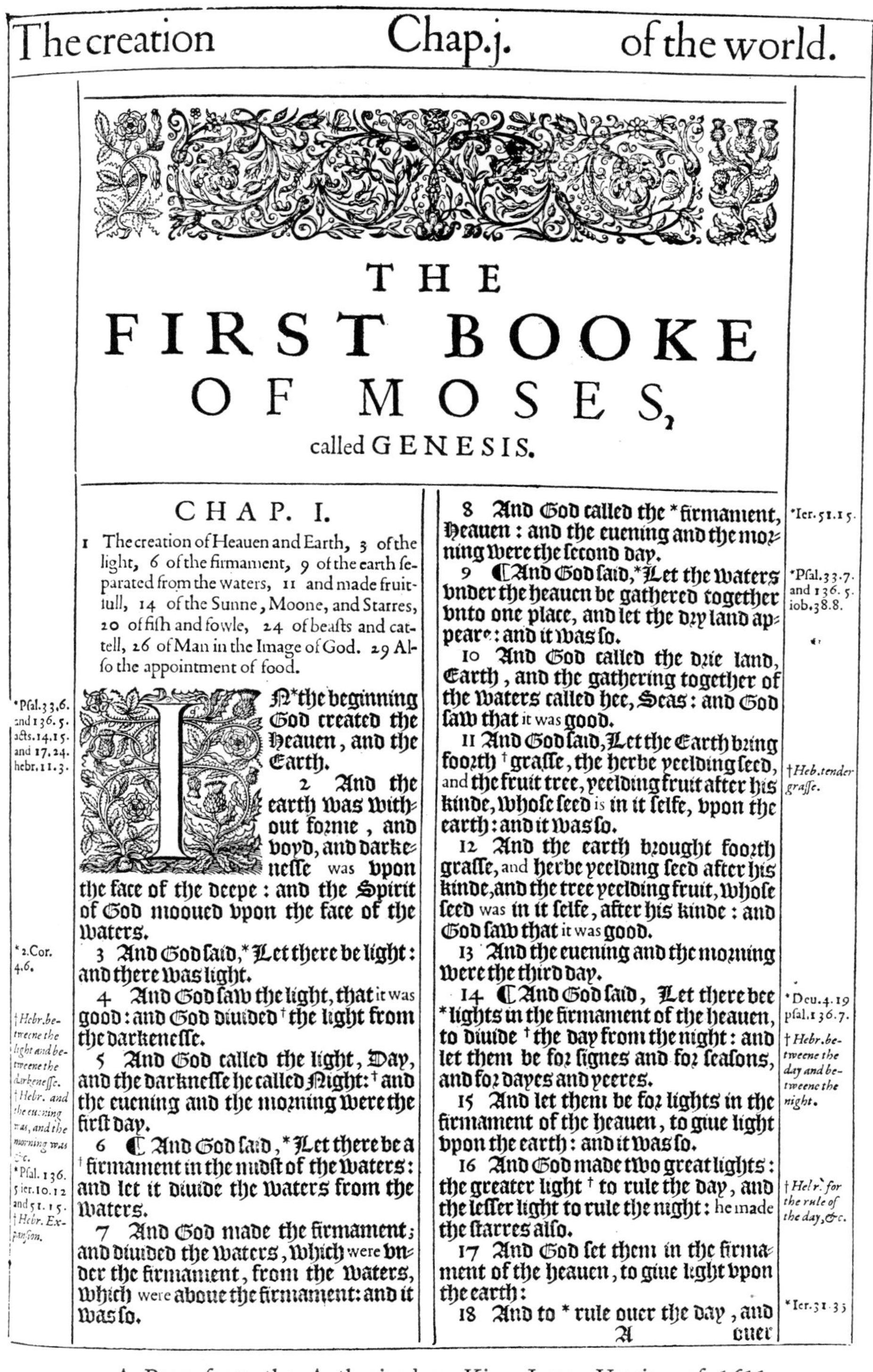

The creation Chap.j. of the world.

THE
FIRST BOOKE
OF MOSES,
called GENESIS.

CHAP. I.

1 The creation of Heauen and Earth, 3 of the light, 6 of the firmament, 9 of the earth separated from the waters, 11 and made fruitfull, 14 of the Sunne, Moone, and Starres, 20 of fish and fowle, 24 of beasts and cattell, 26 of Man in the Image of God. 29 Also the appointment of food.

IN* the beginning God created the Heauen, and the Earth.

2 And the earth was without forme, and voyd, and darkenesse was vpon the face of the deepe: and the Spirit of God mooued vpon the face of the waters.

3 And God said,* Let there be light: and there was light.

4 And God saw the light, that it was good: and God diuided † the light from the darkenesse.

5 And God called the light, Day, and the darknesse he called Night: † and the euening and the morning were the first day.

6 ¶ And God said, * Let there be a † firmament in the midst of the waters: and let it diuide the waters from the waters.

7 And God made the firmament; and diuided the waters, which were vnder the firmament, from the waters, which were aboue the firmament: and it was so.

8 And God called the * firmament, Heauen: and the euening and the morning were the second day.

9 ¶ And God said, * Let the waters vnder the heauen be gathered together vnto one place, and let the dry land appeare: and it was so.

10 And God called the drie land, Earth, and the gathering together of the waters called hee, Seas: and God saw that it was good.

11 And God said, Let the Earth bring foorth † grasse, the herbe yeelding seed, and the fruit tree, yeelding fruit after his kinde, whose seed is in it selfe, vpon the earth: and it was so.

12 And the earth brought foorth grasse, and herbe yeelding seed after his kinde, and the tree yeelding fruit, whose seed was in it selfe, after his kinde: and God saw that it was good.

13 And the euening and the morning were the third day.

14 ¶ And God said, Let there bee * lights in the firmament of the heauen, to diuide † the day from the night: and let them be for signes and for seasons, and for dayes and yeeres.

15 And let them be for lights in the firmament of the heauen, to giue light vpon the earth: and it was so.

16 And God made two great lights: the greater light † to rule the day, and the lesser light to rule the night: he made the starres also.

17 And God set them in the firmament of the heauen, to giue light vpon the earth:

18 And to * rule ouer the day, and ouer

A ouer

*Psal.33.6. and 136.5. acts.14.15. and 17.24. hebr.11.3.
*2.Cor. 4.6.
†Hebr. betweene the light and betweene the darkenesse.
†Hebr. And the euening was, and the morning was &c.
*Psal.136.5. ier.10.12 and 51.15.
†Hebr. Expansion.
*Ier.51.15.
*Psal.33.7. and 136.5. iob.38.8.
†Heb. tender grasse.
*Deu.4.19 psal.136.7.
†Hebr. betweene the day and betweene the night.
†Hebr. for the rule of the day, &c.
*Ier.31.35.

A Page from the Authorized or King James Version of 1611, the Most Widely Read Translation of the Bible in the English-Speaking World.

WILLIAM BRADFORD (1590–1657)

Before the final but short-lived triumph of Puritanism under Cromwell, a group of English Separatists, unable to endure the persecution any longer, fled to Holland and in 1620 migrated on the "Mayflower" to New England. Here, known to posterity as the "Pilgrims," they founded the Plymouth Colony. One of the leaders of this group was William Bradford, a Separatist since his early youth. He was selected governor of the Plymouth Colony in 1621, an office which he held, with short interruptions, for thirty years until his death. From his pen we have the story of this group's venture into the American "wilderness." Bradford's account of the beginnings of Plymouth Colony is one of the noblest documents of Puritan piety and character.

Of Plymouth Plantation*

When, as by the travail and diligence of some godly and zealous preachers and God's blessing on their labours, as in other places of the land, so in the North parts, many became enlightened by the Word of God, and had their ignorance and sins discovered unto them, and began by His grace to reform their lives, and make conscience of their ways, the work of God was no sooner manifest in them, but presently they were both scoffed and scorned by the profane multitude, and the ministers urged with the yoke of subscription, or else must be silenced. And the poor people were so vexed with apparitors and pursuivants and the commisary courts, as truly their affliction was not small; which, notwithstanding, they bore sundry years with much patience, till they were occasioned (by the continuance and increase of these troubles, and other means which the Lord raised up in those days) to see further into things by the light of the Word of God. How not only these base and beggarly ceremonies were unlawful, but also that the lordly and tyranous power of the prelates ought not to be submitted unto; which thus, contrary to the freedom of the Gospel, would load and burden men's consciences, and by their compulsive power make a profane mixture of persons and things in the worship of God. . . .

So many, therefore, of these professors as saw the evil of these things in these parts, and whose hearts the Lord had touched with heavenly zeal for His truth, they shook off this yoke of anti-Christian bondage and as the Lord's free people joined themselves (by a covenant of the Lord) into a church estate, in the fellowship of the Gospel, to walk in all His ways made known, or to be made known unto them, according to their best endeavours, whatsoever it should cost them, the Lord assisting them. And that it cost them something this ensuing history will declare. . . .

But after these things they could not long continue in any peaceable condition, but were hunted and persecuted on every side, so as their former afflictions were but as flea bitings in comparison of these which now came upon them. For some were taken and clapped up in prison, others had their houses beset and watched night and day and hardly escaped their hands; and the most were fain to flee and leave their houses and habitations and the means of their livelihood. Yet these and many other sharper things which afterward befell them were no other than they looked for, and therefore were the better prepared to bear them by the assistance of God's grace and Spirit. Yet seeing themselves thus molested, and that there was no hope of their continuance there, by a joint consent they resolved to go into the Low Countries, where they heard was freedom of religion for all men; as also how sundry from London and other parts of the land had been exiled and persecuted for the same cause, and

* From William Bradford, *Of Plymouth Plantation,* Boston: Wright & Potter, 1898, pp. 11–15, 29–35, 93–97, and 109–112 (modernized by the editor).

were gone thither, and lived at Amsterdam and in other places of the land. So after they had continued together about a year and kept their meetings every Sabbath in one place or another, exercising the worship of God amongst themselves, notwithstanding all the diligence and malice of their adversaries, they seeing they could no longer continue in that condition, they resolved to get over into Holland as they could; which was in the year 1607 and 1608. . . .

After they had lived in this city about some eleven or twelve years, (which is the more observable being the whole time of that famous truce between that state and the Spaniards,) and sundry of them were taken away by death and many others began to be well stricken in years, the grave mistress Experience having taught them many things, those prudent governors with sundry of the sagest members began both deeply to apprehend their present dangers and wisely to foresee the future and think of timely remedy. In the agitation of their thoughts and much discourse of things hereabout, at length they began to incline to this conclusion, of removal to some other place. Not out of any newfangledness, or other such like giddy humor, by which men are oftentimes transported to their great hurt and danger, but for sundry weighty and solid reasons; some of the chief of which I will here briefly touch.

And first, they saw and found by experience the hardness of the place and country to be such, as few in comparison would come to them, and fewer that would bide it out, and continue with them. For many that came to them, and many more that desired to be with them, could not endure that great labour and hard fare with other inconveniences which they underwent and were contented with. But though they loved their persons, approved their cause, and honoured their sufferings, yet they left them as it were weeping, as Orpah did her mother-in-law Naomi, or as those Romans did Cato in Utica, who desired to be excused and borne with, though they could not all be Catos. For many, though they desired to enjoy the ordinances of God in their purity, and the liberty of the Gospel with them, yet, alas, they admitted of bondage with danger of conscience rather than to endure these hardships; yea, some preferred and chose the prisons in England, rather than this liberty in Holland with these afflictions. But it was thought that if a better and easier place of living could be had, it would draw many and take away these discouragements. Yea, their pastor would often say that many of those who both wrote and preached now against them, if they were in a place where they might have liberty and live comfortably, they would then practice as they did.

Secondly, they saw that though the people generally bore all these difficulties very cheerfully and with a resolute courage, being in the best and strongest of their years, yet old age began to steal on many of them, (and their great and continual labours, with other crosses and sorrows, hastened it before the time,) so as it was not only probably thought, but apparently seen that within a few years more they would be in danger to scatter, by necessities pressing them, or sink under their burdens, or both. And, therefore, according to the divine proverb, that a wise man sees the plague when it cometh, and hides himself (Prov. 22:3), so they like skillful and beaten soldiers were fearful either to be entrapped or surrounded by their enemies, so as they should neither be able to fight nor flee; and, therefore, thought it better to dislodge betimes to some place of better advantage and less danger, if any such could be found.

Thirdly, as necessity was a taskmaster over them, so they were forced to be such, not only to their servants but in a sort to their dearest children, the which as it did not a little wound the tender hearts of many a loving father and mother, so it produced likewise sundry sad and sorrowful effects. For many of their children that were of best dispositions and gracious inclinations, having learned to bear the yoke in their youth and willing to bear part of their parents' burden, were oftentimes so oppressed with their heavy labours that though their minds were free and willing, yet their bodies bowed under the weight of the same and became decrepit in their early youth; the vigour of nature being consumed in the very bud, as it were. But that which was more lamentable and of all sorrows most heavy to be borne, was that many of their children, by these occasions and the great licentiousness of youth in that country and the manifold temptations of the place, were drawn away by evil examples into extravagant and dangerous courses, getting the reins off their necks and departing from their parents. Some became soldiers, others took upon them far voyages by sea, and others some worse courses, tending to dissoluteness and the danger of their souls, to the great grief of their parents and dishonor of God. So that they saw their posterity would be in danger to degenerate and be corrupted.

Lastly, (and which was not least,) a great hope and inward zeal they had of laying some good foundation, or at least to make some way thereunto, for the propagation and advancement of the Gospel of the kingdom of Christ in those remote parts of the world; yea, though they should be but even as stepping-stones unto others for the performing of so great a work.

These, and some other like reasons, moved them to undertake this resolution of their removal; the which they afterward prosecuted with so great difficulties, as by the sequel will appear.

The place they had thoughts on was some of those vast and unpeopled countries of America, which are fruitful and fit for habitation, being devoid of all civil inhabitants, where there are only savage and brutish men which range up and down, little otherwise than the wild beasts of the same. This proposition being made public and coming to the scanning of all, it raised many variable opinions amongst men and caused many fears and doubts amongst themselves. Some, from their reasons and hopes conceived, laboured to stir up and encourage the rest to undertake and prosecute the same; others, again, out of their fears objected against it and sought to divert from it, alleging many things, and those neither unreasonable nor improbable; as that it was a great design and subject to many unconceivable perils and dangers; as, besides the casualties of the seas (which none can be freed from) the length of the voyage was such, as the weak bodies of women and other persons worn out with age and travail (as many of them were) could never be able to endure. And yet if they should, the miseries of the land which they should be exposed unto would be too hard to be borne; and likely, some or all of them together, to consume and utterly to ruin them. For there they should be liable to famine and nakedness and the want, in a manner, of all things. The change of air, diet, and drinking of water would affect their bodies with sore sickness and grievous diseases. And also those which should escape or overcome these difficulties should yet be in continual danger of the savage people who are cruel, barbarous, and most treacherous, being most furious in their rage and merciless where they overcome; not being content only to kill and take away life, but delight to torment men in the most bloody manner that may be; flaying some alive with the shells of fishes, cutting of the members and joints of others by piecemeal, and broiling on the coals, eat the collops of their flesh in their sight while they live; with other cruelties horrible to be related. And surely it could not be thought but the very hearing of these things could not but move the very bowels of men to grate within them and make the weak to quake and tremble. It was further objected that it would require greater sums of money to furnish such a voyage and to fit them with necessities, than their consumed estates would amount to; and yet they must as well look to be seconded with supplies, as presently to be transported. Also many precedents of ill success and lamentable miseries befallen others in the like designs were easy to be found and not forgotten to be alleged; besides their own experience, in their former troubles and hardships in their removal into Holland, and how hard a thing it was for them to live in that strange place, though it was a neighbour country and a civil and rich commonwealth.

It was answered that all great and honourable actions are accompanied with great difficulties and must be both enterprised and overcome with answerable courages. It was granted the dangers were great, but not desperate; the difficulties were many, but not invincible. For though there were many of them likely, yet they were not certain; it might be sundry of the things feared might never befall; others by provident care and the use of good means might in a great measure be prevented; and all of them, through the help of God, by fortitude and patience might either be borne, or overcome. True it was that such attempts were not to be made and undertaken without good ground and reason; not rashly or lightly as many have done for curiosity or hope of gain, etc. But their condition was not ordinary; their ends were good and honourable; their calling lawful and urgent; and, therefore, they might expect the blessing of God in their proceeding. Yea, though they should lose their lives in this action, yet might they have comfort in the same, and their endeavours would be honourable. . . .

But to omit other things, (that I may be brief,) after long beating at sea they fell with that land which is called Cape Cod; the which being made and certainly known to be it, they were not a little joyful. After some deliberation had amongst themselves and with the master of the ship, they tacked about and resolved to stand for the southward (the wind and weather being fair) to find some place about Hudson's River for their habitation. But after they had sailed that course about half the day, they fell amongst dangerous shoals and roaring breakers, and they were so far entangled therewith as they conceived themselves in great danger; and the wind shrinking upon them withal, they resolved to bear up again for the Cape and thought themselves happy to get out of those dangers before night overtook them, as by God's providence they did. And the next day they got into the Cape-harbor where they rid in safety. . . .

Being thus arrived in a good harbor and brought safe to land, they fell on their knees and blessed the God of Heaven who had brought them over the vast and furious ocean and delivered them from all the perils and miseries thereof, again to set their feet on the firm and stable earth, their proper element. . . .

But here I cannot but stay and make a pause and stand half amazed at this poor people's present condition; and so I think will the reader, too, when he well considers the same. Being thus passed the vast ocean, and a sea of troubles before in their preparation (as may be remembered by that which went before), they had now no friends to welcome them, nor inns to entertain or refresh their weatherbeaten bodies, no houses or much less towns to repair to, to seek for succour. It is recorded in Scripture as a mercy to the Apostle and his shipwrecked company, that the barbarians showed them no small kindness in refreshing them, but these savage barbarians, when they met with them (as after will appear) were readier to fill their sides full of arrows than otherwise. And for the season it was winter, and they that know the winters of that country know them to be sharp and violent and subject to cruel and fierce storms, dangerous to travel to known places, much more to search an unknown coast. Besides, what could they see but a hideous and desolate wilderness, full of wild beasts and wild men? and what multitudes there might be of them they knew not. Neither could they, as it were, go up to the top of Pisgah, to view from this wilderness a more goodly country to feed their hopes; for which way soever they turned their eyes (save upwards to the heavens) they could have little solace or content in respect of any outward objects. For summer being done, all things stand upon them with a weatherbeaten face; and the whole country, full of woods and thickets, represented a wild and savage hue. If they looked behind them, there was the mighty ocean which they had passed and was now as a main bar and gulf to separate them from all the civil parts of the world. If it be said they had a ship to succour them, it is true; but what heard they daily from the master and company? but that with speed they should look out a place with their shallop, where they would be at some near distance; for the season was such as he would not stir from thence till a safe harbor was discovered by them where they would be, and he might go without danger; and that victuals consumed space, but he must and would keep sufficient for themselves and their return. Yea, it was muttered by some that if they got not a place in time, they would turn them and their goods ashore and leave them. Let it also be considered what weak hopes of supply and succour they left behind them that might bear up their minds in this sad condition and trials they were under; and they could not but be very small. It is true, indeed, the affections and love of their brethren at Leiden was cordial and entire towards them, but they had little power to help them, or themselves; and how the case stood between them and the merchants at their coming away hath already been declared. What could now sustain them but the Spirit of God and His grace? May not and ought not the children of these fathers rightly say: "Our fathers were Englishmen which came over this great ocean and were ready to perish in this wilderness; but they cried unto the Lord, and He heard their voice and looked on their adversity, etc. Let them, therefore, praise the Lord because He is good and His mercies endure forever. Yea let them which have been redeemed of the Lord show how He hath delivered them from the hand of the oppressor. When they wandered in the desert wilderness out of the way and found no city to dwell in, both hungry and thirsty, their soul was overwhelmed in them. Let them confess before the Lord His loving kindness and His wonderful works before the sons of men." . . .

I shall a little return back and begin with a combination made by them before they came ashore, being the first foundation of their government in this place, occasioned partly by the discontented and mutinous speeches that some of the strangers amongst them had let fall from them in the ship. That when they came ashore they would use their own liberty; for none had power to command them, the patent they had being for Virginia, and not for New England, which belonged to another government with which the Virginia Company had nothing to do. And partly that such an act by them done (this their condition considered) might be as firm as any patent, and in some respects more sure.

The form was as follows:

In the name of God, Amen. We whose names are underwritten, the loyal subjects of our dread Sovereign Lord, King James, by the Grace of God, of Great Britain, France, and Ireland, King, Defender of the Faith, etc., having undertaken, for the glory of God, and advancement of the Christian faith and honour of our king and country, a voyage to plant the first colony in the Northern parts of Virginia, do by these presents solemnly and mutually in the presence of God, and of one another, Covenant and Combine ourselves together into a civil body politic, for our better ordering and preservation and furtherance of the ends aforesaid; and by virtue hereof to enact, constitute, and frame such just and equal laws, ordinances, acts, constitutions, and offices, from time to time, as shall be thought most meet and convenient for the general good of the colony, unto which we promise all due submission and obedience. In witness whereof we have hereunder subscribed our names at Cape Cod the 11. of November, in the year of the reign of our Sovereign Lord, King James, of England, France, and Ireland the eighteenth, and of Scotland the fifty-fourth. *Anno Domino* 1620.

After this they chose, or rather confirmed, Mr. John Carver (a man godly and well approved amongst them) their governor for that year. And after they had provided a place for their goods, or common store, (which were long in unloading for want of boats, foulness of winter weather, and sickness of diverse,) and begun some small cottages for their habitation, as time would admit, they met and consulted of laws and orders, both for their civil and military government, as the necessity of their condition did require, still adding thereunto as urgent occasion in several times and as cases did require.

In these hard and difficult beginnings they found some discontents and murmuring arise amongst some, and mutinous speeches and carriages in other; but they were soon quelled and overcome by the wisdom, patience, and just and equal carriage of things by the governour and better part which clave faithfully together in the main. But that which was most sad and lamentable was, that in two or three months' time half of their company died, especially in January and February, being the depth of the winter, and wanting houses and other comforts, being infected with the scurvy and other diseases which this long voyage and their inaccomodate condition had brought upon them; so as there died sometimes two or three of a day in the foresaid time, that of one hundred and odd persons scarce fifty remained. And of these, in the time of most distress, there was but six or seven sound persons who to their great commendations, be it spoken, spared no pains night nor day, but with abundance of toil and hazard of their own health fetched them wood, made them fires, dressed them meat, made their beds, washed their loathsome clothes, clothed and unclothed them—in a word, did all the homely and necessary offices for them which dainty and queasy stomachs cannot endure to hear named; and all this willingly and cheerfully, without any grudging in the least, showing herein their true love unto their friends and brethren; a rare example and worthy to be remembered. Two of these seven were Mr. William Brewster, their reverend elder, and Myles Standish, their captain and military commander, unto whom myself and many others were much beholden in our low and sick condition. And yet the Lord so upheld these persons as in this general calamity they were not at all infected either with sickness or lameness. And what I have said of these I may say of many others who died in this general visitation, and others yet living, that while they had health, yea, or any strength continuing, they were not wanting to any that had need of them. And I doubt not but their recompense is with the Lord. . . .

JOHN WINTHROP (1588–1649)

The small band of Separatists which in 1620 had founded the Plymouth Colony was joined ten years later by the more numerous Puritan groups who settled Massachusetts Bay. When these Puritans left England, they had no intention of withdrawing from the Church of England. They merely desired to be free to reform the English Church along stricter Biblical lines and to replace the Episcopal church order by the Congregational. The leader of this group was John Winthrop, a successful lawyer, who in 1629 agreed, under certain conditions, to supervise and join the Great Migration to New England. Twelve times he was chosen governor of the Massachusetts Bay Colony, whose early history therefore is closely interwoven with his own.

The following selection is taken from a sermon which Winthrop, acting both as the governor of the Massachusetts Bay Colony and as a lay preacher of his church, delivered on board the "Arbella," the flagship of the Great Migration. As they approached the New World, he set forth the ideal of the Puritan theocracy in which both the civil community and the church are subject to the law of God. As Winthrop's sermon shows, the Puritans found this ideal implied in the fundamental Calvinist idea of the covenant between God and man.

A Model of Christian Charity*

God Almighty in His most holy and wise providence hath so disposed of the condition of mankind as in all times some must be rich, some poor, some high and eminent in power and dignity, others mean and in subjection.

The reason hereof:

First, to hold conformity with the rest of His works, being delighted to show forth the glory of His wisdom in the variety and difference of the creatures and the glory of His power, in ordering all these differences for the preservation and good of the whole and the glory of His greatness; that as it is the glory of princes to have many officers, so this great King will have many stewards, counting Himself more honored in dispensing His gifts to man by man than if He did it by His own immediate hand.

Secondly, that He might have the more occasion to manifest the work of His Spirit: first, upon the wicked in moderating and restraining them, so that the rich and mighty should not eat up the poor, nor the poor and despised rise up against their superiors and shake off their yoke; secondly, in the regenerate, in exercising His graces in them: as in the great ones, their love, mercy, gentleness, temperance, etc., in the poor and inferior sort, their faith, patience, obedience, etc.

* From *Winthrop Papers,* The Massachusetts Historical Society, Vol II (1931), pp. 282–284 and 292–295 (modernized by the editor).

Thirdly, that every man might have need of other, and from hence they might be all knit more nearly together in the bond of brotherly affection; from hence it appears plainly that no man is made more honorable than another or more wealthy, etc., out of any particular and singular respect to himself, but for the glory of his creator and the common good of the creature, man. Therefore God still reserves the property of these gifts to Himself (Ezek. 16, 17). He there calls wealth His gold and His silver, etc. (Prov. 3, 9). He claims their service as His due, "Honor the Lord with thy riches, etc." All men being thus (by divine providence) ranked into two sorts, rich and poor; under the first are comprehended all such as are able to live comfortably by their own means duly improved, and all others are poor, according to the former distribution.

There are two rules whereby we are to walk one towards another: *justice* and *mercy*. These are always distinguished in their act and in their object, yet may they both concur in the same subject in each respect; as sometimes there may be an occasion of showing mercy to a rich man in some sudden danger of distress, and also doing of mere justice to a poor man in regard of some particular contract, etc.

There is likewise a double law by which we are regulated in our conversation one towards another: in both the former respects, the law of nature and the law of grace, or the moral law or the law of the Gospel—to omit the rule of justice as not properly belonging to this purpose, otherwise than it may fall into consideration in some particular cases. By the first of these laws, man, as he was enabled so, withal [is] commanded to love his neighbour as himself; upon this ground stand all the precepts of the moral law, which concerns our dealings with men. To apply this to the works of mercy, this law requires two things: first, that every man afford his help to another in every want or distress; secondly, that he perform this out of the same affection which makes him careful of his own good according to that of our saviour, "Whatsoever ye would that men should do to you" (Matt. 7, 12). This was practiced by Abraham and Lot in entertaining the angels and the old man of Gibea.

The law of grace or the Gospel hath some difference from the former as in these respects: first, the law of nature was given to man in the estate of innocency, this of the Gospel in the estate of regeneracy. Secondly, the former propounds one man to another as the same flesh and image of God, this as a brother in Christ also, and in the communion of the same spirit, and so teacheth us to put a difference between Christians and others. "Do good to all, especially to the household of faith." Upon this ground the Israelites were to put a difference between the brethren of such as were strangers though not of the Canaanites. Thirdly, the law of nature could give no rules for dealing with enemies, for all are to be considered as friends in the state of innocency; but the Gospel commands love to an enemy. Proof: "If thine enemy hunger, feed him; love your enemies, do good to them that hate you" (Matt. 5, 44).

This law of the Gospel propounds likewise a difference of seasons and occasions; there is a time when a Christian must sell all and give to the poor as they did in the apostles' times; there is a time also when a Christian (though they give not all yet) must give beyond their ability, as they of Macedonia (II Cor. 8). Likewise, community of perils calls for extraordinary liberality, and so doth community in some special service for the church. Lastly, when there is no other means whereby our Christian brother may be relieved in this distress, we must help him beyond our ability, rather than tempt God in putting him upon help by miraculous or extraordinary means. . . .

First, for the persons, we are a company professing ourselves fellow members of Christ, in which respect only, though we were absent from each other many miles and had our employments as far distant, yet we ought to account ourselves knit together by this bond of love and live in the exercise of it, if we would have comfort of our being in Christ. This was notorious in the practice of the Christians in former times, as is testified of the Waldenses from the mouth of one of the adversaries, Aeneas Sylvius: *Mutuo* [*solent amare*] *pene antequam norint*—they use to love any of their own religion even before they were acquainted with them.

Secondly, for the work we have in hand, it is by mutual consent through a special overruling providence and a more than an ordinary approbation of the churches of Christ, to seek out a place of cohabitation and consortship under a due form of government both civil and ecclesiastical. In such cases as this, the care of the public must oversway all private respects by which not only conscience but mere civil policy doth bind us; for it is a true rule that particular estates cannot subsist in the ruin of the public.

Thirdly, the end is to improve our lives to do more service to the Lord, the comfort and increase of the body of Christ whereof we are members, that ourselves and posterity may be the better preserved from the common corruptions of this evil world to serve the Lord and work out our salvation under the power and purity of His holy ordinances.

Fourthly, for the means whereby this must be effected, they are twofold: a conformity with the work and the end we aim at; these we see are extraordinary, therefore we must not content ourselves with usual ordinary means. Whatsoever we did or ought to have done when we lived in England, the same must we do and more also where we go. That which the most in their churches maintain as a truth in profession only, we must bring into familiar and constant practice; as in this duty of love we must love brotherly without dissimulation, we must love one another with a pure heart fervently, we must bear one another's burden, we must not look only on our own things but also on the things of our brethren. Neither must we think that the Lord will bear with such failings at our hands as He doth from those among whom we have lived, and that for three reasons. (1) In regard of the more near bond of marriage between Him and us, wherein He hath taken us to be His after a most strict and peculiar manner which will make Him the more jealous of our love and obedience. So He tells the people of Israel: "You only have I known of all the families of the earth, therefore will I punish you for your transgressions." (2) Because the Lord will be sanctified in them that come near Him. We know that there were many that corrupted the service of the Lord, some setting up altars before His own, others offering both strange fire and strange sacrifice also; yet there came no fire from heaven, or other sudden judgment upon them, as did upon Nadab and Abihu who yet we may think did not sin presumptuously. (3) When God gives a special commission, He looks to have it strictly observed in every article. When He gave Saul a commission to destroy Amaleck, He indented with him upon certain articles, and because he failed in one of the least, and that upon fair pretence, it lost him the kingdom, which should have been his reward, if he had observed his commission.

Thus stands the cause between God and us: we are entered into covenant with Him for this work, we have taken out a commission, the Lord hath given us leave to draw our own articles. We have professed to enterprise these actions upon these and these ends, we have hereupon besought Him of favor and blessing. Now if the Lord shall please to hear us and bring us in peace to the place we desire, then hath He ratified this covenant and sealed our Commission [and] will expect a strict performance of the articles contained in it; but if we shall neglect the observation of these articles which are the ends we have propounded, and dissembling with our God, shall fall to embrace this present world and prosecute our carnal intentions, seeking great things for ourselves and our posterity, the Lord will surely break out in wrath against us, be revenged of such a perjured people, and make us know the price of the breach of such a covenant.

Now the only way to avoid this shipwreck and to provide for our posterity is to follow the counsel of Micah: to do justly, to love mercy, to walk humbly with our God. For this end, we must be knit together in this work as one man; we must entertain each other in brotherly affection; we must be willing to abridge ourselves of our superfluities, for the supply of others' necessities; we must uphold a familiar commerce together in all meekness, gentleness, patience and liberality; we must delight in each other, make others' conditions our own, rejoice together, mourn together, labor and suffer together, always having before our eyes our commission and community in the work, our community as members of the same body. So shall we keep the unity of the spirit in the bond of peace. The Lord will be our God and delight to dwell among us, as His own people, and will command a blessing upon us in all our ways, so that we shall see much more of His wisdom, power, goodness, and truth than formerly we have been acquainted with. We shall find that the God of Israel is among us, when ten of us shall be able to resist a thousand of our enemies, when He shall make us a praise and glory that men shall say of succeeding plantations: "The Lord make it like that of New England." For we must consider that we shall be as a city upon a hill, the eyes of all people are upon us. So that if we shall deal falsely with our God in this work we have undertaken and so cause Him to withdraw His present help from us, we shall be made a story and a by-word through the world; we shall open the mouths of enemies to speak evil of the ways of God and all professors for God's sake; we shall shame the faces of many of God's worthy servants and cause their prayers to be turned into curses upon us, till we be consumed out of the good land whither we are going. And to shut up this discourse with that exhortation of Moses, that faithful servant of the Lord, in his last farewell to Israel (Deut. 30): Beloved, there is now set before us life and good, death and evil, in that we are commanded this day to love the Lord our God, and to love one another, to walk in His ways and to keep His commandments and ordinance and His laws and the articles of our covenant with Him, that we may live and be multiplied, and that the Lord our God may bless us in the land whither we go to possess it; but if our hearts shall turn away so that we will not obey, but shall be seduced and worship . . . other gods, our pleasures and profits, and serve them, it is propounded unto us this day, we shall surely perish out of the good land whither we pass over this vast sea to possess it.

Therefore, let us choose life,
that we, and our seed,
may live; by obeying His
voice and cleaving to Him,
for He is our life and
our prosperity.

ROGER WILLIAMS (1603?–1684)

When in 1631, probably at the age of twenty-eight, Roger Williams arrived in New England, he was a Puritan minister with the strict Calvinistic convictions which he retained to the end of his life. After he had held several pastorates he was banished in 1636 by the Puritan authorities from the Massachusetts Bay Colony. He then founded the Colony of Rhode Island, became for a while a Baptist, and finally, being a "seeker" by nature, was led to believe that the true Church of Christ is not identifiable with any of the existing churches. There were several reasons for his banishment from the Massachusetts Bay Colony, but the most important one was that Williams had renounced the Puritan ideal of a Holy Commonwealth and instead had advocated the principle of the separation of church and state. The following selections from his greatest work, *The Bloudy Tenent of Persecution* (1644), beginning with a summary of the book's main arguments, show that Williams derived the principle of religious liberty not from religious indifference as later centuries would do. One of his basic arguments was rather that the Church which consists only of regenerate Christians could best be protected from contamination by the unregenerate world if the separation of the religious and the civil communities were strictly enforced and liberty of worship granted to all.

Roger Williams must be counted foremost among those who, on religious grounds, prepared the minds of Protestants for the principles of the separation of church and state and of religious liberty. Those Protestants who adhered to the ideas of Williams and Penn eventually succeeded, in the favorable political climate of the newly born United States, and with the help of statesmen like Madison and Jefferson, in establishing the principle of religious liberty on firm constitutional grounds.

The Bloody Tenet of Persecution*

First, that the blood of so many hundred thousand souls of Protestants and Papists, spilt in the wars of present and former ages, for their respective consciences, is not required nor accepted by Jesus Christ the Prince of Peace.

Secondly, pregnant scriptures and arguments are throughout the work proposed against the doctrine of persecution for cause of conscience.

Thirdly, satisfactory answers are given to scriptures, and objections produced by Mr. Calvin, Beza, Mr. Cotton, and the ministers of the New England churches and others former and later, tending to prove the doctrine of persecution for cause of conscience.

Fourthly, the doctrine of persecution for cause of conscience, is proved guilty of all the blood of the souls crying for vengeance under the altar.

Fifthly, all civil states with their officers of justice in their respective constitutions and administrations are proved essentially civil, and therefore not judges, governors or defenders of the spiritual or Christian state and worship.

Sixthly, it is the will and command of God, that, since the coming of His Son the Lord Jesus, a permission of the most pagan, Jewish, Turkish, or anti-christian consciences and worships, be granted to all men in all nations and countries; and they are only to be fought against with that sword which is only (in soul matters) able to conquer, to wit, the sword of God's Spirit, the Word of God.

Seventhly, the state of the land of Israel, the kings and people thereof in peace and war, is proved figurative and ceremonial, and no pattern nor precedent for any kingdom or civil state in the world to follow.

Eighthly, God requires not a uniformity of religion to be enacted and enforced in any civil state, which enforced uniformity, sooner or later, is the greatest occasion of civil war, ravishing of conscience, persecution of Christ Jesus in his servants, and of the hypocrisy and destruction of millions of souls.

Ninthly, in holding an enforced uniformity of religion in a civil state, we must necessarily disclaim our desires and hopes of the Jews' conversion to Christ.

Tenthly, an enforced uniformity of religion throughout a nation or civil state confounds the civil and religious, denies the principles of Christianity and civility, and that Jesus Christ is come in the flesh.

Eleventhly, the permission of other consciences and worships than a state professes only can (according to God) procure a firm and lasting peace, (good assurance being taken according to the wisdom of the civil state for uniformity of civil obedience from all sorts).

Twelfthly, lastly, true civility and Christianity may both flourish in a state or kingdom, not withstanding the permission of divers and contrary consciences, either of Jew or Gentile. . . .

Truth. My ears have long been filled with a threefold doleful outcry.

First, of one hundred forty-four thousand virgins (Rev. 14) forced and ravished by emperors, kings and governors to their beds of worship and religion, set up (like Absalom's) on high in their several states and countries.

Secondly, the cry of those precious souls under the altar (Rev. 6), the souls of such as have been persecuted and slain for the testimony and witness of Jesus, whose blood has been spilt like water upon the earth, and that because they have held fast the truth and witness of Jesus, against the worship of the states and times, compelling to an uniformity of state religion.

These cries of murdered virgins who can sit still and hear? Who but can run with zeal inflamed to prevent the deflowering of chaste souls and spilling of the blood of the innocents? Humanity stirs up and prompts the sons of men to draw material swords for a virgin's chastity and life against a ravishing murderer. And piety and Christianity must needs awaken the sons of God to draw the spiritual sword (the Word of God) to preserve the chastity and life

* From Roger Williams, "The Bloudy Tenent of Persecution for Cause of Conscience Discussed in a Conference Betweene Truth and Peace," *Publications of the Narragansett Club,* Providence, Rhode Island, First Series, Vol. III (1867), pp. 3 f., 59–61, 63, 73 f., 138 f., 147, 333–335, and 399 f., (modernized by the editor).

of spiritual virgins, who abhor the spiritual defilements of false worship (Rev. 14).

Thirdly, the cry of the whole earth, made drunk with the blood of its inhabitants, slaughtering each other in their blinded zeal, for conscience, for religion, against the Catholics, against the Lutherans, etc.

What fearful cries within these twenty years of hundreds of thousands men, women, children, fathers, mothers, husbands, wives, brethren, sisters, old and young, high and low, plundered, ravished, slaughtered, murdered, famished. And hence these cries, that men fling away the spiritual sword and spiritual artillery (in spiritual and religious causes) and rather trust for the suppressing of each other's God, conscience and religion (as they suppose) to an arm of flesh and sword of steel. . . .

I acknowledge that to molest any person, Jew or Gentile, for either professing doctrine, or practising worship merely religious or spiritual, it is to persecute him, and such a person (whatever his doctrine or practice be, true or false) suffers persecution for conscience. . . .

O, how lost are the sons of men in this point. To illustrate this: The church or company of worshippers (whether true or false) is like unto a body or college of physicians in a city; like unto a corporation, or company of East Indian or Turkish merchants, or any other society or company in London: which companies may hold their courts, keep their records, hold disputations; and in matters concerning their society may dissent, divide, break into schisms and factions, sue and implead each other at the law, yea wholly break up and dissolve into pieces and nothing, and yet the peace of the city not be in the least measure impaired or disturbed; because the essence or being of the city, and so the well-being and peace thereof is essentially distinct from those particular societies; the city courts, city laws, city punishments distinct from theirs. The city was before them, and stands absolute and entire, when such a corporation or society is taken down. For instance further, the city or civil state of Ephesus was essentially distinct from the worship of Diana in the city, or of the whole city. Again, the church of Christ in Ephesus (which were God's people, converted and called out from the worship of that city unto Christianity or worship of God in Christ) was distinct from both.

Now suppose that God remove the candlestick from Ephesus, yea though the whole worship of the city of Ephesus should be altered: yet (if men be true and honestly ingenious to city covenants, combinations and principles) all this might be without the least impeachment or infringement of peace of the city of Ephesus.

Thus in the city of Smyrna was the city itself or civil state one thing, the spiritual or religious state of Smyrna another; the church of Christ in Smyrna, distinct from them both; and the synagogue of the Jews, whether literally Jews (as some think) or mystically, false Christians, (as others) called the Synagogue of Satan (Rev. 2), distinct from all these. And notwithstanding these spiritual oppositions in point of worship and religion, yet hear we not the least noise (nor need we, if men keep but the bond of civility) of any civil breach, or breach of civil peace amongst them: and to persecute God's people there for religion, that only was a breach of civility itself. . . .

A carnal weapon or sword of steel may produce a carnal repentance, a show, an outside, an uniformity through a state or kingdom: but it has pleased the Father to exalt the Lord Jesus only, to be a prince (armed with power and means sufficient) to give repentance to Israel (Acts 5:31).

Accordingly an unbelieving soul being dead in sin (although he be changed from one worship to another, like a dead man shifted into several changes of apparel) cannot please God (Heb. 11), and consequently, whatever such an unregenerate and unbelieving person acts in worship or religion, it is but sin (Rom. 14). Preaching sin; praying (though without beads or books) sin; breaking of bread, or Lord's Supper, sin; yea as odious as the oblation of swine's blood, a dog's neck, or killing of a man (Isa. 66).

But faith, it is that gift which proceeds alone from the Father of light, (Phil. 1:29) and till he please to make his light arise and open the eyes of blind sinners, their souls shall be fast asleep (and the faster, in that a sword of steel compels them to a worship in hypocrisy) in the dungeons of spiritual darkness and Satan's slavery.

Peace. I add that a civil sword (as woeful experience in all ages has proved) is so far from bringing or helping forward an opposite in religion to repentance, that magistrates sin grievously against the work of God and blood of souls by such proceedings. Because as (commonly) the sufferings of false and antichristian teachers harden their followers, who being blind, by this means are occasioned to tumble into the ditch of Hell after their blind leaders, with more inflamed zeal of lying confidence. So secondly, violence and a sword of steel begets such an impression in the sufferers that certainly they conclude (as indeed that religion cannot be true which needs such instruments of violence to uphold it so) that persecutors are far from soft and gentle commiseration of the blindness of others. To this purpose it pleased the Father of spirits, of old, to constrain the emperor of Rome, Antonius Pius, to write to all the governors of his province to forbear to persecute the Christians, because such dealing must needs be so far from converting the Christians from their way, that it rather begat in their minds an opinion of their cruelty, etc. . . .

I hence observe, that there being in this scripture held forth a two-fold state, a civil state and a spiritual, civil officers and spiritual, civil weapons and spiritual weapons, civil vengeance and punishment, and a spiritual vengeance and punishment; although the spirit speaks not here expressly of civil magistrates and their civil weapons, yet these states being of different natures and considerations, as far differing as spirit from flesh, I first observe, that civil weapons are most improper and unfitting in matters of the spiritual state and kingdom, through in the civil state most proper and suitable. . . .

Peace. By these weights we may try the weight of that commonly received and not questioned opinion, *viz.,* that the civil state and the spiritual, the Church and Commonwealth, they are like Hippocrates' twins; they are born together, grow up together, laugh together, weep together, sicken and die together.

Truth. A witty, yet a most dangerous fiction of the father of lies, who hardened in rebellion against God, persuades God's people to drink down such deadly poison, though he knows the truth of these five particulars, which I shall remind you of.

First, many flourishing states in the world have been and are at this day, which hear not of Jesus Christ, and therefore have not the presence and concurrence of a church of Christ with them.

Secondly, there have been many thousands of God's people, who in their personal estate and life of grace were awake to God, but in respect of church estate they knew no other than a church of dead stones, the parish church; or though some light be of late come in through some cranny, yet they seek not after, or least of all are joined to any true church of God, consisting of living and believing stones.

So that by these New England minister's principles, not only is the door of calling to magistracy shut against natural and unregenerate men (though excellently fitted for civil offices) but also against the best and ablest servants of God, except they be entered into church estate, so that thousands of God's own people (excellently qualified) not knowing, or not entering into such a church estate, shall not be accounted fit for civil services.

Thirdly, admit that a civil magistrate be neither a member of a true Church of Christ (if any be in his dominions) nor in his person fear God, yet may he possibly give free permission without molesting, yea and sometimes encouragement and assistance to the service and Church of God. Thus we find Abraham permitted to build and set up an altar to his God wheresoever he came amongst the idolatrous nations in the land of Canaan. Thus Cyrus proclaims liberty to all the people of God in his dominions, freely to go up and build the Temple of God at Jerusalem, and Artaxerxes after him confirmed it.

Thus the Roman emperors and governors under him permitted the Church of God, the Jews in the Lord Christ's time, their temple and worship, although in civil things they were subject to the Romans.

Fourthly, the scriptures of truth and the records of time concur in this, that the first churches of Christ Jesus, the lights, patterns, and precedents to all succeeding ages, were gathered and governed without the aid, assistance, or countenance of any civil authority, from which they suffered great persecutions for the name of the Lord Jesus professed among them.

The nations, rulers, and kings of the earth tumultuously rage against the Lord and his Anointed (Psalms 2:1–2). Yet (verse 6) it hath pleased the Father to set the Lord Jesus King upon his holy hill of Zion. Christ Jesus would not be pleased to make use of the civil magistrate to assist Him in his spiritual kingdom: nor would he yet be daunted or discouraged in his servants by all their threats and terrors: for love is strong as death, and the coals thereof give a most vehement flame, and are not quenched by all the waters and floods of mightiest opposition (Cant. 8).

Christ's Church is like a chaste and loving wife, in whose heart is fixed her husband's love, who hath found the tenderness of his love towards her, and has been made fruitful by him, and therefore seeks she not the smiles, nor fears the frowns of all the emperors in the world to bring her Christ unto her, or keep him from her. . . .

A pagan or antichristian pilot may be as skillfull to carry the ship to its desired port, as any Christian mariner or pilot in the world, and may perform that work with as much safety and speed: yet have they not command over the souls and consciences of their passengers or mariners under them, although they may justly see to the labor of the one, and the civil behavior of all in the ship. A Christian pilot, he performs the same work, (as likewise does the metaphorical pilot in the ship of the commonweal) from a principle of knowledge and experience: but more than this, he acts from a root of the fear of God and love to mankind, in his whole course. Secondly, his aim is more to glorify God than to gain his pay, or make his voyage. Thirdly, he walks heavenly with men and God in a constant observation of God's hand in storms, calms, etc. So that the thread of navigation being equally spun by a believing or unbelieving pilot, yet is it drawn over with the gold of godliness and Christianity by a Christian pilot, while he is holy in all manner of Christianity, (1. Peter 1:15). But lastly, the Christian pilot's power over the souls and consciences of his sailors and passengers is not greater than that of the antichristian, otherwise than he can subdue the souls of any by the two-edged sword of the Spirit, the Word of God, and by his holy demeanor in his place, etc. . . .

JOHN WESLEY (1703–1791)

Among those who initiated a revival of the evangelical spirit in eighteenth century Protestantism, John Wesley stands out as the most influential leader, equally gifted as a preacher of vital religion and an organizer of the following he won. He was born in 1703 at Epworth Rectory, the son of an Anglican priest and one of 19 children. To his mother Susanna, one of the most remarkable women in the history of the modern Church, he owed a Christian upbringing that determined his character. He was educated at Oxford, and in 1728 he was ordained a priest in the Church of England. After his conversion in 1738 which gave him the evangelical faith he longed for, he became the acknowledged leader of the evangelical revival in Great Britain. The break between the Methodist movement and the Church of England grew unavoidable when Wesley, toward the end of his life, decided to ordain some of his associates to the ministry. He justified this action on biblical grounds, for he had become convinced that there was no basic difference in New Testament times between a bishop and a presbyter.

Methodism in England was concurrent with the Pietistic movement in Germany and the beginning of the "Great Awakenings" in America. Wesley's account of the Methodist revival clearly indicates the pattern of thought and action common to these movements in the eighteenth century, which aimed at the revival of the religious life and left a lasting imprint on Protestantism.

A Plain Account of the People Called Methodist*

About ten years ago, my brother and I were desired to preach in many parts of London. We had no view therein but, so far as we were able (and we knew God could work by whomsoever it pleased him) to convince those who would hear what true Christianity was and to persuade them to embrace it.

The points we chiefly insisted upon were four: First, that orthodoxy or right opinions is, at best, but a very slender part of religion if it can be allowed to be any part of it at all; that neither does religion consist in negatives, in bare harmlessness of any kind; nor merely in externals, in doing good, or using the means of grace, in works of piety (so called) or of charity; that it is nothing short of, or different from, "the mind that was in Christ;" the image of God stamped upon the heart; inward righteousness, attended with the peace of God; and "joy in the Holy Ghost." Secondly, that the only way under heaven to this religion is to "repent and believe the gospel;" or (as the Apostle words it), "repentance towards God, and faith in our Lord Jesus Christ." Thirdly, that by this faith "he that worketh not, but believeth on him that justifieth the ungodly, is justified freely by his grace, through the redemption which is in Jesus Christ." And, lastly, that "being justified by faith" we taste of the heaven to which we are going; we are holy and happy; we tread down sin and fear, and "sit in heavenly places with Christ Jesus."

Many of those who heard this began to cry out that we brought "strange things to their ears;" that this was doctrine which they never heard before, or at least never regarded. They "searched the Scriptures, whether these things were so," and acknowledged "the truth as it is in Jesus." Their hearts also were influenced as well as their understandings, and they determined to follow "Jesus Christ, and him crucified."

Immediately they were surrounded with difficulties;—all the world rose up against them; neighbours, strangers, acquaintance, relations, friends, began to cry out amain, "Be not righteous overmuch; why shouldest thou destroy thyself?" Let not "much religion make thee mad."

One and another and another came to us, asking what they should do, being distressed on every side; as every one strove to weaken, and none to strengthen, their hands in God. We advised them, "Strengthen you one another. Talk together as often as you can. And pray earnestly with and for one another, that you may 'endure to the end, and be saved.' " Against this advice we presumed there could be no objection; as being grounded on the plainest reason, and on so many scriptures both of the Old Testament and New, that it would be tedious to recite them.

They said, "But we want you likewise to talk with us often, to direct and quicken us in our way, to give us the advices which you well know we need, and to pray with us, as well as for us." I asked, Which of you desire this? Let me know your names and places of abode. They did so. But I soon found they were too many for me to talk with severally so often as they wanted it. So I told them, "If you will all of you come together every Thursday, in the evening, I will gladly spend some time with you in prayer and give you the best advice I can."

Thus arose, without any previous design on either side, what was afterwards called a Society; a very innocent name, and very common in London, for any number of people associating themselves together. The thing proposed in their associating themselves together was obvious to every one. They wanted to "flee from the wrath to come," and to assist each other in so doing. They therefore united themselves "in order to pray together, to receive the word of exhortation, and to watch over one another in love, that they might help each other to work out their salvation."

There is one only condition previously required in those who desire admission into this society,—"a desire to flee from the wrath to come, to be saved from their sins."

They now likewise agreed that as many of them as had an opportunity would meet together every Friday and spend the dinner hour

* From *The Works of John Wesley,* 3rd ed. London: John Mason, 1830, Vol. VIII, pp. 248–253, and 257.

in crying to God, both for each other and for all mankind.

It quickly appeared that their thus uniting together answered the end proposed therein. In a few months the far greater part of those who had begun to "fear God, and work righteousness," but were not united together, grew faint in their minds, and fell back into what they were before. Meanwhile the far greater part of those who were thus united together continued "striving to enter in at the strait gate" and to "lay hold on eternal life."

Upon reflection I could not but observe, This is the very thing which was from the beginning of Christianity. In the earliest times, those whom God had sent forth "preached the gospel to every creature." And "the body of hearers" were mostly either Jews or Heathens. But as soon as any of these were so convinced of the truth as to forsake sin and seek the gospel salvation, they immediately joined them together, took an account of their names, advised them to watch over each other, and met these "catechumens" (as they were then called), apart from the great congregation, that they might instruct, rebuke, exhort, and pray with them, and for them, according to their several necessities.

But it was not long before an objection was made to this, which had not once entered into my thought:—"Is not this making a schism? Is not the joining these people together, gathering churches out of churches?"

It was easily answered, If you mean only gathering people out of buildings called churches, it is. But if you mean, dividing Christians from Christians and so destroying Christian fellowship, it is not. For, (1) These were not Christians before they were thus joined. Most of them were barefaced Heathens. (2) Neither are they Christians, from whom you suppose them to be divided. You will not look me in the face and say they are. What! drunken Christians! cursing and swearing Christians! lying Christians! cheating Christians! If these are Christians at all, they are devil Christians, as the poor Malabarians term them. (3) Neither are they divided any more than they were before, even from these wretched devil Christians. They are as ready as ever to assist them and to perform every office of real kindness towards them. (4) If it be said, "But there are some true Christians in the parish, and you destroy the Christian fellowship between these and them," I answer, That which never existed, cannot be destroyed. But the fellowship you speak of never existed. Therefore it cannot be destroyed. Which of those true Christians had any such fellowship with these? Who watched over them in love? Who marked their growth in grace? Who advised and exhorted them from time to time? Who prayed with them and for them as they had need? This, and this alone, is Christian fellowship: but, alas! where is it to be found? Look east or west, north or south; name what parish you please: Is this Christian fellowship there? Rather, are not the bulk of the parishioners a mere rope of sand? What Christian connexion is there between them? What intercourse in spiritual things? What watching over each other's souls? What bearing of one another's burdens? What a mere jest is it then to talk so gravely of destroying what never was! The real truth is just the reverse of this: We introduce Christian fellowship where it was utterly destroyed. And the fruits of it have been peace, joy, love, and zeal for every good word and work.

But as much as we endeavoured to watch over each other, we soon found some who did not live the gospel. I do not know that any hypocrites were crept in; for indeed there was no temptations: But several grew cold, and gave way to the sins which had long easily beset them. We quickly perceived there were many ill consequences of suffering these to remain among us. It was dangerous to others; inasmuch as all sin is of an infectious nature. It brought such a scandal on their brethren as exposed them to what was not properly the reproach of Christ. It laid a stumbling-block in the way of others, and caused the truth to be evil spoken of.

We groaned under these inconveniences long before a remedy could be found. The people were scattered so wide in all parts of the town, from Wapping to Westminster, that I could not easily see what the behaviour of each person in his own neighbourhood was: So that several disorderly walkers did much hurt before I was apprised of it.

At length, while we were thinking of quite another thing, we struck upon a method for which we have cause to bless God ever since. I was talking with several of the society in Bristol concerning the means of paying the debts there, when one stood up and said, "Let every member of the society give a penny a week till all are paid." Another answered, "But many of them are poor and cannot afford to do it." "Then," said he, "put eleven of the poorest with me; and if they can give anything, well: I will call on them weekly; and if they can give nothing, I will give for them as well as for myself. And each of you call on eleven of your neighbours weekly; receive what they give, and make up what is wanting." It was done. In a while, some of these informed me they found such and such an one did not live as he ought. It struck me immediately, "This is the thing, the very thing we have wanted so long." I called together all the Leaders of the classes (so we used to term them and their companies,) and desired, that each would make a particular inquiry into the behaviour of those whom he saw weekly. They did so. Many disorderly walkers were detected. Some turned from the evil of their ways. Some were put away from us. Many saw it with fear and rejoiced unto God with reverence.

As soon as possible the same method was used in London and all other places. Evil men were detected and reproved. They were borne with for a season. If they forsook their sins, we received them gladly; if they obstinately persisted therein, it was openly declared that they were not of us. The rest mourned and prayed for them and yet rejoiced that, as far as in us lay, the scandal was rolled away from the society. . . .

The thing which I was greatly afraid of all this time and which I resolved to use every possible method of preventing, was a narrowness of spirit, a party zeal, a being straitened in our own bowels; that miserable bigotry which makes many so unready to believe that there is any work of God but among themselves. I thought it might be a help against this, frequently to read to all who were willing to hear the accounts I received from time to time of the work which God is carrying on in the earth, both in our own and other countries, not among us alone, but among those of various opinions and denominations. For this I allotted one evening in every month; and I find no cause to repent my labour. It is generally a time of strong consolation to those who love God and all mankind for his sake; as well as of breaking down the partition walls which either the craft of the devil or the folly of men has built up; and of encouraging every child of God to say (O when shall it once be!), "Whosoever doeth the will of my Father which is in heaven, the same is my brother, and sister, and mother." . . .

Selected Readings on the Reformation

GENERAL

Bainton, R. H., *The Reformation of the Sixteenth Century*. Boston: Beacon Press, 1952 (also in paperback).

Dillenberger, J., and C. Welch, *Protestant Christianity Interpreted Through Its Development*. New York: Charles Scribner's Sons, 1954, Chapters I–VI (also in paperback).

Fosdick, H. E., *Great Voices of the Reformation*. New York: Random House, 1952.

Grimm, H. J., *The Reformation Era, 1500–1650*. New York: The Macmillan Company, 1954.

Harbison, E. H., *The Age of the Reformation*. Ithaca, N.Y.: Cornell University Press, 1955.

———, *The Christian Scholar in the Age of the Reformation.* New York: Charles Scribner's Sons, 1956.

McGiffert, A. C., *Protestant Thought Before Kant.* New York: Charles Scribner's Sons, 1917.

Pauck, W., *The Heritage of the Reformation,* 2nd ed. Glencoe, Ill.: Free Press, 1961.

Whale, J. S., *The Protestant Tradition.* New York: Cambridge University Press, 1955 (also in paperback).

LUTHERANISM

Bainton, R. H., *Here I Stand: The Life of Martin Luther.* Nashville: Abington Press, 1950 (also in paperback).

Boehmer, H., *Martin Luther: Road to Reformation.* Philadelphia: Muhlenberg Press, 1946 (also in paperback).

Fife, R. H., *The Revolt of Martin Luther.* New York: Columbia University Press, 1957.

Kerr, H. T. (ed.), *A Compend of Luther's Theology.* Philadelphia: Westminster Press, 1943.

Mackinnon, J., *Luther and the Reformation,* 4 vols. London: Longmans, Green and Company, 1925–1930.

Manschreck, C., *Melanchthon, The Quiet Reformer.* Nashville: Abingdon Press, 1958.

Rupp, E. G., *The Righteousness of God.* London: Hodder and Stoughton, 1953.

Schwiebert, E. G., *Luther and His Times.* St. Louis: Concordia Publishing House, 1950.

Watson, P., *Let God Be God: An Interpretation of the Theology of Martin Luther.* London: Epworth Press, 1947.

CALVINISM

Farner, O., *Zwingli the Reformer.* New York: Philosophical Library, 1952.

Hunter, A. M., *The Teaching of Calvin,* 2nd ed., London: Clarke, 1950.

Mackinnon, J., *Calvin and the Reformation.* London: Longmans, Green and Company, 1936.

McNeill, J. T., *The History and Character of Calvinism.* New York: Oxford University Press, 1954.

———, (ed.), *Calvin: Institutes of the Christian Religion* (The Library of Christian Classics, Vols. XX and XXI). Philadelphia: Westminster Press, 1961.

Niesel, W., *The Theology of Calvin.* Philadelphia: Westminster Press, 1956.

Parker, T. H. L., *Portrait of Calvin.* Philadelphia: Westminster Press, 1955.

Tawney, R. H., *Religion and the Rise of Capitalism,* 2nd ed. New York: Harcourt, Brace and Company, 1937 (also in paperback).

Walker, W., *John Calvin.* New York: G. P. Putnam's Sons, 1906.

Weber, M., *The Protestant Ethic and the Spirit of Capitalism.* New York: Charles Scribner's Sons, 1930 (also in paperback).

THE ANABAPTISTS

"Anabaptism," in *Encyclopaedia for Religion and Ethics,* ed. by J. Hasting, Vol. I.

Bender, H. S., *Conrad Grebel: The Founder of the Swiss Brethren.* Scottsdale, Pa.: Mennonite Publishing House, 1950.

Horsch, J., *The Mennonites in Europe.* Scottsdale, Pa.: Mennonite Publishing House, 1942.

Littell, F. H., *The Anabaptist View of the Church,* 2nd ed. Boston: Starr King Press, 1958.

Smithson, R. J., *The Anabaptists.* London: Clarke, 1935.

Williams, G. H., and A. M. Mergal, eds., *Spiritual and Anabaptist Writers* (The Library of Christian Classics, Vol. XXV). Philadelphia: Westminster Press, 1957.

THE REFORMATION IN ENGLAND

Bromiley, G. W., *Thomas Cranmer Theologian.* New York: Oxford University Press, 1956.

Constant, G., *The Reformation in England,* 2 vols. New York: Sheed and Ward, 1934–1941.

George, Ch. H., and K. George, *The Protestant Mind of the English Reformation.* Princeton, N. J.: Princeton University Press, 1961.

Hopf, C., *Martin Bucer and the English Reformation.* Oxford: Blackwell, 1946.

More, P. E., and F. L. Cross, eds., *Anglicanism.* London: S.P.C.K., 1935.

Parker, T. M., *The English Reformation to 1558.* New York: Oxford University Press, 1950.

Powicke, F. M., *The Reformation in England.* New York: Oxford University Press, 1949.

Rupp, E. G., *The English Protestant Tradition.* New York: Cambridge University Press, 1949.

Watson, E. W., *The Church of England.* New York: Oxford University Press, 1950.

THE PURITAN REVOLUTION

Davies, H., *The English Free Churches.* New York: Oxford University Press, 1952.

Haller, W., *The Rise of Puritanism.* New York: Columbia University Press, 1938 (also in paperback).

Miller, P., *The New England Mind: The Seventeenth Century.* New York: The Macmillan Company, 1939.

———, and T. H. Johnson (eds.), *The Puritans.* New York: American Book Company, 1938.

Payne, E. A., *The Free Church Tradition in the Life of England,* 3rd ed. London: S. C. M. Press, 1951.

Russell, E., *The History of Quakerism.* New York: The Macmillan Company, 1942.

Schneider, H. W., *The Puritan Mind.* New York: Holt, Rinehart, and Winston, Inc., 1930 (also in paperback).

Torbet, R. G., *A History of the Baptists.* Philadelphia: Judson Press, 1950.

METHODISM

Brailsford, M. R., *A Tale of Two Brothers: John and Charles Wesley.* New York: Oxford University Press, 1954.

Burtner, R. W., and R. E. Chiles, eds., *A Compend of Wesley's Theology.* Nashville: Abingdon Press, 1954.

Cameron, R. M., *The Rise of Methodism.* New York: Philosophical Library, 1954.

Hildebrandt, F., *Christianity According to the Wesleys.* London: Epworth Press, 1956.

Lindstrom, H., *Wesley and Sanctification: A Study in the Doctrine of Salvation.* Stockholm: Nya Bokförlags Aktiebolaget, 1946.

McConnell, F. J., *John Wesley.* Nashville: Abingdon Press, 1939 (also in paperback).

THE STRUGGLE FOR RELIGIOUS LIBERTY

Bainton, R. H., *Hunted Heretic: The Life and Death of Michael Servetus.* Boston: Beacon Press, 1953 (also in paperback).

————, *The Travail of Religious Liberty.* Philadelphia: Westminster Press, 1951 (also in paperback).

Jordan, W. K., *The Development of Religious Toleration in England,* 4 vols. London: Allen and Unwin, 1932–1940.

Leclerc, J., *Toleration and the Reformation,* Vol. 1. New York: Association Press, 1960.

PART FOUR

THE MODERN PERIOD

Chapel of the Holy Cross, Sedona, Arizona.

Seder Service.

Interior of Christ Evangelical Church, Minneapolis.

Camp Meeting Scene. Lithograph, 1858.

Religion in the Modern Period

As we have seen (p. 249), the major denominational developments of the West were completed before 1750. The influence of groups which have arisen since that time hardly compare in their general cultural significance with the impact of new philosophic ideas, new social forces connected with industrialization, and scientific and technological advances.

We must remember that in the sixteenth century Europe was quite small in population and in cultural influence. In size, political influence, power, and civilization western Europe was in many ways inferior to India, the Ottoman Empire, or China. In the next 400 years, however, western Europe expanded in every respect with almost explosive force. She explored and colonized all over the world. Her population increased eight-fold. She gave birth to the industrial revolution and, as a result of her new productivity, grew enormously in power, prestige, and standard of living. Most significant of all, perhaps, she brought new zest to the ancient biblical mandate: "Be fruitful, and multiply, and replenish the earth, and subdue it; and have dominion over the fish of the sea, and over the fowl of the air, and over every living thing that moveth upon the earth." (Gen. 1:28) To this task she brought not only her new productivity and learning, but also the most potent instrument yet known to human history—modern science. (See p. 333.)

In short, the religious institutions and concepts of the West had for their environment in the modern period the most dynamic, growing and changing civilization in history. This makes the task of comprehending religion in the modern period exceedingly complex, for as we know religion is deeply influenced by its environment. We cannot even pretend, therefore, to survey all of the interesting developments of the modern period. The student may consult one of the books suggested at the end of this section for information on the variety of sects and denominations.

Religion in America

Although the 1960 *Yearbook of American Churches* listed some 250 different religious groups, we must not allow this figure to distort our perspective. The overwhelming majority of people, insofar as they are religious at all, belong to one of the major Jewish or Christian groups. Within Protestantism, where we find most of the splinter groups, approximately 80 per cent of the people belong to nine major bodies*—and, with few exceptions, cooperation between these bodies, through such agencies as The National Council of Churches of Christ in America, is reasonably good. In the limited space at our disposal we shall, for the most part, present thinkers representative of these major groups.

The English movements which we have mentioned (pp. 245 f.), together with the other established Christian groups which came as immigrants, formed the basic structure of Christianity in America. It would be well, were there space, to mention all of the indigenous groups which sprang up on American soil. Some of them were essentially subdivisions of bodies already mentioned. Thus, the Baptists have been divided in this country into 27 groups, most of them quite small. There are 14 different branches of the Mennonites. Though there are 21 different Methodist bodies, approximately 8,790,000 of the total number of Methodists (approximately 8,887,000) belong to The Methodist Church (until 1940 called the Methodist Episcopal Church).

The Lutherans tended to organize along national lines, in terms of the countries from which they had emigrated. Several groups, such as the Disciples of Christ, were founded in the hope that they would become the rallying point for all Christians; but they ended by becoming one more denomination.

Christian Science represents an indigenous American movement. The First Church of Christ Scientist was founded in Boston in 1879 by Mary Baker Eddy. The movement has flourished since that time, numbering now

* According to the report of the Department of Research of the National Council of Churches of Christ in the United States of America, a survey conducted between 1956 and 1958 showed that there were somewhat more than 39,000,000 Protestants. More than 30,000,000 of these belonged to the following groups, in descending numerical order: Methodist, Southern Baptist, Episcopalian, Presbyterian, United Lutheran, Disciples of Christ, Missouri Synod Lutheran, American Baptist (Northern), and Congregational Christian.

perhaps 400,000 adherents.* In theology it diverges from traditional Christianity at a number of fundamental points. It is best known for its great stress upon spiritual healing.

In the early part of the 18th century, both in England and America, the Unitarian movement sprang up. (See the selection from William Ellery Channing, p. 404.) Originally it was a protest against certain Christian doctrines, particularly in their Calvinistic forms. This group denied the doctrine of the Trinity, insisted upon the humanity, and denied the deity, of Jesus, and utterly rejected the notion that our sins were forgiven through the sacrifice of Christ. In more recent times, Unitarianism has become increasingly liberal in its theology, to the extent that many of its members today would regard themselves as humanists or naturalists.

The Church of Jesus Christ of Latter-day Saints (popularly called "Mormon") is another significant native American development. Based upon a revelation to Joseph Smith in 1820, a revelation which urged him to restore the Gospel of Jesus Christ to its original purity, the new group underwent severe persecution and was forced to move several times. Finally, under the leadership of Brigham Young, they migrated to the valley of the Great Salt Lake in Utah, arriving there in 1847. The practice of polygamy which was once practiced by some of the group, and which was no doubt in large part responsible for the hostility towards them, was outlawed by a decree of Wilford Woodruff, then president of the Church, in 1890. The 1960 Yearbook of American Churches lists their number as approximately 846,000.

Judaism

Judaism in the modern world has been deeply affected by the same factors as Protestantism. In America, for example, it is customary to discuss the synagogue in terms of three major branches: Orthodox, Reform, and Conservative (see p. 343, p. 349, and p. 347, respectively). With reservations one may say that these differences are similar to the conservativism, liberalism and neo-orthodoxy which developed in Protestantism (see p. 335). One of the most important factors differentiating these groups is their response to the challenge of modern science. Orthodox Judaism wishes to retain its whole tradition and tends to regard its Scripture as inerrant. Reform Judaism, particularly in its early days, wished to bring every item of tradition before the bar of modern experience and reason, and to discard or modify whatever could not be justified in this court.

Conservative Judaism has typically held that Judaism must remain true

* Recent surveys do not contain figures for The Church of Christ Scientist, because a regulation of that body forbids the numbering of the people. The Census of Religious Bodies, 1936, published by the U. S. Bureau of the Census, reports 268,915 members, but there is reason to believe that this figure is low.

to her historic tradition; but this has been interpreted in a dynamic way which leaves room for critical biblical studies and certain modern alterations or innovations.

However, in considering modern Judaism, at least three special factors must be remembered. First, European Jews lived largely in ghetto conditions, almost completely isolated from the general culture, until the late 18th century. In 1791, under the influence of the Revolution, Jews in France were for the first time granted full civil equality. Emancipation in other western European countries followed swiftly. In America, their freedom had come earlier in such colonies as Pennsylvania and Rhode Island. And with the Bill of Rights they received full legal equality everywhere in the nation.

Before emancipation Judaism was largely cut off from the currents of modern thought, though there were some brilliant exceptions, like Spinoza. Nor did emancipation change things overnight. Most Jews until fairly recently were educated in classical Talmudic studies and knew little of modern rationalism or science. In the United States, immigrants from eastern Europe, in particular, lived in the closed society of orthodoxy. Their children, however, in their eagerness to become Americans, often went to extremes in repudiating the past (see the selection from Will Herberg, p. 366).

Particularly in Germany, and then later in the United States, emancipated Jews quickly assimilated modern learning. In this environment, Reform Judaism was born. Partly in reaction to what they regarded as the excesses of Reform, a group under the leadership of Solomon Schechter began the Conservative movement.

A second thing to be remembered in considering modern Judaism is the fact that Judaism has no official creed. Philosophy and theology seem much less central to Judaism than are history and the celebration of festivals and holy days. Therefore, in spite of the differences noted above, there has been little tendency for radical splits to develop in Judaism. This same factor has meant that, in some ways, the rise of empiricism (see p. 334) has not been a serious threat to Judaism. Judaism has been less concerned with the rational proof of certain theological statements than with living its cultural heritage.

Finally, there can be little doubt that a feeling of solidarity has bound all Jews together, regardless of degree of "orthodoxy," both because of their cultural and historical orientation and because of the hardships and persecutions many of them have faced. The plight of European Jews, particularly under Hitler, gave rise to heroic efforts of common aid. These trials, also, gave a new urgency to the Zionist objectives (see p. 351) which resulted in the establishment of the State of Israel in 1948.

Roman Catholicism

It is common to suggest that, by comparison with other western religious groups, Roman Catholicism has changed little in the modern period. The Council of Trent (see p. 218) reformed certain abuses of the late medieval period and also gave definite direction to the theological work of the future. For the most part, modern Roman Catholicism has gloried in the domination of her theological efforts by the system and spirit of St. Thomas Aquinas (see p. 129 and pp. 185 f.). With this firm foundation, she has seemed better able than other religious groups to meet with equanimity the challenges of modern secular science.

Nevertheless, significant developments have not been lacking. For one thing, the Virgin Mary, who always held a lofty place in Roman Catholic piety, has been the center of a new doctrinal pronouncement. In 1950, Pope Pius XII defined the dogma of the Bodily Assumption of Mary.

Also, the relations of church and state have been intensively discussed both within and outside of Roman Catholicism. On the one hand, the hierarchical structure within the Church has been more precisely defined, especially in the dogma of 1870, proclaiming the infallibility of the Pope as head of the Church on earth and Vicar of Christ. On the other hand, the popular development of democratic institutions in civil life has provided a fresh context for the discussion of the proper relations between church and state.

Some New Social Factors

Historians and sociologists of religion have demonstrated how deeply religious movements are affected by changing social conditions, as well as how great an influence religion has had upon other aspects of life. In the modern period industrialization, urbanization, the democratic revolutions, and the technological advances, to mention a few factors, have so transformed the cultural environment that people tend to look at religion with new eyes and bring to it a whole new set of aspirations and presuppositions. We may single out for special mention two developments which have had perhaps the greatest effect upon religion. For convenience, these may be labeled "secularism" and "pluralism." Though distinguishable, the two are closely related.

SECULARISM

"Secularism" is used here to refer both to an attitude and to a certain type of social organization. The difference in attitude between the Middle Ages, or the Reformation, and the modern world is fundamental, even if it is difficult to describe. For pre-modern man, religious categories were central and all-pervasive in a way which no longer seems to be true. Not only did religion give him his understanding of his ultimate origins and destiny, but it also provided the explanation for the events of daily life. His food was a gift of the Creator, his work was his "calling" from God, his misfortunes were somehow sent as chastisements or as trials, and his blessings were signs of divine grace.

In the modern period, even the religious man typically and spontaneously gives "natural" explanations for such matters. Illness is due to germs or to bodily weakness of some sort. An advance in one's job or profession is due to hard work and skill, or to the influence of one's friends. Though the religious man still feels that ultimately God is the source of all things and the ruler of history, he is more inclined to turn to science for any detailed explanation of particular events.

And what are we to say of those moderns who are non-religious, or only vaguely religious? In their case, the tendency is even stronger to understand their lives without reference to God. This is the meaning of secularism: leaving God out of the understanding of one's life.

Secularism is perhaps partly caused by, and is unquestionably compounded with, the typical fascination of modern people with the good things of this life. Increasingly people act as though the chief end of life were to enjoy good health, prosperity and a good reputation—not to "glorify God and enjoy Him forever" (as Calvin had phrased it). Furthermore, many people not only *act* this way but philosophically defend such goals as the only ones which reasonable men can understand or that anyone can really hope to attain.

The attitude of secularism is by no means confined to a few humanists or atheists. It pervades every aspect of our culture, including church and synagogue. Therefore, it presents a subtle challenge to the whole of the Judaeo-Christian tradition. It tempts Jews and Christians to modify the understanding of their faith in a subtle yet profound way. Thus there is a tendency on the part of those who regard themselves as religious to treat their faith as one of the good things of life, one factor among others which is conducive to full happiness. Does not religious faith reduce our anxieties? Does it not support our democratic way of life? Does it not help our children to acquire certain essential social values?

These questions are perhaps susceptible of empirical answers. Perhaps religion does, in fact, do these things. If so, people who are concerned with these values can hardly be blamed for "being religious." Yet it is fair to ask whether, in the process, we have not turned upside down the very religious faith whose name we attach to such concerns. For now the focus seems to be on the self and its desire for a happy life, the self which naturally uses any instrument likely to promote its ends. In this process the God of judgment, known to the prophets, is not mentioned. One might almost say that it is no longer God, but the happy life, which is worshipped. God is reduced to a means to an end—and it is of such a "god" that traditional Judaism and Christianity have always applied the concept "idol."

Secularism may also refer to a new phenomenon in history—the so-called "omnicompetent state." Most states or kingdoms known to us in history have represented themselves as based upon the will or favor of the "gods"—or, at least, of some divine higher law. The American Declaration of Independence reflects the same concept, even if only in the somewhat vague terms of Deism (see p. 334). Certainly, so far as both Judaism and Christianity are concerned, the state or nation is not the source or ultimate judge of law. Yet, increasingly, the tendency is to refer our laws and our judicial judgments only to human factors—to "the Constitution," to legal precedent, or to the welfare of "the people."

Religious groups or ideologies are, of course, isolated from direct influence upon government wherever the doctrine of "separation of church and state" is adopted. But secularism means more than this. It means, first, that the state ought to consider only the temporal welfare of its people in its laws and decisions, and, second, that there is no higher authority than the law of the state to which a citizen might appeal.

There can be no doubt that secularism, in both senses, has seemed to many people the inevitable correlary of another modern social phenomenon, which might be called "pluralism."

PLURALISM

The bloody Thrity Years' War, ended by the Peace of Westphalia in 1648, demonstrated the futility of the medieval ideal of a unified Christendom. Yet the various religious groups were slow to learn the lesson. The notion of a pluralistic society, where men were not only free but encouraged to criticize every orthodoxy, was unheard of.

Today pluralism is a fact, and we can perhaps even say that its emergence was inescapable. The diffusion of populations, the bringing together in vast urban areas of a variety of peoples, the spread of the democratic ideal, the decrease of certainty regarding religious matters on the part of large segments of society affected by modern rationalism, the dedication of certain sectarian religious groups to the principle of "voluntary association," and perhaps above all the bloodshed and misery caused by intolerance—all of these factors combined to usher in an age of toleration.

Not only is such toleration supported by the democratic and liberal ideals, but it is guaranteed by the secular state. Conversely, the ideal of toleration has contributed indirectly to the growth of secularism. With the freedom to believe as one chooses, an impressive array of divergent religious sects has developed. Faced with such a bewildering variety of opinions, many sensitive people have asked, "How can anyone be sure that *his* faith is right?" Although "subjectivism" does not *logically* follow from the fact of variety, the degree of pluralism has had the psychological effect of increasing the feeling that all religious matters are somehow "relative." For anyone who feels this way, religion begins to appear as one aspect of life which happens to be important for some individuals, but which cannot be a principle of coherence for a whole society. For such common principles one must then turn to secular sources.

Pluralism creates a strange paradox for Judaism or Christianity. On the one hand, most Jews and Christians today not only embrace the principle of toleration but feel that it is implied in the notion of the universal God who loves all his children. Yet, on the other hand, the Jew or Christian cannot admit that it does not matter what an individual believes. Such an admission, not an uncommon fruit of toleration, implies indifference to religious faith. No, the Jew or the Christian believes that there is objective *truth* in his faith. Though he may tolerate other viewpoints, is he not bound to regard them as at least partially wrong? Apparently it is difficult for human beings to combine tolerance and commitment. The danger is that one will slip either into fanaticism or into indifference.

The Impact of Science

The current religious scene cannot be understood without an assessment of the impact of modern science. Both theoretically and practically it has transformed the cultural situation. We cannot discuss in detail the practical repercussions of the advances of science, but we may mention three very briefly. First, it was the fruits of science which made industrialization possible, which in turn radically altered the living habits of the people. Living in vast urban areas and working for a wage in a large, impersonal organization disrupted traditional religious ties for many people, just as it put new strains on traditional family structure. Second, applied science has made it possible to raise our living standard enormously, and thus seems to be closely related to a growing "secularism" (see p. 330). Many people seem more inclined to define their life purposes in terms of economic and social success than in terms of religious values. Third, science has delivered into our hands vast new powers, powers to alter our environment, to blow it up, and even (through medical research) to influence certain personality characteristics of the individual. On the one hand, this new power has tempted modern man to think that he is sufficient to every need and that he no longer needs divine guidance. On the other hand, it has posed fateful and pressing ethical problems with which contemporary religious groups must deal.

Our chief concern is with the impact of science upon the world of ideas. In discussing this matter we touch more upon philosophy than upon science itself. Individual scientists, perfectly competent in their fields, have taken a variety of positions philosophically, insofar as they have been concerned with speculative matters. Science, itself, is neither idealistic nor materialistic, for or against "free will," nor is it committed to any one general theory of knowledge. Nevertheless, especially in England and America, the rise of modern science has been closely connected with a powerful tendency towards empiricism (see below).

Nor can there be much doubt that the triumphs of science largely determined the mood of the so-called Enlightenment. Prepared for by Renaissance humanism and the scientific revolution, and closely associated with the democratic revolutions, the Enlightenment of the eighteenth century glorified the powers of man's reason. Its mood was optimistic and expansive. It seemed that mankind, long dependent upon natural forces which he could not understand, was on the verge of rational control of his own destiny. Many thinkers felt that the same methods used by the physical scientists could be extended to the study of man and society. The expectation was that this would enable man to plan and contrive a just, harmonious and comfortable social existence. No longer was man dependent upon unseen forces, or upon God. Indeed, belief in a providential deity was thought to detract from man's dignity. Therefore, insofar as the Enlightenment displayed any religious feeling at all, it tended to take the form known as Deism. According to Deism, God's function was simply to create the world of nature originally. Once created, the world ran its own course according to immutable natural laws. There was no room for divine intervention of any kind, and therefore the task fell to man to bring in the era of righteousness. According to this view, "salvation" lay not in a crucified savior from the past but in the future which man would make for himself. The Jeffersonian doctrine of religious freedom, incidentally, was an expression of the Deism of the Enlightenment.

EMPIRICISM

Much of this Enlightenment temper is to be found in modern empiricism, though the latter does not necessarily involve the optimistic notion of progress. Broadly speaking, "empiricism" is the view that all knowledge comes by way of rational analysis of experience—and the modern empiricists have as a rule limited this to sense experience. Thus empiricism is not a broad "world view" but a theory of knowledge; yet, as such, it has had the most profound effect upon religious thought in our time. The empiricists were struck by the fact that in science a method had been developed whereby differing theories could be put to the test of experience. In many cases this test resulted in complete public agreement as to the truth of the matter; in other cases there was at least a commonly agreed upon method for attempting to resolve differences. This was in marked contrast with the methods employed in much philosophy, in theology, and in ethics, where history seemed to show a constant parade of different interpretations, with no method for resolving them.

Wherein lies the superiority of the method of science? It lies, according to empiricism, in the interplay of reason and sense observations. On the basis of careful observations, a theory is proposed which, if true, would account for what has been observed. Then by reason or logic, predictions are made of further events which might be expected under given conditions, if the theory were true. Then, one returns to careful observation to see if the expected events do in fact occur. If they do, the theory is to that extent confirmed. Crudely speaking, we may state the principle of empiricism as follows: a statement represents true knowledge if and only if it can be confirmed by sense observations. Such knowledge, resting upon experience, is never regarded as infallible, but its reliability increases with the degree of confirmatory experimental data.

There is a further, perhaps even more consequential implication of this position. What are we to say of a statement for which we cannot devise any method of testing (by sense observations) whether it is true or false? The implication drawn by most modern empiricists is that such a statement is "meaningless." It is meaningless, at least so far as knowledge is concerned, though they might concede to it a kind of "emotional" meaning, like an expression of one's wishes or a spontaneous exclamation.

It has seemed to many modern philosophers who have adopted the empiricist position that religious language has little or nothing to do with knowledge. The reliability of "faith" or "revelation" is brought into radical questioning, since statements of faith do not seem to lend themselves to confirmation by sense observations. Many such philosophers have conceded that religion may have something to do with moral judgments, which seem also to fall into the shadow land beyond the realm of knowledge. Yet, on the whole, the empiricist position, if adopted, has seemed to place religious claims in an unfavorable light, reducing them to a kind of "subjective" basis.

No doubt the vast majority of people have never troubled their heads with such considerations. Nevertheless, in subtle ways the influence of this position has spread. Particularly among educated people there seems to be a kind of crude empiricist axiom at work: *one ought not to commit himself in belief on any matter until it has been proven.* And "proof" generally means verification by sense observation.

LIBERALISM, FUNDAMENTALISM, NEO-ORTHODOXY

It is not our function here to discuss the merits of empiricism. The comments below (p. 337 and p. 338) on positivism and existentialism may, however, suggest certain critical points. A vast literature is growing up among philosophers of religion on this subject. Our purpose is to describe very briefly how the major religious groups have been affected by this trend. There were those who favored radical revision of ancient traditions in the light of modern scientific thought: these are usually called "liberals." There were those who fought for the preservation of the ancient faith in all its particulars. These maintained, as the basis for all other matters of faith, the literal inerrancy of the Bible, and they are often called "fundamentalists" or "conservatives." Yet another tendency found increasing favor among the majority of the older and well-established protestant groups, as well as in conservative Judaism: this was the attempt to harmonize the methods and results of modern thought, including the critical study of the Bible, with the fundamental theological insights of orthodoxy. We have no good name to suggest for this broad tendency. Sometimes it has been dubbed "neo-orthodoxy."

It is very important for the student to realize that these movements—liberalism, fundamentalism, and neo-orthodoxy—cut across denominational lines. Some groups, such as the Unitarians, are wholly in the liberal camp; some, such as various Pentecostal groups, are wholly in the fundamentalist camp; some, such as the Baptists (particularly in the South), are predominantly conservative if not fundamentalist. But among many of our major denominations—Episcopalian, Lutheran, Methodist, Presbyterian, Congregationalist, and to some extent Baptist—one finds a variety of theological stances. A neo-orthodox Methodist has much more in common with a neo-orthodox Presbyterian than with a conservative or fundamentalist member of his own denomination.

Broadly speaking, the European and American religious situation has been deeply influenced by liberalism. What does this mean, the dawn of a "liberal" era? It means that for vast numbers of religious people ancient religious documents, such as the Bible and the creeds, need not be taken literally. Once this feeling is abroad, the doors are open to much revision. If the tides of liberalism continue to run strong, we must reckon with the possibility that the Christianity and the Judaism of the future will display significant differences from what we have known in the past.

ROMAN CATHOLICISM

The above discussion of the impact of science upon religion does not do justice, however, to the situation of Roman Catholicism, which in this respect constitutes a special case. There can be no doubt that some individuals left the Roman Catholic faith because of liberal or skeptical doubts. The Church, herself, met the challenge in a calm and stable way. The great system of St. Thomas Aquinas (see p. 185) proved invaluable in this respect. For, in some ways, St. Thomas himself was an empiricist. He insisted that all natural knowledge was mediated by sense experience and subject to the principles of logical reasoning. But he also held that above our knowledge of nature there is another realm, which in no way conflicts with the former. And this is the realm of revelation, faith, and grace. In addition, Roman Catholicism was aided by its central authority, which was able to guide its members in doctrinal matters.

Does the West Face a Crisis?

A number of philosophers and theologians have been suggesting recently that Western culture faces a crisis. By this they mean that the fundamental concepts underlying the Enlightenment (see p. 334), concepts which tended to produce optimism concerning progress through science, have been so radically questioned that their survival is in doubt. It is certainly true that since the Second World War the mood of the West, as reflected in its art and its philosophic tendencies, has become introspective and skeptical—uncertain of its own principles.

POSITIVISM

One prominent philosophic movement of recent years is usually referred to as "positivism" or "logical empiricism." In one sense, it simply carries further the implications of "empiricism" (see p. 334). But even to many who are sympathetic with its doctrines, it has seemed to imply a basic skepticism concerning the older hopes for progress through science. This is certainly not due to any anti-scientific bias. On the contrary, positivism holds that the methods of science are the only ones which yield knowledge; yet it suggests that fundamental standards of value and questions concerning the purposes of life fall outside the scope of such knowledge and are, therefore, without any objective foundation.

This conclusion is related to the principle of meaning discussed above (see p. 335). Unless a statement can in principle be confirmed by sense observations, it lacks objective significance—even though it may have a subjective meaning, expressing, for example, the feelings of the speaker. Standards of value, norms by which to evaluate things or actions and in terms of which social objectives might be determined, do not seem to be susceptible of such confirmation by sense observation. No matter how accurately we may describe what *is* the case, or predict what will be the case under given circumstances, we cannot derive from such descriptions the conclusion that such states of affairs *ought* to be the case. Fact and value seem to be incommensurate. Indeed, most moralists, as well as the great biblical prophets, would insist that the ideal (what men *ought* to do) is unfortunately quite different from the facts (what men actually do).

The positivists hold that science is concerned with the accurate description of the laws under which events do in fact occur, but that it does not attempt to settle questions of value. Furthermore, they would insist that there is *no* rational procedure for settling value issues, since science is the only method for obtaining reliable knowledge. Many a positivist describes this situation poignantly, recognizing that man apparently *needs* some common standard of values by which to determine his individual and social purposes, but reluctantly concluding that it is beyond his rational grasp.

Once men looked to religion for a definition of the goals or ends they and their societies should seek; and, of course, many men still do look in this direction. But modern rationalism and empiricism led many to replace this old source of moral directives with a new source: reason and science. Now the competence of the new source is being radically questioned. This is one of the reasons for the philosophical skepticism, and even despair, which have risen to prominence in recent years.

EXISTENTIALISM

Along with positivism, existentialism stands as one of the most widespread and serious philosophic movements of the postwar period. It is common to trace its roots back to the Danish thinker, Sören Kierkegaard (d. 1855), but it has come into prominence only recently.

For entirely different reasons, the existentialists also attack the notion that reason is a safe guide outside the realm of experimental science or formal logic. The existentialists offer the following grounds for such a judgment: (1) reason, which understands through classification and abstraction, cannot ever understand the uniqueness of the individual; (2) in any case, the individual is not "pure reason" but a creature passionately concerned for his own survival and the protection of his own interests, and the passionate and biased interests of the individual distort his perceptions and reasoning; (3) the most important aspects of life, such as determining one's basic objectives or deciding upon one's relation to God, cannot be based upon reason, for we know the good only through choosing it concretely; or we can know God, since He is a Person, only by giving ourselves to Him in trust; for God is not an "object" exposed to the gaze of the disinterested observer.

With the existentialists the notions of "crisis" and "despair" are made explicit. Indeed, they are descriptive of the fundamental human situation. Man dreams of arranging his life in the world in an orderly, reasonable, way. He dreams, in short, of security. But again and again his dreams are destroyed, or transformed into nightmares. His concepts come into conflict both with reality—which is composed not of rational laws but of individual things whose uniqueness defies complete rational analysis—and with the concepts of other men—who, like himself, fashion their "world" in part to conform to their hearts' desires and whose personal desires conflict with his. Furthermore, his basic desire for security confronts the fact of death, which he can never quite dismiss. Every individual, and every society, is finite, subject to change and ultimate decay. This, for man who desires eternity, is the basis of despair.

A TIME OF CONFLICT

So we may say that the present time is one of conflict—not only between nations and political ideologies but also between philosophies.

Empiricism remains strong. And there are still many who have confidence that man can solve his problems, insofar as any solution is possible, through reason and science.

Yet many are experiencing doubts on this matter. And two of the most vigorous philosophies of recent times seem to give substance to such doubts.

Many theologians are saying that the time is ripe for a return to faith—not just faith in general, but faith in the God of Abraham, Isaac, and Jacob. Our dream, so they say, of unlimited knowledge and our hope of managing everything for ourselves have been disclosed as illusions. Now, as in every age, the way forward is discerned only by faith.

Issues such as those which we have briefly mentioned are everywhere apparent in their influence upon religion in the modern period, and they lie in the background, or more typically the foreground, of the thinking of those men to whose writings we now turn. The selection from John Dewey opens this section for two reasons. Dewey himself would not wish to be regarded as a representative of any one of the traditions we are discussing. Though he came out of a Protestant background, it would be misleading to place him in that group. John Dewey expresses very clearly the kind of liberal rationalism which has seemed to many men the proper fruit of the rise of modern science.

JOHN DEWEY (1859–1952)

John Dewey gained eminence both as an educator and as a philosopher. His name is usually associated with "progressive education," for he firmly believed that ideas gain significance chiefly through their implications for practical action. He revolted from all forms of absolutism, whether in philosophy or in religion. The fallible but progressively potent methods of science are, he felt, our best hope in the human struggle for truth and goodness.

Though he has had a great influence upon religious "liberals" (see p. 335), he did not regard himself as standing within the tradition of Christianity or Judaism. The following selection is included here, at the beginning of the modern section, because it illustrates the concern with science and reason which have preoccupied so many contemporary writers; and it also shows how these concerns have had a dramatic effect upon traditional religion.

Religion Versus the Religious*

Never before in history has mankind been so much of two minds, so divided into two camps, as it is today. Religions have traditionally been allied with ideas of the supernatural, and often have been based upon explicit beliefs about it. Today there are many who hold that

* From John Dewey, *A Common Faith*. New Haven: Yale University Press, 1934. Pages 1–6, 13–15, and 22–28 are reproduced by permission of the publisher.

nothing worthy of being called religious is possible apart from the supernatural. Those who hold this belief differ in many respects. They range from those who accept the dogmas and sacraments of the Greek and Roman Catholic church as the only sure means of access to the supernatural to the theist or mild deist. Between them are the many Protestant denominations who think the Scriptures, aided by a pure conscience, are adequate avenues to supernatural truth and power. But they agree in one point: the necessity for a Supernatural Being and for an immortality that is beyond the power of nature.

The opposed group consists of those who think the advance of culture and science has completely discredited the supernatural and with it all religions that were allied with belief in it. But they go beyond this point. The extremists in this group believe that with elimination of the supernatural not only must historic religions be dismissed but with them everything of a religious nature. When historical knowledge has discredited the claims made for the supernatural character of the persons said to have founded historic religions; when the supernatural inspiration attributed to literatures held sacred has been riddled, and when anthropological and psychological knowledge has disclosed the all-too-human source from which religious beliefs and practices have sprung, everything religious must, they say, also go.

There is one idea held in common by these two opposite groups: identification of the religious with the supernatural. The question I shall raise in these chapters concerns the ground for and the consequences of this identification: its reasons and its value. In the discussion I shall develop another conception of the nature of the religious phase of experience, one that separates it from the supernatural and the things that have grown up about it. I shall try to show that these derivations are encumbrances and that what is genuinely religious will undergo an emancipation when it is relieved from them; that then, for the first time, the religious aspect of experience will be free to develop freely on its own account. . . .

The heart of my point, as far as I shall develop it in this first section, is that there is a difference between religion, *a* religion, and the religious; between anything that may be denoted by a noun substantive and the quality of experience that is designated by an adjective. It is not easy to find a definition of religion in the substantive sense that wins general acceptance. However, in the *Oxford Dictionary* I find the following: "Recognition on the part of man of some unseen higher power as having control of his destiny and as being entitled to obedience, reverence and worship." . . .

The "unseen powers" referred to have been conceived in a multitude of incompatible ways. Eliminating the differences, nothing is left beyond the bare reference to something unseen and powerful. . . . There is no greater similarity in the ways in which obedience and reverence have been expressed. There has been worship of animals, of ghosts, of ancestors, phallic worship, as well as of a Being of dread power and of love and wisdom. . . .

Finally, there is no discernible unity in the moral motivations appealed to and utilized. They have been as far apart as fear of lasting torture, hope of enduring bliss in which sexual enjoyment has sometimes been a conspicuous element; mortification of the flesh and extreme asceticism; prostitution and chastity; wars to extirpate the unbeliever; persecution to convert or punish the unbeliever, and philanthropic zeal; servile acceptance of imposed dogma, along with brotherly love and aspiration for a reign of justice among men. . . .

I gladly admit that historic religions have been relative to the conditions of social culture in which peoples lived. Indeed, what I am concerned with is to press home the logic of this method of disposal of outgrown traits of past religions. Beliefs and practices in a religion that now prevails are by this logic relative to the present state of culture. If so much flexibility has obtained in the past regarding an unseen power, the way it affects human destiny, and the attitudes we are to take toward it, why should it be assumed that change in conception and action has now come to an end? The logic involved in getting rid of inconvenient aspects of past religions . . . compels us to ask what conception of unseen powers and our relations to them would be consonant with the best achievements and aspirations of the present. It demands that in imagination we wipe the slate clean and start afresh by asking what would be the idea of the unseen, of the manner of its control over us and the ways in which reverence and obedience would be manifested, if whatever is basically religious in experience had the opportunity to express itself free from all historic encumbrances. . . .

My purpose is to indicate what happens when religious experience is already set aside as something *sui generis*. The actual religious quality in the experience described is the *effect* produced, the better adjustment in life and its conditions, not the manner and cause of its production. The way in which the experience operated, its function, determines its religious value. If the reorientation actually occurs, it, and the sense of security and stability accompanying it, are forces on their own account. It takes place in different persons in a multitude of ways. It is sometimes brought about by devotion to a cause; sometimes by a passage of poetry that opens a new perspective; sometimes as was the case with Spinoza—deemed an atheist in his day—through philosophical reflection.

The difference between an experience having a religious force because of what it does in and to the processes of living and religious experience as a separate kind of thing gives me occasion to refer to a previous remark. If this function were rescued through emancipation from dependence upon specific types of beliefs and practices, from those elements that constitute a religion, many individuals would find that experiences having the force of bringing about a better, deeper and enduring adjustment in life are not so rare and infrequent as they are commonly supposed to be. They occur frequently in connection with many significant moments of living. The idea of invisible powers would take on the meaning of all the conditions of nature and human association that support and deepen the sense of values which carry one through periods of darkness and despair to such an extent that they lose their usual depressive character.

I do not suppose for many minds the dislocation of the religious from a religion is easy to effect. Tradition and custom, especially when emotionally charged, are a part of the habits that have become one with our very being. But the possibility of the transfer is demonstrated by its actuality. . . .

What has been said does not imply that all moral faith in ideal ends is by virtue of that fact religious in quality. The religious is "morality touched by emotion" only when the ends of moral conviction arouse emotions that are not only intense but are actuated and supported by ends so inclusive that they unify the self. The inclusiveness of the end in relation to both self and the "universe" to which an inclusive self is related is indispensable. According to the best authorities, "religion" comes from a root that means being bound or tied. Originally, it meant being bound by vows to a particular way of life—as *les religieux* were monks and nuns who had assumed certain vows. The religious attitude signifies something that is bound through imagination to a *general* attitude. This comprehensive attitude, moreover, is much broader than anything indicated by "moral" in its usual sense. The quality of attitude is displayed in art, science and good citizenship.

If we apply the conception set forth to the terms of the definition earlier quoted, these terms take on a new significance. An unseen power controlling our destiny becomes the power of an ideal. All possibilities, as possibilities, are ideal in character. The artist, scientist, citizen, parent, as far as they are actuated by the spirit of their callings, are controlled by the unseen. For all endeavor for the better is moved by faith in what is possible, not by adherence to the actual. Nor does this faith depend for its moving power upon intellectual assurance or belief that the things worked for must surely prevail and come into embodied existence. For the authority of the object to determine our attitude and conduct, the right that is given it to claim our allegiance and devotion is based on the intrinsic nature of the ideal. The outcome, given our best endeavor, is not with us. The inherent vice of all intellectual schemes of idealism is that they convert the idealism of action into a system of beliefs about antecedent reality. The character assigned this reality is so different from that which observation and reflection lead to and support that these schemes inevitably glide into alliance with the supernatural.

All religions, marked by elevated ideal quality, have dwelt upon the power of religion to introduce perspective into the piecemeal and shifting episodes of existence. Here too we need to reverse the ordinary statement and say that whatever introduces genuine perspective is religious, not that religion is something that introduces it. There can be no doubt (referring to the second element of the definition) of our dependence upon forces beyond our control. Primitive man was so impotent in the face of these forces that, especially in an unfavorable natural environment, fear became a dominant attitude, and, as the old saying goes, fear created the gods.

With increase of mechanisms of control, the element of fear has, relatively speaking, subsided. Some optimistic souls have even concluded that the forces about us are on the whole essentially benign. But every crisis, whether of the individual or of the community, reminds man of the precarious and partial nature of the control he exercises. When man, individually and collectively, has done his uttermost, conditions that at different times and places have given rise to the ideas of Fate and Fortune, of Chance and Providence, remain. It is the part of manliness to insist upon the capacity of mankind to strive to direct natural and social forces to humane ends. But unqualified absolutistic statements about the omnipotence of such endeavors reflect egoism rather than intelligent courage.

The fact that human destiny is so interwoven with forces beyond human control renders it unnecessary to suppose that dependence and the humility that accompanies it have to find the particular channel that is prescribed by traditional doctrines. What is especially significant is rather the form which the sense of dependence takes. Fear never gave stable perspective in the life of anyone. It is dispersive and withdrawing. Most religions have in fact added rites of communion to those of expiation and propitiation. For our dependence is manifested in those relations to the environment that support our undertakings and aspirations as much as it is in the defeats inflicted upon us. The essentially unreligious attitude is that which attributes human achievement and purpose to man in isolation from the world of physical nature and his fellows. Our successes are dependent upon the cooperation of nature. The sense of the dignity of human nature is as religious as is the sense of awe and reverence when it rests upon a sense of human nature as a co-operating part of a larger whole. Natural piety is not of necessity either a fatalistic acquiescence in natural happenings or a romantic idealization of the world. It may rest upon a just sense of nature as the whole of which we are parts, while it also recognizes that we are parts that are marked by intelligence and purpose, having the capacity to strive by their aid to bring conditions into greater consonance with what is humanly desirable. Such piety is an inherent constituent of a just perspective in life.

Understanding and knowledge also enter into a perspective that is religious in quality. Faith in the continued disclosing of truth through directed co-operative human endeavor is more religious in quality than is any faith in a completed revelation. It is of course now usual to hold that revelation is not completed in the sense of being ended. But religions hold that the essential framework is settled in its significant moral features at least, and that new elements that are offered must be judged by conformity to this framework. Some fixed doctrinal apparatus is necessary for *a* religion. But faith in the possibilities of continued and rigorous inquiry does not limit access to truth to any channel or scheme of things. It does not first say that truth is universal and then add there is but one road to it. It does not depend for assurance upon subjection to any dogma or item of doctrine. It trusts that the natural interactions between man and his environment will breed more intelligence and generate more knowledge provided the scientific methods that define intelligence in operation are pushed further into the mysteries of the world, being themselves promoted and improved in the operation. There is such a thing as faith in intelligence becoming religious in quality—a fact that perhaps explains the efforts of some religionists to disparage the possibilities of intelligence as a force. They properly feel such faith to be a dangerous rival.

Lives that are consciously inspired by loyalty to such ideals as have been mentioned are still comparatively infrequent to the extent of that comprehensiveness and intensity which arouse an ardor religious in function. But before we infer the incompetency of such ideals and of the actions they inspire, we should at least ask ourselves how much of the existing situation is due to the fact that the religious factors of experience have been drafted into supernatural channels and thereby loaded with irrelevant encumbrances. A body of beliefs and practices that are apart from the common and natural relations of mankind must, in the degree in which it is influential, weaken and sap the force of the possibilities inherent in such relations. Here lies one aspect of the emancipation of the religious from religion.

Any activity pursued in behalf of an ideal end against obstacles and in spite of threats of personal loss because of conviction of its general and enduring value is religious in quality. Many a person, inquirer, artist, philanthropist, citizen, men and women in the humblest walks of life, have achieved, without presumption and without display, such unification of themselves and of their relations to the conditions of existence. It remains to extend their spirit and inspiration to ever wider numbers. If I have said anything about religions and religion that seems harsh, I have said those things because of a firm belief that the claim on the part of religions to possess a monopoly of ideals and of the supernatural means by which alone, it is alleged, they can be furthered, stands in the way of the realization of distinctively religious values inherent in natural experience. For that reason, if for no other, I should be sorry if any were misled by the frequency with which I have employed the adjective "religious" to conceive of what I have said as a disguised apology for what have passed as religions. The opposition between religious values as I conceive them and religions is not to be bridged. Just because the release of these values is so important, their identification with the creeds and cults of religions must be dissolved.

Judaism in the Modern World

Orthodox Judaism

MOSES BEN MAIMON (1135–1204)

Though hardly a modern writer, Moses ben Maimon, often known as "Maimonides," is included here because his "Thirteen Principles" have been held in such high regard by modern Jews. They may be regarded as a classic summary of the orthodox faith. Maimonides was one of the great philosophers of the late Middle Ages. In fact, it was in part through him that Aristotelianism came to have such a role to play among Christian thinkers. In addition to such philosophical works as *The Guide to the Perplexed,* he produced extensive commentaries on the Mishnah and Torah. While carrying great prestige, the following principles were neither intended nor received as dogmatic pronouncements.

The Thirteen Principles*

1. I believe with perfect faith that the Creator, blessed be his name, is the Author and Guide of everything that has been created, and that he alone has made, does make, and will make all things.

2. I believe with perfect faith that the Creator, blessed be his name, is a Unity, and that there is no unity in any manner like unto his, and that he alone is our God, who was, and is, and will be.

3. I believe with perfect faith that the Creator, blessed be his name, is not a body, and that he is free from all the accidents of matter, and that he has not any form whatsoever.

4. I believe with perfect faith that the Creator, blessed be his name, is the first and the last.

5. I believe with perfect faith that to the Creator, blessed be his name, and to him alone it is right to pray, and that it is not right to pray to any being besides him.

6. I believe with perfect faith that all the words of the prophets are true.

7. I believe with perfect faith that the prophecy of Moses our teacher, peace be unto him, was true, and that he was the chief of the prophets, both of those that preceded and of those that followed him.

8. I believe with perfect faith that the whole Law, now in our possession, is the same that was given to Moses our teacher, peace be unto him.

9. I believe with perfect faith that this Law will not be changed, and that there will never be any other law from the Creator, blessed be his name.

10. I believe with perfect faith that the Creator, blessed be his name, knows every deed of the children of men, and all their thoughts, as it is said, It is he that fashioneth the hearts of them all, that giveth heed to all their deeds.

11. I believe with perfect faith that the Creator, blessed be his name, rewards those that keep his commandments, and punishes those that transgress them.

12. I believe with perfect faith in the coming of the Messiah, and, though he tarry, I will wait daily for his coming.

13. I believe with perfect faith that there will be a resurrection of the dead at the time when it shall please the Creator, blessed be his name, and exalted be the remembrance of him for ever and ever.

ISIDORE EPSTEIN (1894–)

Born in Russia, Isidore Epstein was educated in England at the University of London. As a scholar, he has made great contributions to the understanding of medieval Judaism and also to the interpretation of the total Jewish tradition. Since 1928 he has taught at Jew's College, London, and has served as Principal of that institution since 1948. Dr. Epstein is widely regarded as one of the most incisive living exponents of Orthodox Judaism.

* From Moses ben Maimon, as found in the *Authorized Daily Prayer Book,* tr. by S. Singer, Ninth American Edition. New York: Hebrew Publishing Company, pp. 89–90.

Israel as Instrument of Divine Purpose*

The unfolding of divine purpose in history, which Judaism bids us to discern, is nowhere made so manifest as in the history of the Jewish people, the people whom God has chosen as the special instrument for the fulfilment of His purpose. The whole history of Israel is shot through with the presence of the Divine. "Here," in the words of Professor Peake, "God who is never absent from history strikes into its stream with an intense energy." How else are we to account for the unique place this small nation has come to occupy in the history of mankind, and for the all-pervasive influence of its religious thought and moral teaching? . . .

Abraham gladly submits to the divine call to him to become the instrument of God's purpose. Wherever he goes, he brings with him the knowledge of the Lord and His ways—the practice of righteousness and justice (Genesis xviii:19). His work for God is carried on after him by Isaac, and after Isaac by Jacob. With Jacob's sons, God's long-laid plan begins to take clearer shape. Through a combination of wondrous events and circumstances, Joseph is set over the affairs of the mightiest Empire of the time, and thus serves the high ends of God. Driven by hunger, his family joins him, and after years of sojourn in Egypt, Israel is enslaved. Through the painful discipline of bondage, and the miraculous deliverance that follows, the people—at least part of it—becomes conscious that it is called to be a vehicle of divine knowledge to the world, and an instrument for the fulfilment of God's redemptive purpose for humanity. . . .

This was the moment chosen by God to make Israel His chosen people, to become His special instrument, not only for bringing down the rotten edifice of Egyptian tyranny, but also for the promotion of the ideals of justice and righteousness, for the redemption of mankind. What this selection implied was communicated to them in the call "And ye shall be unto me a kingdom of priests and a holy nation" (Exodus xix:6).

Priesthood in Judaism is defined not by social status, but by the functions involved: "And they shall teach my people the difference between holy and profane, and make known to them the difference between what is clean and unclean" (Ezekiel xliv:23).

What is true of the priests in Israel applies to the nation as a whole in its priestly mission. As a kingdom of priests, Israels' divinely appointed vocation was that of teaching. . . .

Israel were thus not chosen for themselves. The mission they received carried no distinction with it. It was part of God's design that they were to serve His righteous purpose. It is His work they were called upon to do in the whole world, transforming the darkest corners of God's earth. "I the Lord have called thee in righteousness and have taken hold of thy hand and set thee for a covenant of the peoples, for a light of the nations" (Isaiah xlii:6). "And I will give thee for a light unto the nations, that My salvation may be unto the end of the earth" (*ibid.*, xlix:6). . . . Viewed in this light, the selection of Israel is not unfair in the way it was first suspected, nor an anomaly to the exceptionless universal love of God for man. . . .

But in order to fit themselves for their universal priestly calling for which they had been chosen, Israel had to be a "holy nation." The significance of this charge is to be found in the root meaning of the Hebrew word for "holy"—to be separate, distinct from. Israel had to be a "holy nation," that is a nation set apart, separate and distinct from other nations, with its own peculiar way of life and conduct.

This separation was essential for Israel alike in the domain of religion and morals. The relentless struggle which the Jewish people, by virtue of their selection, were called upon, from their earliest days, to wage against idolatry was not only because it was a false religion, but also because it was a false morality. . . . For this reason the Jews had to keep themselves separate from the idolatrous nations, alike in matters of worship and moral conduct.

* From Isidore Epstein, *The Faith of Judaism*. London: Soncino Press, 1954. Pages 278–289 and 291–298 are reproduced by permission of the publisher.

With this end in view, the Jewish people were given the Torah. By means of the Torah, they were to develop a way of life which was to be distinct from the way of life of surrounding nations. Instead of a ritual which was debasing and degrading, the Torah was to offer them a system of religious observances which were conducive in a unique manner to their moralisation and perfection. Instead of a morality which was selfcentered, the Torah was to provide them with an ethic which placed service to others at the centre of its system. In and through the Torah, Israel was thus to become a holy nation, distinct and separate, morally and religiously, from all other nations of the world.

How was the Torah designed to achieve this end? The Torah is distinguished from all other systems regulating human conduct both by its method and its scope. The cause of the human failure lay, as we have seen, in the heart rather than in the head. It was moral rather than intellectual. This problem how to make man's impulses keep pace with his ethical knowledge is one that has perplexed moralists of all ages: it is one thing to teach man what is right and good, but it is another to make him disposed and willing to obey and live up to the ideal. As Lecky remarks, "Simply to tell men what is virtue, and to extol its beauty, is insufficient. Something more must be done if the characters . . . are to be moulded, and the inveterate vices eradicated."

This moral problem which philosophy is incapable of meeting is taken over by religion. At this point both Judaism and Christianity step in, each with its distinct method of dealing with the human situation. . . .

Judaism, in accord with Divine purpose, has faith in human nature, and turns with confidence to man, as once God turned with confidence to Israel, though they were corrupted by slavery in Egypt. Judaism embraces the highest and the lowest—the body and the soul—with the same solicitude, conferring upon them both the same rights and linking them both to a common purpose, in co-operation towards a higher plane. . . .

Separation, however, is not the only purpose of the Torah. There are in the innumerable forms and usages of the Torah, so many channels of communion and worship, with the positive power of inspiring and deepening the love of man for his creator, realising thereby for himself a true purpose which imparts true and absolute value to his being and existence. This is a fact which cannot be understood in all its depth by an outsider. Only he who has lived the life of the Torah knows what a heaven's ladder it is.

With the rise of Christianity a new conception was attached to the Torah, in order to discredit it. The opposition to the Torah, of which there are already indications in the teachings of Jesus, reached its full vehemence with Paul. To Paul, Torah, which, following the Greek mistranslation, he called "Nomos," the Law, was the most formidable enemy obstructing the dissemination and progress of the "good news." He therefore relentlessly disparaged the Law as worthless and obsolete, contrasting the slavery of those who live under the Law with the freedom of those who believe in Jesus. All that the Law can do, according to Paul, is to make man conscious of sin. For if it had not been for the Law, he says, in effect, I should never have learnt what sin was. I should not have known what it was to covet if the Law had not said you must not covet (see Romans vii:7–8). This strange argument led Paul to conclude that the Law was a curse, engendering sin and working wrath. It was given to man because of the sin of Adam, and from this curse there was only one way of escape: faith in Jesus. The argument was that just as the heathen cannot escape the wrath of God owing to the horrible sin he is urged to commit by clinging to idols, so the Jew can as little escape by the Law the wrath of God. Instead of removing the germ of death brought to the world by Adam, the Law was given only to increase sin, to make all the greater the need of divine mercy, which was to come through faith in Christ, the new Adam.

Paul's attitude to the Law was determined, of course, by his doctrine of salvation through Christ. He had committed himself to the belief that Jesus had died on the cross to atone for the sins of mankind. This was in opposition to the teachings of Judaism that atonement and consequent salvation are procured through observance of the Law; he thus had to disown the

Law. For, as he correctly remarked, if righteousness came by the Law, then Christ is dead in vain (Galatians ii:21).

However this may be, Paul in his polemic is guilty of deliberate perversion of the significance of the Law. In the conception of Judaism the Law, far from being an instrument of sin, has been given as a means of conquering sin; or, as the Talmudic Sages express it, "as an antidote to the Evil Urge." Nor was the Torah given as a mark of divine wrath. On the contrary, it was vouchsafed to Israel as a token of divine love, designed to train them in moral holiness, in order to make them all the more worthy in the eyes of the Holy One, Blessed be He. . . .

The attack against the Law, begun with Christianity, has assumed a new form in modern times. It has become fashionable in certain quarters to look upon the ceremonial laws as mere empty formalism, of a barren and unprofitable character, and what is more, as subversive of the true religious spirit. . . .

The fact is that, fundamentally, there is no quarrel between prophet and priest, nor did any conflict of any sort ever exist. As servants of God, they both cherished common ideals. The task of the prophet was to enunciate moral and religious principles; the priest had charge of the ceremonial of devotion and worship. They thus both complemented each other. The prophet did much to deepen the ideas which the ritual conveyed; and the priest helped to intensify the people's religious consciousness. The prophet did not exalt the ethical at the expense of the ritual, nor did the priest exalt external observances at the expense of moral values. . . .

While of course it is desirable—nay, important—that the conscious attention to the motive should be present while the religious act is being performed, the value of the mere mechanical performance should not be underrated. However loosely and perfunctorily one may address himself to the fulfilment of a ritual, the supreme thought of "One above" cannot be absent from his mind; and the psychological effect of that thought multiplied and intensified by the daily fulfilment of the multifarious rites required in the life of the Jew can hardly be exaggerated. . . .

But that is not all. The religious observances have a corporate-national significance of incalculable importance and value. The Jewish religious precepts have proved throughout the ages up to the present day the greatest preservative force of the Jewish religion and the Jewish people. For thousands of years they have served as a visible unifying bond, welding the Jews throughout the world into one community by means of common experiences, interests and ideals. The religious precepts were the links which prevented a break in the endless succession of generations. Thanks to them, the Jewish people is the only one which, in the four thousand years of its history, has never had to begin afresh. The unvarying character of the religious precepts, the undeviating form of the ritual observed and celebrated, down all the ages and all over the globe, by Jews of different shades of thought, loyalties and philosophies, constitute the outward evidence of a continuity of spirit unexampled in history. On the soil of this continuity the efforts of generations had time to come to fruition. While thus connecting the present with the past, the observance of religious precepts affords the guarantee for the preservation of this continuity in the future.

Conservative Judaism

SOLOMON SCHECHTER (1847–1915)

Prior to his immigration to the United States, Solomon Schechter had already established a reputation as a brilliant Talmudist and philologist, and become the leading spokesman for Conservative Judaism. From 1902 until

1915 he served as President of the Jewish Theological Seminary in New York City. The history of the Conservative movement is closely associated with that of the seminary, and Dr. Schechter's address on the charter of that institution presents a good introduction to the spirit of this branch of modern Judaism.

The selection by Abraham Heschel (p. 361) may also be read by the student as an example of the attitude of Conservative Judaism.

The Charter of the Seminary*

Let me say a few words about the general religious tendency this Seminary will follow. I am not unaware that this is a very delicate point, and prudence would dictate silence or evasion. But life would hardly be worth living without occasional blundering, "the only relief from dull correctness." Besides, if there be in American history one fact more clearly proved than any other it is that "know-nothing-ism" was an absolute and miserable failure. I must not fall into the same error. And thus, sincerely asking forgiveness of all my dearest friends and dearest enemies with whom it may be my misfortune to differ, I declare, in all humility, but most emphatically, that I do know something. And this is that the religion in which the Jewish ministry should be trained must be specifically and purely Jewish, without any alloy or adulteration. Judaism must stand or fall by that which distinguishes it from other religions as well as by that which it has in common with them. Judaism is not a religion which does not oppose itself to anything in particular. Judaism is opposed to any number of things, and says distinctly "thou shalt not." It permeates the whole of your life. It demands control over all your actions, and interferes even with your menu. It sanctifies the seasons, and regulates your history, both in the past and in the future. Above all, it teaches that disobedience is the strength of sin. It insists upon the observance both of the spirit and of the letter; spirit without letter belongs to the species known to the mystics as "nude souls" wandering about in the universe without balance and without consistency, the play of all possible currents and changes in the atmosphere. In a word Judaism is absolutely incompatible with the abandonment of the Torah. Nay, the very prophet or seer must bring his imprimatur from the Torah. The assertion that the destruction of the Law is its fulfillment is a mere paradox, and recalls strongly the doctrines of Sir Boyle Roche, "the inimitable maker of Irish bulls." He declared emphatically that he "would give up a part, and, if necessary, the whole of the constitution, to preserve the remainder!"

President Abraham Lincoln, the wisest and greatest of rulers, addressed Congress on some occasion of great emergency with the words: "Fellow citizens, we cannot escape history." Nor can we, my friends. The past, with its long chain of events, with its woes and joy, with its tragedies and romances; with its customs and usages, and above all; with its bequest of the Torah, the great entail of the children of Israel, has become an integral and inalienable part of ourselves, bone of our bone and flesh of our flesh. We must make an end to these constant amputations if we do not wish to see the body of "Israel" bleed to death before our very eyes. We must leave off talking about Occidentalizing our religion—as if the occident has ever shown the least genius for religion—or freeing the conscience by abolishing various laws. These, and similar platitudes and stock phrases borrowed from Christian apologetics, must be abandoned entirely, if we do not want to drift slowly but surely into Paulinism, which entered the world as the deadliest enemy of Judaism, pursued it through all its course and is still finding its abettors among us, working for their own destruction. Lord, forgive them, for they know nothing. Those who are entrusted with carrying out the

* From Solomon Schechter, "The Charter of the Seminary," *Tradition and Change: The Development of Conservative Judaism,* ed. by Mordecai Waxman. New York: The Burning Bush Press, 1958. Pages 102–104 are reproduced by permission of the Rabbinical Assemb'y of America.

purpose of this institution, which, as you have seen, aims at the perpetuation of the tenets of the Jewish religion, both pupils and masters, must faithfully and manfully maintain their loyalty to the Torah. There is no other Jewish religion but that taught by the Torah and confirmed by history and tradition, and sunk into the conscience of Catholic Israel.

I have just hinted at the desirability of masters and pupils working for one common end. You must not think that our intention is to convert this school of learning into a drill ground where young men will be forced into a certain groove of thinking, or, rather, not thinking; and after being equipped with a few devotional texts, and supplied with certain catchwords, will be let loose upon an unsuspecting public to proclaim their own virtues and the infallibility of their masters. Nothing is further from our thoughts. I once heard a friend of mine exclaim angrily to a pupil: "Sir, how dare you always agree with me?" I do not even profess to agree with myself always, and I would consider my work, to which, with the help of God, I am going to devote the rest of my life, a complete failure if this institution would not in the future produce such extremes as on the one side a raving mystic who would denounce me as a sober Philistine; on the other side, an advanced critic, who would rail at me as a narrow-minded fanatic, while a third devotee of strict orthodoxy would raise protest against any critical views I may entertain. "We take," says Montaigne, "other men's knowledge on trust, which is idle and superficial learning. We must make it our own." The Rabbis express the same thought with allusion to Ps. 1:2 which they explain to mean that what is first at the initiation of man into the Law—God's Torah, becomes, after a sufficient study, man's own Torah. Nay, God even deigns to descend to man's own level so as not to interfere with his individuality and powers of conception. I reproduce in paraphrase a passage from a Midrash: "Behold now how the voice of Sinai goes forth to all in Israel attuned to the capacity of each; appealing to the sages according to their wisdom: to the virile according to their strength; to the young according to their aspiring youthfulness, and the children and babes according to their innocence; aye, even to the women according to their motherhood." All that I plead for is that the voice should come from Sinai, not from Golgotha; that it should be the voice of Jacob, not of Esau. The Torah gave spiritual accommodation for thousands of years to all sorts and conditions of men, sages, philosophers, scholars, mystics, casuists, schoolmen and skeptics; and it should also prove broad enough to harbor the different minds of the present century. Any attempt to place the centre of gravity outside of the Torah must end in disaster. We must not flatter ourselves that we shall be allowed to land somewhere midway, say in some Omar Khayyam cult or in some Positivists' society or in some other agnostic makeshift. No, my friends, there are laws of gravitation in the spiritual as there are in the physical world; we cannot create halting places at will. We must either remain faithful to history or go the way of all flesh, and join the great majority. The teaching in the Seminary will be in keeping with this spirit, and thus largely confined to the exposition and elucidation of historical Judaism in its various manifestations.

Reform Judaism

Reform Judaism had its beginnings in the late eighteenth century in Germany but has reached its fullest development in the United States. The most important American leaders were Isaac M. Wise (1819–1900), the founder of Hebrew Union College in Cincinnati and the leader of the Central Conference of American Rabbis; and Kaufmann Kohler (1843–1926), whose writings were devoted to the theological basis of the Reform movement. These two men were influential in organizing a meeting of Reform rabbis in Pittsburgh in 1885, from which emerged the famous "Pittsburgh Platform," given below.

The Pittsburgh Platform*

1. We recognize in every religion an attempt to grasp the Infinite, and in every mode, source, or book of revelation held sacred in any religious system the consciousness of the indwelling of God in man. We hold that Judaism presents the highest conception of the God-idea as taught in our Holy Scriptures and developed and spiritualized by the Jewish teachers, in accordance with the moral and philosophical progress of their respective ages. We maintain that Judaism preserved and defended, midst continual struggles and trials and under enforced isolation, this God-idea as the central religious truth for the human race.

2. We recognize in the Bible the record of the consecration of the Jewish people to its mission as the priest of the one God, and value it as the most potent instrument of religious and moral instruction. We hold that the modern discoveries of scientific researches in the domain of nature and history are not antagonistic to the doctrines of Judaism, the Bible reflecting the primitive ideas of its own age, and at times clothing its conception of divine Providence and Justice dealing with man in miraculous narrative.

3. We recognize in the Mosaic legislation a system of training the Jewish people for its mission during its national life in Palestine, and today we accept as binding only its moral laws, and maintain only such ceremonies as elevate and sanctify our lives, but reject all such as are not adapted to the views and habits of modern civilization.

4. We hold that all such Mosaic and rabbinical laws as regulate diet, priestly purity, and dress originated in ages and under the influence of ideas entirely foreign to our present mental and spiritual state. They fail to impress the modern Jew with a spirit of priestly holiness; their observance in our days is apt rather to obstruct than to further modern spiritual elevation.

5. We recognize, in the modern era of universal culture of heart and intellect, the approaching of the realization of Israel's great Messianic hope for the establishment of the kingdom of truth, justice, and peace among all men. We consider ourselves no longer a nation, but a religious community, and therefore expect neither a return to Palestine, nor a sacrificial worship under the sons of Aaron, nor the restoration of any of the laws concerning the Jewish State.

6. We recognize in Judaism a progressive religion, ever striving to be in accord with the postulates of reason. We are convinced of the utmost necessity of preserving the historical identity with our great past. Christianity and Islam being daughter religions of Judaism, we appreciate their providential mission to aid in the spreading of monotheistic and moral truth. We acknowledge that the spirit of broad humanity of our age is our ally in the fulfillment of our mission, and therefore we extend the hand of fellowship to all who operate with us in the establishment of the reign of truth and righteousness among men.

7. We reassert the doctrine of Judaism that the soul is immortal, grounding this belief on the divine nature of the human spirit, which forever finds bliss in righteousness and misery in wickedness. We reject as ideas not rooted in Judaism, the beliefs both in bodily resurrection and in Gehenna and Eden (Hell and Paradise) as abodes for everlasting punishment and reward.

8. In full accordance with the spirit of Mosaic legislation, which strives to regulate the relation between rich and poor, we deem it our duty to participate in the great task of modern times, to solve, on the basis of justice and righteousness, the problems presented by the contrasts and evils of the present organization of society.

* From *The Jewish Encyclopedia*, edited by I. Singer. New York and London: Funk and Wagnalls Company, 1907, Vol. IV, page 215.

Other Representative Jewish Authors

THEODOR HERZL (1860–1904)

Although never interested in Judaism as a religion, Theodor Herzl was deeply affected by the wave of anti-semitism which spread across Europe in the latter part of the nineteenth century. He was trained as a lawyer, but he eventually became a correspondent for a Vienna newspaper. In 1896 he wrote *Der Judenstaat* (The Jewish State), which has become a classic exposition of the Zionist cause, in spite of the fact that his original proposals have been modified in a number of important ways. Not only did Herzl write about this issue, but he was extremely active in diplomatic circles and among Jewish groups in promoting the idea of a Jewish homeland.

The Jewish State*

Preface

The idea which I have developed in this pamphlet is a very old one: it is the restoration of the Jewish State.

The world resounds with outcries against the Jews, and these outcries have awakened the slumbering idea. . . .

The present scheme . . . includes the employment of an existent propelling force. In consideration of my own inadequacy, I shall content myself with indicating the cogs and wheels of the machine to be constructed, and I shall rely on more skilled mechanicians than myself to put them together.

Everything depends on our propelling force. And what is that force? The misery of the Jews. . . .

The Jewish question still exists. It would be foolish to deny it. It is a remnant of the Middle Ages, which civilized nations do not even yet seem able to shake off, try as they will. They certainly showed a generous desire to do so when they emancipated us. The Jewish question exists wherever Jews live in perceptible numbers. Where it does not exist, it is carried by Jews in the course of their migrations. We naturally move to those places where we are not persecuted, and there our presence produces persecution. This is the case in every country, and will remain so, even in those highly civilized—for instance, France—until the Jewish question finds a solution on a political basis. The unfortunate Jews are now carrying the seeds of Anti-Semitism into England; they have already introduced it into America.

I believe that I understand Anti-Semitism, which is really a highly complex movement. I consider it from a Jewish standpoint, yet without fear or hatred. I believe that I can see what elements there are in it of vulgar sport, of common trade jealousy, of inherited prejudice, of religious intolerance and also of pretended self-defence. I think the Jewish question is no more a social than a religious one, notwithstanding that it sometimes takes these and other forms. It is a national question, which can only be solved by making it a political world-question to be discussed and settled by the civilized nations of the world in council.

We are a people—one people.

* From Theodor Herzl, *The Jewish State: An Attempt at a Modern Solution of the Jewish Question*. New York: American Zionist Council, 1946. Pages 69–70, 75–83, 92–96, 146–147, 153, and 156–157 are reproduced by permission of the publisher.

We have honestly endeavored everywhere to merge ourselves in the social life of surrounding communities and to preserve the faith of our fathers. We are not permitted to do so. In vain are we loyal patriots, our loyalty in some places running to extremes; in vain do we make the same sacrifices of life and property as our fellow citizens; in vain do we strive to increase the fame of our native land in science and art, or our wealth by trade and commerce. In countries where we have lived for centuries we are still cried down as strangers, and often by those whose ancestors were not yet domiciled in the land where Jews had already had experience of suffering. . . .

Oppression and persecution cannot exterminate us. No nation on earth has survived such struggles and sufferings as we have gone through. Jew-baiting has merely stripped off our weaklings; the strong among us were invariably true to their race when persecution broke out against them. . . .

Assimilation, by which I understand not only external conformity in dress, habits, custom, and language but also identity of feeling and manner—assimilation of Jews could be effected only by intermarriage. But the need for mixed marriages would have to be felt by the majority; their mere recognition by law would certainly not suffice. . . .

Those who really wished to see the Jews disappear through intermixture with other nations, can only hope to see it come about in one way. The Jews must previously acquire economic power sufficiently great to overcome the old social prejudice against them. The aristocracy may serve as an example of this, for in its ranks occur the proportionately largest numbers of mixed marriages. The Jewish families which regild the old nobility with their money become gradually absorbed. But what form would this phenomenon assume in the middle classes, where (the Jews being a bourgeois people) the Jewish question is mainly concentrated? A previous acquisition of power could be synonymous with that economic supremacy which they are already erroneously declared to possess. And if the power they now possess creates rage and indignation among the Anti-Semites, what outbreaks would such an increase of power create? Hence the first step towards absorption will never be taken, because this step would involve the subjection of the majority to a hitherto scorned minority, possessing neither military nor administrative power of its own. I think, therefore, that the absorption of Jews by means of their prosperity is unlikely to occur. . . .

Because I have drawn this conclusion with complete indifference to everything but the quest of truth, I shall probably be contradicted and opposed by Jews who are in easy circumstances . . . It might more reasonably be objected that I am giving a handle to Anti-Semitism when I say we are a people—one people; that I am hindering the assimilation of Jews where it is about to be consummated, and endangering it where it is an accomplished fact, insofar as it is possible for a solitary writer to hinder or endanger anything.

This objection will be especially brought forward in France. It will probably also be made in other countries, but I shall answer only the French Jews beforehand, because, these afford the most striking example of my point. . . .

If all or any of the French Jews protest against this scheme on account of their own "assimilation," my answer is simple: The whole thing does not concern them at all. They are Jewish Frenchmen, well and good! This is a private affair for the Jews alone.

The movement towards the organization of the State I am proposing would, of course, harm Jewish Frenchmen no more than it would harm the "assimilated" of other countries. It would, on the contrary, be distinctly to their advantage. For they would no longer be disturbed in their "chromatic function," as Darwin puts it, but would be able to assimilate in peace, because the present Anti-Semitism would have been stopped for ever. They would certainly be credited with being assimilated to the very depths of their souls, if they stayed where they were after the new Jewish State, with its superior institutions, had become a reality.

The "assimilated" would profit even more than Christian citizens by the departure of faithful Jews; for they would be rid of the disquieting, incalculable, and unavoidable rivalry of a Jewish proletariat, driven by poverty and political pressure from place to place, from land to land. This floating proletariat would become stationary. Many Christian citizens—whom we call Anti-Semites—can now offer determined resistance to the immigration of foreign Jews. Jewish citizens cannot do this, although it affects them far more directly; for on them they feel first of all the keen competition of individuals carrying on similar branches of industry, who, in addition, either introduce Anti-Semitism where it does not exist, or intensify it where it does. The "assimilated" give expression to this secret grievance in "philanthropic" undertakings. They organize emigration societies for wandering Jews. There is a reverse to the picture which would be comic, if it did not deal with human beings. For some of these charitable institutions are created not for, but against, persecuted Jews; they are created to despatch these poor creatures just as fast and far as possible. And thus, many an apparent friend of the Jews turns out, on careful inspection, to be nothing more than an Anti-Semite of Jewish origin, disguised as a philanthropist.

But the attempts at colonization made even by really benevolent men, interesting attempts though they were, have so far been unsuccessful . . . These attempts were interesting, in that they represented on a small scale the practical fore-runners of the idea of a Jewish State. They were even useful, for out of their mistakes may be gathered experience for carrying the idea out successfully on a larger scale . . . What is unpractical or impossible to accomplish on a small scale, need not necessarily be so on a larger one. A small enterprise may result in loss under the same conditions which would make a large one pay. A rivulet cannot even be navigated by boats, the river into which it flows carries stately iron vessels.

No human being is wealthy or powerful enough to transplant a nation from one habitation to another. An idea alone can achieve that: and this idea of a State may have the requisite power to do so. The Jews have dreamt this kingly dream all through the long nights of their history. "Next year in Jerusalem" is our old phrase. It is now a question of showing that the dream can be converted into a living reality.

For this, many old, outgrown, confused and limited notions must first be entirely erased from the minds of men. Dull brains might, for instance, imagine that this exodus would be from civilized regions into the desert. That is not the case. It will be carried out in the midst of civilization. We shall not revert to a lower stage, we shall rise to a higher one. We shall not dwell in mud huts; we shall build new more beautiful and more modern houses, and possess them in safety. We shall not lose our acquired possessions; we shall realize them. We shall surrender our well earned rights only for better ones. We shall not sacrifice our beloved customs; we shall find them again. We shall not leave our old home before the new one is prepared for us. Those only will depart who are sure thereby to improve their position; those who are now desperate will go first, after them the poor; next the prosperous, and, last of all, the wealthy. Those who go in advance will raise themselves to a higher grade, equal to that whose representatives will shortly follow. Thus the exodus will be at the same time an ascent of the class.

The departure of the Jews will involve no economic disturbances, no crises, no persecutions; in fact, the countries they abandon will revive to a new period of prosperity. There will be an inner migration of Christian citizens into the positions evacuated by Jews. The outgoing current will be gradual, without any disturbance, and its initial movement will put an end to Anti-Semitism. The Jews will leave as honored friends, and if some of them return, they will receive the same favorable welcome and treatment at the hands of civilized nations as is accorded to all foreign visitors. Their exodus will have no resemblance to a flight, for it will be a well-regulated movement under control of public opinion. The movement will not only be inaugurated with absolute conformity to law, but it cannot even be carried out without the friendly cooperation of interested Governments, who would derive considerable benefits from it.

Security for the integrity of the idea and the vigor of its execution will be found in the creation of a body corporate, or corporation. This corporation will be called "The Society of Jews." In addition to it there will be a Jewish company, an economically productive body.

An individual who attempted even to undertake this huge task alone, would be either an impostor or a madman. The personal character of the members of the corporation will guarantee its integrity, and the adequate capital of the Company will prove its stability. . . .

The Plan

The whole plan is in its essence perfectly simple, as it must necessarily be if it is to come within the comprehension of all.

Let the sovereignty be granted us over a portion of the globe large enough to satisfy the rightful requirements of a nation; the rest we shall manage for ourselves. . . .

The plan, simple in design, but complicated in execution, will be carried out by two agencies: The Society of Jews and the Jewish Company.

The Society of Jews will do the preparatory work in the domains of science and politics, which the Jewish Company will afterwards apply practically.

The Jewish Company will be the liquidating agent of the business interests of departing Jews, and will organize commerce and trade in the new country. . . .

Those Jews who agree with our idea of a State will attach themselves to the Society, which will thereby be authorized to confer and treat with Governments in the name of our people. The Society will thus be acknowledged in its relations with Governments as a State-creating power. This acknowledgment will practically create the State. . . .

Palestine Or Argentine?

Shall we choose Palestine or Argentine? We shall take what is given us, and what is selected by Jewish public opinion. The Society will determine both these points.

Argentine is one of the most fertile countries in the world, extends over a vast area, has a sparse population and a mild climate. The Argentine Republic would derive considerable profit from the cession of a portion of its territory to us. The present infiltration of Jews has certainly produced some discontent, and it would be necessary to enlighten the Republic on the intrinsic difference of our new movement.

Palestine is our ever-memorable historic home. The very name of Palestine would attract our people with a force of marvellous potency. If his Majesty the Sultan were to give us Palestine, we could in return undertake to regulate the whole finances of Turkey. We should there form a portion of a rampart of Europe against Asia, an outpost of civilization as opposed to barbarism. We should as a neutral State remain in contact with all Europe, which would have to guarantee our existence. The sanctuaries of Christendom would be safeguarded by assigning to them an extra-territorial status such as is well-known to the law of nations. We should form a guard of honor about these sanctuaries, answering for the fulfilment of this duty with our existence. This guard of honor would be the great symbol of the solution of the Jewish Question after eighteen centuries of Jewish suffering. . . .

Theocracy

Shall we end by having a theocracy? No, indeed. Faith unites us, knowledge gives us freedom. We shall therefore prevent any theocratic tendencies from coming to the fore on the part of our priesthood. We shall keep our priests within the confines of their temples in the same way as we shall keep our professional army within the confines of their barracks. Army and priesthood shall receive honors high as their valuable functions deserve. But they must not interfere in the administration of the State which confers distinction upon them, else they will conjure up difficulties without and within.

Every man will be as free and undisturbed in his faith or his disbelief as he is in his nationality. And if it should occur that men of other creeds and different nationalities come to live amongst us, we should accord them honorable protection and equality before the law. We have learnt toleration in Europe. This is not sarcastically said; for the Anti-Semitism of today could only in a very few places be taken for old religious intolerance. It is for the most part a movement among civilized nations by which they try to chase away the spectres of their own past.

Conclusion

How much has been left unexplained, how many defects, how many harmful superficialities, and how many useless repetitions in this pamphlet, which I have thought over so long and so often revised!

But a fair-minded reader, who has sufficient understanding to grasp the spirit of my words, will not be repelled by these defects. He will rather be roused thereby to cooperate with his intelligence and energy in a work which is not one man's task alone, and to improve it. . . .

Here it is, fellow Jews! Neither fable nor deception! Every man may test its reality for himself, for every man will carry over with him a portion of the Promised Land—one in his head, another in his arms, another in his acquired possessions. . . .

But we must first bring enlightenment to men's minds. The idea must make its way into the most distant, miserable holes where our people dwell. They will awaken from gloomy brooding, for into their lives will come a new significance. Every man need think only of himself, and the movement will assume vast proportions.

And what glory awaits those who fight unselfishly for the cause!

Therefore I believe that a wondrous generation of Jews will spring into existence. The Maccabeans will rise again.

Let me repeat once more my opening words: The Jews who wish for a State will have it.

We shall live at last as free men on our own soil, and die peacefully in our own home.

The world will be freed by our liberty, enriched by our wealth, magnified by our greatness.

And whatever we attempt there to accomplish for our own welfare, will react powerfully and beneficially for the good of humanity.

MARTIN BUBER (1878–)

Early in life Martin Buber came into close contact with the Hasidism, a group of pious and mystically inclined Jews of eastern Europe. He was destined not only to write about them but to develop their characteristic concern for the spiritual aspect of Judaism. An ardent Zionist, and an immigrant to Jerusalem in 1938, Buber has stressed the inner rebirth of Jewish life rather than the sovereignty of the State of Israel as such. An amazingly productive writer, he has contributed to many fields, and with Franz Rosenzweig wrote a much-beloved translation of the Hebrew Bible into German. His most famous book, *I and Thou,* has perhaps had as much influence among Christian as among Jewish thinkers.

The first selection below is in the form of a commentary upon the biblical books of Jeremiah and Job. One's reading will be enriched if he consults the specific biblical passages cited by Buber in parentheses.

The Prophetic Faith*

[Just prior to the passage given here, the author had been discussing the efforts under King Josiah to reform the religion of Israel. This good king, after a short reign, was killed in the battle of Megiddo (609 B.C.).]

* From Martin Buber, *The Prophetic Faith,* translated from the Hebrew by Carlyle Witton-Davies. New York: The Macmillan Company, 1949. Pages 170–172 and 175–180 are reproduced by permission of the publisher.

Only a few months had passed since the battle at Megiddo. These months mark a most important incision in Israelite religious history. The question "Why?" presses upon all hearts. Why has the king, who unlike his predecessors did YHVH's will in everything, been snatched away in the prime of his life and in the midst of his plans for the realization of God's word, at the hour when he went forth undismayed, trusting in God's word (Deut. 20, 1), to fight the superior force? . . . "Wherefore does the way of the wicked prosper?" The ready teaching about reward and punishment in the life of individual and community is shaken. This deity is no more to be formulated. What Isaiah and Micah regarded as the characteristic of the coming age (Is. 8, 17, Mic. 3, 4), what the book of Deuteronomy announced most emphatically for the day of wrath, has happened now: YHVH "hides His face," He has become an enigma. And it is the same thing that God's answer expresses, which Jeremiah may have felt already at that time and later noted in his diary (Jer. 12, 5) in connection with personal matters: "If thou hast run with footmen and they have wearied thee, how wilt thou contend with the horses?" As life, so history will lead to even deeper suffering and mystery. The prophet sees a barrier stretched across his prophetic outlook.

One thing indeed now becomes clearer to him than ever: the reform that did not reform the life of the people is nothing in God's eyes. But the people have no knowledge of this, the people calm the anguish of their hearts for the coming fate with the possession of the indestructible temple; they run to the house and cry (7, 10), "We are delivered!" As the fugitive, seeking asylum, "seizes the horns of the altar" (1 Kgs. 1, 50f; 2, 28), so they cling to the delusive idea of the inviolability of God's house and city: "YHVH's temple, YHVH's temple, YHVH's temple, are these!" (Jer. 7, 4). Jeremiah sees himself as sent to the temple gate to combat this illusion.

His words here simply mean this, that God does not attach decisive importance to "religion." Other gods are dependent on a house, an altar, sacrificial worship, because without these things they have no existence, their whole nature consisting only of what the creatures give them; whereas "the living God and eternal king" (10, 10; a post-Jeremianic saying, but in his spirit) is not dependent upon any of these things, since He is. He desires no religion, He desires a human people, men living together, the makers of decision vindicating their right to those thirsting for justice, the strong having pity on the weak (7, 5f), men associating with men. He rejects this people here, which "enter these gates to throw themselves down before YHVH" (v. 2), He rejects them, because by the iniquity they commit one with another they frustrate the divine order of the people and profane God's name, as the name of Israel's Lord, and therefore He also rejects the desecrated sanctuary (v. 11); "Is this house, upon which My name is called, become a den of robbers in your eyes?! Behold, I too have seen (that this is truly so)." . . .

Over against the "lying words" of false confidence (v. 4 and 8)—and here we are forced to recall that "lying style of scribes"—the prophet sets the decalogue. It is as if he, standing at the gate of the temple, put forth his hand into the innermost room and took from the ark the tablets in order to show them in a changed order to the people. Opposite the self-reliant, spirit-forsaken civilization religion there stands here for all to see God's ancient instruction of the nomad tribes. . . . From the beginning of his prophesying he had been fighting against the priests who "handle" the Torah but do not ask after God's presence and do not know Him (2, 8), against the degeneration of the priestly station, not against the station itself, just as his fight against the cult was directed against its deterioration. He was indeed, more than all his predecessors, inclined to feel that, for the sake of hallowing the whole life, the partition between sacred and profane should be removed; but it was certainly clear to him that this was not the appropriate hour to obtain a picture of the future order of the relationship between God and man. With the expectation of a new covenant which would come after the end of the distress, and in which God's living word would be written on the heart of the people, there was no place to foretell the forms in which the changed heart would express itself . . . The pure prophet is not imaginative or, more precisely, he has no other imagination than the full grasping of the present, actual and potential. His God is the God of a truth which, as far as it is open to mortal man, enters really into time, interwoven with human deeds and misdeeds, that is, it can never be depicted beforehand. "For there is no divination in Jacob, nor soothsaying in Israel," so it is put basically in Balaam's speech (Num. 23, 23). "It will be said in time to Jacob and Israel, what God is working." The true prophet, this quivering magnet needle, pointing the way to God, is altogether bound by this "time." He is bound by the situation of the hour in which God is preparing the work He has in mind, and therefore the decision is not yet made, but is being made. . . . The false prophets misuse and pervert the manifestation of God itself, by declaring the wishful vision of their heart as proceeding from YHVH's mouth (23, 16) . . . Over against such confusion the true word is almost powerless, in no respect here appearing as endowed by the heavenly Lord with supernatural might. God does not corroborate it; He leaves to man the choice of opening his heart to the hard truth or of accepting the easy fraud as truth; He does not in any way lighten this choice for man; He does not endow His declaration with energy; He does not throw onto the scales of man's soul even a particle of His limitless power. . . . It is not whether salvation or disaster is prophesied, but whether the prophecy, whatever it is, agrees with the divine demand meant by a certain historical situation, that is important. In days of false security a shaking and stirring word of disaster is befitting, the outstretched finger pointing to the historically approaching catastrophe, the hand beating upon hardened hearts; whereas in times of great adversity, out of which liberation is liable now or again to occur, in times of regret and repentance, a strengthening and unifying word of salvation is appropriate. Jeremiah opposes the dogmatics of a guardian deity, Deutero-Isaiah the dogmatics of a punishing deity; both of them venerate the living God Who is exalted above all dogmatic wont, and His historically expressed will, which they interpret. Jeremiah, who announces the disaster, and Deutero-Isaiah, who announces the salvation, both prophesy so for the sake of the covenant between godhead and manhood. . . . And so in the life and prophecy of Jeremiah, Moses' word in Deuteronomy (18, 15) comes exactly true that YHVH will raise up for Israel—that is from generation to generation—a prophet like himself. In both—and in no other prophet—in the man Moses of the tradition and in the man Jeremiah of his own confession, we find this conquest by God, this intensive dialogue with Him, this ardor of intercession, and this suffering for the rebellious people and their lot.

* * *

Be the secret of reward and punishment what it may, in the actual reality of the catastrophe, as in that threatening saying of Ezekiel (21, 8f) about the extirpation of "righteous and wicked," "honest and wicked" (Job 9, 22) are destroyed together by God, and in the outer reality the wicked left alive knew how to assert themselves successfully in spite of all the difficulties, "they lived, became old, and even thrived mightily" (21, 7), whereas the pious, endowed with weaker elbows and more sensitive hearts, their days "were swifter than a weaver's shuttle, and were spent without hope" (7, 6); "the robbers' tents are peaceful, and they that anger God have secure abodes" (12, 6), whereas the upright is "become a brother of jackals" (30, 29). This is the experience out of which the book of Job was born, a book opposed to the dogmatics of Ezekiel, a book of the question which then was new and has persisted ever since.

* * *

I cannot ascribe this book—which clearly has only slowly grown to its present form—in its basic kernel to a time later (or earlier) than the beginning of the exile. Its formulations of the question bear the stamp of an intractable directness—the stamp of a first expression. The world, in which they were spoken, had certainly not yet heard the answers of Psalm 73 or Deutero-Isaiah. The author finds before him dogmas in process of formation, he clothes them in grand language, and sets over against them the force of the new question, the question brought into being out of *experience;* in his time these growing dogmas had not yet found their decisive opponents. The book in spite of its thorough rhetoric—the product of a long drawn-out literary process—is one of the special events in world literature, in which we witness the first clothing of a human quest in form of speech.

It has rightly been said[3] that, behind the treatment of Job's fate in this discussion, lie "very bitter experiences of a supra-individual kind." When the sufferer complains, "He breaks me around, and I am gone" (Job 19, 10), this seems no longer the complaint of a single person. When he cries, "God delivers me to the wicked, and hurls me upon the hands of the evil-doers" (16, 11), we think less of the sufferings of an individual than of the exile of a people. It is true it is a personal fate that is presented here, but the stimulus to speaking out, the incentive to complaint and accusation, bursting the bands of the presentation, are the fruit of supra-personal sufferings. Job's question comes into being as the question of a whole generation about the sense of its historic fate. Behind this "I," made so personal here, there still stands the "I" of Israel.

The question of the generation, "Why do we suffer what we suffer?" had from the beginning a religious character; "why?" here is not a philosophical interrogative asking after the nature of things, but a religious concern with the acting of God. With Job, however, it becomes still clearer; he does not ask, "Why does God *permit* me to suffer these things?" but "Why does God *make* me suffer these things?" That everything comes from God is beyond doubt and question; the question is, How are these sufferings compatible with His godhead?

In order to grasp the great inner dialectic of the poem, we must realize that here not two, but four answers stand over against each other; in other words, we find here four views of God's relationship to man's sufferings.

The first view is that of the Prologue. In order to make it clear whether Job serves him "gratuitously" (1, 9), that is to say, not for the sake of receiving a reward, God smites him and brings suffering upon him, as He Himself confesses (2, 3), "gratuitously," that is to say, without sufficient cause. Here God's acts are questioned more critically than in any of Job's accusations, because here we are informed of the true motive, which is one not befitting to deity.

The second view of God is that of the friends. This is the dogmatic view of the cause and effect in the divine system of requital: sufferings point to sin. God's punishment is manifest and clear to all. Job's sufferings testify to his guilt. The inner infinity of the suffering soul is here changed into a formula, and a wrong formula.

The third view of God is that of Job in his complaint and protest. It is the view of a God Who contradicts His revelation by "hiding His face" (13, 24). He is at one and the same time fearfully noticeable and unperceivable (9, 11), and this hiddenness is particularly sensible in face of the excessive presence of the "friends," who are ostensibly God's advocates. All their attempts to cement the rent in Job's world show him that this is the rent in the heart of the world. Clearly the thought of both Job and the friends proceeds from the question about justice. But unlike his friends, Job knows of justice only as a human activity, willed by God, but opposed by His acts. The truth of being just and the reality caused by the unjust acts of God are irreconcilable. Job cannot forego either his own truth or God. God torments him "gratuitously" (9, 17; it is not without purpose that here the word recurs, which in the Prologue Satan uses and God repeats); He "deals crookedly" with him (19, 6). All man's supplications will avail nothing: "there is no justice" (v. 7). Job does not regard himself as free from sin (7, 20; 14, 16f), in contradistinction to God's words about him in the Prologue (1, 8; 2, 3). But his sin and his sufferings are incommensurable. For Job, justice is not a scheme of compensation. Its content is simply this, that one must not cause suffering gratuitously. Job feels himself isolated by this feeling, far removed from God and men. It is true, Job does not forget that God seeks just such justice as this from man. But he cannot understand how God Himself violates it, how He inspects His creature every morning (7, 18), searching after his iniquity (10, 6), and instead of forgiving his sin (7, 21) snatches at him stormily (9, 17)—how He, being infinitely superior to man, thinks it good to reject the work of His hands (10, 3). And in spite of this Job knows that the friends, who side with God (13, 8), do not contend for the true God.

[3] Hempel, Die althebraeische Literatur (1930), 179.

He has recognized before this the true God as the near and intimate God. Now he only experiences Him through suffering and contradiction, but even in this way he does experience God. And even if He draw near to him again only in death, he will again "see" God (19, 26) as His "witness" (16, 19) against God Himself, he will see Him as the avenger of his blood (19, 25) which must not be covered by the earth until it is avenged (16, 18) by God on God. The absurd duality of a truth known to man and a reality sent by God must be swallowed up somewhere, sometime, in a unity of God's presence. How will it take place? Job does not know this, nor does he understand it, he only believes in it.

The fourth view of God is that expressed in the speech of God Himself. The extant text is apparently a late revision, as is the case with many other sections of this book, and we cannot restore the original text. But there is no doubt that the speech is intended for more than the mere demonstration of the mysterious character of God's rule in nature to a greater and more comprehensive extent than had already been done by the friends and Job himself; for more than the mere explanation to Job: "Thou canst not understand the secret of any thing or being in the world, how much less the secret of man's fate." It is also intended to do more than teach by examples taken from the world of nature about the "strange and wonderful" character of the acts of God, which contradict the whole of teleological wisdom, and point to the "playful riddle of the eternal creative power" as to an "inexpressible positive value."[10] The poet does not let his God disregard the fact that it is a matter of *justice*. The speech declares in the ears of man, struggling for justice, another justice than his own, a divine justice. Not *the* divine justice, which remains hidden, but *a* divine justice, namely that manifest in creation. The creation of the world is justice, not a recompensing and compensating justice, but a distributing, a giving justice. God the Creator bestows upon each what belongs to him, upon each thing and being, in so far as He allows it to become entirely itself. Not only for the sea (Job 38, 10), but for every thing and being God "breaks" in the hour of creation "His boundary," that is to say, He cuts the dimension of this thing or being out of "all," giving it its fixed measure, the limit appropriate to this gift. Israel's ancient belief in creation, which matured slowly only in its formulations, has here reached its completion: it is not about a "making" that we are told here, but about a "founding" (v. 4), a "setting" (v. 5, 9f), a "commanding" and "appointing" (v. 12). The creation itself already means communication between Creator and creature. The just Creator gives to all His creatures His boundary, so that each may become fully itself. Designedly man is lacking in this presentation of heaven and earth, in which man is shown the justice that is greater than his, and is shown that he with his justice, which intends to give to everyone what is due to him, is called only to emulate the divine justice, which gives to everyone what he is. In face of such divine teaching as this it would be indeed impossible for the sufferer to do aught else than put "his hand upon his mouth" (40, 4), and to confess (42, 3) that he had erred in speaking of things inconceivable for him. And nothing else could have come of it except this recognition—if he had heard only a voice "from the tempest" (38, 1; 40, 6). But the voice is the voice of *Him Who answers,* the voice of Him that "heard" (31, 35), and appeared so as to be "found" of him (23, 3). In vain Job had tried to penetrate to God through the divine remoteness; now God draws near to him. No more does God hide Himself, only the storm cloud of His sublimity still shrouds Him, and Job's eye "sees" Him (42, 5). The absolute power is for human personality's sake become personality. God offers Himself to the sufferer who, in the depth of his despair, keeps to God with his refractory complaint; He offers Himself to him as an answer.

[10] Rudolf Otto, Das Heilige, 23–25 edn. (1936), 99f; cf. also Vischer, Hiob ein Zeuge Jesu Christi (1934), 29ff; Eichrodt, Theologie des Alten Testaments III (1939), 145f.

The Dialogue between Heaven and Earth*

The most important of all that the biblical view of existence has opened up for all times is clearly recognized by a comparison of Israel's Holy Writ with those holy books of the nations that originated independently of it. None of those books is, like it, full of a dialogue between Heaven and earth. It tells us how again and again God addresses man and is addressed by him . . . The basic doctrine which fills the Hebrew Bible is that our life is a dialogue between the above and the below.

But does this still apply to our present-day life? Believers and unbelievers deny it. A view common among believers is that though everything contained in Scripture is literally true, though God did certainly speak to the men chosen by Him, yet, since then, the holy spirit has been taken from us, heaven is silent to us, and only through the books of the written and oral tradition is God's will made known to us as to what we shall do or not do; certainly, even today, the worshipper stands immediately before his Creator, but how could he dare, like the Psalmist, to report to the world words of personal reply, of personal granting as spoken immediately to him? And as for the unbelievers, it goes without saying that the atheists need not be mentioned at all, but only the adherents of a more or less philosophic God-concept, with which they cannot reconcile the idea of God's addressing, and being addressed by, man; to them, the entire dialogics of Scripture is nothing but a mythical figment, instructive from the point of view of the history of the human mind, but inapplicable to our life.

As against either opinion, a faithful and unprepossessed reader of Scripture must endorse the view he has learnt from it: what happened once happens now and always, and the fact of its happening to us is a guarantee of its having happened. The Bible has, in the form of a glorified remembrance, given vivid, decisive expression to an ever-recurrent happening. In the infinite language of events and situations, eternally changing, but plain to the truly attentive, transcendence speaks to our hearts at the essential moments of personal life. And there is a language in which we can answer it; it is the language of our actions and attitudes, our reactions and our abstentions; the totality of these answers is what we may call our answering-for-ourselves in the most proper sense of the expression. This fundamental interpretation of our existence we owe to the Hebrew Bible; and whenever we truly read it, our self-understanding is renewed and deepened.

But in Scripture, not only the individual, the community too, is addressed from above, in such a manner as is found in no other of the holy books of mankind.

Here the people, as a people, confronts God and receives, as a people, His never-ceasing instruction. It, too, like the individual, is called upon to participate in the realization of the divine will on earth. Just as the individual is to hallow himself in his personal life, the people is to hallow itself in its communal life; it is to become a "holy people." Like the individual, it is free as to its answer to the divine call, free to say yes or no to God by its doing and its not-doing. . . .

This is also why in Scripture the divine voice addresses man not as an isolated individual but always as an individual member of the people. Even before there is a people of Israel, its father-to-be, Abraham, is addressed as such: he is to become "a blessing" in his seed. And in the legislation, both in the Decalogue and in the injunctions supplementing it, God again and again addresses Himself to a "thou" which is certainly the "thou" of each individual in each generation of the people, but as conceived in his connection with the people, at whose communal life that legislation is aimed, so that everyone, when a commandment conveys to him the will of God with regard to his own life, conceives himself as the individual condensation of the people. This basic view unfolds itself up to the highest level of human existence: "Thou art my servant, the Israel in

* From Martin Buber, *At the Turning*. New York: Farrar, Straus and Young, 1952. Pages 47–50, 52–53, and 55–56 are reproduced by permission of the publisher.

whom I will be glorified," says God (Isa. 49) to His elect: the man who fulfills the mandate given to the people embodies the truth of the people's existence.

From here, modern life, both of peoples and of persons, is judged and its sentence passed. This life is split in two: what is thought reprehensible in the relations between persons is thought commendable in the relations between peoples. This is contrary to the prophetic demand: the prophet (Amos 1.2) accuses a people of sinning against another people because it "remembered not the brotherly covenant." . . .

If the first biblical axiom is: "Man is addressed by God in his life," the second is: "The life of man is meant by God as a unit." . . .

Postbiblical thinkers have pondered how the freedom of the human will and the resultant indetermination of the future can be reconciled with divine foresight and predetermination. Outstanding among all that has been said in the effort to overcome this contradiction is the well-known saying of Akiba's ("All is surveyed, and the power is given"), whose meaning is that to God, Who sees them together, the times do not appear in succession but in progress-less eternity, while in the progression of times, in which man lives, freedom reigns, at any given time, in the concrete moment of decision; beyond that, human wisdom has not attained. In the Bible itself, there is no pondering; it does not deal with the essence of God but with His manifestation to mankind; the reality of which it treats is that of the human world, and in it, the immutable truth of decision applies.

For guilty man, this means the decision to turn from his wrong way to the way of God. Here we see most clearly what it means in the biblical view that our answering-for-ourselves is essentially our answering to a divine address. The two great examples are Cain and David. Both have murdered (for so the Bible understands also David's deed, since it makes God's messenger say to him that he "slew Uriah the Hittite with the sword,") and both are called to account by God. Cain attempts evasion: "Am I my brother's keeper?" He is the man who shuns the dialogue with God. Not so David. He answers: "I have sinned against the Lord." This is the true answer: whomsoever one becomes guilty against, in truth one becomes guilty against God. David is the man who acknowledges the relation between God and himself, from which his answerability arises, and realizes that he has betrayed it.

The Hebrew Bible is concerned with the terrible and merciful fact of the *immediacy* between God and ourselves. Even in the dark hour after he has become guilty against his brother, man is not abandoned to the forces of chaos. God Himself seeks him out, and even when He comes to call him to account, His coming is salvation.

ABRAHAM JOSHUA HESCHEL (1907–)

The early life of Abraham Joshua Heschel was spent in Warsaw under the influence of the Hasidic movement (see the introductory note on M. Buber, p. 355). After a thorough grounding in Talmudic studies, he went to the University of Berlin where he studied philosophy. He is now Professor of Jewish Ethics and Mysticism at the Jewish Theological Seminary in New York City. His book, *God in Search of Man,* has been widely acclaimed as one of the most important contributions to the philosophy of religion from the Jewish standpoint.

The Presence of God*

Two sources of religious thinking are given us: *memory* (tradition) and *personal* insight. We must rely on our memory and we must strive for fresh insight. We *hear* from tradition, we also *understand* through our own seeking. The prophets appeal to the spiritual power in man: "Know, therefore, this day, and lay it to your heart, that the Lord is God in heaven above and on the earth beneath; there is no other" (Deuteronomy 4:39). The psalmist calls on us "O taste and see that the Lord is good" (34:9). How does one know? How does one taste? . . .

Out of his own insight a person must first arrive at the understanding: *This is my God, and I will glorify Him,* and subsequently he will attain the realization that He is *the God of my father, and I will exalt Him.* . . .

How does one seek Him? How does one find in this world, within one's own human existence and response to this world, ways that lead to the certainty of His presence? . . .

There are three starting points of contemplation about God; three trails that lead to Him. The first is the way of sensing the presence of God in the world, in things; the second is the way of sensing His presence in the Bible; the third is the way of sensing His presence in sacred deeds. . . .

These three ways correspond in our tradition to the main aspects of religious existence: worship, learning, and action. The three are one, and we must go all three ways to reach the one destination. For this is what Israel discovered: the God of nature is the God of history, and the way to know Him is to do His will. . . .

How does one find the way to an awareness of God through beholding the world here and now? To understand the Biblical answer, we must try to ascertain what the world means and to comprehend the categories in which the Bible sees the world: the sublime, wonder, mystery, awe, and glory.

Lift up your eyes and see. How does a man lift up his eyes to see a little higher than himself? *The grand premise* of religion is that *man is able to surpass himself;* that man who is part of this world may enter into a relationship with Him who is greater than the world . . .

Small is the world that most of us pay attention to, and limited is our concern. What do we see when we see the world? There are three aspects of nature that command our attention: its *power,* its *beauty,* and its *grandeur.* Accordingly, there are three ways in which we may relate ourselves to the world—we may exploit it, we may enjoy it, we may accept it in awe. In the history of civilization, different aspects of nature have drawn forth the talent of man; sometimes its power, sometimes its beauty and occasionally its grandeur have attracted his mind. Our age is one in which usefulness is thought to be the chief merit of nature; in which the attainment of power, the utilization of its resources is taken to be the chief purpose of man in God's creation. Man has indeed become primarily a tool-making animal, and the world is now a gigantic tool box for the satisfaction of his needs. . . .

Wonder or radical amazement is the chief characteristic of the religious man's attitude toward history and nature. One attitude is alien to his spirit: taking things for granted, regarding events as a natural course of things. To find an approximate cause of a phenomenon is no answer to his ultimate wonder. He knows that there are laws that regulate the course of natural processes; he is aware of the regularity and pattern of things. However, such knowledge fails to mitigate his sense of perpetual surprise at the fact that there are facts at all. Looking at the world he would say, "This is the Lord's doing, it is marvelous in our eyes" (Psalms 118:23).

That "wonder is the feeling of a philosopher, and philosophy begins in wonder" was stated by Plato and maintained by Aristotle: "For it is owing to their wonder that men both now begin and at first began to philosophize." To this day, rational wonder is appreciated as *"semen scientiae,"* as the seed of knowledge, as something conducive, not indigenous to cogni-

* From Abraham Joshua Heschel, *God in Search of Man.* New York: Farrar, Straus and Cudahy, 1955. Pages 27, 30–34, 43, 45–47, and 114–122 are reproduced by permission of the publisher.

tion. Wonder is the prelude to knowledge; it ceases, once the cause of a phenomenon is explained.

But does the worth of wonder merely consist in its being a stimulant to the acquisition of knowledge? Is wonder the same as curiosity? To the prophets wonder is *a form of thinking*. It is not the beginning of knowledge but an act that goes beyond knowledge; it does not come to an end when knowledge is acquired; it is an attitude that never ceases. There is no answer in the world to man's radical amazement.

"Stand Still and Consider"

As civilization advances, the sense of wonder declines. Such decline is an alarming symptom of our state of mind. Mankind will not perish for want of information; but only for want of appreciation. The beginning of our happiness lies in the understanding that life without wonder is not worth living. What we lack is not a will to believe but a will to wonder.

Awareness of the divine begins with wonder. It is the result of what man does with his higher incomprehension. The greatest hindrance to such awareness is our adjustment to conventional notions, to mental clichés. Wonder or radical amazement, the state of maladjustment to words and notions, is therefore a prerequisite for an authentic awareness of that which is.

Radical amazement has a wider scope than any other act of man. While any act of perception or cognition has as its object a selected segment of reality, radical amazement refers to all of reality; not only to what we see, but also to the very act of seeing as well as to our own selves, to the selves that see and are amazed at their ability to see.

The grandeur or mystery of being is not a particular puzzle to the mind, as, for example, the cause of volcanic eruptions. We do not have to go to the end of reasoning to encounter it. Grandeur or mystery is something with which we are confronted everywhere and at all times. Even the very act of thinking baffles our thinking, just as every intelligible fact is, by virtue of its being a fact, drunk with baffling aloofness. Does not mystery reign within reasoning, within perception, within explanation? Where is the self-understanding that could unfurl the marvel of our own thinking, that could explain the grace of our emptying the concrete with charms of abstraction? What formula could explain and solve the enigma of the very fact of thinking? Ours is neither thing nor thought but only the subtle magic blending the two.

What fills us with radical amazement is not the relations in which everything is embedded but the fact that even the minimum of perception is a maximum of enigma. The most incomprehensible fact is the fact that we comprehend at all. . . .

But how can we ever reach an understanding of Him who is beyond the mystery? How do we go from the intimations of the divine to a sense for the realness of God? Certainty of the realness of God comes about:

As a response of the whole person to the mystery and transcendence of living.

As a response, it is an act of raising from the depths of the mind an *ontological presupposition* which makes that response intellectually understandable.

The meaning and verification of the ontological presupposition are attained in rare *moments of insight*.

It is the mystery that evokes our religious concern, and it is the mystery where religious thinking must begin . . .

Indeed, knowledge does not come into being only as the fruit of thinking. Only an extreme rationalist or solipsist would claim that knowledge is produced exclusively through the combination of concepts. Any genuine encounter with reality is an encounter with the unknown, is an intuition in which an awareness of the object is won, a rudimentary, *preconceptual* knowledge. Indeed, no object is truly known, unless it was first experienced in its unknownness.

It is a fact of profound significance that we sense more than we can say. When we stand face to face with the grandeur of the world, any formulation of thought appears as an anticlimax. It is in the awareness that the mystery which we face is incomparably deeper than what we know that all creative thinking begins.

Preconceptual Thinking

The encounter with reality does not take

place on the level of concepts through the channels of logical categories; concepts are second thoughts. All conceptualization is symbolization, an act of accommodation of reality to the human mind. The living encounter with reality takes place on a level that precedes conceptualization, on a level that is responsive, *immediate, preconceptual,* and *presymbolic.* Theory, speculation, generalization, and hypothesis, are efforts to clarify and to validate the insights which preconceptual experience provides . . .

Particularly in religious and artistic thinking, the disparity between that which we encounter and that which is expressed in words and symbols, no words and symbols can adequately convey. In our religious situation we do not comprehend the transcendent; we are present at it, we witness it. Whatever we know is inadequate; whatever we say is an understatement. We have an awareness that is deeper than our concepts; we possess insights that are not accessible to the power of expression.

Knowledge is not the same as awareness, and expression is not the same as experience. By proceeding from awareness to knowledge we gain in clarity and lose in immediacy. What we gain in distinctness by going from experience to expression we lose in genuineness. The difference becomes a divergence when our preconceptual insights are lost in our conceptualizations, when the encounter with the ineffable is forfeited in our symbolizations, when the dogmatic formulation becomes more important than the religious situation.

The entire range of religious thought and expression is a sublimation of a presymbolic knowledge which the awareness of the ineffable provides. That awareness can only partly be sublimated into rational symbols.

Philosophy of religion must be an effort to recall and to keep alive *the meta-symbolic relevance of religious terms.* Religious thinking is in perpetual danger of giving primacy to concepts and dogmas and to forfeit the immediacy of insights, to forget that the known is but a reminder of God, that the dogma is a token of His will, the expression the inexpressible at its minimum. Concepts, words must not become screens; they must be regarded as windows.

The roots of ultimate insights are found, as said above, not on the level of discursive thinking, but on the level of wonder and radical amazement, in the depth of awe, in our sensitivity to the mystery, in our awareness of the ineffable. It is the level on which the great things happen to the soul, where the unique insights of art, religion, and philosophy come into being.

It is not from experience but *from our inability to experience* what is given to our mind that certainty of the realness of God is derived. It is not the order of being but the transcendent in the contingency of all order, the allusions to transcendence in all acts and all things that challenge our deepest understanding.

Our certainty is the result of wonder and radical amazement, of awe before the mystery and meaning of the totality of life beyond our rational discerning. Faith is *the response* to the mystery, shot through with meaning; the response to a challenge which no one can forever ignore. "The heaven" is a challenge. When you "lift up your eyes on high," you are faced with the question. Faith is an act of man who *transcending himself* responds to Him who *transcends the world.*

To Rise Above Our Wisdom

Such response is a sign of man's essential dignity. For the essence and greatness of man do not lie in his ability to please his ego, to satisfy his needs, but rather in his ability to stand above his ego, to ignore his own needs; to sacrifice his own interests for the sake of the holy. The soul's urge to judge its own judgments, to look for meaning beyond the scope of the tangible and finite—in short, the soul's urge *to rise above its own wisdom*—is the root of religious faith.

God is the great mystery, but our faith in Him conveys to us more understanding of Him than either reason or perception is able to grasp. . . .

To have faith is not to capitulate but to rise to a higher plane of thinking. To have faith is not to defy human reason but rather to share divine wisdom.

Lift up your eyes on high and see: Who created these. One must rise to a higher plane of thinking in order to see, in order to sense the allusions, the glory, the presence. One must rise to a higher plane of living and learn to sense the urgency of the ultimate question, the supreme relevance of eternity. He who has not arrived at the highest realm, the realm of the mystery; he who does not realize he is living at the edge of the mystery; he who has only a sense for the obvious and apparent, will not be able to lift up his eyes, for whatever is apparent is not attached to the highest realm; what is highest is hidden. Faith, believing in God, is attachment to the highest realm, the realm of the mystery. This is its essence. Our faith is capable of reaching the realm of the mystery.

The sense of wonder, awe, and mystery does not give us a knowledge of God. It only leads to a plane where the question about God becomes an inescapable concern, to a situation in which we discover that we can neither place our anxiety in the safe deposit of opinions nor delegate to others the urgent task of answering the ultimate question.

Such ultimate concern is *an act of worship,* an act of acknowledging in the most intense manner the supremacy of the issue. It is not an act of choice, something that we can for ever ignore. It is the manifestation of a fundamental fact of human existence, the fact of worship.

Every one of us is bound to have an ultimate object of worship, yet he is free to choose the object of his worship. He cannot live without it; it may be either a fictitious or a real object, God or an idol. . . .

Since our concern with the question about God is an act of worship, and since worship posits the realness of its object, our very concern involves by implication the acceptance of His realness.

Just as supreme worship of an ultimate object is indigenous to human existence, so is explicit denial of the realness of an ultimate object absurd. . . .

There can be no honest denial of the existence of God. There can only be faith or the honest confession of inability to believe—or arrogance. Man could maintain inability to believe or suspend his judgment, if he were not driven by the pressure of existence into a situation in which he must decide between yes and no; in which he must decide what or whom to worship. He is driven toward some sort of affirmation. In whatever decision he makes he implicitly accepts either the realness of God or the absurdity of denying Him.

We Praise Before We Prove

Understanding God is not attained by calling into session all arguments for and against Him, in order to debate whether He is a reality or a figment of the mind. God cannot be sensed as a second thought, as an explanation of the origin of the universe. He is either the first and the last, or just another concept.

Speculation does not precede faith. The antecedents of faith are the premise of wonder and the premise of praise. Worship of God precedes affirmation of His realness. We *praise* before we *prove*. We respond before we question.

Proofs for the existence of God may add strength to our belief; they do not generate it. Human existence implies the realness of God. There is a certainty without knowledge in the depth of our being that accounts for our asking the ultimate question, a preconceptual certainty that lies beyond all formulation or verbalization.

An Ontological Presupposition

It is *the assertion* that God is real, independent of our preconceptual awareness, that presents the major difficulty. Subjective awareness is not always an index of truth. What is subjectively true is not necessarily trans-subjectively real. All we have is the awareness of allusions to His concern, intimations of His presence. To speak of His reality is to transcend awareness, to surpass the limits of thinking. It is like springing clear of the ground. Are we intellectually justified in inferring from our awareness a reality that lies beyond it? Are we entitled to rise from the realm of this world to a realm that is beyond this world?

We are often guilty of misunderstanding the nature of an assertion such as "God is." Such an assertion would constitute a leap if the assertion constituted an addition to our ineffable awareness of God. The truth, however, is that to say "God is" means less than what our immediate awareness contains. *The statement "God is" is an understatement.*

Thus, the certainty of the realness of God does not come about as a corollary of logical premises, as a leap from the realm of logic to the realm of ontology, from an assumption to a fact. It is, on the contrary, a transition from an immediate apprehension to a thought, from a preconceptual awareness to a definite assurance, from being overwhelmed by the presence of God to an awareness of His existence. What we attempt to do in the act of reflection is to raise that preconceptual awareness to the level of understanding.

In sensing the spiritual dimension of all being, we become aware of the absolute reality of the divine. In formulating a creed, in asserting: God is, we merely bring down overpowering reality to the level of thought. Our thought is but an after-belief.

In other words, our belief in the reality of God is not a case of first possessing an idea and then postulating the ontal counterpart of it; or, to use a Kantian phrase, of first having the idea of a hundred dollars and then claiming to possess them on the basis of the idea. What obtains here is first the actual possession of the dollars and then the attempt to count the sum. There are possibilities of error in counting the notes, but the notes themselves are here.

In other words, our belief in His reality is not a leap over a missing link in a syllogism but rather *a regaining,* giving up a view rather than adding one, going behind self-consciousness and questioning the self and all its cognitive pretensions. *It is an ontological presupposition.*

In the depth of human thinking we all presuppose some ultimate reality which on the level of discursive thinking is crystallized into the concept of a power, a principle or a structure. This, then, is the order in our thinking and existence: The ultimate or God comes first and our reasoning about Him second. Metaphysical speculation has reversed the order: reasoning comes first and the question about His reality second; either He is proved or He is not real.

However, just as there is no thinking about the world without the premise of the reality of the world, there can be no thinking about God without the premise of the realness of God.

WILL HERBERG (1906–)

Educated at Columbia University, Will Herberg has written widely on social, political and religious topics. For years he served as research analyst for a large labor union. His book, *Protestant, Catholic, Jew,* established him as a leading interpreter of the sociology of American religious life. Since 1958 he has been Professor of Judaic Studies and Social Philosophy at Drew University. His most influential theological treatise has been *Judaism and Modern Man.*

Religious Trends in American Jewry*

The past twenty years have witnessed a remarkable change in the religious situation of the Jews in America. Trends that had prevailed since the earlier days of immigration and that seemed to be part of the very "nature" of American Jewry have been reversed, and new tendencies have emerged that are shaping the American Jewish community in ways undreamed of a generation ago. There can be no doubt that we have entered a significantly

* From Will Herberg, "Religious Trends in American Jewery," *Judaism,* Vol. III, 1954. Pages 229–230, 230–232 are reprinted with the permission of the publisher.

new period in the history of American Jewry. It is the purpose of this paper to examine the new situation in its major aspects and to assess the significance of the new trends for Jewish life in America.

I

The outstanding fact defining the new situation is the reversal of the two major trends that characterized the pattern of American Jewish life well through the 1920's—the trend toward the dissolution of Jewishness and the trend toward the abandonment of the Jewish religious tradition and of all religious concern whatsoever. Assimilation and secularism marked the pattern of American Jewish life from the beginning of the great immigration at the end of the last century, although for decades these tendencies, particularly the former, were masked by the continuous influx of new immigrants. When large-scale immigration came to an end during the first world war, the logic of the underlying social and cultural pattern became evident: American Jews were abandoning their Jewishness and losing all interest in their religious heritage. There were not wanting those who were already sounding the knell of American Jewry and confidently relegating the synagogue, along with the church, to the limbo of obsolescent institutions.

The situation is obviously very different today. The trend toward dissolution and secularism, so marked through the twenties, has been halted, even reversed. Among all sections of American Jewry, but particularly among the younger generation, there is a movement of "return." "Return" to what? It is hard to say exactly: return to a new sense of Jewishness, return to the synagogue, return to personal religious concern. These various aspects are often fused and compounded in the movement of "return"; yet they sometimes also exhibit a certain tension, which shows that the underlying forces and motives are not of one piece but reflect different facets of the experience of the American Jew in mid-twentieth century America.

The return to Jewishness, to self-affirmation as a Jew and to self-identification with Jewry, is perhaps the most obvious sign of the times. The young people in the colleges—who, let us remember, make up the next generation of American Jews—as well as those out of school who are setting up homes for themselves, recognize and affirm their Jewishness in a way that would have seemed unbelievable some thirty years ago, and to a greater or less degree this is also true of other sections of American Jewry . . . This trend is signalized by the emergence of the "third generation" of American Jewry. The first generation, the immigrant generation, came with their Jewishness as part of their immigrant heritage; it was embedded in their life and culture. The younger members of that generation, and of the next, revolted against this heritage, and in the process of establishing their independence and adjusting themselves to their new environment, they strove to cast off their Jewishness as part of the immigrant baggage they were so eager to abandon. They were intent—quite naturally and properly intent—upon becoming Americans, and to become Americans they had to cease to be foreigners, which to them only too often meant to cease to be Jews. The third generation is in a very different position; it is secure in its Americanness and does not have an immigrant burden which it is anxious to throw off. It can therefore face the problem of its Jewishness in a new and creative manner, free from many of the anxieties and compulsions that afflicted the earlier generations. How it is coping with the problems of its Jewishness we are only just beginning to discern in vague outline.

But here a question arises that leads us to the heart of the matter. This phenomenon of the "third generation" is common to all of the many immigrant groups that came to these shores in the past century and that have entered into the making of the American people. But in every other case, the emergence of the "third generation"—I refer here to the sociological category; in some cases, it may actually be a fourth or a fifth generation—in every other case, I say, the emergence of the "third generation" has meant the dissolution of the ethnic-immigrant group from which it came and its absorption into the developing mainstream of American life; that is precisely how the American people and American culture have come into being. With the Jews it has been different. The first and second generations of Jews in America repeated the common immigrant pattern: immigrant foreignness followed by an anxious effort to get rid of that foreignness and become American. But the "third generation" of American Jews, instead of somehow finally getting rid of their separateness and dissolving completely into the general community, which is what all other "third generations" have done or are doing, the "third generation" of American Jews are actually returning to Jewishness. How are we to account for this strange anomaly which distinguishes Jews from all other immigrant groups that have gone into the making of America?

We can account for this anomaly only by recognizing that American Jewry cannot be understood if it is taken to be merely one of the many ethnic groups that left the old world for the new in the course of the great migrations of the past century. The Jews who came to America did of course constitute an immigrant group, but their Jewishness was apparently something that transcended their immigrant character in a way that was not true of the merely ethnic or national character of the other immigrant groups. Their Jewishness was apparently something very different from the kind of ethnic or cultural foreignness that tends to disappear with the emergence of the third generation. Had it not been something very different, we would not now be witnessing a return of the "third generation" to Jewishness.

The fact of the matter seems to be that just when the immigrant-cultural basis of American Jewish existence was beginning to disappear with the emergence of a thoroughly American "third generation," American Jewry was becoming transformed into what sociologists call a "religious community." The religious community has, in fact, become the primary context of social location in contemporary American life. When an American asks of a new family in town, "What does he do?" he means the occupation or profession of the head of the family; when he asks, "What are they?" he means to what religious community do they belong—Protestant, Catholic, or Jewish. A century ago, the question, "What are they?" would have been answered in terms of immigrant-ethnic origin, and today it is still answered in some such terms for Negroes as well as for Americans of Oriental or recent Latin American origin. But increasingly, the great mass of Americans understand themselves and their place in American society in terms of the religious community with which they are identified. And "religious community" in this usage refers not so much to the particular denomination, of which there are scores in this country, but to the three great divisions, Catholics, Protestants, and Jews. America is the land of the "triple melting pot," for it is within these three religious communities that the process of ethnic and cultural integration so characteristic of American life takes place.

We can restate all this by saying that while the unity of American life is indeed a unity in multiplicity, the pluralism that this implies is of a very special kind. America recognizes no permanent national or cultural minorities; what Europe knows under this head are in this country regarded as "foreign language" or "foreign culture" groups, whose separateness is merely temporary, the consequence of recent immigration, destined to be overcome with increasing integration into American life. America does indeed know and acknowledge the separateness of so-called minority "races," but such separateness has always involved some degree of segregation and consequent relegation to an inferior status in the social hierarchy. The only kind of separateness or diversity that America recognizes as permanent and yet also as involving no status of inferiority is the diversity or separateness of religious communities. In short, while America knows no national or cultural minorities except as temporary, transitional phenomena, it does know a free variety and plurality of religions, and it is as a member of a religious group that the great mass of Americans understand the status of the Jew in this country and that the American Jew understands himself. This is particularly true of the younger generation of Jews. When they are moved to affirm their Jewishness, and they must do so if only to identify themselves to themselves and to others, they can conceive of no way of doing so except in religious terms. The many substitutes for Jewish religious identification, which were open to earlier generations, are no longer viable to them. It is simply a fact that the average American Jew —I mean the Jew who is acculturated to America—if he thinks of himself as a Jew at all, tends almost automatically to think of himself as belonging to a religious community, even if he himself does not have personal faith. In the Vilna of the 1920's, it was possible for a militantly anti-religious Jewish doctor to assert himself as a Jew by sending his children to a secular Yiddish school, and for a time this pattern was familiar among Jewish immigrants in this country. For some time, too, one could "be a Jew" simply by being a Zionist or by identifying oneself with some Jewish philanthropic cause. All this is becoming increasingly untenable. Today, if the American Jew is to regard himself as a Jew, and if he is to be so regarded by his non-Jewish neighbors and friends, some religious association, however vague, is necessary. The only way in which the Jew can integrate himself into American society is in terms of a religious community.

That is one reason why the "return" to Jewishness of which I have spoken has also meant a return to the synagogue. It is beyond dispute that synagogue construction, synagogue membership, and even synagogue attendance are growing at an unprecedented rate in this country. This is part of a larger movement characterizing the entire American people today, for the growth of religious bodies and the increase in religious affiliation on the part of the American people is one of the most striking facts about the present situation in the United States. In 1900, 36 percent of the American people were reported as religiously affiliated; by 1930, the figure had risen to 47 percent; and by 1950, to 57 percent. In the quarter of a century from 1926 to 1950, the population of the United States rose 28.6 percent; church membership, however, jumped nearly 60 percent. There are no comparable figures applying specifically to the Jews, but all evidence goes to show that the movement of American Jews into the synagogue in recent years has been at least as sweeping and as vigorous as the movement of Americans generally into the church. Many of the older people, who had once broken away and had never thought of the possibility of returning, are back again, but it is primarily the trend of the younger generation that is decisive. For them, the "return" to Jewishness which we are witnessing is in great measure a return to the synagogue, for not only is the synagogue the one enduring and representative Jewish institution; not only is it the unique embodiment through the ages of Jewish spirituality: it is also the characteristically American vehicle of Jewish self-identification.

Roman Catholicism in the Modern World

POPE LEO XIII (1810–1903)

No modern pope has had a greater influence on the social teachings of the Roman Catholic Church than Pope Leo XIII. He was born Vincent Joachim Pecci and educated at the College of Rome in the natural sciences and philosophy. Ordained in 1837, he was elected pope in 1878. His encyclical letters covered such topics as Christian marriage, human liberty, slavery, the Christian philosophy of the state, socialism, and democracy. His most famous encyclical,

De Rerum Novarum, (see p. 375) gave a solid foundation to the attitude of the church toward the problems of labor and capital.

Selections are given from two encyclicals. In *Aeterni Patris* (August 4, 1879), he condemns the errors of modern philosophy and directs the faithful to study the works of St. Thomas Aquinas (see pp. 185f.). In *Immortale Dei* (November 1, 1885) he discusses the relations of church and state.

Aeterni Patris*

The only-begotten Son of the Eternal Father, who came on earth to bring salvation and the light of divine wisdom to men, conferred a great and wonderful blessing on the world when, about to ascend again into heaven, He commanded the Apostles to go and teach all nations, and left the Church which He had founded to be the common and supreme teacher of the peoples. For men whom the truth had set free were to be preserved by the truth; nor would the fruits of heavenly doctrines by which salvation comes to men have long remained had not the Lord Christ appointed an unfailing teaching authority to train the minds to faith. And the Church built upon the promises of its own divine Author, whose charity it imitated, so faithfully followed out His commands that its constant aim and chief wish was this: to teach religion and contend forever against errors. . . .

. . . We do not, indeed, attribute such force and authority to philosophy as to esteem it equal to the task of combating and rooting out all errors; for, when the Christian religion was first constituted, it came upon earth to restore it to its primeval dignity by the admirable light of faith, diffused "not by persuasive words of human wisdom, but in the manifestation of spirit and of power"; so also at the present time we look above all things to the powerful help of Almighty God to bring back to a right understanding the minds of men and dispel the darkness of error. But the natural helps with which the grace of the divine wisdom, strongly and sweetly disposing all things, has supplied the human race are neither to be despised nor neglected, chief among which is evidently the right use of philosophy. For, not in vain did God set the light of reason in the human mind; and so far is the super-added light of faith from extinguishing or lessening the power of the intelligence that it completes it rather, and by adding to its strength renders it capable of greater things. . . .

But in order that philosophy may be found equal to the gathering of those precious fruits which we have indicated, it behooves it above all things never to turn aside from that path which the Fathers have entered upon from a venerable antiquity, and which the Vatican Council solemnly and authoritatively approved. As it is evident that very many truths of the supernatural order which are far beyond the reach of the keenest intellect must be accepted, human reason, conscious of its own infirmity, dare not affect to itself too great powers, nor deny those truths, nor measure them by its own standard, nor interpret them at will; but receive them, rather, with a full and humble faith, and esteem it the highest honor to be allowed to wait upon heavenly doctrines like a handmaid and attendant, and by God's goodness attain to them in any way whatsoever. But in the case of such doctrines as the human intelligence may perceive, it is equally just that philosophy should make use of its own method, principles, and arguments—not, indeed, in such fashion as to seem rashly to withdraw from the divine authority. But, since it is established that those things which become known by revelation have the force of certain truth, and that those things which war against

* From Pope Leo XIII, "On Christian Philosophy" in *The Church Speaks to the Modern World: The Social Teaching of Leo XIII,* edited, with an introduction by Etienne Gilson. New York: Doubleday and Company Image Books, 1954. Pages 31–33, 37–38, 43–44, and 46–48 are reproduced by permission of the Paulist Press, New York.

faith war equally against right reason, the Catholic philosopher will know that he violates at once faith and the laws of reason if he accepts any conclusion which he understands to be opposed to revealed doctrine.

We know that there are some who, in their overestimate of the human faculties, maintain that as soon as man's intellect becomes subject to divine authority it falls from its native dignity, and, hampered by the yoke of this species of slavery, is much retarded and hindered in its progress toward the supreme truth and excellence. Such an idea is most false and deceptive, and its sole tendency is to induce foolish and ungrateful men wilfully to repudiate the most sublime truths, and reject the divine gift of faith, from which the fountains of all good things flow out upon civil society. For the human mind, being confined within certain limits, and those narrow enough, is exposed to many errors and is ignorant of many things; whereas the Christian faith, reposing on the authority of God, is the unfailing mistress of truth, whom whoso followeth he will be neither enmeshed in the snares of error nor tossed hither and thither on the waves of fluctuating opinion. . . .

Among the Scholastic Doctors, the chief and master of all, towers Thomas Aquinas, who, as Cajetan observes, because "he most venerated the ancient doctors of the Church, in a certain way seems to have inherited the intellect of all." The doctrines of those illustrious men, like the scattered members of a body, Thomas collected together and cemented, distributed in wonderful order, and so increased with important additions that he is rightly and deservedly esteemed the special bulwark and glory of the Catholic faith. . . .

Moreover, the Angelic Doctor pushed his philosophic inquiry into the reasons and principles of things, which because they are most comprehensive and contain in their bosom, so to say, the seeds of almost infinite truths, were to be unfolded in good time by later masters and with a goodly yield. And as he also used this philosophic method in the refutation of error, he won this title to distinction for himself: that, single-handed, he victoriously combated the errors of former times, and supplied invincible arms to put those to rout which might in after-times spring up. Again, clearly distinguishing, as is fitting, reason from faith, while happily associating the one with the other, he both preserved the rights and had regard for the dignity of each; so much so, indeed, that reason, borne on the wings of Thomas to its human height, can scarcely rise higher, while faith could scarcely expect more or stronger aids from reason than those which she has already obtained through Thomas. . . .

Therefore, venerable brethren, as often as We contemplate the good, the force, and the singular advantages to be derived from his philosophic discipline which Our Fathers so dearly loved, We think it hazardous that its special honor should not always and everywhere remain, especially when it is established that daily experience, and the judgment of the greatest men, and, to crown all, the voice of the Church, have favored the Scholastic philosophy. Moreover, to the old teaching a novel system of philosophy has succeeded here and there, in which We fail to perceive those desirable and wholesome fruits which the Church and civil society itself would prefer. For it pleased the struggling innovators of the sixteenth century to philosophize without any respect for faith, the power of inventing in accordance with his own pleasure and bent being asked and given in turn by each one. Hence, it was natural that systems of philosophy multiplied beyond measure, and conclusions differing and clashing one with another arose about those matters even which are the most important in human knowledge. From a mass of conclusions men often come to wavering and doubt; and who knows not how easily the mind slips from doubt to error. . . .

With wise forethought, therefore, not a few of the advocates of philosophic studies, when turning their minds recently to the practical reform of philosophy, aimed and aim at restoring the renowned teaching of Thomas Aquinas and winning it back to its ancient beauty.

We have learned with great joy that many members of your order, venerable brethren, have taken this plan to heart; and while We earnestly commend their efforts, We exhort them to hold fast to their purpose, and remind each and all of you that Our first and most cherished idea is that you should all furnish to studious youth a generous and copious supply of those purest streams of wisdom flowing inexhaustibly from the precious fountainhead of the Angelic Doctor.

Immortale Dei*

The Catholic Church, that imperishable handiwork of our all-merciful God, has for her immediate and natural purpose the saving of souls and securing our happiness in heaven. Yet, in regard to things temporal, she is the source of benefits as manifold and great as if the chief end of her existence were to ensure the prospering of our earthly life. And, indeed, wherever the Church has set her foot she has straightway changed the face of things, and has attempered the moral tone of the people with a new civilization and with virtues before unknown. All nations which have yielded to her sway have become eminent by their gentleness, their sense of justice, and the glory of their high deeds.

And yet a hackneyed reproach of old date is leveled against her, that the Church is opposed to the rightful aims of the civil government, and is wholly unable to afford help in spreading that welfare and progress which justly and naturally are sought after by every well-regulated State. . . . Many, indeed, are they who have tried to work out a plan of civil society based on doctrines other than those approved by the Catholic Church. Nay, in these latter days a novel conception of law has begun here and there to gain increase and influence, the outcome, as it is maintained, of an age arrived at full stature, and the result of progressive liberty. But, though endeavors of various kinds have been ventured on, it is clear that no better mode has been devised for the building up and ruling the State than that which is the necessary growth of the teachings of the Gospel. We deem it, therefore, of the highest moment, and a strict duty of Our apostolic office, to contrast with the lessons taught by Christ the novel theories now advanced touching the State. By this means We cherish hope that the bright shining of the truth may scatter the mists of error and doubt, so that one and all may see clearly the imperious law of life which they are bound to follow and obey.

It is not difficult to determine what would be the form and character of the State were it governed according to the principles of Christian philosophy. Man's natural instinct moves him to live in civil society, for he cannot, if dwelling apart, provide himself with the necessary requirements of life, nor procure the means of developing his mental and moral faculties. Hence, it is divinely ordained that he should lead his life—be it family, or civil—with his fellow men, amongst whom alone his several wants can be adequately supplied. But, as no society can hold together unless some one be over all, directing all to strive earnestly for the common good, every body politic must have a ruling authority, and this authority, no less than society itself, has its source in nature, and has, consequently, God for its Author. Hence, it follows that all public power must proceed from God. For God alone is the true and supreme Lord of the world. Everything, without exception, must be subject to Him, and must serve Him, so that whosoever holds the right to govern holds it from one sole and single source, namely, God, the sovereign Ruler of all. "There is no power but from God."

The right to rule is not necessarily, however, bound up with any special mode of government. It may take this or that form, provided only that it be of a nature to insure the general welfare. But, whatever be the nature of the government, rulers must ever bear in mind that God is the paramount ruler of the world,

* From Pope Leo XIII, "On The Christian Constitution of States," in *The Church Speaks to the Modern World: The Social Teachings of Leo XIII, op. cit.* Pages 161–168, 172–173, and 178–180 are reproduced by permission of the Paulist Press, New York.

and must set Him before themselves as their exemplar and law in the administration of the State. . . .

They, therefore, who rule should rule with even-handed justice, not as masters, but rather as fathers, for the rule of God over man is most just, and is tempered always with a father's kindness. Government should, moreover, be administered for the well-being of the citizens, because they who govern others possess authority solely for the welfare of the State. Furthermore, the civil power must not be subservient to the advantage of any one individual or of some few persons, inasmuch as it was established for the common good of all. . . .

As a consequence, the State, constituted as it is, is clearly bound to act up to the manifold and weighty duties linking it to God, by the public profession of religion. Nature and reason, which command every individual devoutly to worship God in holiness, because we belong to Him and must return to Him, since from Him we came, bind also the civil community by a like law. For, men living together in society are under the power of God no less than individuals are, and society, no less than individuals, owes gratitude to God who gave it being and maintains it and whose ever-bounteous goodness enriches it with countless blessings. Since, then, no one is allowed to be remiss in the service due to God, and since the chief duty of all men is to cling to religion in both its teaching and practice—not such religion as they may have a preference for, but the religion which God enjoins, and which certain and most clear marks show to be the only one true religion—it is a public crime to act as though there were no God. So, too, is it a sin for the State not to have care for religion, as a something beyond its scope, or as of no practical benefit; or out of many forms of religion to adopt that one which chimes in with the fancy; for we are bound absolutely to worship God in that way which He has shown to be His will. . . .

Now, it cannot be difficult to find out which is the true religion, if only it be sought with an earnest and unbiased mind; for proofs are abundant and striking. We have, for example, the fulfillment of prophecies, miracles in great numbers, the rapid spread of the faith in the midst of enemies and in face of overwhelming obstacles, the witness of the martyrs, and the like. From all these it is evident that the only true religion is the one established by Jesus Christ Himself, and which He committed to His Church to protect and to propagate. . . .

This society is made up of men, just as civil society is, and yet is supernatural and spiritual, on account of the end for which it was founded, and of the means by which it aims at attaining that end. Hence, it is distinguished and differs from civil society, and, what is of highest moment, it is a society chartered as of right divine, perfect in its nature and in its title, to possess in itself and by itself, through the will and loving kindness of its Founder, all needful provisions for its maintenance and action. And just as the end at which the Church aims is by far the noblest of ends, so is its authority the most exalted of all authority, nor can it be looked upon as inferior to the civil power, or in any manner dependent upon it. . . .

The Almighty, therefore, has given the charge of the human race to two powers, the ecclesiastical and the civil, the one being set over divine, and the other over human, things. Each in its kind is supreme, each has fixed limits within which it is contained, limits which are defined by the nature and special object of the province of each, so that there is, we may say, an orbit traced out within which the action of each is brought into play by its own native right. . . .

. . . There must, accordingly, exist between these two powers a certain orderly connection, which may be compared to the union of the soul and body in man. The nature and scope of that connection can be determined only, as We have laid down, by having regard to the nature of each power, and by taking account of the relative excellence and nobleness of their purpose. One of the two has for its proximate and chief object the well-being of this mortal life; the other, the everlasting joys of heaven. Whatever, therefore, in things human is of a sacred character, whatever belongs either of its own nature or by reason of the end to which it is referred, to the salvation of souls, or to the worship of God, is subject to the power and judgment of the Church. Whatever is to be ranged under the civil and political order is rightly subject to the civil authority. Jesus Christ has Himself given command that what is Caesar's is to be rendered to Caesar, and that what belongs to God is to be rendered to God. . . .

But that harmful and deplorable passion for innovation which was aroused in the sixteenth century threw first of all into confusion the Christian religion, and next, by natural sequence, invaded the precincts of philosophy, whence it spread amongst all classes of society. From this source, as from a fountain-head, burst forth all those later tenets of unbridled license which, in the midst of the terrible upheavals of the last century, were wildly conceived and boldly proclaimed as the principles and foundation of that new conception of law which was not merely previously unknown, but was at variance on many points with not only the Christian, but even the natural law.

Amongst these principles the main one lays down that as all men are alike by race and nature, so in like manner all are equal in the control of their life; that each one is so far his own master as to be in no sense under the rule of any other individual; that each is free to think on every subject just as he may choose, and to do whatever he may like to do; that no man has any right to rule over other men. In a society grounded upon such maxims all government is nothing more nor less than the will of the people, and the people, being under the power of itself alone, is alone its own ruler. It does choose, nevertheless, some to whose charge it may commit itself, but in such wise that it makes over to them not the right so much as the business of governing, to be exercised, however, in its name.

The authority of God is passed over in silence, just as if there were no God; or as if He cared nothing for human society; or as if men, whether in their individual capacity or bound together in social relations, owed nothing to God; or as if there could be a government of which the whole origin and power and authority did not reside in God Himself. Thus, as is evident, a State becomes nothing but a multitude which is its own master and ruler. And since the people is declared to contain within itself the spring-head of all rights and of all power, it follows that the State does not consider itself bound by any kind of duty toward God. Moreover, it believes that it is not obliged to make public profession of any religion; or to inquire which of the very many religions is the only one true; or to prefer one religion to all the rest; or to show to any form of religion special favor; but, on the contrary, is bound to grant equal rights to every creed, so that public order may not be disturbed by any particular form of religious belief.

And it is a part of this theory that all questions that concern religion are to be referred to private judgment; that every one is to be free to follow whatever religion he prefers, or none at all if he disapprove of all. From this the following consequences logically flow: that the judgment of each one's conscience is independent of all law; that the most unrestrained opinions may be openly expressed as to the practice or omission of divine worship; and that every one has unbounded license to think whatever he chooses and to publish abroad whatever he thinks.

Now, when the State rests on foundations like those just named—and for the time being they are greatly in favor—it readily appears into what and how unrightful a position the Church is driven. For, when the management of public business is in harmony with doctrines of such a kind, the Catholic religion is allowed a standing in civil society equal only, or inferior, to societies alien from it; no regard is paid to the laws of the Church, and she who, by the order and commission of Jesus Christ, has the duty of teaching all nations, finds herself forbidden to take any part in the instruction of the people. With reference to matters that are of twofold jurisdiction, they who administer the civil power lay down the law at their own will, and in matters that appertain to religion defiantly put aside the most sacred decrees of the Church. . . . The Church, indeed, deems it unlawful to place the various forms of divine worship on the same footing as the true religion, but does not, on that account, condemn those rulers who, for the sake of securing some great good or of hindering some great evil, allow patiently custom or usage to be a kind of sanction for each kind of religion having its place in the State. And, in fact, the Church is wont to take earnest heed that no one shall be forced to embrace the Catholic faith against his will, for, as St. Augustine wisely reminds us, "Man cannot believe otherwise than of his own will." . . .

All this, though so reasonable and full of counsel, finds little favor nowadays when States not only refuse to conform to the rules of Christian wisdom, but seem even anxious to recede from them further and further on each successive day. Nevertheless, since truth when brought to light is wont, of its own nature, to spread itself far and wide, and gradually take possession of the minds of men, We, moved by the great and holy duty of Our apostolic mission to all nations, speak, as We are bound to do, with freedom. Our eyes are not closed to the spirit of the times. We repudiate not the assured and useful improvements of our age, but devoutly wish affairs of State to take a safer course than they are now taking, and to rest on a more firm foundation without injury to the true freedom of the people; for the best parent and guardian of liberty among men is truth. "The truth shall make you free." . . .

POPE PIUS XI (1857–1939)

Achille Amborgio Damiano Ratti was ordained to the priesthood of the Roman Catholic Church in 1879. Following posts as teacher and librarian he was raised to the Cardinalate in 1921 and elected Pope in 1922. His long pontificate, which ended on the eve of World War II, saw many drastic social and political upheavals in both East and West.

The encyclical letter, "Quadragesimo Anno," was written in 1931 and reflects the Pontiff's deep concern for a social reconstruction which would be carried out on the basis of Leo XIII's famous encyclical, "De Rerum Novarum."

Reconstructing the Social Order*

Forty years have passed since Leo XIII of happy memory issued his incomparable encyclical, *Rerum Novarum,* which grateful Catholics all over the world are now preparing to commemorate with due solemnity. . . .

Occasion of Rerum Novarum

Toward the close of the nineteenth century, new economic methods and new development of industry had in most nations led to such consequences that human society appeared more and more divided into two classes. The first, small in numbers, enjoyed practically all the comforts so plentifully supplied by modern invention. The second class, comprising immense multitudes of workingmen, strove in vain to escape from the pressure of dire want under which they were living.

This state of things was quite satisfactory to the wealthy, who looked upon it as the consequence of inevitable and natural economic laws, and who therefore were content to abandon to charity alone the full care of relieving the unfortunate, *as though it were the task of charity to make amends for the open violation of justice, a violation not merely tolerated but sanctioned at times by legislators.* On the other hand, the working classes, victims of these harsh conditions, submitted to them with extreme reluctance, and became more and more unwilling to bear the galling yoke. Some, carried away by the heat of evil counsels, went so far as to seek the disruption of the whole social fabric. Others, whom Christian training restrained from such misguided excesses, convinced themselves nevertheless that there was much in all this that needed a radical and speedy reform. . . .

* From Pope Pius XI, *Reconstructing the Social Order.* New York: The America Press. Pages 1–8, 12, 14–16, 31–37, 40–41, 43, and 46–47.

You know, Venerable Brethren and beloved children, and are familiar with the admirable teaching which has made the encyclical *Rerum Novarum* forever memorable. In this document the Supreme Shepherd, grieving for "the misery and wretchedness" pressing on such a large proportion of mankind, boldly took in his own hands the cause of workingmen, "surrendered, isolated and defenseless, to the callousness of employers and the greed of unrestrained competition" (*R.N.*, 2). He sought help neither from liberalism nor socialism. The former had already shown its utter impotence to find a right solution of the social question, while the latter would have exposed human society to still graver dangers by offering a remedy much more disastrous than the evil it designed to cure.

But the Sovereign Pontiff, exercising his manifest rights, and justly maintaining that on him primarily devolved the guardianship of religion and the charge of whatever was intimately connected with it, approached the question as one to which no solution could be found apart from the assistance of religion and of the Church (*R.N.*, 13). Basing his doctrine solely upon the unchangeable principles drawn from right reason and divine revelation, he indicated and proclaimed with confidence, and "as one having authority" (Matt. 7:29), *"the relative rights and mutual duties of the wealthy and of the poor, of capital and of labor,"* and at the same time the part that was to be taken by the Church, by the state and by the parties immediately concerned (*R.N.*, 1). . . .

In the first place, Leo himself clearly stated what could be expected from the Church. "It is the Church that proclaims from the gospel those teachings whereby the conflict can be brought to an end, or at least made far less bitter. The Church improves the condition of the workingman by numerous useful organizations. She does her best, moreover, to enlist the services of all ranks in discussing and endeavoring to meet, in the most practical way, the claims of the working classes" (*R. N.*, 13). . . .

It is not surprising, therefore, that under the teaching and guidance of the Church, many learned priests and laymen earnestly devoted themselves to the problem of elaborating social and economic science in accordance with the conditions of our age, for the chief purpose of adapting to modern needs the unchanging and unchangeable doctrine of the Church. . . .

With regard to the public authority, Leo XIII passed beyond the restrictions imposed by liberalism, and fearlessly proclaimed the doctrine that *the civil power is more than the mere guardian of law and order, and that it must strive with all zeal "to make sure that the laws and institutions, the general character and administration of the commonwealth, shall be such as to produce of themselves public well-being and private prosperity"* (*R.N.*, 26). It is true, indeed, that a just freedom of action should be left to individual citizens and families: but this principle is valid only as long as the common good is secure and no injustice is entailed. *The duty of rulers is to protect the community and its various elements; in protecting the rights of individuals they must have special regard for the weak and needy.* "For the rich have many ways of protecting themselves and stand less in need of help from the state; the masses of the needy have no resources of their own to fall back upon, and must chiefly depend upon the assistance of the state. And for this reason wage earners, who are, undoubtedly, among the weak and needy, should be especially cared for and protected by the commonwealth" (*R. N.*, 29). . . .

In the course of these years, however, doubts have arisen concerning the correct interpretation of certain passages of the encyclical or the conclusions to be drawn from them, and these doubts have led to controversies even among Catholics, not always of a peaceful character. On the other hand, the new needs of our age and the changed conditions of society have rendered necessary a more precise application and amplification of Leo's doctrine. We, therefore, gladly seize this opportunity of answering their doubts, so far as in Us lies, and of satisfying the demands of the present day. This We do in virtue of Our Apostolic office, by which We are a debtor to all (Rom. 2:14). . . .

Descending now to details, We commence with ownership, or the right of property. You are aware, Venerable Brethren and beloved children, how strenuously Our predecessor of happy memory defended the right of property against the teachings of the Socialists of his time, showing that the abolition of private ownership would not prove to be beneficial, but grievously harmful to the working classes. . . .

That We may keep within bounds the controversies which have arisen concerning ownership and the duties attaching to it, We reassert in the first place the fundamental principle laid down by Leo XIII, that *the right of property must be distinguished from its use* (*R. N.*, 19). It belongs to what is called commutative justice faithfully to respect the possessions of others and not to encroach on the rights of another by exceeding one's own rights of ownership. The putting of one's own possessions to proper use, however, does not fall under this form of justice, but under certain other virtues, and therefore it is "a duty which is not enforced by human laws" (*R. N.*, 19). Hence it is false to contend that the right of ownership and its proper use are bounded by the same limits; and it is even less true that the very misuse or even the nonuse of ownership destroys or forfeits the right to it.

Most helpful, therefore, and worthy of all praise are the efforts of those who, in a spirit of harmony and with due regard for the traditions of the Church, seek to determine the precise nature of these duties and to define the limitations imposed by the requirements of social life upon the right of ownership itself or upon its use. On the contrary, it is a grievous error so to weaken the individual character of ownership as actually to destroy it.

It follows from the twofold character of ownership, which We have termed individual and social, that men must take into account in this matter not only their own advantage but also the common good. *To define in detail these duties, when the need occurs and when the natural law does not do so, is the function of government. Provided that the natural and divine law be observed, the public authority, in view of the true necessity of the common good, may specify more accurately what is licit and what is illicit for property owners in the use of their possessions.* Moreover, Leo XIII had wisely taught that "the limits of private possession have been left to be fixed by man's own industry and by the laws of individual peoples" (*R. N.*, 7). . . .

It is plain, however, that the state may not discharge this duty in an arbitrary manner. Man's natural right of privately possessing and transmitting property by inheritance must be kept intact and cannot be taken away by the state, for "man is older than the state" (*R. N.*, 6), and "the domestic household is anterior both in idea and in fact to the gathering of men into a commonwealth" (*R. N.*, 10). Hence the prudent Pontiff had already declared it unlawful for the state to exhaust the means of individuals by crushing taxes and tributes: "The right to possess private property is from nature, not from man; and the state has only the right to regulate its use in the interest of the public good, but by no means to abolish it altogether" (*R. N.*, 35).

However, when civil authority adjusts ownership to meet the needs of the public good, it acts not as an enemy but as the friend of private owners; for thus it effectively prevents the possession of private property, intended by nature's Author in His wisdom for the support of human life, from creating intolerable evils and so rushing to its own destruction. It does not, therefore, abolish but protects private ownership, and far from weakening the right of private property, it gives it new strength. . . .

Great Changes Since the Time of Leo

Since the time of Leo XIII important changes have taken place both in the economic regime and in socialism. . . .

In the first place, then, *it is patent that in our days not alone is wealth accumulated, but immense power and despotic economic domination are concentrated in the hands of a few, and that those few are frequently not the owners, but only the trustees and directors of invested funds, who administer them at their good pleasure.*

This power becomes particularly irresistible when exercised by those who, *because they hold and control money, are able also to govern credit and determine its allotment, for that reason supplying, so to speak, the life-blood to the entire economic body, and grasping, as it were, in their hands the very soul of production, so that no one dare breathe against their will.*

This accumulation of resources and power, the characteristic note of the modern economic order, *is a natural result of limitless free competition which permits the survival of those only who are the strongest, which often means those who fight most relentlessly, who pay least heed to the dictates of conscience.*

This concentration of power has led to a threefold struggle: first, there is *the struggle for dictatorship in the economic sphere itself;* then, *the fierce battle to acquire control of the state,* so that its resources and authority may be abused in the economic struggle; finally, *the clash between states themselves.*

This latter arises from two causes: because the nations apply their power and political influence, regardless of circumstances, to promote every economic advantage of their citizens; but also because they seek to decide political controversies that arise among nations through the use of their economic supremacy and control of economic forces.

You assuredly know, Venerable Brethren and beloved children, and you lament the ultimate consequences of this individualistic spirit in economic affairs. *Free competition has killed itself. Economic domination has taken its place.*

Unbridled ambition for domination has succeeded the desire for gain; the whole economic life has become hard, cruel and relentless in a ghastly way. . . .

The remedies for these great evils We have exposed in the second part of the present encyclical, where We explicitly dwelt upon their doctrinal aspect. It will, therefore, be sufficient to recall them briefly here. Since the present economic regime is based mainly upon capital and labor, it follows that the principles of right reason and Christian social philosophy regarding capital, labor and their mutual cooperation must be accepted in theory and reduced to practice. In the first place, due consideration must be had for the double character, individual and social, of capital and labor, in order that the dangers of individualism and of collectivism be avoided. *The mutual relations between capital and labor must be determined according to the laws of the strictest justice, called commutative justice, supported however by Christian charity. Free competition, kept within just and definite limits* and, still more, economic domination, must be brought under the effective control of the public authority, in matters appertaining to this latter's competence. The public institutions of the nations must be such as to make the whole of human society conform to the common good, that is, to the standard of social justice. If this is done, the economic system, that most important branch of social life, will necessarily be restored to sanity and right order.

Since the days of Leo XIII, socialism, too, the great enemy against which his battles were waged, has undergone profound changes, no less than economics. At that time socialism could fairly be termed a single system, which defended certain definite and mutually coherent doctrines. Nowadays it has in the main become divided into two opposing and often bitterly hostile camps, neither of which, however, has abandoned the principle peculiar to socialism, namely, opposition to the Christian faith.

One section of socialism has undergone approximately the same change through which, as We have described, the capitalistic economic regime has passed; it has degenerated into communism. *Communism teaches and pursues a twofold aim: merciless class warfare and complete abolition of private ownership, and this it does, not in secret and by hidden methods, but openly, frankly and by every means, even the most violent.* To obtain these ends, Communists shrink from nothing and fear nothing; and when they have attained power it is beyond belief how cruel and inhuman they show themselves to be. . . . *We cannot contemplate without profound sorrow the heedlessness of those who seem to make light of these imminent dangers and with stolid indifference allow the propagation far and wide of those doctrines which seeks by violence and bloodshed the destruction of all society. Even more severely must be condemned the foolhardiness of those who neglect to remove or modify such conditions as exasperate the minds of the people, and so prepare the way for the overthrow and ruin of the social order.*

The other section, which has retained the name of socialism, is much less radical in its views. Not only does it condemn recourse to physical force; it mitigates and moderates to some extent, if it does not reject entirely, class warfare and the abolition of private property. It would seem as if socialism were afraid of its own principles and of the conclusions drawn therefrom by the Communists, and in consequence were drifting toward the truths which Christian tradition has always held in respect; for it cannot be denied that its programs often strikingly approach the just demands of Christian social reformers. . . .

Just demands and desires of this kind contain nothing opposed to Christian truth, nor are they in any sense peculiar to socialism. Those, therefore, who look for nothing else, have no reason for becoming Socialists. . . .

. . . We pronounce as follows: *whether socialism be considered as a doctrine, or as a historical fact, or as a movement, if it really remain socialism, it cannot be brought into harmony with the dogmas of the Catholic Church,* even after it has yielded to truth and justice in the points We have mentioned, the reason being that it conceives human society in a way utterly alien to Christian truth.

For according to Christian doctrine, man, endowed with a social nature, is placed here on earth in order that, spending his life in society and under an authority ordained by God, he may develop and evolve to the full all his faculties to the praise and glory of his Creator; and that, by fulfilling faithfully the duties of his station, he may attain to temporal and eternal happiness. Socialism, on the contrary, entirely ignorant of and unconcerned about this sublime end both of individuals and of society, affirms that human society was instituted merely for the sake of material advantages. . . .

We have passed in review, Venerable Brethren and beloved children, the state of the modern economic world, and have found it suffering from the greatest evils. We have investigated a new socialism and communism, and have found them, even in their mitigated forms, far removed from the precepts of the gospel.

"And if society is to be healed now"—We use the words of Our predecessor—"in no way can it be healed save by a return to Christian life and Christian institutions" (*R. N., 22*). *For Christianity alone can apply an efficacious remedy for the excessive solicitude for transitory things, which is the origin of all vices.* When men are fascinated and completely absorbed in the things of the world, it alone can draw away their attention and raise it to heaven. And who will say that this remedy is not urgently needed by society?

For most men are affected almost exclusively by temporal upheavals, disasters and ruins. Yet if we view things with Christian eyes—and we should—what are they all in comparison with the ruin of souls? Nevertheless, it may be said with all truth that nowadays the conditions of social and economic life are such that vast multitudes of men can only with great difficulty pay attention to that one thing necessary, namely, their eternal salvation. . . .

The fundamental cause of this defection from the Christian law in social and economic matters, and of the apostasy of many workingmen from the Catholic faith which has resulted from it, is the disorderly affection of the soul, a sad consequence of original sin. By original sin the marvelous harmony of man's faculties has been so deranged that now he is easily led astray by low desires, and strongly tempted to prefer the transient goods of this world to the lasting goods of heaven. Hence comes that unquenchable thirst for riches and temporal possessions, which at all times has impelled men to break the law of God and trample on the rights of their neighbors. . . .

For this pitiable ruin of souls, which, if it continues, will frustrate all efforts to reform society, there can be no other remedy than a frank and sincere return to the teachings of the gospel. Men must observe anew the precepts of Him who alone has the words of eternal life (John 6:70), words which, even though heaven and earth be changed, shall not pass away (Matt. 24:35). . . .

Present circumstances, therefore, Venerable Brethren and beloved children, indicate clearly the course to be followed. Nowadays, as more than once in the history of the Church, we are confronted with a world which in large measure has almost fallen back into paganism. In order to bring back to Christ these whole classes of men who have denied Him, we must gather and train from amongst their very ranks auxiliary soldiers of the Church, men who know well their mentality and their aspirations, and who with kindly fraternal charity will be able to win their hearts. *Undoubtedly the first and immediate apostles of the workingmen must themselves be workingmen, while the apostles of the industrial and commercial world should themselves be employers and merchants.*

It is your chief duty, Venerable Brethren, and that of your clergy, to seek diligently, to select prudently and train fittingly these lay apostles, among workingmen and among employers.

No easy task is here imposed upon the clergy, wherefore *all candidates for the sacred priesthood must be adequately prepared to meet it by intense study of social matters.* It is particularly necessary, however, that they whom you specially select and devote to this work show themselves endowed with a keen sense of justice, ready to oppose with real, manly constancy unjust claims and unjust actions; that they avoid every extreme with consummate prudence and discretion; above all, that they be thoroughly imbued with the charity of Christ, which alone has power to incline men's hearts and wills firmly and gently to the laws of equity and justice. This course, already productive of success in the past, we must follow now with alacrity.

POPE PIUS XII (1876–1958)

Eugenio Pacelli was born into a Roman family which had long served the papacy. He was educated in philosophy and theology at the Gregorian University and at the Pontifical Institute of the Appolinare. Shortly after his ordination in 1899, he began to work in the office of the papal secretary of state. Here he had a brilliant career, culminating in his own appointment to that secretaryship. He ascended the papal throne in 1939. In 1950 he solemnly pronounced the Dogma of the Bodily Assumption of the Virgin Mary.

Mystici Corporis*

Introduction

Venerable Brothers: health and apostolic benediction. We first learned of the Mystical Body of Christ, which is the Church, from the lips of the Redeemer Himself. Illustrating, as it does, the grand and inestimable privilege of our intimate union with a Head so exalted, this doctrine is certainly calculated by its sublime dignity to draw all spiritual-minded men to deep and serious study, and to give them, in the truths which it unfolds to the mind, a strong incentive to such virtuous conduct as is conformable to its lessons. This is why We have thought it fitting to speak with you on this subject through this encyclical letter, examining and explaining above all what concerns the Church militant. The surpassing magnificence of the argument attracts Us; the circumstances of the present hour urge Us on.

For We intend to speak of the riches hidden in a Church which Christ hath purchased with His own blood, and whose members glory in a thorn-crowned Head. Striking proof is this that the greatest glory and exaltation are born only of sufferings, and hence that we should rejoice if we partake of the sufferings of Christ, so that when His glory shall be revealed, we may also be glad with exceeding joy. . . .

When one reflects on this doctrine, one recalls immediately the words of the apostle: "Where sin abounded, grace did more abound." All know that the father of the whole human race was constituted by God in a state so exalted that he was to hand on to his posterity, together with earthly existence, the heavenly life of divine grace. But after the unhappy fall of Adam, the universal progeny of mankind, infected by a hereditary stain, lost their sharing of the divine nature, and we were all children of wrath. But God, all merciful, "so loved the world as to give his only-begotten Son": and the Word of the eternal Father, through this same divine love, assumed human nature from the race of Adam—but an innocent and spotless nature it was—so that He, as a new Adam, might be the source whence the grace of the

* From Pope Pius XII, *The Mystical Body of Christ,* with introduction and notes by Joseph Bluett, S.J. New York: The American Press, 3rd ed., 1957. Pages 11, 15–16, 17–18, 24–25, 26, 40, and 51–52.

Holy Spirit should flow unto all the children of the first parent. Through the sin of the first man they had been excluded from adoption into the children of God; through the Word Incarnate, made brothers according to the flesh of the only-begotten Son of God, they would receive the power to become the sons of God.

As He hung upon the Cross, Christ Jesus not only avenged the justice of the eternal Father that had been flouted, but He also won for us, His brothers, an unending flow of graces. It was possible for Him personally, immediately to impart these graces to men; but He wished to do so only through a visible Church that would be formed by the union of men, and thus through the Church every man would perform a work of collaboration with Him in dispensing the graces of redemption. The Word of God willed to make use of our nature, when in excruciating agony He would redeem mankind; in much the same way throughout the centuries He makes use of the Church that the work begun might endure.

If we would define and describe this true Church of Jesus Christ—which is the One, Holy, Catholic, Apostolic, Roman Church—we shall find no expression more noble, more sublime or more divine than the phrase which calls it "the Mystical Body of Jesus Christ." This title is derived from and is, as it were, the fair flower of the repeated teaching of Sacred Scripture and the holy fathers.

That the Church is a body is frequently asserted in Sacred Scripture. "Christ," says the apostle, "is the Head of the Body of the Church." If the Church is a body, it must be an unbroken unity, according to those words of Paul: "Though many, we are one body in Christ." But it is not enough that the Body of the Church be an unbroken unity; it must also be something definite and perceptible to the senses, as Our predecessor of happy memory, Leo XIII, in his encyclical *Satis cognitum* asserts: "The Church is visible because it is a Body." Hence they err in a matter of divine truth, who imagine the "Church to be invisible, intangible, a something merely 'pneumatological'," as they say, by which many Christian communities, though they differ from each other in their profession of faith, are united by a bond that eludes the senses.

But a body calls also for a multiplicity of members, which are linked together in such a way as to help one another. And as in our mortal composite being when one member suffers, all other members share its pain, and the healthy members come to the assistance of those ailing; so in the Church the individual members do not live for themselves alone, but also help their fellows, and all work in mutual collaboration for their common effort and for the more perfect building up of the whole Body.

Again, as in nature a body is not formed by any haphazard grouping of members but must be constituted of organs, that is, members that have not the same function and are arranged in due order; so for this reason above all the Church is called a body, that it is constituted by the coalescence of structurally united parts, and that it has a variety of members reciprocally dependent. It is thus the apostle describes the Church when he writes: "As in one body we have many members, but all the members have not the same office; so we being many are one body in Christ, and every one members one of another." . . .

Now we see how the human body is given its own means to provide for its own life, health and growth and for that of all its members. Similarly the Saviour of mankind, out of His infinite goodness, has provided in a marvelous way for His Mystical Body, endowing it with the sacraments; so that by so many consecutive, graduated graces, as it were, its members should be supported from the cradle to life's last breath, and that the social needs of the Church might also be generously provided for.

As all know, through the waters of baptism those who are born into this world, being dead in sin, are not only born again and made members of the Church, but, being stamped with a spiritual seal, they become capable and fit to receive the other sacraments. By the chrism of confirmation, the faithful are given added strength to protect and defend the Church, their Mother, and the faith she has given them. In the sacrament of penance a saving medicine is offered to the Church's members who have fallen into sin, not only to provide for their own health, but to remove from other members of the Mystical Body all danger of contagion, or rather to afford them the tonic of virtuous example.

Nor is that enough; for in the Holy Eucharist

the faithful are nourished and grow strong at the same table, and in a divine, ineffable way are brought into union with each other and with the divine Head of the whole Body. Finally, like a devoted mother, the Church is at the bedside of those who are sick unto death; and if it be not always God's will that by the sacred anointing of the sick she restore health to this mortal body, yet she does minister supernatural medicine for wounded souls, and sends new citizens on to heaven to enjoy forever the happiness of God—new advocates assigned to her.

For the social needs of the Church, Christ has provided in a particular way by two sacraments which He instituted. Through matrimony, when the contracting parties are ministers of grace to each other, provision is made for the external and properly regulated increase of Christian society and, what is of greater importance, for the correct religious education of the offspring, without which this Mystical Body would be in grave danger. Through holy orders men are set aside and consecrated to God, to offer in sacrifice the Eucharistic Victim, to feed the flock of the faithful with the Bread of Angels and the food of doctrine, to guide them in the way of God's commandments and counsels, to strengthen them with all the other supernatural helps. . . .

But our divine Saviour governs and guides His community also directly and personally. For it is He who reigns within the minds and hearts of men and bends and subjects to His purpose their wills even when rebellious. . . .

We must not think that He rules only in a hidden or extraordinary way. On the contrary, our divine Redeemer also governs His Mystical Body in a visible way and ordinarily, through His Vicar on earth. You know, Venerable Brothers, that after He had ruled the "little flock" Himself during His mortal pilgrimage, when about to leave this world and return to the Father, Christ our Lord entrusted to the chief of the apostles the visible government of the entire community He had founded. He was all wise; and how could He leave without a visible head the body of the Church He had founded as a human society?

Nor against this may one argue that the primacy of jurisdiction established in the Church gives such a Mystical Body two heads. For Peter in virtue of his primacy is only Christ's vicar; so that there is only one chief Head of this Body, namely Christ. He never ceases personally to guide the Church by an unseen hand, though at the same time He rules it externally, visibly through him who is His representative on earth. After His glorious Ascension into heaven, this Church rested not on Him alone, but on Peter, too, its visible foundation stone. That Christ and His vicar constitute one only Head is the solemn teaching of Our predecessor of immortal memory, Boniface VIII, in the apostolic letter *Unam Sanctam;* and his successors have never ceased to repeat the same.

They, therefore, walk the path of dangerous error who believe that they can accept Christ as the Head of the Church, while they reject genuine loyalty to His vicar on earth. They have taken away the visible head, broken the visible bonds of unity, and they leave the Mystical Body of the Redeemer in such obscurity and so maimed that those who are seeking the haven of eternal salvation cannot see it and cannot find it. . . .

Because Christ the Head holds such an eminent position, one must not think that He does not require the Body's help. What Paul said of the human organism is to be applied likewise to this Mystical Body: "The head cannot say to the feet: I have no need of you." It is manifestly clear that the faithful need the help of the divine Redeemer, for He has said: "Without me you can do nothing," and in the teaching of the apostle, every advance of this Body toward its perfection derives from Christ the Head. Yet, this, too, must be held, marvelous though it appear: Christ requires His members. . . . This is not because He is indigent and weak, but rather because He has so willed it for the greater glory of His unspotted Spouse. Dying on the cross, He left to His Church the immense treasury of the redemption; toward this she contributed nothing. But when those graces come to be distributed, not only does He share this task of sanctification with His Church, but He wants it in a way to be due to her action. Deep mystery this, subject of inexhaustible meditation: that the salvation of many depends on the prayers and voluntary penances which the members of the Mystical Body of Jesus Christ offer for this intention, and on the assistance of pastors of souls and of the faithful, especially of fathers and mothers of families, which they must offer to our divine Saviour as though they were His associates. . . .

It seems to Us that something would be lacking to what We have thus far proposed concerning this close union of the Mystical Body of Jesus Christ with its Head, if We did not add here a few words on the Holy Eucharist, wherein this union during this mortal life reaches, as it were, a climax. Through the Eucharistic Sacrifice, Christ our Lord wishes to give to the faithful special evidence of our union among ourselves and with our divine Head, marvelous as it is and beyond all praise. For here the sacred ministers act in the person, not only of our Saviour, but of the whole Mystical Body and of every one of the faithful. In this act of sacrifice through the hands of the priest, whose word alone has brought the Immaculate Lamb to be present on the altar, the faithful themselves with one desire and one prayer offer It to the eternal Father—the most acceptable victim of praise and propitiation for the Church's universal needs. And just as the divine Redeemer, dying on the cross, offered Himself as Head of the whole human race to the eternal Father, so "in this pure oblation" He offers not only Himself as Head of the Church to the heavenly Father, but in Himself His mystical members as well. He embraces them all, even the weak and ailing ones, in the tenderest love of His Heart. . . .

Conclusion

MARY, MOTHER OF THE MYSTICAL BODY

Venerable Brothers, may the Virgin Mother of God grant the prayers of Our paternal heart—and they are yours, too—and obtain for all a true love of the Church. Her sinless soul, more than all other created souls together, was filled with the divine Spirit of Jesus Christ; and "in the name of the whole human race" she gave her consent for a "spiritual marriage between the Son of God and human nature." Within her virginal womb, Christ our Lord already bore the exalted title of Head of the Church; in a marvelous birth she brought Him forth as source of all supernatural life, and presented Him, new born, as Prophet, King and Priest to those who came the first of Jews and Gentiles to adore Him. Her only Son, yielding to a mother's prayer in "Cana of Galilee," performed the miracle by which "His disciples believed in Him." Free from all sin, original and personal, always most intimately united with her Son, as another Eve she offered Him on Golgotha to the eternal Father for all the children of Adam sin-stained by his fall, and her mother's rights and mother's love were included in the holocaust. Thus she, who corporally was the mother of our Head, through the added title of pain and glory became spiritually the mother of all His members. She it was who through her powerful prayers obtained the grace that the Spirit of our divine Redeemer, already given to the Church on the cross, should be bestowed through miraculous gifts on the newly founded hierarchy on Pentecost. Bearing with courage and confidence the tremendous burden of her sorrows and desolation, truly the Queen of Martyrs, she more than all the faithful "filled up those things that are wanting of the sufferings of Christ . . . for his body, which is the Church" and she continued to show for the Mystical Body of Christ, born from the pierced Heart of the Saviour, the same mother's care and ardent love with which she clasped the infant Jesus to her warm and nourishing breast.

INVOCATION OF MARY

May she, then, most holy mother of all Christ's members, to whose immaculate heart We have trustingly consecrated all men, her body and soul refulgent with the glory of heaven where she reigns with her Son—may she never cease to beg from Him that a continuous, copious flow of graces may pass from its glorious Head into all the members of the Mystical Body. May she throw about the Church today, as in times gone by, the mantle of her protection and obtain from God that now at last the Church and all mankind may enjoy more peaceful days.

With full confidence in this hope, from an overflowing heart We impart to you all, Venerable Brothers, and to the flocks confided to your care, as a promise of heavenly graces and a token of Our special affection the apostolic benediction.

JACQUES MARITAIN (1882–)

One of the most influential contemporary Roman Catholic philosophers, Jacques Maritain was born in France and educated at the Sorbonne, where in the course of his studies of the natural sciences and philosophy he was converted to the Roman Catholic faith. Since 1948 he has worked and taught at Princeton University. A prodigious writer, he has won great success in introducing to a wide audience in this country the fundamental ideas of St. Thomas Aquinas. Yet he does not simply restate the concepts of his medieval mentor but rather brings them into fruitful conversation with modern thought. Maritain has been one of the leading spokesmen for the concept that Roman Catholicism is not only compatible with the liberal, pluralistic state but actually flourishes better in this environment.

Approaches to God*

The Primordial Way of Approach:

NATURAL OR PREPHILOSOPHIC KNOWLEDGE OF GOD

From Plato and Aristotle to St. Anselm and St. Thomas Aquinas, to Descartes and Leibniz, philosophers have proposed proofs or demonstrations of the existence of God, or, as Thomas Aquinas more modestly puts it, *ways* through which the intellect is led to the certitude of His existence. All are highly conceptualized and rationalized proofs, specifically philosophic ways of approach. . . .

However, it is not these highly conceptualized, rationalized and specifically philosophical way of approach which I should like to consider at present. When St. Paul affirmed that:

> that which is known of God is manifest in them. For God hath manifested it unto them. For the invisible things of Him, from the creation of the world, are clearly seen, being understood by the things that are made; His eternal power also, and divinity . . . (Romans I:19–20)

he was thinking not only of scientifically elaborated or specifically philosophical ways of establishing the existence of God. He had in mind also and above all the natural knowledge of the existence of God to which the vision of created things leads the reason of every man, philosopher or not. It is this doubly *natural* knowledge of God I wish to take up here. It is natural not only in the sense that it belongs to the rational order rather than to the supernatural order of faith, but also in the sense that it is *prephilosophic*. . . .

Before entering into the sphere of completely formed and articulated knowledge, in particular the sphere of metaphysical knowledge, the human mind is indeed capable of a prephilosophical knowledge which is *virtually metaphysical*. Therein is found the first, the primordial way of approach through which men become aware of the existence of God.

Here everything depends on the natural intuition of being. . . .

Let us rouse ourselves, let us stop living in dreams or in the magic of images and formulas, of words, of signs and practical symbols. Once a man has been awakened to the reality of existence and of his own existence, when he has really perceived that formidable, sometimes elating, sometimes sickening or maddening fact *I exist,* he is henceforth possessed by the intuition of being and the implications it bears with it.

Precisely speaking, this primordial intuition is both the intuition of *my* existence and of the

* From *Approaches to God,* by Jacques Maritain. Copyright 1954 by Jacques Maritain. Reprinted by permission of Harper & Brothers. Pages 1, 2, 3–7, 84–85, 49–50, 50–52, 109–111, and 112–114.

existence *of things,* but first and foremost of the existence of things. When it takes place, I suddenly realize that a given entity—man, mountain or tree—exists and exercises this sovereign activity *to be* in its own way, in an independence of *me* which is total, totally self-assertive and totally implacable. And at the same time I realize that *I* also exist, but as thrown back into my loneliness and frailty by this other existence by which things assert themselves and in which I have positively no part, to which I am exactly as naught. And no doubt, in face of my existence others have the same feeling of being frail and threatened. As for me, confronted with others, it is my own existence that I feel to be fragile and menaced, exposed to destruction and death. Thus the primordial intuition of being is the intuition of the solidity and inexorability of existence; and, second, of the death and nothingness to which *my* existence is liable. And third, in the same flash of intuition, which is but my becoming aware of the intelligible value of being, I realize that this solid and inexorable existence, perceived in anything whatsoever, implies—I do not yet know in what form, perhaps in the things themselves, perhaps separately from them—some absolute, irrefragable existence, completely free from nothingness and death. These three leaps—by which the intellect moves first to actual existence as asserting itself independently of me; and then from this sheer objective existence to my own threatened existence; and finally from my existence spoiled with nothingness to absolute existence—are achieved within the same unique intuition, which philosophers would explain as the intuitive perception of the essentially analogical content of the first concept, the concept of Being.

Next—this is the second stage—a prompt, spontaneous reasoning, as natural as this intuition (and as a matter of fact more or less involved in it), immediately springs forth as the necessary fruit of such a primordial apperception, and as enforced by and under its light. It is a reasoning without words, which cannot be expressed in articulate fashion without sacrificing its vital concentration and the rapidity with which it takes place. I see first that my being is liable to death; and second, that it is dependent on the totality of nature, on the universal whole of which I am a part. I see that Being-with-nothingness, such as my own being, implies, in order that it should be, Being-without-nothingness—that absolute existence which I confusedly perceived from the beginning as involved in my primordial intuition of existence. But then the universal whole of which I am a part itself Being-with-nothingness, by the very fact that I am part of it. And from this it follows finally that since this universal whole does not exist by virtue of itself, it must be that Being-without-nothingness exists apart from it. There is another Whole—a separate one—another Being, transcendent and self-sufficient and unknown in itself and activating all beings, which is Being-without-nothingness, that is, self-subsisting Being, Being existing through itself.

Thus the internal dynamism of the intuition of existence, or of the intelligible value of Being, causes me to see that absolute existence or Being-without-nothingness transcends the totality of nature. And there I am, confronted with the existence of God. . . .

The Ways of the Practical Intellect

Poetic Experience and Creation in Beauty. The practical intellect also has its ways of approach towards God—which are not demonstrations at all but belong to an existential and prephilosophic order. I shall give here some brief indications concerning them.

There is first, in the line of artistic creation, what one might call the analogy of the approach to God in poetic experience, or the poetic knowledge of the mirrors of God.

The artist is held in the grip of a twofold absolute, which is not the Absolute, but which draws the soul toward it. The demands of that beauty which must pass into his work, and the demands of that poetry which incites him to create, claim him so entirely that, in a certain way, they cut him off from the rest of men.

Beauty is a transcendental, a perfection in things which transcends things and attests their kinship with the infinite, because it makes them fit to give joy to the spirit. It is a reflection in things of the Spirit from which they proceed, and it is a divine name: God is subsistent Beauty, and "the being of all things derives from the divine beauty." Knowing this, we realize that it is impossible that the artist, devoted as he is to created beauty which is a mirror of God, should not tend at the same time—but by a more profound and more secret urge than all that he can know of himself—toward the principle of beauty. . . .

Knowledge, not rational and conceptual, but affective and nostalgic, the knowledge through connaturality which the artist has of beauty in his creative experience, is *in itself* (I do not say for him or for his own consciousness) an advance toward God, a spiritual inclination in the direction of God. . . .

The "Fourth Way" of St. Thomas. [The author here offers his interpretation and defense of one of the proofs for the existence of God as found in Aquinas, see pp. 192f.]

It is a fact that there is a qualitative "more or less," that there are degrees of value or perfection in things. There are degrees in the beauty of things (Plato saw this better than anyone); degrees in their goodness; in fine, things *are* to a greater or lesser degree. Knowledge is more highly and more perfectly knowledge in intelligence than in sense; life is more highly and more perfectly life in the free and thinking living thing than in the animal living thing, and in the animal living thing than in the vegetative living thing. . . .

Since goodness, beauty, life, knowledge, love and ultimately Being are in things in divers degrees, it is necessary that there exist somewhere a maximum or a supreme degree of these values.

But the progressive or ascending ensemble of the values in question, inasmuch as they can exist in things, is an infinite ensemble, in which consequently there is no actually supreme degree. One thing is good and another is better, but there can always be another still better. In other words, goodness exceeds or transcends every category of beings, and is not in its fullness in any one of them. Each good or beautiful thing is beautiful or good partially or by participation. It is not, then, unto itself the reason for its goodness. For *that* it would be necessary that it be good *by reason of itself* or *in essence* (then it would have goodness in all its plenitude. But such is not the case). Therefore, it derives its goodness from another thing; it is caused in goodness.

But whatever cause be considered, if it is itself caused in goodness, it derives its goodness from something else. Here again it is necessary to come to a stop at a First Cause which is good in essence and by reason of itself.

In other words it is necessary that there exist somewhere a maximum or a supreme degree of goodness (and of the other transcendental values of which we spoke). But this maximum or supreme degree, because it is the First Cause of all that there is of goodness in things, is a peak beyond the infinite series of all possible degrees of goodness in things. It is a supreme degree beyond the whole series. It is a transcendent First Cause which is good by reason of itself, which, therefore, does not *have* goodness but *is* goodness—it is Goodness that subsists by reason of itself. . . .

The Desire to See God

It is as First Cause of things that all the proofs of the existence of God make us know God. Whether they be philosophical or prephilosophical, the approaches to God of which our nature is capable lead us to God, known in and through His effects or in the mirror of the things which proceed from Him.

But how could the intellect, knowing God in His effects, fail to aspire to know Him in Himself? It is natural and normal that, knowing a reality—and the most important of all—from without and by means of signs, we should desire to know it in itself and to grasp it without any intermediary. Such a desire follows from the very nature of that quest of being which essentially characterizes the intellect. There is in the human intellect a natural desire to see in His essence that very God whom it knows through the things which He has created.

But this desire to know the *First Cause through its essence* is a desire which does not know what it asks. . . . For to know the First Cause in its essence, or without the intermediary of any other thing, is to know the First Cause otherwise than as First Cause; it is to know it by ceasing to attain it by the very means by which we attain it, by ceasing to exercise the very act which bears us up to it. The natural desire to know the First Cause in its essence envelops within itself the indication of the impossibility in which nature is placed to satisfy it.

To know God in His essence is evidently something which transcends the powers of every created or creatable nature, for it is to possess God intuitively, in a vision in which there is no mediation of any idea, but in which the divine essence itself replaces every idea born in our mind, so that it immediately forms and determines our intellect. This is to know God divinely, as He Himself knows Himself and as He knows us, in His own uncreated light.

Nothing is more human than for man to desire naturally things impossible to his nature. It is, indeed, the property of a nature which is not closed up in matter like the nature of physical things, but which is intellectual or infinitized by the spirit. It is the property of a *methaphysical* nature. Such desires reach for the infinite, because the intellect thirsts for being and being is infinite. . . .

To say that our intellect naturally desires to see God is to say that it naturally desires a knowledge of which nature itself is incapable. . . .

And because this desire which asks for what is impossible to nature is a desire of nature in its profoundest depths, St. Thomas Aquinas asserts that it cannot issue in an absolute impossibility. It is in no wise necessary that it *be* satisfied, since it asks for what is impossible for nature. But it is necessary that by some means (which is not nature) it *be able* to be satisfied, since it necessarily emanates from nature. In other words it is necessary that an order superior to nature be possible in which man is capable of that of which nature is incapable but which it necessarily desires. It is necessary that there be in man an "obediential potency" which, answering to the divine omnipotence, renders him apt to receive a life which surpasses infinitely the capacities of his nature. It is necessary that we be able to know God in His essence through a gift which transcends all the possibilities of our natural forces. It is necessary that this knowledge, impossible to nature alone, to which nature inevitably aspires, be possible through a gratuitous gift.

Shall we go beyond philosophy in order to get our answer? Through the night of faith it is given us to attain in His inner life—on the testimony of His Word—the very God who will be intuitively grasped when faith gives way to vision. And in the intellect elevated to the life of faith, the natural desire to see God supernaturally becomes a desire which knows what it asks for—a knowledge of God through His essence, *such as He gives Himself, in His own uncreated light*—and which from now on has *in germ* the wherewithal to attain what it asks for.

Thus the natural desire to see that First Cause whose existence is shown to us through the natural approaches to God is, in human reason, the mark of the possibility—through a gift which transcends the whole order of nature, and in which God communicates what belongs only to Himself—of a knowledge of God superior to reason, which is not due to reason, but to which reason aspires.

Church and State*

The Human Person and the Body Politic

From a philosophical point of view, the first thing, it seems to me, that we have to stress is the relationship between the human person and the body politic, namely the fact that the human person is both part of the body politic and superior to it through what is supratemporal, or eternal, in him, in his spiritual interests and his final destination.

That very superiority of what is eternal in man over the political society can already be seen in the merely natural realm. We know that the whole man is engaged in the common good of civil society. But we also know that in respect to things *which are not Caesar's,* both society itself and its common good are indirectly subordinated to the perfect accomplishment of the person and his supra-temporal aspirations as to an end of another order—an end which transcends the body politic. . . .

Now the Christian knows that there is a

* Reprinted from *Man and the State* by Jacques Maritain by permission of the University of Chicago Press. Copyright 1951 by the University of Chicago. Copyright under the International Copyright Union. Pages 148, 149–154, 159, 160–164, 169–170, and 173.

supernatural order, and that the ultimate end—the absolute ultimate end—of the human person is God causing His own personal life and eternal bliss to be participated in by man. The direct ordination of the human person to God transcends every created common good—both the common good of the political society and the intrinsic common good of the universe. Here is the rock of the dignity of the human person as well as of the unshakeable requirements of the Christian message. Thus the indirect subordination of the body politic,—not as a mere means, but as an end worthy in itself yet of lesser dignity—to the supratemporal values to which human life is appendent, refers first and foremost, as matter of fact, to the supernatural end to which the human person is directly ordained. To sum up all this in one single expression, let us say that the law we are faced with here is the law of the *primacy of the spiritual.*

The Freedom of the Church

Let us now go one step further, and consider the Church in her own realm or order. What is the Church? To begin with, what is the Church *for the unbeliever?* In the eyes of the unbeliever, the Church is, or the Churches are, organized bodies or associations especially concerned with the religious needs and creeds of a number of his fellow-men, that is, with spiritual values to which they have committed themselves, and to which their moral standards are appendent. These spiritual values are part—in actual fact the most important part, as history shows it—of those supra-temporal goods with respect to which, even in the natural order, the human person transcends, as we have seen, political society, and which constitute the moral heritage of mankind, the spiritual common good of civilization or of the community of minds. Even though the unbeliever does not believe in these particular spiritual values, he has to respect them. In his eyes the Church, or the Churches, are in the social community particular bodies which must enjoy that *right to freedom* which is but one, not only with the right to free association naturally belonging to the human person, but with the right freely to believe the truth recognized by one's conscience, that is, with the most basic and inalienable of all human rights. Thus, the unbeliever, from his own point of view—I mean, of course, the unbeliever who, at least, is not an unbeliever in reason, and, furthermore, who is a democratically-minded unbeliever—acknowledges as a normal and necessary thing the freedom of the Church, or of the Churches.

But what is the Church *for the believer?* For the believer the Church is a supernatural society, both divine and human—the very type of perfect or achieved-in-itself, self-sufficient, and independent society—which unites in itself men as co-citizens of the Kingdom of God and leads them to eternal life, already begun here below; which teaches them the revealed truth received in trust from the Incarnate Word Himself; and which is the very body of which the head is Christ, a body *visible,* by reason of its essence, in its professed creed, its worship, its discipline and sacraments, and in the refraction of its supernatural personality through its human structure and activity, *invisible* in the mystery of the divine grace and charity vivifying human souls, even those which belong to that body without knowing it and only through the inner movement of their hearts, because they live outside the sphere of explicit faith but seek for God in truth. For the believer the Church is the body of Christ supernaturally made up of the human race, or, as Bossuet put it, *le Christ répandu et communiqué,* Christ Himself diffused and communicated.

In such a perspective, not only is the freedom of the Church to be recognized as required by freedom of association and freedom of religious belief without interference from the State, but that freedom of the Church appears as grounded on the very rights of God and as identical with His own freedom in the face of any human institution. The freedom of the Church does express the very independence of the Incarnate Word. As a result, the first general principle to be stated, with respect to the problems we are examining, is *the freedom of the Church to teach and preach and worship, the freedom of the Gospel, the freedom of the word of God.*

The Church and the Body Politic

We come now to a further point, namely the relation between the Church and the body politic. It is clear, on the one hand, that the freedom and independence of which I just spoke, since they belong to a true and genuine society, imply for the Church the freedom of developing her own institutions and governing herself without interference by the body politic. . . .

There is no distinction without an order of values. If the things that are God's are distinct from the things that are Caesar's, that means that they are better. The said distinction, developing its virtualities in the course of human history, has resulted in the notion of the intrinsically *lay* or *secular* nature of the body politic. I do not say that the body politic is by nature irreligious or indifferent to religion ("lay" and "laicized," "secular" and "secularized" are two quite different things); I say that by nature the body politic, which belongs strictly to the natural order, is only concerned with the temporal life of men and their temporal common good. In that temporal realm the body politic, as Pope Leo XIII has insisted, is fully autonomous; the State, the modern State, is under the command of no superior authority in its own order. But the order of eternal life is superior in itself to the order of temporal life.

The Kingdom of God is essentially spiritual, and by the very fact that its own order is not of this world, it in no way threatens the kingdoms and republics of the earth. . . .

On the other hand it is clear that, as sharply distinct as they may be, the Church and the body politic cannot live and develop in sheer isolation from the ignorance of one another. This would be simply anti-natural. From the very fact that the same human person is simultaneously a member of that society which is the Church and a member of that society which is the body politic, an absolute division between those two societies would mean that the human person must be cut in two. The third general principle to be stated with respect to the problems we are examining is *the necessary cooperation between the Church and the body politic or the State*. . . .

The Historical Climate of Modern Civilization

The modern age is not a sacral, but a secular age. The order of terrestrial civilization and of temporal society has gained complete differentiation and full autonomy, which is something normal in itself, required by the Gospel's very distinction between God's and Caesar's domains. But that normal process was accompanied—and spoiled—by a most aggressive and stupid process of insulation from, and finally rejection of, God and the Gospel in the sphere of social and political life. The fruit of this we can contemplate today in the theocratic atheism of the Communist State. . . .

. . . The historical climate of modern civilization, in contradistinction to mediaeval civilization, is characterized by the fact that it is a "lay" or "secular," not a "sacral" civilization. On the one hand the dominant dynamic idea is not the idea of strength or fortitude at the service of justice, but rather that of the conquest of freedom and the realization of human dignity. On the other hand the root requirement for a sound mutual cooperation between the Church and the body politic is not the unity of a religio-political body, as the *respublica Christiana* of the Middle Ages was, but the very unity of the human person, simultaneously a member of the body politic and of the Church, if he freely adheres to her. The unity of religion is not a prerequisite for political unity, and men subscribing to diverse religious or non-religious creeds have to share in and work for the same political or temporal common good. Whereas "medieval man," as Father Courtney Murray puts it, "entered the State (what State there was) to become a 'citizen,' through the Church and his membership in the Church, modern man is a citizen with full civic rights whether he is a member of the Church or not."

Hence many consequences derive. First, the political power is not the secular arm of the spiritual power, the body politic is autonomous and independent within its own sphere. Second, the equality of all members of the body politic has been recognized as a basic tenet. Third, the importance of the inner forces at work in the human person, in contradistinction to the external forces of coercion; the freedom of individual conscience with regard to the State; the axiom—always taught by the Catholic Church, but disregarded as a rule by the princes and kings of old—that faith cannot be imposed by constraint—all these assertions have become, more explicitly than before, crucial assets to civilization, and are to be especially emphasized if we are to escape the worst dangers of perversion of the social body and of state totalitarianism. Fourth, a reasoned-out awareness has developed, at least in those parts of the civilized world where love for freedom is still treasured —and is growing all the keener as freedom is more threatened—with regard to the fact that nothing more imperils both the common good of the earthly city and the supra-temporal interests of truth in human minds than a weakening and breaking down of the internal springs of conscience. Common consciousness has also become aware of the fact that freedom of inquiry, even at the risk of error, is the normal condition for men to get access to truth, so that freedom to search for God in their own way, for those who have been brought up in ignorance or semi-ignorance of Him, is the normal condition in which to listen to the message of the Gospel and the teachings of the Church, when grace will illumine their hearts.

Given such an existential frame of reference, what can be the ways of applying and realizing, in our historical age, the supreme principles that hold sway over the relationship between Church and State? Let us say that in a new Christianly inspired civilization, as far as we are able to see it, those principles would in general be applied less in terms of the social power than in terms of the vivifying inspiration of the Church. The very modality of her action upon the body politic has been spiritualized, the emphasis having shifted from power and legal constraints (which the Church exercises, now as ever, in her own spiritual sphere over her own subjects, but not over the State) to moral influence and authority; in other words, to a fashion or "style," in the external relations of the Church, more appropriate to the Church herself, and more detached from the modalities that had inevitably been introduced by the Christian Empire of Constantine. Thus the superior dignity of the Church is to find its ways of realization in the full exercise of her *superior strength of all-pervading inspiration.*

The Principle of the Superiority of the Church

The supreme, immutable principle of the superiority of the Kingdom of God over the earthly kingdoms can apply in other ways than in making the civil government the secular arm of the Church, in asking kings to expel heretics, or in using the rights of the spiritual sword to seize upon temporal affairs for the sake of some spiritual necessity (for instance in releasing the subjects of an apostate prince from their oath of allegiance). These things we can admire in the Middle Ages; they are a dead letter in our age. The supreme, immutable principle of the primacy of the spiritual and the superiority of the Church can apply otherwise—but not less truly, and even more purely—when, from the very fact that the State has become secular, the supreme functions of moral enlightenment and moral guidance of men, even as concerns the standards and principles which deal with the social and political order, are exercised by the Church in a completely free and autonomous manner, and when the moral authority of the Church freely moves human consciences in every particular case in which some major spiritual interest is at stake. Then the superior dignity and authority of the Church asserts itself, not by virtue of a coercion exercized on the civil power, but by virtue of the spiritual enlightenment conveyed to the souls of the citizens, who must freely bear judgment, according to their own personal conscience, on every matter pertaining to the political common good.

. . .

I would say, therefore, that in the matters we are considering, civil legislation should adapt itself to the variety of moral creeds of the diverse spiritual lineages which essentially bear on the common good of the social body—not by endorsing them or approving of them, but rather by giving allowance to them. In other words, civil law would only lay down the regulations concerned with the allowance of the actions sanctioned by those various moral codes, or grant such actions the juridical effects requested by their nature; and consequently the State would not take upon itself the responsibility for them, or make them valid by its own pronouncement, but only register (when the matter is of a nature to require a decision of civil authorities) the validity acknowledged to them by the moral codes in question.

Thus, in the sense which I just defined, a sound application of the pluralist principle and of the principle of the lesser evil would require from the State a juridical recognition of the moral codes peculiar to those minorities comprised in the body politic whose rules of morality, though defective in some regard with respect to perfect Christian morality, would prove to be a real asset in the heritage of the nation and its common trend toward good human life. . . .

The Specific Forms of Mutual Cooperation

With respect to the . . . specific forms of mutual help between the body politic and the Church . . . it is obvious that it is the spiritual mission of the Church which is to be helped, not the political power or the temporal advantages to which certain of her members might lay claim in her name. In the stage of development and self-awareness which modern societies have reached, a social or political discrimination in favor of the Church, or the granting of juridical privileges to her ministers or to her faithful, would be precisely of a nature to jeopardize, rather than to help, this spiritual mission.

ROMANO GUARDINI (1885–)

Though born in Italy, Romano Guardini grew up and was educated in Germany. In 1910 he was ordained a priest in the Roman Catholic Church. He was one of the leaders of the German Catholic Youth Movement. Several of his books, of which *The Spirit of the Liturgy* is perhaps best known, have contributed greatly to the revival of scholarly and pious interest in the forms and content of Christian worship. During World War II Romano Guardini wrote a number of brief essays on fundamental religious questions which people were asking. These were printed as tiny pamphlets which could be sent as letter enclosures, thus for a time escaping the attention of the authorities. The selection given below was originally written for such distribution.

God's Dominion and Man's Freedom*

There is a group of questions which occurs and re-occurs in Christian thinking. The questions run somewhat as follows: If God knows everything, He knows the future and what man will do; how, then, can man be free? If God is the cause of every thing, and all that happens is His work, how can man be a cause? If God is good, desires the good, and is able to accomplish what He desires, how is evil possible? Can there be such a thing as evil, and to the frightful degree which our experience often forces us to believe? Is God really all-powerful, and if so, to what extent does He participate in evil-doing? Can He really be good? Is He not, rather, a frightful being? . . . These questions are difficult and depressing. Many times in history, notably during the Renaissance, they have been asked very insistently. Moreover, certain serious-minded, over-sensitive people fall easily under their sway. Clergymen and physicians know well what power these questions can exercise over the lives of such people, a power sometimes so great as to render their victims unfit for useful living. They know, too, how hard, if not impossible, it is to set such people straight.

Let us examine the questions now, as far as the limits of this essay permit, for it would be a positive gain to find an answer to them, or even a clear position in their regard. Aside from this, we have another purpose in view. We need to be clear in our minds not only concerning the subject matter of such problems, but also their nature, not only about the truth of them, but how these difficult, even dangerous

* From Romano Guardini, *The Faith and Modern Man,* translated from the German by Charlotte Forsyth. New York: Pantheon Books, and London: Burns and Oates, Ltd., 1952. Pages 27–35 are reproduced by permission of the publisher.

questions must be approached if we are to derive any useful results.

First of all we must reduce this tangled web of questions to a simple form. To do so would be a great gain, for (we shall return to this point later) much of the difficulty in questions of this kind arises from the confusion caused by the intermingling of points of view, of thoughts with feeling, of concepts with inner unrest. Let us express what lies at the root of the matter by this question: If God is all-knowing and all-powerful, how can there be any genuine human freedom?

We can now isolate this question and discuss it. We can examine how, in man's actions, God's will and man's will stand in relation to one another; what part each plays in the act; how, if the expression be allowed, the responsibility is shared. The task will be difficult, and even if some good were to come of it, the final result will be disappointing. But should a so-called solution be found, and reason feel satisfied, this would indeed be a cause for misgivings. Actually, something would have gone awry. Either the human will would have been repressed and the answer given in terms of the pure, perfect efficacy of the divine will, which would altogether eliminate human freedom, or human freedom would have been given its due, but in a way that would limit the divine will, which, in turn, eliminates the divine character of that will. And a "solution" satisfactory to every aspect of the problem might well correspond to the old saying, "God does not cause evil, He merely permits it," which, on closer examination, reveals itself as meaningless, a mere sedative for our emotions. The question remains as before, awaiting an answer.

Such a line of argument gets us nowhere. To avoid wasting our intellectual efforts and the ever-ready danger of falling into the wrangling and dogmatizing which, alas, runs through the whole course of Christian thought, we must try another approach. A prize was once offered for the solution of equations of a highly complicated character. A talented young mathematician answered the question by giving the reasons for its insolubility. Something similar must apply here. For whenever we approach the problem directly, we find ourselves baffled. We must therefore try to find where the special difficulty lies and see whether it is at all possible to overcome it. At the instant we find ourselves faced with a task utterly beyond our powers. For in order to understand how the human will can subsist along with the divine will, we should have to place both "quantities" on the same plane under a common denominator, and this cannot possibly be done. Thus we are unable to "solve" this or any similar problem directly. The only honest answer consists in admitting this fact and explaining why it is so. Any other answer either evades the problem, or the alleged solution covers up the difficulty without mastering it. Our question concerns the nature of man's finite existence before God, the way the created subsists as created. It is unanswerable because our human reason is unable to grasp the relationship between the glorious self-subsisting of God and the finite human creature. Recognition of this fact is part of the truth of existence. We must accept the insolubility, make of it a confession of humility and a form of adoration. In so doing the problem is "solved," not intellectually, but in the form of a vital act.

But what if someone were to reply that this "insolubility" was sheer nonsense. That a faith which expected acceptance of such a thing would insult honor and reason, and that a man would have the right, indeed, the duty, to break with it. And what if the objector would go on to show that at the root of these age-old questions lurked a deep-seated denial of life, the causes of which had been worked out by psychologists. Also, that a person disturbed by these questions has no more urgent duty than to rid himself of them, to realize their essentially unreal character, and to spend the strength hitherto wasted upon them upon things more real, more rewarding. The psychological argument is impressive, especially when it can be shown that concern over such questions is often associated with certain grave manifestations,—scruples, violent forms of impatience, fanaticism and religious depression. But is it true? Are there not phenomena in our daily lives which, while they cannot answer our question, do at least indicate that the puzzle which they present is not caused by lack of reason—more than that, that it rests upon a genuine reason? There are such. Let us now look closely at one of them.

Whenever a physical force acts upon an inanimate object, as, for instance, when pressure is exerted by a lever on a stone, necessity enters in. The lever will raise the stone to a height which is in exact proportion to the power applied to it. Thus it invariably acts, at all times, in all places. What, on the other hand, is the relation between the sun and a grain of wheat buried in the earth? Warmth and light affect the seed so that it opens and, in the course of time, sends roots downward and shoots upward. Would you say that warmth and light act upon the seed in exactly the same way that the lever acts upon the stone? Obviously not. We express the difference in our everyday speech by saying that the lever "lifts" the stone; the sun "awakens" the seed. In the latter case, the light is directed toward the property of life inherent in the organism. The sun arouses the grain's initiative. The processes of growth, now set in motion, proceed from the organism's own living center. What then happens is not an immediate transformation of the object by the operating power, but a gradual response on the part of the object's own life principle.

How does mind act upon mind? When a man wants to win another over to his point of view, he can influence him psychologically by making threats or promises, by exercising his power of sympathy, by arousing his pride and thereby guiding the other's judgment. He does not really overcome the other's objections but talks him out of them, and by continually repeating his own point of view, acts upon his emotions and imagination until the other gives in and simply agrees. The operation resembles the lifting of the stone by the lever, or even the skillful manipulation of his plants by the gardener. It is not an intelligent but a psychic influence. It is suggestion, the application of mental force.

True intellectual influence is altogether different. It consists in setting forth the truth so clearly, so profoundly, so effectively, relying so entirely on reason, that the hearer is affected inwardly, and genuinely convinced. Here no force has been exerted, but rather the depths of the other man's mind have been moved in such a way that he recognizes the truth and responds to it. Truth is the life of the intellect. Through words the mind's natural relation to truth is touched, and the mind responds naturally. The speaker must curb his enthusiasm and his persuasiveness out of respect for the hearer, out of the obligation not to influence him directly, but rather to awaken him to himself. The influence of light on the grain of wheat releases an innate power; here the same happens, to an even greater degree, and differently; genuine intellectual influence is possible only through acting freely upon a comprehending, creative center.

And now a final illustration. The love which one person bestows upon another exercises a powerful influence in the life of the one loved. There are different ways of loving. Love of an immediate, instinctive kind seeks physical gratification. Another kind, not physical in origin, seeks ultimately to make the loved one dependent and to dominate him. An observer of human relationships will grant that this latter way of loving is the most common. Fundamentally selfish, it is a devious way of securing the upper hand; it forces, makes dependent, subjugates. But there is such a thing as genuine love which is always considerate. Its distinguishing characteristic is, in fact, regard for personal dignity. Its effect is to stimulate self-respect in the other person. Its concern is to help the one loved to become his true self. It seeks him for his own sake. In a mysterious way such love finds its purest realization in its power to stimulate the other to attain his highest self-realization. Thus its effect is to draw the other out into freedom. And if the loved one were called upon to give an account of what that love had meant to him, he would say: "I owe everything to it, most of all the fact that through it, alone, have I become my real self." A marvelous paradox! Truly, life's ultimate mystery!

What have we just been doing? We have been going from one form of influence to another, from the lower to the higher. In each case there has been a decisive difference. Each time an effect has been produced. Step by step the influence has become stronger, more essential, more radical. For the effect of light on the grain of wheat is greater than that of the lever on the stone; greater still the effect of mind on mind; greatest of all the power of love in the life of one loved. At the same time the influence has more and more assumed the attitude of reserve. More and more strongly has it seemed to be directed toward some property inherent in the object—toward freedom. Not as if it were consciously intending to effect freedom for the object, but as if it were by nature related to freedom and concerned with awakening it.

Does this process end with man? In the human sphere alone there are innumerable degrees. From this point of view how greatly men vary in their behavior—in respect for others, in magnanimity, in unselfishness, in creative mental ability, in the generative power of love. The list is endlessly long and runs through the whole of creation—why not beyond creation? Why should it not have significance for God Himself? And not because He is involved in, and is part of, world processes, but because what we have been observing seems to be but a reflection of something found essentially and perfectly in Him alone. Is it not in this direction that the "insolubility" of our problem points? God is pure power. Not a power like that exercised by the lever, nor like that of instinctual urges, but intellectual power; and not simply undifferentiated power of knowledge and will, but individual, personal power. Our use of the words "I" and "you" is but a reflection of God's being. Holy Scripture tells us that God is love. Not merely that He is loving, which might imply that He loves as we love, only more and better; not even that He is the embodiment of love, the fountainhead of that which is evident whenever one being turns lovingly to another. It means more than all that. It means that Love is God Himself, that what a man does when he loves is but a reflection of what God is. And whenever a man speaks simply of "Love," he means God, whether he realizes the fact or not. If this be true—and that it is true constitutes a mystery of the Christian Faith—must not freedom emerge in fullest measure under the dominion of divine love? No, not simply in fullest measure, but actually there alone, so that the earthly phenomena which we have been observing will serve as hints and preparation for what can exist essentially only in the relationship between God and His creature.

In this must be found the true source of that paradox of love of which we have been speaking. For God's power is love. God's will is love. By directing His love toward man, God enables man to become what he essentially was meant to be, a free person. The more actually a man is led by God's love, the more fully he realizes his true self; the more immediately a man's acts spring from love, the more completely they become his own.

But though this is the mystic's blessed answer, let us not misunderstand it. Such an answer cannot be a "solution" to the problem we are considering, it can only give us a hint that the word "insolubility" is a term for a mystery of profound reality.

But truth must be tested in living. And if this doctrine is true, what will be its effects in our lives?

Chesterton, in a brilliant passage, says: "The sun is the one created thing which one cannot look at: it is the one thing in the light of which one looks at everything else: Like the sun at noon-day, mystery explains everything by its own invisibility. Detached intellectualism is (in the exact sense of a popular phrase) all moonshine, for it is light without heat; it is secondary light reflected from a dead world."

Dogma is a mystery into which we cannot look directly. If it is taken as a starting point from which to approach the world, if it is, so to speak, behind us so that its light can fall upon the objects before us, these objects will stand out clearly, and we can make our way among them. If the light itself could be looked at, it would lack the illuminating quality necessary for seeing things properly. The world is rightly seen only in the light that comes from above, and that light must itself be invisible to human sight.

The problem we are considering involves the dogma of grace. Whatever a man does, he does through God's power; whatever of eternal worth he is able to achieve, he achieves by God's help. Everything, therefore, is a gift—everything, even our work. It is our work, indeed, because it is a gift. Man is a creature, his essence and being are given to him, he exists by receiving them continually from God. He can effect something real only through something received, that is to say through grace. God working in man enables man to work, and to be responsible to Him for that work. Proprietorship and responsibility come not by the limitation of God's dominion, not by what might be called a counterplay to the divine will, but as the fruits of that will. This is the doctrine of grace. How does it affect the life of one who believes?

Let us review the question of God's dominion

and man's freedom in reverse order. It is a mystery. It transcends the power of human comprehension. We may try to dispense with the mystery by suppressing the one or the other side of the paradox. Then, apparently, the problem clears up. We may argue, for example, as the proponents of the sole, absolute dominion of God, the so-called Predestinarians, have done, that God effects everything, and that man is but His tool. The mind can take hold of this statement. But as soon as a man tries to apply the teaching to his life, he loses the powers which make for courageous Christian action. He becomes a fatalist, that is, a slave. And his sons, or at any rate his grandsons, will consider his views untenable and unworthy, they will rebel against the "enslaving God" and rely wholly upon their own reason and natural impulses.

We may adduce the enlightenment on the other side, as the so-called Pelagians and other defenders of human autonomy have done, and declare that man is his own master, that he acts merely by his own means, and that what he achieves is exclusively his own work. This statement also is clear and applicable, only on the opposite side. God is now relegated to the outer edge of existence; man has a free hand. But if a man adopts this view in earnest, he will overstrain himself. He will forget about reverence and moderation and become superficial and self-seeking. He will no longer try to live as a man, but as some kind of god. And that mystery which he has betrayed will eventually penetrate into his life. He will become a pantheist, one who sees man merely as a fleeting manifestation of the divine; or a biologist who sees man merely as an organ, a cell or a pulse-beat of the universal life; or a materialist who regards man as merely an accidental form of matter—unless he fall prey to superstition and put his faith in things which a religious man would be ashamed to believe.

However, if a man will accept the mystery and allow it to become a living influence in his life, he will be enabled to do that hardest thing of all, namely, to live in the truth, to make his way along that narrow ridge assigned to mankind. He will achieve that inner balance which will enable him to act with confidence, yet to take everything as coming from God. This, in turn, will give him a sense of responsibility and help him to realize that he lives by grace. It will also safeguard that soundness of the emotions which is more important, even, than soundness of body—soundness of mind, of heart, of being.

RONALD KNOX (1888–1957)

Son of an Anglican Bishop, and for five years an ordained clergyman of the Church of England, Ronald Knox was converted to Roman Catholicism in 1917. Two years later he became a priest in that Church. A man of many gifts, he has written not only theological treatises but several satires, an autobiography, and a gripping murder mystery. His greatest achievement was the translation of the entire Holy Bible into excellent modern English. The following selection states concisely one of the major criticisms of protestantism which Roman Catholics often make.

Where Protestantism Goes Wrong*

When we have come so far upon our journey with regard to matters discussed in previous chapters, we have already parted company with a great portion of mankind; with the atheists, who deny God's existence, and with the pagans or pantheists, who misconceive his Nature; with the Jews, Mohammedans, and Unitarians, who refuse Divine honours to Jesus Christ. It is, if I may pursue my metaphor, at the very next turning that we have to take leave of our Protestant friends. For the next step on our journey is the step they never take. The next stage in our argument, after establishing the authority of Jesus Christ, is one which, if they are to be consistent with their own principles, they must needs disallow. We proceed immediately to the proof that our Lord Jesus Christ founded, before he left us, a single, visible and invisible Church.

Before we proceed to that proof, it will be well to consider the consequences which are involved if we ignore it. I say, if we ignore it; for it is a matter of common experience that Protestants differ from us not so much because they disagree with us on this head, as because they refuse, most of them, to enter into the discussion at all. They are not clear-headed enough to perceive that a proper notion of the Church is a necessary stage before we argue from the authority of Christ to any other theological doctrine whatever. The infallibility of the Church is, for us, the true induction from which all our theological conclusions are derived. . . . We derive from our apprehension of the living Christ the apprehension of a living Church; it is from that living Church that we take our guidance. Protestantism claims to take its guidance immediately from the living Christ. But what is the guidance he gives us, and where are we to find it? That is the question over which Protestantism has always failed to answer the Catholic challenge, over which it finds it increasingly difficult, nowadays, to answer the challenge of its own children.

We may be pardoned, perhaps, for making a distinction here in parenthesis. Protestants, especially old-fashioned Protestants, often talk as if, for Catholics, the Church came between Christ and the soul. That is a falsehood; only ignorance can excuse them for repeating it. For the Catholic, as for the Protestant, sanctification is the direct work of Christ; it is Christ, not the Church, who gives us (as Priest and as Victim) his Body and Blood in Communion. It is Christ who forgives us our sins, sometimes when we submit them to the Church in Confession, sometimes before. The Catholic, no less than the Protestant, hopes to be saved through the merits of Christ's Blood shed for him, and for no other consideration. The Church, then, in the order of worship, does not come between Christ and the individual soul. But in the order of intellectual conviction, the Church does, if you will, come between Christ and the individual mind. It is through the Church that the Catholic finds out what he is to believe and why he is to believe it. . . . For three centuries the true issue between the two parties was obscured, owing to the preposterous action of the Protestants in admiring Biblical inspiration. The Bible, it appeared, was common ground between the combatants, the Bible, therefore, was the arena of the struggle; from it the controversialist, like David at the brook, must pick up texts to sling at his adversary. In fact, of course, the Protestant had no conceivable right to base any arguments on the inspiration of the Bible, for the inspiration of the Bible was a doctrine which had been believed, before the Reformation, on the mere authority of the Church; it rested on exactly the same basis as the doctrine of Transubstantiation. Protestantism repudiated Transubstantiation, and in doing so repudiated the authority of the Church; and then, without a shred of logic, calmly went on believing in the inspiration of the Bible, as if nothing had happened! Did they suppose that Biblical inspiration was a self-evident fact, like the axioms of Euclid? or did they derive it from some words of our Lord? If so, what words? What authority have we, apart from that of the Church, to say that the Epistles of Paul are inspired, and the Epistle of Barnabas is not? It is, perhaps, the most amazing and the most tragic spectacle in the history of thought, the picture of blood flowing, fires blazing, and kingdoms changing hands for a century and a half, all in defence of a vicious circle.

The only logic which succeeded in convincing the Protestants of their fallacy was the logic of facts. So long as nobody except scoffers and atheists challenged the truth of the scriptural narratives, the doctrine of inspiration maintained its curiously inflated credit. Then Christians, nay, even clergymen, began to wonder about Genesis, began to have scruples about the genuineness of 2 Peter. And then, quite suddenly, it became apparent that there was no reason why Protestants should not doubt the inspiration of the Bible; it violated no principle of their system. . . . For three centuries the inspired Bible had been a handy stick to beat Catholics with; then it broke in the hand that wielded it, and Protestantism flung it languidly aside.

I do not mean, of course, that modern Protestants do not affirm, and affirm sincerely, their belief in Biblical inspiration *of some sort*. But if you examine the affirmation, you will find that the whole meaning of the term has changed; it was once a literal inspiration that was acknowledged, now it is only a literary inspiration. If you need tangible proof of this, you have only to consider the amount of literary flattery which is lavished upon certain Biblical authors by modern scholarships; how they belaud the fierce independence of Amos, the profound spiritual insight of St. Paul. It was all one to our great-grandfathers; Amos, for them, was no more of a figure than Habacuc, or Paul than the author of the Apocalypse; what did it matter? It was all inspired. . . .

In our time, we are beginning to reap the whirlwind. Even men of moderate opinions will not, to-day, vouch for the authenticity of the Fourth Gospel; will not quote the threefold invocation of Matthew xxviii. 19 as certainly representing the views of the apostolic age; will not attach any importance to the story of our Lord's Ascension. And these things are done in the green tree; what of the dry? If these are the hesitations which Protestantism cultivates, what of those it tolerates? We have seen in our time Oxford—the Oxford that flamed with controversy over the case of Dr. Hampden—vaguely discussing whether anything could be done about a clergyman who denied the Resurrection.

I do not mean to suggest, what these criticisms might at sight appear to suggest, that Biblical study, unguided by any belief in the doctrines of a teaching Church, is certain to lead men to wrong conclusions. I mean that such study is humanly certain to lead different men to different conclusions, even on subjects of the highest moment. If they belonged to a living Church, its traditions, or its instincts, the unconscious fruit of its traditions, would act as a corrective; one view would be ruled out as inadequate. "No," the Church would say, "my child, the Evangelist cannot have meant that." The dead letter and the living instinct support and correct one another. But the Protestant critics have no such arbiter to adjudge their theological awards; two different doctrines are held, and therefore neither doctrine is certain. . . .

. . . Consider the bearing of this difficulty even on a purely doctrinal, not a disciplinary point. The question whether there is or is not eternal punishment for impenitent sinners beyond the grave is one, surely, which a revelation might have been expected to settle for us. It is a belief which has been constantly affirmed by the Church; it is a belief which Protestants found no difficulty in accepting, so long as Protestants believed in the inerrancy of the Bible. On the other hand, it is a belief which seems to most free-thinkers in our day a superstition, and a superstition which taxes Almighty God with systematic cruelty. There could hardly be a subject on which, you would think, a preacher would be more anxious to deliver a clear message, one way or the other. Once again let us remit the question to the tribunal of Protestant scholarship; what is the verdict?

Here it must be confessed that the common-sense inquirer would be disposed to say that the words of the Gospel left our Lord's sentiments in no kind of doubt. "To be cast into Gehenna, where the worm does not die, and the fire is not quenched", "Depart from me, ye wicked, into the everlasting fire which is prepared for the devil and his angels"—such language might be considered plain enough, yet not all scholars are convinced by these apparently unequivocal declarations. One will say that the words must be understood metaphorically; another, that our Lord was accommodating his expressions to suit the notions of his own day; another, that those who reported his words have misrepresented him, and so on. So long as these rival possibilities hold the field, there can be no certainty whether hell is a fact or not. Those who assert the doctrine can only assert it as a pious opinion, and at the risk of finding their preaching flatly contradicted by Bishops of their own Communion.

It will be objected, however, that contemporary Anglicanism, whatever the practice of the other Christian bodies, does not confine itself to this Scriptural appeal. Many, at all events, of its most distinguished apologists supplement this appeal to the Bible—that is, to the critics of the Bible—by an appeal to the Church—that is, to the historians of the Church. The Anglicans of the seventeenth century, the Tractarians of the nineteenth century, pointed us to the first six centuries of Christendom as authoritative; others would point us to the first thirteen, the first fifteen, or even the first eighteen, but the difference is one of detail; it is not the Church, but the history of the Church that we are invited by these controversialists to accept as the criterion of orthodoxy. But this fresh appeal involves us in fresh embarrassments, no less serious than those already mentioned. . . .

The appeal to the Church of the Historians, like the appeal to the Bible of the Critics, is one which fails to produce certainty. No subject, I suppose, could have been more carefully investigated by Christian scholars than the history of the ministry—had the Church originally Bishops as part of its constitution, or only priests and deacons? Even on such a question, Presbyterian scholars still find room for disagreement with their Anglican brethren. Auricular confession, which is preached as obligatory by some Anglicans, cannot be traced to the primitive Church with a certainty which would convince all historians. Even doctrines such as that of the Trinity or that of the two Natures in the Incarnation appear in a strictly defined form only in the third or fourth century. Now, it is true that you escape from these particular difficulties by appealing to six centuries instead of one or two; but who told you that there should be six, no less and no more? Is it a mystical number, that it should be credited with this strange finality?

But the essential weakness of this appeal to antiquity is that it resolutely shuts its eyes to the really salient fact about Christendom; I mean that it was essentially *one*. The unity and the uniqueness of the Christian Church are assumed in the language of its writers from the very earliest times of which we have record. St. Ignatius sees in the local bishop the representative of that college of bishops scattered throughout the world, whose unity is the unity of the faith. St. Paul, writing in days when it would hardly seem possible that heresies should have become a serious threat, stigmatises heretics as having made shipwreck of the faith, and urges his converts to abide in the unity of the doctrine. The modern Christianities, be they what they may, are the relics of schism; not one of them dares to represent itself as the one Church of Christ. Consequently, in appealing to the early Church, with its instinct of inviolable unity, they are appealing to an arbiter who has already given the award against them.

Protestantism in the Modern World

HARRY EMERSON FOSDICK (1878–)

For years pastor of the Riverside Church and also Professor at Union Theological Seminary in New York City, Harry Emerson Fosdick has been one of the most eloquent and popular voices of liberal Protestantism. Though not himself a technical biblical scholar, he very effectively communicated to a wide audience the spirit and the results of modern criticism in this area. Our brief selection illustrates the attitude towards the Bible taken by many liberals.

The Impact of Biblical Scholarship*

One major result of the last half-century of Biblical scholarship is the ability to arrange the documents of Scripture in their approximately chronological order. The typical questions asked by scholars concerning Biblical writings —Who wrote them? When, to whom, and why were they written?—while still presenting many baffling difficulties, have been answered sufficiently to clarify the broad outlines of the Bible's chronological development.

An important result of thus seeing the Biblical writings in sequence is ability to study the development of Biblical ideas. Upon this problem some of the best scholarly work in recent years has been expended. Seen as informed students now regard it, the Bible is the record of an incalculably influential development of religious thought and life, extending from the primitive faith of early Hebraism into the Christianity of the second century. Such a bald statement, however, does scant justice to the illumination which has thus fallen on the Jewish-Christian writings. The first results of critical research into the Bible seemed disruptive, tearing the once unified Book into many disparate and often contradictory documents. The final result has turned out to be constructive, putting the Bible together again, not indeed on the old basis of a level, infallible inspiration, but on the factually demonstrable basis of a coherent development. The Scriptures reflect some twelve centuries and more of deepening and enlarging spiritual experience and insight, in the written record of which nothing is without significance, and everything is illumined by its genetic relationships.

In general, this view of the Scriptures has become the common property of the well-informed, but it still remains, in many minds, a mere framework without substantial content. That the Bible is the record of centuries of religious change, that its early concepts are allied with primitive, animistic faiths, that between such origins and the messages of Hebrew prophets and Christian evangelists an immensely important development is reflected in the Book—this general view is the familiar possession of many in both synagogue and church. All too few, however, have any clear and specific conception of the ways in which the Biblical ideas unfolded from their beginnings until they became one of the most potent influences in Western culture.

The chronological fallacy haunts such a study as this and is difficult to avoid. The very fact that six historically influential ideas are presented in terms of development, with their later formulations on an altitude immeasurably higher than the lowlands from which they came, may produce the illusion of constant ascent, as though being posterior in time always meant being superior in quality. But truth and chronology are incommensurable terms. A poet writing in the twentieth century A.D. may be a puny figure compared with the titanic stature of a Greek dramatist five centuries before Christ, and ethical insight cannot be graded on the basis of the calendar. The fact that one Biblical book is later in time than another is in itself not the slightest indication that it is superior in quality—Nahum is on a much lower spiritual level than Amos, and the Book of Revelation in the New Testament is morally inferior to the writings of the Great Isaiah in the Old Testament. Of this fact the reader is continually reminded in this book, and no statement, I think, denies or neglects it. I have tried to make plain the retrogressions in Biblical thought, the irregularities of change, with its ups and downs, its persistent lags, and its moral surrenders. There is no smooth and even ascent in the Book. There are, instead, long detours, recrudescences of primitivism, lost ethical gains, and lapses in spiritual insight. There are even vehement denials of nascent truth, and high visions that go neglected for centuries. At this point I am solicitous that my desire for clarity in tracing development may not beguile any reader into the illusions of the chronological fallacy.

Modernization dogs the footsteps of any one who endeavors to make ancient developments of thought live for contemporary readers. By subtle, unnoticed gradations the presentation

* From Harry Emerson Fosdick, *A Guide to Understanding the Bible*. New York: Harper & Brothers, 1938. Pages ix–x and xiii–xv are reproduced by permission of the publisher.

of old patterns of thinking slips over into twentieth-century categories and phrases. The more one perceives in ancient literature, whether of Judea or Greece, values of permanent validity, the more one tends to lift them out of their original frameworks of concept and present them in modern terms and ways of thinking. But "corporate personality," demonology, Messiahship, apocalypticism, the Logos-doctrine, and many other mental categories in the Bible are not modern. It requires a difficult thrust of historic imagination to understand at all what they meant to their original users. It may be comforting to translate them into present-day equivalents but that always involves an historic fallacy. This difficulty is everywhere present in this book and I wish the reader to be aware of it. I have honestly tried never to picture an ancient way of conceiving facts as though it were identical with modern thinking, but always to portray the Biblical writers as using their own mental forms of thought in their own way, however diverse from ours those forms may be. Such is the difficulty involved, however, in making modern language serve this purpose that in this regard the co-operation of the reader is imperative.

The implications of this book with regard to theories about the Bible are not discussed in the text. Obviously, any idea of inspiration which implies equal value in the teachings of Scripture, or inerrancy in its statements, or conclusive infallibility in its ideas, is irreconcilable with such facts as this book presents. The inspirations of God fortunately have not been thus stereotyped and mechanical. There is, however, nothing in the process of development itself, whether in the organic world in general or in the realm of mind and morals, to call in question the creative and directive activity of God.

Needless to say, the author is a theist. The process of spiritual development reflected in the Bible seems to him to involve not only human discovery but divine self-disclosure. Indeed, the unfolding of ideas which the Scripture records would represent not so much discovery as illusion, were there not an objective spiritual world to be discovered. Any one, therefore, holding a religious rather than a materialistic philosophy, will think of the process of Biblical development as dual—seen from one side, a human achievement; seen from the other, a divine self-revelation.

Nevertheless, there is no finality about it in the sense that the ideas which the Scriptures opened up were finished when the Scriptures stopped. Neither Judaism nor Christianity, despite their theories, has in practice succeeded in so treating the Book. Every one of the six lines of unfolding thought traced in this volume has had a long subsequent history of continuing development, and the end is not yet in sight. The God of the Bible has proved his quality as "the living God," who has not said his last word on any subject or put the finishing touch on any task. The supreme contribution of the Bible is not that it finished anything but that it started something. Its thinking is not so much a product as a process, issuing from a long precedent process and inaugurating an immeasurably important subsequent development.

WALTER RAUSCHENBUSCH (1861–1918)

Among the achievements of liberal Protestantism is its rediscovery of the social responsibility of the Christian churches. Preceding generations of American Christians, with some notable exceptions, had been content to cultivate personal piety, with emphasis either on its doctrinal or emotional aspects, while they had neglected to relate their faith to the social structures of life. Toward the end of the 19th century, however, liberal Protestantism under the leadership of such men as Gladden and Rauschenbusch became possessed by "an interfering spirit of righteousness" and began to develop the so-called Social Gospel, a Christian answer to the burning issues with which Western society then was faced by the emergence of industrial capitalism.

Rauschenbusch had his first encounter with the disastrous conditions under which men were forced to live and to work when he assumed his pastorate in Hell's Kitchen on Manhattan's west side. There his social philosophy matured and began shortly afterwards to bear fruit in a number of great books.

Wanted: A Faith For A Task*

A great task demands a great faith. To live a great life a man needs a great cause to which he can surrender, something divinely large and engrossing for which he can live and, if need be, die. A great religious faith will lift him out of his narrow grooves and make him the inspired instrument of the universal will of God. It is the point at which the mind of man coincides with the mind of the Eternal. A vital faith will gradually saturate a man's whole life and master not only his conscious energies, but his subconscious drifts. The religious revolution in Paul's life was due to a new faith which seized him and made him over, and ever after he knew that a man is justified by a faith more than by any doings. He had made proof of the fact.

Our entire generation needs a faith, for it is confronting the mightiest task ever undertaken consciously by any generation of men. Our civilization is passing through a great historic transition. We are at the parting of the ways. The final outcome may be the decay and extinction of Western civilization, or it may be a new epoch in the evolution of the race, compared with which our present era will seem like a modified barbarism. We now have such scientific knowledge of social laws and forces, of economics, of history that we can intelligently mold and guide the evolution in which we take part. Our fathers cowered before the lightning; we have subdued it to our will. Former generations were swept along more or less blindly toward a hidden destiny; we have reached the point where we can make history make us. Have we the will to match our knowledge? Can we marshal the moral forces capable of breaking what must be broken, and then building what must be built? What spiritual hosts can God line up to rout the Devil in the battle of Armageddon?

Our moral efficiency depends on our religious faith. The force of will, of courage, of self-sacrifice liberated by a living religious faith is so incalculable, so invincible, that nothing is impossible when that power enters the field. The author of the greatest revolution in history made the proposition that even the slightest amount of faith is competent to do the unbelievable; faith as tiny as a mustard seed can blast away mountains. . . .

The chief purpose of the Christian Church in the past has been the salvation of individuals. But the most pressing task of the present is not individualistic. Our business is to make over an antiquated and immoral economic system; to get rid of laws, customs, maxims, and philosophies inherited from an evil and despotic past; to create just and brotherly relations between great groups and classes of society; and thus to lay a social foundation on which modern men individually can live and work in a fashion that will not outrage all the better elements in them. Our inherited Christian faith dealt with individuals; our present task deals with society.

The Christian Church in the past has taught us to do our work with our eyes fixed on another world and a life to come. But the business before us is concerned with refashioning this present world, making this earth clean and sweet and habitable.

Here is the problem for all religious minds: we need a great faith to serve as a spiritual basis for the tremendous social task before us, and the working creed of our religion, in the form in which it has come down to us, has none. Its theology is silent or stammers where we most need a ringing and dogmatic message. It has no adequate answer to the fundamental moral questions of our day. It has manifestly furnished no sufficient religious motives to bring the unregenerate portions of our social order under the control of the Christian law. Its hymns, its ritual, its prayers, its books of devotion, are so devoid of social thought that the

* From W. Rauschenbusch, *Christianizing the Social Order*. New York: The Macmillan Company, 1912. Pages 40–44 and 46–47 are reproduced by permission of the Macmillan Company.

most thrilling passions of our generation lie in us half stifled for lack of religious utterance. The whole scheme of religion which tradition has handed down to us was not devised for such ends as we now have in hand and is inadequate for them. We need a new foundation for Christian thought. . . .

With true Christian instinct men have turned to the Christian law of love as the key to the situation. If we all loved our neighbor, we should "treat him right," pay him a living wage, give sixteen ounces to the pound, and not charge so much for beef. But this appeal assumes that we are still living in the simple personal relations of the good old times, and that every man can do the right thing when he wants to do it. But suppose a businessman would be glad indeed to pay his young women the twelve dollars a week which they need for a decent living, but all his competitors are paying from seven dollars down to five dollars. Shall he love himself into bankruptcy? . . .

The old advice of love breaks down before the hugeness of modern relations. We might as well try to start a stranded ocean liner with the oar which poled our old dory from the mud banks many a time. It is indeed love that we want, but it is socialized love. Blessed be the love that holds the cup of water to thirsty lips. We can never do without the plain affection of man to man. But what we most need today is not the love that will break its back drawing water for a growing factory town from a well that was meant to supply a village, but a love so large and intelligent that it will persuade an ignorant people to build a system of waterworks up in the hills, and that will get after the thoughtless farmers who contaminate the brooks with typhoid bacilli, and after the lumber concern that is denuding the watershed of its forest. We want a new avatar of love. . . .

What great word of faith does historic Christianity offer to express and hallow and quicken this spiritual passion which is so evidently begotten of the spirit of Christ? Must he go to materialistic socialism to find a dogmatic faith large enough to house him, and intellectual food nutritious enough to feed his hunger? Thousands have left the Church and have gone to socialism, not to shake off a faith, but to get a faith.

I raise this challenge because I believe Christianity can meet it. My purpose is not critical, but wholly constructive. If I did not believe in the vitality and adaptability of the Christian faith, I should sit down with Job on the ashes and keep silence.

But let no one take the challenge lightly. It points to no superficial flaw in the working machinery of the Church, but to the failure of our religious ideas to connect with our religious needs, and that is fundamental. Religion, to have power over an age, must satisfy the highest moral and religious desires of that age. If it lags behind, and presents outgrown conceptions of life and duty, it is no longer in the full sense the Gospel.

The Kingdom of God*

If theology is to offer an adequate doctrinal basis for the social gospel, it must not only make room for the doctrine of the Kingdom of God, but give it a central place and revise all other doctrines so that they will articulate organically with it. . . .

Jesus always spoke of the Kingdom of God. Only two of his reported sayings contain the word "Church," and both passages are of questionable authenticity. It is safe to say that he never thought of founding the kind of institution which afterward claimed to be acting for him. . . .

When the doctrine of the Kingdom of God shriveled to an undeveloped and pathetic remnant in Christian thought, this loss was bound to have far-reaching consequences. . . .

The Church is primarily a fellowship for worship; the Kingdom is a fellowship of righteousness. When the latter was neglected in theology, the ethical force of Christianity was weakened; when the former was emphasized in theology,

* From W. Rauschenbusch, *A Theology for the Social Gospel*. New York: The Macmillan Company, 1917. Pages 131–137 and 139–140 are reproduced by permission of the Macmillan Company.

the importance of worship was exaggerated. The prophets and Jesus had cried down sacrifices and ceremonial performances, and cried up righteousness, mercy, solidarity. Theology now reversed this, and by its theoretical discussions did its best to stimulate sacramental actions and priestly importance. Thus the religious energy and enthusiasm which might have saved mankind from its great sins, were used up in hearing and endowing masses, or in maintaining competitive church organizations, while mankind is still stuck in the mud. There are nations in which the ethical condition of the masses is the reverse of the frequency of the masses in the churches. . . .

The Kingdom ideal is the test and corrective of the influence of the Church. When the Kingdom ideal disappeared, the conscience of the Church was muffled. It became possible for the missionary expansion of Christianity to halt for centuries without creating any sense of shortcoming. It became possible for the most unjust social conditions to fasten themselves on Christain nations without awakening any consciousness that the purpose of Christ was being defied and beaten back. The practical undertakings of the Church remained within narrow lines, and the theological thought of the Church was necessarily confined in a similar way. The claims of the Church were allowed to stand in theology with no conditions and obligations to test and balance them. If the Kingdom had stood as the purpose for which the Church exists, the Church could not have fallen into such corruption and sloth. Theology bears part of the guilt for the pride, the greed, and the ambition of the Church.

The Kingdom ideal contains the revolutionary force of Christianity. When this ideal faded out of the systematic thought of the Church, it became a conservative social influence and increased the weight of the other stationary forces in society. If the Kingdom of God had remained part of the theological and Christian consciousness, the Church could not, down to our times, have been salaried by autocratic class governments to keep the democratic and economic impulses of the people under check. . . .

When the doctrine of the Kingdom of God is lacking in theology, the salvation of the individual is seen in its relation to the Church and to the future life, but not in its relation to the task of saving the social order. Theology has left this important point in a condition so hazy and muddled that it has taken us almost a generation to see that the salvation of the individual and the redemption of the social order are closely related, and how. . . .

In the following brief propositions I should like to offer a few suggestions, on behalf of the social gospel, for the theological formulation of the doctrine of the Kingdom. Something like this is needed to give us "a theology for the social gospel."

The Kingdom of God is divine in its origin, progress, and consummation. It was initiated by Jesus Christ, in whom the prophetic spirit came to its consummation, it is sustained by the Holy Spirit, and it will be brought to its fulfillment by the power of God in his own time. The passive and active resistance of the Kingdom of Evil at every stage of its advance is so great, and the human resources of the Kingdom of God so slender, that no explanation can satisfy a religious mind which does not see the power of God in its movements. The Kingdom of God, therefore, is miraculous all the way, and is the continuous revelation of the power, the righteousness, and the love of God. The establishment of a community of righteousness in mankind is just as much a saving act of God as the salvation of an individual from his natural selfishness and moral inability. The Kingdom of God, therefore, is not merely ethical, but has a rightful place in theology. This doctrine is absolutely necessary to establish that organic union between religion and morality, between theology and ethics, which is one of the characteristics of the Christian religion. . . .

The Kingdom of God contains the theology of the Christian religion. It translates theology from the static to the dynamic. It sees, not doctrines or rites to be conserved and perpetuated, but resistance to be overcome and great ends to be achieved. Since the Kingdom of God is the supreme purpose of God, we shall understand the Kingdom so far as we understand God, and we shall understand God so far as we understand his Kingdom. As long as organized sin is in the world, the Kingdom of God is characterized by conflict with evil. But if there were no evil, or after evil has been overcome, the Kingdom of God will still be the end to which God is lifting the race. It is realized not only by redemption, but also by the education of mankind and the revelation of his life within it.

WILLIAM ELLERY CHANNING (1780–1842)

Not all "liberals" (see p. 335) are Unitarians, but nowhere are the tendencies of liberalism more clearly to be seen than in this movement, which, broke away from the prevailing calvinistic orthodoxy early in the nineteenth century. Directly influenced by the enlightenment (see p. 334), the Unitarians contended for the place of reason in religion, for the concept of Jesus as a moral teacher rather than a divine person, and for a program of educating the natural moral propensities of mankind.

William Ellery Channing is often called the spiritual father of American Unitarianism. Educated at Harvard, he was ordained as a Congregational clergyman in 1803. By 1819, however, he had emerged as a leading spokesman of the Unitarian group. It was in that year that the sermon, from which our selection is taken, was delivered.

Unitarian Christianity*

. . . There are two natural divisions under which my thoughts will be arranged. I shall endeavor to unfold, first, The principles which we adopt in interpreting the Scriptures. And secondly, Some of the doctrines, which the Scriptures, so interpreted, seem to us clearly to express.

I. We regard the Scriptures as the records of God's successive revelations to mankind, and particularly of the last and most perfect revelation of his will by Jesus Christ. Whatever doctrines seem to us to be clearly taught in the Scriptures, we receive without reserve or exception. We do not, however, attach equal importance to all the books in this collection. Our religion, we believe, lies chiefly in the New Testament. The dispensation of Moses, compared with that of Jesus, we consider as adapted to the childhood of the human race, a preparation for a nobler system, and chiefly useful now as serving to confirm and illustrate the Christian Scriptures. Jesus Christ is the only master of Christians, and whatever he taught, either during his personal ministry, or by his inspired Apostles, we regard as of divine authority, and profess to make the rule of our lives. . . .

The principles adopted by the class of Christians in whose name I speak, need to be explained, because they are often misunderstood. We are particularly accused of making an unwarrantable use of reason in the interpretation of Scripture. We are said to exalt reason above revelation, to prefer our own wisdom to God's. . . .

Our leading principle in interpreting Scripture is this, that the Bible is a book written for men, in the language of men, and that its meaning is to be sought in the same manner as that of other books. We believe that God, when he speaks to the human race, conforms, if we may so say, to the established rules of speaking and writing. . . .

Now all books, and all conversation, require in the reader or hearer the constant exercise of reason; or their true import is only to be obtained by continual comparison and inference. . . .

We find, too, that some of these books are

* From William E. Channing, "Unitarian Christianity," *A Selection from the Works of William E. Channing*. Boston: American Unitarian Association, 1855. Pages 180–181, 183–191, 194–195, 202–203, 205–206, and 210–212.

strongly marked by the genius and character of their respective writers, that the Holy Spirit did not so guide the Apostles as to suspend the peculiarities of their minds, and that a knowledge of their feelings, and of the influences under which they were placed, is one of the preparations for understanding their writings. With these views of the Bible, we feel it our bounden duty to exercise our reason upon it perpetually, to compare, to infer, to look beyond the letter to the spirit, to seek in the nature of the subject, and the aim of the writer, his true meaning; and, in general, to make use of what is known, for explaining what is difficult, and for discovering new truths.

Need I descend to particulars, to prove that the Scriptures demand the exercise of reason? Take, for example, the style in which they generally speak of God, and observe how habitually they apply to him human passions and organs. Recollect the declarations of Christ, that he came not to send peace, but a sword; that unless we eat his flesh, and drink his blood, we have no life in us; that we must hate father and mother, and pluck out the right eye; and a vast number of passages equally bold and unlimited. Recollect the unqualified manner in which it is said of Christians, that they possess all things, know all things, and can do all things. Recollect the verbal contradiction between Paul and James, and apparent clashing of some parts of Paul's writings with the general doctrines and end of Christianity. I might extend the enumeration indefinitely; and who does not see, that we must limit all these passages by the known attributes of God, of Jesus Christ, and of human nature, and by the circumstances under which they were written, so as to give the language a quite different import from what it would require, had it been applied to different beings, or used in different connexions. . . .

We object strongly to the contemptuous manner in which human reason is often spoken of by our adversaries, because it leads, we believe, to universal skepticism. If reason be so dreadfully darkened by the fall, that its most decisive judgments on religion are unworthy of trust, then Christianity, and even natural theology, must be abandoned; for the existence and veracity of God, and the divine original of Christianity, are conclusions of reason, and must stand or fall with it. . . .

The true inference from the almost endless errors, which have darkened theology, is, not that we are to neglect and disparage our powers, but to exert them more patiently, circumspectly, uprightly . . . the worst errors, after all, having sprung up in that church, which proscribes reason, and demands from its members implicit faith. The most pernicious doctrines have been the growth of the darkest times, when the general credulity encouraged bad men and enthusiasts to broach their dreams and inventions, and to stifle the faint remonstrances of reason, by the menaces of everlasting perdition. Say what we may, God has given us a rational nature, and will call us to account for it. We may let it sleep, but we do so at our peril. Revelation is addressed to us as rational beings. . . .

II. Having thus stated the principles according to which we interpret Scripture, I now proceed to the second great head of this discourse, which is, to state some of the views which we derive from that sacred book, particularly those which disinguish us from other Christians.

In the first place, we believe in the doctrine of God's *unity,* or that there is one God, and one only. To this truth we give infinite importance, and we feel ourselves bound to take heed, lest any man spoil us of it by vain philosophy. The proposition, that there is one God, seems to us exceedingly plain. We understand by it, that there is one being, one mind, one person, one intelligent agent, and one only, to whom underived and infinite perfection and dominion belong. . . .

We object to the doctrine of the Trinity, that, whilst acknowledging in words, it subverts in effect, the unity of God. According to this doctrine, there are three infinite and equal persons, possessing supreme divinity, called the Father, Son, and Holy Ghost. Each of these persons, as described by theologians, has his own particular consciousness, will, and perceptions. They love each other, converse with each other, and delight in each other's society. They perform different parts in man's redemption, each having his appropriate office, and neither doing the work of the other. The Son is mediator and not the Father. The Father sends the Son, and is not himself sent; nor is he conscious, like the Son, of taking flesh. Here, then, we have three intelligent agents, possessed of different consciousness, different will, and different perceptions, performing different acts, and sustaining different relations; and if these things do not imply and constitute three minds or beings, we are utterly at a loss to know how three minds or beings are to be formed. . . .

With Jesus, we worship the Father, as the only living and true God. We are astonished, that any man can read the New Testament, and avoid the conviction, that the Father alone is God. We hear our Saviour continually appropriating this character to the Father. We find the Father continually distinguished from Jesus by this title. . . .

We also think, that the doctrine of the Trinity injures devotion, not only by joining to the Father other objects of worship, but by taking from the Father the supreme affection, which is his due, and transferring it to the Son. This is a most important view. That Jesus Christ, if exalted into the infinite Divinity, should be more interesting than the Father, is precisely what might be expected from history, and from the principles of human nature. Men want an object of worship like themselves, and the great secret of idolatry lies in this propensity. A God, clothed in our form, and feeling our wants and sorrows, speaks to our weak nature more strongly, than a Father in heaven, a pure spirit, invisible and unapproachable, save by the reflecting and purified mind. . . .

We do believe, that the worship of a bleeding, suffering God, tends strongly to absorb the mind, and to draw it from other objects, just as the human tenderness of the Virgin Mary has given her so conspicuous a place in the devotions of the Church of Rome. We believe, too, that this worship, though attractive, is not most fitted to spiritualize the mind, that it awakens human transport, rather than that deep veneration of the moral perfections of God, which is the essence of piety. . . .

Having thus given our belief on two great points, namely, that there is one God, and that Jesus Christ is a being distinct from, and inferior to, God, I now proceed to another point, on which we lay still greater stress. We believe in the moral perfection of God. We consider no part of theology so important as that which treats of God's moral character; and we value our views of Christianity chiefly as they assert his amiable and venerable attributes.

It may be said, that, in regard to this subject, all Christians agree, that all ascribe to the Supreme Being infinite justice, goodness, and holiness. We reply, that it is very possible to speak of God magnificently, and to think of him meanly; to apply to his person high sounding epithets, and to his government, principles which make him odious. . . .

We conceive that Christians have generally leaned towards a very injurious view of the Supreme Being. They have too often felt, as if he were raised, by his greatness and sovereignty, above the principles of morality, above those eternal laws of equity and rectitude, to which all other beings are subjected. We believe, that in no being is the sense of right so strong, so omnipotent, as in God. We believe that his almighty power is entirely submitted to his perceptions of rectitude; and this is the ground of our piety. It is not because He is our Creator merely, but because He created us for good and holy purposes; it is not because his will is irresistible, but because his will is the perfection of virtue, that we pay him allegiance. We cannot bow before a being, however great and powerful, who governs tyrannically. We respect nothing but excellence, whether on earth or in heaven. We venerate not the loftiness of God's throne, but the equity and goodness in which it is established. . . .

Now, we object to the systems of religion, which prevail among us, that they are adverse, in a greater or less degree, to these purifying, comforting, and honorable views of God; that they take from us our Father in heaven, and substitute for him a being, whom we cannot love if we would, and whom we ought not to love if we could. We object, particularly on this ground, to that system, which arrogates to itself the name of Orthodoxy, and which is now industriously propagated through our country. This system indeed takes various shapes, but in all it casts dishonor on the Creator. According to its old and genuine form, it teaches, that God brings us into life wholly depraved, so that under the innocent features of our childhood is hidden a nature averse to all good and propense to all evil, a nature which exposes us to God's displeasure and wrath, even before we have acquired power to understand our duties, or to reflect upon our actions. . . . Now, according to the plainest principles of morality, we maintain, that a natural constitution of the mind, unfailingly disposing it to evil and to evil alone, would absolve it from guilt; that to give existence under this condition would argue unspeakable cruelty; and that to punish the sin of this unhappily constituted child with endless ruin, would be a wrong unparalleled by the most merciless despotism.

This system also teaches, that God selects from this corrupt mass a number to be saved, and plucks them, by a special influence, from the common ruin; that the rest of mankind, though left without that special grace which their conversion requires, are commanded to repent, under penalty of aggravated woe; and that forgiveness is promised them, on terms which their very constitution infallibly disposes them to reject, and in rejecting which they awfully enhance the punishments of hell. These proffers of forgiveness and exhortations of amendment, to beings born under a blighting curse, fill our minds with a horror which we want words to express. . . .

We farther agree in rejecting, as unscriptural and absurd, the explanation given by the popular system, of the manner in which Christ's death procures forgiveness for men. . . . The system teaches, that sin, of whatever degree, exposes to endless punishment, and that the whole human race, being infallibly involved by their nature in sin, owe this awful penalty to the justice of their Creator. It teaches, that this penalty cannot be remitted, in consistency with the honor of the divine law, unless a substitute be found to endure it or to suffer an equivalent. It also teaches, that, from the nature of the case, no substitute is adequate to this work, save the infinite God himself; and accordingly, God, in his second person, took on him human nature, that he might pay to his own justice the debt of punishment incurred by men, and might thus reconcile forgiveness with the claims and threatenings of his law. . . .

We believe . . . that this system is unfavorable to the character. It naturally leads men to think, that Christ came to change God's mind rather than their own; that the highest object of his mission was to avert punishment, rather than to communicate holiness; and that a large part of religion consists in disparaging good works and human virtue, for the purpose of magnifying the value of Christ's vicarious sufferings. In this way, a sense of the infinite importance and indispensable necessity of personal improvement is weakened, and high-sounding praises of Christ's cross seem often to be substituted for obedience to his precepts. For ourselves, we have not so learned Jesus. Whilst we gratefully acknowledge, that he came to rescue us from punishment, we believe, that he was sent on a still nobler errand, namely, to deliver us from sin itself, and to form us to a sublime and heavenly virtue. We regard him as a Saviour, chiefly as he is the light, physician, and guide of the dark, diseased, and wandering mind. No influence in the universe seems to us so glorious, as that over the character; and no redemption so worthy of thankfulness, as the restoration of the soul to purity.

WILLIAM JENNINGS BRYAN (1860–1925)

The modern-fundamentalist controversy, which so greatly agitated the American Protestant Churches in the first quarter of the present century, came to a spectacular head in the now-famous Scopes trial ("monkey trial") in Dayton, Tennessee. The Scopes case involved the indictment and prosecution of a young science teacher in the Dayton, Tennessee, High School. The State of Tennessee had passed a statute which forbade the teaching of evolution in the public schools. In defiance of this statute John Scopes taught some of Darwin's theories in the classroom. He was promptly indicted and the ensuing trial became one of the most famous and bizarre of the twentieth century.

The noted trial lawyer (and free-thinker), Clarence Darrow, defended Scopes. William Jennings Bryan, already famous as a political reformer and twice-defeated candidate for the Presidency, offered his services to the Prosecution. Bryan was an orthodox-fundamentalist Christian of deep sincerity and conviction. To him, evolution was the greatest danger facing Christianity. He viewed the Scopes trial as the great test of Orthodox Christianity against all the perils of modernism. Although Scopes was found guilty, the trial ended in confusion and the religious question so important to Bryan was not really resolved.

Orthodox Christianity versus Modernism*

The Fundamentals

I respond with pleasure to your request for an article on the orthodox side of the controversy that brought forth the reaffirmation of the position of the Presbyterian Church (Northern) last May on the five points mentioned in your letter,—the same pronouncement having been made by the General Assembly held in 1910, and repeated in 1916. The text of the resolution reads as follows:

1. "It is an essential doctrine of the Word of God and our standards that the Holy Spirit did so inspire, guide and move the writers of Holy Scripture as to keep them from error."
2. "It is an essential doctrine of the Word of God and our standards that our Lord Jesus Christ was born of the Virgin Mary."
3. "It is an essential doctrine of the Word of God and our standards that Christ offered up Himself a sacrifice to satisfy Divine Justice and to reconcile us to God."
4. "It is an essential doctrine of the Word of God and of our standards concerning our Lord Jesus Christ, that on the third day He rose again from the dead with the same body with which He suffered, with which also He ascended into heaven, and there sitteth at the right hand of His Father, making intercession."
5. "It is an essential doctrine of the Word of God as the supreme standard of our faith that our Lord Jesus showed His power and love by working mighty miracles. This working was not contrary to nature, but superior to it."

The questions at issue are so vital and the differences of opinion so great,—in fact, so irreconcilable,—that it is due to the general public, as well as to the church, that the opposing views should be stated with clearness and candour.

I do not mean to bind anyone else either by my conclusions or by the reasons given for them, but I am quite sure that my views on this subject are in harmony with the views of a large majority of the members, not only of the Presbyterian church, but of all the churches that call themselves Christian.

The First Proposition

The first proposition deals with the doctrine that necessarily comes first, namely, the inerrancy of the Bible. It is declared to be not only true, but "an essential doctrine of the Word of God and our standards, that the Holy Spirit did so inspire, guide and move the writers of Holy Scripture as to keep them from error."

The Bible is either the Word of God or merely a man-made book. If time permitted, I might defend the Christian position and point out as conclusive proof of the Bible's divine origin the fact that the wisest men living today, with an inheritance of all the learning of the past, with countless books to consult and great universities on every hand, cannot furnish the equal of, or a substitute for, this book which was compiled from the writings of men largely unlettered, scattered through many centuries and yet producing an unbroken story,—men of a single race and living in a limited area, without the advantages of swift ships or telegraph wires. . . .

When one asserts that the Bible is not infallible, he must measure it by some standard which he considers better authority than the Bible itself. If the Bible is to be rejected as an authority, upon whose authority is it to be condemned? We must have a standard; where shall we find it? When one decides that the Bible is, as a whole or in part, erroneous, he sits in judg-

* From Bryan, *Orthodox Christianity versus Modernism*. New York: Fleming H. Revell Company, 1923. Pages 7–13, 16–18, 20–21, and 23.

ment upon it and, looking down from his own infallibility, declares it fallible,—that is, that it contains falsehoods or errors. As no two of the critics of the Bible fully agree as to what part is myth and what part is authentic history, each one, in fact, transfers the presumption of infallibility from the Bible to himself.

Upon the first proposition all the rest depend. If the Bible is true,—that is, so divinely inspired as to be free from error,—then the second, third, fourth and fifth propositions follow inevitably, because they are based upon what the Bible actually says in language clear and unmistakable. If, on the other hand, the Bible is not to be accepted as true, there is no reason why anybody should believe anything in it that he objects to, no matter upon what his objection is founded. He need not go to the trouble of giving a reason for it; if he is at liberty to eliminate any passage which he does not like, then no reason is necessary. When the Bible ceases to be an authority—a divine authority—the Word of God can be accepted, rejected, or mutilated, according to the whim or mood of the reader.

The Second Proposition

The second proposition, which declares it to be "an essential doctrine of the Word of God and our standards that our Lord Jesus Christ was born of the Virgin Mary," is really the pivotal point in the present controversy between the so-called liberals and those who are described as conservatives. The action of the General Assembly has so exasperated a number of Presbyterian preachers that they have openly declared that they do not believe in the virgin birth. Why? Because there is any uncertainty in the record of the Savior's birth as given in Matthew and Luke? No, the account is written in simple language and in detail. Mary was the first one to inquire whether such a birth was possible. The atheists, the agnostics, the infidels, and the doubters, were all anticipated by the Virgin herself. . . .

The virgin birth is no more mysterious than the birth of each of us,—it is simply different. No one without revelation has ever solved the mystery of life, whether it be the life found in man, or in the beast or in the plant. The God who can *give* life can certainly give it in any way or through any means that may please Him. It was just as easy for God to bring Christ into the world as He did, according to Matthew and Luke, as to bring us into the world as He did. Shall we doubt the *power of* God? If so, we do not believe in God. Or, relying upon our own wisdom, shall we deny that God would *want* to do what He is reported to have done? Who dares to make himself equal in wisdom with God,—as one must be if he claims to know, without possibility of mistake, what God would or would not do?

If Christ came down from the Father for the purpose of saving the people from their sins, is it *unreasonable* that His birth should have been different from the birth of others?

The task that Christ came to perform was more than a man's task. No man aspiring to be a God could have done what He did; it required a God condescending to be a man. Is it *unreasonable* that one who offered himself as a sacrifice for sin, revealed God to man, and guides man by His heaven-born wisdom, should have been conceived of the Holy Ghost and born of the Virgin Mary? The rejection of the virgin birth not only condemns the Bible record on this subject as false, but it changes one's whole conception of Christ and makes it difficult, if not impossible, to present Him as the Bible presents Him. . . .

The Third Proposition

But to return to the five points. The third proposition deals with the sacrificial character of the death of Christ. Those who reject the virgin birth quite naturally and for the same reason reject the doctrine of the atonement. They deny that man ever fell; on the contrary, they contend that man has been rising from the beginning and, therefore, needs no Saviour. To such, Christ is just an example, differing in value to different individuals according to the estimate that they place upon His wisdom. Those who reject the atonement and simply search Christ's teachings for advice (if at any time they feel they need His advice) describe the Nazarene in different ways. Some say that He was the most perfect man known to history; others say that He was a man of extraordinary merit; still others believe Him an unusual man for His time; while some would simply put the title "Mr." before His name and class Him among the well-meaning visionaries. To those who strip Christ of His deity, He can mean but little. If they will only take Him out of the *man* class and put Him in the *God* class all that the Bible says of Him will be easily understood and gladly accepted. . . .

The Fourth Proposition

The fourth proposition, like the second and third, stands or falls with the first. The only information that we have regarding the bodily resurrection of Christ is found in the Bible, and the only reason for rejecting it is the same given for the rejection of the virgin birth and the doctrine of the atonement, namely, that it is *different* from anything else known among men. The resurrection of Christ—the bodily resurrection—is declared in the General Assembly pronouncement to be not only true, but an *essential* doctrine. "If Christ be not raised, your faith is vain," exclaims the great apostle, Paul. The denial of Christ's resurrection, taken in connection with the denial of the virgin birth and the denial of the atonement, completes His degradation. . . .

The Fifth Proposition

The fifth proposition asserts that belief in the miracles performed by Christ is an essential doctrine of the Word of God. This proposition might well have come second because the veracity of the Word of God must be denied before the miracles can be disputed and the miracles must be discarded before objection can be made to the second, third, and fourth propositions. The natural order with those who depart from the Faith of our Fathers is first to deny the infallibility of the Bible, then to deny the authenticity of the miracles, then to deny the virgin birth, the atonement, and the resurrection, because they are miracles. When all the miracles and all the supernatural are eliminated from the Bible it becomes a "scrap of paper." . . .

Evolution

But what is it that thus, progressively, whittles away the Word of God and destroys its vitality? I venture to assert that the unproven hypothesis of evolution is the root cause of nearly all the dissension in the church over the five points under discussion. "Liberalism," however you define it, is built upon the guess to which the euphonious name of "evolution" has been given. . . .

Will the Christian church admit that there is anything in education that naturally or necessarily weakens faith? This cannot be admitted. The church has been the greatest patron of learning,—the greatest friend that education has ever had. What is there, then, in our colleges that undermines faith and paralyzes religion? Only one thing: namely, an hypothesis that links man in blood relationship with every other form of life, animal and vegetable, and makes him cousin to brute and bird and fish and reptile,—to flower and fruit and vegetable and weed. Even in Christian colleges the student is asked to substitute the hypothesis of evolution for the Bible record of creation, although *not one species has ever* yet been traced to another species. The "missing links" between a million species,—Darwin estimated the number at from two to three millions,—are yet to be found; not one has been produced. . . .

BENJAMIN B. WARFIELD (1851–1921)

Born in Kentucky and educated at Princeton Theological Seminary, to which he was destined to return as a professor of theology, Benjamin Warfield proved to be one of the most eloquent and gifted defenders of conservative Protestantism. His writings in the field of biblical studies were extensive, scholarly and influential. Though it would be a mistake to classify him as a "fundamentalist" (see p. 335), he had certain affinities with their critique of liberalism. In Warfield we find one of the clearest statements of the belief that the Scriptures contain no error.

Christian Supernaturalism*

Somewhere between the two extremes of a consistent naturalism and an exclusive supernaturalism we shall assuredly find the center of gravity of the thinking of the ages—the point on which philosophy rests all the more stably that on both sides wings stretch themselves far beyond all support and hang over the abyss. Precisely where, between the two extremes, this stable center is to be found, it may be more difficult to determine—our instruments of measurement are not always "implements of precision." Assuredly, however, it will not be found where either the purely supernatural or the purely natural is excluded, and in any case it is much to know that it lies somewhere between the two extremes, and that it is as unphilosophical as it is inhuman to deny or doubt either the natural or the supernatural.

It is not to be gainsaid, of course, that from time to time, strong tendencies of thought set in to this direction or to that; and, for a while, it may seem as if the whole world were rushing to one extreme or the other. A special type of philosophizing becomes temporarily dominant and its conceptions run burning over the whole thinking world. At such times men are likely to fancy that the great problem of the ages is settled, and to felicitate themselves upon the facility with which they see through what to men of other times were clouds of great darkness. Such a period visited European thought in the last century, when English Deism set the supernatural so far off from the world that French Atheism thought it an easy thing to dispense with it altogether. "Down with the infamy!" cried Voltaire, and actually thought the world had hearkened to his commandment. The atheistic naturalism of the eighteenth century has long since taken up its abode with the owls and bats; but the world has not yet learned its lesson. An even more powerful current seems to have seized the modern world, and to be hurling it by a very different pathway to practically the same conclusion. It is to be feared that it cannot be denied that we are today in the midst of a very strong drift away from frank recognition of the supernatural as a factor in human life. . . .

It may not be amiss, however, to recall the anti-supernaturalistic root and the anti-supernaturalistic effects of the dominance of this mode of conceiving things; and thus to identify in it the cause of the persistent anti-supernaturalism which at present characterizes the world's thought. The recognition of the supernatural is too deeply intrenched in human nature ever to be extirpated; man is not a brute, and he differs from the brutes in nothing more markedly or more ineradicably than in his correlation with an unseen world. But probably there never was an era in which the thinking of the more or less educated classes was more deeply tinged with an anti-supernatural stain than at present. Even when we confess the supernatural with our lips and look for it and find it with our reasons, our instincts as modern men lead us unconsciously to neglect and in all practical ways to disallow and even to scout it.

It would be impossible that what we call specifically Christian thought should be unaffected by such a powerful trend in the thinking of the world. Christian men are men first and Christians afterwards: and therefore their Christian thinking is superinduced on a basis of world-thinking. Theology accordingly in each age is stamped with the traits of the philosophy ruling at the time. The supernatural is the very breath of Christianity's nostrils and an anti-supernaturalistic atmosphere is to it the deadliest miasma. An absolutely anti-supernaturalistic Christianity is therefore a contradiction in terms. Nevertheless, immersed in an anti-supernaturalistic world-atmosphere, Christian thinking tends to become as anti-supernaturalistic as is possible to it. And it is indisputable that this is the characteristic of the Christian thought of our day. As Dr. Bascom puts it, the task that has been set themselves by those who would fain be considered the "bolder thinkers of our time" is "to curb the supernatural, to bring it into the full service of reason." The real question with them seems to be, not what kind and

* From Benjamin B. Warfield, *Bibical and Theological Studies*. Philadelphia: Presbyterian and Reformed Publishing Company, 1952. Pages 3–8, 15–18, and 20 are reproduced by permission of the publisher.

measure of supernaturalism does the Christianity of Christ and His apostles recognize and require; but, how little of the supernatural may be admitted and yet men continue to call themselves Christians. The effort is not to Christianize the world-conception of the age, but specifically to desupernaturalize Christianity so as to bring it into accord with the prevailing world-view.

The effects of the adoption of this point of view are all about us. This is the account to give, for example, of that speculative theism which poses under the name of "non-miraculous Christianity" and seeks to convince the world through reasoners like Pfleiderer and to woo it through novels like "Robert Elsmere." This is also the account to give of that odd positivistic religion offered us by the followers of Albrecht Ritschl, who, under color of a phenomenalism which knows nothing of "the thing in itself," profess to hold it not to be a matter of serious importance to Christianity whether God be a person, or Christ be God, or the soul have any persistence, and to find it enough to bask in the sweet impression which is made on the heart by the personality of the man Jesus, dimly seen through the mists of critical history. This is the account again to give of the growing disbelief and denial of the virgin-birth of our Lord; of the increasingly numerous and subtle attempts to explain away His bodily resurrection; and, in far wider circles, of the ever renewed and constantly varying efforts that positively swarm about us to reduce His miracles and those of His predecessors and followers—the God-endowed prophets and apostles of the two Testaments—to natural phenomena, the product of natural forces, though these forces may be held to be as yet undiscovered or even entirely undiscoverable by men. This also is the account to give of the vogue which destructive criticism of the Biblical books has gained in our time; and it is also the reason why detailed refutations of the numerous critical theories of the origin of the Biblical writings, though so repeatedly complete and logically final, have so little effect in abolishing destructive criticism. Its roots are not set in its detailed accounts of the origin of the Biblical writings, but in its antisupernaturalistic bias: and so long as its two fixed points remain to it—its starting point in unbelief in the supernatural and its goal in a naturalistic development of the religion of Israel and its record—it easily shifts the pathway by which it proceeds from one to the other, according to its varying needs. . . . In every way, in a word, and in every sphere of Christian thought, the Christian thinking of our time is curbed, limited, confined within unnatural bounds by doubt and hesitation before the supernatural. In wide circles the reality of direct supernatural activity in this world is openly rejected: in wider circles still it is doubted: almost everywhere its assertion is timid and chary. . . .

It is certainly to be allowed that it is no light task for a Christian man to hold his anchorage in the rush of such a current of antisupernaturalistic thought. We need not wonder that so many are carried from their moorings. How shall we so firmly brace ourselves that, as the flood of the world's thought beats upon us, it may bring us cleansing and refreshment, but may not sweep us away from our grasp on Christian truth? How, but by constantly reminding ourselves of what Christianity is, and of what as Christian men we must needs believe as to the nature and measure of the supernatural in its impact on the life of the world? For this nature and measure of the supernatural we have all the evidence which gives us Christianity. And surely the mass of that evidence is far too great to be shaken by any current of the world's thought whatever. Christian truth is a rock too securely planted to go down before any storm. Let us attach ourselves to it by such strong cables, and let us know so well its promontories of vantage and secure hiding-places, that though the waters may go over us we shall not be moved. To this end it will not be useless to recall continually the frankness of Christianity's commitment to the absolute supernatural. And it may be that we shall find profit in enumerating at this time a few of the points, at least, at which, as Christian men, we must recognize, with all heartiness, the intrusion of pure supernaturalism into our conception of things.

The Christian man, then, must, first of all, give the heartiest and frankest recognition to *the supernatural fact*. "God," we call it. But it is not enough for us to say "God." The pantheist, too, says "God," and means this universal frame: for him accordingly the supernatural is but the more inclusive natural. When the Christian says "God," he means, and if he is to remain Christian he must mean, a *super*natural God—a God who is not entangled in nature, is not only another name for nature in its co-ordinated activities, or for that mystery which lies beneath and throbs through the All; but who is above nature and beyond, who existed, the Living God, before nature was, and should nature cease to be would still exist, the Everlasting God, and so long as this universal frame endures exists above and outside of nature as its Lord, its Lawgiver, and its Almighty King.

No Christian man may allow that the universe, material and spiritual combined, call it infinite if you will, in all its operations, be they as myriad as you choose, sums up the being or the activities of God. Before this universe was, God was, the one eternal One, rich in infinite activities: and while this universe persists, outside and beyond and above it God is, the one infinite One, ineffably rich in innumerable activities inconceivable, it may be, to the whole universe of derived being. He is not imprisoned within His works: the laws which He has ordained for them express indeed His character, but do not compass the possibilities of His action. The Apostle Paul has no doubt told us that "in Him we live and move and have our being," but no accredited voice has declared that in the universe He lives and moves and has His being. No, the heaven of heavens cannot contain Him; and what He has made is to what He is only as the smallest moisture-particle of the most attenuated vapor to the mighty expanse of the immeasurable sea. . . .

Nevertheless, inconceivable as it would appear, there are many voices raised about us which would fain persuade us, in the professed interest of Christianity itself, to attenuate or evacuate the supernatural even in redemption. That supernatural history of preparation for the Redeemer, we are asked, did it indeed all happen as it is there recorded by the simple-minded writers? Are we not at liberty to read it merely as the record of what pious hearts, meditating on the great past, fancied ought to have occurred, when God was with the fathers; and to dig out from beneath the strata of its devout imaginations, as veritable history, only a sober narrative of how Israel walked in the felt presence of God and was led by His providence to ever clearer and higher conceptions of His Holy Being and of its mission as His chosen people? And that supernatural figure which the evangelists and apostles have limned for us, did it indeed ever walk this sin-stricken earth of ours? Are we not bound to see in it, we are asked, merely the projection of the hopes and fears swallowed up in hope of His devoted followers, clothing with all imaginable heavenly virtues the dead form of their Master snatched from their sight—of whom they had "hoped that it was He who should deliver Israel"? And are we not bound reverently to draw aside the veil laid by such tender hands over the dead face, that we may see beneath it the real Jesus, dead indeed, but a man of infinite sweetness of temper and depth of faith, from whose holy life we may even yet catch an inspiration and receive an impulse for good? And Peter and Paul and John and the rest of those whose hearts were set on fire by the spectacle of that great and noble life, are we really to take their enthusiasm as the rule of our thought? Are we not bound, we are asked, though honoring the purity of their fine hero-worship, to curb the extravagance of their assertions; and to follow the faith quickened in them by the Master's example while we correct the exuberance of their fancy in attributing to Him superhuman qualities and performances? In a word—for let us put it at length plainly—are we not at liberty, are we not bound, to eviscerate Christianity of all that makes it a redemptive scheme, of all that has given it power in the earth, of all that has made it a message of hope and joy to lost men, of all that belongs to its very heart's blood and essence, as witnessed by all history and all experience alike, and yet claim still to remain Christians? No, let our answer be: as Christian men, a thousand times, no! When the antisupernaturalistic bias of this age attacks the supernatural in the very process of redemption, and seeks to evaporate it into a set of platitudes about the guiding hand of God in history, the power of the man Jesus' pure faith over His followers' imaginations, and the imitation by us of the religion of Jesus—it has assaulted Christianity in the very citadel of its life. As Christian men we must assert with all vigor the purity and the absoluteness of the supernatural in redemption.

And let us add at once, further, that as Christian men we must retain a frank and hearty faith in a *supernatural revelation*. For how should we be advantaged by a supernatural redemption of which we knew nothing? Who is competent to uncover to us the meaning of this great series of redemptive acts but God Himself? It is easy to talk of revelation by deed. But how little is capable of being revealed by even the mightiest deeds, unaccompanied by the explanatory word? Two thousand years ago a child was born in Bethlehem, who throve and grew up nobly, lived a live of poverty and beneficence, was cruelly slain and rose from the dead. What is that to us? After a little, as His followers sat waiting in Jerusalem, there was a rush as of a mighty wind, and an appearance of tongues of fire descending upon their heads. Strange: but what concern have we in it all? We require the revealing word to tell us who and what this goodly child was, why He lived and what He wrought by His death, what it meant that He could not be holden of the grave, and what those cloven tongues of flame signified—before they can avail as redemptive facts to us. No earthly person knew, or could know, their import. No earthly insight was capable of divining it. No earthly authority could assure the world of any presumed meaning attached to them. None but God was in a position to know or assert their real significance. Only, then, as God spake through His servants, the prophets and apostles, could the mighty deeds by which He would save the world be given a voice and a message—be transformed into a gospel. And so the supernatural word receives its necessary position among the redemptive acts as their interpretation and their complement. . . .

The Christian man is not the product of the regenerative forces of nature under however divine a direction; he is not an "evolution" out of the natural man: he is a new creation. He has not made himself by however wary a walk, letting the ape and tiger die and cherishing his higher ideals until they become dominant in his life; he is not merely the old man improved: he is a new man, recreated in Christ Jesus by the almighty power of the Holy Spirit—by a power comparable only to that by which God raised Jesus Christ from the dead. As well might it be contended that Lazarus, not only came forth from the tomb, but rose from the dead by his own will and at his own motion, as that the Christian man not only of his own desire works out his salvation with fear and trembling, in the knowledge that it is God who is working in him both the willing and the doing according to His own good pleasure, but has even initiated that salvation in his soul by an act of his own will and accord. He lives by virtue of the life that has been given him, and prior to the inception of that life, of course, he has no power of action: and it is of the utmost importance that as Christian men we should not lower our testimony to this true supernaturalness of our salvation. We confess that it was God who made us men: let us confess with equal heartiness that it is God who makes us Christians.

The Inspiration of Scripture*

Inspiration is that extraordinary, supernatural influence (or, passively, the result of it,) exerted by the Holy Ghost on the writers of our Sacred Books, by which their words were rendered also the words of God, and, therefore, perfectly infallible. In this definition, it is to be noted: 1st. That this influence is a supernatural one—something different from the inspiration of the poet or man of genius. Luke's accuracy is not left by it with only the safeguards which "the diligent and accurate Suetonius" had. 2d. That it is an extraordinary influence—something different from the ordinary action of the Spirit in the conversion and sanctifying guidance of believers. Paul had some more prevalent safeguard against false-teaching than Luther or even the saintly Rutherford. 3d. That it is such an influence as makes the words written under

* From Benjamin B. Warfield, *The Inspiration and Authority of the Bible*. Philadelphia: Presbyterian and Reformed Publishing Company, 1948. Pages 420–422 are reproduced by permission of the publisher.

its guidance, the words of God; by which is meant to be affirmed an absolute infallibility (as alone fitted to divine words), admitting no degrees whatever—extending to the very word, and to all the words. So that every part of Holy Writ is thus held alike infallibly true in all its statements, of whatever kind.

Fencing around and explaining this definition, it is to be remarked further:

1st. That it purposely declares nothing as to the mode of inspiration. The Reformed Churches admit that this is inscrutable. They content themselves with defining carefully and holding fast the effects of the divine influence, leaving the mode of divine action by which it is brought about draped in mystery.

2d. It is purposely so framed as to distinguish it from revelation;—seeing that it has to do with the communication of truth not its acquirement.

3d. It is by no means to be imagined that it is meant to proclaim a mechanical theory of inspiration. The Reformed Churches have never held such a theory: though dishonest, careless, ignorant or over eager controverters of its doctrine have often brought the charge. Even those special theologians in whose teeth such an accusation has been oftenest thrown (e.g., Gaussen) are explicit in teaching that the human element is never absent. The Reformed Churches hold, indeed, that every word of the Scriptures, without exception, is the word of God; but, alongside of that, they hold equally explicitly that every word is the word of man. And, therefore, though strong and uncompromising in resisting the attribution to the Scriptures of any failure in absolute truth and infallibility, they are before all others in seeking, and finding, and gazing on in loving rapture, the marks of the fervid impetuosity of a Paul—the tender saintliness of a John—the practical genius of a James, in the writings which through them the Holy Ghost has given for our guidance. Though strong and uncompromising in resisting all effort to separate the human and divine, they distance all competitors in giving honor alike to both by proclaiming in one breath that all is divine and all is human. As Gaussen so well expresses it, "We all hold that every verse, without exception, is from men, and every verse, without exception, is from God"; "every word of the Bible is as really from man as it is from God."

4th. Nor is this a mysterious doctrine—except, indeed, in the sense in which everything supernatural is mysterious. We are not dealing in puzzles, but in the plainest facts of spiritual experience. How close, indeed, is the analogy here with all that we know of the Spirit's action in other spheres! Just as the first act of loving faith by which the regenerated soul flows out of itself to its Saviour, is at once the consciously-chosen act of that soul and the direct work of the Holy Ghost; so, every word indited under the analogous influence of inspiration was at one and the same time the consciously self-chosen word of the writer and the divine-inspired word of the Spirit. I cannot help thinking that it is through failure to note and assimilate this fact, that the doctrine of verbal inspiration is so summarily set aside and so unthinkingly inveighed against by divines otherwise cautious and reverent. Once grasp this idea, and how impossible is it to separate in any measure the human and divine. It is all human—every word, and all divine. The human characteristics are to be noted and exhibited; the divine perfection and infallibility, no less.

This, then, is what we understand by the church doctrine:—a doctrine which claims that by a special, supernatural, extraordinary influence of the Holy Ghost, the sacred writers have been guided in their writing in such a way, as while their humanity was not susperseded, it was yet so dominated that their words became at the same time the words of God, and thus, in every case and all alike, absolutely infallible.

KARL BARTH (1886–)

Karl Barth, though educated in Germany, has had his pastoral and teaching career primarily in Switzerland. Since 1935 he has been Professor of Theology at the University of Basel. There he has attracted students from all over the Protestant world. The publication of his *Roemerbrief (Commentary on Romans)* in 1919 proved to be a theological bombshell. The very strong tendency in contemporary Protestant theology to return to the categories and insights of the Reformation is usually dated by the appearance of that book. With his insistence upon revelation as the only avenue to knowledge of God, and upon grace as the only cure for sin, Karl Barth has been a consistent and potent critic of liberalism in theology. These themes are present in all his writings and are worked out thoroughly in his most important contribution, the massive *Church Dogmatics.*

Revelation and Faith*

[In the passage given below Barth speaks of *dogmatics;* this term is not very familiar in America, where one would perhaps say "systematic theology." Also, note that the German term *Wissenschaft* (here translated "science") means systematic human knowledge generally and is not confined to the natural sciences. Barth holds that in every science the fundamental axioms used to guide its investigations and judge its results *cannot be proven;* so in theology, for example, it is axiomatic that the Holy Scriptures constitute the regulative norm.]

The Task

Dogmatics is the science in which the Church, in accordance with the state of its knowledge at different times, takes account of the content of its proclamation critically, that is, by the standard of Holy Scripture and under the guidance of its Confessions.

Dogmatics is a science. What science really is has already been pondered, discussed and written about infinitely often and at all periods. We cannot develop this discussion even allusively here. I offer you a concept of science which is at any rate discussible and may serve as the basis for our expositions. I propose that by science we understand an attempt at comprehension and exposition, at investigation and instruction, which is related to a definite object and sphere of activity. No act of man can claim to be more than an attempt, not even science. By describing it as an attempt, we are simply stating its nature as preliminary and limited. Wherever science is taken in practice completely seriously, we are under no illusion that anything man can do can ever be an undertaking of supreme wisdom and final art, that there exists an absolute science, one that as it were has fallen from Heaven. Even Christian dogmatics is an attempt—an attempt to understand and an attempt to expound, an attempt to see, to hear and to state definite facts, to survey and co-ordinate these facts, to present them in the form of a doctrine. In every science an object is involved and a sphere of activity. In no science is it a matter of pure theory or pure practice; on the one hand, theory comes in, but also, on the other hand, practice guided by this theory. So by dogmatics, too, we understand this twofold activity of investigation and doctrine in relation to an object and a sphere of activity.

In the science of dogmatics the Church draws up its reckoning in accordance with the state of its knowledge at different times. It might be

* From Karl Barth, *Dogmatics in Outline,* translated from the German by G. T. Thomson. New York: Philosophical Library, 1947. Pages 9–13, 15, 17–18 and 22–24 are reproduced by permission of the publisher.

said that this is quite obvious, given the premised concept of science. But it is not so automatically obvious, according to certain ideas about dogmatics which many have in their heads. I repeat that dogmatics is not a thing which has fallen from Heaven to earth. And if someone were to say that it would be wonderful if there were such an absolute dogmatics fallen from Heaven, the only possible answer would be: "Yes, if we were angels." But since by God's will we are not, it will be good for us to have just a human and earthly dogmatics. The Christian Church does not exist in Heaven, but on earth and in time. And although it is a gift of God, He has set it right amid earthly and human circumstances, and to that fact corresponds absolutely everything that happens in the Church. The Christian Church lives on earth and it lives in history, with the lofty good entrusted to it by God. In the possession and administration of this lofty good it passes on its way through history, in strength and in weakness, in faithfulness and in unfaithfulness, in obedience and in disobedience, in understanding and in misunderstanding of what is said to it. Amid the history unfolded upon earth, for example, that of nature and civilization, of morals and religion, of art and science, of society and the State, there is also a history of the Church. It too is a human, earthly history; and so it is not quite indefensible for Goethe to say of it that in all periods it has been a hotchpotch of error and power. If we Christians are sincere, we have to concede that this holds no less of Church history than of world history. That being so, we have cause to speak modestly and humbly of what the Church is capable of, and therefore also of the Church work that we are doing here—namely, dogmatics. Dogmatics will always be able to fulfill its task only in accordance with the state of the Church at different times. It is because the Church is conscious of its limitations that it owes a reckoning and a responsibility to the good it has to administer and to cherish, and to the good One who has entrusted this good to it. . . .

As a science dogmatics takes account of the content of proclamation in the Christian Church. There would be no dogmatics and there would perhaps be no theology at all, unless the Church's task consisted centrally in the proclamation of the Gospel in witness to the Word spoken by God. What as Christians do we really have to say? For undoubtedly the Church should be the place where a word reverberates right into the world. . . .

Dogmatics is a critical science. So it cannot be held, as is sometimes thought, that it is a matter of stating certain old or even new propositions that one can take home in black and white. On the contrary, if there exists a critical science at all, which is constantly having to begin at the beginning, dogmatics is that science. Outwardly, of course, dogmatics arises from the fact that the Church's proclamation is in danger of going astray. Dogmatics is the testing of Church doctrine and proclamation, not an arbitrary testing from a freely chosen standpoint, but from the standpoint of the Church which in this case is the solely relevant standpoint. The concrete significance of this is that dogmatics measures the Church's proclamation by the standard of the Holy Scriptures, of the Old and New Testaments. Holy Scripture is the document of the basis, of the innermost life of the Church, the document of the manifestation of the Word of God in the person of Jesus Christ. We have no other document for this living basis of the Church; and where the Church is alive, it will always be having to reassess itself by this standard. We cannot pursue dogmatics without this standard being kept in sight. We must always be putting the question, "What is the evidence?" Not the evidence of my thoughts, or my heart, but the evidence of the apostles and prophets, as the evidence of God's self-evidence. Should a dogmatics lose sight of this standard, it would be an irrelevant dogmatics. . . .

Faith as Trust

Christian faith is the gift of the meeting in which men become free to hear the word of grace which God has spoken in Jesus Christ in such a way that, in spite of all that contradicts it, they may once for all, exclusively and entirely, hold to His promise and guidance. . . .

. . . Freedom is God's great gift, the gift of meeting with Him. Why a gift, and why a gift of freedom? What it means is that this meeting of which the Creed speaks does not take place in vain. It rests not upon a human possibility and human initiative, nor on the fact that we men bear in us a capacity to meet God, to hear His Word. Were we to reckon up for ourselves what we men are capable of, we should strive in vain to discover anything which might be termed a disposition toward the Word of God. Without any possibility on our side God's great possibility comes into view, making possible what is impossible from our side. It is God's gift, God's free gift, not prepared for by anything on our side, if we meet Him and in meeting with Him hear His Word. The Creed of the Father, Son and Holy Spirit speaks in all three articles of a nature and work absolutely new to us men, inaccessible and inconceivable to us. And as this nature and work of God the Father, the Son and the Holy Spirit is His free grace towards us, it is grace all over again if our eyes and ears are opened to this grace. As it is the mystery of God of which the Creed speaks, we are set in its midst when it is disclosed to us, when we become free to know it and to live in it. "I believe that not of my own reason and power do I believe in my Lord or am able to come to Him," says Luther. I believe; so then, it is itself a recognition of faith, to recognize that God is to be known only through God Himself. . . . That which I do in believing is the only thing left me, to which I have been invited, to which I have been made free by Him who can do what I can neither begin nor accomplish of myself. I make use of the gift in which God has given me Himself. I breathe, and now I breathe joyfully and freely in the freedom which I have not taken to myself, which I have not sought nor found by myself, but in which God has come to me and adopted me. . . .

Faith as Knowledge

Christian faith is the illumination of the reason in which men become free to live in the truth of Jesus Christ and thereby to become sure also of the meaning of their own existence and of the ground and goal of all that happens.

Possibly you may be struck by the emergence of the concept of reason. I use it deliberately. The saying, "Despise only reason and science, man's supremest power of all," was uttered not by a prophet, but by Goethe's Mephisto. Christendom and the theological world were always ill-advised in thinking it their duty for some reason or other, either of enthusiasm or of theological conception, to betake themselves to the camp of an opposition to reason. Over the Christian Church, as the essence of revelation and of the work of God which constitues its basis, stands the Word: "The Word was made flesh," The Logos became man. Church proclamation is language, and language not of an accidental, arbitrary, chaotic and incomprehensible kind, but language which comes forward with the claim to be true and to uphold itself as the truth against the lie. Do not let us be forced from the clarity of this position. . . . Church proclamation, theology, is no talk or babbling; it is not propaganda unable to withstand the claim. Is it then true as well, this that is said? Is it really so? . . .

But once this is established, it must also be said that Christian faith is concerned with an illumination of the reason. Christian faith has to do with the object, with God the Father, the Son, and the Holy Spirit, of which the Creed speaks. Of course it is of the nature and being of this object, of God the Father, the Son, and the Holy Spirit, that He cannot be known by the powers of human knowledge, but is apprehensible and apprehended solely because of His own freedom, decision and action. What man can know by his own power according to the measure of his natural powers, his understanding, his feeling, will be at most something like a supreme being, an absolute nature, the idea of an utterly free power, of a being towering over everything. This absolute and supreme being, the ultimate and most profound, this "thing in itself," has nothing to do with God. It is part of the intuitions and marginal possibilities of man's thinking, man's contrivance. Man is able to think this being; but he has not thereby thought God. God is thought and known when in His own freedom God makes Himself apprehensible. We shall have to speak later about God, His being and His nature, but we must now say that God is always the One who has made Himself known to man in His own revelation, and not the one man thinks out for himself and describes as God.

The Humanity of God*

Who God is and what He is in His deity He proves and reveals not in a vacuum as a divine being-for-Himself, but precisely and authentically in the fact that He exists, speaks, and acts as the *partner* of man, though of course as the absolutely superior partner. He who does *that* is the living God. And the freedom in which He does *that* is His deity. It is the deity which as such also has the character of humanity. . . . It is precisely God's *deity* which, rightly understood, includes his *humanity*.

How do we come to know that? What permits and requires this statement? It is a *Christological* statement, or rather one grounded in and to be unfolded from Christology. . . . Certainly in *Jesus Christ,* as He is attested in Holy Scripture, we are not dealing with man in the abstract: not with the man who is able with his modicum of religion and religious morality to be sufficient unto himself without God and thus himself to be God. But neither are we dealing with *God* in the abstract: not with one who in His deity exists only separated from man, distant and strange and thus a non-human if not indeed an inhuman God. In Jesus Christ there is no isolation of man from God or of God from man. Rather, in Him we encounter the history, the dialogue, in which God and man meet together and are together, the reality of the covenant *mutually* contracted, preserved, and fulfilled by them. Jesus Christ is in His one Person, as true *God, man's* loyal partner, and as true *man, God's*. He is the Lord humbled for communion with man and likewise the Servant exalted to communion with God. He is the Word spoken from the loftiest, most luminous transcendence and likewise the Word heard in the deepest, darkest immanence. He is both, without their being confused but also without their being divided; He is wholly the one and wholly the other. Thus in this oneness Jesus Christ is the Mediator, the Reconciler, between God and man. Thus He comes forward to *man* on behalf of *God* calling for and awakening faith, love, and hope, and to *God* on behalf of *man,* representing man, making satisfaction and interceding. Thus He attests and guarantees to man God's free *grace* and at the same time attests and guarantees to God man's free *gratitude*. Thus He establishes in His Person the justice of God vis-à-vis man and also the justice of man before God. Thus He is in His Person the covenant in its fullness, the Kingdom of heaven which is at hand, in which God speaks and man hears, God gives and man receives, God commands and man obeys, God's glory shines in the heights and thence into the depths, and peace on earth comes to pass among men in whom He is well pleased. Moreover, exactly in this way Jesus Christ, as this Mediator and Reconciler between God and man, is also the *Revealer* of them both. We do not need to engage in a free-ranging investigation to seek out and construct who and what God truly is, and who and what man truly is, but only to read the truth about both where it resides, namely, in the fullness of their togetherness, their covenant which proclaims itself in Jesus Christ.

Who and what *God* is—this is what in particular we have to learn better. . . . But the question must be, who and what is God *in Jesus Christ,* if we here today would push forward to a better answer.

Beyond doubt God's *deity* is the first and fundamental fact that strikes us when we look at the existence of Jesus Christ as attested in the Holy Scripture. And God's deity in Jesus Christ consists in the fact that God Himself in Him is the *subject* who speaks and acts with sovereignty. *He* is the free One in whom all freedom has its ground, its meaning, its prototype. *He* is the initiator, founder, preserver, and fulfiller of the covenant. . . . In the existence of Jesus Christ, the fact that God speaks, gives, orders, comes absolutely first—that man hears, receives, obeys, can and must only follow this first act. In Jesus Christ man's freedom is wholly enclosed in the freedom of God. Without the condescension of God there would be

* From Karl Barth, *The Humanity of God,* translated by John Newton Thomas and Thomas Wieser. Richmond, Virginia: John Knox Press, 1960. Pages 45–49, 51, and 52–55 are reproduced by permission of the publisher.

no exaltation of man. As the Son of God and not otherwise, Jesus Christ is the Son of Man. This sequence is irreversible. . . . Thus we have here no universal deity capable of being reached conceptually, but this concrete deity—real and recognizable in the *descent* grounded in that sequence and peculiar to the existence of Jesus Christ.

But here there is something even more concrete to be seen. God's high freedom in Jesus Christ is His freedom for *love*. The divine capacity which operates and exhibits itself in that superiority and subordination is manifestly also God's capacity to bend downwards, to attach Himself to another and this other to Himself, to be together with him. This takes place in that irreversible sequence, but in it is completely real. In that sequence there arises and continues in Jesus Christ the highest communion of God with man. God's deity is thus no prison in which He can exist only in and for Himself. It is rather His freedom to be in and for Himself but also with and for us, to assert but also to sacrifice Himself, to be wholly exalted but also completely humble, not only almighty but also almighty mercy, not only Lord but also servant, not only judge but also Himself the judged, not only man's eternal king but also his brother in time. . . .

In this divinely free volition and election, in this sovereign decision (the ancients said, in His decree), God is *human*. His free affirmation of man, His free concern for him, His free substitution for him—this is God's humanity. We recognize it exactly at the point where we also first recognize His deity. Is it not true that in Jesus Christ, as He is attested in the Holy Scripture, genuine deity includes in itself genuine humanity? There is the father who cares for his lost son, the king who does the same for his insolvent debtor, the Samaritan who takes pity on the one who fell among robbers and in his thoroughgoing act of compassion cares for him in a fashion as unexpected as it is liberal. And this is the act of compassion to which all these parables as parables of the Kingdom of heaven refer. The very One who speaks in these parables takes to His heart the weakness and the perversity, the helplessness and the misery, of the human race surrounding Him. He does not despise men, but in an inconceivable manner esteems them highly just as they are, takes them into His heart and sets Himself in their place. He perceives that the superior will of God, to which He wholly subordinates Himself, requires that He sacrifice Himself for the human race, and seeks His honor in doing this. . . .

From the fact that God is human in the sense described, there follows first of all a quite definite *distinction* of *man* as such. It is a distinction of every being which bears the human countenance. This includes the whole stock of those capacities and possibilities which are in part common to man and to other creatures, and in part peculiar to him, and likewise man's work and his productions. The acknowledgment of this distinction has nothing to do with an optimistic judgment of man. It is due him because he is the being whom God willed to exalt as His covenant-partner, not otherwise. But just because God is human in this sense, it is actually *due* man and may not be denied him through any pessimistic judgment, whatever its basis. On the basis of the eternal will of God we have to think of *every human being*, even the oddest, most villainous or miserable, as one to whom Jesus Christ is Brother and God is Father; and we have to deal with him on this assumption. If the other person knows that already, then we have to strengthen him in the knowledge. If he does not know it yet or no longer knows it, our business is to transmit this knowledge to him. On the basis of the knowledge of the humanity of God no other attitude to any kind of fellow man is possible. It is identical with the practical acknowledgment of his human rights and his human dignity. To deny it to him would be for us to renounce having Jesus Christ as Brother and God as Father.

The distinction due to man as such through the humanity of God, however, extends also to everything with which man as man is endowed and equipped by God, his Creator. This gift, his humanity, is not blotted out through the fall of man, nor is its goodness diminished. Man is not elected to intercourse with God because, by virtue of his humanity, he deserved such preference. He is elected through God's grace alone. He is elected, however, as the being especially endowed by God. This is manifest in his special bodily nature, in which he of course has ever so much in common with plant and animal, and also in the fact that he is a rationally thinking, willing, and speaking being destined for responsible and spontaneous decision. Above all, however, it is shown in the fact that from the beginning he is constituted, bound, and obligated as a fellow man. God concerns Himself with, loves, and calls him as *this* being in his particular totality. In bringing into action his particular nature man, as *this* being, may and should praise Him and be submissive to His grace in thankfulness. It would not do even partially to cast suspicion upon, undervalue, or speak ill of his humanity, the gift of God, which characterizes him as this being. We can meet God only within the limits of humanity determined by Him. But in these limits we may meet Him. He does not reject the human! Quite the contrary! We must hold fast to this.

The distinction of man, however, goes still further. It extends itself indeed even to the particular human activity based on his endowment, to what one is accustomed to call human *culture* in its higher and lower levels. . . . What is culture in itself except the attempt of man to be man and thus to hold the good gift of his humanity in honor and to put it to work? That in this attempt he ever and again runs aground and even accomplishes the opposite is a problem in itself, but one which in no way alters the fact that this attempt is inevitable. Above all, the fact remains that the *man* who, either as the creator or as the beneficiary, somehow participates in this attempt is the being who interests God. Finally, it also remains true that God, as Creator and Lord of man, is always free to produce even in human activity and its results, in spite of the problems involved, *parables* of His own eternal good will and actions. It is more than ever true, then, that with regard to these no proud abstention but only reverence, joy, and gratitude are appropriate.

RUDOLF BULTMANN (1884–)

No single New Testament scholar has had a greater influence in recent years than Rudolf Bultmann. He was educated and has taught in Germany. As one of the founders of "form criticism" in biblical research, he challenged many traditional concepts regarding the Scriptures. Since 1940 Protestant thinking about the Bible has been much occupied with a problem raised in acute form by Bultmann: how is a modern man to understand the Bible in view of the fact that it relies so heavily upon ancient mythological concepts? It is to this question that the following selection addresses itself.

Mythology and the Message of Jesus*

The Message of Jesus and the Problem of Mythology

The heart of the preaching of Jesus Christ is the Kingdom of God. During the nineteenth century exegesis and theology understood the Kingdom of God as a spiritual community consisting of men joined together by obedience to the will of God which ruled in their wills. By such obedience they sought to enlarge the sphere of His rule in the world. They were building, it was said, the Kingdom of God as a realm which is spiritual but within the world, active and effective in this world, unfolding in the history of this world.

The year 1892 saw the publication of *The Preaching of Jesus about the Kingdom of God* by Johannes Weiss. This epoch-making book refuted the interpretation which was hitherto generally accepted. Weiss showed that the King-

* Reprinted with the permission of Charles Scribner's Sons from *Jesus Christ and Mythology*, pp. 11–12, 12–13, 14–15, 16, 17–18, 19, 20, 20–21, 21–23, 25–26, 29, 31–32, 33–36, 38–39, 39–40, 43–44, by Rudolf Bultmann.

dom of God is not immanent in the world and does not grow as part of the world's history, but is rather eschatological; i.e., the Kingdom of God transcends the historical order. It will come into being not through the moral endeavour of man, but solely through the supernatural action of God. God will suddenly put an end to the world and to history, and He will bring in a new world, the world of eternal blessedness. . . .

Jesus expected that this would take place soon, in the immediate future, and he said that the dawning of that age could already be perceived in the signs and wonders which he performed, especially in his casting out of demons. Jesus envisaged the inauguration of the Kingdom of God as a tremendous cosmic drama. The Son of Man will come with the clouds of heaven, the dead will be raised and the day of judgment will arrive; for the righteous the time of bliss will begin, whereas the damned will be delivered to the torments of hell. . . .

This hope of Jesus and of the early Christian community was not fulfilled. The same world still exists and history continues. The course of history has refuted mythology. For the conception "Kingdom of God" is mythological, as is the conception of the eschatological drama. Just as mythological are the presuppositions of the expectation of the Kingdom of God, namely, the theory that the world, although created by God, is ruled by the devil, Satan, and that his army, the demons, is the cause of all evil, sin and disease. The whole conception of the world which is presupposed in the preaching of Jesus as in the New Testament generally is mythological; i.e., the conception of the world as being structured in three stories, heaven, earth and hell; the conception of the intervention of supernatural powers in the course of events; and the conception of miracles, especially the conception of the intervention of supernatural powers in the inner life of the soul, the conception that men can be tempted and corrupted by the devil and possessed by evil spirits. This conception of the world we call mythological because it is different from the conception of the world which has been formed and developed by science since its inception in ancient Greece and which has been accepted by all modern men. In this modern conception of the world the cause-and-effect nexus is fundamental. Although modern physical theories take account of chance in the chain of cause and effect in subatomic phenomena, our daily living, purposes and actions are not affected. In any case, modern science does not believe that the course of nature can be interrupted or, so to speak, perforated, by supernatural powers. . . .

Then the question inevitably arises: is it possible that Jesus' preaching of the Kingdom of God still has any importance for modern men and the preaching of the New Testament as a whole is still important for modern men? . . .

. . . Is it possible to expect that we shall make a sacrifice of understanding, *sacrificium intellectus,* in order to accept what we cannot sincerely consider true—merely because such conceptions are suggested by the Bible? Or ought we to pass over those sayings of the New Testament which contain such mythological conceptions and to select other sayings which are not such stumbling-blocks to modern man? In fact, the preaching of Jesus is not confined to eschatological sayings. He proclaimed also the will of God, which is God's demand, the demand for the good. Jesus demands truthfulness and purity, readiness to sacrifice and to love. He demands that the whole man be obedient to God, and he protests against the delusion that one's duty to God can be fulfilled by obeying certain external commandments. If the ethical demands of Jesus are stumbling-blocks to modern man, then it is to his selfish will, not to his understanding, that they are stumbling-blocks.

What follows from all this? Shall we retain the ethical preaching of Jesus and abandon his eschatological preaching? Shall we reduce his preaching of the Kingdom of God to the so-called social gospel? Or is there a third possibility? We must ask whether the eschatological preaching and the mythological sayings as a whole contain a still deeper meaning which is concealed under the cover of mythology. If that is so, let us abandon the mythological conceptions precisely because we want to retain their deeper meaning. This method of interpretation of the New Testament which tries to recover the deeper meaning behind the mythological conceptions I call *de-mythologizing*—an unsatisfactory word, to be sure. Its aim is not to eliminate the mythological statements but to interpret them. . . .

Mythology expresses a certain understanding of human existence. It believes that the world and human life have their ground and their limits in a power which is beyond all that we can calculate or control. Mythology speaks about this power inadequately and insufficiently because it speaks about it as if it were a worldly power. It speaks of gods who represent the power beyond the visible, comprehensible world. It speaks of gods as if they were men and of their actions as human actions, although it conceives of the gods as endowed with superhuman power and of their actions as incalculable, as capable of breaking the normal, ordinary order of events. It may be said that myths give to the transcendent reality an immanent, this-worldly objectivity. Myths give worldly objectivity to that which is unworldly. . . .

All this holds true also of the mythological conceptions found in the Bible. According to mythological thinking, God has his domicile in heaven. What is the meaning of this statement? The meaning is quite clear. In a crude manner it expresses the idea that God is beyond the world, that He is transcendent. The thinking which is not yet capable of forming the abstract idea of transcendence expresses its intention in the category of space; the transcendent God is imagined as being at an immense spatial distance, far above the world: for above this world is the world of the stars, of the light which enlightens and makes glad the life of men. . . .

Another example is the conception of Satan and the evil spirits into whose power men are delivered. This conception rests upon the experience, quite apart from the inexplicable evils arising outside ourselves to which we are exposed, that our own actions are often so puzzling; men are often carried away by their passions and are no longer master of themselves, with the result that inconceivable wickedness breaks forth from them. Again, the conception of Satan as ruler over the world expresses a deep insight, namely, the insight that evil is not only to be found here and there in the world, but that all particular evils make up one single power which in the last analysis grows from the very actions of men, which form an atmosphere, a spiritual tradition, which overwhelms every man. . . .

Now the question arises: is it possible to demythologize the message of Jesus and the preaching of the early Christian community? Since this preaching was shaped by the eschatological belief, the first question is this: *What is the meaning of eschatology in general?*

The Interpretation of Mythological Eschatology

In the language of traditional theology eschatology is the doctrine of the last things, and "last" means last in the course of time, that is, the end of the world which is imminent as the future is to our present. But in the actual preaching of the prophets and of Jesus this "last" has a further meaning. As in the conception of heaven the transcendence of God is imagined by means of the category of space, so in the conception of the end of the world, the idea of the transcendence of God is imagined by means of the category of time. However, it is not simply the idea of transcendence as such, but of the importance of the transcendence of God, of God who is never present as a familiar phenomenon but who is always the coming God, who is veiled by the unknown future. Eschatological preaching views the present time in the light of the future and it says to men that this present world, the world of nature and history, the world in which we live our lives and make our plans is not the only world; that this world is temporal and transitory, yes, ultimately empty and unreal in the face of eternity.

. . . It is possible that the Biblical eschatology may rise again. It will not rise in its old mythological form but from the terrifying vision that modern technology, especially atomic science, may bring about the destruction of our earth through the abuse of human science and technology. When we ponder this possibility, we can feel the terror and the anxiety which were evoked by the eschatological preaching of the imminent end of the world. To be sure, that preaching was developed in conceptions which are no longer intelligible today, but they do express the knowledge of the finiteness of the world, and of the end which is imminent to us all because we all are beings of this finite world. This is the insight to which as a rule we turn a blind eye, but which may be brought to light by modern technology. It is precisely the intensity of this insight which explains why Jesus, like the Old Testament prophets, expected the end of the world to occur in the immediate future. The majesty of God and the inescapability of His judgment, and over against these the emptiness of the world and of men were felt with such an intensity that it seemed that the world was at an end, and that the hour of crisis was present. Jesus proclaims the will of God and the responsibility of man, pointing towards the eschatological events, but it is not because he is an eschatologist that he proclaims the will of God. On the contrary, he is an eschatologist because he proclaims the will of God.

The difference between the Biblical and the Greek understanding of the human situation regarding the unknown future can now be seen in a clearer light. It consists in the fact that in the thinking of the prophets and of Jesus the nature of God involves more than simply His omnipotence and His judgment touches not only the man who offends Him by presumption and boasting. For the prophets and for Jesus God is the Holy One, who demands right and righteousness, who demands love of neighbour and who therefore is the judge of all human thoughts and actions. The world is empty not only because it is transitory, but because men have turned it into a place in which evil spreads and sin rules. The end of the world, therefore, is the judgment of God; that is, the eschatological preaching not only brings to consciousness the emptiness of the human situation and calls men, as was the case among the Greeks, to moderation, humility and resignation; it calls men first and foremost to responsibility toward God and to repentance. . . .

In Christian thinking freedom is not the freedom of a spirit who is satisfied with perceiving the truth; it is the freedom of man to be himself. Freedom is freedom from sin, from wickedness, or as St. Paul says, from the flesh, from the old self, because God is Holy. Thus, obtaining bliss means obtaining grace and righteousness by God's judgment. . . .

This, then, is the deeper meaning of the mythological preaching of Jesus—to be open to God's future which is really imminent for every one of us; to be prepared for this future which can come as a thief in the night when we do not expect it; to be prepared, because this future will be a judgment on all men who have bound themselves to this world and are not free, not open to God's future.

The eschatological preaching of Jesus was retained and continued by the early Christian community in its mythological form. But very soon the process of de-mythologizing began, partially with Paul, and radically with John. . . .

. . . John de-mythologized the eschatology in a radical manner. For John the coming and departing of Jesus is the eschatological event. "And this is the judgment, that the light has come into the world, and men loved darkness rather than light, because their deeds were evil" (John 3:19). "Now is the judgment of this world, now shall the ruler of this world be cast out" (12:31). For John the resurrection of Jesus, Pentecost and the *parousia* of Jesus are one and the same event, and those who believe have already eternal life. "He who believes in him is not condemned; he who does not believe is condemned already" (3:18). "He who believes in the Son has eternal life; he who does not obey the Son shall not see life, but the wrath of God rests upon him" (3:36). "Truly, truly, I say to you, the hour is coming, and now is, when the dead will hear the voice of the Son of God, and those who hear will live" (5:25). "I am the resurrection and the life; he who believes in me, though he die, yet shall he live; and whoever lives and believes in me shall never die" (11:25f.).

As in Paul, so in John de-mythologizing may be further observed in a particular instance. In Jewish eschatological expectations we find that the figure of the anti-Christ is a thoroughly mythological figure as it is described, for example, in II Thessalonians (2:7–12). In John false teachers play the role of this mythological figure. Mythology has been transposed into history. These examples show, it seems to me, that de-mythologizing has its beginning in the New Testament itself, and therefore our task of de-mythologizing today is justified.

The Christian Message and the Modern World-View

An objection often heard against the attempt

to de-mythologize is that it takes the modern world-view as the criterion of the interpretation of the Scripture and the Christian message and that Scripture and Christian message are not allowed to say anything that is in contradiction with the modern world-view.

It is, of course, true that de-mythologizing takes the modern world-view as a criterion. To de-mythologize is to reject not Scripture or the Christian message as a whole, but the world-view of Scripture, which is the world-view of a past epoch, which all too often is retained in Christian dogmatics and in the preaching of the Church. To de-mythologize is to deny that the message of Scripture and of the Church is bound to an ancient world-view which is obsolete.

. . . It is mere wishful thinking to suppose that the ancient world-view of the Bible can be renewed. It is the radical abandonment and the conscious critique of the mythological world-view of the Bible which bring the real stumbling-block into sharp focus. This stumbling-block is that the Word of God calls man out of all man-made security. The scientific world-view engenders a great temptation, namely, that man strive for mastery over the world and over his own life. He knows the laws of nature and can use the powers of nature according to his plans and desires. . . . Thus modern man is in danger of forgetting two things: first, that his plans and undertakings should be guided not by his own desires for happiness and security, usefulness and profit, but rather by obedient response to the challenge of goodness, truth and love, by obedience to the commandment of God which man forgets in his selfishness and presumption; and secondly, that it is an illusion to suppose that real security can be gained by men organizing their own personal and community life. There are encounters and destinies which man cannot master. He cannot secure endurance for his works. His life is fleeting and its end is death. History goes on and pulls down all the towers of Babel again and again. There is no real, definitive security, and it is precisely this illusion to which men are prone to succumb in their yearning for security.

What is the underlying reason for this yearning? It is the sorrow, the secret anxiety which moves in the depths of the soul at the very moment when man thinks that he must obtain security for himself.

It is the word of God which calls man away from his selfishness and from the illusory security which he has built up for himself. It calls him to God, who is beyond the world and beyond scientific thinking. At the same time, it calls man to his true self. For the self of man, his inner life, his personal existence is also beyond the visible world and beyond rational thinking. The Word of God addresses man in his personal existence and thereby it gives him freedom from the world and from the sorrow and anxiety which overwhelm him when he forgets the beyond. By means of science men try to take possession of the world, but in fact the world gets possession of men. We can see in our times to what degree men are dependent on technology, and to what degree technology brings with it terrible consequences. To believe in the Word of God means to abandon all merely human security and thus to overcome the despair which arises from the attempt to find security, an attempt which is always vain.

. . . Thus it follows that the objection is raised by a mistake, namely, the objection that de-mythologizing means rationalizing the Christian message, that de-mythologizing dissolves the message into a product of human rational thinking, and that the mystery of God is destroyed by de-mythologizing. Not at all! On the contrary, de-mythologizing makes clear the true meaning of God's mystery. The incomprehensibility of God lies not in the sphere of theoretical thought but in the sphere of personal existence. Not what God is in Himself, but how he acts with men, is the mystery in which faith is interested. This is a mystery not to theoretical thought, but to the natural wills and desires of men.

God's Word is not a mystery to my understanding. On the contrary, I cannot truly believe in the Word without understanding it. But to understand does not mean to explain rationally. I can understand, for example, what friendship, love and faithfulness mean, and precisely by genuinely understanding I know that the friendship, love and faithfulness which I personally enjoy are a mystery which I cannot but thankfully receive. For I perceive them neither by my rational thinking, nor by psychological, nor by anthropological analysis but only in open readiness to personal encounters. In this readiness I can understand them in a certain way already before I am given them because my personal existence needs them. Then I understand them in searching for them, in asking for them. Nevertheless, the fact itself that my yearning is fulfilled, that a friend comes to me, remains a mystery.

In the same manner I can understand what God's grace means, asking for it as long as it does not come to me, accepting it thankfully when it does come to me. The fact that it comes to me, that the gracious God is my God, remains forever a mystery, not because God performs in an irrational manner something that interrupts the natural course of events, but because it is inconceivable that He should encounter me in His Word as the gracious God.

PAUL TILLICH (1886–)

The relation of theology to various aspects of modern culture has been a special contribution of Paul Tillich. He was trained in Germany in both philosophy and theology, has gained a wide and deep acquaintance with modern art and with depth psychology, and has actively participated in social and political activities. After the First World War he became one of the leaders of the "Christian Socialist" movement in Germany. Because of these activities as well as the whole tenor of his thought, he was regarded as an enemy by the Nazis and forced to leave Germany. In 1933 he came to Union Theological Seminary in New York City, where he remained until 1954. Since then he has taught as University Professor at Harvard University.

The Dynamics of Faith*

What Faith Is

Faith is the state of being ultimately concerned: the dynamics of faith are the dynamics of man's ultimate concern. Man, like every living being, is concerned about many things, above all about those which condition his very existence, such as food and shelter. But man, in contrast to other living beings, has spiritual concerns—cognitive, aesthetic, social, political. Some of them are urgent, often extremely urgent, and each of them as well as the vital concerns can claim ultimacy for a human life or the life of a social group. If it claims ultimacy it demands the total surrender of him who accepts this claim, and it promises total fulfillment even if all other claims have to be subjected to it or rejected in its name. If a national group makes the life and growth of the nation its ultimate concern, it demands that all other concerns, economic well-being, health and life, family, aesthetic and cognitive truth, justice and humanity, be sacrificed. The extreme nationalisms of our century are laboratories for the study of what ultimate concern means in all aspects of human existence, including the smallest concern of one's daily life. Everything is centered in the only god, the nation—a god who certainly proves to be a demon, but who shows clearly the unconditional character of an ultimate concern.

But it is not only the unconditional demand made by that which is one's ultimate concern, it is also the promise of ultimate fulfillment which is accepted in the act of faith. The content of this promise is not necessarily defined. It can be expressed in indefinite symbols or in concrete symbols which cannot be taken literally, like the "greatness" of one's nation in which one participates even if one has died for it, or the conquest of mankind by the "saving race," etc. In each of these cases it is "ultimate

* From *Dynamics of Faith* by Paul Tillich. Copyright © 1957 by Paul Tillich. Reprinted by permission of Harper & Brothers. Pages 1–4, 41–52, and 99–105.

fulfillment" that is promised, and it is exclusion from such fulfillment which is threatened if the unconditional demand is not obeyed.

An example—and more than an example—is the faith manifest in the religion of the Old Testament. It also has the character of ultimate concern in demand, threat and promise. The content of this concern is not the nation—although Jewish nationalism has sometimes tried to distort it into that—but the content is the God of justice, who, because he represents justice and every nation, is called the universal God, the God of the universe. He is the ultimate concern of every pious Jew, and therefore in his name the great commandment is given: "You shall love the Lord your God with all your heart, and with all your soul, and with all your might" (Deut. 6:5). This is what ultimate concern means and from these words the term "ultimate concern" is derived. . . .

Another example—almost a counter-example, yet nevertheless equally revealing—is the ultimate concern with "success" and with social standing and economic power. It is the god of many people in the highly competitive Western culture and it does what every ultimate concern must do: it demands unconditional surrender to its laws even if the price is the sacrifice of genuine human relations, personal conviction, and creative *eros* [love]. Its threat is social and economic defeat, and its promise—indefinite as all such promises—the fulfillment of one's being. It is the breakdown of this kind of faith which characterizes and makes religiously important most contemporary literature. Not false calculations but a misplaced faith is revealed in novels like *Point of No Return.* When fulfilled, the promise of this faith proves to be empty.

Faith is the state of being ultimately concerned. The content matters infinitely for the life of the believer, but it does not matter for the formal definition of faith. And this is the first step we have to make in order to understand the dynamics of faith. . . .

Symbols of Faith

Man's ultimate concern must be expressed symbolically, because symbolic language alone is able to express the ultimate. This statement demands explanation in several respects. In spite of the manifold research about the meaning and function of symbols which is going on in contemporary philosophy, every writer who uses the term "symbol" must explain his understanding of it.

Symbols have one characteristic in common with signs; they point beyond themselves to something else. The red sign at the street corner points to the order to stop the movement of cars at certain intervals. A red light and the stopping of cars have essentially no relation to each other, but conventionally they are united as long as the convention lasts. The same is true of letters and numbers and partly even words. They point beyond themselves to sounds and meanings. They are given this special function by convention within a nation or by international conventions, as the mathematical signs. Sometimes such signs are called symbols; but this is unfortunate because it makes the distinction between signs and symbols more difficult. Decisive is the fact that signs do not participate in the reality of that to which they point, while symbols do. Therefore, signs can be replaced for reasons of expediency or convention, while symbols cannot.

This leads to the second characteristic of the symbol: It participates in that to which it points: the flag participates in the power and dignity of the nation for which it stands. Therefore, it cannot be replaced except after an historic catastrophe that changes the reality of the nation which it symbolizes. An attack on the flag is felt as an attack on the majesty of the group in which it is acknowledged. Such an attack is considered blasphemy.

The third characteristic of a symbol is that it opens up levels of reality which otherwise are closed for us. All arts create symbols for a level of reality which cannot be reached in any other way. A picture and a poem reveal elements of reality which cannot be approached scientifically. In the creative work of art we encounter reality in a dimension which is closed for us without such works. The symbol's fourth characteristic not only opens up dimensions and elements of reality which otherwise would remain unapproachable but also unlocks dimensions and elements of our soul which correspond to the dimensions and elements of reality. A great play gives us not only a new vision of the human scene, but it opens up hidden depths of our own being. Thus we are able to receive what the play reveals to us in reality. There are within us dimensions of which we cannot become aware except through symbols, as melodies and rhythms in music. . . .

We have discussed the meaning of symbols generally because, as we said, man's ultimate concern must be expressed symbolically! One may ask: Why can it not be expressed directly and properly? If money, success or the nation is someone's ultimate concern, can this not be said in a direct way without symbolic language? Is it not only in those cases in which the content of the ultimate concern is called "God" that we are in the realm of symbols? The answer is that everything which is a matter of unconditional concern is made into a god. If the nation is someone's ultimate concern, the name of the nation becomes a sacred name and the nation receives divine qualities which far surpass the reality of the being and functioning of the nation. The nation then stands for and symbolizes the true ultimate, but in an idolatrous way. . . .

The reason for this transformation of concepts into symbols is the character of ultimacy and the nature of faith. That which is the true ultimate transcends the realm of finite reality infinitely. Therefore, no finite reality can express it directly and properly. . . . Faith, understood as the state of being ultimately concerned, has no language other than symbols. When saying this I always expect the question: Only a symbol? He who asks this question shows that he has not understood the difference between signs and symbols nor the power of symbolic language, which surpasses in quality and strength the power of any nonsymbolic language. One should never say "only a symbol," but one should say "not less than a symbol." With this in mind we can now describe the different kinds of symbols of faith.

The fundamental symbol of our ultimate concern is God. It is always present in any act of faith, even if the act of faith includes the denial of God. Where there is ultimate concern, God can be denied only in the name of God. One God can deny the other one. Ultimate concern cannot deny its own character as ultimate. Therefore, it affirms what is meant by the word "God." Atheism, consequently, can only mean the attempt to remove any ultimate concern—to remain unconcerned about the meaning of one's existence. Indifference toward the ultimate question is the only imaginable form of atheism. Whether it is possible is a problem which must remain unsolved at this point. In any case, he who denies God as a matter of ultimate concern affirms God, because he affirms ultimacy in his concern. God is the fundamental symbol for what concerns us ultimately. Again it would be completely wrong to ask: So God is nothing but a symbol? Because the next question has to be: A symbol for what? And then the answer would be: For God! God is symbol for God. . . .

It is obvious that such an understanding of the meaning of God makes the discussions about the existence or non-existence of God meaningless. It is meaningless to question the ultimacy of an ultimate concern. This element in the idea of God is in itself certain. The symbolic expression of this element varies endlessly through the whole history of mankind. Here again it would be meaningless to ask whether one or another of the figures in which an ultimate concern is symbolized does "exist." If "existence" refers to something which can be found within the whole of reality, no divine being exists. The question is not this, but: which of the innumerable symbols of faith is most adequate to the meaning of faith? In other words, which symbol of ultimacy expresses the ultimate without idolatrous elements? This is the problem, and not the so-called "existence of God"—which is in itself an impossible combination of words. God as the ultimate in man's ultimate concern is more certain than any other certainty, even that of oneself. God as symbolized in a divine figure is a matter of daring faith, of courage and risk.

God is the basic symbol of faith, but not the only one. All the qualities we attribute to him, power, love, justice, are taken from finite experiences and applied symbolically to that which is beyond finitude and infinity. If faith calls God "almighty," it uses the human experience of power in order to symbolize the content of its infinite concern, but it does not describe a highest being who can do as he pleases. So it is with all the other qualities and with all the actions, past, present and future, which men attribute to God. They are symbols taken from our daily experience, and not information about what God did once upon a time or will do sometime in the future. Faith is not the belief in such stories, but it is the acceptance of symbols that express our ultimate concern in terms of divine actions.

Another group of symbols of faith are manifestations of the divine in things and events, in persons and communities, in words and documents. This whole realm of sacred objects is a treasure of symbols. Holy things are not holy in themselves, but they point beyond themselves to the source of all holiness, that which is of ultimate concern.

The symbols of faith do not appear in isolation. They are united in "stories of the gods," which is the meaning of the Greek word "mythos"—myth. . . .

Myths are always present in every act of faith, because the language of faith is the symbol. They are also attacked, criticized and transcended in each of the great religions of mankind. The reason for this criticism is the very nature of the myth. It uses material from our ordinary experience. It puts the stories of the gods into the framework of time and space although it belongs to the nature of the ultimate to be beyond time and space. . . .

A myth which is understood as a myth, but not removed or replaced, can be called a "broken myth." Christianity denies by its very nature any unbroken myth, because its presupposition is the first commandment: the affirmation of the ultimate as ultimate and the rejection of any kind of idolatry. All mythological elements in the Bible, and doctrine and liturgy should be recognized as mythological, but they should be maintained in their symbolic form and not be replaced by scientific substitutes. For there is no substitute for the use of symbols and myths: they are the language of faith.

The radical criticism of the myth is due to the fact that the primitive mythological consciousness resists the attempt to interpret the myth of myth. It is afraid of every act of demythologization. It believes that the broken myth is deprived of its truth and of its convincing power. Those who live in an unbroken mythological world feel safe and certain. They resist, often fanatically, any attempt to introduce an element of uncertainty by "breaking the myth," namely, by making conscious its symbolic character. Such resistance is supported by authoritarian systems, religious or political, in order to give security to the people under their control and unchallenged power to those who exercise the control. The resistance against demythologization expresses itself in "literalism." The symbols and myths are understood in their immediate meaning. The material, taken from nature and history, is used in its proper sense. The character of the symbol to point beyond itself to something else is disregarded. Creation is taken as a magic act which happened once upon a time. The fall of Adam is localized on a special geographical point and attributed to a human individual. The virgin birth of the Messiah is understood in biological terms, resurrection and ascension as physical events, the second coming of the Christ as a telluric, or cosmic, catastrophe. The presupposition of such literalism is that God is a being, acting in time and space, dwelling in a special place, affecting the course of events and being affected by them like any other being in the universe. Literalism deprives God of his ultimacy and, religiously speaking, of his majesty. It draws him down to the level of that which is not ultimate, the finite and conditional. In the last analysis it is not rational criticism of the myth which is decisive but the inner religious criticism. Faith, if it takes its symbols literally, becomes idolatrous! It calls something ultimate which is less than ultimate. Faith, conscious of the symbolic character of its symbols, gives God the honor which is due him. . . .

The Life of Faith

Everything said about faith in the previous chapters is derived from the experience of actual faith, of faith as a living reality, or in a metaphoric abbreviation, of the life of faith. This experience is the subject of our last chapter. The "dynamics of faith" are present not only in the inner tensions and conflicts of the content of faith, but also present in the life of faith, and of course the one is dependent on the other.

Where there is faith there is tension between participation and separation, between the faithful one and his ultimate concern. We have used the metaphor "being grasped" for describing the state of ultimate concern. And being grasped implies that he who is grasped and that by which he is grasped are, so to speak, at the same place. Without some participation in the object of one's ultimate concern, it is not possible to be concerned about it. In this sense every act of faith presupposes participation in that toward which it is directed. Without a preceding experience of the ultimate no faith in the ultimate can exist. The mystical type of faith has emphasized this point most strongly. Here lies its truth which no theology of "mere faith" can destroy. Without the manifestation of God in man the question of God and faith in God are not possible. There is no faith without participation!

But faith would cease to be faith without separation—the opposite element. He who has faith is separated from the object of his faith. Otherwise he would possess it. It would be a matter of immediate certainty and not of faith. The "in-spite-of element" of faith would be lacking. But the human situation, its finitude and estrangement, prevents man's participation in the ultimate without both the separation and the promise of faith. Here the limit of mysticism becomes visible: it neglects the human predicament and the separation of man from the ultimate. There is no faith without separation.

Out of the element of participation follows the certainty of faith; out of the element of separation follows the doubt in faith. And each is essential for the nature of faith. Sometimes certainty conquers doubt, but it cannot eliminate doubt. The conquered of today may become the conqueror of tomorrow. Sometimes doubt conquers faith, but it still contains faith. Otherwise it would be indifference. Neither faith nor doubt can be eliminated, though each of them can be reduced to a minimum, in the life of faith. Since the life of faith is life in the state of ultimate concern and no human being can exist completely without such a concern, we can say: Neither faith nor doubt can be eliminated from man as man.

Faith and doubt have been contrasted in such a way that the quiet certainty of faith has been praised as the complete removal of doubt. There is, indeed, a serenity of the life in faith beyond the disturbing struggles between faith and doubt. To attain such a state is a natural and justified desire of every human being. But even if it is attained—as in people who are called saints or in others who are described as firm in their faith—the element of doubt, though conquered, is not lacking. In the saints it appears, according to holy legend, as a temptation which increases in power with the increase of saintliness. In those who rest on their unshakable faith, pharisaism and fanaticism are the unmistakable symptoms of doubt which has been repressed. Doubt is overcome not by repression but by courage. Courage does not deny that there is doubt, but it takes the doubt into itself as an expression of its own finitude and affirms the content of an ultimate concern. Courage does not need the safety of an unquestionable conviction. It includes the risk without which no creative life is possible. For example, if the content of someone's ultimate concern is Jesus as the Christ, such faith is not a matter of a doubtless certainty, it is a matter of daring courage with the risk to fail. Even if the confession that Jesus is the Christ is expressed in a strong and positive way, the fact that it is a confession implies courage and risk.

All this is said of living faith, of faith as actual concern, and not of faith as a traditional attitude without tensions, without doubt and without courage. Faith in this sense, which is the attitude of many members of the churches as well as of society at large, is far removed from the dynamic character of faith as described in this book. One could say that such conventional faith is the dead remnant of former experiences of ultimate concern. It is dead but it can become alive. For even nondynamic faith lives in symbols. In these symbols the power of original faith is still embodied. . . .

To the state of separated finitude belong faith and the courage to risk. The risk of faith is the concrete content of one's ultimate concern. But it may not be the truly ultimate about which one is concerned. Religiously speaking, there may be an idolatrous element in one's faith. It may be one's own wishful thinking which determines the content; it may be the interest of one's social group which holds us in an obsolete tradition; it may be a piece of reality which is not sufficient to express man's ultimate concern, as in old and new polytheism; it may be an attempt to use the ultimate for one's own purposes, as in magic practices and prayers in all religions. It may be the confusion of the bearer of the ultimate with the ultimate itself. This is done in all types of faith and has been, from the first gospel stories on, the permanent danger of Christianity. A protest against such a confusion is found in the Fourth Gospel, which has Jesus say: "He who believes in me does not believe in me but in him who has sent me." But the classical dogma, the liturgies and the devotional life are not kept free from it. Nevertheless, the Christian can have the courage to affirm his faith in Jesus as the Christ. He is aware of the possibility and even the inevitability of idolatrous deviations, but also of the fact that in the picture of the Christ itself the criterion against its idolatrous abuse is given—the cross.

Out of this criterion comes the message which is the very heart of Christianity and makes possible the courage to affirm faith in the Christ, namely, that in spite of all forces of separation between God and man this is overcome from the side of God. One of these forces of separation is a doubt which tries to prevent the courage to affirm one's faith. In this situation faith still can be affirmed if the certainty is given that even the failure of the risk of faith cannot separate the concern of one's daring faith from the ultimate. This is the only absolute certainty of faith which corresponds with the only absolute content of faith, namely, that in relation to the ultimate we are always receiving and never giving. We are never able to bridge the infinite distance between the infinite and the finite from the side of the finite. This alone makes the courage of faith possible. The risk of failure, of error and of idolatrous distortion can be taken, because the failure cannot separate us from what is our ultimate concern.

REINHOLD NIEBUHR (1892–)

After graduating from Yale Divinity School in 1915, Reinhold Niebuhr served as pastor of the Bethel Church in Detroit. Here his profound concern with social and political problems was deepened, and he was led to question the adequacy of the religious liberals' approach to these problems. Increasingly he felt the need of the categories of sin and grace to account for what he saw. Since 1928 Niebuhr has taught at Union Theological Seminary in New York City. Many regard him as the greatest American spokesman of the so-called "neo-Reformation" movement, a tendency to return to the stress on God's sovereignty and on faith as the only avenue to knowledge of Him.

The Christian View of Man*

Man has always been his own most vexing problem. How shall he think of himself? Every affirmation which he may make about his stature, virtue, or place in the cosmos becomes involved in contradictions when fully analyzed. The analysis reveals some presupposition or implication which seems to deny what the proposition intended to affirm.

If man insists that he is a child of nature and that he ought not to pretend to be more than the animal, which he obviously is, he tacitly admits that he is, at any rate, a curious kind of animal who has both the inclination and the capacity to make such pretensions. If on the other hand he insists upon his unique and distinctive place in nature and points to his rational faculties as proof of his special eminence, there is usually an anxious note in his avowals of uniqueness which betrays his unconscious sense of kinship with the brutes. This note of anxiety gives poignant significance to the heat and animus in which the Darwinian controversy was conducted and the Darwinian thesis was resisted by the traditionalists. Furthermore the very effort to estimate the significance of his rational faculties implies a degree of transcendence over himself which is not fully defined or explained in what is usually connoted by "reason." For the man who weighs the importance of his rational faculties is in some sense more than "reason" and has capacities which transcend the ability to form general concepts.

If man takes his uniqueness for granted he is immediately involved in questions and contradictions on the problem of his virtue. If he believes himself to be essentially good and attributes the admitted evils of human history to specific social and historical causes he involves himself in begging the question; for all these specific historical causes of evil are revealed, upon close analysis, to be no more than particular consequences and historical configurations of evil tendencies in man himself. They cannot be understood at all if a capacity for, and inclination toward, evil in man himself is not presupposed. If, on the other hand, man comes to pessimistic conclusions about himself, his capacity for such judgments would seem to negate the content of the judgments. How can man be "essentially" evil if he knows himself to be so? What is the character of the ultimate subject, the quintessential "I," which passes such devastating judgments upon itself as object?

If one turns to the question of the value of human life and asks whether life is worth living, the very character of the question reveals that the questioner must in some sense be able to stand outside of, and to transcend the life which is thus judged and estimated. Man can reveal this transcendence more explicitly not only by actually committing suicide but by elaborating religions and philosophies which negate life and regard a "lifeless" eternity, such as Nirvana, as the only possible end of life.

Have those who inveigh so violently against otherworldliness in religion, justified as their criticisms may be, ever fully realized what the error of denying life implies in regard to the stature of man? The man who can negate "life" must be something other than mere vitality. Every effort to dissuade him from the neglect of natural vitality and historic existence implies a vantage point in him above natural vitality and history; otherwise he could not be tempted to the error from which he is to be dissuaded.

Man's place in the universe is subject to the same antinomies. Men have been assailed periodically by qualms of conscience and fits of dizziness for pretending to occupy the centre of the universe. Every philosophy of life is touched with anthropocentric tendencies. Even theocentric religions believe that the Creator of the world is interested in saving man from his unique predicament. But periodically man is advised and advises himself to moderate his pretensions and admit that he is only a little animal living a precarious existence on a second-rate planet, attached to a second-rate sun. There are moderns who believe that this modesty is the characteristic genius of modern man and the fruit of his discovery of the vastness of interstellar spaces; but it was no modern astronomer who confessed, "When I consider thy heavens, the work of thy fingers, the moon and the stars, which thou hast ordained; What is man that thou art mindful of him?" (Ps. 8:4). Yet the vantage point from which man judges his insignificance is a rather significant vantage point. . . .

While these paradoxes of human self-knowledge are not easily reduced to simpler formulæ, they all point to two facts about man: one of them obvious and the other not quite so obvious. The two are not usually appreciated with equal sympathy. The obvious fact is that man is a child of nature, subject to its vicissitudes, compelled by its necessities, driven by its impulses, and confined within the brevity of the years which nature permits its varied organic forms, allowing them some, but not too much, latitude. The other less obvious fact is that man is a spirit who stands outside of nature, life, himself, his reason and the world. . . .

How difficult it is to do justice to both the uniqueness of man and his affinities with the world of nature below him is proved by the almost unvarying tendency of those philosophies, which describe and emphasize the rational faculties of man or his capacity for self-transcendence to forget his relation to nature and to identify him, prematurely and unqualifiedly, with the divine and the eternal; and of naturalistic philosophies to obscure the uniqueness of man. . . .

. . . As the classical view is determined by

Greek metaphysical presuppositions, so the Christian view is determined by the ultimate presuppositions of Christian faith. The Christian faith in God as Creator of the world transcends the canons and antinomies of rationality, particularly the antinomy between mind and matter, between consciousness and extension. God is not merely mind who forms a previously given formless stuff. God is both vitality and form and the source of all existence. He creates the world. This world is not God; but it is not evil because it is not God. Being God's creation, it is good.

The consequence of this conception of the world upon the view of human nature in Christian thought is to allow an appreciation of the unity of body and soul in human personality which idealists and naturalists have sought in vain. Furthermore it prevents the idealistic error of regarding the mind as essentially good or essentially eternal and the body as essentially evil. But it also obviates the romantic error of seeking for the good in man-as-nature and for evil in man-as-spirit or as reason. Man is, according to the Biblical view, a created and finite existence in both body and spirit. . . .

The second important characteristic of the Christian view of man is that he is understood primarily from the standpoint of God, rather than the uniqueness of his rational faculties or his relation to nature. He is made in the "image of God." It has been the mistake of many Christian rationalists to assume that this term is no more than a religious-pictorial expression of what philosophy intends when it defines man as a rational animal. . . . The human spirit has the special capacity of standing continually outside itself in terms of indefinite regression. Consciousness is a capacity for surveying the world and determining action from a governing centre. Self-consciousness represents a further degree of transcendence in which the self makes itself its own object in such a way that the ego is finally always subject and not object. The rational capacity of surveying the world, of forming general concepts and analysing the order of the world is thus but one aspect of what Christianity knows as "spirit." The self knows the world, insofar as it knows the world, because it stands outside both itself and the world, which means that it cannot understand itself except as it is understood from beyond itself and the world.

This essential homelessness of the human spirit is the ground of all religion; for the self which stands outside itself and the world cannot find the meaning of life in itself or the world. It cannot identify meaning with causality in nature; for its freedom is obviously something different from the necessary causal links of nature. Nor can it identify the principle of meaning with rationality, since it transcends its own rational processes, so that it may, for instance, ask the question whether there is a relevance between its rational forms and the recurrences and forms of nature. It is this capacity of freedom which finally prompts great cultures and philosophies to transcend rationalism and to seek for the meaning of life in an unconditional ground of existence. But from the standpoint of human thought this unconditioned ground of existence, this God, can be defined only negatively. . . .

. . . To understand himself truly means to begin with a faith that he is understood from beyond himself, that he is known and loved of God and must find himself in terms of obedience to the divine will. This relation of the divine to the human will makes it possible for man to relate himself to God without pretending to be God; and to accept his distance from God as a created thing, without believing that the evil of his nature is caused by this finiteness. Man's finite existence in the body and in history can be essentially affirmed, as naturalism wants to affirm it. Yet the uniqueness of man's spirit can be appreciated even more than idealism appreciates it, though always preserving a proper distinction between the human and divine. Also the unity of spirit and body can be emphasized in terms of its relation to a Creator and Redeemer who created both mind and body. These are the ultra-rational foundations and presuppositions of Christian wisdom about man.

This conception of man's stature is not, however, the complete Christian picture of man. The high estimate of the human stature implied in the concept of "image of God" stands in paradoxical juxtaposition to the low estimate of human virtue in Christian thought. Man is a sinner. His sin is defined as rebellion against God. The Christian estimate of human evil is so serious precisely because it places evil at the very centre of human personality: in the will. This evil cannot be regarded complacently as the inevitable consequence of his finiteness or the fruit of his involvement in the contingencies and necessities of nature. Sin is occasioned precisely by the fact that man refuses to admit his "creatureliness" and to acknowledge himself as merely a member of a total unity of life. He pretends to be more than he is. Nor can he, as in both rationalistic and mystic dualism, dismiss his sins as residing in that part of himself which is not his true self, that is, that part of himself which is involved in physical necessity. In Christianity it is not the eternal man who judges the finite man; but the eternal and holy God who judges sinful man. Nor is redemption in the power of the eternal man who gradually sloughs off finite man. Man is not divided against himself so that the essential man can be extricated from the nonessential. Man contradicts himself within the terms of his true essence. His essence is free self-determination. His sin is the wrong use of his freedom and its consequent destruction.

Man is an individual but he is not self-sufficing. The law of his nature is love, a harmonious relation of life to life in obedience to the divine centre and source of his life. This law is violated when man seeks to make himself the centre and source of his own life. His sin is therefore spiritual and not carnal, though the infection of rebellion spreads from the spirit to the body and disturbs its harmonies also. Man, in other words, is a sinner not because he is one limited individual within a whole but rather because he is betrayed by his very ability to survey the whole to imagine himself the whole.

The fact that human vitality inevitably expresses itself in defiance of the laws of measure can be observed without the presuppositions of the Christian faith. The analysis of this fact in Greek tragedy has already been observed. But it is impossible without the presuppositions of the Christian faith to find the source of sin within man himself. Greek tragedy regards human evil as the consequence of a conflict between vitality and form, between Dionysian and Olympian divinities. Only in a religion of revelation, whose God reveals Himself to man from beyond himself and from beyond the contrast of vitality and form, can man discover the root of sin to be within himself. The essence of man is his freedom. Sin is committed in that freedom. Sin can therefore not be attributed to a defect in his essence. It can only be understood as a self-contradiction, made possible by the fact of his freedom but not following necessarily from it.

Christianity, therefore, issues inevitably in the religious expression of an uneasy conscience. Only within terms of the Christian faith can man not only understand the reality of the evil in himself but escape the error of attributing that evil to any one but himself. It is possible of course to point out that man is tempted by the situation in which he stands. He stands at the juncture of nature and spirit. The freedom of his spirit causes him to break the harmonies of nature and the pride of his spirit prevents him from establishing a new harmony. The freedom of his spirit enables him to use the forces and processes of nature creatively; but his failure to observe the limits of his finite existence causes him to defy the forms and restraints of both nature and reason. Human self-consciousness is a high tower looking upon a large and inclusive world. It vainly imagines that it is the large world which it beholds and not a narrow tower insecurely erected amidst the shifting sands of the world.

Faith and History*

The sovereignty of God establishes the general frame of meaning for life and history, according to Biblical faith. But the first specific content of the drama of history is furnished by the assertion of divine sovereignty against man's rebellious efforts to establish himself as the perverse center of existence. Biblical faith does not deny the fact of evil in history. On the con-

* Reprinted with the permission of Charles Scribner's Sons and James Nisbet & Co. Ltd. from *Faith and History,* pp. 120–123, 123–124, 132, 132–133, 135–137, by Reinhold Niebuhr. Copyright 1949 Charles Scribner's Sons.

trary it discerns that men are capable of such bold and persistent defiance of the laws and structures of their existence that only the resource of the divine power and love is finally able to overcome this rebellion. The patterns of human existence are filled with obscurities and abysses of meaninglessness because of this possibility of evil in human life.

The obscurities and incoherences of life are, according to Biblical faith, primarily the consequence of human actions. The incoherences and confusions, usually defined as "natural" evil, are not the chief concern of the Christian faith. Natural evil represents the failure of nature's processes to conform perfectly to human ends. It is the consequence of man's ambiguous position in nature. As a creature of nature he is subject to necessities and contingencies, which may be completely irrelevant to the wider purposes, interests, and ambitions which he conceives and elaborates as creative spirit. The most vivid symbol of natural evil is death. Death is a simple fact in the dimension of nature; but it is an irrelevance and a threat of meaninglessness in the realm of history. Biblical faith is, however, only obliquely interested in the problem of natural evil. It does not regard death, as such, as an evil. "The sting of death," declares St. Paul, "is sin."

Nor does it regard moral evil as due to man's involvement in natural finiteness. On the contrary, moral or historical evil is the consequence of man's abortive effort to overcome his insecurity by his own power, to hide the finiteness of his intelligence by pretensions of omniscience and to seek for emancipation from his ambiguous position by his own resources. Sin is, in short, the consequence of man's inclination to usurp the prerogatives of God, to think more highly of himself than he ought to think, thus making destructive use of his freedom by not observing the limits to which a creaturely freedom is bound.

Man is at variance with God through this abortive effort to establish himself as his own Lord; and he is at variance with his fellowmen by the force of the same pride which brings him in conflict with God. The prophets of Israel seemed to sense this primary form of historical evil most immediately in its collective form. They felt that Israel was guilty of it, because it drew complacent conclusions from the fact of its special covenant with God. The great nations and empires which encircled Israel were guilty because they imagined that their power made them immortal and secure. The myth of the Fall of Adam universalizes, as well as individualizes, this theme of man's revolt against God. The influence of this myth upon the Christian imagination is not primarily due to any literalistic illusions of Christian orthodoxy. The myth accurately symbolizes the consistent Biblical diagnosis of moral and historical evil. Adam and, together with him, all men seek to overstep the bounds which are set by the Creator for man as creature. St. Paul's definition of sin is in perfect conformity with this theme, even when he makes no specific reference to the Fall. Man's sin, declares St. Paul, is that he "changes the glory of the uncorruptible God into an image of corruptible man" (Romans 1:23). If men fail to penetrate to the mystery of the divine, the fault lies, according to the Bible, not so much in the finiteness of their intelligence as in the "vanity" of their imagination. They are, declares St. Paul, "without excuse" in their ignorance of God. For "the invisible things of him from the creation of the world are clearly seen, being understood by the things that are made" (Romans 1:20). It is obvious, in other words, that the world is not self-derived. It points beyond itself to its Creator. The failure to recognize this fact is not the fault of the mind but of the person who usurps the central position in the scheme of things and thereby brings confusion into his own life and into the whole order of history. Biblical faith has always insisted upon the embarrassing truth that the corruption of evil is at the heart of the human personality. It is not the inertia of its natural impulses in opposition to the purer impulses of the mind. The fact that it is a corruption which has a universal dominion over all men, though it is not by nature but in freedom that men sin, is the "mystery" of "original sin," which will always be an offense to rationalists. But it has the merit of being true to the facts of human existence. A scientific age will seek, and also find, specific reasons and causes for the jealousy of children, or the power lusts in mature individuals, or the naive egotism of even the saintly individual, or the envies and hatreds which infect all human relations. The discovery of specific causes of specific forms of these evils has obscured and will continue to obscure the profounder truth, that all men, saints and sinners, the righteous and the unrighteous, are inclined to use the freedom to transcend time, history, and themselves in such a way as to make themselves the false center of existence. Thus the same freedom which gives human life a creative power, not possessed by the other creatures, also endows it with destructive possibilities not known in nature. The two-fold possibility of creativity and destruction in human freedom accounts for the growth of both good and evil through the extension of human powers. The failure to recognize this obvious fact in modern culture accounts for most of its errors in estimating the actual trends of history.

The tendency of modern culture to see only the creative possibilities of human freedom makes the Christian estimate of the human situation seem morbid by contrast. . . . Is it not true that men are able by increasing freedom to envisage a larger world and to assume a responsible attitude toward a wider and wider circle of claims upon their conscience? Does the Christian faith do justice, for instance, to the fact that increasing freedom has set the commandment, "Thou shalt love thy neighbor as thyself," in a larger frame of reference than ever before in history? Is it not significant that we have reached a global situation in which we may destroy ourselves and each other if we fail to organize a new global "neighborhood" into a tenable brotherhood?

Such misgivings fail to recognize how intimately the dignity and the misery of man are related in the Christian conception. The dignity of man, which modern culture is ostensibly so anxious to guard and validate, is greater than the modern mind realizes. For it consists of a unique freedom which is able, not only to transcend the "laws" of nature or of reason to which classical and modern culture would bind it, but also to defy and outrage the very structure of man's existence. The dignity of man is therefore no proof of his virtue; nor is the misery of man a proof of his "bestiality." Both the destructive and the creative powers of man are unique because of the special quality of freedom which he possesses.

If the destructive, rather than the creative, possibilities of freedom seem unduly emphasized in Biblical thought, that is because in the ultimate instance (that is when men are not judging themselves but feel themselves under a divine judgement) they become conscious of the self's persistent self-centeredness. When they are judging themselves they are inclined to be impressed by the self's virtuous inclination to consider interests, other than its own.

It is worth noting that the behaviour of a man or nation, viewed from the standpoint of a critical rival or observer is invariably assessed, not as the morally complacent self judges its own actions but as the devout and contrite self judges it. The Christian interpretation of the human situation corresponds to what men and nations say about each other, even without Christian insight. But without Christian insights they bring even greater confusion into the affairs of men by assuming that only their rivals and competitors are guilty of the pride and lust for power which they behold. Only under the judgement of God do they recognize the universality of this human situation of sin and guilt. . . . The prophets of the Old Testament correctly measured the moral problem of life in its dimensions of both height and breadth. They discerned that man, in his individual and collective experience, is finally confronted by the divine source and end of his existence; and that this experience inevitably contains the contrite sense of being judged. The conscience is guilty because the individual or the nation is discovered in this final experience of faith and revelation to be involved in a defiance of God by reason of its pride and self-seeking. The prophets saw, secondly, that this experience of judgement is neither irrelevant nor simply relevant to the experiences of history. It is relevant insofar as the individual and the collective ego is subject to pressures, punishments, vicissitudes and catastrophes which are, and which may be interpreted as, justified forms of judgement upon its sins. If they are not so interpreted the catastrophes of history are, or may become, a source of confusion and despair. If they are recognized as related to the divine sovereignty over life, they may become the occasion for the renewal of life. The prophets also recognized that the historical process represents no exact execution of a divine justice. Perhaps it would be more correct to say that it does not conform to any human notion of what the divine justice should be. . . .

The prophetic interpretation of the relation of the divine to historical judgements is true to constant human experience in its discernment of two facets of the problem of man's rebellion. The moral obscurity of history is recognized as due partly to the fact that all men have the inclination and the capacity to defy the laws and structures of their existence. This fact raises the question whether there is a power great enough and good enough to overcome the confusion of this rebellion. This is the problem of redemption in its profoundest form. The moral obscurity of history is, on the other hand, recognized as partly due to the fact that rewards and punishments are not exactly proportioned to relative guilt and innocency of men and nations. This is the problem of the quality of justice in the historical process. . . .

The New Testament faith is radically different from Old Testament messianism. That fact is signified by the rejection, by those who expect the Messiah, of a Messiah who died upon a Cross. This Messiah, whom the church accepts as the true Messiah, does not correct the moral disbalances of history. He does not establish the triumph of the righteous over the unrighteous. The perfect love which His life and death exemplify is defeated, rather than triumphant, in the actual course of history. Thus, according to the Christian belief, history remains morally ambiguous to the end. The perfect love of Christ is both the ultimate possibility of all historic virtues and a contradiction to them. Justice remains imperfect unless it culminates in this perfect love of self-giving. But every form of historic justice contains elements which place it in contradiction to such perfect love.

For the Christian faith the enigma of life is resolved by the confidence that this same love has more than an historical dimension. This love is the revelation of a divine mercy which overcomes the contradictions of human life. Suffering innocence, which reveals the problem of moral ambiguity of history, becomes in the Christian faith the answer to the problem at the point, when it is seen as a revelation of a divine suffering which bears and overcomes the sins of the world.

Thus the Christian faith does not promise to overcome the fragmentary and contradictory aspects of man's historic existence. It does claim to have apprehended by faith the divine power and mercy which will ultimately resolve life's ambiguities and purge men of the evil into which they fall because they seek so desperately to overcome them. Insofar as men abandon themselves to this power and mercy in faith and repentance, this destruction of selfhood through a too desperate effort to preserve and realize it may be overcome. New life is possible by dying to self, even as death results from a too desperate effort to live. In that sense the Christian faith promises indeterminate renewals of life in history. But on the other hand the total historical enterprise is not progressively emancipated from evil. The Christian faith expects some of the most explicit forms of evil at the end of history. But nothing can happen in history to shake the confidence in the meaning of existence, to those who have discerned by faith the revelation of the ultimate power and love which bears and guides men through their historic vicissitudes.

Thus the final revelation of the divine sovereignty in New Testament faith transfigures the moral perplexity about suffering innocence into the ultimate light of meaning. It gives life a final meaning without promising the annullment of history's moral obscurities. Above all it holds out the hope of redemption from evil, upon the basis of a humble acceptance of human finiteness and a contrite recognition of the evil in which men are involved when they seek to deny their finitude.

The points of reference for the structure of the meaning of history in the Christian faith are obviously not found by an empirical analysis of the observable structures and coherences of history. They are "revelations," apprehended by faith, of the character and purposes of God. The experience of faith by which they are apprehended is an experience at the ultimate limits of human knowledge; and it requires a condition of repentance which is a possibility for the individual, but only indirectly for nations and collectives.

The character of these points of reference or these foundations for a structure of meaning make it quite clear that it is not possible to speak simply of a "Christian philosophy of history." Perhaps it is not possible to have any adequate "philosophy" of history at all because a philosophy will reduce the antinomies, obscurities and the variety of forms in history to a too simple form of intelligibility. Yet a Christian theology of history is not an arbitrary construct. It "makes sense" out of life and history.

That the final clue to the mystery of the divine power is found in the suffering love of a man on the Cross is not a proposition which follows logically from the observable facts of history. But there are no observable facts of history which can not be interpreted in its light. When so interpreted the confusions and catastrophes of history may become the source of the renewal of life.

W. A. VISSER 'T HOOFT (1900–)

Though Christians have always hoped for unity, it has not been until recently that a formal organization, embracing various Church bodies, has been developed to seek this end. The "ecumenical movement" ("ecumenical" meaning "universal") resulted in the formation in 1948 of the World Council of Churches. Most of the world's Protestant, Anglican, and Orthodox bodies have affiliated with this Council, whose General Secretary is W. A. Visser 't Hooft. This Dutch theologian and churchman became interested in the ecumenical movement while he was still a student involved in a number of international conferences and projects. Visser 't Hooft has not only given practical guidance to the movement but has contributed a number of books and articles setting forth its theological basis.

The Significance of the World Council of Churches*

I. *Introduction*

The plan of forming a World Council of Churches was conceived in 1937. The draft constitution was elaborated in the following year. The invitations to the churches to participate in the formation of the Council were sent out in the winter 1938–1939. Then came the war, during which thorough theological discussion between the churches proved impossible. It is, therefore, not astonishing that the fundamental questions concerning the nature of the Council and its function have not yet been clarified and that we approach the first Assembly without having arrived at a clear common conception of the precise nature of the body which we are setting up together. . . .

The Council cannot, of course, adopt one specific ecclesiology as its basic conception of the nature of the Church and of church unity. If such a generally acceptable ecclesiology were available the ecumenical problem would be solved, and there would be no need for an ecumenical "movement." The present situation is characterized precisely by the fact that churches with very divergent conceptions of the Church seek to live and work together in spite of their differences. But while it is impossible to force this situation, it is equally impossible to go forward without some tentative principles and definitions concerning the nature of the new body which the churches together have decided to set up. . . .

It is then not surprising that the question; "What is the World Council?" is being raised in different quarters, sometimes in a tone of expectation and sometimes in a tone of suspicion.

Already in 1935 Dietrich Bonhoeffer, who since proved by his witness and death how deeply his life was rooted in the *Una Sancta* [the One Holy Church], had warned the ecumenical movement that the struggle of the confessing church involved a decisive question for the ecumenical movement: *Ist die Oekumene*

* From W. A. Visser 't Hooft, "The Significance of the World Council of Churches," *Man's Disorder and God's Design: the Amsterdam Assembly Series,* 1949, Vol. I, pages 177–188.

Kirche? ["Is the ecumenical movement the Church?"]. The Church is only there where men witness to the lordship of Christ and against His enemies. And there is no true unity where unity in confessing the faith is lacking. Has the ecumenical movement that unity? Does it seek that unity? And if not, is it truly the Church of Christ? . . .

II. *Background*

It may be useful to begin with a short summary of ecumenical developments leading up to the formation of the World Council.

As a result of the untiring efforts of a small group of pioneers the ecumenical conferences of Stockholm and Lausanne are convened. For the first time in centuries the churches meet together. But what do these meetings mean? Are they intended to demonstrate the oneness of the Church of Christ and to declare the common faith? Are they a visible representation of the *Una Sancta?* In trying to answer these questions, we are confronted by a fundamental dualism in the definitions and statements which these conferences make and which are made concerning them. For on the one hand both conferences deny (in different ways) that they intend to speak on behalf of the churches and to represent the Church Universal. But both speak to the churches and to the world in such a way that they are inevitably regarded as claiming to represent, though in a very provisional and imperfect way, that unity which in New Testament language is the unity of the one Body, the one Church of Christ. . . .

Now this dualism has remained characteristic of the ecumenical movement. At times it has spoken of itself as an agency of the churches to prepare the way for unity; at other times it has acted as an organ which declares the unity already achieved. This is even more clearly seen in the Oxford and Edinburgh Conferences. For the Oxford Conference spoke in its message, in its substantial reports and in its word to the German Church, much more definitely as a voice of "the Church" than the Stockholm Conference had done. In its message, it declared clearly that "God has done great things through His Church," and that "one of the greatest" is that "there exists an actual world-fellowship," so that "our unity in Christ is not a theme for aspiration; it is an experienced fact," of which the Conference itself is an illustration. Similarly the Edinburgh Conference in its "Affirmation of Unity" goes further than the Lausanne Conference in defining the nature of the unity which already exists and "which is deeper than our divisions." In the opening service of the Conference, the President (Archbishop Temple) said: "The occurrence of the two world conferences in one summer is itself a manifestation of the *Una Sancta,* the holy fellowship of those who worship God in Jesus Christ." But both conferences maintain the principle that they do not speak authoritatively for the churches and do not, therefore, speak as the Church Universal. . . .

III. *What the World Council is Not*

It is true that the ecumenical conferences have been able to give expression to a common mind, but the scope of their witness has been very limited. And the fact remains that the teaching of the churches in the Council is not a common *kerygma* [proclamation] with different aspects or emphases, but in many respects a confusion of tongues. The churches contradict each other on points which they consider, and must consider, as essential parts of their message. In joining with churches of other confessions in the fellowship of the Council they recognize that Christ is at work in these other churches; they accept, therefore, the duty of discussion and co-operation with these churches, but they continue to look upon these other churches as churches whose teaching is incomplete, distorted or even heretical. It is impossible to claim that this provisional and tentative relationship between the churches is itself the *Una Sancta*. . . . .

It is, however, not only in the realm of these easily observable conditions of its life, but in the less tangible realm of the spiritual situation that one discovers strong reasons why the Council should not make too exalted claims for itself. The churches are at the moment not able to manifest the *Una Sancta* in a way which corresponds to the reality of its nature. The unity which would be seen, if the issue of unity were forced now, would be far too much a unity of compromise. There is still in much of our present ecumenism a strong element of relativism and of lack of concern for the truth of God. And so our unity would not be the biblical unity in truth. There can be no real representation of the *Una Sancta* until the churches have turned in a new way to the Word of God, until they have discovered their sickness, until they have found something of that clarity and certainty of preaching and witness which characterized the New Testament Church, until they are truly "becoming the Church" and meet each other on the level of that *metanoia* [change of heart]. In the providence of God signs are not wanting that some of these things are beginning to happen. But we are yet far away from the time of harvest. Until that time it will be well for us to be very modest in our claims.

Is the World Council then just an organization? If it cannot be considered as a visible representation of the *Una Sancta,* must it be considered as a man-made organ which may have a very noble and useful function to perform and which may render great services to the cause of the Church but which is not itself an expression and representation of "the Church"? . . .

It is a fact that the World Council is often presented in such purely organizational terms. Thus, many "practically minded" supporters of the Council speak of it as just an agency of collaboration in concrete tasks. Now the Council is certainly such an agency, but its origins show clearly that it cannot be satisfied with that role. However grateful we may be to the pioneers of Stockholm, we cannot and dare not go back to the "as if" theology which demands that we shall act "as if" we were one in faith. We have discovered that our witness to the common faith is our first and foremost duty to the world and that without that witness our unity in "life and work" is impotent. When churches meet together they cannot leave on one side the question of their common confession of allegiance to their common Lord. It is not by accident that the ecumenical conferences have borne that witness in spite of all canonical obstacles to their doing so. The inner dynamic of the Church forced them to do so.

The same applies to the view that the exclusive purpose of the council is the fostering of common study. Study is indispensable and common study on an ecumenical level is one of the great needs of the hour, but a Council of Churches cannot possibly consider study as an aim in itself. In the setting of the Church's mission study can have meaning only as a preparation for action, that is, for decisions of faith. When this is forgotten study may even become a danger, for study without decision fosters a theology-for-the-sake-of-theology rather than for the sake of the Church. If the ecumenical movement meant that all possible Christian standpoints were to be set permanently side by side on equal pedestals, it would become a museum and cease to have any relevance for the living Church.

The World Council cannot be content to be a federation of bodies, each of which watches jealously over its own sovereignty. A fellowship of churches which know that there is no sovereignty save that of their common Lord must differ essentially from a pragmatic combination of sovereign states. The gathering together of the churches can have spiritual relevance only if these churches desire in some way to become members of the one Body, and if, even in the early stages of their meeting, they give evidence of that desire. But if they do so, their relationships cannot possibly remain of a purely organizational character.

The World Council cannot be a mere organization simply because it is a council *of churches*. For the Church in the churches insists on asserting itself. Wherever two or three churches are gathered together, the *Una Sancta* is in the midst of them and demands to be manifested.

IV. *What then is the World Council?*

We have seen that the World Council cannot claim to be the *Una Sancta*. We have also seen that it cannot be satisfied to be a more or less permanent conference about church unity or an organization for practical purposes. On the one hand it dare not minimize the very real disunity within its membership; on the other hand it may not refuse the gift of unity which the Lord has actually given and gives to the churches, when He enables them to speak and act together. The Council may not anticipate that unity which belongs only to the truly reunited Church, but neither can it refuse to follow the call to speak with one voice and to act as one body whenever that call is addressed to it. The Council cannot create the Church out of the churches, but neither can it stand aside as an observer when the Church in the churches affirms and expresses itself.

This is the dilemma which dominates the whole existence of the Council. Its member churches are as yet unable to be together the one Church of God, but they are no longer able to regard their fellow-members as being outside the Church of God. They cannot unite, but neither can they let each other go. They know that there is no unity outside truth, but they realize also that truth demands unity.

Is there any way out of this dilemma? Only a way of faith. Only a way which takes its point of departure not in man-made syntheses or theoretical schemes, but in the simple truth that the unity of the Church is the work of the Lord of the Church. This truth has been clearly expressed at both the Oxford and Edinburgh Conferences. The Oxford Message says: "The source of unity is not the consenting movement of men's wills; it is Jesus Christ whose one life flows through the Body and subdues the many wills to His." And the Edinburgh Affirmation says: "Thus unity does not consist in the agreement of our minds or the consent of our wills. It is founded in Jesus Christ Himself."

In his opening sermon at the Edinburgh Conference, Archbishop Temple said:

> "It is not we who can heal the wounds of His Body. We confer and deliberate, and that is right. But it is not by contrivance and adjustment that we can unite the Church of God. It is only by coming closer to Him that we come nearer to one another. . . . Only when God has drawn us closer to Himself shall we be truly united together; and then our task will be, not to consummate our endeavour, but to register His achievement."

Karl Barth puts the same truth in a different way. He states that: "all efforts towards unity depend altogether on an act of recognition by the Church," namely, the recognition of the fact that this particular unity is willed by God. When this is really the case "we must obediently do our share so that we do not contradict on earth what is God's will in heaven."

And is not this also the true significance of the basis of the World Council? It means that the living Christ—God and Saviour—alone can create the unity which we seek. Thus it gives the Council the indispensable foundation for its existence.

Unity is received, but that does not mean that man's role is purely passive. We are to look out for it and to be constantly ready to receive it. The unity which is given to us must become visible and effective in our midst. . . .

Who shall say when this is the case? Certainly not the World Council itself. For as we have seen, it can only try to express the mind of the *Una Sancta,* but not claim to be the *Una Sancta.* Rather it is open to any member church, and indeed to every church member to decide whether, in each given case, it recognizes in the World Council a manifestation of the one Body which fulfills the will of the Head. The World Council does not claim any authority for itself. But it must realize that it may *Deo volente,* ["God willing"] suddenly take on the formidable authority of an organ of the Holy Spirit.

Its whole life must be a constant counting with that possibility and a constant watching for that intervention from above. If it lives in that attitude, it will not become a mere ecclesiastical bureaucracy and will have true relevance for the life of the churches.

Selected Readings on Religion in the Modern Period

GENERAL SURVEYS

Brinton, C., *The Shaping of the Modern Mind*. New York: New American Library, 1958.

Latourette, K. S., *A History of Christianity*. New York: Harper and Brothers, 1953.

McGiffert, A. C., *The Rise of Modern Religious Ideas*. New York: The Macmillan Company, 1915.

McNeill, J. T., *Modern Christian Movements*. Philadelphia: Westminster, 1954.

Moore, E. C., *An Outline of the History of Christian Thought since Kant*. New York: Charles Scribner's Sons, 1912.

Nichols, J. H., *History of Christianity: 1650–1950: Secularization of the West*. New York: Ronald Press, 1956.

Norwood, F. A., *The Development of Modern Christianity since 1500*. Nashville: Abingdon, 1956.

Randall, J. H., *The Making of the Modern Mind*, rev. ed. Boston: Houghton Mifflin, 1940.

JUDAISM IN THE MODERN PERIOD

Agus, J. B., *Modern Philosophies of Judaism*. New York: Behrman, 1941.

Finkelstein, Louis (ed.), *The Jews: Their History, Culture and Religion,* 4 vols. Philadelphia: Jewish Publication Society, 1949.

Margolis, M., and A. Marx, *A History of the Jewish People*. New York: Meridian Books, Inc., 1927.

Philipson, D., *The Reform Movement in Judaism*. New York: The Macmillan Company, 1931.

Sachar, A. L., *A History of the Jews*. New York: A. A. Knopf, Inc., 1943.

ROMAN CATHOLICISM IN THE MODERN PERIOD

Adam, K., *The Spirit of Catholicism*. New York: Sheed and Ward, Inc., 1929.

Clark, W. H., *The Oxford Group: Its History and Significance*. New York: Bookman Associates, 1951.

Gilson, E. (ed.), *The Church Speaks to the Modern World*. New York: Image Books, 1958.

Guardini, R., *The Faith and Modern Man*. New York: Pantheon Books, 1954.

Gurian, W., and M. A. Fitzsimons, *The Caltholic Church in World Affairs*. Notre Dame: University of Notre Dame Press, 1954.

Janelle, P., *The Catholic Reformation.* Milwaukee: Bruce Publishing Company, 1949.

McCaffrey, J., *History of the Catholic Church in the Nineteenth Century.* St. Louis: Herder, 1909.

PROTESTANTISM IN THE MODERN PERIOD

Barth, K., *Protestant Thought from Rousseau to Ritschl.* New York: Harper and Brothers, 1959.

Dillenberger, J., and C. Welch, *Protestant Christianity Interpreted Through Its Development.* New York: Charles Scribner's Sons, 1954.

Mackintosh, H. R., *Types of Modern Theology: Schleiermacher to Barth.* New York: Charles Scribner's Sons, 1937.

Nash, A. S. (ed.), *Protestant Thought in the Twentieth Century.* New York: The Macmillan Company, 1951.

Williams, D. D., *What Present Day Theologians Are Thinking,* rev. ed. New York: Harper and Brothers, 1959.

RELIGION IN AMERICA

Blau, J. L. (ed.), *Cornerstones of Religious Liberty in America.* Boston: Beacon Press, 1949.

Brauer, J. C., *Protestantism in America: A Narrative History.* Philadelphia: Westminster, 1953.

Clark, E. T., *The Small Sects in America,* rev. ed. Nashville: Abingdon, 1949.

Ellis, J. T., *American Catholicism.* Chicago: University of Chicago Press, 1956.

Glazer, N., *American Judaism.* Chicago: University of Chicago Press, 1957.

Handlin, O., *Adventure in Freedom: 300 Years of Jewish Life in America.* New York: McGraw-Hill Book Company, Inc., 1954.

Herberg, W., *Protestant, Catholic, Jew,* rev. ed. New York: Harper Torchbook, 1959.

Mayer, F. E., *The Religious Bodies of America.* St. Louis: Concordia Publishing House, 1956.

Maynard, T., *The Story of American Catholicism.* New York: The Macmillan Company, 1941.

Miller, P., *Jonathan Edwards.* New York: W. Sloane Associates, 1949.

Mode, P. G., *The Frontier Spirit in American Christianity.* New York: The Macmillan Company, 1923.

Niebuhr, H. Richard, *The Social Sources of Denominationalism.* Hamden, Conn.: Shoestring Press, 1954.

———, *The Kingdom of God in America.* New York: Willett Clark, 1937.

Olmstead, C. E., *History of Religion in the United States.* Englewood Cliffs, N. J.: Prentice-Hall, Inc., 1960.

Smith, H. S., R. T. Handy, and L. A. Loetscher, *American Christianity: An Historical Interpretation with Representatives Documents,* Vol. I. New York: Charles Scribner's Sons, 1960.

Stokes, A. P., *Church and State in the United States.* New York: Harper and Brothers, 1950.

Sweet, W. W., *The Story of Religion in America,* rev. ed. New York: Harper and Brothers, 1950.

SPECIAL TOPICS

Baillie, J., *The Belief in Progress.* New York: Charles Scribner's Sons, 1951.

———, *The Idea of Revelation in Recent Thought.* New York: Columbia University Press, 1956.

Bainton, R. H., *The Travail of Religious Liberty.* Philadelphia: Westminster, 1951.

Balthasar, H., *Science, Religion and Christianity.* Westminster, Md.: Newman Press, 1958.

Bulgakov, S., *The Orthodox Church.* London: Centenary Press, 1953.

Burtt, E. A., *The Metaphysical Foundations of Modern Physical Science,* rev. ed. Garden City, N. Y.: Doubleday and Company, 1954.

Coulson, C. A., *Science and Christian Belief.* New York: Oxford University Press, 1955.

Davis, H. J., and R. C. Good (eds.), *Reinhold Niebuhr on Politics.* New York: Charles Scribner's Sons, 1960.

Edwards, M., *John Wesley and the Eighteenth Century.* Nashville: Abingdon Press, 1933.

Furniss, N. F., *The Fundamentalist Controversy.* New Haven, Conn.: Yale University Press, 1954.

Hopkins, C. H., *The Rise of the Social Gospel in American Protestantism.* New Haven, Conn.: Yale University Press, 1940.

Machen, J. G., *Christianity and Liberalism.* New York: The Macmillan Company, 1923.

Maritain, J., *True Humanism.* New York: Charles Scribner's Sons, 1938.

McNeill, J. T., *The History and Character of Calvinism.* New York: Oxford University Press, 1954.

Roberts, D. E., *Existentialism and Religious Belief.* New York: Oxford University Press, 1957.

———, *Psychotherapy and a Christian View of Man.* New York: Charles Scribner's Sons, 1950.

Sweet, W. W., *Revivalism in America.* New York: Charles Scribner's Sons, 1944.

Tawney, R. H., *Religion and the Rise of Capitalism.* New York: Harcourt Brace and Company, 1926.

Tillich, P., *The Courage To Be.* New Haven, Conn.: Yale University Press, 1952.

Van Dusen, H. P., and D. E. Roberts (eds.), *Liberal Theology.* New York: Charles Scribner's Sons, 1942.

Welch, C., *In This Name* (the "Trinity" in recent thought). New York: Charles Scribner's Sons, 1952.

Wild, J., *The Challenge of Existentialism.* Bloomington, Indiana: Indiana University Press, 1955.